KB100518

2학기 전과정

적중 100 plus

영어 **기출문제집**

중**2**

동아 | 윤정미

Best Collection

구성과 특징

교과서의 주요 학습 내용을 중심으로 학습 영역별 특성에 맞춰 단계별로 다양한 학습 기회를 제공하여
단원별 학습능력 평가는 물론 중간 및 기말고사 시험 등에 완벽하게 대비할 수 있도록 내용을 구성

Words & Expressions

Step1　Key Words 단원별 핵심 단어 설명 및 풀이
　　　　　Key Expression 단원별 핵심 숙어 및 관용어 설명
　　　　　Word Power 반대 또는 비슷한 뜻 단어 배우기
　　　　　English Dictionary 영어로 배우는 영어 단어

Step2　실력평가 단원별 수시평가 대비 주관식, 객관식 문제풀이

Step3　서술형 대비 학업성취도 및 수행능력평가 대비 서술형 문제풀이

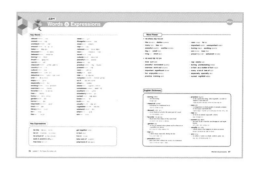

Conversation

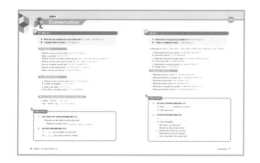

Step1　핵심 의사소통 소통에 필요한 주요 표현 방법 요약
　　　　　핵심 Check 기본적인 표현 방법 및 활용능력 확인

Step2　대화문 익히기 교과서 대화문 심층 분석 및 확인

Step3　교과서 확인학습 빈칸 채우기를 통한 문장 완성 능력 확인

Step4　기본평가 시험대비 기초 학습 능력 평가

Step5　실력평가 단원별 수시평가 대비 주관식, 객관식 문제풀이

Step6　서술형 대비 학업성취도 및 수행능력평가 대비 서술형 문제풀이

Grammar

Step1　주요 문법 단원별 주요 문법 사항과 예문을 알기 쉽게 설명
　　　　　핵심 Check 기본 문법사항에 대한 이해 여부 확인

Step2　기본평가 시험대비 기초 학습 능력 평가

Step3　실력평가 단원별 수시평가 대비 주관식, 객관식 문제풀이

Step4　서술형 대비 학업성취도 및 수행능력평가 대비 서술형 문제풀이

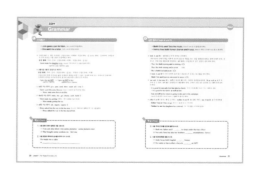

Reading

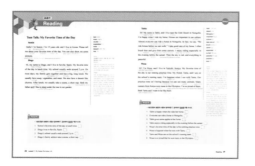

Step1　구문 분석 단원별로 제시된 문장에 대한 구문별 분석과 내용 설명
　　　　　확인문제 문장에 대한 기본적인 이해와 인지능력 확인

Step2　확인학습A 빈칸 채우기를 통한 문장 완성 능력 확인

Step3　확인학습B 제시된 우리말을 영어로 완성하여 작문 능력 키우기

Step4　실력평가 단원별 수시평가 대비 주관식, 객관식 문제풀이

Step5　서술형 대비 학업성취도 및 수행능력평가 대비 서술형 문제풀이
　　　　　교과서 구석구석 교과서에 나오는 기타 문장까지 완벽 학습

Composition

|영역별 핵심문제|

단어 및 어휘, 대화문, 문법, 독해 등 각 영역별 기출문제의 출제 유형을 분석하여 실전에 대비하고 연습할 수 있도록 문제를 배열

|단원별 예상문제|

기출문제를 분석한 후 새로운 시험 출제 경향을 더하여 새롭게 출제될 수 있는 문제를 포함하여 시험에 완벽하게 대비할 수 있도록 준비

|서술형 실전 및 창의사고력 문제|

학교 시험에서 점차 늘어나는 서술형 시험에 집중 대비하고 고득점을 취득하는데 만전을 기하기 위한 학습 코너

|단원별 모의고사|

영역별, 단계별 학습을 모두 마친 후 실전 연습을 위한 모의고사

교과서 파헤치기

- **단어Test1~3** 영어 단어 우리말 쓰기, 우리말을 영어 단어로 쓰기, 영영풀이에 해당하는 단어와 우리말 쓰기
- **대화문Test1~2** 대화문 빈칸 완성 및 전체 대화문 쓰기
- **본문Test1~5** 빈칸 완성, 우리말 쓰기, 문장 배열연습, 영어 작문하기 복습 등 단계별 반복 학습을 통해 교과서 지문에 대한 완벽한 습득
- **구석구석지문Test1~2** 지문 빈칸 완성 및 전문 영어로 쓰기

Contents

이책의 차례

Lesson 5

Living Healthily and Safely

 의사소통 기능

- 문제점이나 증상을 묻고 답하기
  A: What's wrong?
  B: I have a headache.

- 당부하기
  Make sure you take some medicine.

언어 형식

- 목적격 관계대명사
  Another problem **(which/that)** you can have is neck pain.

- call *A B*
  We **call** such people smombies.

Words & Expressions

교과서

Key Words

- accident[ǽksidənt] 명 사고
- addiction[ədíkʃən] 명 중독
- advice[ædváis] 명 충고
- another[ənʌ́ðər] 형 또 다른
- around[əráund] 부 주위에
- author[ɔ́ːθər] 명 작가, 저자
- back[bæk] 명 등
- blink[bliŋk] 동 눈을 깜박이다
- cause[kɔːz] 동 야기하다
- celebrity[səlébrəti] 명 유명인사, 유명인
- delicious[dilíʃəs] 형 맛있는
- dentist[déntist] 명 치과의사
- difficult[dífikʌlt] 형 어려운
- dry[drai] 형 건조한, 마른
- during[djúəriŋ] 전 ~ 동안
- example[igzǽmpl] 명 예, 사례
- exercise[éksərsàiz] 명 운동
- fever[fíːvər] 명 열, 열병
- headache[hédeik] 명 두통
- health[helθ] 명 건강
- hole[houl] 명 구덩이, 구멍
- hurt[həːrt] 동 다치다
- increase[inkríːs] 동 증가하다
- intelligent[intélədʒənt] 형 똑똑한, 지적인
- meal[miːl] 명 식사
- medicine[médisn] 명 약
- nervous[nə́rvəs] 형 초조한, 불안한
- pain[pein] 명 아픔, 고통
- prevent[privént] 동 막다, 예방하다
- promise[prámis] 명 약속
- regularly[régjulərli] 부 규칙적으로
- safety[séifti] 명 안전
- sign[sain] 명 표지판
- simple[símpl] 형 단순한
- skin[skin] 명 피부
- smart[smɑːrt] 형 현명한, 말쑥한
- sore[sɔːr] 형 아픈, 쓰린
- subject[sʌ́bdʒikt] 명 과목
- such[sətʃ] 형 그러한
- terrible[térəbl] 형 끔찍한, 무서운
- text[tekst] 동 문자를 보내다
- throat[θrout] 명 목구멍
- thumb[θʌm] 명 엄지손가락
- tip[tip] 명 조언
- toothache[túːθeik] 명 치통
- unwise[ənwáiz] 형 현명하지 않은
- various[véəriəs] 형 다양한
- while[hwail] 접 ~하는 동안
- without[wiðáut] 전 ~ 없이
- zombie[zámbi] 명 좀비, 반쯤 죽은 것 같은 사람

Key Expressions

- a few 몇몇의
- a heating pad 찜질 패드
- all over the world 전 세계적으로
- be good at ~ ~을 잘하다
- eye level 눈높이
- fall asleep 잠들다
- for example 예를 들어
- from now on 지금부터
- get hurt 다치다
- get into ~ (~한 상태에) 처하다
- have a cold 감기에 걸리다
- have a fever 열이 나다
- have a runny nose 콧물이 흐르다
- have a sore throat 목이 아프다
- Here are+복수 명사 여기에 ~가 있다
- instead of ~ ~ 대신에
- look well 건강해 보이다
- take a rest 휴식을 취하다, 쉬다
- take medicine 약을 먹다
- talk to ~ ~에게 말하다
- text message 문자 메시지
- these days 요즘
- traffic light 교통 신호등
- try to+동사원형 ~하려고 애쓰다[노력하다]
- turn off ~을 끄다
- Why don't you+동사원형 ~? ~하는 게 어때?

Word Power

※ 서로 반대되는 뜻을 가진 단어

- □ **wise** (현명한) ↔ **unwise** (현명하지 않은)
- □ **nervous** (초조한) ↔ **calm** (차분한)
- □ **dry** (건조한) ↔ **wet** (젖은)
- □ **without** (~ 없이) ↔ **with** (~을 가지고)
- □ **increase** (증가하다) ↔ **decrease** (감소하다)
- □ **careful** (조심하는) ↔ **careless** (부주의한)

- □ **well** (건강한) ↔ **ill** (아픈)
- □ **cheap** (싼) ↔ **expensive** (비싼)
- □ **interesting** (흥미로운) ↔ **uninteresting** (재미없는)
- □ **difficult** (어려운) ↔ **easy** (쉬운)
- □ **turn off** (끄다) ↔ **turn on** (켜다)
- □ **intelligent** (똑똑한) ↔ **stupid** (어리석은)

※ 서로 비슷한 뜻을 가진 단어

- □ **sore** : **painful** (아픈)
- □ **well** : **healthy** (건강한)
- □ **advice** : **tip** (조언, 충고)
- □ **prevent** : **inhibit** (막다)

- □ **terrible** : **awful** (끔찍한, 지독한)
- □ **nervous** : **anxious** (초조한, 불안한)
- □ **various** : **varied** (다양한)
- □ **pain** : **suffering** (고통)

English Dictionary

- □ **addiction** 중독
  → the problem when someone cannot stop doing something, or does something too much
  어떤 일을 하는 것을 멈출 수 없거나 너무 많이 할 때의 문제

- □ **blink** 눈을 깜박이다
  → to open and close your eyes very quickly
  매우 빨리 눈을 뜨고 감다

- □ **cause** 야기하다
  → to make something happen
  어떤 일이 발생하도록 하다

- □ **medicine** 약, 약물
  → a pill or a liquid that you take when you are sick to help you get better
  아플 때 나아지도록 하기 위해 복용하는 알약 또는 액체

- □ **pad** 패드
  → a thick piece of soft material
  부드러운 소재의 두꺼운 조각

- □ **pain** 고통
  → the feeling you have when a part of your body hurts
  신체의 일부가 아플 때 가지는 느낌

- □ **prevent** 막다, 예방하다
  → to stop something from happening, or stop someone from doing
  어떤 일이 일어나거나 누군가가 하는 것을 막다

- □ **regularly** 규칙적으로
  → at the same time every day, every week, etc.
  매일, 매주 등의 같은 시간에

- □ **rest** 휴식
  → a time when you relax or sleep
  쉬거나 잠을 자는 시간

- □ **safety** 안전
  → the state of being safe and protected from danger or harm
  위험이나 해로부터 안전하고 보호받는 상태

- □ **text** 문자를 보내다
  → to send someone a written message using a cell phone
  휴대전화를 이용하여 누군가에게 문자 메시지를 보내다

- □ **throat** 목구멍
  → the passage at the back of your mouth, where you swallow
  음식을 삼키는 입의 뒤쪽에 있는 통로

- □ **thumb** 엄지손가락
  → the short thick finger on your hand that helps you hold things
  물건을 집는 데 도움이 되는 손에 있는 짧고 두꺼운 손가락

서답형

01 다음 문장의 빈칸에 주어진 영어 설명에 해당하는 말을 쓰시오.

> used when one thing replaces another, or when you do a different thing

> • Turn off your smartphone during meals or meetings. You can talk to people _____ _____ texting them.

➡ _____

02 다음 빈칸에 공통으로 들어갈 말은? (대 · 소문자 무시)

> • I think you have a cold. _____ this medicine and make sure you _____ a good rest.

① take   ② get   ③ go
④ make   ⑤ look

서답형

03 다음 우리말에 맞게 빈칸에 알맞은 단어를 쓰시오.

> 너는 스마트폰을 볼 때 자주 눈을 깜박이지 않는다.

➡ When you look at your smartphone, you do not _____ often.

04 다음 글의 흐름상 빈칸에 들어갈 가장 적절한 단어는?

> Do you feel sad when you check your smartphone and there is no text message? If your answers are "yes," you may have smartphone _____.

① pain   ② author
③ addiction   ④ promise
⑤ celebrity

[05~06] 다음 영영풀이에 해당하는 단어를 고르시오.

05

> the feeling you have when a part of your body hurts

① sour   ② hurt
③ pain   ④ addiction
⑤ stress

06

> at the same time every day, every week, etc.

① sometimes   ② always
③ carefully   ④ simply
⑤ regularly

서답형

07 다음 짝지어진 단어의 관계가 같도록 빈칸에 알맞은 말을 쓰시오.

> well : healthy = anxious : _____

08 다음 빈칸에 들어갈 말이 알맞게 짝지어진 것은?

> • Unwise or too much use of smartphones can _____ various problems.
> • When you look down at your smartphone, the stress on your neck _____s.

① prevent – decrease
② prevent – increase
③ hurt – prevent
④ cause – increase
⑤ cause – decrease

01 다음 빈칸에 들어갈 말을 〈보기〉에서 찾아 쓰시오. (필요하면 변형하여 쓰시오.)

┌─ 보기 ─┐
nervous　well　have　smombie
└────────┘

(1) I think he _____ a headache.

(2) You don't look _____. What's wrong?

(3) If you are a _____, you can have various safety problems.

(4) I get _____ when my smartphone is not around.

02 다음 영영풀이에 알맞은 단어를 〈보기〉에서 찾아 첫 번째 칸에 쓰고, 두 번째 칸에는 우리말 뜻을 쓰시오.

┌─ 보기 ─┐
pad　medicine　addiction　text
blink　fever　　nervous　　prevent
└────────┘

(1) _____ : to stop something from happening, or stop someone from doing: _____

(2) _____ : a pill or a liquid that you take when you are sick to help you get better: _____

(3) _____ : the problem when someone cannot stop doing something, or does something too much: _____

03 다음 빈칸에 들어갈 알맞은 단어를 주어진 철자로 시작하여 쓰시오.

• Many people like sending t_____ messages more than calling.

• Too much use of smartphones can c_____ dry eyes.

04 다음 우리말과 같은 표현이 되도록 문장의 빈칸을 채우시오.

(1) 스마트폰 없이 사는 것은 요즘 많은 사람들에게 어렵다.
　➡ Living _____ smartphones is difficult for many of us these days.

(2) 우리는 그러한 사람들을 스몸비, 즉 스마트폰 좀비라고 부른다.
　➡ We call _____ people smombies, smartphone zombies.

(3) 지금부터, 나는 매일 30분 동안 걸으려고 노력할 것이다.
　➡ _____ _____ _____, I will try to walk for 30 minutes every day.

(4) 잠자리에서 스마트폰을 사용하면, 쉽게 잠들지 못할 거야.
　➡ If you use your smartphone in bed, you may not _____ _____ easily.

05 다음 빈칸에 들어갈 말을 〈보기〉에서 골라 알맞은 형태로 고쳐 쓰시오.

┌─ 보기 ─┐
regular　nerve　addict　vary　text
└────────┘

(1) People may have smartphone _____ if they feel anxious when their smartphones are not around.

(2) Make sure you exercise _____.

(3) Unwise or too much use of smartphones can cause _____ problems.

(4) He did not notice the car because he was _____.

Conversation

1 문제점이나 증상을 묻고 답하기

> **A** What's wrong? 무슨 일이니?
> **B** I have a headache. 머리가 아파요.

■ 상대방이 기분이 좋지 않거나 어딘가 아파 보일 때 What's wrong (with you)?라고 묻는다. What's the matter (with you)?라고 물을 수도 있다.

■ **문제점이나 증상을 묻는 다양한 표현들**
"무슨 일 있니?"라는 의미로 What's wrong with you? / What's the matter? / Is there anything wrong? / What happened? / What's the problem? 등을 사용한다.

■ **증상 답하기**
'나는 ~가 아프다.'는 'I have a/an+명사'로 나타내는데, 명사 자리에 아픈 증상이나 병명을 써서 어디가 아픈지를 표현한다. 아픈 증상을 나타내는 말은 주로 신체 부위 뒤에 '아픔, 통증'을 뜻하는 'ache'를 붙여 쓴다. 예를 들면 head(머리)에 ache를 붙이면 '두통'이라는 뜻의 'headache'가 된다. 이와 같은 형태로 요통 'backache', 귀앓이 'earache', 치통 'toothache' 등의 표현을 쓴다.

• A: You don't look well. 너 몸이 안 좋아 보여.
  What's wrong? 무슨 일 있니?
  B: I have a headache. 머리가 아파.

• A: What's the matter? 무슨 일 있니?
  B: My dog ate my homework. 내 개가 내 숙제를 먹어 버렸어.

• A: What's wrong, Peter? 무슨 일이니, Peter?
  B: I don't know, Ms. Kim, but my back hurts a lot. 모르겠어요, 김 선생님, 하지만 등이 매우 아파요.

핵심 Check

1. 다음 대화의 빈칸에 알맞은 말을 쓰시오.

   A: _____ _____ with your leg, Sam?

   B: I fell and hurt my foot while I was playing soccer.

2. 다음 주어진 문장과 같은 의미가 되도록 빈칸에 알맞은 말을 쓰시오.

   What's wrong?

   = Is there _____ _____?

2 당부하기

Make sure you take some medicine. 약을 꼭 먹도록 하렴.

■ 상대방에게 당부하는 표현으로 '반드시 ~하도록 해라, ~을 확실히 해라'라는 의미의 'make sure ~'를 사용한다. make sure 다음에 접속사 that을 생략할 수 있고 당부하고자 하는 내용을 주어와 동사를 갖춘 문장으로 쓴다. 즉, sure 다음에는 '(that+)주어+동사'를 쓴다. 유사한 의미를 가진 표현으로 'You had better+동사원형 ~', 'Don't forget to+동사원형 ~', 'Remember to+동사원형 ~' 등이 있다.

당부하기 표현

- A: Well, make sure you take a warm bath. 음. 꼭 따뜻하게 목욕을 하도록 하렴.

  B: OK. Thanks a lot. 알았어요. 고마워요.
- A: I think I caught a cold. 나 감기에 걸린 것 같아.

  B: That's too bad. Make sure you take some medicine and relax. 안됐구나. 꼭 약을 먹고 쉬렴.
- Remember to call me when you leave. 떠날 때 나에게 전화하는 것을 기억해라.
- Don't forget to call me when you arrive. 도착하면 나에게 전화하는 것을 잊지 마.
- You had better call me when you arrive. 너는 도착하면 나에게 전화하는 것이 좋겠다.

■ 상대방의 당부를 받아들일 때 make sure 다음에 긍정문이 오면 'OK. I will.'로 답하고, 부정문이 오면 'OK. I won't.'로 답한다.

- A: Make sure you give me a call when you get home. 집에 도착하면 내게 꼭 전화해.

  B: Okay, I will. 응. 그렇게 할게.
- A: Make sure you won't be late for the class again. 다시는 수업에 지각하지 마.

  B: Okay, I won't. 네. 안 할게요.

핵심 Check

3. 다음 대화의 빈칸에 들어갈 알맞은 것은?

A: Mom, can I play soccer with my friends after school?

B: Sure, but _____.

① you don't have to play soccer

② you can't

③ you had better not play soccer

④ don't forget to stay home after school

⑤ make sure you come home before dinner

A. Listen and Talk A-1

W: You ❶look sick. ❷What's wrong, Inho?

B: ❸I have a sore throat. I have a fever, too.

W: I think you have a cold. ❹Take this medicine and ❺make sure you take a good rest.

B: OK. Thank you.

W: 너 아파 보인다. 무슨 일이니, 인호야?
B: 목이 아파요. 열도 나요.
W: 감기에 걸린 것 같구나. 이 약을 먹고 좀 쉬도록 하렴.
B: 알겠어요. 감사합니다.

❶ 'look+형용사'는 '~처럼 보인다'는 의미이다.
❷ 문제점이나 증상을 묻는 표현으로 Is there anything wrong?, What happened?, What's the problem? 등으로 물을 수 있다.
❸ '나는 ~가 아프다.'는 표현으로 'I have a/an+명사'로 나타내는데, 명사 자리에 아픈 증상이나 병명을 써서 어디가 아픈지 표현한다.
❹ '약을 복용하다'라는 의미로 동사 take를 사용한다.
❺ 'make sure ~'는 상대방에게 당부하는 표현으로 '반드시 ~하도록 해라, ~을 확실히 해라'라는 의미다. '쉬다, 휴식을 취하다'는 표현에 동사 take를 사용한다.

Check(√) True or False

(1) Inho has a cold.　　　　　　　　　　　　　　　T ☐ F ☐

(2) The woman may be a school nurse.　　　　　　　T ☐ F ☐

B. Listen and Talk C

W: ❶What's wrong, Andy?

B: Hello, Ms. Kim. My right thumb hurts.

W: Hmm. Do you use your smartphone a lot?

B: Yes, ❷I text a lot. Why?

W: I think you have texting thumb.

B: Texting thumb? What's texting thumb?

W: It's pain in your thumb. You can get it from ❸texting too much.

B: Oh, I didn't know that.

W: ❹Why don't you do some finger stretching exercises?

B: OK, I will.

W: And ❺make sure you don't text too much.

W: 무슨 일이니, Andy?
B: 안녕하세요, 김 선생님. 제 오른손 엄지손가락이 아파요.
W: 음. 너 스마트폰을 많이 사용하니?
B: 네, 저 문자를 많이 해요. 왜요?
W: 내 생각에 너는 texting thumb인 것 같아.
B: texting thumb이요? texting thumb이 뭐예요?
W: 엄지손가락에 통증이 있는 거야. 문자를 너무 많이 하면 생길 수 있어.
B: 오, 그건 몰랐네요.
W: 손가락 스트레칭 운동을 좀 하는 게 어떠니?
B: 네, 그럴게요.
W: 그리고 문자를 너무 많이 하지 않도록 하렴.

❶ 문제점이나 증상을 물어볼 때 사용하는 표현으로 'What's the matter?'로 바꾸어 쓸 수 있다.
❷ text는 동사로 '문자를 보내다'는 의미다.
❸ 전치사 from 뒤의 texting은 전치사의 목적어로 사용된 동명사이다.
❹ 'Why don't you+동사원형 ~?'은 '~하는 게 어때?'라는 뜻으로 제안이나 권유를 할 때 사용하는 표현이다.
❺ 상대방에게 당부하는 표현으로 '반드시 ~하도록 해라, ~을 확실히 해라'라는 의미이다.

Check(√) True or False

(3) Andy's right thumb hurts.　　　　　　　　　　　T ☐ F ☐

(4) Andy won't do any finger stretching exercises.　　T ☐ F ☐

Listen and Talk A-2

W: ❶What's wrong, Peter?

B: I don't know, Ms. Kim, but ❷my back hurts a lot.

W: ❸Put a heating pad on it.

B: OK, I will.

W: And ❹make sure you do some stretching exercises.

❶ Is there anything wrong?, What happened?, What's the problem? 등과 같은 표현으로 문제점이나 증상을 물어볼 때 사용한다.

❷ 여기서 back은 명사로 '등'을 의미한다. a lot은 동사 hurts를 수식하는 부사구로 '많이'의 의미다.

❸ put A on B 형태로 'A를 B에 놓다'는 의미다.

❹ 상대방에게 당부하는 표현으로 '반드시 ~하도록 해라, ~을 확실히 해라'라는 의미다.

Listen and Talk A-3

W: ❶What's the matter, Chris?

B: I have a terrible toothache.

W: ❷Here is some medicine. Take this.

B: Thank you.

W: And make sure you ❸go to the dentist.

B: OK, I will.

❶ 문제점이나 증상을 물어볼 때 사용하는 표현이다.

❷ 'Here is+단수 명사'로 '여기에 ~가 있다'는 의미다

❸ go to the dentist는 '치과에 가다'는 의미다.

Listen and Talk A-4

W: What's wrong with your leg, Sam?

B: I fell and hurt my foot ❶while I was playing soccer.

W: Can you walk?

B: Yes, but it hurts a lot.

W: ❷Why don't you put some ice on it? And make sure you don't play soccer until next week.

❶ while은 접속사로 '~하는 동안'의 의미다.

❷ 'Why don't you+동사원형 ~?'은 '~하는 게 어때?'라는 의미이다.

Listen and Talk B-1

A: You don't ❶look well. What's wrong?

B: I have a headache.

A: ❷That's too bad. Make sure you ❸take some medicine.

B: OK, I will.

❶ 'look+형용사'로 여기서 well은 형용사로 '건강한'의 의미다.

❷ 상대방의 안 좋은 일이나 소식에 대해 '안 됐다'라는 의미다.

❸ take는 '복용하다, 먹다'는 의미다.

Listen and Talk B-2

A: You don't look well. What's wrong?

B: I have a cold.

A: That's too bad. Make sure you ❶go see a doctor.

B: OK, I will.

❶ 'go see a doctor'는 '병원에 가다'는 의미로 해석한다.

Review 1

G: ❶What's wrong, Mike?

B: ❷I have a terrible headache.

G: I think you ❸should take some medicine.

B: OK, I will.

❶ Is there anything wrong?, What happened?, What's the problem? 등과 같은 표현으로 문제점이나 증상을 물어볼 때 사용한다.

❷ '나는 ~가 아프다.'는 표현으로 'I have a/an+명사'로 나타내는데, 명사 자리에 아픈 증상이나 병명을 써서 어디가 아픈지 표현한다.

❸ 상대방에게 조언을 할 때 조동사 should를 사용한다.

Review 2

M: What's the matter, Mina?

G: I ❶have a sore throat. I also ❷have a runny nose.

M: I think you have a cold. Make sure you get some rest.

G: OK, I will.

❶ 'have a sore throat'는 '목이 아프다'는 의미다.

❷ 'have a runny nose'는 '콧물이 난다'는 의미다.

● 다음 우리말과 일치하도록 빈칸에 알맞은 말을 쓰시오.

Listen and Talk A-1

W: You look sick. _____ _____, Inho?
B: I _____ _____ _____ _____. I _____ _____ _____, too.
W: I think you _____ _____ _____. _____ this medicine and _____ _____ you _____ a good rest.
B: OK. Thank you.

해석
W: 너 아파 보인다. 무슨 일이니, 인호야?
B: 목이 아파요. 열도 나요.
W: 감기에 걸린 것 같구나. 이 약을 먹고 좀 쉬도록 하렴.
B: 알겠어요. 감사합니다.

Listen and Talk A-2

W: What's _____, Peter?
B: I don't know, Ms. Kim, but my back _____ a lot.
W: _____ a heating pad _____ it.
B: OK, I will.
W: And _____ _____ you do some stretching exercises.

W: 무슨 일이니, Peter?
B: 모르겠어요, 김 선생님, 등이 아파요.
W: 그곳에 찜질 패드를 올려놓으렴.
B: 네, 그럴게요.
W: 그리고 스트레칭 운동을 하렴.

Listen and Talk A-3

W: What's the _____, Chris?
B: I _____ _____ terrible toothache.
W: _____ _____ some medicine. _____ this.
B: Thank you.
W: And _____ _____ you go to the dentist.
B: OK, I will.

W: 무슨 일이니, Chris?
B: 저는 심한 치통이 있어요.
W: 여기 약이 있단다. 이것을 먹으렴.
B: 감사합니다.
W: 그리고 치과에 가도록 하렴.
B: 네, 알겠어요.

Listen and Talk A-4

W: What's _____ _____ your leg, Sam?
B: I fell and hurt my foot _____ I was playing soccer.
W: Can you walk?
B: Yes, but it _____ a lot.
W: _____ _____ _____ put some ice on it? And _____ _____ you don't play soccer _____ next week.

W: 다리에 무슨 문제가 있니, Sam?
B: 축구를 하다가 넘어져서 발을 다쳤어요.
W: 걸을 수는 있겠니?
B: 네, 하지만 많이 아파요.
W: 얼음을 그 위에 올려놓는 게 어떠니? 그리고 다음 주까지는 축구를 하지 않도록 하렴.

Listen and Talk B

1. **A:** You don't _____ _____. What's wrong?

   B: I _____ a headache.

   A: _____ _____ _____. Make sure you _____ some medicine.

   B: OK, I _____.

2. **A:** You _____ _____ _____. What's _____?

   B: I have a _____.

   A: That's too bad. _____ _____ you go see a doctor.

   B: OK, I will.

Listen and Talk C

W: What's _____, Andy?

B: Hello, Ms. Kim. My right _____ hurts.

W: Hmm. Do you use your smartphone _____ _____?

B: Yes, I _____ a lot. Why?

W: I think you _____ texting thumb.

B: Texting thumb? What's texting thumb?

W: It's _____ in your thumb. You can _____ it from _____ too much.

B: Oh, I didn't know that.

W: _____ _____ _____ do some finger stretching exercises?

B: OK, I will.

W: And _____ _____ you don't text too much.

Review 1

G: What's wrong, Mike?

B: I _____ _____ _____ headache.

G: I think you _____ _____ some medicine.

B: OK, I will.

Review 2

M: What's _____ _____, Mina?

G: I _____ _____ _____ _____ _____. I also have a _____ nose.

M: I think you have a cold. _____ _____ you get some rest.

G: OK, I will.

해석

1. A: 너 몸이 안 좋아 보여. 무슨 일 있니?
   B: 머리가 아파.
   A: 안됐다. 약을 먹으렴.
   B: 응, 그렇게.

2. A: 너 몸이 안 좋아 보여. 무슨 일 있니?
   B: 감기에 걸렸어.
   A: 안됐다. 병원에 가도록 하렴.
   B: 응, 그렇게.

W: 무슨 일이니, Andy?
B: 안녕하세요, 김 선생님. 제 오른손 엄지손가락이 아파요.
W: 음. 너 스마트폰을 많이 사용하니?
B: 네, 저 문자를 많이 해요. 왜요?
W: 내 생각에 너는 texting thumb인 것 같아.
B: texting thumb이요? texting thumb이 뭐예요?
W: 엄지손가락에 통증이 있는 거야. 문자를 너무 많이 하면 생길 수 있어.
B: 오, 그건 몰랐네요.
W: 손가락 스트레칭 운동을 좀 하는 게 어떠니?
B: 네, 그럴게요.
W: 그리고 문자를 너무 많이 하지 않도록 하렴.

G: 무슨 일 있니, Mike?
B: 머리가 너무 아파.
G: 너는 약을 먹는 것이 좋겠다.
B: 알겠어, 그럴게.

M: 무슨 일 있니, 미나야?
G: 목이 아파요. 그리고 콧물도 나요.
M: 내 생각에 네가 감기에 걸린 것 같구나. 좀 쉬도록 하렴.
G: 네, 그럴게요.

01 다음 우리말에 맞도록 빈칸에 들어갈 알맞은 말을 쓰시오.

> 좀 쉬도록 하렴.

➡ _____ _____ you get some rest.

02 다음 대화의 빈칸에 들어갈 말로 어색한 것은?

> W: _____, Sam?
> B: I fell and hurt my foot while I was playing soccer.

① What's wrong with you
② What's the matter with you
③ What happened
④ What do you mean
⑤ What's wrong with your leg

03 다음 대화의 빈칸에 들어갈 말로 어색한 것은?

> W: You look sick. What's wrong, Inho?
> B: I have a sore throat. I have a fever, too.
> W: I think you have a cold. _____
> B: OK. Thank you.

① Don't forget to go see a doctor.
② Make sure you take a good rest.
③ Remember to go to the dentist.
④ You should drink a lot of water.
⑤ Take this medicine.

04 다음 대화의 밑줄 친 우리말에 맞게 문장의 빈칸을 채우시오.

> A: You don't look well. What's wrong?
> B: 머리가 아파요.

➡ I _____ _____ headache.

[01~02] 다음 대화를 읽고 물음에 답하시오.

W: _____(A)_____, Chris?

B: I have a terrible toothache.

W: Here is some medicine. ___(B)___ this.

B: Thank you.

W: And make sure you go to the dentist.

B: OK, I will.

01 위 대화의 빈칸 (A)에 들어갈 말로 <u>어색한</u> 것은?

① What's wrong

② What's the problem

③ What's the matter

④ How's it going

⑤ Is there anything wrong

02 위 대화의 빈칸 (B)에 들어갈 말로 알맞은 것은?

① Want   ② Bring

③ Leave   ④ Make

⑤ Take

03 다음 대화의 순서를 바르게 배열한 것은?

(A) I have a sore throat. I also have a runny nose.

(B) I think you have a cold. Make sure you get some rest.

(C) OK, I will.

(D) What's the matter, Mina?

① (A) – (B) – (C) – (D)

② (B) – (A) – (C) – (D)

③ (B) – (C) – (A) – (D)

④ (D) – (A) – (B) – (C)

⑤ (D) – (B) – (A) – (C)

[04~06] 다음 대화를 읽고 물음에 답하시오.

G: (A)What's wrong, Mike?

B: I ___ⓐ___ a terrible headache.

G: (B)You should take some medicine.

B: OK, I will.

04 위 대화의 빈칸 ⓐ에 들어갈 말로 알맞은 것은?

① take   ② make

③ catch   ④ explain

⑤ have

서답형
05 위 대화의 밑줄 친 (A)와 같은 뜻이 되도록 다음 문장의 빈칸을 채우시오.

= What's _____ _____ with you

= What _____

06 위 대화의 밑줄 친 (B)와 바꾸어 쓸 수 <u>없는</u> 것은?

① You had better take some medicine.

② Make sure you take some medicine.

③ Don't forget to take some medicine.

④ Remember to take some medicine.

⑤ Don't remember to take some medicine.

07 다음 대화의 밑줄 친 부분의 의도로 알맞은 것은?

A: You don't look well. What's wrong?

B: I have a headache.

A: That's too bad. <u>Make sure you take some medicine.</u>

B: OK, I will.

① 안부 묻기   ② 의무 표현하기

③ 요청하기   ④ 당부하기

⑤ 의견 묻기

[08~10] 다음 대화를 읽고 물음에 답하시오.

W: What's the matter, Chris?
B: I have a terrible (A)toothache.
W: (B)여기 약이 있단다. Take this.
B: Thank you.
W: And _____ (C) _____.
B: OK, I will.

서답형

08 다음 문장은 밑줄 친 (A)에 대한 영어 설명이다. 빈칸에 알맞은 단어를 쓰시오.

a _____ in a tooth

➡ _____

서답형

09 위 대화의 밑줄 친 (B)의 우리말에 맞게 다음 문장의 빈칸을 완성하시오.

➡ _____ _____ some medicine.

10 위 대화의 빈칸 (C)에 들어갈 말로 가장 적절한 것은?

① make sure you do some exercises
② don't play soccer
③ make sure you go to the dentist
④ make sure you don't text too much
⑤ you need to eat well

[11~13] 다음 대화를 읽고 물음에 답하시오.

W: (A)무슨 일이니, Andy?
B: Hello, Ms. Kim. My right thumb hurts.
W: Hmm. (①) Do you use your smartphone a lot?
B: Yes, I text a lot. Why?
W: (②) I think you have texting thumb.
B: Texting thumb? (③) What's texting thumb?
W: (④) You can get it from texting too much.
B: Oh, I didn't know that. (⑤)

W: Why don't you do some finger stretching exercises?
B: OK, I will.
W: And make sure you don't text too much.

서답형

11 위 대화의 밑줄 친 (A)의 우리말에 맞게 주어진 단어를 이용하여 영어로 쓰시오.

what, matter, with

➡ _____

서답형

12 다음 주어진 문장이 들어갈 위치로 알맞은 것은?

It's pain in your thumb.

①   ②   ③   ④   ⑤

13 위 대화의 내용과 일치하지 <u>않는</u> 것은?

① Andy uses his smartphone a lot.
② Andy texts a lot.
③ Andy feels pain in his right thumb.
④ Ms. Kim advises Andy to do some finger stretching exercises.
⑤ Ms. Kim doesn't text too much.

중요

14 다음 중 짝지어진 대화가 <u>어색한</u> 것은?

① A: What's wrong?
   B: I have a headache.
② A: What's the matter, Chris?
   B: I have a terrible toothache.
③ A: Here is some medicine. Take this.
   B: Thank you.
④ A: You don't look well. Is there anything wrong?
   B: No problem. I have a headache.
⑤ A: I have a sore throat. I have a fever, too.
   B: I think you have a cold.

[01~02] 다음 대화를 읽고 물음에 답하시오.

W: You look sick. What's ⓐ , Inho?

B: I ⓑ a sore throat. I have a fever, too.

W: I think you ⓒ a cold. (A)이 약을 먹고 꼭 충분히 쉬도록 하렴.

B: OK. Thank you.

01 위 대화의 흐름상 빈칸 ⓐ~ⓒ에 알맞은 말을 쓰시오.

➡ ⓐ _____ ⓑ _____ ⓒ _____

02 위 대화의 밑줄 친 (A)의 우리말에 맞게 주어진 어구를 이용하여 영어로 쓰시오.

> medicine, and, make, take you, a, good rest

➡ _____

03 다음 대화의 밑줄 친 우리말에 맞게 주어진 단어를 이용하여 빈칸을 채우시오.

> W: (A)다리에 무슨 문제가 있니, Sam?
>
> B: I fell and hurt my foot (B)축구를 하다가.
>
> W: Can you walk?
>
> B: Yes, but it hurts a lot.
>
> W: Why don't you put some ice on it? And (C)축구를 하지 않도록 하렴 until next week.

➡ (A) _____
　　　(wrong, with, leg)
　　(B) _____
　　　(while, was, soccer)
　　(C) _____
　　　(make, sure, play)

[04~05] 다음 대화를 읽고 물음에 답하시오.

W: What's wrong, Andy?

B: Hello, Ms. Kim. My right thumb hurts.

W: Hmm. Do you use your smartphone a lot?

B: Yes, I text a lot. Why?

W: I think you have texting thumb.

B: Texting thumb? What's texting thumb?

W: _____ (A) _____ You can get it from texting too much.

B: Oh, I didn't know that.

W: Why don't you do some finger stretching exercises?

B: OK, I will.

W: And _____ (B) _____ .

04 위 대화의 내용으로 보아 Andy의 질문에 대한 답으로 (A)에 들어갈 알맞은 말을 완성하시오.

➡ It's _____ in your _____ .

05 위 대화의 빈칸 (B)에 들어갈 Ms. Kim의 충고를 완성하시오.

➡ _____ _____ you _____ _____ too much

06 다음 대화의 충고를 읽고, 빈칸에 들어갈 말을 주어진 단어를 이용하여 완성하시오.

> A: What's wrong, Peter?
>
> B: _____
>
> A: I think you need to eat well. Try to eat lots of fresh fruit and vegetables. And make sure you exercise regularly.
>
> B: OK, I will.

➡ _____ (get, tire, easily)

Grammar

교과서

• Another problem **(which/that)** you can have is neck pain.
네가 가질 수 있는 또 다른 문제는 목 통증이다.

■ 관계대명사절에서 관계대명사의 역할이 목적어일 때 이것을 목적격 관계대명사라고 하며, 관계대명사 절의 첫머리에 위치해야 한다.

■ 목적격 관계대명사는 수식하는 선행사가 사람이면 who나 whom, that을, 사람이 아니면 which나 that 을 쓴다. 목적격 관계대명사는 생략될 수 있다.

• I know the man **(who/whom/that)** you met yesterday. 나는 네가 어제 만난 그 남자를 알아.

• This is the book **(which/that)** I have chosen. 이것이 내가 고른 책이다.

■ 목적격 관계대명사절을 만들 때 특히 주의할 것은 동사 뒤에 목적어가 없다는 것인데, 이것은 앞에 있 는 관계대명사가 동사의 목적어 역할을 하기 때문이다.

• The person is my father. I respect **him(=the person)** the most.

= The person **(who/whom/that)** I respect the most is my father.

• John is reading the book. He bought **it(=the book)** last Saturday.

= John is reading the book **(which/that)** he bought last Saturday.

■ 목적격 관계대명사가 전치사의 목적어인 경우 전치사는 관계대명사절의 끝에 오거나 관계대명사 앞에 올 수 있다. 전치사가 관계대명사절의 끝에 올 경우에는 관계대명사를 생략할 수 있다. 전치사가 관계 대명사 앞에 올 경우에는 관계대명사 that을 쓸 수 없으며, 관계대명사를 생략하지 않는다.

• This is the pen **(which/that)** he wrote the novel with. 이것은 그가 그 소설을 쓰는 데 썼던 펜이다.

= This is the pen with **which** he wrote the novel.

= This is the pen with that he wrote the novel. (×)

핵심 Check

1. 다음 우리말에 맞게 빈칸에 알맞은 말을 쓰시오.

(1) 나는 John이 말한 그 사람을 알고 있어요.

➡ I know the man _____ John mentioned.

(2) 그는 엄마가 만들어 주는 피자를 먹는 것을 좋아한다.

➡ He likes to eat the pizza _____ his mom makes.

2 call A B

- We **call** such people smombies. 우리는 그런 사람들을 스몸비라고 부른다.
- We **elected** her chairman. 우리는 그녀를 의장으로 선출했다.

■ 'call A B'는 'A를 B라고 부르다'라는 의미로, 문법적으로는 call 다음의 명사[대명사] A를 목적어, 그리고 B에 해당하는 명사를 목적격 보어로 볼 수 있는 5형식 구문이다.

- They will **call** their daughter Sophie. 그들은 그들의 딸을 Sophie라고 부를 것이다.

■ call A B와 유사하게 목적격 보어 자리에 명사가 올 수 있는 동사로는 make, name, elect, consider 등이 있다.

call A B	A를 B라고 부르다
name A B	A를 B라고 이름 짓다
make A B	A를 B로 만들다
elect A B	A를 B로 선출하다
consider A B	A를 B로 여기다[생각하다]

- I **consider** him a friend. 나는 그를 친구로 생각한다.

■ 동사 다음에 두 개의 명사가 목적어, 목적격 보어로 쓰인다는 점에서는 consider, believe 등의 동사와 유사해 보이지만, call은 목적격 보어로 형용사나 to부정사를 취하지 않는다는 점에 유의한다.

- Can we **call** it a success? 우리가 그것을 성공이라고 부를 수 있느냐?
- We **named** her Mina. 우리는 그녀를 Mina라고 이름 지었다.
- She **made** her son a teacher. 그녀는 그녀의 아들을 선생님으로 만들었다.
- I **believe** him honest. 나는 그가 정직하다고 생각한다.

핵심 Check

2. 다음 우리말에 맞게 빈칸에 알맞은 말을 쓰시오.

(1) 우리는 이것을 text neck이라고 부른다.

➡ We _____ this _____ _____.

(2) 그의 발명은 그를 부자로 만들었다.

➡ His invention _____ him a _____ _____.

Grammar 시험대비 기본평가

01 다음 빈칸에 들어갈 말로 알맞지 <u>않은</u> 것을 <u>모두</u> 고르시오.

> The friend _____ I met yesterday is Sue.

① who ② whose ③ whom
④ that ⑤ which

02 다음 문장에서 어법상 어색한 부분을 바르게 고쳐 쓰시오.

beast: 짐승 the king of beasts: 백수(百獸)의 왕

(1) He showed me the photos who he had taken in Spain.

_____ ➡ _____

(2) The children which Ms. Collins is teaching are smart.

_____ ➡ _____

(3) We call the lion to be the king of beasts.

_____ ➡ _____

03 다음 우리말에 맞게 괄호 안에 주어진 단어를 바르게 배열하시오.

(1) 이것이 어제 내가 산 신발들이다. (I, the shoes, yesterday, are, bought, these, which)

➡ _____

(2) 우리는 우리 물고기를 Ernie라고 불렀다. (we, Ernie, our, fish, called)

➡ _____

04 다음 우리말을 영어로 옮길 때, 빈칸에 알맞은 말이 순서대로 짝지어진 것은?

> 우리는 화면의 화살표를 커서라고 부른다.
>
> ➡ We call _____ _____.

① the arrow on the screen – a cursor
② a cursor – the arrow on the screen
③ the arrow – a cursor on the screen
④ a cursor on the screen – the arrow
⑤ on the screen a cursor – the arrow

01 다음 〈보기〉의 밑줄 친 부분과 다르게 쓰인 것은?

> ┤ 보기 ├
>
> There are various things that you can do to prevent this.

① Tom bought the book that he wanted to read.

② Wayne met the girl who looked very intelligent at the party.

③ Susan is the girl who I gave some flowers yesterday.

④ The skirt which she is wearing is pretty.

⑤ I want to marry a woman that I love.

02 다음 빈칸에 들어갈 수 있는 말이 다른 하나는?

① Mr. Lee was my teacher _____ taught me math.

② A computer is a thing _____ people do many things with.

③ This is the pen _____ was on the table.

④ Are there any students _____ name hasn't been called?

⑤ Christina Rossetti is the poet _____ I like most.

03 다음 빈칸에 알맞지 않은 것은?

> We _____ him our class president.

① elected   ② made

③ appointed   ④ considered

⑤ took

04 서답형 다음 괄호 안에서 알맞은 말을 고르시오.

(1) I know the boy (which / that) everyone likes.

(2) Monica wants to see *the Mona Lisa* (who / which) Leonardo da Vinci painted.

(3) There was a program in (that / which) I really wanted to take part.

(4) Sharon wore the earrings (whom / which) I gave to her.

(5) We (call / consider) her to be a genius.

➡ (1) _____ (2) _____ (3) _____

(4) _____ (5) _____

05 서답형 다음 우리말을 주어진 어휘를 이용하여 영어로 쓰시오.

> 나는 할아버지께서 내게 해 주신 이야기들을 아직 기억한다. (the stories, still, my grandfather, tell)

➡ _____

_____

06 중요 다음 중 어법상 바르지 않은 것은?

① The movie made her a star.

② Which do you consider to be the most important?

③ They elected Obama President of the USA.

④ They named their baby James.

⑤ We call such music as hip hop.

07 다음 중 어법상 옳은 문장은?

① This is the book who my sister bought last night.

② We sometimes have to eat side dishes whom we don't like.

③ This is the house which she lives.

④ This is something that you should bear in mind.

⑤ James is the only friend which he can trust.

08 다음 밑줄 친 that의 용법이 나머지 넷과 다른 것은?

① My opinion is that he really doesn't understand you.

② This is an animal that has a long nose.

③ The movie that Mike and I watched yesterday was interesting.

④ The cookies that she made were very delicious.

⑤ Jerry never touched the food that he didn't like.

09 다음 중 〈보기〉와 문장의 형식이 다르게 쓰인 것은?

─┤ 보기 ├─
They called their dog Lucky.

① As it is very cold outside, please keep yourself warm.

② We elected him President.

③ Jeff made his son a desk.

④ We found the boy asleep in the sofa.

⑤ Ms. Han named her cat Willow.

10 다음 문장에서 생략할 수 있는 것을 찾아 쓰시오.

(1) The sport that Frank can play well is basketball.

(2) The girl whom you met last night is my sister.

(3) *Annie* is the story of an 11-year-old girl who is named Annie.

➡ (1) _____ (2) _____ (3) _____

11 다음 두 문장을 한 문장으로 바르게 바꾼 것은?

• BJ is a rap singer.
• I like BJ the most.

① BJ is whom a rap singer I like the most.

② BJ is a rap singer which I like the most.

③ BJ is a rap singer who like the most.

④ BJ is a rap singer who I like him the most.

⑤ BJ is a rap singer whom I like the most.

12 다음 중 밑줄 친 부분의 쓰임이 잘못된 것은?

① His success abroad has made him a national hero in Korea.

② They call it strange.

③ I consider it to be the best novel I have written in my life.

④ The students elected her as president of their class.

⑤ The town chose Mr. White as mayor.

서답형

13 다음 두 문장을 관계대명사를 사용하여 한 문장으로 바꾸시오.

(1) • New York is a big city.
   • Many people visit New York every year.

➡ _____

_____

(2) • My favorite subject is math.
   • I'm good at math.

➡ _____

_____

(3) • The man was my math teacher.
   • I saw the man at the mall.

➡ _____

_____

(4) • She is a famous movie star.
   • Many people like her.

➡ _____

_____

(5) • I was surprised at the speed.
   • He learned to speak with the speed.

➡ _____

_____

(6) • Do you know the girl?
   • Anne is talking to the girl.

➡ _____

_____

14 다음 빈칸에 자연스러운 의미가 되도록 들어갈 알맞은 것은?

We _____ Chicago the Windy City.

① call
② want
③ give
④ regard
⑤ have

중요

15 다음 밑줄 친 부분의 쓰임이 어색한 것은?

① This is the road which leads to the library.
② Fall is the season which comes after summer.
③ Philip loves the girl who I love.
④ The young boy to that Jane is talking is Alex.
⑤ The famous man lives in the town which Tom visited last year.

서답형

16 우리말에 맞게 괄호 안의 어휘를 바르게 배열하시오.

(1) 우리는 셰익스피어를 영국의 국민 시인이라고 부른다. (we, Shakespeare, poet, England's, call, national)

➡ _____

(2) 나는 그를 겁쟁이라고 생각한다. (I, him, coward, be, consider, a, to)

➡ _____

17 주어진 문장의 밑줄 친 부분과 용법이 같은 것을 두 개 고르시오.

The spaghetti that Suji made for me yesterday was delicious.

① There was no hope that she would recover her health.
② The actor who I like the most is Robert.
③ I didn't know who you were talking about.
④ The movie which I want to watch is *Alita*.
⑤ They must be swallows that have come back from the south.

01 다음 두 문장을 관계대명사를 이용하여 한 문장으로 연결하여 쓰시오.

(1) • I bought the snack.
   • Everyone likes the snack.

➡ _____

   _____

(2) • *Romeo and Juliet* is the movie.
   • Helen saw *Romeo and Juliet*.

➡ _____

   _____

(3) • The person is my sister.
   • I love the person the most.

➡ _____

   _____

(4) • The author is C. S. Lewis.
   • I like the author the most.

➡ _____

   _____

(5) • Look at the boy.
   • Mary is talking to the boy.

➡ _____

   _____

(6) • Look at Chris and his dog.
   • Bella is playing with them.

➡ _____

   _____

02 다음 괄호 안에 주어진 말을 바르게 배열하여 문장을 완성하시오.

(1) (people / New York City / the Big Apple / call)

➡ _____

(2) (people / hero / him / consider / may / some / a / as / not)

➡ _____

(3) (they / her / the Boxer of the Year / named)

➡ _____

(4) (ability / him / his / person / made / famous / a)

➡ _____

(5) (leader / him / we / be / elected / to / a)

➡ _____

(6) (followers / a genius / him / his / be / believed / to)

➡ _____

(7) (they / Mike / fool / regard / as / a)

➡ _____

03 다음 그림을 보고 괄호 안에 주어진 어휘를 이용하여 문장을 완성하시오.

(the park in the sky / the rooftop garden / call)

➡ We _____.

04 다음 문장에서 잘못된 부분을 바르게 고쳐 문장을 다시 쓰시오.

(1) Andy is the boy which Hajun met in Canada.

➡ _____

_____

(2) The table who my dad made for me is sturdy.

➡ _____

(3) Hemingway is the author whom I like him the most.

➡ _____

(4) The book which he wrote it is fun.

➡ _____

_____

(5) Can I borrow the book about that you told me?

➡ _____

_____

05 두 문장을 관계대명사를 사용하여 한 문장으로 썼을 때, 빈칸에 해당하는 문장을 쓰시오.

(1) • I ate the chocolate cake.

+ • _____

➡ I ate the chocolate cake which my grandmother made.

(2) • Do you remember the people?

+ • _____

➡ Do you remember the people whom we met on the plane?

(3) • _____

+ • He will drive the car while he stays in New York.

➡ He wants to rent a car that he will drive while he stays in New York.

(4) • _____

+ • You can depend on the friend.

➡ Do you have a friend whom you can depend on?

06 다음 문장을 어법에 맞게 고쳐 쓰시오.

(1) They called him to be Mr. Long.

➡ _____

(2) They regarded him their leader.

➡ _____

07 괄호 안에 주어진 어휘를 이용하여 우리말에 맞게 영작하시오.

(1) 우리는 그곳에 매우 바람이 많이 불기 때문에 Chicago를 the Windy City라고 부른다. (it, there, call, windy, because, very) (we로 시작할 것)

➡ _____

_____

(2) 나는 나의 엄마가 내게 만들어 주신 과자를 좋아한다. (like, the cookies, for, make)

➡ _____

_____

(3) 내가 가장 방문하고 싶은 나라는 프랑스이다. (the country, visit, the most)

➡ _____

_____

(4) Harry는 작년에 나와 함께 일했던 파트너였다. (the partner, that, worked)

➡ _____

_____

Reading

Be Smart with Your Smartphones!

without: '～ 없이' (전치사)

Living without smartphones is difficult for many of us these days.
동명사(주어): 단수로 취급 → 단수 동사 is를 쓴다.   요즈음

However, unwise or too much use of smartphones can cause various
unwise와 too much가 or로 연결, 뒤에 나온 use를 수식

problems.

Are you a smombie?

All over the world, people are walking around like zombies. Their
전 세계에 걸쳐   좀비처럼

heads are down, and their eyes are on their smartphones. We call such
그들의 눈은 스마트폰을 향하고 있다   call A B: A를 B라고 부르다

people smombies, smartphone zombies. If you are a smombie, you
smombies와 smartphone zombies는 동격

can have various safety problems. You may not see a hole in the street,
추측(～일지도 모른다)

so you may fall and get hurt. You may get into a car accident, too. So
그래서   다치다

what can you do to prevent these problems? It's simple. Do not look at
to부정사의 부사적 용법(목적)   앞에 나온 다양한 안전 관련 문제들

your smartphone while you are walking!
～하는 동안

Do you have dry eyes or text neck?

Smartphones can cause various health problems. One example is dry
스마트폰이 야기할 수 있는 건강 문제의 한 예

eyes. When you look at your smartphone, you do not blink often. Then
when 이하는 시간의 부사절로 '～할 때'라는 의미

your eyes will feel dry.
feel은 감각동사로 형용사가 보어로 쓰였다.

---

without ～ 없이

cause 일으키다, 야기하다

various 다양한, 여러 가지의

such 그런, 그러한

zombie 좀비 (반쯤 죽은 것 같은 사람)

hole 구덩이

prevent 방지하다, 막다

simple 간단한

text neck 거북목 증후군

dry eye 안구 건조증

text 문자 메시지; (휴대 전화로) 문자를 보내다

📎 **확인문제**

● 다음 문장이 본문의 내용과 일치하면 T, 일치하지 않으면 F를 쓰시오.

1 Living without smartphones is difficult for many of us these days. ☐

2 Smombies are smart zombies. ☐

3 Smombies can have various social problems. ☐

4 Smombies may not see a hole in the street, so they may fall and get hurt. ☐

Another problem you can have is neck pain. When you look down at
problem과 you 사이에 목적격 관계대명사 which/that이 생략되어 있다.
~을 내려다보다

your smartphone, the stress on your neck increases. Too much use of
형용사구

your smartphone, for example, too much texting, can cause neck pain.
Too much use of your smartphone의 한 예

We call this text neck.
call A B: A를 B라고 부르다

Here are some tips for these problems. For dry eyes, try to blink
여기 ~이 있다   try to+동사원형: ~하려고 노력하다. cf. try +-ing: 한번 ~해 보다

often. For text neck, move your smartphone up to your eye level. You
~까지

can also do some neck stretching exercises.

How do you feel when you don't have your smartphone with you?

Do you feel nervous when your smartphone is not around? Do
when 이하는 시간의 부사절로 '~할 때'라는 의미   주위에(부사)

you feel sad when you check your smartphone and there is no text
feel은 감각동사로 형용사가 보어로 쓰였다.   ~이 없다

message? If your answers are "yes," you may have smartphone
things와 you 사이에는 목적격 관계대명사 that 또는 which 생략   추측(~일지도 모른다)   = smartphone addiction:

addiction. There are various things you can do to prevent this. For
~이 있다   to부정사의 부사적 용법(목적)

example, turn off your smartphone during meals or meetings. You can
~을 끄다   ~ 중에

talk to people instead of texting them.
~ 하는 대신에, 뒤에 동명사가 온다.   = people

---

blink (눈을) 깜박거리다

pain 통증, 고통

look down at ~을 내려다보다

increase 증가하다

eye level 눈높이

stretch 늘이다, 뻗다

nervous 초조한

around 주위에

addiction 중독

meal 식사

instead of ~ 대신에

확인문제

- 다음 문장이 본문의 내용과 일치하면 T, 일치하지 <u>않으면</u> F를 쓰시오.

1 When you look at your smartphone, your eyes will feel dry,
   so you should not blink often. ☐

2 When you look down at your smartphone, the stress on your back increases. ☐

3 Too much texting can cause neck pain called text neck. ☐

4 If you feel nervous when your smartphone is not around, you may have smartphone
   addiction. ☐

5 There are few things you can do to prevent smartphone addiction. ☐

6 You can talk to people instead of texting them to prevent smartphone addiction. ☐

● 우리말을 참고하여 빈칸에 알맞은 말을 쓰시오.

1 ＿＿＿＿＿ ＿＿＿＿＿ ＿＿＿＿＿ Your Smartphones!

2 ＿＿＿＿＿ ＿＿＿＿＿ ＿＿＿＿＿ is difficult for many of us these days.

3 However, ＿＿＿＿＿ ＿＿＿＿＿ ＿＿＿＿＿ ＿＿＿＿＿ ＿＿＿＿＿ of smartphones can cause various problems.

4 Are you ＿＿＿＿＿ ＿＿＿＿＿?

5 All over the world, people are walking around ＿＿＿＿＿ ＿＿＿＿＿.

6 Their heads are down, and their eyes are ＿＿＿＿＿ ＿＿＿＿＿ ＿＿＿＿＿.

7 We call ＿＿＿＿＿ ＿＿＿＿＿ smombies, smartphone zombies.

8 If you are a smombie, you can have ＿＿＿＿＿ ＿＿＿＿＿ ＿＿＿＿＿.

9 You ＿＿＿＿＿ ＿＿＿＿＿ ＿＿＿＿＿ a hole in the street, ＿＿＿＿＿ you may fall and get hurt.

10 You may ＿＿＿＿＿ ＿＿＿＿＿ a car accident, too.

11 So what can you do ＿＿＿＿＿ ＿＿＿＿＿ these problems?

12 It's ＿＿＿＿＿.

13 Do not look at your smartphone ＿＿＿＿＿ you are ＿＿＿＿＿!

14 Do you have ＿＿＿＿＿ ＿＿＿＿＿ or ＿＿＿＿＿ ＿＿＿＿＿?

15 Smartphones can cause various ＿＿＿＿＿ ＿＿＿＿＿.

16 One example is ＿＿＿＿＿ ＿＿＿＿＿.

---

1 스마트폰을 현명하게 사용하라!

2 스마트폰 없이 사는 것은 요즘 많은 사람들에게 어렵다.

3 하지만 스마트폰을 현명하지 않게 사용하거나 너무 과도하게 사용하는 것은 다양한 문제를 야기할 수 있다.

4 당신은 스몸비인가요?

5 전 세계적으로 사람들이 좀비처럼 걸어다니고 있다.

6 그들의 머리는 아래를 향하고, 그들의 눈은 스마트폰을 향하고 있다.

7 우리는 그런 사람들을 스몸비, 즉 스마트폰 좀비라고 부른다.

8 만약 당신이 스몸비라면, 당신은 다양한 안전 관련 문제들을 겪을 수 있다.

9 당신은 거리에 있는 구덩이를 보지 못할 수도 있고, 그래서 넘어져서 다칠지도 모른다.

10 당신은 또한 교통사고를 당할지도 모른다.

11 그렇다면 이런 문제들을 방지하기 위해 무엇을 할 수 있을까?

12 간단하다.

13 걷고 있는 동안에는 스마트폰을 보지 마라!

14 당신은 안구 건조증이나 거북목 증후군이 있나요?

15 스마트폰은 다양한 건강상의 문제를 일으킬 수 있다.

16 한 가지 예가 안구 건조증이다.

17 When you _____ _____ your smartphone, you do not _____ often.

18 Then your eyes will _____ _____ .

19 _____ _____ you can have is neck pain.

20 When you _____ _____ _____ your smartphone, the stress _____ your neck increases.

21 _____ _____ _____ of your smartphone, for example, _____ _____ _____ , can cause neck pain.

22 We call this _____ _____ .

23 Here are _____ _____ for these problems.

24 For dry eyes, _____ _____ _____ often.

25 For text neck, move your smartphone _____ _____ _____ _____ _____ .

26 You can also do some _____ _____ _____ .

27 _____ _____ _____ _____ when you don't have your smartphone with you?

28 Do you _____ _____ when your smartphone is not _____ ?

29 Do you _____ _____ when you check your smartphone and there is _____ _____ _____ ?

30 If your answers are "yes," you may have _____ _____ .

31 There are various things you can do _____ _____ _____ .

32 For example, _____ _____ your smartphone _____ meals or meetings.

33 You can talk to people _____ _____ _____ them.

17 스마트폰을 볼 때, 당신은 눈을 자주 깜박거리지 않는다.

18 그러면 눈이 건조하다고 느낄 것이다.

19 일어날 수 있는 또 다른 문제는 목 통증이다.

20 스마트폰을 내려다볼 때, 목에 가해지는 압박이 증가한다.

21 스마트폰을 너무 많이 사용하는 것은, 예를 들어, 너무 많이 문자를 하는 것은 목 통증을 일으킬 수 있다.

22 이런 증상을 거북목 증후군이라고 부른다.

23 여기에 이런 문제들을 위한 몇 가지 조언이 있다.

24 안구 건조증에는, 눈을 자주 깜박이려고 노력해라.

25 거북목 증후군에는 당신의 눈높이까지 스마트폰을 위로 올려라.

26 목 스트레칭 운동 또한 할 수 있다.

27 스마트폰이 없을 때 어떤 기분이 드나요?

28 스마트폰이 주위에 없을 때 당신은 초조한 기분이 드는가?

29 스마트폰을 확인했을 때 아무런 문자 메시지가 없으면 슬픈 기분이 드는가?

30 만약 당신의 대답이 '그렇다'이면, 당신은 스마트폰 중독일지도 모른다.

31 이것을 방지하기 위해 할 수 있는 일은 여러 가지가 있다.

32 예를 들어, 식사나 회의 중에는 스마트폰을 꺼라.

33 문자를 보내는 대신에 사람들과 이야기를 할 수 있다.

● 우리말을 참고하여 본문을 영작하시오.

1 스마트폰을 현명하게 사용하라!

➡ _____

2 스마트폰 없이 사는 것은 요즘 많은 사람들에게 어렵다.

➡ _____

3 하지만 스마트폰을 현명하지 않게 사용하거나 너무 과도하게 사용하는 것은 다양한 문제를 야기할 수 있다.

➡ _____

4 당신은 스몸비인가요?

➡ _____

5 전 세계적으로 사람들이 좀비처럼 걸어다니고 있다.

➡ _____

6 그들의 머리는 아래를 향하고, 그들의 눈은 스마트폰을 향하고 있다.

➡ _____

7 우리는 그런 사람들을 스몸비, 즉 스마트폰 좀비라고 부른다.

➡ _____

8 만약 당신이 스몸비라면, 당신은 다양한 안전 관련 문제들을 겪을 수 있다.

➡ _____

9 당신은 거리에 있는 구덩이를 보지 못할 수도 있고, 그래서 넘어져서 다칠지도 모른다.

➡ _____

10 당신은 또한 교통사고를 당할지도 모른다.

➡ _____

11 그렇다면 이런 문제들을 방지하기 위해 무엇을 할 수 있을까?

➡ _____

12 간단하다.

➡ _____

13 걷고 있는 동안에는 스마트폰을 보지 마라!

➡ _____

14 당신은 안구 건조증이나 거북목 증후군이 있나요?

➡ _____

15 스마트폰은 다양한 건강상의 문제를 일으킬 수 있다.

➡ _____

16 한 가지 예가 안구 건조증이다.

➡ _____

17 스마트폰을 볼 때, 당신은 눈을 자주 깜박거리지 않는다.

➡ _____

18 그러면 눈이 건조하다고 느낄 것이다.

➡ _____

19 일어날 수 있는 또 다른 문제는 목 통증이다.

➡ _____

20 스마트폰을 내려다볼 때, 목에 가해지는 압박이 증가한다.

➡ _____

21 스마트폰을 너무 많이 사용하는 것은, 예를 들어, 너무 많이 문자를 하는 것은 목 통증을 일으킬 수 있다.

➡ _____

22 이런 증상을 거북목 증후군이라고 부른다.

➡ _____

23 여기에 이런 문제들을 위한 몇 가지 조언이 있다.

➡ _____

24 안구 건조증에는, 눈을 자주 깜박이려고 노력해라.

➡ _____

25 거북목 증후군에는 당신의 눈높이까지 스마트폰을 위로 올려라.

➡ _____

26 목 스트레칭 운동 또한 할 수 있다.

➡ _____

27 스마트폰이 없을 때 어떤 기분이 드나요?

➡ _____

28 스마트폰이 주위에 없을 때 당신은 초조한 기분이 드는가?

➡ _____

29 스마트폰을 확인했을 때 아무런 문자 메시지가 없으면 슬픈 기분이 드는가?

➡ _____

30 만약 당신의 대답이 '그렇다'이면, 당신은 스마트폰 중독일지도 모른다.

➡ _____

31 이것을 방지하기 위해 할 수 있는 일은 여러 가지가 있다.

➡ _____

32 예를 들어, 식사나 회의 중에는 스마트폰을 꺼라.

➡ _____

33 문자를 보내는 대신에 사람들과 이야기를 할 수 있다.

➡ _____

[01~03] 다음 글을 읽고 물음에 답하시오.

Living without smartphones is difficult for many of us these days. ___ⓐ___, unwise or too much use of smartphones can cause various problems.

Are you a smombie?

All over the world, people are walking around like zombies. Their heads are down, and their eyes are on their smartphones. ⓑ We call such people smombies, smartphone zombies. If you are a smombie, you can have various safety problems. You may not see a hole in the street, so you may fall and get hurt. You may get into a car accident, too. So what can you do to prevent these problems? It's simple. Do not look at your smartphone while you are walking!

01 위 글의 빈칸 ⓐ에 들어갈 알맞은 것은?

① Therefore   ② However
③ In addition   ④ For example
⑤ In other words

02 위 글의 밑줄 친 ⓑ와 문장의 형식이 같은 것을 모두 고르시오.

① We elected him President.
② She always keeps her word.
③ He made Jane a box.
④ I found it easy.
⑤ Father bought me a camera.

03 위 글의 내용과 일치하지 <u>않는</u> 것은?

① 스마트폰 없이 사는 것은 요즘 많은 사람들에게 어렵다.
② 스마트폰을 현명하지 않게 사용하거나 너무 과도하게 사용하는 것은 다양한 문제를 야기할 수 있다.
③ 전 세계적으로 사람들이 좀비처럼 걸어다니고 있다.
④ 스몸비들은 다양한 안전 관련 문제들을 겪을 수 있다.
⑤ 안전 관련 문제들을 예방하는 것은 어렵다.

[04~07] 다음 글을 읽고 물음에 답하시오.

Do you have dry eyes or text neck?

Smartphones can cause various health problems. One example is dry eyes. When you look at your smartphone, you do not blink often. Then your eyes will feel dry.

ⓐOther problem you can have is neck pain. When you look down at your smartphone, the stress on your neck increases. (①) Too much use of your smartphone, for example, too much texting, can cause neck pain. (②) We call this text neck.

(③) For dry eyes, try ⓑto blink often. (④) For text neck, move your smartphone up to your eye level. (⑤) You can also do some neck stretching exercises.

04 위 글의 흐름으로 보아, 주어진 문장이 들어가기에 가장 적절한 곳은?

> Here are some tips for these problems.

①   ②   ③   ④   ⑤

서답형

05 위 글의 밑줄 친 ⓐ에서 어법상 틀린 부분을 찾아 고쳐 쓰시오.

⟶ _____ ➡ _____

06 아래 〈보기〉에서 위 글의 밑줄 친 ⓑto blink와 to부정사의 용법이 같은 것의 개수를 고르시오.

┌─ 보기 ├─

① I found it useless to teach you math.

② She came here to have a talk with you.

③ It is dangerous to play with matches.

④ Your fault is to talk too much.

⑤ I decided to help those young children.

① 1개　② 2개　③ 3개　④ 4개　⑤ 5개

중요

07 위 글의 주제로 알맞은 것은?

① the cause of dry eyes and the tips to prevent them

② health problems from smartphones and tips for them

③ some tips for avoiding text neck caused by smartphones

④ the increase of the stress due to smartphones

⑤ the importance of neck stretching for a healthy life

[08~10] 다음 글을 읽고 물음에 답하시오.

How do you feel when you don't have your smartphone with you?

Do you feel (A)[nervous / nervously] when your smartphone is not around? Do you feel (B)[sad / sadly] when you check your smartphone and there is no text message?

If your answers are "yes," you may have smartphone ____ⓐ____. There are various things you can do (C)[preventing / to prevent] this. For example, turn off your smartphone during meals or meetings. You can talk to people instead of texting ⓑthem.

서답형

08 위 글의 괄호 (A)~(C)에서 어법상 알맞은 것을 골라 쓰시오.

➡ (A) _____ (B) _____ (C) _____

서답형

09 주어진 영영풀이를 참고하여 빈칸 ⓐ에 철자 a로 시작하는 단어를 쓰시오.

┌──────────────────────────┐
│ 1. the condition of taking harmful drugs and being unable to stop taking them
│
│ 2. a very strong desire or need for something
└──────────────────────────┘

➡ _____

서답형

10 위 글의 밑줄 친 ⓑthem이 가리키는 것을 본문에서 찾아 쓰시오.

➡ _____

[11~14] 다음 글을 읽고 물음에 답하시오.

ⓐLiving without smartphones is difficult for many of us these days. However, unwise or too much use of smartphones can cause various problems.

ⓑ_____

All over the world, people are walking around like zombies. Their heads are down, and their eyes are on their smartphones. We call such people smombies, smartphone zombies. If you are a smombie, you can have various safety problems. You may not see a hole in the street, so you may fall and get hurt. You may get into a car accident, too. So what can you do to prevent these problems? It's simple. Do not look at your smartphone while you are walking!

11 위 글의 밑줄 친 ⓐLiving과 문법적 쓰임이 같은 것을 모두 고르시오.

① The boy reading a book is my son.
② I saw you running on the ground.
③ My brother is good at dancing.
④ My hobby is watching movies.
⑤ Look at the flying bird.

12 위 글의 빈칸 ⓑ에 들어갈 문장으로 알맞은 것은?

① Living without smartphones is difficult.
② Are you a smombie?
③ See a hole in the street!
④ You should prevent a car accident.
⑤ A smombie isn't a troublemaker!

서답형
13 위 글의 내용과 일치하도록 다음 빈칸 (A)와 (B)에 알맞은 단어를 본문에서 찾아 쓰시오.

> You must not look at your (A)_____ while you are walking to prevent various (B)_____ problems.

14 위 글을 읽고 대답할 수 없는 질문은?

① Is it easy for many of us to live without smartphones these days?
② Can too much use of smartphones cause problems?
③ What does a smombie mean?
④ What problems do smombies have?
⑤ What is the most dangerous problem that smombies may have?

[15~17] 다음 글을 읽고 물음에 답하시오.

Do you have dry eyes or text neck?

Smartphones can cause various health problems. One example is dry eyes. When you look ___ⓐ___ your smartphone, you do not blink often. Then your eyes will feel dry.

ⓑAnother problem you can have is neck pain. When you look down ___ⓐ___ your smartphone, the stress on your neck increases. Too much use of your smartphone, for example, too much texting, can cause neck pain. We call this text neck.

Here are some tips for these problems. ___ⓒ___ dry eyes, try to blink often. ___ⓒ___ text neck, move your smartphone ⓓup to your eye level. You can also do some neck stretching exercises.

중요

15 위 글의 빈칸 ⓐ와 ⓒ에 각각 공통으로 들어갈 전치사가 바르게 짝지어진 것은?

① for – From ② at – For
③ at – From ④ for – To
⑤ on – For

서답형

16 위 글의 밑줄 친 문장 ⓑ에 생략된 단어를 넣어 문장을 다시 쓰시오.

➡ _____

17 위 글의 밑줄 친 ⓓup to와 같은 의미로 쓰인 것은?

① He's not up to the job.
② It's up to you.
③ The temperature went up to 35℃.
④ What's she up to?
⑤ She is looking up to you.

[18~21] 다음 글을 읽고 물음에 답하시오.

How do you feel when you don't have your smartphone with you?

ⓐDo you feel nervous when your smartphone is around? Do you feel sad when you check your smartphone and there is no text message?

If your answers are "yes," you may have smartphone addiction. There are various things you can do to prevent ⓑthis. For example, turn off your smartphone during meals or meetings. You can talk to people instead of texting them.

서답형

18 위 글의 밑줄 친 ⓐ에서 흐름상 어색한 부분을 찾아 고치시오.

➡ _____

서답형

19 위 글의 밑줄 친 ⓑthis가 가리키는 것을 본문에서 찾아 영어로 쓰시오.

➡ _____

서답형

20 다음 질문에 대한 알맞은 대답을 영어로 쓰시오. (두 가지)

Q: What can you do to prevent smartphone addiction?

➡ (1) _____
  (2) _____

21 위 글의 주제로 알맞은 것을 고르시오.

① living without your smartphone
② feeling sad when using a smartphone
③ how to get many text messages
④ smartphone addiction and its prevention
⑤ the danger of smartphone addiction

[22~24] 다음 글을 읽고 물음에 답하시오.

Minho: Yesterday, I fell on the street and got hurt. I was texting and I didn't see a hole.
  ↳Reply: Do not use your smartphone while you are walking.

Emma: My eyes feel dry when I use my smartphone.
  ↳Reply: Try to blink often.

Suji: I have neck pain ⓐwhen I text a lot.
  ↳Reply: Move your smartphone up to your eye level and do some neck stretching exercises.

Eric: I think I have smartphone addiction.
  ↳Reply: Turn off your smartphone during meals or meetings and talk to people instead of texting them.

서답형

22 다음 질문에 대한 알맞은 대답을 주어진 단어로 시작하여 쓰시오. (8~9 단어)

> Q: Why did Minho fall on the street and get hurt yesterday?

A: Because _____.

23 위 글의 밑줄 친 ⓐwhen과 같은 의미로 쓰인 것을 모두 고르시오.

① When I was a boy, I was very smart.
② I don't know when I should go.
③ Time goes very fast when I'm busy.
④ When did she promise to meet him?
⑤ When can you come?

24 위 글의 내용과 일치하지 <u>않는</u> 것은?

① 민호는 걷는 동안에는 스마트폰을 사용하지 말아야 한다.
② Emma는 스마트폰을 사용할 때 눈이 건조하다고 느낀다.
③ 수지는 문자를 많이 보낼 때 목 통증이 있다.
④ Eric은 스마트폰을 눈높이까지 들고, 목 스트레칭 운동을 해야 한다.
⑤ Eric은 식사나 회의 중에는 스마트폰을 끄고 문자를 보내는 대신에 사람들과 이야기해야 한다.

[25~27] 다음 글을 읽고 물음에 답하시오.

How do you feel when you don't have your smartphone with you?

  Do you feel nervous when your smartphone is not around? (①) Do you feel sad when you check your smartphone and there is no text message?
  (②) If your answers are "yes," you may have smartphone (A)[addition / addiction]. (③) ____ⓐ____, turn (B)[on / off] your smartphone during meals or meetings. (④) You can talk to people (C)[instead of / because of] texting them. (⑤)

25 위 글의 ①~⑤ 중 다음 주어진 문장이 들어갈 알맞은 곳은?

> There are various things you can do to prevent this.

① 　② 　③ 　④　⑤

26 위 글의 빈칸 ⓐ에 들어갈 알맞은 것은?

① For example　　② Thus
③ Moreover　　④ However
⑤ On the other hand

27 위 글의 괄호 (A)~(C)에서 문맥상 알맞은 낱말을 골라 쓰시오.

➡ (A) _____ (B) _____ (C) _____

[28~30] 다음 글을 읽고 물음에 답하시오.

　Living without smartphones is difficult for many of us these days. However, unwise or too much use of smartphones can cause various problems.

Are you a smombie?

　All over the world, people are ⓐwalking around like zombies. Their heads are down, and their eyes are on their smartphones. We call such people smombies, smartphone zombies. If you are a smombie, you can have various ___(A)___ problems. You may not see a hole in the street, so you may fall and get hurt. You may get into a car accident, too. So what can you do to prevent these problems? It's simple. Do not look at your smartphone while you are walking!

28 위 글의 빈칸 (A)에 들어갈 알맞은 것은?

① health　　② mental
③ economical　　④ safety
⑤ physical

29 아래 〈보기〉에서 위 글의 밑줄 친 ⓐwalking과 문법적 쓰임이 다른 것의 개수를 고르시오.

　보기
① Look at the boy singing on the street.
② Thank you for helping me solve it.
③ My hobby is taking pictures.
④ She is making an apple pie.
⑤ Keeping a diary every day is difficult.

① 1개　② 2개　③ 3개　④ 4개　⑤ 5개

30 위 글의 주제로 알맞은 것은?

① the comfortable living by using smartphones
② the difficulty of living without using smartphones
③ the increase of people like zombies all over the world
④ a car accident which is caused by smombies
⑤ various safety problems due to unwise use of smartphones

[01~03] 다음 글을 읽고 물음에 답하시오.

Living without smartphones (A)[is / are] difficult for many of us these days. However, unwise or too much use of smartphones can cause various problems.

Are you a smombie?

All over the world, people are walking around (B)[like / alike] zombies. Their heads are down, and their eyes are on their smartphones. We call such people smombies, smartphone zombies. If you are a smombie, you can have various ⓐsafety problems. You may not see a hole in the street, so you may fall and get hurt. You may get into a car accident, too. So what can you do to prevent these problems? (C)[Its / It's] simple. Do not look at your smartphone while you are walking!

01 위 글의 괄호 (A)~(C)에서 어법상 알맞은 낱말을 골라 쓰시오.

➡ (A) _____ (B) _____ (C) _____

02 다음 빈칸 (A)~(C)에 알맞은 단어를 넣어 smombies에 대한 설명을 완성하시오.

> They are people who are walking around like (A)_____ with their (B)_____ hanging down, and their (C)_____ on their smartphones.

03 위 글의 밑줄 친 ⓐ의 예 두 가지를 본문에서 찾아 우리말로 쓰시오.

➡ (1) _____
　　(2) _____

[04~06] 다음 글을 읽고 물음에 답하시오.

Do you have dry eyes or text neck?

Smartphones can cause various health problems. One example is dry eyes. When you look at your smartphone, you do not _____ⓐ_____ often. Then your eyes will feel dry.

Another problem you can have is neck pain. ⓑ스마트폰을 내려다볼 때, 목에 가해지는 압박이 증가한다. Too much use of your smartphone, for example, too much texting, can cause neck pain. We call this ⓒtext neck.

Here are some tips for these problems. For dry eyes, try to _____ⓓ_____ often. For text neck, move your smartphone up to your eye level. You can also do some neck stretching exercises.

04 주어진 영영풀이를 참고하여 빈칸 ⓐ와 ⓓ에 공통으로 들어갈 단어를 철자 b로 시작하여 쓰시오.

> to shut your eyes and very quickly open them again

➡ _____

05 위 글의 밑줄 친 ⓑ의 우리말에 맞게 한 단어를 보충하여, 주어진 어휘를 알맞게 배열하시오. (when으로 시작할 것)

> your neck / down / the stress / when / look / your smartphone / at / you / increases / ,

➡ _____
　_____

06 What does the underlined ⓒtext neck mean? Fill in the blanks with the suitable words.

> It means the neck pain which is caused by (A)_____ _____ _____ of your smartphone like too much (B)_____.

[07~09] 다음 글을 읽고 물음에 답하시오.

Living without smartphones is difficult for many of us these days. However, ⓐunwise or too much use of smartphones can cause various problems.

Are you a smombie?

All over the world, people are walking around like zombies. Their heads are down, and their eyes are on their smartphones. ⓑ우리는 그런 사람들을 스몸비, 즉 스마트폰 좀비라고 부른다. If you are a smombie, you can have various safety problems. ⓒYou may not see a hole in the street, so you may fall and get hurt. You may get into a car accident, too. So what can you do to prevent these problems? It's simple. Do not look at your smartphone while you are walking!

07 위 글의 밑줄 친 ⓐ의 예를 본문에서 찾아 우리말로 쓰시오. (30~35자)

➡ _____

_____

08 위 글의 밑줄 친 ⓑ의 우리말에 맞게 주어진 어휘를 이용하여 7 단어로 영작하시오.

> such, smombies

➡ _____

09 위 글의 밑줄 친 ⓒ를 다음과 같이 바꿔 쓸 때 빈칸에 들어갈 알맞은 말을 쓰시오.

➡ _____ you may not see a hole in the street, you may fall and get hurt.

[10~11] 다음 글을 읽고 물음에 답하시오.

Do you have dry eyes or text neck?

Smartphones can cause various health problems. One example is ⓐdry eyes. When you look at your smartphone, you do not blink often. Then your eyes will feel dry.

Another problem you can have is neck pain. When you look down at your smartphone, the stress on your neck increases. Too much use of your smartphone, ⓑfor example, too much texting, can cause neck pain. We call this text neck.

Here are some tips for these problems. For dry eyes, try to blink often. For text neck, move your smartphone up to your eye level. You can also do some neck stretching exercises.

10 위 글의 밑줄 친 ⓐdry eyes의 원인과 이 문제를 위한 조언을 우리말로 쓰시오.

➡ 원인: _____

조언: _____

11 위 글의 밑줄 친 ⓑfor example과 바꿔 쓸 수 있는 단어를 두 단어로 쓰시오.

➡ _____

Talk and Play

A: What's wrong?
상대방이 기분이 좋지 않거나 어딘가 아파 보일 때 사용함.(= What's the matter?)

B: I have a fever.
'나는 ~가 아프다'는 표현으로 'have+a/an+병명/증상' 형태를 사용.

A: That's too bad. Make sure you get some rest.
상대방이 안 좋은 일을 당했을 때 사용하는 표현.(= I'm sorry to hear that.)

B: OK, I will. 상대방에게 당부하는 표현.(반드시 ~하도록 하다, ~을 확실히 하다)

구문해설 • **fever**: 열 • **make sure**: 확실히 ~하다 • **rest**: 휴식

A: 무슨 일이니?
B: 나는 열이 나.
A: 안됐다. 좀 쉬도록 하렴.
B: 응, 알겠어.

After You Read B

Be Smart with Your Smartphones!

Minho: Yesterday, I fell on the street and got hurt. I was texting and I didn't
현재분사
see a hole.

└, Reply: Do not use your smartphone while you are walking.

Emma: My eyes feel dry when I use my smartphone.
feel은 감각동사로 형용사가 보어로 쓰였다.
└, Reply: Try to blink often.
명사적 용법(목적어)

Suji: I have neck pain when I text a lot.
때(접속사)
└, Reply: Move your smartphone up to your eye level and do some
~까지
neck stretching exercises.

Eric: I think I have smartphone addiction.
스마트폰 중독
└, Reply: Turn off your smartphone during meals or meetings and
~을 끄다 ↔ turn on
talk to people instead of texting them.
~ 대신에 (뒤에 명사 또는 동명사가 온다.) = people

구문해설 • **hole**: 구덩이 • **blink**: (눈을) 깜박거리다 • **text**: 문자 메시지; (휴대 전화로) 문자를 보내다
• **stretch**: 늘이다, 뻗다 • **addiction**: 중독 • **meal**: 식사 • **instead of**: ~ 대신에

스마트폰을 현명하게 사용하라!
민호: 어제, 나는 길에서 넘어져서 다쳤다. 나는 문자를 보내고 있었고 구덩이를 보지 못했다.
→ 대답: 걷는 동안에는 스마트폰을 사용하지 마라.
Emma: 나는 스마트폰을 사용할 때 눈이 건조하다고 느낀다.
→ 대답: 눈을 자주 깜박이도록 노력해라.
수지: 나는 문자를 많이 보낼 때 목 통증이 있다.
→ 대답: 스마트폰을 눈높이까지 들고, 목 스트레칭 운동을 해라.
Eric: 나는 스마트폰 중독인 것 같다.
→ 대답: 식사나 회의 중에는 스마트폰을 끄고 문자를 보내는 대신에 사람들과 이야기해라.

Around the World

This sign says, "Be careful of using your smartphone while you are walking."
전치사 of의 목적어로 동명사   접속사(~하는 동안)
There are traffic lights on the ground, so people can see them while they are
그래서   = traffic lights
using their smartphones.
현재분사
This sign on the ground means, "This side of the street is for people who are
형용사구   주격 관계대명사
texting."

구문해설 • **say**: (신문 · 게시 · 편지 · 책 따위가) ~라고 씌어져 있다 • **mean**: 의미하다

이 표지판은 "걷는 동안 스마트폰 사용을 주의하세요."라는 의미이다.
땅바닥에 신호등이 있어서, 사람들이 스마트폰을 사용하는 동안에도 신호등을 볼 수 있다.
땅바닥에 있는 이 표지판은 "길의 이쪽은 문자를 보내고 있는 사람들을 위한 곳입니다."라는 의미이다.

01 다음 주어진 두 단어의 관계가 같도록 빈칸에 알맞은 단어를 쓰시오. (주어진 철자로 시작할 것)

> expensive : cheap = stupid : i_____

02 다음 글의 빈칸 ⓐ와 ⓑ에 들어갈 단어가 바르게 짝지어진 것은?

> Living ____ⓐ____ smartphones is difficult for many of us these days. However, unwise or too much use of smartphones can ____ⓑ____ various problems.

① with – prevent
② with – cause
③ without – prevent
④ without – cause
⑤ without – decrease

[03~04] 다음 영영풀이에 해당하는 것을 고르시오.

03
> to spread out your arms, legs, or body as far as possible

① text   ② blink
③ stretch   ④ cause
⑤ prevent

04
> in the state of sleep; sleeping

① asleep   ② sour
③ intelligent   ④ various
⑤ simple

05 빈칸에 공통으로 들어갈 말을 주어진 철자로 시작하여 쓰시오.

> • The c_____ of the accident is not clear. The police are still looking into it.
> • Too much use of smartphones can c_____ dry eyes.

➡ _____

06 다음 밑줄 친 부분의 뜻이 잘못된 것은?

① Make sure you get some rest. (확실히 ~하라)
② I think you have computer game addiction! (중독)
③ My eyes are so dry. I try to blink often. (눈을 감다)
④ Don't look at your smartphone while you are walking! (~ 하는 동안)
⑤ When you look down at your smartphone, the stress on your neck increases. (압박)

07 다음 대화의 빈칸에 들어갈 말로 알맞지 않은 것은?

> W: _____, Chris?
> B: I have a terrible toothache.
> W: Here is some medicine. Take this.
> B: Thank you.

① What's the matter
② What's the problem
③ Is there anything wrong
④ What do you mean
⑤ What's wrong with you

[08~10] 다음 대화를 읽고 물음에 답하시오.

> W: @What's wrong, Andy?
>
> B: Hello, Ms. Kim. My right thumb hurts.
>
> W: Hmm. (①) Do you use your smartphone a lot?
>
> B: Yes, I ⓑtext a lot. Why? (②)
>
> W: I think you have texting thumb.
>
> B: Texting thumb? (③)
>
> W: It's ⓒpain in your thumb. You can get it from texting too much. (④)
>
> B: Oh, I didn't know (A)that.
>
> W: Why don't you ⓓdo some finger stretching exercises?
>
> B: OK, I will. (⑤)
>
> W: And make sure ⓔyou text too much.

08 주어진 문장이 들어갈 위치로 알맞은 것은?

> What's texting thumb?

①   ②   ③   ④   ⑤

09 밑줄 친 (A)that이 가리키는 것을 우리말로 쓰시오.

➡ _____

10 위 대화의 밑줄 친 @~ⓔ 중, 흐름상 어색한 것은?

① @   ② ⓑ   ③ ⓒ   ④ ⓓ   ⑤ ⓔ

11 다음 대화의 밑줄 친 부분 중 어법상 어색한 것은?

> W: What's @wrong with your leg, Sam?
>
> B: I fell and hurt my foot ⓑwhile I was playing soccer.
>
> W: Can you walk?
>
> B: Yes, but it ⓒhurts a lot.
>
> W: ⓓWhy don't you put some ice on it? And ⓔmake sure don't play soccer until next week.

① @   ② ⓑ   ③ ⓒ   ④ ⓓ   ⑤ ⓔ

12 다음 중 짝지어진 대화가 어색한 것은?

① A: I have a headache.
   B: That's too bad.

② A: Make sure you take some medicine.
   B: OK, I will.

③ A: What's the matter, Chris?
   B: I have a terrible toothache.

④ A: I fell and hurt my foot while I was playing soccer.
   B: That sounds good.

⑤ A: Here is some medicine. Take this. And make sure you go to the dentist.
   B: OK, I will.

13 다음 대화의 밑줄 친 부분에 대한 설명으로 적절하지 않은 것은?

> W: @What's the matter, Chris?
>
> B: I ⓑhave a terrible toothache.
>
> W: Here is some medicine. ⓒTake this.
>
> B: Thank you.
>
> W: And ⓓmake sure you go to the dentist.
>
> B: ⓔOK, I will.

① @: 문제점에 대해 물어볼 때 사용하는 표현이다.

② ⓑ: 이가 매우 아프다는 뜻이다.

③ ⓒ: '가져가다'라는 의미로 사용되었다.

④ ⓓ: 상대방에게 당부할 때 사용하는 표현이다.

⑤ ⓔ: 상대방의 조언에 '그렇게 하겠다'는 긍정의 표현이다.

> Grammar

14 다음 밑줄 친 부분 중 어법상 어색한 것은?

> He was very ①intelligent, ②so we ③all called ④him ⑤to be Einstein.

①   ②   ③   ④   ⑤

15 다음 중 두 문장을 한 문장으로 만들 때 의미가 <u>다른</u> 하나는?

① This is the book.
   + John read the book last week.
   ➡ This is the book which John read last week.

② Grace sent an email to the boy.
   + Grace loved him.
   ➡ Grace sent an email to the boy whom she loved.

③ The card was sent to Sue.
   + I bought the card yesterday.
   ➡ Sue sent the card that I bought yesterday.

④ Remember to include all the expenses.
   + You spent the expenses.
   ➡ Remember to include all the expenses that you spent.

⑤ Those are the flowers.
   + Rachel planted them this spring.
   ➡ Those are the flowers Rachel planted this spring.

16 〈보기〉의 밑줄 친 which와 용법이 <u>다른</u> 하나는?

> ┌─── 보기 ───┐
> Yesterday I watched the movie <u>which</u> he recommended.

① Herold is the only person <u>that</u> I want to meet now.

② I like the dog <u>which</u> my friend gave to me.

③ I employed a young man <u>who</u> Jenny liked a lot.

④ He is wearing a jacket <u>which</u> has two pockets.

⑤ The teacher <u>whom</u> I like most teaches math.

17 다음 문장의 빈칸에 알맞지 <u>않은</u> 것은?

> They _____ him to be their leader.

① called   ② chose
③ considered   ④ wanted
⑤ elected

18 다음 밑줄 친 부분 중 생략할 수 있는 것은?

① Nick Larson is the man <u>that</u> lives in this town.

② Where did you buy <u>that</u> watch?

③ It is certain <u>that</u> he will come.

④ I like the robot <u>that</u> Kirk bought for me.

⑤ His dress is <u>that</u> of a gentleman.

19 괄호 안에 주어진 어휘를 사용해 다음을 영작하시오. (that 사용 금지)

(1) *Jane Eyre*는 Yumi가 어제 읽은 책이다. (the book, read)

   ➡ _____

(2) 내가 입고 있는 재킷은 나의 할머니로부터의 선물이다. (jacket, wear, a present)

   ➡ _____
   _____

(3) 사람들은 그러한 음식을 fajitas라고 부른다. (call, such, fajitas)

   ➡ _____
   _____

(4) 그 축제는 그 도시를 방문하기에 인기 있는 장소로 만들었다. (a, popular, visit)

   ➡ _____
   _____

Reading

[20~22] 다음 글을 읽고 물음에 답하시오.

Are you a smombie?

All over the world, people are walking around like zombies. Their heads are down, and their eyes are ___ⓐ___ their smartphones. We call such people smombies, smartphone zombies. (①) You may not see a hole in the street, so you may fall and get hurt. (②) You may get ___ⓑ___ a car accident, too. (③) So what can you do ©to prevent these problems? (④) It's simple. (⑤) Do not look at your smartphone while you are walking!

20 위 글의 흐름으로 보아, 주어진 문장이 들어가기에 가장 적절한 곳은?

If you are a smombie, you can have various safety problems.

①   ②   ③   ④   ⑤

21 위 글의 빈칸 ⓐ와 ⓑ에 들어갈 전치사가 바르게 짝지어진 것은?

① from – into   ② in – at
③ on – into   ④ from – to
⑤ on – for

22 위 글의 밑줄 친 ©to prevent와 to부정사의 용법이 다른 것을 고르시오. (2개)

① She was pleased to see her son.
② He was the first man to land on the moon.
③ You are too young to understand it.
④ He is studying English to get a good job.
⑤ He promised me to come back soon.

[23~25] 다음 글을 읽고 물음에 답하시오.

ⓐ

Smartphones can cause various health problems. One example is dry eyes. When you look at your smartphone, you do not blink often. Then your eyes will feel dry.

(A)[Another / The other] problem you can have is neck pain. When you look down at your smartphone, the stress on your neck (B)[decreases / increases]. Too much use of your smartphone, ___ⓑ___, too much texting, can cause neck pain. We call this text neck.

Here are some (C)[advices / tips] for these problems. For dry eyes, try to blink often. For text neck, move your smartphone up to your eye level. You can also do some neck stretching exercises.

23 위 글의 빈칸 ⓐ에 들어갈 문장으로 알맞은 것은?

① Blink often when using a smartphone!
② Does the stress on the neck increase?
③ What is the main reason of text neck?
④ Do you have dry eyes or text neck?
⑤ Do some neck stretching exercises!

24 위 글의 빈칸 ⓑ에 들어갈 알맞은 것은?

① in addition   ② for example
③ however   ④ in fact
⑤ as a result

25 위 글의 괄호 (A)~(C)에서 문맥이나 어법상 알맞은 낱말을 골라 쓰시오.

➡ (A) _____ (B) _____ (C) _____

[26~27] 다음 글을 읽고 물음에 답하시오.

How do you feel when you don't have your smartphone with you?

ⓐ스마트폰이 주위에 없을 때 당신은 초조한 기분이 드는가? Do you feel sad when you check your smartphone and there is no text message?

If your answers are "yes," you may have smartphone addiction. There are various things you can do to prevent this. ⓑFor example, turn off your smartphone while meals or meetings. You can talk to people instead of texting them.

26 위 글의 밑줄 친 ⓐ의 우리말에 맞게 주어진 어휘를 이용하여 10 단어로 영작하시오. (Do로 시작할 것)

nervous, around

➡ _____

_____

27 위 글의 밑줄 친 ⓑ에서 어법상 틀린 부분을 찾아 고치시오.

_____ ➡ _____

[28~29] 다음 글을 읽고 물음에 답하시오.

Minho: Yesterday, I fell on the street and got hurt. I was texting and I didn't see a hole.
∟ Reply: Do not use your smartphone while you are walking.
Emma: My eyes feel dry when I use my smartphone.
∟ Reply: Try to blink often.
Suji: I have neck pain when I text a lot.
∟ Reply: Move your smartphone up to your eye level and do some neck stretching exercises.
Eric: I think I have smartphone addiction.
∟ Reply: Turn off your smartphone during meals or meetings and talk to people ___ⓐ___ .

28 위 글의 빈칸 ⓐ에 들어갈 알맞은 말은?

① instead of looking at them
② besides texting them
③ through SNS
④ instead of texting them
⑤ besides emailing them

29 Fill in the blanks with the suitable words.

Q1: Who should try to blink often?
Q2: Why should he[she] try to blink often?

➡ Q1: _____ should try to blink often.

Q2: Because the eyes _____ _____ when he[she] uses the smartphone.

[30~31] 다음 글을 읽고 물음에 답하시오.

How do you feel when you don't have your smartphone with you?

Do you feel nervous when your smartphone is not around? Do you feel sad when you check your smartphone and there is no text message?

If your answers are "yes," you may have smartphone addiction. There are various things you can do to prevent this. For example, turn off your smartphone during meals or meetings. You can talk to people instead of ___ⓐ___ them.

30 위 글을 읽고 스마트폰 중독이라고 생각할 수 있는 경우 두 가지를 우리말로 쓰시오.

➡ (1) _____

(2) _____

_____

31 위 글의 빈칸 ⓐ에 text를 알맞은 형태로 쓰시오.

➡ _____

01 다음 짝지어진 단어의 관계가 같도록 빈칸에 알맞은 말을 쓰시오.

출제율 90%

> sore : painful = varied : _____

02 다음 영영풀이에 해당하는 단어는?

출제율 95%

> a famous person

① author   ② promise

③ celebrity   ④ zombie

⑤ hole

03 다음 빈칸에 우리말에 맞게 알맞은 단어를 쓰시오. (주어진 철자로 시작하시오.)

출제율 85%

> • 여기에 이런 문제에 대한 몇 가지 조언이 있다.
>
> (A) _____ _____ some tips for these problems.
>
> • 스마트폰이 주위에 없을 때 당신은 초조한 기분이 드는가?
>
> (B) Do you feel n_____ when your smartphone is not around?

[04~05] 다음 대화를 읽고 물음에 답하시오.

> A: (A)너 몸이 안 좋아 보여. What's wrong?
> B: I have a headache.
> A: _____ (B) _____ Make sure you take some medicine.
> B: OK, I will.

04 위 대화의 밑줄 친 (A)의 우리말에 맞게 주어진 문장을 채우시오.

출제율 95%

➡ You don't _____ _____.

05 위 대화의 (B)에 들어갈 말로 알맞은 것을 모두 고르시오.

출제율 95%

① That sounds good.

② I'm sorry to hear that.

③ I'm pleased to hear that.

④ That's too bad.

⑤ How are you doing?

06 다음 (A)~(C)에 알맞은 말이 바르게 짝지어진 것은?

출제율 95%

> Smartphones can cause (A)[simple / various] health problems. One example is dry eyes. When you look at your smartphone, you do not blink often. Then your eyes will feel (B)[dry / wet]. Another problem you can have is neck pain. When you look down at your smartphone, the stress on your neck [decreases / increases].

	(A)	(B)	(C)
①	simple	wet	increases
②	simple	dry	decreases
③	various	wet	decreases
④	various	dry	increases
⑤	various	dry	decreases

07 다음 대화의 밑줄 친 부분 중 어법상 어색한 것은?

출제율 95%

> W: You ⓐlook sick. What's wrong, Inho?
> B: I ⓑhave a sore throat. I ⓒhave a fever, too.
> W: I think you ⓓhave cold. Take this medicine and ⓔmake sure you take a good rest.
> B: OK. Thank you.

① ⓐ   ② ⓑ   ③ ⓒ   ④ ⓓ   ⑤ ⓔ

[08~09] 다음 대화를 읽고 물음에 답하시오.

W: _____(A)_____, Andy?

B: Hello, Ms. Kim. My right thumb hurts.

W: Hmm. Do you use your smartphone a lot?

B: Yes, I text a lot. Why?

W: I think you have texting thumb.

B: Texting thumb? What's texting thumb?

W: _____(B)_____. You can get it from texting too much.

B: Oh, I didn't know that.

W: ⓐ손가락 스트레칭 운동을 좀 하는 게 어떠니?

B: OK, I will.

W: And _____(C)_____.

08 위 대화의 빈칸 (A)~(C)에 들어갈 말로 알맞은 것을 〈보기〉에서 찾아 쓰시오.

┌─── 보기 ───┐
- What can I do for you
- What's wrong
- It's pain in your thumb
- don't forget to text message to me
- make sure you don't text too much
└────────────┘

➡ (A) _____

(B) _____

(C) _____

09 위 대화의 밑줄 친 ⓐ의 우리말에 맞게 주어진 단어를 이용하여 영어로 쓰시오.

┌────────────────────────────┐
why, you, do, some, stretching exercises
└────────────────────────────┘

➡ _____

10 다음 대화의 빈칸에 들어갈 말로 알맞은 것은?

┌────────────────────────────┐
W: What's wrong, Peter?

B: I don't know, Ms. Kim, but my back hurts a lot.

W: Put a heating pad on it.

B: OK, I will.

W: And _____.
└────────────────────────────┘

① you should not forget to lock the door

② you had better text a lot

③ make sure you do some stretching exercises

④ make sure you give me a call when you get home

⑤ make sure you get enough sleep tonight

11 다음 문장에서 어법상 어색한 것을 바르게 고쳐 문장을 다시 쓰시오.

(1) The pizza who my dad made was really delicious.

➡ _____
_____

(2) I know the girl which you are talking about.

➡ _____
_____

(3) We elected class president Chris.

➡ _____

(4) The game that we saw it was very boring.

➡ _____

(5) He called me as Queen.

➡ _____

12 다음 빈칸에 들어갈 말을 **모두** 고르시오.

> Jane is the girl _____ Peter met in the park.

① who　　　　　② whose

③ whom　　　　④ which

⑤ that

13 다음 중 어법상 바르지 **않은** 것은?

① Do you like the hat you bought yesterday?

② Arnold calls his daughter *My Little Princess*.

③ I met the lady with whom you had dinner last Saturday.

④ They called the ship to be Titanic.

⑤ *Yesterday* is the song that I can sing in English.

14 다음 우리말을 괄호 안에 주어진 어휘를 이용하여 영작하시오. (that 사용 금지)

(1) 우리는 그러한 춤을 Salsa라고 부른다. (such, call, a dance, 6 단어)

➡ _____

(2) 아무도 Nicole이 만든 스파게티를 좋아하지 않았다. (spaghetti, make, 7 단어)

➡ _____

(3) 우리는 Alex를 우리 동아리의 회장으로 선출했다. (elect, president, club, 7 단어)

➡ _____

(4) 그녀는 내가 가장 좋아하는 가수이다. (the singer, most, 8 단어)

➡ _____

[15~17] 다음 글을 읽고 물음에 답하시오.

Are you a smombie?

 All over the world, people are walking around ⓐlike zombies. Their heads are down, and their eyes are on their smartphones. We call such people smombies, smartphone zombies. If you are a smombie, you can have various safety problems. You may not see a hole in the street, so you may fall and get hurt. You may get into a car accident, too. So what can you do to prevent ⓑthese problems? It's simple. Do not look at your smartphone while you are ___(A)___!

15 위 글의 빈칸 (A)에 들어갈 가장 알맞은 것은?

① talking　　　② walking

③ studying　　 ④ eating

⑤ playing

16 위 글의 밑줄 친 ⓐlike와 의미가 **다른** 것은?

① He ran like the wind.

② You do it like this.

③ I had a chance to meet people of like mind.

④ Don't look at me like that.

⑤ Students were angry at being treated like children.

17 위 글의 밑줄 친 ⓑthese problems와 바꿔 쓸 수 있는 말을 본문에서 찾아 쓰시오.

➡ _____

[18~19] 다음 글을 읽고 물음에 답하시오.

Do you have dry eyes or text neck?

Smartphones can cause various ⓐ_____ problems. One example is dry eyes. When you look at your smartphone, you do not blink often. Then your eyes will feel dry.

Another problem you can have is neck pain. When you look down at your smartphone, the stress on your neck increases. Too much use of your smartphone, for example, too much texting, can cause neck pain. We call this text neck.

Here are some tips for these problems. For dry eyes, try to blink often. For text neck, move your smartphone up to your eye level. You can also do some neck stretching exercises.

🖉 출제율 95%

18 위 글의 빈칸 ⓐ에 들어갈 알맞은 것은?

① safety   ② social
③ environment   ④ mental
⑤ health

🖉 출제율 90%

19 위 글의 내용과 일치하지 <u>않는</u> 것은?

① 스마트폰 사용은 안구 건조증을 일으킬 수 있다.
② 스마트폰 사용은 목 통증을 일으킬 수 있다.
③ 스마트폰을 내려다볼 때, 목에 가해지는 압박이 감소한다.
④ 안구 건조증에는, 눈을 자주 깜박이려고 노력해야 한다.
⑤ 거북목 증후군에는 당신의 눈높이까지 스마트폰을 위로 올려야 한다.

[20~22] 다음 글을 읽고 물음에 답하시오.

There are a few things I need to change to have a ⓐ_____ life.

First, I don't exercise much. From now on, I will try to walk for 30 minutes every day.

Second, I think I eat too much fast food. I will eat fast food only once a week.

Third, I often eat at night. I will not eat after 10 o'clock.

I will try my best ⓑ<u>to keep</u> these promises.

🖉 출제율 95%

20 위 글의 빈칸 ⓐ에 healthy의 비교급을 쓰시오.

➡ _____

🖉 출제율 100%

21 위 글을 읽고 더 건강한 생활을 하기 위해 필자가 바꾸어야 할 세 가지를 우리말로 쓰시오.

(1) _____
    ➡ _____
(2) _____
    ➡ _____
(3) _____
    ➡ _____

🖉 출제율 90%

22 아래 〈보기〉에서 위 글의 밑줄 친 ⓑto keep과 to부정사의 용법이 <u>다른</u> 것의 개수를 고르시오.

┌─── 보기 ───┐

① This chair seems comfortable <u>to sit</u> on.
② I have no friends <u>to help</u> me.
③ I found it difficult <u>to persuade</u> them.
④ I was shocked <u>to hear</u> the tragic news.
⑤ What a fool he is <u>to say</u> such a foolish thing!

① 1개   ② 2개   ③ 3개   ④ 4개   ⑤ 5개

01 다음 그림을 보고 아래 대화의 빈칸에 알맞은 단어를 쓰시오.

G: What's _____, Mike?

B: I _____ _____ terrible _____.

G: I think you _____ _____ some medicine.

B: OK, I _____.

02 다음 대화를 읽고 아래의 표를 완성하시오.

W: What's wrong, Andy?

B: Hello, Ms. Kim. My right thumb hurts.

W: Hmm. Do you use your smartphone a lot?

B: Yes, I text a lot. Why?

W: I think you have texting thumb.

B: Texting thumb? What's texting thumb?

W: It's pain in your thumb. You can get it from texting too much.

B: Oh, I didn't know that.

W: Why don't you do some finger stretching exercises?

B: OK, I will.

W: And make sure you don't text too much.

• Problem: _____ _____ (_____ in your thumb)

• Advice: (1) do some _____ _____
 _____ (2) don't _____ too much

03 괄호 안에 주어진 단어를 이용하여 다음 대화를 완성하시오.

M: _____ (A) _____, Mina?

G: I _____ (B) _____. I also have a runny nose.

M: I think you have a cold. _____ (C) _____

G: OK, I will.

➡ (A) _____ (what, matter)

(B) _____ (a sore throat)

(C) _____ (make, you, some rest)

04 다음 두 문장을 관계대명사를 사용하여 한 문장으로 바꾸시오.

(1) • The book is about nature.
 • I'm reading the book.
 ➡ _____

(2) • Kenya is the country.
 • John wants to visit the country.
 ➡ _____

(3) • J. K. Rowling is a famous novelist.
 • Many people like her.
 ➡ _____
 _____

(4) • I want to know the name of the girl.
 • I met her at the party.
 ➡ _____
 _____

(5) • Start by identifying the people.
 • You want to work with the people.
 ➡ _____
 _____

(6) • The rate can be very slow.
 • Hair grows at the rate.
 ➡ _____
 _____

[05~07] 다음 글을 읽고 물음에 답하시오.

Living (A)[with / without] smartphones is difficult for many of us these days. However, unwise or too much use of smartphones can cause various problems.

Are you a smombie?

All over the world, people are walking around like zombies. ⓐ그들의 머리는 아래를 향하고, 그들의 눈은 스마트폰을 향하고 있다. We call such people smombies, smartphone zombies. If you are a smombie, you can have various safety problems. You may not see a (B)[hole / whole] in the street, so you may fall and get hurt. You may get into a car accident, too. So what can you do to (C)[prevent / protect] these problems? It's simple. Do not look at your smartphone while you are walking!

05 위 글의 괄호 (A)~(C)에서 문맥상 알맞은 낱말을 골라 쓰시오.

➡ (A) _____ (B) _____ (C) _____

06 위 글의 밑줄 친 ⓐ의 우리말에 맞게 한 단어를 보충하여, 주어진 어휘를 알맞게 배열하시오.

their smartphones / are / on / are / their eyes / and / their heads / ,

➡ _____

_____

07 다음 빈칸 (A)와 (B)에 알맞은 단어를 넣어 질문에 답하시오.

Q: Why may smombies fall and get hurt in the street?

A: Because they look at their (A)_____ while they are walking and may not see a (B)_____ in the street.

[08~10] 다음 글을 읽고 물음에 답하시오.

Do you have dry eyes or text neck?

Smartphones can cause various health problems. One example is dry eyes. When you look at your smartphone, you do not blink often. Then your eyes will feel dry.

Another problem you can have is neck pain. ⓐWhen you look up at your smartphone, the stress on your neck increases. Too much use of your smartphone, for example, too much texting, can cause ⓑneck pain. We call this text neck.

Here are some tips for these problems. For dry eyes, try to blink often. For text neck, move your smartphone up to your eye level. You can also do some neck stretching exercises.

08 위 글의 내용과 일치하도록 다음 빈칸 (A)와 (B)에 알맞은 단어를 쓰시오.

One of the health problems smartphones can cause is (A)_____ _____ and another problem is (B)_____ _____.

09 위 글의 밑줄 친 ⓐ에서 흐름상 어색한 부분을 찾아 고치시오.

_____ ➡ _____

10 위 글의 밑줄 친 ⓑneck pain의 원인과 이 문제를 위한 조언을 우리말로 쓰시오.

➡ 원인: _____

_____

조언: (1) _____

(2) _____

01 다음 주어진 문제점과 그에 맞는 충고를 찾아서 〈보기〉와 같이 적절한 대화를 완성하시오.

Problem	Advice
• headache　• toothache • cold　• sore throat • fever　• runny nose	• take some medicine　• get some rest • go see a doctor　• drink a lot of water • go to the dentist　• take a warm bath

┤ 보기 ├

A: You don't look well. What's wrong?

B: I have a headache.

A: That's too bad. Make sure you take some medicine.

B: OK, I will.

(1) _____

_____

(2) _____

_____

02 다음은 Big Ben의 사진이다. 그림을 참고하고 괄호 안에 주어진 어휘를 이용하여 문장을 완성하시오.

(the clock tower / call)

➡ People _____.

03 다음 내용을 바탕으로 건강한 생활을 위한 다짐을 하는 글을 쓰시오.

My problems are that	I'll try to ....
e.g. I don't exercise much	e.g. walk for 30 minutes every day

There are a few things I need (A)_____ to have a healthier life.

First, I don't exercise much. (B)_____, I will try to walk for 30 minutes every day.

Second, I think I eat too much fast food. I will eat fast food only (C)_____.

Third, I often eat at night. I will not eat (D)_____ 10 o'clock.

I will try (E)_____ to keep these promises.

단원별 모의고사

01 다음 단어에 대한 영어 설명이 <u>어색한</u> 것은?

① zombie: in stories and movies, a dead body that moves by magic
② blink: to open and close your eyes very quickly
③ prevent: to try to allow something to happen
④ simple: not difficult or complicated
⑤ traffic light: a set of colored lights at the side of the road that show when cars are allowed to move

02 다음 짝지어진 단어의 관계가 같도록 빈칸에 알맞은 말을 쓰시오.

well : healthy = suffering: _____

03 다음 영영풀이에 해당하는 단어는?

able to learn and understand things quickly

① intelligent   ② various
③ careful   ④ dry
⑤ stupid

04 다음 대화의 빈칸에 공통으로 들어갈 말은?

W: You look sick. What's wrong, Inho?
B: I _____ sore throat. I _____ fever, too.
W: I think you _____ cold. Take this medicine and make sure you take a good rest.
B: OK. Thank you.

① catch   ② take a   ③ make
④ turn a   ⑤ have a

05 다음 대화의 순서가 바르게 배열된 것은?

(A) I fell and hurt my foot while I was playing soccer.
(B) Yes, but it hurts a lot.
(C) Can you walk?
(D) What's wrong with your leg, Sam?

① (A) – (C) – (B) – (D)
② (B) – (C) – (D) – (A)
③ (C) – (D) – (A) – (B)
④ (D) – (A) – (C) – (B)
⑤ (D) – (B) – (A) – (C)

06 다음 중 짝지어진 대화가 <u>어색한</u> 것은?

① A: What's wrong, Peter?
   B: I don't know, Ms. Kim, but my back hurts a lot.
② A: What's the matter with you, Jenny? You don't look well.
   B: I won first prize in the singing contest.
③ A: What's wrong with your legs, Andy?
   B: I fell and hurt them while I was playing soccer.
④ A: I have a runny nose. I have a fever, too.
   B: Take this medicine and make sure you take a good rest.
⑤ A: You don't look well. What's wrong?
   B: I couldn't sleep well last night. I'm so tired.

07 다음 대화의 빈칸에 들어갈 말로 어색한 것은?

> A: What's the matter, Inho?
> B: _____

① I have a headache.
② I have a fever.
③ I have a stomachache.
④ I hurt my back.
⑤ Make sure you take some medicine.

[08~09] 다음 대화를 읽고 물음에 답하시오.

> W: What's wrong, Peter?
> B: I don't know, Ms. Kim, but my back hurts a lot.
> W: Put a heating pad on ⓐit.
> B: OK, I will.
> W: And _____ (A) _____.

08 밑줄 친 ⓐit이 가리키는 것을 Ms. Kim의 입장에서 영어로 쓰시오.

➡ _____

09 위 대화의 빈칸 (A)에 들어갈 말로 어색한 것은?

① don't remember to do some stretching exercises
② make sure you do some stretching exercises
③ remember to do some stretching exercises
④ don't forget to do some stretching exercises
⑤ you had better do some stretching exercises

10 다음 대화의 빈칸 (A)에 들어갈 당부의 표현으로 가장 어색한 것은?

> A: You don't look well. What's wrong?
> B: I have a runny nose.
> A: That's too bad. Make sure ____(A)____.
> B: OK, I will.

① you go see a doctor
② you take some medicine
③ you get some rest
④ you go to the dentist
⑤ you take a warm bath

[11~12] 다음 대화를 읽고 물음에 답하시오.

> W: What's wrong, Andy?
> B: Hello, Ms. Kim. My right thumb hurts.
> W: Hmm. Do you use your smartphone a lot?
> B: Yes, I text a lot. Why?
> W: I think you have texting thumb.
> B: Texting thumb? What's texting thumb?
> W: It's pain in your thumb. You can get (A)it from texting too much.
> B: Oh, I didn't know that.
> W: Why don't you do some finger stretching exercises?
> B: OK, I will.
> W: And make sure you don't text too much.

11 Andy가 Ms. Kim을 만난 이유로 알맞은 것은?

① Because he texted a lot.
② Because his right thumb hurt.
③ Because he lost his smartphone.
④ To ask her what exercises to do.
⑤ To make sure he would not text too much.

12 위 대화의 밑줄 친 (A)it이 가리키는 것을 영어로 쓰시오.

➡ _____

13 괄호 안에 주어진 어휘를 이용하여 우리말을 영작하시오.

(1) Cameron은 Gillian이 가장 좋아하는 감독이다. (the director, best)

➡ _____

(2) 우리는 Jason이 우리에게 해준 이야기를 좋아했다. (the story, tell, 7단어)

➡ _____

(3) 그의 사업은 그를 백만장자로 만들었다. (business, a millionaire)

➡ _____

(4) 우리는 Bali를 신들의 섬이라고 부른다. (the island of gods)

➡ _____

14 다음 빈칸에 공통으로 들어갈 단어는?

> • Let's _____ the world a better place.
> • I will _____ him do his homework.

① call   ② make
③ elect   ④ consider
⑤ name

15 두 문장을 관계대명사를 사용하여 한 문장으로 썼을 때 빈칸의 문장을 쓰시오.

(1) • Mr. Lee is the teacher.

  • _____

➡ Mr. Lee is the teacher whom every student respects.

(2) • There are various things.

  • _____

➡ There are various things that you can do to prevent this.

16 다음 중 어법상 바르지 않은 것은?

① His music has made him a citizen of the world.
② They elected Jane club leader.
③ They considered their son to be a genius.
④ She named him after Harry Porter.
⑤ We want to call this cup as Cookie Eater.

17 어법상 어색한 것을 바르게 고쳐 문장을 다시 쓰시오.

(1) He is a gentleman which I built a good trust on.

➡ _____
_____

(2) These are the pants who I bought yesterday.

➡ _____

(3) She doesn't consider an artist him.

➡ _____

(4) This is the issue about that we need to express our opinion.

➡ _____
_____
_____

(5) Ella received some flowers that her boy friend had sent them to her.

➡ _____
_____

(6) They call it as 'Non La'.

➡ _____

[18~20] 다음 글을 읽고 물음에 답하시오.

Do you have dry eyes or text neck?

Smartphones can cause various health problems. One example is dry eyes. When you look at your smartphone, you do not blink often. Then your eyes will feel (A)[dry / drily].

Another problem you can have (B)[is / are] neck pain. When you look down at your smartphone, the stress on your neck increases. Too much use of your smartphone, for example, too much texting, can cause neck pain. ⓐWe call this text neck.

Here are some tips for ⓑthese problems. For dry eyes, try to blink often. For text neck, move your smartphone up to your eye level. You can also do some neck (C)[stretching / stretched] exercises.

18 위 글의 괄호 (A)~(C)에서 어법상 알맞은 낱말을 골라 쓰시오.

➡ (A) _____ (B) _____ (C) _____

19 위 글의 밑줄 친 ⓐ와 문장의 형식이 <u>다른</u> 것을 모두 고르시오.

① I painted the door green.
② She sent me a long letter.
③ He found this book easily.
④ Each girl kept her love a secret.
⑤ I gave her the book.

20 위 글의 밑줄 친 ⓑthese problems에 해당하지 <u>않는</u> 것을 고르시오.

① Your eyes will feel dry.
② You often blink.
③ You can have neck pain.
④ The stress on your neck increases.
⑤ Too much texting can cause text neck.

[21~22] 다음 글을 읽고 물음에 답하시오.

How do you feel when you don't have your smartphone with you?

Do you feel nervous when your smartphone is not around? Do you feel sad when you check your smartphone and there is no text message?

If your answers are "yes," you may have smartphone addiction. ⓐThere are various things you can do to prevent this. For example, turn off your smartphone during meals or meetings. You can talk to people instead of texting them.

21 위 글의 밑줄 친 ⓐ에서 things와 you 사이에 생략된 단어를 <u>모두</u> 고르시오.

① which   ② who
③ what   ④ that
⑤ whom

22 위 글의 내용과 일치하지 <u>않는</u> 것은?

① 스마트폰이 주위에 없을 때 초조한 기분이 들면 스마트폰 중독일지도 모른다.
② 스마트폰을 확인했을 때 아무런 문자 메시지가 없을 경우 슬픈 기분이 들면 스마트폰 중독일지도 모른다.
③ 스마트폰 중독을 예방하기 위해 할 수 있는 일은 별로 없다.
④ 스마트폰 중독을 예방하기 위해 식사나 회의 중에는 스마트폰을 꺼야 한다.
⑤ 스마트폰 중독을 예방하기 위해 문자를 보내는 대신에 사람들과 이야기를 할 수 있다.

Lesson

6

Different People, Different Views

 의사소통 기능

- 계획 말하기
  I'm planning to see a movie this Saturday.
- 약속 정하기
  A: What time and where should we meet?
  B: How about meeting at 2:30 in front of Star Movie Theater?
  A: OK. See you then.

 언어 형식

- 지각동사＋목적어＋-ing
  Daedalus **saw** birds **flying**.

- so ～ that ...
  Icarus was **so** excited **that** he forgot his father's warning.

Words & Expressions

Key Words

- **adventurous** [ædvéntʃərəs] 형 모험심이 강한
- **beauty** [bjúːti] 명 아름다움, 미
- **brave** [breiv] 형 용감한
- **concert** [káːnsərt] 명 콘서트
- **creative** [kriéitiv] 형 창의적인
- **detail** [ditéil] 명 세부 사항
- **different** [dífərənt] 형 다른
- **difference** [dífərəns] 명 차이
- **dynamic** [dainǽmik] 형 역동적인
- **escape** [iskéip] 동 달아나다, 탈출하다
- **example** [igzǽmpl] 명 예, 사례
- **exhibition** [èksəbíʃən] 명 전시회
- **fall** [fɔːl] 동 떨어지다 (-fell-fallen)
- **favorite** [féivərit] 형 가장 좋아하는
- **feather** [féðər] 명 (새의) 털, 깃털
- **flight** [flait] 명 비행, 날기
- **foolish** [fúːliʃ] 형 어리석은
- **forever** [fərévər] 부 영원히
- **forget** [fərgét] 동 잊어버리다, 잊다
- **furthermore** [fə́ːrðərmɔ̀ːr] 부 게다가, 더욱이
- **gather** [gǽðər] 동 모으다
- **glue** [gluː] 동 붙이다
- **Greek** [griːk] 형 그리스의
- **imaginative** [imǽdʒənətiv] 형 상상력이 풍부한
- **inventor** [invéntər] 명 발명가
- **library** [láibrèri] 명 도서관
- **melt** [melt] 동 녹다
- **myth** [miθ] 명 신화
- **outline** [áutlain] 명 윤곽, 외형
- **plan** [plæn] 동 계획하다, 계획을 세우다
- **ready** [rédi] 형 준비된
- **romantic** [rouméntik] 형 로맨틱한, 낭만적인
- **sci-fi movie** 공상 과학 영화
- **sentence** [séntəns] 명 문장
- **shout** [ʃaut] 동 외치다, 소리치다
- **simple** [símpl] 형 단순한
- **skip** [skip] 동 빼먹다, 거르다
- **special** [spéʃəl] 형 특별한
- **subject** [sʌ́bdʒikt] 명 주제
- **style** [stail] 명 화풍, 스타일
- **tea** [tiː] 명 차, 홍차
- **ticket office** 매표소
- **title** [táitl] 명 제목
- **tower** [táuər] 명 탑
- **violinist** [vàiəlínist] 명 바이올린 연주자
- **warn** [wɔːrn] 동 경고하다
- **warning** [wɔ́ːrniŋ] 명 경고, 주의
- **wax** [wæks] 명 밀랍, 왁스
- **whole** [houl] 형 전부의, 전체의
- **wing** [wiŋ] 명 날개

Key Expressions

- **be planning to+동사원형** ~할 계획이다
- **be interested in ~** ~에 관심이 있다
- **be proud of ~** ~을 자랑스러워하다
- **come from ~** ~로부터 오다
- **deal with** ~을 다루다
- **fall in love with ~** ~와 사랑에 빠지다
- **focus on ~** ~에 초점을 맞추다
- **How about -ing?** ~하는 게 어때?
- **higher and higher** 점점 더 높이
- **in addition to** ~에 더하여, ~일 뿐 아니라
- **in contrast** 그에 반해서
- **in front of ~** ~ 앞에
- **so 형용사 that ...** 너무 ~해서 …하다
- **try to+동사원형** ~하려고 시도하다
- **Why don't you+동사원형 ~?** ~하는 게 어때?

Word Power

※ 서로 반대되는 뜻을 가진 어휘

□ **different** (다른) ↔ **same** (같은)

□ **brave** (용감한) ↔ **timid** (겁 많은, 소심한)

□ **simple** (단순한) ↔ **complicated** (복잡한)

□ **romantic** (낭만적인) ↔ **unromantic** (낭만적이지 않은)

□ **foolish** (어리석은) ↔ **wise** (현명한)

□ **interested** (관심 있는) ↔ **uninterested** (무관심한)

※ 서로 비슷한 뜻을 가진 어휘

□ **gather** : **collect** (모으다)

□ **shout** : **yell** (외치다)

□ **glue** : **paste** (붙이다)

□ **foolish** : **silly** (어리석은)

□ **melt** : **thaw** (녹다)

□ **furthermore** : **moreover** (게다가)

English Dictionary

□ **adventurous** 모험심이 강한
→ willing to try new or exciting things
새롭고 흥미로운 일을 기꺼이 시도하려고 하는

□ **detail** 세부 사항
→ a small fact, feature, or piece of information
사소한 사실, 특징 또는 정보

□ **escape** 달아나다
→ to get away from a place or person
어떤 장소나 사람으로부터 멀리 벗어나다

□ **exhibition** 전시회
→ a public show of something
어떤 것을 공개적으로 보여주는 것

□ **feather** 깃털
→ one of the light soft things that cover a bird's body
새의 몸을 덮고 있는 가볍고 부드러운 것 중 하나

□ **flight** 비행
→ the act of flying through the air
공중을 나는 행위

□ **foolish** 어리석은
→ silly or not sensible
어리석거나 현명하지 않은

□ **furthermore** 게다가
→ used when adding another piece of information
또 다른 정보를 더할 때 사용되는

□ **gather** 모으다
→ to come together in a group
한 무리로 합치다

□ **glue** 붙이다
→ to join things together using glue
풀을 사용하여 물건을 결합하다

□ **in addition to** ~에 더하여
→ used for saying that something extra exists
추가적인 무언가가 존재한다는 것을 말하기 위해 사용되는

□ **myth** 신화
→ an old story about gods, brave people, magical creatures, etc.
신이나 용감한 사람들, 마법의 생물 등에 관한 오래된 이야기

□ **outline** 윤곽, 외형
→ a line that shows the shape of something
어떤 것의 모양을 보여주는 선

□ **romantic** 낭만적인
→ showing a strong feeling of love
강한 사랑의 감정을 드러내는

□ **shout** 소리치다
→ to say something very loudly
매우 크게 무언가를 말하다

□ **skip** 빼먹다, 거르다
→ to avoid something or not to do something
무언가를 피하거나 하지 않다

□ **tea** 차, 홍차
→ a hot drink that you make by pouring boiling water onto dried leaves
말린 잎에 끓는 물을 부어 만든 뜨거운 음료

□ **warn** 경고하다
→ to tell someone that something bad might happen, so that he or she can avoid it
그 혹은 그녀가 그것을 피할 수 있도록 누군가에게 어떤 나쁜 일이 일어날 수 있다고 말하다

□ **wax** 왁스, 밀랍
→ a substance used for making candles and crayons
양초와 크레용을 만드는 데 사용되는 물질

□ **wing** 날개
→ one of the parts of bird's or insect's body that it uses to fly
날기 위해 사용하는 새나 곤충의 몸의 한 부분

01 다음 빈칸에 들어갈 말로 알맞은 것은?

We often find different paintings with the _____ subject. An example is *The Flight of Icarus* by Henri Matisse and *The Fall of Icarus* by Marc Chagall.

① different ② brave
③ foolish ④ same
⑤ fallen

서답형
02 다음 영어 설명을 읽고 빈칸에 알맞은 말을 쓰시오.

In Greek _____, Icarus is the son of Daedalus, a great inventor.

an old story about gods, brave people, magical creatures, etc.

[03~04] 다음 영어 설명에 해당하는 단어를 고르시오.

03

one of the light soft things that cover a bird's body

① feature ② wing
③ feather ④ further
⑤ beak

중요
04

to say something very loudly

① escape ② gather
③ skip ④ warn
⑤ shout

서답형
05 다음 우리말에 맞게 빈칸에 알맞은 단어를 쓰시오.

Matisse와 Chagall 둘 다 그들의 그림에서 같은 주제를 다루지만, 그것들은 다르다.
➡ Matisse and Chagall both _____ _____ the same subject in their paintings, but they are different.

중요
06 다음 빈칸에 들어갈 말로 알맞은 것은?

Matisse thought that Icarus was brave and adventurous. _____, Chagall thought that Icarus was foolish.

① In addition ② In contrast
③ For example ④ Furthermore
⑤ In addition to

서답형
07 다음 짝지어진 단어의 관계가 같도록 빈칸에 알맞은 말을 쓰시오.

shout – yell : collect – _____

08 다음 빈칸에 들어갈 말로 알맞게 짝지어진 것은?

• Matisse's painting is very simple, but Chagall's painting has many _____.
• Don't fly too close to the sun. The wax will _____.

① differences – freeze
② differences – melt
③ details – freeze
④ details – melt
⑤ details – gather

01 다음 빈칸에 들어갈 말을 〈보기〉에서 찾아 쓰시오. (필요하면 변형하여 쓰시오.)

> ┤ 보기 ├
>
> flight   gather   adventurous   wax
> warn   detail   simple   outline

(1) When the wings were ready, he _____ his son, "Don't fly too close to the sun."

(2) Daedalus then _____ bird feathers and glued them together with _____.

(3) Matisse's painting is very _____. In his painting, Icarus' body has just a simple outline.

(4) Matisse thought that Icarus was brave and _____. In contrast, Chagall thought that Icarus was foolish.

02 영영풀이에 해당하는 단어를 〈보기〉에서 찾아 첫 번째 칸에 쓰고, 두 번째 칸에는 우리말 뜻을 쓰시오.

> ┤ 보기 ├
>
> adventurous   foolish   glue
> skip   escape   shout

(1) _____ : silly or not sensible : _____

(2) _____ : to avoid something or not to do something : _____

(3) _____ : willing to try new or exciting things: _____

(4) _____ : to join things together using glue: _____

03 두 그림의 특징을 설명하는 다음 글의 빈칸에 알맞은 단어를 〈보기〉에서 골라 쓰시오. (필요하면 어형을 변화시키시오.)

> ┤ 보기 ├
>
> detail   however   furthermore   outline
> in addition to   difference   title

Matisse's painting is very simple, but Chagall's painting has many (1)_____. In Matisse's painting, there are only Icarus and some stars. (2)_____, Icarus' body has just a simple (3)_____. In contrast, Chagall painted many people and houses (4)_____ _____ _____ Icarus.

04 다음 우리말과 같은 표현이 되도록 문장의 빈칸을 채우시오.

(1) Daedalus는 탈출하고 싶었다.
➡ Daedalus wanted to _____.

(2) Icarus는 매우 흥분해서 아버지의 경고를 잊었다.
➡ Icarus was so excited that he forgot his father's _____.

Conversation

1 계획 말하기

> I'm planning to see a movie this Saturday. 나는 이번 주 토요일에 영화를 볼 계획이야.

- 'be planning to+동사원형'은 '~할 계획이다'라는 의미로 미래의 계획을 말할 때 쓰며, '~할 예정이다' 라는 뜻의 'be going to+동사원형', 'be trying to+동사원형', 'be supposed to+동사원형' 등으로 바꿔 말할 수 있다.

- be going to+동사원형
  'be going to+동사원형' 구문은 현재 시점에서 실현 가능성을 확인할 수 있는 미래의 행위를 언급할 때 쓴 다. 즉, 이미 계획했거나 결정된 일 등에 주로 쓰이며 의도한 일이거나 이미 결정된 사실임을 강조한다.
  - I'm going to eat out tonight. 나는 오늘밤 외식을 할 것이다.
  - We're going to buy a new car soon. 우리는 곧 새 차를 구입할 것이다.
  - I'm planning to visit my grandparents this weekend. 나는 이번 주말에 조부모님을 방문할 계획이야.

- 계획을 묻는 표현
  - A: Are you planning to take a dance class? 너는 무용 수업을 받을 계획이니?
    B: Yes, I am. 응. 그래.

- Are you planning to invite him to your birthday party?
  = Are you going to invite him to your birthday party?
  = Are you trying to invite him to your birthday party? 너는 너의 생일 파티에 그를 초대할 거니?

핵심 Check

1. 다음 대화의 빈칸에 들어갈 말로 알맞은 것은?

   A: What are you planning to do this weekend?
   B: I'm _____ a trip with my family.

   ① plan to taking
   ② planning to taking
   ③ planning to take
   ④ plan to take
   ⑤ go to take

② 약속 정하기

A What time and where should we meet? 몇 시에 어디에서 만날까?

B How about meeting at 2:30 in front of Star Movie Theater?
Star 영화관 앞에서 2시 30분에 만나는 게 어때?

A OK. See you then. 좋아. 그때 보자.

■ 함께 하자고 제안을 할 때는 Do you want to go with me?, How about joining me? 등으로 말한다. 약속 시간이나 장소를 정할 때는 When/Where should we meet?, Can you make it at 5?, Shall we meet at the library? 등의 표현을 사용한다.

약속 시간 정하기

- When should we meet?
- Let's meet at 5.
- How about five o'clock?
- What time should we meet?
- Can you make it at 5?

■ 시간 약속을 정하는 표현에 알맞은 응답

- 수락할 때
  Sure. / Okay. / Yeah. / Sounds great. / All right. 좋아.
  See you then. 그때 보자.

- 거절할 때
  I'm afraid, I can't. How about at four? 미안하지만 안 돼. 4시는 어떨까?
  I'm sorry, but I can't make it at 3. 미안하지만 3시는 안되겠어.

■ 약속 장소 정하기
  - Where should we meet? 어디에서 만날까?
  - Let's meet at the library. 도서실에서 만나자.

핵심 Check

2. 다음 대화의 빈칸에 알맞은 것은?

A: _____ should we meet at the ballpark?

B: How about meeting at two?

① What   ② How

③ Where   ④ How many

⑤ What time

Listen and Talk A-1

G: ❶I'm planning to go to a piano concert tomorrow. ❷Do you want to go with me, Kevin?

B: Sure. ❸What time should we meet?

G: The concert begins at 7 o'clock, so ❹let's meet at 6 at the bus stop.

B: OK. See you then.

G: 나는 내일 피아노 콘서트에 갈 예정이야. 나랑 같이 갈래, Kevin?
B: 물론이지. 몇 시에 만날까?
G: 콘서트는 7시에 시작하니까 6시에 버스 정류장에서 만나자.
B: 좋아. 그때 보자.

❶ 'be planning to+동사원형'은 '~할 계획이다'라는 의미로 미래의 계획을 말할 때 사용하는 표현이다.
❷ 함께 하자고 제안을 할 때 사용하는 표현으로 How about joining me?로 바꾸어 표현할 수 있다.
❸ 약속 시간을 정할 때 사용하는 표현으로 '몇 시에 만날까?'로 해석한다. When should we meet?으로 표현할 수 있다.
❹ 'let's+동사원형'은 '~하자'라는 제안이나 권유의 의미로 사용된다.

Check(√) True or False

(1) Kevin is going to go to a piano concert with the girl. T ☐ F ☐

(2) They will meet at 7 o'clock at the bus stop. T ☐ F ☐

Listen and Talk A-2

G: ❶I'm planning to go see *Cats* this Saturday. Do you want to go with me?

B: Sure. ❷What time and where should we meet?

G: The musical starts at 3 o'clock. ❸Let's meet at 2 at Dream Art Hall.

B: Great. See you on Saturday.

G: 나는 이번 주 토요일에 'Cats'를 보러 갈 계획이야. 나랑 같이 갈래?
B: 좋아. 몇 시에 어디서 만날까?
G: 뮤지컬은 3시에 시작해. 2시에 Dream 아트 홀에서 만나자.
B: 좋아. 토요일에 만나자.

❶ 'be planning to+동사원형'은 '~할 계획이다'라는 의미이며 미래의 계획을 말할 때 사용하는 표현으로, '~할 예정이다'라는 뜻의 'be going to+동사원형', 'be trying to+동사원형', 'be supposed to+동사원형' 등으로 바꿔 말할 수 있다.
❷ 약속 시간과 장소를 정할 때 사용하는 표현이다. what time은 when으로 바꾸어 쓸 수 있다.
❸ 'let's+동사원형'은 '~하자'라는 약속 시간을 제안할 때 사용된다.

Check(√) True or False

(3) The girl wants to go to see the musical *Cats* with the boy. T ☐ F ☐

(4) The boy is going to meet the girl at 2 on Saturday. T ☐ F ☐

Listen and Talk A-3

G: I'm planning to go see a soccer game next Friday. ❶What about joining me, Jinho?

B: That sounds great. ❷What time should we meet?

G: Let's meet at 10:30 in front of Green Stadium.

B: OK. See you then.

❶ 함께 하자고 제안하는 표현으로 How about joining me?로 바꾸어 말할 수 있다.
❷ 약속 시간을 정할 때 사용하는 표현으로 '몇 시에 만날까?'라는 의미다.

Listen and Talk A-4

B: ❶What are you going to do this Sunday?

G: I'm planning to go to Dream Amusement Park with my brother. ❷You can go with us if you want to.

B: ❸I'd love to. When should we meet?

G: I want to go early, so let's meet at 9 at the subway station.

B: Sounds good. I'll see you then.

❶ 미래의 계획을 물어보는 표현이다.
❷ 함께 하자고 제안하는 표현으로 if you want to 뒤에는 go with us가 생략되어 있다.
❸ 제안을 승낙하는 표현으로 I'd love to go with you.를 줄여 쓴 말이다.

Listen and Talk B

A: I'm planning to see a movie this Saturday. Do you want to go with me?

B: Sure. What time and where should we meet?

A: ❶How about meeting at 2:30 in front of Star Movie Theater?

B: OK. See you then.

❶ 약속 시간을 제안하는 표현으로 '~하는 게 어때?'의 뜻이다.

Listen and Talk C

(*Smartphone rings.*)

B: Hi, Kate. What's up?

G: Hi, Minho. ❶What are you going to do this Saturday?

B: ❷Nothing special. Why?

G: ❸I'm planning to go to the Van Gogh exhibition at the National Art Museum. Do you want to go

with me?

B: I'd love to! He's my favorite painter. ❹What time should we meet?

G: How about meeting at 11?

B: OK. ❺Where should we meet?

G: Let's meet in front of the ticket office.

B: Sounds good. I'll see you there at 11.

❶ 미래의 계획을 물어보는 표현이다.
❷ nothing은 형용사가 뒤에서 수식을 한다.
❸ '~할 계획이다'라는 의미로 미래의 계획을 말할 때 사용하는 표현이다.
❹ 시간 약속을 정하는 표현이다.
❺ 장소를 정할 때 사용하는 표현이다.

Review 1

G: I'm planning to go to a piano concert this Friday. ❶Why don't you join me, Kevin?

B: Sure. What time should we meet?

G: ❷Let's meet at 10:30 at the bus stop.

B: OK. See you then.

❶ 함께 하자고 제안하는 표현으로 What about joining me, Kevin?과 같은 표현이다.
❷ 약속 시간을 제안할 때 사용하는 표현이다.

Review 2

B: ❶I'm planning to go to a soccer game tomorrow. Do you want to go with me, Susan?

G: Sure. ❷What time should we meet?

B: The game begins at 7, so let's meet at 6 in front of Dream Stadium.

G: OK. See you then.

❶ 미래의 계획을 물어보는 표현으로, 'I'm going to go ~'와 같은 의미로 사용된다.
❷ 약속 시간을 제안할 때 사용하는 표현이다.

Review 3

B: Sumi, I'm planning to go shopping with Jenny this Saturday. ❶Will you join us?

G: Sounds great. ❷What time should we meet?

B: ❸How about meeting at 12:30?

G: OK. Where should we meet?

B: Let's meet in front of the shopping mall.

❶ 함께 하자고 제안하는 표현이다.
❷ 시간 약속을 정하는 표현이다.
❸ 시간을 제안할 때 사용하는 표현이다.

● 다음 우리말과 일치하도록 빈칸에 알맞은 말을 쓰시오.

Listen and Talk A-1

G: I'm _____ _____ _____ to a piano concert tomorrow. Do you want _____ _____ _____ me, Kevin?

B: Sure. _____ _____ should we meet?

G: The concert begins at 7 o'clock, so _____ meet at 6 at the bus stop.

B: OK. _____ you then.

Listen and Talk A-2

G: I'm _____ to go see *Cats* this Saturday. Do you _____ to go with me?

B: Sure. _____ _____ and _____ _____ we meet?

G: The musical starts at 3 o'clock. _____ _____ at 2 at Dream Art Hall.

B: Great. See you _____ Saturday.

Listen and Talk A-3

G: I'm planning _____ _____ _____ a soccer game next Friday. _____ _____ _____ me, Jinho?

B: That _____ great. What time _____ _____ _____?

G: _____ _____ at 10:30 _____ _____ Green Stadium.

B: OK. See you then.

Listen and Talk A-4

B: _____ are you _____ _____ _____ this Sunday?

G: I'm _____ _____ _____ to Dream Amusement Park with my brother. You can go with us _____ you _____ _____.

B: I'd _____ _____. _____ _____ we meet?

G: I want to go early, so _____ _____ at 9 at the subway station.

B: _____ good. I'll see you then.

Listen and Talk B

A: I'm _____ to see a movie this Saturday. Do you _____ _____ go with me?

B: Sure. _____ _____ and _____ should we meet?

A: _____ about _____ at 2:30 in front of Star Movie Theater?

B: OK. See you then.

해석

G: 나는 내일 피아노 콘서트에 갈 예정이야. 나랑 같이 갈래, Kevin?
B: 물론이지. 몇 시에 만날까?
G: 콘서트는 7시에 시작하니까 6시에 버스 정류장에서 만나자.
B: 좋아. 그때 보자.

G: 나는 이번 주 토요일에 'Cats'를 보러 갈 계획이야. 나랑 같이 갈래?
B: 좋아. 몇 시에 어디서 만날까?
G: 뮤지컬은 3시에 시작해. 2시에 Dream 아트 홀에서 만나자.
B: 좋아. 토요일에 만나자.

G: 나는 다음 주 금요일에 축구 경기를 보러 갈 계획이야. 나랑 같이 가는 게 어떠니, 진호야?
B: 좋은 생각이다. 몇 시에 만날까?
G: Green 경기장 앞에서 10시 30분에 만나자.
B: 좋아. 그때 보자.

B: 이번 주 일요일에 무엇을 할 계획이니?
G: 나는 내 남동생과 Dream 놀이동산에 갈 예정이야. 만약 네가 원한다면 우리와 함께 가도 돼.
B: 그러고 싶어. 언제 만날까?
G: 나는 일찍 가고 싶어, 그래서 9시에 지하철역에서 만나자.
B: 좋아. 그때 보자.

A: 나는 이번 주 토요일에 영화를 볼 계획이야. 나랑 같이 갈래?
B: 물론이지. 몇 시에 어디에서 만날까?
A: Star 영화관 앞에서 2시 30분에 만나는 게 어때?.
B: 좋아. 그때 보자.

Listen and Talk C

(*Smartphone rings.*)

B: Hi, Kate. What's up?

G: Hi, Minho. What are you _____ _____ _____ this Saturday?

B: Nothing _____. Why?

G: I'm _____ _____ _____ to the Van Gogh exhibition at the National Art Museum. Do you want to go with me?

B: I'd _____ _____! He's my favorite painter. _____ _____ _____ we meet?

G: _____ _____ meeting at 11?

B: OK. _____ _____ we meet?

G: _____ meet in front _____ the ticket office.

B: Sounds good. I'll see you there at 11.

Review 1

G: I'm planning to go to a piano concert this Friday. _____ _____ _____ join me, Kevin?

B: Sure. What time _____ _____ _____?

G: _____ _____ at 10:30 at the bus stop.

B: OK. See you _____.

Review 2

B: I'm planning to go to a soccer game tomorrow. _____ _____ _____ to go with me, Susan?

G: Sure. What time _____ we meet?

B: The game begins at 7, so _____ meet at 6 in _____ of Dream Stadium.

G: OK. See you then.

Review 3

B: Sumi, _____ _____ _____ go shopping with Jenny this Saturday. Will you _____ us?

G: Sounds great. What time should we meet?

B: How about _____ at 12:30?

G: OK. _____ should we meet?

B: Let's meet _____ _____ _____ the shopping mall.

해석

(스마트폰이 울린다.)
B: 안녕, Kate. 무슨 일이야?
G: 안녕, 민호야. 이번 토요일에 뭐 할 거야?
B: 특별한 일은 없어. 왜?
G: 나는 국립 미술관에서 하는 반 고흐 전시회에 갈 계획이야. 나와 함께 갈래?
B: 그러고 싶어! 그는 내가 가장 좋아하는 화가거든. 몇 시에 만날까?
G: 11시에 만나는 게 어때?
B: 좋아. 어디에서 만날까?
G: 매표소 앞에서 만나자.
B: 좋아. 11시에 거기에서 봐.

G: 나는 이번 주 금요일에 피아노 콘서트에 갈 계획이야. 나랑 같이 가는 게 어때, Kevin?
B: 물론이지. 몇 시에 만날까?
G: 10시 30분에 버스 정류장에서 만나자.
B: 좋아. 그때 보자.

B: 나는 내일 축구 경기에 갈 계획이야. 나랑 같이 갈래, Susan?
G: 물론이지. 몇 시에 만날까?
B: 경기는 7시에 시작하니까, Dream 경기장 앞에서 6시에 만나자.
G: 좋아. 그때 보자.

B: 수미야, 나 이번 주 토요일에 Jenny와 쇼핑을 갈 계획이야. 너도 같이 갈래?
G: 좋은 생각이야. 몇 시에 만날까?
B: 12시 30분에 만나는 게 어때?
G: 좋아. 어디서 만날까?
B: 쇼핑몰 앞에서 만나자.

01 우리말에 맞게 주어진 단어를 이용하여 빈칸에 알맞은 말을 쓰시오.

> 나는 이번 주 토요일에 영화를 볼 계획이야. (plan)
> ➡ I'm _____ _____ _____ a movie this Saturday.

02 다음 대화의 빈칸에 들어갈 말이 바르게 짝지어진 것은?

> A: __(A)__ should we meet?
> B: How about meeting at 5:30?
> A: OK. __(B)__ should we meet?
> B: Let's meet in front of the library.
> A: Sounds good. See you then.

① When – What time   ② Why don't we – Where
③ Where – When   ④ What time –Where
⑤ Why – When

03 다음 대화의 빈칸에 들어갈 말로 알맞은 것은?

> A: _____
> B: I'm planning to go to the Van Gogh exhibition at the National Art Museum.

① What are you doing now?
② Where are you going?
③ Where should we meet?
④ What were you doing last night?
⑤ What are you going to do this Saturday?

04 다음 대화의 빈칸에 들어갈 말로 알맞은 것은?

> A: I'm planning to go to a soccer game tomorrow. Do you want to go with me, Susan?
> B: Sure. _____ should we meet?
> A: Let's meet at 4 after school.

① Who   ② How   ③ When
④ What   ⑤ Where

[01~02] 다음 대화를 읽고 물음에 답하시오.

> Jenny: I'm planning to go to a piano concert tomorrow. _____ (A)
>
> Kevin: Sure. (B)몇 시에 만날까?
>
> Jenny: The concert begins at 7 o'clock, so let's meet at 6 at the bus stop.
>
> Kevin: OK. See you then.

01 위 대화의 빈칸 (A)에 들어갈 말로 어색한 것은?

① What about joining me, Kevin?
② Can you make it around two?
③ Why don't you join me, Kevin?
④ Do you want to go with me, Kevin?
⑤ Will you join me?

서답형

02 위 대화의 밑줄 친 (B)의 우리말에 맞게 주어진 단어를 이용하여 영어로 쓰시오.

> time / should / what / we / meet / ?

➡ _____

서답형

03 자연스러운 대화가 되도록 (A)~(D)를 바르게 배열하시오.

> A: I'm planning to go swimming this Wednesday. Do you want to go with me, Minsu?
>
> (A) OK. Where should we meet?
> (B) Sure. What time should we meet?
> (C) How about meeting at 10:30?
> (D) Let's meet at the bus stop.
>
> B: Sounds good. See you then.

➡ _____

서답형

04 밑줄 친 (A)의 우리말에 맞게 주어진 어구를 이용하여 영어로 쓰시오. (어형 변화 필수)

> A: (A)이번 주 일요일에 하이킹을 갈 계획이야. Do you want to go with me, Jina?
>
> B: I'm sorry, but I have other plans.
>
> A: OK.

> be / plan / go / hike / this Sunday

➡ _____

[05~07] 다음 대화를 읽고 물음에 답하시오.

> B: What are you going to do this Sunday?
>
> G: (A) I'm planning to go to Dream Amusement Park with my brother. You can go with us if you want to.
>
> B: I'd love to. ___(B)___ should we meet?
>
> G: I want to go early, so let's meet at 9 at the subway station.
>
> B: Sounds good. I'll see you then.

중요

05 위 대화의 밑줄 친 (A)의 의도로 알맞은 것은?

① 시간 약속 정하기 ② 경험 말하기
③ 조언 구하기 ④ 취미 말하기
⑤ 계획 말하기

06 위 대화의 빈칸 (B)에 들어갈 말로 알맞은 것은?

① When ② Who ③ What
④ How ⑤ Why

서답형

07 위 대화를 읽고 다음 물음에 대해 영어로 답하시오.

> Q: When and where are the speakers going to meet?

➡ They are going _____.

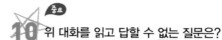

서답형

08 다음 대화의 밑줄 친 우리말에 맞게 주어진 어구를 이용하여 영어로 쓰시오. (어형 변화 필수)

> A: I'm planning to see a movie this Saturday. Do you want to go with me?
> B: Sure. What time and where should we meet?
> A: <u>Star 영화관 앞에서 2시 30분에 만나는 게 어때?</u>
> B: OK. See you then.

> how / meet / 2:30 / Star Movie Theater / front / about / at / ?

➡ _____

_____

[09~10] 다음 대화를 읽고 물음에 답하시오.

> (*Smartphone rings.*)
> B: Hi, Kate. What's up?
> G: Hi, Minho. What are you going to do this Saturday?
> B: (①) Nothing special. Why?
> G: (②) I'm planning to go to the Van Gogh exhibition at the National Art Museum. Do you want to go with me?
> B: (③) What time should we meet?
> G: How about meeting at 11?
> B: (④) OK. Where should we meet?
> G: Let's meet in front of the ticket office.
> B: Sounds good. (⑤) I'll see you there at 11.

09 위 대화의 ①~⑤ 중 다음 문장이 들어갈 위치로 알맞은 것은?

> I'd love to! He's my favorite painter.

①   ②   ③   ④   ⑤

10 위 대화를 읽고 답할 수 <u>없는</u> 질문은?

① What exhibition is Kate planning to go to this Saturday?
② What are Kate and Minho talking about?
③ When are Kate and Minho going to meet?
④ Where are Kate and Minho going to meet?
⑤ Why did Minho invite Kate to the Van Gogh exhibition?

[11~13] 다음 대화를 읽고 물음에 답하시오.

> A: I'm planning to go to the library this Monday. Do you want to go with me, Jiho?
> B: Sure. (a)<u>몇 시에 만날까?</u>
> A: How about ___(A)___ at 5:30?
> B: OK. Where should we meet?
> A: (b)<u>Let's meet in front of the library.</u>
> B: Sounds good. See you then.

11 위 대화의 빈칸 (A)에 들어갈 단어의 형태로 알맞은 것은?

① meet   ② to meet
③ meeting   ④ to meeting
⑤ met

서답형

12 위 대화의 밑줄 친 (a)의 우리말에 맞게 주어진 단어를 이용하여 영어로 쓰시오.

> what / should

➡ _____

서답형

13 위 대화의 밑줄 친 (b)와 같은 의미의 표현을 쓰고자 한다. 주어진 단어로 시작하여 문장을 쓰시오.

➡ Why _____?
     Shall _____?

Conversation 서술형 시험대비

01 다음 대화의 밑줄 친 (A)의 우리말에 맞게 주어진 단어를 이용하여 영작하시오.

> G: (A)나는 이번 주 금요일에 피아노 콘서트에 갈 계획이야. (plan / go / concert / this) Why don't you join me, Kevin?
> B: Sure. What time should we meet?
> G: Let's meet at 10:30 at the bus stop.
> B: OK. See you then.

➡ _____

02 다음 대화의 빈칸 (A)와 (B)에 들어갈 문장을 주어진 〈조건〉에 맞게 완성하시오.

> A: I'm planning to go to the Picasso exhibition this Thursday. _____(A)_____, Sumi?
> B: Sure. What time should we meet?
> A: How about meeting at 4 after school?
> B: OK. _____(B)_____
> A: Let's meet at Sejong Art Hall.
> B: Sounds good. See you then.

┤ (A) 조건 ├
- 함께 하자고 제안하는 표현을 쓸 것.
- want와 with를 이용할 것

➡ _____

┤ (B) 조건 ├
- 약속 장소를 정하는 표현을 쓸 것.
- 조동사 should를 이용할 것

➡ _____

03 다음 대화의 빈칸에 들어갈 말로 자연스러운 것을 〈보기〉에서 찾아 쓰시오.

> B: _____(A)_____
> G: I'm planning to go to Dream Amusement Park with my brother. _____(B)_____
> B: I'd love to. _____(C)_____
> G: I want to go early, so let's meet at 9 at the subway station.
> B: Sounds good. I'll see you then.

┤ 보기 ├
- When should we meet?
- What are you going to do this Sunday?
- You can go with us if you want to.

(A) _____
(B) _____
(C) _____

04 다음 대화의 빈칸 (A)는 밑줄 친 말에 대한 질문이다. 주어진 〈조건〉에 맞게 문장을 완성하시오.

> G: I'm planning to go see *Cats* this Saturday. Do you want to go with me?
> B: Sure. _____(A)_____
> G: The musical starts at 3 o'clock. Let's meet at 2 at Dream Art Hall.
> B: Great. See you on Saturday.

┤ 조건 ├
- 의문사 what과 where를 이용할 것
- 접속사 and를 쓸 것
- 조동사 should를 쓸 것
  (meet)

➡ _____

Grammar

1 지각동사+목적어+-ing

- Daedalus **saw** birds **flying**. Daedalus는 새가 날고 있는 것을 보았다.
- I **heard** him **sing**. 나는 그가 노래하는 소리를 들었다.

■ 지각동사는 '보다, 듣다, 느끼다'의 의미를 갖는 see, look at, watch, hear, listen to, feel 등의 동사를 말하며, 일반적으로 목적어와 함께 3형식 문장을 이루지만, 목적어와 목적격 보어가 있는 5형식 문장으로도 많이 쓰인다. 지각동사가 쓰인 5형식 문장에서 목적격 보어가 될 수 있는 말은 원형부정사와 분사(현재분사 / 과거분사)이다. 원형부정사와 현재분사의 차이는 현재분사에 진행의 의미가 들어간다는 점이다.

- They **saw** him **cross** the street. 그들은 그가 길을 건너는 것을 보았다.
- Did you **hear** Sally **crying**? 너는 Sally가 울고 있는 소리를 들었니?

■ '지각동사+목적어+원형부정사[현재분사]'로 쓰이는 경우, 목적어와 목적격보어는 능동 관계가 된다. '지각동사+목적어+과거분사'로 쓰이는 경우 목적어와 목적격보어의 관계는 수동이다.

- I **felt** someone **touch** my shoulder. 나는 누군가 내 어깨를 만지는 것을 느꼈다.
- I **heard** my name **called**. 나는 내 이름을 부르는 소리를 들었다.

■ 사역동사 make, have, let과 혼동하지 않도록 한다. 사역동사도 5형식 동사로 목적어와 목적격보어를 취하지만, 사역동사의 목적격보어로는 현재분사가 오지 않는다.

- The teacher **made** me **do** it again. 선생님은 나에게 그것을 다시 하라고 시키셨다.
- I **had** my bicycle **fixed** yesterday. 나는 어제 내 자전거가 수리되도록 했다.

핵심 Check

1. 다음 우리말과 일치하도록 빈칸에 알맞은 말을 쓰시오.
   (1) 나는 내 동생이 숙제하고 있는 것을 보았다.
      ➡ I _____ my brother _____ his homework.
   (2) 나는 Amy가 설거지하는 소리를 들었다.
      ➡ I _____ Amy _____ the dishes.
   (3) 난 방을 청소시켜야 한다.
      ➡ I must have the room _____.

2 so ~ that ...

- Icarus was **so** excited **that** he forgot his father's warning.
  Icarus는 너무 흥분해서 아버지의 경고를 잊었다.

- It's **so** cold **that** I want to drink hot tea. 너무 추워서 나는 뜨거운 차를 마시고 싶어요.

- 'so+형용사[부사]+that+주어+동사' 구문은 '너무 ~해서 …하다'라는 뜻으로 so 다음에는 형용사나 부사가 오고 that 다음에는 주어와 동사가 있는 절이 온다. so 다음에 나오는 말이 '원인', that 다음에 나오는 절이 그에 따른 '결과'를 나타낸다.
  - It's **so** cold **that** I don't want to play outside. 너무 추워서 나는 밖에서 놀고 싶지 않다.

- 'so ~ that …' 구문에서 that 앞에 형용사나 부사 대신 명사가 오면 so 대신 such를 쓴다.
  - It gave him **such** a shock **that** his face turned white.
    그는 그것에 큰 충격을 받은 나머지 얼굴이 하얗게 질렸다.

- 'so that+주어+동사'는 목적을 나타내어 '~하기 위해서' 혹은 '~하도록'이라는 의미로 쓰인다. 'so ~ that …'과 혼동하지 않도록 유의한다.
  - He is wearing a baseball cap **so that** his face is hidden.
    그는 야구 모자를 쓰고 있어서 그의 얼굴은 가려 있었다.

- 'so+형용사[부사]+that+주어+can ~'은 '형용사[부사]+enough+to 동사원형'으로 바꿔 쓸 수 있으며, 'so+형용사[부사]+that+주어+can't ~'는 'too+형용사[부사]+to 동사원형'으로 바꿔 쓸 수 있다.
  - He is **so** rich **that** he can hire a driver.
    = He is rich **enough to** hire a driver. 그는 운전사를 고용할 수 있을 만큼 부자다.
  - My sister was **so** young **that** she couldn't ride it by herself.
    = My sister was **too** young **to** ride it by herself. 제 여동생은 너무 어려서 혼자서 탈 수가 없었어요.

핵심 Check

2. 다음 우리말에 맞게 괄호 안의 단어를 바르게 배열하시오.

(1) Emma는 너무 지루해서 혼자 노래를 부르기 시작했다.

(Emma, she, herself, singing, bored, started, was, so, that, by)

➡ _____

(2) 우리 팀은 경기에 이기기 위해 열심히 연습했다.

(Our team, the game, we, could, practiced, win, so, that, hard)

➡ _____

(3) 나는 너무 피곤해서 일을 할 수 없었다.

(I, I, work, was, couldn't, tired, so, that)

➡ _____

01 다음 문장에서 어법상 <u>어색한</u> 부분을 바르게 고치시오.

(1) He heard the bird sang.

_____ ➡ _____

(2) Daedalus saw birds to fly.

_____ ➡ _____

(3) She was very sick that she had to stay in bed.

_____ ➡ _____

(4) Tom was so busy what he couldn't go out.

_____ ➡ _____

02 주어진 단어를 어법에 맞게 빈칸에 쓰시오.

(1) They heard the baby _____. (cry)
(2) They saw the trash _____ away. (throw)
(3) People gathered to watch the house _____. (burn)
(4) She felt the rain _____ on her face. (fall)

03 다음 우리말을 영어로 바르게 옮긴 것은?

> 질문이 너무 쉬워서 모두가 그것에 답했다.

① The question was very easy that everybody answered it.
② The question was too easy that everybody answered it.
③ The question was enough easy that everybody answered it.
④ The question was so easy that everybody answered it.
⑤ The question was easy so that everybody answered it.

04 주어진 단어를 바르게 배열하여 다음 우리말을 영어로 쓰시오. 필요하다면 단어를 추가하거나 변형하시오.

> 그는 너무 늦게 도착해서 비행기를 놓쳤다.
> (he / he / his / plane / late / missed / arrived / that)

➡ _____

01 다음 빈칸에 알맞은 말이 순서대로 바르게 짝지어진 것은?

> • Minsu sees some boys _____ baseball.
> • The bus was _____ late that they had to wait for a long time.

① play – too   ② played – very
③ played – so   ④ playing – very
⑤ playing – so

02 다음 빈칸에 들어갈 말로 가장 적절한 것은?

> I heard someone _____ my name on the street.

① calls   ② call   ③ called
④ to call   ⑤ to calling

03 다음 빈칸에 알맞은 말이 바르게 짝지어진 것을 고르시오.

> Sujin studied _____ hard _____ she got an A on the test.

① so – that   ② that – so
③ very – that   ④ too – that
⑤ too – to

서답형

04 주어진 단어를 이용하여 다음 우리말을 영어로 쓰시오. (10 단어)

> 물고기가 너무 빨라서 나는 잡을 수가 없다.
> (the fish / catch / fast / so)

➡ _____

중요

05 다음 중 어법상 바르지 않은 것은?

① I see a person carrying a box on the street.
② We heard a girl singing on the stage.
③ She could feel somebody pulling her hair.
④ I watched him to sing in his first performance.
⑤ The students listened to Ella introduce herself.

서답형

06 다음 괄호 안에서 알맞은 것을 고르시오.

(1) I was surprised to see him (to touch / touching) the snake.
(2) The teacher heard Minsu (sing / sang) a song.
(3) I listened to the song (repeat / repeated) endlessly in the kitchen.
(4) Are you making her (cleaning / clean) our bathroom?
(5) Brian was (so / very) tired that he didn't go out.
(6) I got up so late (that / what) I was late for class.
(7) The boy was (too / very) small to ride a horse.

중요

07 다음 중 어법상 바르지 <u>않은</u> 것은?

> I ①heard ②my name ③to call ④on the
> street ⑤by my neighbor.

①   ②   ③   ④   ⑤

서답형

08 다음 문장에서 어법상 <u>틀린</u> 부분을 찾아 바르게 고치시오.

> The boy was thirsty so that he drank a
> glass of water.

_____ ➡ _____

[09~10] 다음 우리말을 영어로 바르게 옮긴 것을 <u>모두</u> 고르시오.

09

> 나는 내 남동생이 강에서 수영하고 있는 것을 봤다.

① I saw my brother swam in the river.
② I saw my brother swum in the river.
③ I saw my brother swim in the river.
④ I saw my brother swimming in the river.
⑤ I saw my brother to swim in the river.

10

> 그는 열심히 연습해서 우승할 수 있었다.

① He practiced very hard that he could win
first prize.
② He practiced hard so that he could win
first prize.
③ He practiced so hard that he could win
first prize.
④ He practiced too hard to win first prize.
⑤ He practiced hard enough to win first
prize.

서답형

11 다음 대화의 빈칸에 알맞은 말을 4단어로 쓰시오.

> A: Did Mina open the window?
> B: I think so. I heard _____
> _____ .

12 다음 중 어법상 올바른 문장을 <u>모두</u> 고르시오.

① I heard Somi talked with Yubin.
② Minsu sees an old man reading a book.
③ He was busy so that he skipped lunch.
④ It was so a nice day that we went on a
picnic.
⑤ The room is so dark that I can't see
anything.

중요

13 다음 중 (A)~(C)에서 어법상 옳은 것끼리 바르게 짝지은 것은?

> • Eric saw Sue (A)(painting / to paint) a
> picture.
> • He felt somebody (B)(touch / to touch)
> his hand.
> • Andrew heard his name (C)(calling /
> called) behind his back.

① to paint – touch – calling
② to paint – to touch – called
③ painting – touch – called
④ painting – touch – calling
⑤ painting – to touch – calling

14 다음 우리말을 영어로 바르게 옮기지 <u>않은</u> 것은?

> 그들은 마술이 어떻게 일어나는지를 배우기 위해 열심히 공부해야 한다.

① They must study hard so that they can learn how magic works.
② They must study so hard that they can learn how magic works.
③ They must study hard to learn how magic works.
④ They must study hard in order to learn how magic works.
⑤ They must study hard so as to learn how magic works.

15 다음 주어진 문장의 밑줄 친 부분과 쓰임이 같은 것은?

> I heard her <u>singing</u> in the room.

① <u>Forgetting</u> his father's warning, Icarus flew higher and higher.
② King Minos was <u>keeping</u> Daedalus and Icarus in a tall tower.
③ Mike saw a bird <u>flying</u>.
④ My plan was <u>visiting</u> Paris again.
⑤ I thought she enjoyed <u>eating</u> *bulgogi*.

16 다음 문장을 주어진 어휘를 이용하여 바꿔 쓰시오.

(1) My sister was very tired, so she went to bed early. (so, that)

   ⇒ _____

(2) We had to stay at home because it rained really hard. (so, that)

   ⇒ _____

17 다음 괄호 안에 주어진 어구를 이용하여 우리말을 영어로 옮기시오.

(1) 나는 정원에서 책을 읽고 있을 때, 토끼가 혼잣말을 하고 있는 것을 들었다.
   (a rabbit, a book, hear, talk, to himself)

   ⇒ _____

   _____

(2) 나는 그가 내 머리카락을 잡아당기는 것을 느낄 수 있었다. (feel, pull, my hair)

   ⇒ _____

(3) Somin이는 Minji가 자전거를 타고 있는 것을 보았다. (a bike, see, ride)

   ⇒ _____

(4) 그녀는 너무 천천히 걸어서 모두 그녀를 지나쳐 갔다. (everybody, walk, pass by, slowly, so, that)

   ⇒ _____

(5) 너무 배불러서 더 이상 못 먹겠어.
   (full, can't, so, anymore)

   ⇒ _____

18 다음 문장에서 어법상 어색한 부분을 바르게 고치시오.

(1) I watched my sister to download songs from the Internet.

   _____ ⇒ _____

(2) The library is very big that you may get lost in it.

   _____ ⇒ _____

(3) She was surprised enough to say anything.

   _____ ⇒ _____

01 다음 문장에서 어법상 <u>어색한</u> 부분을 고쳐 다시 쓰시오.

(1) Eric heard Mina played the guitar.

➡ _____

(2) I saw Mike to swim in the lake.

➡ _____

(3) She felt her heart beats fast.

➡ _____

(4) Simpson won the Trophy in 2008 but saw it stealing 10 years ago.

➡ _____

_____

(5) She got up very late that she had to run all the way to school.

➡ _____

_____

(6) She speaks too quietly for me understanding.

➡ _____

(7) I left early enough arriving on time.

➡ _____

02 다음 두 문장을 〈보기〉와 같이 지각동사를 이용하여 한 문장으로 완성하시오.

┌─ 보기 ├─
- I went to the library.
- Sara was studying there.
➡ I saw Sara studying in the library.

- I went to the concert.
- Maryline was singing a song there.

➡ _____

03 다음 문장을 to부정사를 이용하여 바꿔 쓰시오.

(1) Dad was so busy that he couldn't play with us.

➡ _____

(2) The dog was so small that it could go through the hole.

➡ _____

_____

(3) The coffee is so hot that she can't drink it.

➡ _____

(4) The math problem was so easy that Laura could solve it.

➡ _____

_____

04 그림을 보고 주어진 어구를 바르게 배열하여 문장을 완성하시오.

Pandora, she, Zeus, the box, was, had given, opened, that, foolish, which, her, so, to

➡ _____

_____

05 다음 두 문장을 〈보기〉와 같이 한 문장으로 쓰시오.

┌─ 보기 ┐

The boy was very kind. Everyone liked him.

➡ The boy was so kind that everyone liked him.

(1) • It rained really hard.
    • He couldn't play soccer.

➡ _____

(2) • Last night I was very tired.
    • I went to bed early.

➡ _____

(3) • The box was too heavy.
    • I couldn't carry it.

➡ _____

(4) • There were too many people.
    • We didn't get into the sea.

➡ _____
_____

(5) • They had to cancel the game.
    • It rained really heavily.

➡ _____

06 〈보기〉에서 의미상 적절한 단어를 골라 빈칸에 알맞은 형태로 쓰시오.

┌─ 보기 ┐

arrest / carry / take / open

(1) Sally wanted me _____ _____ the box for her.

(2) I saw Mike _____ by the police on my way home.

(3) I heard her _____ the window.

(4) Mom made me _____ the umbrella with me.

07 다음 문장을 so와 that을 이용하여 바꾸어 쓰시오.

(1) It was too dark for us to see anything.

➡ _____

(2) I want to live long enough to see you rise in the world.

➡ _____
_____

08 다음 두 문장을 〈보기〉와 같이 한 문장으로 바꿔 쓰시오.

┌─ 보기 ┐

We saw him. + He was standing still.
= We saw him standing still.

(1) He looked at the violinist.
    + The violinist was dancing.

➡ _____

(2) The teacher heard Somin.
    + She was playing the piano.

➡ _____

09 다음 그림을 참고하여 단어 fall의 알맞은 형태를 빈칸에 알맞게 채우시오.

Daedalus saw Icarus _____ into the sea.

Reading

교과서

Same Story, Different Paintings

We often find different paintings with the same subject. An example
빈도부사 – 일반동사 앞   (그림 · 사진 등의) 대상[소재]
is *The Flight of Icarus* by Henri Matisse and *The Fall of Icarus*
저자 이름 앞의 'by': …가 했[쓴/만든 등]
by Marc Chagall. They are both about the same Greek myth.
둘 다(They와 동격)

The Greek Myth of Icarus

Daedalus was a great inventor. King Minos liked Daedalus' work so
invent+-or   so+부사+that+주어+동사: '매우 ~해서 …하다'
much that he wanted to keep Daedalus with him forever. Daedalus,

however, tried to leave, so the King kept him and his son, Icarus, in a
~하려고 애썼다   ('이유'를 나타내어) 그래서   동격
tall tower. Daedalus wanted to escape.
want는 목적어로 to부정사를 쓴다.

One day, Daedalus saw birds flying. "Wings! I need wings!" he
지각동사 see의 목적격 보어: 동사원형 또는 -ing(진행의 의미를 강조)
shouted. Daedalus then gathered bird feathers and glued them together
                                                        bird feathers
with wax. When the wings were ready, he warned his son, "Don't fly
~으로
too close to the sun. The wax will melt."
너무 가깝게

Daedalus and Icarus began to fly. Icarus was so excited that he forgot
= began flying   so+형용사+that+주어+동사: '매우 ~해서 …하다'
his father's warning. He flew higher and higher, and the wax began to
"Don't fly too close to the sun. The wax will melt." 비교급+and+비교급: '점점 더 ~하게'   = began melting
melt. "Oh, no! I'm falling," Icarus cried out. Icarus fell into the sea and

died.

---

flight 비행, 날기
myth 신화
escape 탈출하다
wing 날개
shout 외치다
gather 모으다
feather 깃털
wax 밀랍, 왁스
warn 경고하다, 주의를 주다

확인문제

● 다음 문장이 본문의 내용과 일치하면 T, 일치하지 않으면 F를 쓰시오.

1 *The Flight of Icarus* by Henri Matisse and *The Fall of Icarus* by Marc Chagall are
both about the same Greek myth. ☐

2 Icarus was a great inventor. ☐

3 Daedalus gathered bird feathers and sewed them together. ☐

4 Daedalus warned his son not to fly too close to the sun. ☐

5 Icarus was so excited that he forgot his father's warning. ☐

6 Icarus flew higher and higher, and succeeded in escaping. ☐

Two Different Paintings

Matisse and Chagall both deal with the same subject in their paintings, but they are different. First, in Matisse's painting, you can see Icarus flying, but in Chagall's painting, the boy is falling. This difference comes from the different ideas that the two painters had. Matisse thought that Icarus was brave and adventurous. In contrast, Chagall thought that Icarus was foolish.

Second, Matisse's painting is very simple, but Chagall's painting has many details. In Matisse's painting, there are only Icarus and some stars. Furthermore, Icarus' body has just a simple outline. In contrast, Chagall painted many people and houses in addition to Icarus. This difference comes from the different painting styles of the two painters.

Whose painting do you like more? People will have different answers because they may see the same thing in different ways.

deal with (주제, 소재로) ~을 다루다

adventurous 모험심이 강한

in contrast 그에 반해서, 반면에

simple 단순한

detail 세부 사항

furthermore 게다가, 더욱이

outline 윤곽

in addition to ~뿐만 아니라, ~에 더하여

확인문제

- 다음 문장이 본문의 내용과 일치하면 T, 일치하지 않으면 F를 쓰시오.

1 Matisse and Chagall deal with the same subject in their paintings in different ways. ☐

2 In Matisse's painting, you can see Icarus falling. ☐

3 In Chagall's painting, Icarus is flying. ☐

4 Matisse thought that Icarus was brave and adventurous. ☐

5 Chagall thought that Icarus was foolish. ☐

6 Matisse painted many people and houses in addition to Icarus. ☐

● 우리말을 참고하여 빈칸에 알맞은 말을 쓰시오.

1 _____ Story, _____ Paintings

2 We often find _____ _____ with _____ _____ _____.

3 An _____ is *The Flight of Icarus* _____ Henri Matisse and *The Fall of Icarus* _____ Marc Chagall.

4 They are both about _____ _____ _____ _____.

5 The _____ _____ of Icarus

6 Daedalus was _____ _____ _____.

7 King Minos liked Daedalus' work _____ much _____ he wanted to _____ Daedalus with him _____.

8 Daedalus, _____, tried _____ _____, so the King _____ him and his son, Icarus, in a tall tower.

9 Daedalus wanted _____ _____.

10 One day, Daedalus saw birds _____.

11 "Wings! _____ _____ _____!" he shouted.

12 Daedalus then gathered bird feathers and _____ _____ _____ with wax.

13 When the wings were ready, he warned his son, "_____ _____ _____ _____ to the sun.

14 The wax will _____."

15 Daedalus and Icarus began _____ _____.

16 Icarus was _____ excited _____ he forgot his father's _____.

17 He flew _____ _____ _____, and the wax began to melt.

18 "Oh, no! I'm falling," Icarus _____ _____.

19 Icarus _____ _____ the sea and died.

1 같은 이야기, 다른 그림

2 우리는 종종 같은 주제의 다른 그림들을 발견한다.

3 한 예가 Henri Matisse가 그린 "The Flight of Icarus(이카로스의 비행)"와 Marc Chagall이 그린 "The Fall of Icarus(이카로스의 추락)"이다.

4 그것들은 둘 다 같은 그리스 신화에 관한 것이다.

5 Icarus에 관한 그리스 신화

6 Daedalus는 훌륭한 발명가였다.

7 Minos왕은 Daedalus의 작품을 매우 좋아해서 Daedalus를 그의 곁에 영원히 두고 싶어 했다.

8 그러나 Daedalus는 떠나려고 했고, 그러자 왕은 그와 그의 아들인 Icarus를 높은 탑에 가두었다.

9 Daedalus는 탈출하고 싶었다.

10 어느 날, Daedalus는 새가 날고 있는 것을 보았다.

11 "날개! 날개가 필요해!" 그가 외쳤다.

12 그 다음에 Daedalus는 새의 깃털을 모아 그것들을 밀랍으로 붙였다.

13 날개가 준비되었을 때, 그는 아들에게 경고했다. "태양에 너무 가까이 날지 마라.

14 밀랍이 녹을 거야."

15 Daedalus와 Icarus는 날기 시작했다.

16 Icarus는 매우 흥분해서 아버지의 경고를 잊었다.

17 그는 점점 더 높이 날았고, 밀랍은 녹기 시작했다.

18 "오, 안 돼! 추락하고 있어." Icarus는 비명을 질렀다.

19 Icarus는 바다로 떨어져서 죽었다.

20 Two _____ Paintings

21 Matisse and Chagall both _____ _____ the _____ _____ in their paintings, but they are _____.

22 First, in Matisse's painting, you can see Icarus _____, but in Chagall's painting, the boy is _____.

23 This difference _____ _____ the _____ _____ that the two painters had.

24 Matisse thought that Icarus was _____ and _____.

25 _____ _____, Chagall thought that Icarus was foolish.

26 Second, Matisse's painting is _____ _____, but Chagall's painting has _____ _____.

27 In Matisse's painting, there are _____ _____ and _____ _____.

28 _____, Icarus' body has just a simple _____.

29 _____ _____, Chagall painted many people and houses _____ _____ _____ Icarus.

30 This _____ comes from the _____ _____ _____ of the two painters.

31 _____ _____ do you like more?

32 People will have different answers because they may see the _____ _____ _____ _____.

20 다른 두 그림

21 Matisse와 Chagall 둘 다 그들의 그림에서 같은 주제를 다루지만, 그것들은 다르다.

22 첫째, Matisse의 그림에서, 여러분은 Icarus가 날고 있는 것을 볼 수 있지만, Chagall의 그림에서는 그 소년이 추락하고 있다.

23 이러한 차이는 두 화가들이 갖고 있던 서로 다른 생각에서 기인한다.

24 Matisse는 Icarus가 용감하고 모험심이 강하다고 생각했다.

25 반면에 Chagall은 Icarus가 어리석다고 생각했다.

26 둘째, Matisse의 그림은 매우 단순하지만, Chagall의 그림에는 세부적인 것들이 많다.

27 Matisse의 그림에는 Icarus와 몇 개의 별들만 있다.

28 게다가 Icarus의 몸은 단지 단순한 윤곽만으로 되어 있다.

29 반면에 Chagall은 Icarus뿐만 아니라 많은 사람들과 집들을 그렸다.

30 이러한 차이는 두 화가의 서로 다른 화풍에서 기인한다.

31 여러분은 누구의 그림이 더 좋은가?

32 사람들은 같은 것을 다른 방식들로 볼 수도 있기 때문에 서로 다른 대답을 할 것이다.

● 우리말을 참고하여 본문을 영작하시오.

1 같은 이야기, 다른 그림
➡ _____

2 우리는 종종 같은 주제의 다른 그림들을 발견한다.
➡ _____

3 한 예가 Henri Matisse가 그린 "*The Flight of Icarus*(이카로스의 비행)"와 Marc Chagall이 그린 "*The Fall of Icarus*(이카로스의 추락)"이다.
➡ _____

4 그것들은 둘 다 모두 같은 그리스 신화에 관한 것이다.
➡ _____

5 Icarus에 관한 그리스 신화
➡ _____

6 Daedalus는 훌륭한 발명가였다.
➡ _____

7 Minos왕은 Daedalus의 작품을 매우 좋아해서 Daedalus를 그의 곁에 영원히 두고 싶어 했다.
➡ _____

8 그러나 Daedalus는 떠나려고 했고, 그러자 왕은 그와 그의 아들인 Icarus를 높은 탑에 가두었다.
➡ _____

9 Daedalus는 탈출하고 싶었다.
➡ _____

10 어느 날, Daedalus는 새가 날고 있는 것을 보았다.
➡ _____

11 "날개! 날개가 필요해!" 그가 외쳤다.
➡ _____

12 그 다음에 Daedalus는 새의 깃털을 모아 그것들을 밀랍으로 붙였다.
➡ _____

13 날개가 준비되었을 때, 그는 아들에게 경고했다. "태양에 너무 가까이 날지 마라.
➡ _____

14 밀랍이 녹을 거야."
➡ _____

15 Daedalus와 Icarus는 날기 시작했다.
➡ _____

16 Icarus는 매우 흥분해서 아버지의 경고를 잊었다.
➡ _____

17 그는 점점 더 높이 날았고, 밀랍은 녹기 시작했다.
➡ _____

18 "오, 안 돼! 추락하고 있어." Icarus는 비명을 질렀다.
➡ _____

19 Icarus는 바다로 떨어져서 죽었다.
➡ _____

20 다른 두 그림

➡ _____

21 Matisse와 Chagall 둘 다 그들의 그림에서 같은 주제를 다루지만, 그것들은 다르다.

➡ _____

22 첫째, Matisse의 그림에서, 여러분은 Icarus가 날고 있는 것을 볼 수 있지만, Chagall의 그림에서는 그 소년이 추락하고 있다.

➡ _____

23 이러한 차이는 두 화가들이 갖고 있던 서로 다른 생각에서 기인한다.

➡ _____

24 Matisse는 Icarus가 용감하고 모험심이 강하다고 생각했다.

➡ _____

25 반면에 Chagall은 Icarus가 어리석다고 생각했다.

➡ _____

26 둘째, Matisse의 그림은 매우 단순하지만, Chagall의 그림에는 세부적인 것들이 많다.

➡ _____

27 Matisse의 그림에는 Icarus와 몇 개의 별들만 있다.

➡ _____

28 게다가 Icarus의 몸은 단지 단순한 윤곽만으로 되어 있다.

➡ _____

29 반면에 Chagall은 Icarus뿐만 아니라 많은 사람들과 집들을 그렸다.

➡ _____

30 이러한 차이는 두 화가의 서로 다른 화풍에서 기인한다.

➡ _____

31 여러분은 누구의 그림이 더 좋은가?

➡ _____

32 사람들은 같은 것을 다른 방식들로 볼 수도 있기 때문에 서로 다른 대답을 할 것이다.

➡ _____

[01~03] 다음 글을 읽고 물음에 답하시오.

We often find ____ⓐ____ paintings with the ____ⓑ____ subject. An example is *The Flight of Icarus* by Henri Matisse and *The Fall of Icarus* by Marc Chagall. They are both about the same Greek ⓒmyth.

The Greek Myth of Icarus

Daedalus was a great inventor. King Minos liked Daedalus' work so much that he wanted to keep Daedalus with him forever. Daedalus, however, tried to leave, so the King kept him and his son, Icarus, in a tall tower. Daedalus wanted to escape.

One day, Daedalus saw birds flying. "Wings! I need wings!" he shouted. Daedalus then gathered bird feathers and glued them together with wax. When the wings were ready, he warned his son, "Don't fly too close to the sun. The wax will melt."

Daedalus and Icarus began to fly. Icarus was so excited that he forgot his father's warning. He flew higher and higher, and the wax began to melt. "Oh, no! I'm falling," Icarus cried out. Icarus fell into the sea and died.

01 위 글의 빈칸 ⓐ와 ⓑ에 들어갈 가장 알맞은 말을 고르시오.

① usual – unusual
② different – same
③ equal – unequal
④ unusual – usual
⑤ same – different

02 위 글의 밑줄 친 ⓒ와 같은 의미로 쓰인 것을 모두 고르시오.

① It's a <u>myth</u> that wolves are dangerous to people.
② I like the story of the heroes of <u>myth</u> and legend.
③ The common belief that Einstein was not an excellent student is a <u>myth</u>.
④ There is a popular <u>myth</u> that women are worse drivers than men.
⑤ He is famous for his study on Dangun <u>myth</u>.

03 위 글의 내용과 일치하지 <u>않는</u> 것은?

① King Minos wanted to keep Daedalus with him forever because he liked Daedalus' work so much.
② King Minos kept Daedalus and Icarus in a tall tower because Daedalus tried to leave.
③ Icarus gathered bird feathers and glued them together with wax.
④ Daedalus warned Icarus not to fly too close to the sun.
⑤ Icarus was excited enough to forget his father's warning.

[04~06] 다음 글을 읽고 물음에 답하시오.

Two Different Paintings

Matisse and Chagall both deal with the same subject in their paintings, but ⓐthey are different.

First, in Matisse's painting, you can see Icarus flying, but in Chagall's painting, the boy is falling. This difference comes from the different ideas that the two painters had. Matisse thought that Icarus was brave and adventurous. ⓑIn contrast, Chagall thought that Icarus was wise.

04 위 글의 주제가 되는 문장으로 알맞은 것을 고르시오.

① Both the painters deal with the same subject in their paintings.
② The paintings of Matisse and Chagall are different.
③ Different ideas of the painters made them draw the same subject differently.
④ Matisse thought that Icarus was brave and adventurous.
⑤ In Chagall's painting, Icarus is falling.

서답형

05 위 글의 밑줄 친 ⓐthey가 가리키는 것을 본문에서 찾아 쓰시오.

➡ _____

서답형

06 위 글의 밑줄 친 ⓑ에서 흐름상 어색한 부분을 찾아 고치시오.

_____ ➡ _____

[07~09] 다음 글을 읽고 물음에 답하시오.

Second, Matisse's painting is very simple, but Chagall's painting has many details. In Matisse's painting, there are only Icarus and some stars. Furthermore, Icarus' body has just a simple outline. In contrast, ⓐChagall painted many people and houses in addition to Icarus. This difference comes from the different painting styles of the two painters.

Whose painting do you like more? People will have different answers because they may see the same thing in different ways.

07 위 글의 마지막 부분의 내용과 어울리는 속담을 고르시오.

① Too many cooks spoil the broth.
② So many men, so many minds.
③ A bad workman always blames his tools.
④ Do to others as you would be done by.
⑤ Two heads are better than one.

08 위 글의 밑줄 친 ⓐ와 의미가 다른 문장을 고르시오.

① Chagall painted not only Icarus but also many people and houses.
② Chagall painted many people and houses besides Icarus.
③ Chagall painted many people and houses as well as Icarus.
④ Chagall painted not Icarus but many people and houses.
⑤ Chagall painted not only Icarus but many people and houses as well

서답형

09 다음 문장에서 위 글의 내용과 다른 부분을 찾아서 고치시오. (두 군데)

> Because their painting styles were different, Matisse and Chagall painted the different subject in the same ways.

_____ ➡ _____
_____ ➡ _____

[10~12] 다음 글을 읽고 물음에 답하시오.

We often find different paintings ___ⓐ___ the same subject. An example is *The Flight of Icarus* ___ⓑ___ Henri Matisse and *The Fall of Icarus* ___ⓑ___ Marc Chagall. They are both about the same Greek myth.

_____ⓒ_____

Daedalus was a great inventor. King Minos liked Daedalus' work so much that he wanted to keep Daedalus with him forever. Daedalus, however, tried to leave, so the King kept him and his son, Icarus, in a tall tower. Daedalus wanted to escape.

(①) One day, Daedalus saw birds flying. (②) "Wings! I need wings!" he shouted. (③) When the wings were ready, he warned his son, "Don't fly too close to the sun. (④) The wax will melt." (⑤)

Daedalus and Icarus began to fly. Icarus was so excited that he forgot his father's warning. He flew higher and higher, and the wax began to melt. "Oh, no! I'm falling," Icarus cried out. Icarus fell into the sea and died.

10 위 글의 빈칸 ⓐ와 ⓑ에 들어갈 전치사가 바르게 짝지어진 것은?

① with – to ② at – from

③ to – from ④ with – by

⑤ at – by

11 위 글의 빈칸 ⓒ에 들어갈 제목으로 가장 알맞은 것을 고르시오.

① The Favorite Inventor of King Minos

② Daedalus Got Ideas from Birds

③ The Greek Myth of Daedalus

④ Look! We are Flying!

⑤ The Greek Myth of Icarus

12 위 글의 흐름으로 보아, 주어진 문장이 들어가기에 가장 적절한 곳은?

Daedalus then gathered bird feathers and glued them together with wax.

① ② ③ ④ ⑤

[13~15] 다음 글을 읽고 물음에 답하시오.

Two Different Paintings

Matisse and Chagall both deal with the same subject in their paintings, but they are different.

First, in Matisse's painting, you can see Icarus flying, but in Chagall's painting, the boy is falling. This ___(A)___ comes from the different ideas ⓐthat the two painters had. Matisse thought ⓑthat Icarus was brave and adventurous. ___(B)___, Chagall thought that Icarus was foolish.

13 서답형 본문의 한 단어를 변형하여 위 글의 빈칸 (A)에 들어갈 알맞은 말을 쓰시오.

➡ _____

14 위 글의 빈칸 (B)에 들어갈 알맞은 말을 고르시오.

① Therefore ② In other words

③ In addition ④ In contrast

⑤ Moreover

15 서답형 다음 〈보기〉에서 위 글의 밑줄 친 ⓐ와 ⓑ의 that과 문법적 쓰임이 같은 것을 각각 고르시오.

① She told me that she was busy.

② I hope that I'll pass the test.

③ This is the book that he was reading.

④ I believe that you'll succeed.

⑤ The watch that you gave me keeps perfect time.

ⓐ _____ ⓑ _____

[16~18] 다음 글을 읽고 물음에 답하시오.

Second, Matisse's painting is very (A) [complex / simple], but Chagall's painting has many details. In Matisse's painting, there are only Icarus and some stars. Furthermore, Icarus' body has just a simple outline. In contrast, Chagall painted many people and houses in addition to Icarus. This difference comes from the different painting styles of the two painters.

Whose painting do you like more? People will have different answers because they may see (B)[different / the same] thing in (C) [different / the same] ways.

서답형

16 위 글의 괄호 (A)~(C)에서 문맥이나 어법상 알맞은 낱말을 골라 쓰시오.

(A) _____ (B) _____ (C) _____

17 위 글의 서술 방식으로 알맞은 것을 고르시오.

① 비유 　　　　② 비교와 대조
③ 분류와 구분 　④ 정의와 지정
⑤ 인과적 분석

18 위 글을 읽고 대답할 수 없는 질문은?

① Whose painting is simple, Matisse's or Chagall's?
② In Matisse's painting, what can you see?
③ Why did Matisse and Chagall paint Icarus?
④ In Chagall's painting, what can you see besides Icarus?
⑤ Why did Matisse and Chagall paint the same subject differently?

[19~22] 다음 글을 읽고 물음에 답하시오.

　The two paintings, *The Green Violinist* by Marc Chagall and *The Violinist at the Window* by Henri Matisse, both deal with a violinist. In both paintings, we see a man ⓐ(play) the violin. The two paintings, however, have (A)some differences. First, in Chagall's painting, we can see the man's face, but in Matisse's painting, we cannot see it. Second, in Chagall's painting, we see the violinist ⓑ(dance) while in Matisse's painting, we see him ⓒ(stand) (B)still. (C)Finally, another difference between the two paintings is that Chagall's painting is more dynamic.

서답형

19 위 글의 괄호 ⓐ~ⓒ에 주어진 단어를 각각 알맞은 형태로 쓰시오.

(A) _____
(B) _____
(C) _____

서답형

20 위 글의 밑줄 친 (A)some differences의 예를 우리말로 쓰시오. (세 가지)

(1) _____
 _____
(2) _____
 _____
(3) _____

21 위 글의 밑줄 친 (B)still과 같은 의미로 쓰인 것을 고르시오.

① Can you sit still there?
② I'm still hungry!
③ She had a still better idea.
④ The weather was cold and wet. Still, we had a great time.
⑤ Do you still live at the same address?

서답형

22 위 글의 밑줄 친 문장 (C)의 맨 뒤에 생략된 말을 쓰시오.

➡ _____

[23~25] 다음 글을 읽고 물음에 답하시오.

Second, Matisse's painting is ⓐvery simple, but Chagall's painting has many details. In Matisse's painting, there are only Icarus and some stars. Furthermore, Icarus' body has just a simple outline. In contrast, Chagall painted many people and houses in addition to Icarus. This difference comes from the different painting styles of the two painters.

Whose painting do you like more? People will have different answers because they may see the same thing in different ways.

서답형

23 위 글에서 Matisse의 그림을 밑줄 친 ⓐ처럼 말한 이유를 우리말로 쓰시오.

➡ _____

_____

서답형

24 다음 영영풀이에 해당하는 단어를 본문에서 찾아 쓰시오.

the main shape or edge of something, without any details

➡ _____

중요

25 다음 빈칸 (A)와 (B)에 알맞은 단어를 넣어 Matisse와 Chagall의 화풍에 대한 소개를 완성하시오.

Matisse painted in a very (A)_____ way, but Chagall painted (B)_____ _____ in his painting.

[26~28] 다음 글을 읽고 물음에 답하시오.

Two Different Paintings

Matisse and Chagall both deal with the same subject in their paintings, but they are different.

First, in Matisse's painting, you can see Icarus flying, but in Chagall's painting, the boy is falling. ⓐThis difference comes from the different ideas that the two painters had. Matisse thought that Icarus was brave and adventurous. ⓑ contrast, Chagall thought that Icarus was foolish.

서답형

26 다음 빈칸 (A)와 (B)에 알맞은 단어를 넣어 ⓐThis difference에 대한 설명을 완성하시오.

Icarus is (A)_____ in Matisse's painting, but he is (B)_____ in Chagall's painting.

중요

27 위 글의 빈칸 ⓑ에 알맞은 것은?

① To   ② Of   ③ In
④ For   ⑤ With

28 위 글을 읽고 대답할 수 <u>없는</u> 질문은?

① Do Matisse and Chagall both deal with the same subject in their paintings?
② What is Icarus doing in Matisse's painting?
③ What is Icarus doing in Chagall's painting?
④ Why did Matisse think that Icarus was brave and adventurous?
⑤ Did Chagall also think that Icarus was brave and adventurous?

[29~30] 다음 글을 읽고 물음에 답하시오.

Second, Matisse's painting is very ___ⓐ___, but Chagall's painting has many details. In Matisse's painting, there are only Icarus and some stars. ___ⓑ___, Icarus' body has just a simple outline. ___ⓒ___, Chagall painted many people and houses in addition to Icarus. This difference comes from the different painting styles of the two painters.

Whose painting do you like more? People will have different answers because they may see the same thing in different ways.

29 위 글의 빈칸 ⓐ에 알맞은 것은?

① clean　　　② difficult
③ bright　　　④ complex
⑤ simple

30 위 글의 빈칸 ⓑ와 ⓒ에 들어갈 알맞은 말을 고르시오.

① Therefore – On the other hand
② Furthermore – In contrast
③ For example – Likewise
④ In other words – In contrast
⑤ Moreover – In addition

서답형

31 위 글의 내용과 일치하도록 다음 빈칸 (A)와 (B)에 알맞은 단어를 쓰시오.

> Because of their (A)_____ _____
> _____, Matisse and Chagall painted
> the same (B)_____ in different ways.

32 다음 미술 작품 설명서와 일치하도록 <보기>에서 알맞은 단어를 골라 두 화가가 그린 그림을 비교·대조하는 벤 다이어그램(Venn Diagram)에 그 번호를 쓰시오.

> Title: The Flight of Icarus
> Painter: Henri Matisse
> 　In Matisse's painting, Icarus is flying. He thought Icarus was brave and adventurous. His painting is very simple. He drew only Icarus and some stars.
>
> Title: The Fall of Icarus
> Painter: Marc Chagall
> 　In Chagall's painting, Icarus is falling. He thought Icarus was foolish. His painting has many details. He painted many people and houses in addition to Icarus.

── 보기 ──
① many details, ② Icarus, ③ falling,
④ brave and adventurous, ⑤ very simple,
⑥ foolish, ⑦ flying

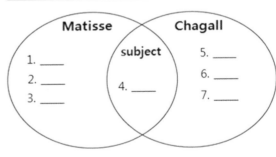

1. _____　2. _____　3. _____　4. _____
5. _____　6. _____　7. _____

[01~03] 다음 글을 읽고 물음에 답하시오.

We often find different paintings with the same (A)[object / subject]. An example is *The Flight of Icarus* by Henri Matisse and *The Fall of Icarus* by Marc Chagall. ⓐThey are both about the same Greek myth.

The Greek Myth of Icarus

Daedalus was a great inventor. King Minos liked Daedalus' work so much that he wanted to keep Daedalus with him (B)[forever / temporarily]. Daedalus, however, tried to leave, so the King kept him and his son, Icarus, in a tall tower. Daedalus wanted to escape.

One day, Daedalus saw birds flying. "Wings! I need wings!" he shouted. Daedalus then gathered bird feathers and glued ⓑthem together with wax. When the wings were ready, he warned his son, "Don't fly too close to the sun. The wax will melt."

Daedalus and Icarus began to fly. Icarus was so (C)[exciting / excited] that he forgot his father's ___Ⓐ___. He flew higher and higher, and the wax began to melt. "Oh, no! I'm falling," Icarus cried out. Icarus fell into the sea and died.

01 본문의 한 단어를 변형하여 위 글의 빈칸 Ⓐ에 들어갈 알맞은 말을 쓰시오.

➡ _____

02 위 글의 밑줄 친 ⓐThey와 ⓑthem이 가리키는 것을 본문에서 찾아 쓰시오.

ⓐ _____
_____
ⓑ _____

03 위 글의 괄호 (A)~(C)에서 문맥이나 어법상 알맞은 낱말을 골라 쓰시오.

(A) _____ (B) _____ (C) _____

[04~06] 다음 글을 읽고 물음에 답하시오.

Two Different Paintings

Matisse and Chagall both deal with ⓐthe same subject in their paintings, but they are different.

First, in Matisse's painting, you can see Icarus flying, but in Chagall's painting, the boy is falling. This difference comes from ⓑthe different ideas that the two painters had them. Matisse thought that Icarus was brave and adventurous. In contrast, Chagall thought that Icarus was foolish.

04 위 글의 밑줄 친 ⓐthe same subject가 가리키는 것을 영어로 쓰시오.

➡ _____

05 위 글의 밑줄 친 ⓑ에서 어법상 틀린 부분을 찾아 고치시오.

_____ ➡ _____

06 본문의 내용과 일치하도록 다음 빈칸 (A)~(D)에 알맞은 단어를 쓰시오.

Matisse thought that Icarus was (A)_____ _____ _____, so in his painting Icarus is (B)_____. But as Chagall thought that Icarus was (C)_____, you can see Icarus (D)_____ in his painting.

[07~09] 다음 글을 읽고 물음에 답하시오.

ⓐSecond, Matisse's painting has many details, but Chagall's painting is very simple. In Matisse's painting, there are only Icarus and some stars. Furthermore, Icarus' body has just a simple outline. In contrast, Chagall painted many people and houses in addition to Icarus. This difference comes from the different painting styles of the two painters.

Whose painting do you like more? People will have different answers ⓑ같은 것을 다른 방식들로 볼 수도 있기 때문에.

07 위 글의 밑줄 친 ⓐ에서 흐름상 어색한 부분을 찾아 고치시오. (두 군데)

➡ _____

_____

_____

08 위 글의 밑줄 친 ⓑ의 우리말에 맞게 주어진 어휘를 이용하여 10 단어로 영작하시오.

because, may see, different ways

➡ _____

09 다음 빈칸 (A)와 (B)에 알맞은 단어를 넣어 Matisse와 Chagall의 그림에 대한 소개를 완성하시오.

In Matisse's painting, you can see only (A)_____ and (B)_____ _____.
Moreover, Icarus' body has just (C)_____
_____ _____. On the other hand, in Chagall's painting, you can see many people and houses as well as (D)_____.

[10~12] 다음 글을 읽고 물음에 답하시오.

We often find different paintings with the same subject. An example is *The Flight of Icarus* by Henri Matisse and *The Fall of Icarus* by Marc Chagall. They are both about the same Greek myth.

The Greek Myth of Icarus

Daedalus was a great inventor. King Minos liked Daedalus' work __(A)__ much __(B)__ he wanted to keep Daedalus with him forever. Daedalus, however, tried to leave, so the King kept him and his son, Icarus, in a tall tower. Daedalus wanted to escape.

ⓐOne day, Daedalus saw birds to fly. "Wings! I need wings!" he shouted. Daedalus then gathered bird feathers and glued them together with wax. When the wings were ready, he warned his son, "Don't fly too close to the sun. The wax will melt."

Daedalus and Icarus began to fly. Icarus was __(A)__ excited __(B)__ he forgot his father's warning. He flew higher and higher, and the wax began to melt. "Oh, no! I'm falling," Icarus cried out. Icarus fell into the sea and died.

10 위 글의 빈칸 (A)와 (B)에 들어갈 알맞은 말을 쓰시오.

(A) _____ (B) _____

11 위 글의 밑줄 친 ⓐ에서 어법상 틀린 부분을 찾아 고치시오.

_____ ➡ _____

12 다음 문장에서 위 글의 내용과 다른 부분을 찾아서 고치시오.

The Flight of Icarus and *The Fall of Icarus* are different paintings but have the different subject.

➡ _____ ➡ _____

Talk and Play

A: I'm planning to go to the library this Monday. Do you want to go with me, Jiho?
~할 계획이다 / 함께 가자고 제안하기

B: Sure. What time should we meet?
약속 시간 정하는 표현

A: How about meeting at 5:30?
How about+-ing?: ~하는 게 어때?

B: OK. Where should we meet?
약속 장소 정하는 표현

A: Let's meet in front of the library.

B: Sounds good. See you then.

구문해설 · How about ~?: ~은 어때?   · in front of ~: ~ 앞에

Around the World

Narcissus

Narcissus was proud of his beauty. One day, he saw his face in the water and fell in love with himself.
~을 자랑스러워했다 / (과거의) 어느 날 / ~와 사랑에 빠졌다 / 주어와 같은 대상이므로 재귀대명사 사용

Pandora

There was a box that had all the bad things in the world inside. Pandora opened it, and they all came out.
주격 관계대명사(= which) / 안에 / = the box / = all the bad things in the world

Orpheus

Orpheus was a great musician. When his wife died, he met Hades and told him, "Please return my wife to me.
시간의 부사절을 이끄는 접속사 / 하데스(죽음과 지하 세계를 관장하는 신)

구문해설 · inside: 내부에[로], 안쪽에[으로]   · return: 돌려주다, 도로 보내다

After You Read D Reading Project

Title: *The Flight of Icarus*

Painter: Henri Matisse

In Matisse's painting, Icarus is flying. He thought Icarus was brave and adventurous. His painting is very simple. He drew only Icarus and some stars.
현재진행시제 / Matisse's / draw–drew–drawn

Title: T*he Fall of Icarus*

Painter: Marc Chagall

In Chagall's painting, Icarus is falling. He thought Icarus was foolish. His painting has many details. He painted many people and houses in addition to Icarus.
현재진행시제 / Chagall's / = besides

구문해설 · adventurous: 모험심이 강한   · simple: 단순한   · drew: draw의 과거
· detail: 세부 사항   · in addition to: ~뿐만 아니라, ~에 더하여

해석

A: 나는 이번 주 월요일에 도서관에 갈 예정이야. 나랑 같이 갈래, 지호야?
B: 물론이지. 몇 시에 만날까?
A: 5시 30분에 만나는 게 어때?
B: 좋아. 어디서 만날까?
A: 도서관 앞에서 만나자.
B: 좋은 생각이야. 그때 보자.

Narcissus
Narcissus는 그의 아름다움을 자랑스러워했다. 어느 날, 그는 물에 비친 그의 얼굴을 보고 자신과 사랑에 빠졌다.

판도라
세상의 온갖 나쁜 것들이 들어 있는 상자가 하나 있었다. 판도라는 그 상자를 열었고, 그것들이 모두 밖으로 나왔다.

오르페우스
오르페우스는 훌륭한 음악가였다. 그는 아내가 죽었을 때 하데스를 만나, "제발 제 아내를 제게 돌려보내 주세요."라고 말했다.

제목: The Flight of Icarus (이카로스의 비행)
화가: Henri Matisse
Matisse의 그림에서, Icarus는 날고 있다. 그는 Icarus가 용감하고 모험심이 강하다고 생각했다. 그의 그림은 매우 단순하다. 그는 Icarus와 몇 개의 별들만 그렸다.

제목: The Fall of Icarus(이카로스의 추락)
화가: Marc Chagall
Chagall의 그림에서, Icarus는 추락하고 있다. 그는 Icarus가 어리석다고 생각했다. 그의 그림에는 세부적인 것들이 많다. 그는 Icarus뿐만 아니라 많은 사람들과 집들을 그렸다.

01 다음 두 단어의 관계가 같도록 빈칸에 알맞은 단어를 주어진 철자로 시작하여 쓰시오.

> melt : thaw = moreover : f_____

02 다음 글의 빈칸 ⓐ와 ⓑ에 들어갈 단어로 바르게 짝지어진 것은?

> • The house is beautiful. ⓐ_____ it's in a great location.
> • Minsu and his brother are very different. Minsu is funny. _____, his brother is very serious.

① However – In addition
② However – In contrast
③ Furthermore – In addition
④ Furthermore – In contrast
⑤ Similarly – However

[03~04] 다음 영영 풀이에 해당하는 것을 고르시오.

03

> a hot drink that you make by pouring boiling water onto dried leaves

① juice   ② beverage   ③ tea
④ coffee   ⑤ milk

04

> the act of flying through the air

① flight   ② float   ③ wing
④ feather   ⑤ form

05 다음 빈칸에 공통으로 들어갈 말을 쓰시오.

> • This week, let's learn how to _____ _____ your anger.
> • The book _____s _____ the subject of love.
> • A: Can you handle the situation by yourself?
>   B: Of course, I can. I can _____ _____ it without any help.

06 다음 중 밑줄 친 부분의 뜻이 잘못된 것은?

① Icarus was so excited that he forgot his father's warning. (경고)
② Daedalus tried to think of ways to escape. (달아나다)
③ I'm planning to go to the Van Gogh exhibition. (전시회)
④ Daedalus then gathered bird feathers and glued them together with wax. (붙였다)
⑤ Chagall painted many people and houses in addition to Icarus. (게다가)

07 다음 대화를 순서에 맞게 바르게 배열하시오.

> (A) Let's meet at 10:30 in front of Green Stadium.
> (B) That sounds great. What time should we meet?
> (C) I'm planning to go see a soccer game next Friday. What about joining me, Jinho?
> (D) OK. See you then.

➡ _____

[08~10] 다음 대화를 읽고 물음에 답하시오.

(*Smartphone rings.*)

B: Hi, Kate. What's up?

G: Hi, Minho. What are you going to do this Saturday?

B: Nothing special. Why? (①)

G: I'm planning to go to the Van Gogh exhibition at the National Art Museum. Do you want to go with me? (②)

B: I'd love to! He's my favorite painter. What time should we meet? (③)

G: How about meeting at 11? (④)

B: OK. (⑤)

G: Let's meet in front of the ticket office.

B: Sounds good. I'll see you there at 11.

08 주어진 문장이 들어갈 위치로 알맞은 것은?

> Where should we meet?

①　　②　　③　　④　　⑤

09 다음 질문에 대한 답을 위 대화에서 찾아 쓰시오.

> Q: What are the speakers going to do this Saturday?

➡ _____

10 위 대화의 내용과 일치하지 <u>않는</u> 것은?

① Kate is planning to go to the Van Gogh exhibition.

② Minho will be busy on Saturday.

③ Van Gogh is Minho's favorite painter.

④ Kate and Minho are going to meet at 11.

⑤ Kate and Minho are going to meet in front of the ticket office.

11 다음에 제시된 〈조건〉에 맞게 아래 대화의 빈칸을 완성하시오.

┌── 조건 ──┐

(1) 수영을 갈 계획을 말하는 표현을 쓸 것. 'plan'을 이용하여 진행형으로 쓸 것.

(2) 'how'를 이용하여 만날 시간을 제안하는 표현을 쓸 것.

(3) 'should'를 이용하여 만날 장소를 묻는 표현을 쓸 것.

A: (1) _____.
　 this Wednesday. Do you want to go with me, Minsu?

B: Sure. What time should we meet?

A: (2) _____ at 10:30?

B: OK. (3) _____

A: Let's meet at the bus stop.

B: Sounds good. See you then.

12 다음 대화의 밑줄 친 부분에 대한 설명으로 적절하지 <u>않은</u> 것은?

B: Sumi, ⓐI'm planning to go shopping with Jenny this Saturday. ⓑWill you join us?

G: Sounds great. ⓒWhat time should we meet?

B: ⓓHow about meeting at 12:30?

G: OK. ⓔWhere should we meet?

B: Let's meet in front of the shopping mall.

① ⓐ: 미래의 계획을 말하는 것으로 'I'm going to go shopping with Jenny this Saturday.'와 같은 표현이다.

② ⓑ: 함께 하자고 제안하는 말로 'How about joining us?'와 같은 표현이다.

③ ⓒ: 약속 시간을 정하는 표현으로 'When should we meet?'으로 바꾸어 쓸 수 있다.

④ ⓓ: 약속 시간을 제안하는 말로 'Can you make it at 12:30?'으로 바꾸어 쓸 수 있다.

⑤ ⓔ: 약속 장소를 정하는 말로 'Do you want to go with me?'와 바꾸어 쓸 수 있다.

13 다음 빈칸에 알맞은 말이 순서대로 짝지어진 것은?

> • Stella smelled something _____ in the kitchen.
> • He saw his mom _____ dinner in the kitchen.

① burn – to make　② burns – making

③ burnt – made　④ to burn – makes

⑤ burning – make

14 다음 그림을 보고 괄호 안에 주어진 어휘를 이용하여 빈칸에 알맞은 말을 쓰시오.

(1) I saw a person _____ the guitar.
(play)
(2) I saw a person _____ his bag.
(carry)
(3) I saw a person _____ the wall.
(paint)

15 다음 중 어법상 바르지 않은 것은?

① The weather was so nice that I went for a walk.

② I was very hungry that I ate a whole pizza.

③ It was such a shock that her face turned white.

④ The music is too loud for me to sleep.

⑤ The water is cold enough to kill an ordinary person.

16 다음 중 어법상 바르지 않은 것은?

① I often watch them talking on the phone.

② He ran so fast that nobody could follow him.

③ I was so busy that I forgot Mia's birthday.

④ Did you see the man walked his dog?

⑤ She had me cook the curry and rice yesterday.

17 괄호 안에 주어진 어휘를 이용하여 다음을 영작하시오.

(1) 나는 누군가가 내 이름을 반복하는 것을 들었다.
(someone, repeat)
➡ _____

(2) 소녀는 소년이 물고기에게 먹이를 주고 있는 것을 보았다. (see, feed)
➡ _____

(3) 너는 그가 그 소식을 말하는 것을 들었니?
(listen, tell, the news)
➡ _____

(4) 그는 너무 배가 고파서 피자 세 조각을 먹었다.
(eat, piece, that)
➡ _____

(5) 음식이 너무 맛이 없어서 우리는 그것을 먹지 않았다. (the food, awful, so, eat)
➡ _____

(6) 이 상자는 너무 무거워서 제가 들 수가 없어요.
(this box, carry, to)
➡ _____

Reading

[18~21] 다음 글을 읽고 물음에 답하시오.

We often find different paintings with the same (a)subject. An example is *The ⓐ of Icarus* by Henri Matisse and *The Fall of Icarus* by Marc Chagall. They are both about the same Greek myth.

The Greek Myth of Icarus

Daedalus was a great inventor. King Minos liked Daedalus' work so much that he wanted to keep Daedalus with him forever. Daedalus, however, tried to leave, so the King kept him and his son, Icarus, in a tall tower. Daedalus wanted to escape.

One day, Daedalus saw birds ⓑ . "Wings! I need wings!" he shouted. Daedalus then gathered bird feathers and glued them together with wax. When the wings were ready, he warned his son, "Don't ⓒ too close to the sun. (A) "

Daedalus and Icarus began ⓓ . Icarus was so excited that he forgot his father's warning. He ⓔ higher and higher, and the wax began to melt. "Oh, no! I'm falling," Icarus cried out. Icarus fell into the sea and died.

18 위 글의 빈칸 ⓐ~ⓔ에 fly를 알맞은 형태로 쓰시오.

ⓐ _____ ⓑ _____ ⓒ _____
ⓓ _____ ⓔ _____

19 위 글의 빈칸 (A)에 들어갈 알맞은 말을 고르시오.

① It will follow you.
② The wax will melt.
③ I won't be able to follow you.
④ You'll become blind.
⑤ You won't be able to fly fast.

20 위 글의 밑줄 친 (a)subject와 같은 의미로 쓰인 것을 고르시오.

① Biology is my favourite subject.
② Children are subject to their parents.
③ We need a male subject between the ages of 18 and 25 for the experiment.
④ What is the subject of this sentence?
⑤ The landscape was a popular subject with many 18th century painters.

21 위 글의 마지막 부분에서 알 수 있는 Icarus의 성격으로 가장 알맞은 것을 고르시오.

① wise   ② patient
③ careless   ④ reasonable
⑤ curious

[22~24] 다음 글을 읽고 물음에 답하시오.

Two Different Paintings

Matisse and Chagall both ⓐdeal with the same subject in their paintings, but ⓑthey are different.

First, in Matisse's painting, you can see Icarus flying, but in Chagall's painting, the boy is falling. This difference comes from the different ideas that the two painters had. Matisse thought that Icarus was brave and adventurous. In contrast, Chagall thought that Icarus was foolish.

22 위 글의 밑줄 친 ⓐdeal with와 바꿔 쓸 수 있는 단어를 모두 고르시오.

① control   ② treat
③ trade   ④ prepare
⑤ handle

23 위 글의 밑줄 친 ⓑthey are different의 구체적인 내용을 우리말로 설명하시오.

➡ _____

_____

24 위 글의 내용과 일치하지 <u>않는</u> 것은?

① Matisse와 Chagall 둘 다 그들의 그림에서 같은 주제를 다루었다.
② Matisse와 Chagall은 같은 주제를 서로 다르게 그렸다.
③ 두 그림의 차이는 두 화가들의 서로 다른 생활에서 기인한다.
④ Matisse는 Icarus가 용감하고 모험심이 강하다고 생각했다.
⑤ Chagall은 Icarus가 어리석다고 생각했다.

[25~27] 다음 글을 읽고 물음에 답하시오.

(①) Second, Matisse's painting is very simple, but Chagall's painting has many details. (②) In Matisse's painting, there are only Icarus and some stars. (③) Furthermore, Icarus' body has just a simple outline. (④) In contrast, Chagall painted many people and houses in addition to Icarus. (⑤)

Whose painting do you like more? People will have different answers because they may see the same thing in different ways.

25 위 글의 흐름으로 보아, 주어진 문장이 들어가기에 가장 적절한 곳은?

> This difference comes from the different painting styles of the two painters.

①   ②   ③   ④   ⑤

26 위 글의 앞에 나왔을 내용으로 가장 알맞은 것을 고르시오.

① Matisse와 Chagall이 같은 주제를 고르게 된 첫 번째 배경
② Matisse의 화풍 설명
③ Chagall의 화풍 설명
④ Matisse와 Chagall이 같은 주제를 다르게 다룬 것에 관한 첫 번째 설명
⑤ Matisse와 Chagall의 그림에 대한 사람들의 선호도

27 다음 중 위 글의 내용과 어울리지 <u>않는</u> 말을 하는 사람을 고르시오.

> 동명: I like Matisse's painting because I like a simple style.
> 창수: I don't like Matisse's painting because there aren't many details in his painting.
> 희진: Chagall's painting looks good to me because I like a painting with many details.
> 준규: I think Matisse and Chagall chose the same subject because they had the same painting style.
> 민지: I like Matisse's painting, but I think there may be someone who doesn't like it.

① 동명   ② 창수   ③ 희진
④ 준규   ⑤ 민지

출제율 85%

01 다음 짝지어진 단어의 관계가 같도록 빈칸에 알맞은 단어를 주어진 철자로 시작하여 쓰시오.

shout : yell = silly : f_____

출제율 90%

02 다음 영영 풀이에 해당하는 단어는?

to tell someone that something bad might happen, so that he or she can avoid it

① escape   ② shout   ③ warn
④ gather   ⑤ skip

출제율 95%

03 다음 글의 빈칸 (A)~(C)에 들어갈 말로 알맞은 것은?

Daedalus, however, tried to leave, so the King kept him and his son, Icarus, in a tall tower. Daedalus wanted to escape. One day, Daedalus saw birds flying. "Wings! I need wings!" he ___(A)___. Daedalus then ___(B)___ bird feathers and glued them together with wax. When the wings were ready, he warned his son, "Don't fly too close to the sun. The ___(C)___ will melt."

① skipped – collected – feathers
② skipped – gathered – wax
③ shouted – gathered – feathers
④ shouted – escaped – feathers
⑤ shouted – gathered – wax

출제율 100%

04 대화의 밑줄 친 ⓐ~ⓔ 중 어법상 어색한 것은?

B: What are you going to do this Sunday?
G: I'm ⓐplanning to go to Dream Amusement Park with my brother. You can go with us ⓑif you want to.
B: ⓒI'd love to. ⓓWhen should we meet?
G: I want to go early, so ⓔlet's to meet at 9 at the subway station.
B: Sounds good. I'll see you then.

① ⓐ   ② ⓑ   ③ ⓒ   ④ ⓓ   ⑤ ⓔ

출제율 95%

05 다음 글의 밑줄 친 (A)~(E)의 해석으로 틀린 것은?

First, in Matisse's painting, you can see Icarus flying, but in Chagall's painting, the boy is falling. This (A)difference comes from the different ideas that the two painters had. Matisse thought that Icarus was (B)brave and adventurous. (C)In contrast, Chagall thought that Icarus was foolish. Second, Matisse's painting is very simple, but Chagall's painting has many (D)details. In Matisse's painting, there are only Icarus and some stars. Furthermore, Icarus' body has just a simple (E)outline.

① (A) 차이   ② (B) 용감한
③ (C) 게다가   ④ (D) 세부 사항
⑤ (E) 윤곽

[06~07] 다음 대화를 읽고 물음에 답하시오.

G: (A)나는 이번 주 금요일에 피아노 콘서트에 갈 계획이야. Why don't you join me, Kevin?
B: Sure. _____(B)_____
G: Let's meet at 10:30.
B: OK. See you then.

06 위 대화의 밑줄 친 (A)의 우리말에 맞게 주어진 문장의 빈칸을 채우시오.

> I'm _____ _____ _____ _____
>
> a piano concert this Friday.

07 위 대화의 빈칸 (B)에 들어갈 말로 알맞은 것을 고르시오.

① Will you join us?

② What time should we meet?

③ Where should we meet?

④ Do you want to go with me?

⑤ Do you have time?

[08~10] 다음 대화를 읽고 물음에 답하시오.

(*Smartphone rings.*)

B: Hi, Kate. What's up?

G: Hi, Minho. (A)<u>이번 토요일에 뭐 할 거야</u>?

B: Nothing special. Why?

G: I'm planning to go to the Van Gogh exhibition at the National Art Museum. Do you want to go with me?

B: (B)<u>I'd love to!</u> He's my favorite painter. ⓐ should we meet?

G: ⓑ meeting at 11?

B: OK. ⓒ should we meet?

G: Let's meet in front of the ticket office.

B: Sounds good. I'll see you there at 11.

08 위 대화의 빈칸 ⓐ~ⓒ에 들어갈 말로 알맞은 것은?

① When – How – Where

② When – How about – Why

③ What time – How about – Where

④ What time – What about – When

⑤ Where – What about – What time

---

09 위 대화의 밑줄 친 (A)의 우리말에 맞게 주어진 어휘를 배열하여 대화를 완성하시오.

> are / going / what / you / to / this / do / Saturday

➡ _____

10 위 대화의 밑줄 친 (B)를 생략되지 않은 문장으로 쓰시오.

➡ _____

11 다음 빈칸에 들어갈 말이 바르게 짝지어진 것은?

> • I saw the moon _____ above the horizon.
>
> • This problem is easy _____ for everybody to solve.

① rising – too

② rising – enough

③ rose – too

④ rose – enough

⑤ rise – too

[12~13] 어법상 올바른 문장을 <u>모두</u> 고르시오.

12 ① I saw Junho taking a picture.

② The teacher saw Hoyeong to dance.

③ I felt somebody watched me.

④ He was looking at the monkey ate bananas.

⑤ I heard two men fight with each other.

13 ① The movie was too sad that I cried a lot.

② The cake was delicious so that I ate it all.

③ Tom was so nervous that he made a big mistake.

④ He was too hungry to get to sleep last night.

⑤ The man is rich enough that he can buy anything he wants.

14 다음 중 어법상 틀린 문장의 개수는?

ⓐ We saw the spider spinning its web.

ⓑ We heard her played the piano.

ⓒ Gabriel listened to her telling him what she did.

ⓓ Jocelyn felt him held her hand.

ⓔ He was so nervous that he made some mistakes on the test.

ⓕ The dog ran too quickly for me to catch it.

ⓖ The sky was enough clear to see stars very well.

① 1개　② 2개　③ 3개　④ 4개　⑤ 5개

[15~17] 다음 글을 읽고 물음에 답하시오.

We often find different paintings with the same subject. An example is *The Flight of Icarus* by Henri Matisse and *The Fall of Icarus* by Marc Chagall. They are both about the same Greek myth.

The Greek Myth of Icarus

Daedalus was a great inventor. King Minos liked Daedalus' work so much that he wanted to keep Daedalus with him forever. Daedalus, ___ⓐ___, tried to leave, so the King kept him and his son, Icarus, in a tall tower. Daedalus wanted to escape.

One day, Daedalus saw birds flying. "Wings! I need wings!" he shouted. Daedalus then gathered bird feathers and glued them together with wax. When the wings were ready, he warned his son, "Don't fly too close to the sun. The wax will melt."

Daedalus and Icarus began ⓑto fly. Icarus was so excited that he forgot his father's warning. He flew higher and higher, and the wax began to melt. "Oh, no! I'm falling," Icarus cried out. Icarus fell into the sea and died.

15 위 글의 빈칸 ⓐ에 들어갈 알맞은 말을 고르시오.

① therefore　② however

③ in addition　④ for example

⑤ as a result

16 위 글의 밑줄 친 ⓑto fly와 to부정사의 용법이 다른 것을 모두 고르시오.

① When did you make the decision to leave here?

② She decided to leave right now.

③ It was the best decision to leave immediately.

④ To leave as soon as possible, he made a quick decision.

⑤ My decision was to leave at once.

17 위 글을 읽고 대답할 수 없는 질문은?

① Are the subjects of *The Flight of Icarus* and *The Fall of Icarus* different?

② What's the subject of *The Flight of Icarus*?

③ Why did King Minos keep Daedalus and Icarus in a tall tower?

④ How did Daedalus gather bird feathers?

⑤ Why did Icarus fly higher and higher?

[18~21] 다음 글을 읽고 물음에 답하시오.

Two Different Paintings

ⓐMatisse와 Chagall 둘 다 그들의 그림에서 같은 주제를 다루지만, 그것들은 다르다.

ⓑFirst, in Matisse's painting, you can see Icarus falling, but in Chagall's painting, the boy is flying. This difference ⓒcomes from the ⓓdifferent ideas that the two painters had. Matisse thought that Icarus was brave and adventurous. In contrast, Chagall thought that Icarus was foolish.

18 위 글의 밑줄 친 @의 우리말에 맞게 한 단어를 보충하여, 주어진 어휘를 알맞게 배열하시오.

출제율 95%

> different / are / but / the same subject / deal / they / Matisse and Chagall both / in their paintings

➡ _____

_____

19 위 글의 밑줄 친 ⓑ에서 흐름상 어색한 부분을 찾아 고치시오. (두 군데)

출제율 100%

_____ ➡ _____

_____ ➡ _____

20 위 글의 밑줄 친 ©comes from과 바꿔 쓸 수 없는 말을 모두 고르시오.

출제율 85%

① is due to ② results from

③ causes ④ arises from

⑤ results in

21 위 글의 밑줄 친 @different ideas의 구체적인 내용을 우리말로 설명하시오.

출제율 90%

➡ _____

_____

[22~24] 다음 글을 읽고 물음에 답하시오.

Second, Matisse's painting is very simple, but Chagall's painting has many details. In Matisse's painting, there are only Icarus and some stars. @Furthermore, Icarus' body has just a simple outline. In contrast, Chagall painted many people and houses in addition to Icarus. ⓑThis difference comes from the ___(A)___ painting styles of the two painters.

Whose painting do you like more? People will have ___(B)___ answers because they may see the same thing in ___(C)___ ways.

22 위 글의 한 단어를 변형하여 위 글의 빈칸 (A)~(C)에 공통으로 들어갈 알맞은 단어를 쓰시오.

출제율 100%

➡ _____

23 위 글의 밑줄 친 @Furthermore와 바꿔 쓸 수 없는 말을 고르시오.

출제율 95%

① Additionally ② Moreover

③ Beside ④ In addition

⑤ Besides

24 다음 빈칸 (A)와 (B)에 알맞은 단어를 넣어 ⓑThis difference에 대한 소개를 완성하시오.

출제율 90%

> Matisse painted only Icarus whose body has just (A)_____ _____ _____ and some stars. But Chagall painted not only Icarus but also (B)_____ _____ like many people and houses.

중요

01 아래 〈조건〉에 맞게 주어진 단어를 이용하여 대화의 빈칸을 완성하시오.

> B: What are you going to do this Sunday?
> G: I'm planning to go to Dream Amusement Park with my brother. _____(A)_____ .
> B: I'd love to. When should we meet?
> G: I want to go early, so _____(B)_____ .
> B: Sounds good. I'll see you then.

┤ 조건 ├
(A) • 함께 가자고 제안하는 표현을 쓸 것.
  • you를 주어로 하는 평서문으로 문장을 시작하고, if절을 쓸 것.
  • 'go with'와 'want to'를 이용할 것
(B) • 지하철역에서 9시에 만나자고 제안하는 표현을 쓸 것.
  • let's로 문장을 시작할 것.

(A) _____
(B) _____

02 다음 대화의 밑줄 친 우리말을 주어진 어휘를 배열하여 완성하시오.

> A: I'm planning to go hiking this Sunday. <u>나와 함께 갈래</u>(you / want / do / to / with / go / me), Jina?
> B: I'm sorry, but I have other plans.
> A: OK.

➡ _____

03 다음 대화를 읽고 아래의 물음에 영어로 답하시오.

> A: I'm planning to go to the library this Monday. Do you want to go with me, Jiho?
> B: Sure. What time should we meet?
> A: How about meeting at 5:30?
> B: OK. Where should we meet?
> A: Let's meet in front of the library.
> B: Sounds good. See you then.

(1) Where are they going to go this Monday?
  ➡ _____
(2) When are they going to meet?
  ➡ _____

중요

04 다음 문장을 to부정사를 이용하여 다시 쓰시오.

(1) The room was so noisy that we couldn't hear him speak.
  ➡ _____
(2) She speaks so fast that I can't understand her.
  ➡ _____
(3) The math problem is so easy that anyone can solve it.
  ➡ _____

05 다음 두 문장을 하나의 문장으로 쓰시오.

(1) • Minsu played soccer.
　　 • Did you see him?
　　➡ _____

(2) • Sophia opened the window.
　　 • Did you hear it?
　　➡ _____

(3) • Your mom touched you on the shoulder.
　　 • Did you feel it?
　　➡ _____
　　 _____

06 그림을 보고 괄호 안에 주어진 어구들을 바르게 배열하여 문장을 완성하시오.

(Orpheus, Hades, musician, his wife, him, a, was, returned, great, that, such, to)

➡ _____
_____

[07~09] 다음 글을 읽고 물음에 답하시오.

ⓐ우리는 종종 같은 주제의 다른 그림들을 발견한다. An example is *The Flight of Icarus* by Henri Matisse and *The Fall of Icarus* by Marc Chagall. They are both about ⓑthe same Greek myth.

The Greek Myth of Icarus

Daedalus was a great inventor. ⓒKing Minos liked Daedalus' work so much that he wanted to keep Daedalus with him forever. Daedalus, however, tried to leave, so the King kept him and his son, Icarus, in a tall tower. Daedalus wanted to escape.

One day, Daedalus saw birds flying. "Wings! I need wings!" he shouted. Daedalus then gathered bird feathers and glued them together with wax. When the wings were ready, he warned his son, "Don't fly too close to the sun. The wax will melt."

Daedalus and Icarus began to fly. Icarus was so excited that he forgot ⓓhis father's warning. He flew higher and higher, and the wax began to melt. "Oh, no! I'm falling," Icarus cried out. Icarus fell into the sea and died.

07 위 글의 밑줄 친 ⓐ의 우리말에 맞게 주어진 어휘를 이용하여 9 단어로 영작하시오.

often, paintings, with

➡ _____
_____

08 위 글의 밑줄 친 ⓑ와 ⓓ가 가리키는 것을 본문에서 찾아 쓰시오.

ⓑ _____
ⓓ _____

09 위 글의 밑줄 친 문장 ⓒ를 다음과 같이 바꿔 쓸 때 빈칸에 들어갈 알맞은 말을 쓰시오.

King Minos wanted to keep Daedalus with him forever _____ he liked Daedalus' work so much.

창의사고력 서술형 문제

01 다음 주어진 정보를 이용하여 대화의 빈칸을 완성하시오.

> plan: go see a soccer game / what time: at 10:00 / where: at the bus stop

A: _____ see a soccer game. Do you want to go with me?
B: Sure. _____?
A: How _____ at 10:00 at the bus stop?
B: OK. See you then.

02 〈보기〉에 주어진 어휘와 so와 that을 이용하여 3 문장 이상 쓰시오.

> ┌─ 보기 ─
> very nervous   very happy   very tired   really sad
> play well   danced   fell asleep on the floor   everybody cried

(1) _____
(2) _____
(3) _____
(4) _____

03 다음 내용을 바탕으로 두 그림을 비교·대조하는 글을 쓰시오.

> • **subject:** a violinist
> ***The Green Violinist* by Marc Chagall**
> • We can see the man's face.
> • We see the violinist dancing.
> • Chagall's painting is more dynamic.
> ***The Violinist at the Window* by Henri Matisse**
> • We cannot see the man's face.
> • We see the violinist standing still.

>   The two paintings, *The Green Violinist* by Marc Chagall and *The Violinist at the Window* by Henri Matisse, both deal with (A) _____. In both paintings, we see a man playing the violin. The two paintings, however, have some differences. First, in Chagall's painting, we (B)_____ the man's face, but in Matisse's painting, we cannot see it. Second, in Chagall's painting, we see the violinist (C)_____ while in Matisse's painting, we see him (D)_____. Finally, another difference between the two paintings is that Chagall's painting is (E)_____.

단원별 모의고사

01 다음 단어에 대한 영어 설명이 <u>어색한</u> 것은?

① in contrast: used when you are comparing two things or people and saying that the second one is very different from the first

② forever: for all of the time in the future

③ wax: a substance used for making candles and crayons

④ skip: to get away from a place or person

⑤ in addition to: used for saying that something extra exists

02 다음 짝지어진 단어의 관계가 같도록 빈칸에 알맞은 말을 쓰시오.

different : same = complicated : _____

[03~04] 다음 대화의 빈칸에 들어갈 말로 알맞은 것을 고르시오.

03

G: I'm planning to go to a piano concert this Friday. Why don't you join me, Kevin?

B: Sure. What time should we meet?

G: _____

B: OK. See you then.

① I'd like to, but I have to take care of my younger brother.

② Did you know Mars has its moons?

③ Let's meet at 10:30 at the bus stop.

④ Let's meet at the bus stop.

⑤ I'm afraid I can't. I'm going on a family trip.

04

B: What are you going to do this Sunday?

G: I'm planning to go to Dream Amusement Park with my brother. You can go with us if you want to.

B: I'd love to. _____

G: I want to go early, so let's meet at 9.

B: Sounds good. I'll see you then.

① How about meeting at the park?

② What is going on?

③ When does it begin?

④ Where should we meet?

⑤ When should we meet?

05 다음 영영풀이에 해당하는 단어를 고르시오.

a small fact, feature, or piece of information

① detail　　② myth　　③ title

④ tea　　⑤ wax

06 다음 중 짝지어진 대화가 <u>어색한</u> 것은?

① A: What time should we meet?

B: How about meeting at 5:30?

② A: Where should we meet?

B: Let's meet in front of the library.

③ A: Do you want to go with me?

B: I'd love to!

④ A: What are you going to do this Saturday?

B: Nothing special. Why?

⑤ A: What time and where should we meet?

B: Sounds good. See you then.

[07~09] 다음 대화를 읽고 물음에 답하시오.

(*Smartphone rings.*)

B: Hi, Kate. What's up?

G: Hi, Minho. What are you going to do this Saturday?

B: Nothing special. Why?

G: I'm planning to go to the Van Gogh exhibition at the National Art Museum. Do you want to go with me?

B: I'd love to! He's my favorite painter.

_____ (A) _____

G: How about meeting at 11?

B: OK. Where should we meet?

G: Let's meet in front of the ticket office.

B: Sounds good. I'll see you there at 11.

07 위 대화의 빈칸 (A)에 들어갈 말로 알맞은 것은?

① What time does the museum open?
② What time should we meet?
③ Where should we meet?
④ Where is the museum?
⑤ How about you?

08 Where are Kate and Minho going to meet? (be going to 를 이용하여 쓸 것)

➡ _____

09 위 대화를 읽고, Kate가 Minho에게 보내는 메시지를 완성하시오.

Minho, don't forget our _____ for this Saturday. I'll see you at 11 _____ _____ _____ the _____ _____ of the National Art Museum.

10 다음 대화의 내용과 일치하면 T, 일치하지 <u>않으면</u> F에 표시하시오.

Minho: Sumi, I'm planning to go shopping with Jenny this Saturday. Will you join us?

Sumi: Sounds great. What time should we meet?

Minho: How about meeting at 12:30?

Sumi: OK. Where should we meet?

Minho: Let's meet in front of the shopping mall.

(1) Miho is planning to go shopping by himself. (T / F)

(2) Minho and Sumi are going to meet at 12:30 in front of the shopping mall. (T / F)

11 다음 대화의 빈칸에 알맞은 것은?

B: I'm planning to go to a soccer game tomorrow. Do you want to go with me, Susan?

G: Sure. What time should we meet?

B: The game begins at 7, so _____.

G: OK. See you then.

① why don't we go to a soccer game?
② I want to meet you tomorrow.
③ let's meet at 6 in front of Dream Stadium.
④ where should we meet?
⑤ we have to make haste.

12 다음 대화를 순서대로 배열하시오.

> (A) The musical starts at 3 o'clock. Let's meet at 2 at Dream Art Hall.
> (B) Sure. What time and where should we meet?
> (C) I'm planning to go see *Cats* this Saturday. Do you want to go with me?
> (D) Great. See you on Saturday.

➡ _____

13 주어진 단어를 이용하여 다음 우리말을 영어로 쓰시오.

(1) 나는 나의 삼촌이 기타를 치는 것을 들었다.
(hear, play, guitar)
➡ _____

(2) 나는 그들이 집안에서 운동화를 신고 있는 것을 보았다. (see, wear, their sneakers)
➡ _____

(3) 나는 한 여왕이 장미의 향기를 맡고 있는 것을 보았다. (see, smell, a rose)
➡ _____

(4) 그 영화가 너무 좋아서 그들은 그것을 두 번 보았다. (good, that, watch, twice)
➡ _____

(5) 날씨가 너무 나빠서 그들은 집에 있었다.
(the weather, bad, that, stay home)
➡ _____

(6) John은 너무 아파서 학교에 갈 수 없다. (too, sick)
➡ _____

14 다음 두 문장을 'so ~ that' 구문을 사용하여 한 문장으로 연결하여 쓰시오.

(1) • This problem is really easy.
• So, everybody can solve it.
➡ _____

(2) • We decided to have dinner at the restaurant once again.
• Because the meal was very good.
➡ _____
_____

15 다음 중 어법상 바르지 <u>않은</u> 것은?

① We heard Joy to talk on the phone.
② Mr. Kim was so full that he couldn't eat anymore.
③ It is interesting to watch her dance to the music.
④ Eric saw Minsu playing soccer.
⑤ The girl was so happy that she jumped up and down.

16 다음 두 문장이 서로 <u>다른</u> 의미를 갖는 것은?

① We felt the ground shaking for a few seconds.
= We felt the ground shake for a few seconds.
② She studied so hard that she could pass the exam.
= She studied hard so that she could pass the exam.
③ We watched the woman getting into the car.
= We watched the woman get into the car.
④ The students were very tired. So, they fell asleep during the movie.
= The students were so tired that they fell asleep during the movie.
⑤ I want to take a nap because I'm very tired.
= I'm so tired that I want to take a nap.

17 다음 문장에서 어법상 어색한 부분을 바르게 고치시오.

(1) I heard him ran down the stairs.

_____ ➡ _____

(2) I felt my heart to beat fast.

_____ ➡ _____

(3) Can you smell something burns?

_____ ➡ _____

(4) The kids were too tired at the end of the race that they just walked.

_____ ➡ _____

(5) The floor was slippery so that I almost fell.

_____ ➡ _____

(6) The box was light enough for the man to carry it.

_____ ➡ _____

[18~21] 다음 글을 읽고 물음에 답하시오.

We often find different paintings with the same subject. An example is *The Flight of Icarus* by Henri Matisse and *The Fall of Icarus* by Marc Chagall. They are both about the same Greek myth.

The Greek Myth of Icarus

Daedalus was a great inventor. King Minos liked Daedalus' work so much that he wanted to keep Daedalus with ⓐhim forever. Daedalus, however, tried to leave, so the King kept him and ⓑhis son, Icarus, in a tall tower. Daedalus wanted to escape.

One day, Daedalus saw birds (A)flying. "Wings! ⓒI need wings!" he shouted. Daedalus then gathered bird feathers and glued them together with wax. When the wings were ready, he warned his son, "Don't fly too close to the sun. The wax will melt."

Daedalus and Icarus began to fly. Icarus was so excited that he forgot ⓓhis father's warning. (B)그는 점점 더 높이 날았고, 밀랍은 녹기 시작했다. "Oh, no! ⓔI'm falling," Icarus cried out. Icarus fell into the sea and died.

18 아래 〈보기〉에서 위 글의 밑줄 친 (A)flying과 문법적 쓰임이 같은 것의 개수를 고르시오.

① They were on a plane flying from London to New York.
② I'm flying to Hong Kong tomorrow.
③ The Wright Brothers dreamed of flying in the sky.
④ Look at the children flying kites there.
⑤ The pilot finished flying the large passenger plane.

① 1개   ② 2개   ③ 3개   ④ 4개   ⑤ 5개

19 위 글의 밑줄 친 ⓐ~ⓔ 중 가리키는 대상이 같은 것끼리 짝 지어진 것은?

① ⓐ와 ⓑ   ② ⓐ와 ⓒ   ③ ⓑ와 ⓓ
④ ⓒ와 ⓓ   ⑤ ⓓ와 ⓔ

20 위 글의 내용과 일치하도록 다음 빈칸 (A)와 (B)에 알맞은 단어를 쓰시오.

Matisse and Chagall drew different paintings with the (A)_____ _____, the Greek Myth of Icarus, who fell into the sea and died because he forgot his father's (B)_____.

21 위 글의 밑줄 친 (B)의 우리말에 맞게 주어진 어휘를 이용하여 11 단어로 영작하시오.

flew, and, the wax

➡ _____

Lesson 7

Life in Space

🎙 의사소통 기능

- 알고 있는지 묻기
  A: Did you hear about the new musical?
  B: Yes, I did. / No, I didn't.

- 궁금증 표현하기
  I'm really curious about it.

🎙 언어 형식

- 현재완료
  I've never seen a blue sky.

- It ~ to부정사
  It's difficult to walk on Earth.

Words & Expressions

교과서

Key Words

- **adventure**[ædvéntʃər] 명 모험
- **air**[ɛər] 명 공기
- **amazing**[əméiziŋ] 형 놀라운
- **arrive**[əráiv] 동 도착하다
- **balloon**[bəlúːn] 명 풍선
- **container**[kəntéinər] 명 그릇, 용기
- **curious**[kjúəriəs] 형 궁금한, 호기심이 많은
- **dessert**[dizə́ːrt] 명 디저트
- **different**[dífərənt] 형 다른
- **difficult**[dífikʌlt] 형 어려운
- **ever**[évər] 부 줄곧, 내내
- **everywhere**[évriwɛ̀ər] 부 모든 곳에
- **excited**[iksáitid] 형 신난, 흥분한
- **exciting**[iksáitiŋ] 형 흥미진진한
- **exploration**[èkspləréiʃən] 명 탐험, 탐사
- **finally**[fáinəli] 부 마침내
- **fix**[fiks] 동 고치다
- **foreign**[fɔ́ːrən] 형 외국의
- **float**[flout] 동 뜨다, 떠가다
- **form**[fɔːrm] 동 형성하다, 만들어 내다
- **French**[frentʃ] 형 프랑스의
- **grass**[græs] 명 풀, 잔디
- **hear**[hiər] 동 듣다 (-heard-heard)
- **hill**[hil] 명 언덕
- **interesting**[íntərəstiŋ] 형 재미있는, 흥미로운
- **land**[lænd] 동 착륙하다
- **laugh**[læf] 동 웃다
- **lie**[lai] 동 눕다 (-lay-lain)
- **little**[lítl] 형 작은
- **marathon**[mǽrəθɑ̀n] 명 마라톤
- **musical**[mjúːzikəl] 명 뮤지컬
- **nearest**[níərist] (near의 최상급) 가장 가까운
- **other**[ʌ́ðər] 형 다른
- **poster**[póustər] 명 포스터
- **recently**[ríːsntli] 부 최근에
- **ride**[raid] 동 타다 (-rode-ridden)
- **save**[seiv] 동 구하다, 절약하다
- **secret**[síːkrit] 명 비밀, 기밀
- **shake**[ʃeik] 동 흔들다 (-shook-shaken)
- **shout**[ʃaut] 동 외치다
- **since**[sins] 접 ~한 이래로
- **soft**[sɔːft] 형 부드러운
- **spaceship**[spéisʃip] 명 우주선
- **space station** 우주 정거장
- **space suit** 우주복
- **swallow**[swɑ́lou] 동 삼키다
- **taste**[teist] 명 맛
- **thirsty**[θə́ːrsti] 형 목마른
- **thrilling**[θríliŋ] 형 아주 신나는
- **type**[taip] 명 종류, 유형
- **towards**[tɔːrdz] 전 ~쪽으로, ~을 향하여
- **vegetable**[védʒətəbl] 명 야채, 채소
- **wet**[wet] 형 젖은
- **wind**[wind] 명 바람

Key Expressions

- **all night** 하룻밤 내내, 밤새도록
- **be born** 태어나다
- **be covered with** ~으로 뒤덮이다
- **be curious about ~** ~에 관해 궁금해 하다
- **don't have to+동사원형** ~할 필요 없다
- **each other** (둘 사이의) 서로
- **for example** 예를 들어
- **get on** ~에 타다
- **get wet** 젖다
- **here it is** (물건을 건네줄 때) 여기 있어
- **in surprise** 놀라서
- **in the air** 공중에
- **lie down** 눕다
- **not ~ anymore** 더 이상 ~ 않다
- **pull down** 아래로 끌어내리다
- **roll down** 굴러 내려가다
- **run up to ~** ~으로 달려가다
- **sound+형용사** ~하게 들리다
- **take a walk** 산책하다
- **talk about ~** ~에 관해 말하다
- **try to+동사원형** ~하려고 시도하다

Word Power

※ 서로 반대되는 뜻을 가진 어휘

□ **different** (다른) ↔ **same** (같은)

□ **arrive** (도착하다) ↔ **depart** (출발하다)

□ **difficult** (어려운) ↔ **easy** (쉬운)

□ **excited** (신나는) ↔ **bored** (지루한)

□ **land** (착륙하다) ↔ **take off** (이륙하다)

□ **interesting** (흥미로운) ↔ **uninteresting** (재미없는)

□ **little** (작은) ↔ **big** (큰)

□ **near** (가까운) ↔ **far** (먼)

□ **soft** (부드러운) ↔ **hard** (딱딱한)

□ **wet** (젖은) ↔ **dry** (마른)

□ **get on** (타다) ↔ **get off** (내리다)

□ **intelligent** (똑똑한) ↔ **stupid** (어리석은)

※ 서로 비슷한 뜻을 가진 어휘

□ **amazing** : **surprising** (놀라운)

□ **fix** : **repair** (고치다, 수리하다)

□ **form** : **build** (형성하다)

□ **recently** : **lately** (최근에)

□ **save** : **rescue** (구하다)

□ **shout** : **yell** (외치다)

□ **exciting** : **thrilling** (신나는)

□ **land** : **touch down** (착륙하다)

English Dictionary

□ **adventure** 모험
 → an unusual, exciting, and possibly dangerous activity, such as a trip
 여행과 같이 특이하고, 흥미진진하며, 위험할 수도 있는 활동

□ **amazing** 놀라운
 → extremely surprising
 매우 놀라운

□ **arrive** 도착하다
 → to reach a place, especially at the end of a journey
 특히 여행이 끝날 때, 어떤 장소에 도착하다

□ **curious** 호기심 많은
 → interested in learning about people or things around you
 주변 사람 또는 사물을 알고자 하는 데 관심이 있는

□ **exploration** 탐험, 탐사
 → the activity of searching and finding out about something
 무언가를 찾고 알아내는 활동

□ **foreign** 외국의
 → belonging or connected to a country that is not your own
 자신의 나라가 아닌 나라와 관련되어 있거나 속해 있는

□ **float** 뜨다
 → to stay on the surface of a liquid and not sink
 액체의 표면에 머무르고 가라앉지 않다

□ **form** 형성하다, 만들다
 → to make something into a particular shape
 어떤 것을 특정한 모양으로 만들다

□ **land** 착륙하다
 → to arrive on the ground or other surface after moving down through the air
 공중에서 아래로 이동한 후 땅이나 다른 표면에 도착하다

□ **swallow** 삼키다
 → to cause food, drink, pills, etc. to move from your mouth into your stomach by using the muscles of your throat
 목의 근육을 사용함으로써 음식, 음료, 약 등을 입에서 배 속으로 움직이도록 하다

□ **secret** 비밀
 → a piece of information that is only known by one person or a few people and should not be told to others
 한 사람이나 몇 사람만 알고 다른 사람에게는 말하지 말아야 하는 정보

□ **spaceship** 우주선
 → a vehicle used for travel in space
 우주에서 여행하기 위해 사용되는 운송 수단

□ **space station** 우주 정거장
 → a place or vehicle in space where people can stay
 사람들이 머물 수 있는 우주에 있는 장소나 탈것

□ **towards** ~을 향해
 → in the direction of, or closer to someone or something
 누군가나 어떤 것의 방향으로 또는 더 가까이

01 다음 문장의 빈칸에 주어진 영어 설명에 해당하는 말을 쓰시오.

Rada and Jonny thought about it all night and didn't tell Mom and Dad about it. It was their _____.

a piece of information that is only known by one person or a few people and should not be told to others

중요

02 다음 빈칸에 들어갈 말로 가장 적절한 것은?

Jonny opened a milk container and shook it. The milk _____ed in the air and formed balls.

① float   ② reach
③ swallow   ④ fix
⑤ look

[03~04] 다음 영영풀이에 해당하는 단어를 고르시오.

03
to move something down, using your hands

① roll down   ② be born
③ in surprise   ④ pull down
⑤ each other

중요

04
covered in or full of water or another liquid

① soft   ② dry
③ near   ④ simple
⑤ wet

05 다음 우리말에 맞게 빈칸에 알맞은 단어를 쓰시오.

언덕들이 있어. 그리고 언덕들은 부드러운 초록색의 잔디로 덮여 있지.
➡ There are hills, and they _____
_____ _____ soft green grass.

06 다음 빈칸에 공통으로 들어갈 말로 알맞은 것은?

• He put a grape into his mouth and _____ed it.
• One _____ doesn't make a summer.

① plan   ② land
③ swallow   ④ throw
⑤ laugh

07 다음 짝지어진 단어의 관계가 같도록 빈칸에 알맞은 말을 쓰시오.

amazing : surprising = lately : _____

중요

08 다음 빈칸에 들어갈 말로 알맞게 짝지어진 것은?

• They looked at _____ other and laughed.
• Rada and Jonny _____ down on the soft green grass and rolled down the hill.

① one – laid   ② each – rolled
③ every – lied   ④ each – lay
⑤ one – pulled

01 다음 빈칸에 들어갈 말을 〈보기〉에서 찾아 쓰시오. (필요하면 변형하여 쓰시오.)

> ┤ 보기 ├
> curious   excite   pull   cover

(1) It's also hard to jump there because Earth _____ you down.

(2) Hills are _____ with soft green grass.

(3) It was _____ to think about all the new things they were going to see and do.

(4) I'm really _____ about the space marathon.

02 다음 그림에 맞게 〈보기〉에서 단어를 골라 알맞은 표현을 쓰시오. (어형 변화 필수)

> ┤ 보기 ├
> cover   pull   roll down   shake   land

(1) (2) (3)

(1) A girl is _____ a bottle.

(2) A ball is _____ _____ the hill.

(3) An airplane is _____.

03 다음 빈칸에 공통으로 알맞은 단어를 주어진 철자로 시작하여 쓰시오.

(1) • You have to fill out a f_____ on their website.
  • The milk floated in the air and f_____ed balls. Jonny swallowed the balls.

(2) • The sailors saw l_____ in the distance.
  • The plane l_____ed safely at last.

04 다음 우리말과 같은 표현이 되도록 문장의 빈칸을 채우시오.

(1) 그들은 우주에서 태어났다.
  ➡ They _____ _____ in space.

(2) Rada와 Jonny는 깜짝 놀라 아빠를 보았고, 그에게 둥둥 떠서 갔다.
  ➡ Rada and Jonny looked at Dad in _____ and floated towards him.

(3) 모든 곳에 공기가 있기 때문에 너는 크고 무거운 우주복을 입을 필요가 없어.
  ➡ You _____ _____ _____ wear your big heavy _____ _____ because there is air _____.

05 다음 영영풀이에 해당하는 단어를 〈보기〉에서 찾아 첫 번째 칸에 쓰고, 두 번째 칸에는 우리말 뜻을 쓰시오.

> ┤ 보기 ├
> space station   exploration   secret
> air   space suit   adventure

(1) _____: the gases around you, which you breathe: _____

(2) _____: a piece of information that is only known by one person or a few people and should not be told to others _____

(3) _____: a special piece of clothing that astronauts wear in space: _____

Conversation

1 알고 있는지 묻기

> **A** Did you hear about the new musical? 새로운 뮤지컬에 대해 들어 봤니?
> **B** Yes, I did. / No, I didn't. 응. 들어 봤어. / 아니, 못 들어 봤어.

■ 'Did you hear about ~?'은 '~에 대해서 들어 봤니?'라는 의미로 새로운 정보에 대해서 알고 있는지 묻는 표현이다. 비슷한 표현으로 'Do you know (about) ~?', 'Are you aware (of) ~?'와 현재완료를 사용해 'Have you heard about ~?'으로 들어 본 적이 있는지 물을 수도 있다.

- A: Did you hear about the new store on Main Street? Main가에 있는 새 가게에 대해 들어 봤니?
  B: Yes, I did. / No, I didn't. 응. 들어 봤어. / 아니. 못 들어 봤어.

- A: Are you aware that ice cream is from China? 너는 아이스크림이 중국에서 왔다는 것을 알고 있니?
  B: No. That's interesting. 아니. 그거 참 흥미롭구나.

- A: Have you heard about the new waffle shop? 새 와플 가게에 대해 들어 본 적 있니?
  B: Yeah. I saw an ad about it on a poster. 응. 포스터에서 그것에 대한 광고를 봤어.

■ 알고 있음을 표현할 때
- I'm aware of the situation. / I've been told about it. / I've heard about it.

핵심 Check

1. 다음 대화의 밑줄 친 ⓐ의 의도로 알맞은 것은?

G: Hojin, ⓐdid you hear about the speaking contest?
B: No, I didn't. Where did you hear about it?
G: From the school newspaper.

① 놀람 표현하기   ② 확신하는지 묻기
③ 알고 있는지 묻기   ④ 도움이 필요한지 묻기
⑤ 대안 묻기

2. 다음 주어진 문장과 같은 의미가 되도록 빈칸에 알맞은 말을 쓰시오.

Did you hear about the accident?

= _____ you _____ _____ the accident?

② 궁금증 표현하기

I'm really curious about it. 나는 그것에 대해 정말 궁금해.

■ 'I'm really curious about ~.'은 '나는 ~에 대해서 정말 궁금해.'라는 의미로 새로운 정보에 대하여 궁금증을 표현하거나 보다 많은 정보를 알고 싶을 때 사용하는 표현이다. 'I'd like to know more about ~.', 'I'm interested in ~, I want to know ~.' 등으로도 표현할 수 있다.

- The cat was naturally curious about its new surroundings. 그 고양이는 원래 새로운 환경에 호기심이 있었다.
- We are curious about why you never called us. 우리는 왜 네가 우리에게 전화를 하지 않았는지가 궁금하다.

■ '~하고 싶다, 궁금해지다'라는 의미는 'be[become] curious to+동사원형'으로 나타낼 수 있다.

- They were curious to find out who won the game. 그들은 누가 게임을 이겼는지 알고 싶다.
- I'm curious to know more about her. 나는 그녀에 관하여 더 알고 싶다.

핵심 Check

3. 다음 대화의 빈칸에 들어갈 알맞은 것은?

A: Why did you borrow the book about Mars?

B: It's because I'm curious _____ the universe.

① in   ② to   ③ for

④ with   ⑤ about

4. 다음 문장과 같은 의미로 사용될 수 있는 것을 <u>모두</u> 고르시오.

I am curious about this movie.

① I'd like to know more about this movie.

② I want to know about this movie.

③ I can tell you about this movie.

④ I don't know much about this movie.

⑤ I'm curious to know more about this movie.

Listen and Talk A-1

B: ❶Did you hear about the first spaceship ❷that went into space?

G: No, I didn't. ❸I'm curious about it.

B: This is a poster of the spaceship.

G: Really? I want to buy it.

B: 너는 우주에 간 첫 번째 우주선에 대해 들어 봤니?

G: 아니, 못 들어 봤어. 궁금하다.

B: 이것이 그 우주선 포스터야.

G: 정말? 그것을 사고 싶다.

❶ '~에 대해서 들어 봤니?'라는 의미로 새로운 정보에 대해서 알고 있는지 묻는 표현이다.

❷ that went into space는 주격 관계대명사절로 선행사인 the first spaceship을 꾸며주는 역할을 한다.

❸ 궁금증을 표현하거나 보다 많은 정보를 알고 싶을 때 사용하는 표현이다. 'I'd like to know more about ~.' 'I'm interested in ~, I want to know ~' 등으로 표현할 수도 있다.

Check(√) True or False

(1) G didn't know about the first spaceship that went into space.　　　T☐ F☐

(2) G has an interest in the spaceship.　　　T☐ F☐

Listen and Talk A-2

G: ❶Did you hear about the new book about Mars?

B: No, I didn't. ❷I'm really curious about Mars.

G: Look. It's ❸right here. ❹It's about Mars and its moons.

B: Great. I think I'll buy the book.

G: 너는 화성에 관한 새로운 책에 관해 들어 봤니?

B: 아니, 못 들어 봤어. 나는 화성에 관해 정말 궁금해.

G: 봐. 바로 여기 있어. 그것은 화성과 그것의 위성들에 관한 내용이야.

B: 멋지다. 이 책을 사야겠어.

❶ '~에 대해서 들어 봤니?'라는 의미로 새로운 정보에 대해서 알고 있는지 묻는 표현으로 'Do you know (about) ~?', 'Are you aware (of) ~?' 등으로 바꾸어 쓸 수 있다.

❷ 궁금증을 표현하거나 보다 많은 정보를 알고 싶을 때 사용하는 표현이다. 'I'd like to know more about ~.', 'I'm interested in ~, I want to know ~' 등으로 표현할 수도 있다.

❸ 여기서 right는 부사로 '바로'라는 뜻이다.

❹ be about은 '~에 관한 것이다'로 해석한다.

Check(√) True or False

(3) B knew about the book about Mars.　　　T☐ F☐

(4) B is going to buy the book about Mars.　　　T☐ F☐

Listen and Talk A-3

G: ❶Did you hear about the space marathon?

B: No, I didn't.

G: It's a marathon on a space station. Look at this video.

B: OK. ❷I'm really curious about it.

❶ '~에 대해서 들어 봤니?'라는 의미로 새로운 정보에 대해서 알고 있는지 묻는 표현으로 'Do you know (about) ~?', 'Are you aware (of) ~?' 등으로 바꾸어 쓸 수 있다.

❷ 궁금증을 표현하거나 보다 많은 정보를 알고 싶을 때 사용하는 표현이다.

Listen and Talk A-4

G: Did you hear about the new space food?

B: Yes, I did. It's ❶a type of ice cream.

G: Yes, and ❷here it is. It looks good.

B: I'm really curious about the taste.

❶ a type of: ~의 일종

❷ 상대방에게 물건을 건네줄 때 사용하는 표현으로 '여기 있다'는 의미이다.

Listen and Talk B

A: Look at this. ❶Did you hear about the new musical?

B: Yes, I did. I heard it has great songs.

A: Oh, I'm really curious about it.

❶ Have you heard about the new musical?로 바꾸어 표현할 수 있다.

Listen and Talk B

A: Look at this. Did you hear about the new musical?

B: No, I didn't.

A: I heard it has great songs.

B: Oh, ❶I'm really curious about it.

❶ 'I'd like to know more about it.'으로 바꾸어 표현할 수 있다.

Listen and Talk C

B: Subin, ❶did you hear about the new movie, *Life on the Moon?*

G: No, I didn't.

B: I heard it's really good.

G: ❷I'm really curious about the movie. What's it about?

B: It's about a man ❸who is trying to live on the moon.

G: ❹That sounds interesting.

B: Look. The movie is playing at the Space Theater here.

G: What time is the movie?

B: It begins at 2:30.

G: Let's eat lunch first and then see the movie.

B: OK. I'm hungry. Let's go!

❶ are you aware of the new movie로 바꾸어 쓸 수 있다.

❷ 궁금증을 표현하거나 보다 많은 정보를 알고 싶을 때 사용하는 표현이다. I'd like to know more about the movie.로 바꾸어 쓸 수 있다.

❸ who 이하의 문장은 선행사 a man을 수식하는 주격 관계대명사절이다.

❹ 'sound+형용사' 형태로 '그거 재미있겠다.'는 뜻이다.

Review 1

G: Tony, ❶did you hear about the movie, *My Hero?*

B: No, I didn't.

G: Well, I heard it's really good.

B: I'm really curious about the movie. What's it about?

G: ❷It's about a father who saves his son.

❶ '~에 대해서 들어 봤니?'라는 의미로 새로운 정보에 대해서 알고 있는지 묻는 표현으로 'Do you know (about) ~?', 'Are you aware (of) ~?' 등으로 바꾸어 쓸 수 있다.

❷ be about은 '~에 관한 것이다'로 해석하고, who saves his son은 선행사 a father를 수식하는 주격 관계대명사절이다.

Review 2

G: Did you hear about the new book, *Living in a Foreign Country?*

B: No, I didn't.

G: Look. It's right here. ❶It's about living in New York.

B: Great. I'm really curious about this book.

G: ❷Me, too.

❶ be about은 '~에 관한 것[내용]이다'는 뜻이고, 전치사 about 뒤에 동명사 living 형태를 사용한다.

❷ '나도 그래.'의 뜻으로 So am I.로 바꿔 쓸 수 있다.

● 다음 우리말과 일치하도록 빈칸에 알맞은 말을 쓰시오.

Listen and Talk A-1

B: Did you _____ _____ the first spaceship _____ went into space?

G: No, I didn't. I'm _____ _____ it.

B: This is a poster of the spaceship.

G: Really? I want _____ _____ it.

해석

B: 너는 우주에 간 첫 번째 우주선에 대해 들어 봤니?
G: 아니, 못 들어 봤어. 궁금하다.
B: 이것이 그 우주선 포스터야.
G: 정말? 그것을 사고 싶다.

Listen and Talk A-2

G: _____ you _____ _____ the new book about Mars?

B: No, I didn't. _____ _____ _____ _____ Mars.

G: Look. It's _____ _____. It's _____ Mars and its moons.

B: Great. I think I'll buy the book.

G: 너는 화성에 관한 새로운 책에 관해 들어 봤니?
B: 아니, 못 들어 봤어. 나는 화성에 관해 정말 궁금해.
G: 봐. 바로 여기 있어. 그것은 화성과 그것의 위성들에 관한 내용이야.
B: 멋지다. 이 책을 사야겠어.

Listen and Talk A-3

G: _____ _____ _____ _____ _____ the space marathon?

B: No, _____ _____.

G: It's a marathon on a space station. _____ _____ this video.

B: OK. _____ _____ _____ _____ it.

G: 너는 우주 마라톤에 대해 들어 봤니?
B: 아니, 못 들어 봤어.
G: 그것은 우주 정거장에서 하는 마라톤이야. 이 비디오를 봐.
B: 알겠어. 정말 궁금하다.

Listen and Talk A-4

G: Did you hear _____ the new space food?

B: Yes, I did. It's _____ _____ of ice cream.

G: Yes, and _____ _____ _____. It looks good.

B: I'm really _____ _____ the taste.

G: 너는 새로운 우주 음식에 대해 들어 봤니?
B: 응, 들어 봤어. 그건 일종의 아이스크림이야.
G: 응, 여기 있어. 맛있어 보인다.
B: 그 맛이 참 궁금하다.

Listen and Talk B

1. A: Look at this. Did you hear _____ the new musical?

   B: Yes, I did. I _____ it has great songs.

   A: Oh, I'm really _____ _____ it.

2. A: _____ _____ this. Did you _____ _____ the new musical?

   B: No, I didn't.

   A: I heard _____ _____ _____ _____ _____.

   B: Oh, I'm really _____ about it.

1. A: 이것 봐. 새 뮤지컬에 대해 들어 봤니?
   B: 응, 들어 봤어. 좋은 노래들이 나온다고 들었어.
   A: 오, 정말 궁금하다.

2. A: 이것 봐. 새 뮤지컬에 대해 들어 봤니?
   B: 아니, 못 들어 봤어.
   A: 좋은 노래들이 나온다고 들었어.
   B: 오, 정말 궁금하다.

Listen and Talk C

B: Subin, did you hear _____ the new movie, *Life on the Moon*?

G: No, I didn't.

B: I heard it's really _____.

G: I'm really _____ _____ the movie. What's it _____?

B: It's _____ a man _____ is trying _____ _____ on the moon.

G: That sounds _____.

B: Look. The movie _____ _____ at the Space Theater here.

G: _____ _____ is the movie?

B: It _____ at 2:30.

G: _____ eat lunch first _____ _____ see the movie.

B: OK. I'm _____. Let's go!

Review 1

G: Tony, _____ _____ hear about the movie, *My Hero*?

B: No, I didn't.

G: Well, I _____ it's really good.

B: I'm really _____ about the movie. What's it _____?

G: It's _____ a father _____ saves his son.

Review 2

G: Did you hear _____ the new book, *Living in a Foreign Country*?

B: No, I didn't.

G: Look. It's _____ here. It's about _____ in New York.

B: Great. I'm really _____ _____ this book.

G: Me, too.

해석

B: 수빈아, "달에서의 생활"이라는 새 영화에 대해서 들어 봤니?

G: 아니.

B: 굉장히 좋다고 들었거든.

G: 그 영화가 정말 궁금하네. 뭐에 관한 거야?

B: 달에서 살기 위해 노력하는 한 남자에 관한 영화래.

G: 그거 재미있겠다.

B: 봐. 그 영화가 여기 우주 극장에서 상영되고 있어.

G: 영화가 몇 시에 상영되는데?

B: 2시 30분에 시작해.

G: 우선 점심부터 먹고 영화를 보자.

B: 좋아. 나 배고파. 가자!

G: Tony, 영화 My Hero에 대해 들어 봤니?

B: 아니, 못 들어 봤어.

G: 음, 정말 좋다고 들었어.

B: 그 영화에 대해 정말 궁금하다. 무엇에 대한 것이니?

G: 그것은 아들을 구하는 아빠에 관한 거야.

G: 새 책인 "Living in a Foreign Country"에 대해 들어 봤니?

B: 아니, 못 들어 봤어.

G: 봐. 바로 여기 있어. 그것은 뉴욕에서의 삶에 관한 거야.

B: 멋지다. 이 책이 정말 궁금해.

G: 나도 그래.

01 다음 우리말에 맞도록 빈칸에 들어갈 알맞은 말을 쓰시오.

나는 화성에 관해 정말 궁금해.
➡ I'm really _____ _____ Mars.

02 다음 대화의 빈칸에 들어갈 말로 알맞은 것은?

A: _____ the new movie, *My Father*?
B: No, I didn't, but I'm curious about it.

① Are you curious about   ② Why don't we see
③ Tell me about   ④ Did you hear about
⑤ Are you interested in

03 다음 대화의 빈칸에 들어갈 말로 알맞은 것은? (2개)

A: What are you looking at?
B: I'm looking at this poster. _____
A: It's Mars.

① I'd like to know where this place is.
② I know where this place is.
③ I want to know where this place is.
④ I have heard where this place is.
⑤ I'm amazed about this place.

04 다음 대화의 밑줄 친 우리말에 맞게 문장의 빈칸을 채우시오.

A: 새 영화 New Moon에 대해 들어 봤니?
B: No, I didn't, but I'm really curious about it.

➡ Did you _____ _____ the new movie, *New Moon*?

[01~02] 다음 대화를 읽고 물음에 답하시오.

B: _____(A)_____ the spaceship that went into space?

G: No, I didn't. I _____(B)_____ it.

B: This is a poster of the spaceship.

G: Really? I want to buy it.

01 위 대화의 빈칸 (A)에 들어갈 말로 알맞은 것은?

① Have you bought
② Have you seen the poster of
③ What do you think of
④ Did you hear about
⑤ Did you want to know about

02 위 대화의 빈칸 (B)에 들어갈 말로 알맞은 것을 모두 고르시오.

① am tired of
② am surprised at
③ am full of
④ am curious about
⑤ want to know about

03 다음 대화의 순서를 알맞게 배열한 것은?

(A) OK. I'm really curious about it.
(B) It's a marathon on a space station. Look at this video.
(C) No, I didn't.
(D) Did you hear about the space marathon?

① (A) – (B) – (C) – (D)
② (B) – (A) – (C) – (D)
③ (B) – (C) – (A) – (D)
④ (C) – (B) – (D) – (A)
⑤ (D) – (C) – (B) – (A)

[04~05] 다음 대화를 읽고 물음에 답하시오.

G: Did you hear ___(A)___ the new space food?

B: Yes, I did. It's a type of ice cream.

G: Yes, and (B)여기 있어. It looks good.

B: I'm really curious ___(A)___ the taste.

04 위 대화의 빈칸 (A)에 공통으로 들어갈 말로 알맞은 것은?

① with　　② about　　③ in
④ for　　⑤ at

05 위 대화의 밑줄 친 (B)의 우리말에 해당하는 표현을 주어진 단어를 포함하여 세 단어로 쓰시오.

➡ _____ (here)

06 다음 두 사람의 대화가 어색한 것은?

① A: What are you looking at?
　 B: This picture. I want to know who the painter is.

② A: Did you hear about the new movie star, William Black?
　 B: No, I didn't, but I'm curious about him.

③ A: Did you hear about the new TV show, *Hip Hop*?
　 B: No, I didn't, but I'm curious about it.

④ A: Look at this. Did you hear about the new musical?
　 B: No, I didn't. I heard it has great songs.

⑤ A: I'm really curious about the movie. What's it about?
　 B: It's about a man who is trying to live on the moon.

07 다음 대화의 밑줄 친 우리말에 맞게 주어진 단어를 이용하여 영어로 쓰시오. (어형 변화 필수)

> G: Tony, did you hear about the movie, *My Hero*?
> B: No, I didn't.
> G: Well, I heard it's really good.
> B: I'm really curious about the movie. What's it about?
> G: 그것은 아들을 구하는 아버지에 관한 거야.

> it / about / a father / who / save / son

➡ _____

08 다음 대화의 밑줄 친 부분의 의도로 알맞은 것은?

> G: Did you hear about the new book about Mars?
> B: No, I didn't. I'm really curious about Mars.

① 알고 있는지 묻기　② 의무 표현하기
③ 확신 표현하기　④ 궁금증 표현하기
⑤ 의견 묻기

[09~10] 다음 대화를 읽고 물음에 답하시오.

> Bin: Subin, ⓐdid you hear about the new movie, *Life on the Moon*?
> Subin: No, I didn't.
> Bin: I heard it's really good.
> Subin: I'm really ⓑcurious about the movie. What's it about?
> Bin: It's about a man ⓒwho are trying to live on the moon.
> Subin: That sounds ⓓinteresting.
> Bin: Look. The movie is playing at the Space Theater here.
> Subin: What time is the movie?
> Bin: It ⓔbegins at 2:30.
> Subin: Let's eat lunch first and then see the movie.

> Bin: OK. I'm hungry. Let's go!

09 위 대화의 밑줄 친 ⓐ~ⓔ 중 어법상 어색한 것은?

① ⓐ　② ⓑ　③ ⓒ　④ ⓓ　⑤ ⓔ

10 위 대화를 읽고 답할 수 없는 질문은?

① What are they talking about?
② Is Subin interested in the new movie?
③ What is the movie, *Life on the Moon*, about?
④ What time does the movie begin?
⑤ What are they going to do after seeing the movie?

[11~12] 다음 대화를 읽고 물음에 답하시오.

> D: Did you hear about the new space food?
> B: ____(A)____ It's a type of ice cream.
> G: Yes, and here it is. It looks good.
> B: I'm really ___(B)___ about the taste.

11 위 대화의 빈칸 (A)에 들어갈 말로 알맞은 것은?

① Yes, I am.　② Yes, I did.
③ No, I don't.　④ No, I haven't.
⑤ Of course not.

12 위 대화의 빈칸 (B)에 들어갈 말에 대한 영어 풀이를 보고 주어진 철자로 시작하여 쓰시오.

> wanting to know something, or to learn about the world

➡ c_____

[01~02] 다음 대화를 읽고 물음에 답하시오.

G: (A)새 책인 "Living in a Foreign Country"에 대해 들어 봤니?
B: No, I didn't.
G: Look. It's right here. It's about living in New York.
B: Great. (B)이 책이 정말 궁금해.
G: Me, too.

01 위 대화의 밑줄 친 (A)의 우리말에 맞게 주어진 단어를 이용하여 영작하시오.

> hear, the new book, *Living in a Foreign Country*

➡ _____

_____

02 위 대화의 밑줄 친 (B)의 우리말에 맞게 'curious'와 'really'를 이용하여 영작하시오.

➡ _____

03 다음 대화의 빈칸에 들어갈 말로 자연스러운 것을 〈보기〉에서 찾아 문장을 쓰시오.

A: _____ (A)
B: No, I didn't. _____ (B)
A: They are comfortable and not that expensive.
B: Oh, _____ (C)

┤ 보기 ├
• What about them?
• I'm curious about them.
• Did you hear about the new running shoes, *Speed*?

(A) _____
(B) _____
(C) _____

04 다음 대화의 밑줄 친 질문에 대한 답을 주어진 단어를 활용하여 조건에 맞게 영작하시오.

G: Tony, did you hear about the movie, *My Hero*?
B: No, I didn't.
G: Well, I heard it's really good.
B: I'm really curious about the movie. (A) What's it about?
G: _____

┤ 조건 ├
• 전치사를 사용할 것
• 관계대명사를 사용할 것
• 현재시제를 사용할 것

> (a father, save, his son)

➡ It's _____.

05 다음 대화들을 순서대로 배열했을 때, 제일 마지막에 오는 문장을 쓰시오.

(A) I heard it's really good.
(B) Subin, did you hear about the new movie, *Life on the Moon*?
(C) I'm really curious about the movie. What's it about?
(D) It's about a man who is trying to live on the moon.
(E) That sounds interesting.
(F) No, I didn't.

➡ _____

Grammar

① 현재완료

- I**'ve** never **seen** a blue sky. 전 한 번도 파란 하늘을 본 적이 없어요.
- **Have** you ever **thought** about becoming a teacher?
  선생님이 되는 것에 대해 생각해 본 적이 있어요?

- 현재완료는 'have[has]+과거분사'의 형태로 과거에 시작된 동작과 그 동작의 현재 상태를 동시에 표현한다.

- 의문문은 'Have[Has]+주어+과거분사 ~?'이며, 부정문은 'have[has]+not[never]+과거분사'로 나타낸다.
  - I **haven't smoked** for ten years. 나는 10년 동안 담배를 안 피우고 있어요.
  - **Have** you **done** your homework already? 숙제를 벌써 했니?

- 현재완료는 '계속(~해 왔다), 경험(~한 적이 있다), 완료(막[벌써] ~했다), 결과(~해 버렸다)'의 네 가지 용법으로 쓰인다. 계속적 용법은 보통 'for(~ 동안)+기간 명사'나 'since(~부터, ~ 이래로)+시간 명사'와 함께 쓰이며, 경험은 'once(한 번), twice(두 번), three times(세 번), ever(이제껏), never(한 번도 ~않다), before(전에)' 등과 같은 부사(구)와 함께 쓰인다. 완료 용법은 보통 'already(이미, 벌써), just(막, 방금), yet(아직, 벌써)' 등과 같은 부사와 쓰이고, 결과 용법은 과거에 발생한 사건이 현재 미치고 있는 결과를 포함한다.
  - Mary **has studied** French for 5 years. 〈계속〉 Mary는 5년 동안 불어를 공부해 오고 있다.
  - I **have** never **heard** such a sad story. 〈경험〉 나는 그런 슬픈 이야기를 들어 본 적이 없다.
  - He **has** already **spent** all his money. 〈완료〉 그는 이미 자신의 돈을 다 써버렸다.
  - The girl **has lost** her dog at the park. 〈결과〉
    그 소녀는 공원에서 그녀의 개를 잃어버렸다. (그 결과 (그녀의 개가) 지금 없다.)

- 현재완료는 과거에 시작된 동작과 그 동작의 현재 상태를 동시에 표현하므로 명백한 과거를 나타내는 yesterday, ~ ago, last week 등의 부사(구)나 의문사 when과는 함께 쓰이지 않는다.
  - He wasn't present at the meeting last week. (○)
    He hasn't been present at the meeting last week. (X) 그는 지난 주 모임에 참석하지 않았다.

  ※ have[has] been to vs. have[has] gone to
  have[has] been to는 '~에 가 본 적이 있다'는 경험을 나타내고, have[has] gone to는 '~에 가고 없다'는 결과를 나타낸다. 그러므로 have[has] gone to는 3인칭만 주어로 쓸 수 있다.

핵심 Check

1. 다음 주어진 동사를 빈칸에 어법에 맞게 쓰시오.
   (1) He _____ _____ English for ten years. (study)
   (2) I have not _____ from her for six years. (hear)
   (3) _____ you _____ a famous person before? (meet)

② It ~ to부정사

> • **It's** difficult **to walk** on Earth. 지구에서는 걷는 것이 어려워요.
>
> • **It** is good **to know** how to say hello. 인사하는 법을 아는 것이 좋다.

■ 비교적 긴 to부정사 부분이 문장의 주어로 쓰일 때 그 to부정사 부분을 일반적인 주어의 자리인 문장의 맨 앞에 두지 않고 문장 제일 뒤에 둔다. 대신 주어 자리에는 it을 넣어주는데 그것을 가주어 it이라고 부르고 문장 뒤로 간 to부정사 부분은 진주어라고 부른다. 이때 쓰인 it은 가주어이므로 구체적인 뜻이 없으며, '…하는 것은 ~하다'로 해석한다.

- **It** is easy **to play** the piano. 피아노를 치는 것은 쉽다.
  = **To play** the piano is easy.

- **It** is interesting **to watch** birds. 조류 관찰은 재미있다.
  = **To watch** birds is interesting.

■ It ~ to부정사의 의미상 주어
to부정사의 동작을 실제로 하는 사람을 to부정사의 의미상 주어라고 한다. to부정사의 의미상 주어는 to부정사 바로 앞에 'for+명사[대명사]의 목적격'의 형태로 쓴다. It ~ to부정사 구문에서 to부정사의 의미상 주어가 없는 경우는 특별한 사람이 아니라 일반적인 사람이기 때문이다. 문장에 쓰인 형용사가 nice, kind, smart, wise, foolish, careful, careless, honest, polite, rude 등과 같이 사람의 성향, 성격을 나타내는 말일 때는 'of+목적격'을 쓴다. 또한 to부정사의 부정은 to부정사 앞에 not[never]을 써서 'not[never]+to V'로 나타내며 '…하지 않는 것은 ~하다'로 해석한다.

- **It** is important for you **to choose** good friends. 네가 좋은 친구를 고르는 것은 중요하다.

- **It** is nice of you **to show** me the way. 길을 가르쳐 주셔서 감사합니다.

- **It** is easy **not to think** outside the box. 새로운 사고를 하지 않는 것은 쉽다.

핵심 Check

2. 다음 우리말과 일치하도록 빈칸에 알맞은 말을 쓰시오.

(1) 운동을 하는 것이 왜 중요할까요?

➡ Why _____ _____ _____ _____ exercise?

(2) 구명 조끼를 입는 것이 안전하다.

➡ _____ is safe _____ wear a life jacket.

(3) 내가 피아노를 치는 것은 쉽다.

➡ It's easy _____ _____ _____ _____ the piano.

01 다음 빈칸에 알맞은 것을 고르시오.

> A: Isn't it good _____ with friends?
> B: Yes, of course.

① to travel in Korea
② travels in Korea
③ to traveling in Korea
④ of you to travel in Korea
⑤ your travel in Korea

02 다음 중 어법상 어색한 문장은?

① Have you ever seen a koala?
② The plane has just left for Seoul.
③ I have gone to Hong Kong.
④ Marianne has played the piano for 10 years.
⑤ I have already washed my hands.

03 다음 문장에서 어법상 어색한 부분을 바르게 고치시오.

(1) My parents have just return from the trip.

_____ ➡ _____

(2) Rada has eaten dinner with Jonny last weekend.

_____ ➡ _____

(3) How long do you have been in Canada?

_____ ➡ _____

(4) They've worked here for last year.

_____ ➡ _____

(5) That is nervous to sing in front of the class.

_____ ➡ _____

(6) It will be helpful reads the book.

_____ ➡ _____

01 다음 중 어법상 바르지 <u>않은</u> 것은?

① Emily has caught a big fish and she is very excited.
② I've never heard her use bad language before.
③ They have lived in that house for more than 20 years.
④ When have you watched the new movie?
⑤ Hermionne has gone back to her country already.

 02 다음 중 어법상 바른 것은?

① It isn't easy studies English every day.
② It is so kind for you to lend me the book.
③ That's necessary to wear a helmet.
④ It's better run your own business if you can.
⑤ It has become common practice to chat online.

 03 다음 빈칸에 알맞은 말이 바르게 짝지어진 것은?

• _____ the team won ten games this year?
• It was hard _____ a science experiment.

① Is – to do   ② Is – done
③ Has – to do   ④ Has – done
⑤ Was – doing

 04 다음 문장의 빈칸에 들어갈 알맞은 것은?

_____ is easy to play musical instruments.

① It   ② This   ③ That
④ What   ⑤ One

05 다음 대화의 빈칸에 들어갈 말로 알맞은 것은?

M: Where's your homework, Peter?
W: I'm sorry, but I have not finished it _____.

① just   ② already   ③ yet
④ for   ⑤ since

서답형
06 다음 괄호 안에서 알맞은 말을 고르시오.

(1) Alex (have / has) decided to visit an art museum in London.
(2) I (don't have / haven't) seen David today.
(3) Jane is not here now. She has (been / gone) to Stockholm to find work.
(4) Bella (has been / went) to the United States in 2011.
(5) It is always exciting (sleeps / to sleep) in a tent.
(6) It is impossible (of / for) them to get lost.

07 다음 중 어법상 옳은 것은?

① Angie has bought a new smartphone yesterday.
② Have she told you the good news yet?
③ I have gone to England once.
④ I have already seen the movie.
⑤ I've been learning English since ten years.

08 다음 중 밑줄 친 부분의 쓰임이 <u>다른</u> 하나는?

① <u>It</u> is impossible to live without air and water.
② <u>It</u> was not accepted in old days.
③ <u>It</u>'s important for the students to do the project in three days.
④ <u>It</u> is dangerous to be in the street after dark.
⑤ <u>It</u> is better to be safe than sorry.

09 다음 질문에 대한 응답으로 알맞은 것은?

> Has he had any serious problems with ear in the past?

① Yes, he has.　② Yes, he is.
③ Yes, he does.　④ No, he isn't.
⑤ No, he doesn't.

서답형

10 주어진 어휘를 이용하여 다음 우리말을 영작하시오.

> 규칙적으로 휴식을 취할 필요가 있다.
> (it, a break, regularly, take, necessary, to)

➡ _____

11 다음 두 문장을 한 문장으로 바르게 연결한 것은?

> • Jack went back to his home.
> • And he is not here now.

① Jack went to his home.
② Jack went to his home already.
③ Jack hasn't been to his home.
④ Jack hasn't come back to his home yet.
⑤ Jack has gone to his home.

12 다음 우리말과 일치하도록 빈칸에 알맞은 단어로 묶은 것은?

> 비행기를 조종하는 것은 내 꿈 중 한 가지이다.
> ➡ _____ is a dream of mine _____ an airplane.

① It – fly　　　② It – to fly
③ That – fly　　④ That – to fly
⑤ This – flying

13 다음 〈보기〉의 밑줄 친 부분과 용법이 같은 것은?

> ┤ 보기 ├
> He <u>has worked</u> for the company for more than 10 years.

① My mom <u>has been</u> sick since last week.
② She <u>has gone</u> to Japan.
③ Judy <u>has been</u> to America five times.
④ Kevin <u>has</u> already <u>heard</u> about the party at school.
⑤ Megan <u>has lost</u> her wallet on the train.

서답형

14 다음 문장에서 어법상 어색한 것을 바르게 고쳐 다시 쓰시오.

(1) It is difficult for me guess the ending of the story.

➡ _____

_____

(2) This is boring to read a science book.

➡ _____

(3) It is important read for an hour every day.

➡ _____

(4) I have worked in the hospital snack bar then.

➡ _____

(5) Jim has had a cat since three years.

➡ _____

(6) Garry has been to New York on business and he stays there now.

➡ _____

_____

서답형

15 다음 두 문장을 비슷한 뜻을 가진 한 문장으로 바꿔 쓰시오.

(1) Josh lost his smartphone. So, he doesn't have any smartphone now.

➡ _____

(2) Sophia started to live in Georgia five years ago. And she still lives there.

➡ _____

[16~17] 다음 우리말에 맞게 영작한 것을 고르시오.

16

> 너는 작년 이후로 아주 키가 컸다.

① You grew very tall since last year.
② You have grown very tall last year.
③ You have grown very tall for last year.
④ You have grown very tall as last year.
⑤ You have grown very tall since last year.

17

> 기말고사 후에 친구들과 어울리는 것은 정말 신이 나.

① It is very exciting hang out with my friends after finals.
② It is very exciting hangs out with my friends after finals.
③ It is very exciting to hang out with my friends after finals.
④ That is very exciting to hang out with my friends after finals.
⑤ That is very exciting hanging out with my friends after finals.

중요

18 다음 중 어법상 어색한 것을 고르시오. (2개)

① It is necessary for Daniel to talk to his parents.
② It's nice for her to take care of her young sister.
③ It is fun to swim in the lake.
④ When have you watched the movie with her?
⑤ We have lived here since I was born.

01 다음 우리말에 맞게 주어진 어구를 바르게 배열하시오.

(1) Kelly는 10살 이후로 LA에서 살고 있다.
(Kelly, she, years, LA, has, was, lived, 10, old, since, in)
➡ _____

(2) 정부는 교육에 더 관심을 가지게 되었다.
(education, the government, interested, become, has, more, in)
➡ _____
_____

(3) 그는 그 소문에 대해 들은 적이 있어.
(the rumor, heard, he, has, about)
➡ _____

(4) 다른 나라들을 여행하는 것은 멋지다.
(countries, it, wonderful, travel, is, other, to, to)
➡ _____

(5) 그가 그 경기의 표를 구하는 것이 가능하니?
(the game, it, tickets, him, possible, get, is, for, for, to)
➡ _____

02 다음 우리말을 (1) to부정사 주어를 써서, (2) 가주어를 써서 영작하시오.

• 밤에 운전하는 것은 위험하다.
(1) _____
(2) _____

• 물건을 훔치는 것은 잘못이다.
(1) _____
(2) _____

03 그림을 보고, 주어진 어휘를 이용하여 자신의 경험에 대해 쓰시오. (현재완료 시제로 주어와 동사를 갖춘 완전한 문장으로 쓸 것.)

(1) (eat, nacho)
➡ _____

(2) (have, to)
➡ _____
_____

04 다음 주어진 두 문장을 한 문장으로 바꿔 쓰시오.

(1) • Sonya visited New York again.
• It is her third visit.
➡ _____

(2) • I ate dinner a moment ago.
• So I am full now.
➡ _____

05 다음 문장을 It으로 시작하여 다시 쓰시오.

(1) To think about all the new things was exciting.

➡ _____

(2) To swim in the cool blue sea was great.

➡ _____

(3) To eat a lot of vegetables is good.

➡ _____

(4) That the pen is mightier than the sword is true.

➡ _____

06 다음 우리말을 괄호 안에 주어진 어휘를 이용하여 영작하시오.

(1) 나는 한 번도 일출을 본 적이 없다.
(a sunrise, see, never, 6 단어)

➡ _____

(2) 그는 영어를 20년 동안 가르쳐 왔다.
(teach, 7 단어)

➡ _____

(3) 이 물을 마셔도 안전한가요?
(this water, safe, drink, 7 단어)

➡ _____

(4) 내가 그 팀에서 축구를 하게 되어 운이 좋다.
(the team, lucky, me, 10 단어)

➡ _____

(5) 이를 매일 닦는 것은 중요하다.
(brush your teeth, important, 9 단어)

➡ _____

07 다음 문장에서 어법상 어색한 것을 고쳐 문장을 다시 쓰시오.

(1) When have you heard from Susan?

➡ _____

(2) Mr. Brown has lived in Jeju-do for 2010.

➡ _____

(3) Have you gone to Canada before?

➡ _____

(4) Use a ticket machine in the theater is easy.

➡ _____
_____

(5) It's important for her understands him.

➡ _____

08 다음 문장을 부정문과 의문문으로 각각 바꿔 쓰시오.

They have already finished their project.

부정문 _____

의문문 _____

09 다음 두 문장의 의미가 같도록 빈칸에 알맞은 말을 쓰시오.

(1) It started raining last Saturday. It is still raining.

➡ It _____ last Saturday.

(2) Aiko went back to Tokyo. She is in Tokyo now.

➡ Aiko _____ to Tokyo.

The Best New Thing

Rada lived on a little world, far out in space. She lived there with
　　　　　　　　　　　　　　　　멀리　　우주에서
her father, mother, and brother Jonny. Rada's father and other people

worked on spaceships. Only Rada and Jonny were children, and they
우주선에서 일했다
were born in space. One day, Dad told Rada and Jonny, "We're going
태어났다　　　　(과거의) 어느 날.　　　　　　are going: 현재진행의 의미가 아니라 가까운 미래를 나타냄
back to Earth tomorrow." Rada and Jonny looked at Dad in surprise
돌아가다　　　　　　　　　　　　　　　　　　　　　　　　　　　　놀라서
and floated towards him. Rada asked Dad, "What's it like on Earth?"

"Everything is different there. For example, the sky is blue," answered
　　　　　　　　　= on Earth 인용문을 먼저 쓰고 '~가 말했다'를 뒤에 쓸 때: 주어와 동사의 순서를 바꾸어 쓸 수 있음
Dad. "I've never seen a blue sky," said Jonny. "The sky is always black
현재완료(경험). never: have와 과거분사 사이에 not 대신에 부정의 의미를 강조　　　　　빈도부사: be동사 뒤에 위치.
here," said Rada. "You don't have to wear your big heavy space suits
　　　　　　　　　　　　～할 필요가 없다
because there is air everywhere. It's also hard to jump there because
　　　　　　　　　　　　　　　　　It은 가주어로서 진주어인 to jump there를 대신한다.
Earth pulls you down," said Dad. "What else?" asked Rada. "There are
너를 끌어당긴다　　　　　　　　　　　　그 밖에
hills, and they are covered with soft green grass. You can roll down the
　　　　= hills.　　～으로 뒤덮여 있다
hills," answered Mom. "Dad, have you ever rolled down a hill?" asked
　　　　　　　　　　　　현재완료(경험)　　　roll down: 굴러 내려가다
Rada. "Yes, it's really amazing!" answered Dad. Jonny was thirsty, so
　　　　　　　　　　　　　　　　　　　　　　　　　　　　　　결과를 나타내는 접속사.
he opened a milk container and shook it. The milk floated in the air and
　　　　　　　　　　　　　　　　　a milk container
formed balls. Jonny swallowed the balls. "Jonny, if you drink milk that
　　　　　　　　　　　　　　　　　　　　　'우유를 먹기 위해 우유 용기를 열어 흔들어서 우유 방울을 만들어 먹는 것'
way on Earth, you'll get wet," said Mom.
젖다

📎 **확인문제**

● 다음 문장이 본문의 내용과 일치하면 T, 일치하지 않으면 F를 쓰시오.

1 Rada and Jonny were born in space. ☐

2 The sky is always black in space. ☐

3 You don't have to wear your big heavy space suits because Earth pulls you down. ☐

4 You can roll down the hills which are covered with soft green grass. ☐

Later that night, Rada and Jonny talked a long time about Earth. It
늦게   =for a long time: 오랫동안   It: 가주어

was exciting to think about all the new things they were going to see
진주어   things와 they 사이에 목적격 관계대명사 which/that이 생략

and do. There was one new thing Rada and Jonny really wanted to do.
thing과 Rada 사이에 목적격 관계대명사 which/that이 생략

They thought about it all night and didn't tell Mom and Dad about it. It
one new thing

was their secret. The next day, Rada's family got on a spaceship. "It's
(교통수단을) 타다

going to be a long trip," said Mom. "That's alright. I'm so excited!"
be going to+동사원형: 미래의 구체적인 계획을 통해 곧 일어날 것이라고 판단할 수 있는 일에 사용   = all right   excited는 과거분사지만 완전히 형용사화되어 so로 수식할 수 있음.

said Rada. The spaceship finally landed. "Dad, it's difficult to walk
가주어   진주어

on Earth," said Rada. "I know. Earth is pulling you down," said Dad.
pull down: 끌어당기다, 지구에 중력이 있음을 의미

Rada and Jonny couldn't float anymore. That was the first new thing.
우주에서는 공중에 떠다녔지만, 지구에서는 중력 때문에 더 이상 떠다닐 수 없음을 의미, 앞 문장 전체

"What's that sound?" asked Rada. "A bird is singing," said Mom. "I've
be동사 현재형+-ing: 현재진행형, 현재 하고 있는 동작을 나타낸다.

never heard a bird sing," said Rada. "And I've never felt the wind,"
현재완료(경험), '결코 들어 본 적이 없다' 지각동사 hear+목적어+동사원형/-ing   현재완료(경험), '바람을 한 번도 느껴 본 적이 없다'

said Jonny. These were all new things. Rada and Jonny ran up the
near의 최상급, '가장 가까운'

nearest hill. At the top, they looked at each other and laughed. Then
laughed 앞에 주어인 they가 중복되어 생략

they lay down on the soft green grass and rolled down the hill. That
lie(눕다)의 과거형, lie-lay-lain / lay-laid-laid: 놓다, 눕히다

was their secret! "This is the best new thing of all!" shouted Rada and
good의 최상급

Jonny. And they ran up to the top of the hill again.
~으로 뛰어 올라갔다

secret 비밀

all night 밤새도록

get on ~에 타다, ~에 오르다

each other 서로

lie 눕다

📎 **확인문제**

● 다음 문장이 본문의 내용과 일치하면 T, 일치하지 않으면 F를 쓰시오.

1 It was exciting for Rada and Jonny to think about all the new things they were going to see and do on Earth. ☐

2 Rada and Jonny thought about one new thing they really wanted to do on Earth and told Mom and Dad about it. ☐

3 Rada has ever heard a bird sing. ☐

4 Rada and Jonny's secret was to lie down on the grass and roll down the hill. ☐

● 우리말을 참고하여 빈칸에 알맞은 말을 쓰시오.

1 The _____ New Thing

2 Rada lived on a little world, _____ _____ _____ _____.

3 She _____ _____ _____ her father, mother, and brother Jonny.

4 Rada's father and other people _____ _____ spaceships.

5 _____ Rada and Jonny were children, and they _____ _____ in space.

6 One day, Dad told Rada and Jonny, "We're _____ _____ Earth tomorrow."

7 Rada and Jonny looked at Dad _____ _____ and floated towards him.

8 Rada asked Dad, "_____ _____ _____ on Earth?"

9 "Everything _____ _____ there.

10 _____ _____, the sky is blue," answered Dad.

11 "_____ _____ _____ a blue sky," said Jonny.

12 "The sky _____ _____ _____ here," said Rada.

13 "You _____ _____ _____ wear your big heavy space suits because _____ _____ _____ everywhere.

14 It's also hard to jump there because Earth _____ _____ _____," said Dad.

15 "_____ _____?" asked Rada.

16 "There are hills, and they _____ _____ _____ soft green grass.

17 You can _____ _____ the hills," answered Mom.

18 "Dad, _____ _____ _____ _____ _____ a hill?" asked Rada.

19 "Yes, it's really _____!" answered Dad.

20 Jonny was thirsty, so he _____ a milk container and _____ it.

21 The milk _____ in the air and _____ balls.

22 Jonny _____ the balls.

23 "Jonny, if you drink milk that way on Earth, you'll _____ _____," said Mom.

1	최고의 새로운 것
2	Rada는 먼 우주의 작은 세계에 살고 있었다.
3	그녀는 아빠, 엄마 그리고 남동생 Jonny와 함께 그곳에서 살고 있었다.
4	Rada의 아빠와 다른 사람들은 우주선에서 일했다.
5	Rada와 Jonny만이 아이들이었고, 그들은 우주에서 태어났다.
6	어느 날, 아빠가 Rada와 Jonny에게, "우리는 내일 지구로 돌아갈 거야."라고 말했다.
7	Rada와 Jonny는 깜짝 놀라 아빠를 바라보았고, 그에게 둥둥 떠서 갔다.
8	Rada가 아빠에게, "지구는 어떤 곳인가요?"라고 물었다.
9	"그곳에선 모든 것이 다르단다.
10	예를 들어, 하늘은 파란색이지."라고 아빠가 대답했다.
11	"전 한 번도 파란 하늘을 본 적이 없어요."라고 Jonny가 말했다.
12	"여기는 하늘이 항상 검은색이잖아요."라고 Rada가 말했다.
13	"그곳에는 모든 곳에 공기가 있기 때문에 크고 무거운 우주복을 입을 필요가 없단다.
14	또한 지구가 너희들을 끌어당기기 때문에 거기에서는 점프하는 것도 어렵단다." 아빠가 말했다.
15	"그 밖에 또 뭐가 있어요?" Rada가 물었다.
16	"언덕들이 있는데 그것들은 부드러운 초록색의 잔디로 뒤덮여 있단다.
17	언덕을 굴러 내려갈 수도 있어." 엄마가 대답했다.
18	"아빠, 언덕을 굴러 내려가 본 적 있어요?" Rada가 물었다.
19	"그럼, 정말 놀라워!" 아빠가 대답했다.
20	Jonny는 목이 말라서 우유 용기를 열어 그것을 흔들었다.
21	우유가 공기 중으로 떠서 방울을 형성했다.
22	Jonny는 그 우유 방울을 삼켰다.
23	"Jonny, 만약 네가 지구에서 그런 식으로 우유를 마신다면, 다 젖을 거야." 엄마가 말했다.

24 _____ _____ _____, Rada and Jonny talked a long time about Earth.

25 It was _____ to think about _____ _____ _____ _____ they were going to see and do.

26 There was _____ _____ _____ Rada and Jonny really wanted to do.

27 They thought about it _____ _____ and didn't tell Mom and Dad about it.

28 It was _____ _____.

29 The next day, Rada's family _____ _____ a spaceship.

30 "_____ _____ _____ _____ a long trip," said Mom.

31 "That's alright. I'm _____ _____!" said Rada.

32 The spaceship _____ landed.

33 "Dad, it's difficult _____ _____ on Earth," said Rada.

34 "I know. Earth is _____ _____ _____," said Dad.

35 Rada and Jonny _____ _____ _____.

36 That was _____ _____ _____ _____.

37 "_____ that sound?" asked Rada.

38 "A bird _____ _____," said Mom.

39 "_____ _____ _____ a bird sing," said Rada.

40 "And _____ _____ _____ the wind," said Jonny.

41 _____ were all new things.

42 Rada and Jonny ran up _____ _____ hill.

43 At the top, they looked at _____ _____ and laughed.

44 Then they _____ _____ on the soft green grass and _____ _____ the hill.

45 That was _____ _____!

46 "This is the _____ _____ _____ of all!" shouted Rada and Jonny.

47 And they ran _____ _____ _____ _____ of the hill again.

24 그날 밤 늦게, Rada와 Jonny는 지구에 대해서 오랜 시간 이야기했다.

25 그들이 보고, 하게 될 모든 새로운 것들을 생각하는 것은 흥미로웠다.

26 Rada와 Jonny가 정말로 하고 싶었던 한 가지 새로운 것이 있었다.

27 그들은 밤새 그것에 대해서 생각했고 엄마와 아빠에게는 그것을 말하지 않았다.

28 그것은 그들의 비밀이었다.

29 다음날, Rada의 가족은 우주선에 올랐다.

30 "긴 여행이 될 거야." 엄마가 말했다.

31 "괜찮아요. 정말 신나요!" Rada가 말했다.

32 우주선이 마침내 착륙했다.

33 "아빠, 지구에서는 걷는 것이 어려워요." Rada가 말했다.

34 "그래. 지구가 너를 끌어당기고 있거든." 아빠가 말했다.

35 Rada와 Jonny는 더 이상 떠다닐 수 없었다.

36 그것이 첫 번째 새로운 것이었다.

37 "저건 무슨 소리죠?"라고 Rada가 물었다.

38 "새가 노래하는 거야." 엄마가 말했다.

39 "새가 노래하는 것을 들어 본 적이 없어요."라고 Rada가 말했다.

40 "그리고 저는 바람을 느껴 본 적도 없어요."라고 Jonny가 말했다.

41 이러한 것들이 모두 새로운 것들이었다.

42 Rada와 Jonny는 가장 가까운 언덕으로 뛰어 올라갔다.

43 꼭대기에서, 그들은 서로를 쳐다보고 웃었다.

44 그리고 나서 그들은 부드러운 초록 잔디에 누워서 언덕 아래로 굴러 내려갔다.

45 그것이 그들의 비밀이었다!

46 "이것이 모든 것들 중에서 최고의 새로운 것이에요!" Rada와 Jonny는 외쳤다.

47 그리고 그들은 언덕 꼭대기로 다시 뛰어 올라갔다.

● 우리말을 참고하여 본문을 영작하시오.

1 최고의 새로운 것
➡ _____

2 Rada는 먼 우주의 작은 세계에 살고 있었다.
➡ _____

3 그녀는 아빠, 엄마 그리고 남동생 Jonny와 함께 그곳에서 살고 있었다.
➡ _____

4 Rada의 아빠와 다른 사람들은 우주선에서 일했다.
➡ _____

5 Rada와 Jonny만이 아이들이었고, 그들은 우주에서 태어났다.
➡ _____

6 어느 날, 아빠가 Rada와 Jonny에게, "우리는 내일 지구로 돌아갈 거야."라고 말했다.
➡ _____

7 Rada와 Jonny는 깜짝 놀라 아빠를 바라보았고, 그에게 둥둥 떠서 갔다.
➡ _____

8 Rada가 아빠에게, "지구는 어떤 곳인가요?"라고 물었다.
➡ _____

9 "그곳에선 모든 것이 다르단다.
➡ _____

10 예를 들어, 하늘은 파란색이지."라고 아빠가 대답했다.
➡ _____

11 "전 한 번도 파란 하늘을 본 적이 없어요."라고 Jonny가 말했다.
➡ _____

12 "여기는 하늘이 항상 검은색이잖아요."라고 Rada가 말했다.
➡ _____

13 "그곳에는 모든 곳에 공기가 있기 때문에 크고 무거운 우주복을 입을 필요가 없단다.
➡ _____

14 또한 지구가 너희들을 끌어당기기 때문에 거기에서는 점프하는 것도 어렵단다." 아빠가 말했다.
➡ _____

15 "그 밖에 또 뭐가 있어요?" Rada가 물었다.
➡ _____

16 "언덕들이 있는데 그것들은 부드러운 초록색의 잔디로 뒤덮여 있단다.
➡ _____

17 언덕을 굴러 내려갈 수도 있어." 엄마가 대답했다.
➡ _____

18 "아빠, 언덕을 굴러 내려가 본 적 있어요?" Rada가 물었다.
➡ _____

19 "그럼, 정말 놀라워!" 아빠가 대답했다.
➡ _____

20 Jonny는 목이 말라서 우유 용기를 열어 그것을 흔들었다.
➡ _____

21 우유가 공기 중으로 떠서 방울을 형성했다.
➡ _____

22 Jonny는 그 우유 방울을 삼켰다.
➡ _____

23 "Jonny, 만약 네가 지구에서 그런 식으로 우유를 마신다면, 다 젖을 거야." 엄마가 말했다.
➡ _____

24 그날 밤 늦게, Rada와 Jonny는 지구에 대해서 오랜 시간 이야기했다.
➡ _____

25 그들이 보고, 하게 될 모든 새로운 것들을 생각하는 것은 흥미로웠다.
➡ _____

26 Rada와 Jonny가 정말로 하고 싶었던 한 가지 새로운 것이 있었다.
➡ _____

27 그들은 밤새 그것에 대해서 생각했고 엄마와 아빠에게는 그것을 말하지 않았다.
➡ _____

28 그것은 그들의 비밀이었다.
➡ _____

29 다음날, Rada의 가족은 우주선에 올랐다.
➡ _____

30 "긴 여행이 될 거야." 엄마가 말했다.
➡ _____

31 "괜찮아요. 정말 신나요!" Rada가 말했다.
➡ _____

32 우주선이 마침내 착륙했다.
➡ _____

33 "아빠, 지구에서는 걷는 것이 어려워요." Rada가 말했다.
➡ _____

34 "그래. 지구가 너를 끌어당기고 있거든." 아빠가 말했다.
➡ _____

35 Rada와 Jonny는 더 이상 떠다닐 수 없었다.
➡ _____

36 그것이 첫 번째 새로운 것이었다.
➡ _____

37 "저건 무슨 소리죠?"라고 Rada가 물었다.
➡ _____

38 "새가 노래하는 거야." 엄마가 말했다.
➡ _____

39 "새가 노래하는 것을 들어 본 적이 없어요."라고 Rada가 말했다.
➡ _____

40 "그리고 저는 바람을 느껴 본 적도 없어요."라고 Jonny가 말했다.
➡ _____

41 이러한 것들이 모두 새로운 것들이었다.
➡ _____

42 Rada와 Jonny는 가장 가까운 언덕으로 뛰어 올라갔다.
➡ _____

43 꼭대기에서, 그들은 서로를 쳐다보고 웃었다.
➡ _____

44 그러고 나서 그들은 부드러운 초록 잔디에 누워서 언덕 아래로 굴러 내려갔다.
➡ _____

45 그것이 그들의 비밀이었다!
➡ _____

46 "이것이 모든 것들 중에서 최고의 새로운 것이에요!" Rada와 Jonny는 외쳤다.
➡ _____

47 그리고 그들은 언덕 꼭대기로 다시 뛰어 올라갔다.
➡ _____

[01~04] 다음 글을 읽고 물음에 답하시오.

Rada lived on a little world, far out ___ⓐ___ space. She lived there with her father, mother, and brother Jonny. Rada's father and other people worked on spaceships. Only Rada and Jonny were children, and they were born in space.

One day, Dad told Rada and Jonny, "We're going back to Earth tomorrow."

Rada and Jonny looked at Dad in surprise and floated towards him.

Rada asked Dad, "What's (A)it like ___ⓑ___ Earth?"

"Everything is different there. For example, the sky is blue," answered Dad.

"I've never seen a blue sky," said Jonny.

"The sky is always black here," said Rada.

01 위 글의 빈칸 ⓐ와 ⓑ에 들어갈 전치사가 바르게 짝지어진 것은?

① for – to
② in – for
③ in – on
④ from – to
⑤ for – on

02 위 글의 밑줄 친 (A)it과 문법적 쓰임이 같은 것을 모두 고르시오.

① I think it strange that she wants them.
② How's it going with you?
③ It was wine, not water, that you drank.
④ It is impossible to get there in time.
⑤ As it happened, I left the book at home.

03 위 글의 종류로 알맞은 것을 고르시오.

① book report
② article
③ biography
④ essay
⑤ science fiction

04 위 글의 내용과 일치하지 <u>않는</u> 것은?

① Rada lived far out in space with her family.
② Rada and Jonny were born in space.
③ When Rada and Jonny heard they were returning to space, they were surprised.
④ Dad said everything was different on Earth.
⑤ The sky was always black in space.

[05~08] 다음 글을 읽고 물음에 답하시오.

"You don't have to wear your big heavy space suits because there is air everywhere. It's also hard to jump there because Earth pulls you down," said Dad.

"What else?" asked Rada.

"There are hills, and they are covered with soft green grass. You can roll down the hills," answered Mom.

"Dad, ⓐhave you ever rolled down a hill?" asked Rada.

"Yes, it's really amazing!" answered Dad.

Jonny was thirsty, so he opened a milk container and ___(A)___ it. The milk floated in the air and formed balls. Jonny swallowed the balls.

"Jonny, ⓑ만약 네가 지구에서 그런 식으로 우유를 마신다면, 다 젖을 거야," said Mom.

서답형

05 위 글의 빈칸 (A)에 shake를 알맞은 형태로 쓰시오.

➡ _____

06 아래 〈보기〉에서 위 글의 밑줄 친 ⓐ의 현재완료와 용법이 같은 것의 개수를 고르시오.

① He has lost his pen.
② We have visited Paris before.
③ I have learned English since 2015.
④ She hasn't cleaned her room yet.
⑤ How many times have you seen it?

① 1개　② 2개　③ 3개　④ 4개　⑤ 5개

서답형

07 위 글의 밑줄 친 ⓑ의 우리말에 맞게 주어진 어휘를 이용하여 11 단어로 영작하시오.

drink, that way, get wet

➡ _____

중요

08 다음 중 Rada와 Jonny가 지구에서 처음 경험하게 될 일이 **아닌** 것을 고르시오.

① 우주복을 입을 필요가 없는 것
② 점프를 쉽게 할 수 있는 것
③ 부드러운 초록색의 잔디로 뒤덮여 있는 언덕을 보는 것
④ 언덕을 굴러 내려가는 것
⑤ 우유 방울을 삼키는 대신 마시는 것

[09~11] 다음 글을 읽고 물음에 답하시오.

Later that night, Rada and Jonny talked a long time about Earth. ⓐIt was (A)[exciting / excited] to think about all the new things they were going to see and do. There was one new thing Rada and Jonny really wanted to do. They thought about ⓑit all (B)[night / nights] and didn't tell Mom and Dad about ⓒit. It was their secret.

The next day, Rada's family got (C)[on / off] a spaceship.

"It's going to be a long trip," said Mom.

"That's alright. I'm so excited!" said Rada.

서답형

09 위 글의 밑줄 친 ⓐit, ⓑit, ⓒit이 가리키는 것을 본문에서 찾아 영어로 쓰시오.

(A) _____
_____
(B) _____
(C) _____

서답형

10 위 글의 괄호 (A)~(C)에서 문맥이나 어법상 알맞은 낱말을 골라 쓰시오.

(A) _____ (B) _____ (C) _____

11 위 글에서 알 수 있는 Rada와 Jonny의 심경으로 가장 알맞은 것을 고르시오.

① upset　　　　② confused
③ worried　　　④ disappointed
⑤ expectant

[12~15] 다음 글을 읽고 물음에 답하시오.

The spaceship finally (A)[landed / took off].

"Dad, it's difficult to walk on Earth," said Rada.

"I know. Earth is (B)[pulling / pushing] you down," said Dad.

Rada and Jonny couldn't float anymore. That was the first new thing.

"What's that sound?" asked Rada.

"A bird is singing," said Mom.

"I've never heard a bird sing," said Rada.

"And I've never felt the wind," said Jonny.

These were all new things.

Rada and Jonny ran up the nearest hill. At the top, they looked at each other and laughed. ⓐThen they lie down on the soft green grass and rolled down the hill. That was their secret!

"This is the best (C)[familiar / new] thing of all!" shouted Rada and Jonny.

And they ran up to the top of the hill again.

서답형
12 위 글의 괄호 (A)~(C)에서 문맥상 알맞은 낱말을 골라 쓰시오.

(A) _____ (B) _____ (C) _____

서답형
13 위 글의 밑줄 친 ⓐ에서 어법상 틀린 부분을 찾아 고치시오.

_____ ➡ _____

14 위 글의 제목으로 알맞은 것을 고르시오.

① Oh, It's Difficult to Walk on Earth!

② Be Careful! Earth Is Pulling You Down!

③ Guess What? I Can't Float Anymore!

④ New Things They Experienced on Earth

⑤ How to Roll Down the Hill

15 위 글의 내용과 일치하지 <u>않는</u> 것은?

① 지구에서는 걷는 것이 어렵다고 Rada가 아빠에게 말했다.

② 지구에서 Rada와 Jonny는 더 이상 떠다닐 수 없었다.

③ Rada는 새가 노래하는 것을 들어 본 적이 있다.

④ Jonny는 바람을 느껴 본 적이 없다.

⑤ Rada와 Jonny는 부드러운 초록 잔디에 누워서 언덕 아래로 굴러 내려갔다.

[16~18] 다음 글을 읽고 물음에 답하시오.

"You don't have to wear your big heavy space suits because there is air everywhere. (①) It's also hard to jump there because Earth pulls you down," said Dad.

(②) "There are hills, and they are covered with soft green grass. (③) You can roll down the hills," answered Mom.

(④) "Dad, have you ever rolled down a hill?" asked Rada.

(⑤) "Yes, it's really amazing!" answered Dad.

Jonny was thirsty, so he opened a milk container and shook it. The milk floated in the air and formed balls. Jonny swallowed the balls.

"Jonny, if you drink milk that way on Earth, you'll get wet," said Mom.

16 위 글의 흐름으로 보아, 주어진 문장이 들어가기에 가장 적절한 곳은?

> "What else?" asked Rada.

①   ②   ③   ④   ⑤

서답형

17 다음 빈칸 (A)~(C)에 알맞은 단어를 넣어 우주에서 우유 먹는 법을 완성하시오.

> In space, you can't drink milk in the same way as people do on Earth. First, you open a milk container and _____(A)_____ it. Then, the milk floats in the air and forms _____(B)_____. Finally, you can _____(C)_____ the balls.

(A) _____ (B) _____ (C) _____

18 위 글을 읽고 대답할 수 <u>없는</u> 질문은?

① Why is there no need to wear your big heavy space suits on Earth?
② Why is it difficult to jump on Earth?
③ What can you do on the hills that are covered with soft green grass?
④ When did Dad roll down a hill?
⑤ When Jonny was thirsty, what did he do?

[19~21] 다음 글을 읽고 물음에 답하시오.

The spaceship finally landed.
"Dad, it's difficult to walk on Earth," said Rada.
"I know. Earth is pulling you down," said Dad.
Rada and Jonny couldn't float anymore. That was the first new thing.
"What's that sound?" asked Rada.
"A bird is singing," said Mom.
"I've never heard a bird sing," said Rada.
"And I've never felt the wind," said Jonny.
ⓐThese were all familiar things.
Rada and Jonny ran up to the nearest hill. At the top, they looked at each other and laughed. Then ⓑ그들은 부드러운 초록 잔디에 누워서 언덕 아래로 굴러 내려갔다. That was their secret!
"This is the best new thing of all!" shouted Rada and Jonny.
And they ran up to the top of the hill again.

서답형

19 What was the first new thing to Rada and Jonny? Fill in the blanks with suitable words. (6 words)

➡ It was that _____.

서답형

20 위 글의 밑줄 친 ⓐ에서 흐름상 <u>어색한</u> 부분을 찾아 고치시오.

_____ ➡ _____

서답형

21 위 글의 밑줄 친 ⓑ의 우리말에 맞게 주어진 어휘를 이용하여 13 단어로 영작하시오.

> on the soft green grass

➡ _____

_____

[22~24] 다음 글을 읽고 물음에 답하시오.

> The next morning, Rada's family went to a park. Rada said to Dad, "Dad, I've never ___ⓐ___ a bike before." "Let's ___ⓑ___ bikes, then," said Dad. They then ___ⓒ___ bikes together. The weather was great, and it was so fun.
>
> In the afternoon, Rada's family went to the beach. Jonny said to Mom, "I've never swum before." "Let's swim, then," said Mom. It was great to swim in the cool blue sea.
>
> At night, Rada and Jonny talked about living on Earth. "It's wonderful to live on Earth," Rada said to Jonny. "Yes. It's great to be here," Jonny said.

서답형

22 위 글의 빈칸 ⓐ~ⓒ에 ride를 알맞은 형태로 쓰시오.

ⓐ _____ ⓑ _____ ⓒ _____

서답형

23 위 글을 읽고 Rada의 가족이 한 일을 우리말로 쓰시오.

오전: _____

오후: _____

밤: _____

서답형

24 What did Rada and Jonny think about living on Earth? Answer in English in a full sentence.

➡ _____

_____

[25~27] 다음 글을 읽고 물음에 답하시오.

> Later that night, Rada and Jonny talked a long time about Earth. ⓐIt was exciting ⓑto think about all the new things they were going to see and do them. There was one new thing Rada and Jonny really wanted to do. They thought about it all night and didn't tell Mom and Dad about it. It was their secret.
>
> The next day, Rada's family got on a spaceship. "It's going to be a long trip," said Mom. "That's alright. I'm so excited!" said Rada.

25 아래 〈보기〉에서 위 글의 밑줄 친 ⓐIt과 문법적 쓰임이 같은 것의 개수를 고르시오.

> ① It is warmer than yesterday.
> ② It is important to choose good friends.
> ③ Look! It's going up that tree.
> ④ It is impossible to master English in a month or two.
> ⑤ I think it necessary that you should do it at once.

① 1개　② 2개　③ 3개　④ 4개　⑤ 5개

서답형

26 위 글의 밑줄 친 ⓑ에서 어법상 틀린 부분을 찾아 고치시오.

_____ ➡ _____

서답형

27 What was Rada and Jonny's secret? Answer in English. (8 words)

➡ _____

[28~30] 다음 글을 읽고 물음에 답하시오.

The spaceship finally landed.

"Dad, it's difficult to walk on Earth," said Rada.

"I know. Earth is pulling you down," said Dad.

Rada and Jonny couldn't float anymore. That was the first new thing.

"What's that sound?" asked Rada.

"A bird is singing," said Mom.

"ⓐI've never heard a bird to sing," said Rada.

"And I've never felt the wind," said Jonny.

These were all new things.

Rada and Jonny ran up the nearest hill. At the top, they looked at each other and laughed. Then they lay down on the soft green grass and rolled down the hill. That was their secret!

"This is the best new thing of all!" shouted Rada and Jonny.

And they ran up to the top of the hill again.

28 위 글의 주제로 알맞은 것을 고르시오.

① final landing of the spaceship
② new things Rada and Jonny experienced on Earth
③ the gravity of the Earth
④ the way Rada heard a bird sing and Jonny felt the wind
⑤ Rada and Jonny who enjoyed rolling down the hill

서답형

29 위 글의 밑줄 친 ⓐ에서 어법상 틀린 부분을 찾아 고치시오.

_____ ➡ _____

30 위 글을 읽고 대답할 수 없는 질문은?

① Why is it difficult to walk on Earth?
② Was it possible for Rada and Jonny to float on Earth?
③ Has Jonny ever felt the wind?
④ What did Rada and Jonny do at the top of the hill?
⑤ How many times will Rada and Jonny run up to the top of the hill?

[01~03] 다음 글을 읽고 물음에 답하시오.

Rada lived on a little world, far out in space. She lived there with her father, mother, and brother Jonny. Rada's father and other people worked on spaceships. Only Rada and Jonny were children, and they were born in space.

One day, Dad told Rada and Jonny, "We're going back to Earth tomorrow."

ⓐRada와 Jonny는 깜짝 놀라 아빠를 바라보았고, 그에게 둥둥 떠서 갔다.

Rada asked Dad, "What's it like on Earth?"

"Everything is different there. For example, the sky is blue," answered Dad.

"I've never seen a blue sky," said Jonny.

"The sky is always black here," said Rada.

01 위 글의 내용과 일치하도록 다음 빈칸 (A)와 (B)에 알맞은 단어를 쓰시오.

> In space, there were no (A)_____ except Rada and Jonny (B)_____ were born there.

02 위 글의 밑줄 친 ⓐ의 우리말에 맞게 한 단어를 보충하여, 주어진 어휘를 알맞게 배열하시오.

> surprise/ towards / looked / him / and / Rada and Jonny / floated / Dad / at

➡ _____

_____

03 다음 빈칸에 알맞은 단어를 넣어 우주와 지구의 차이점을 완성하시오.

> The _____ of the sky in space is different from that on Earth.

[04~06] 다음 글을 읽고 물음에 답하시오.

"You don't have to wear your big heavy space suits because there is air everywhere. It's also hard to jump there because Earth pulls you down," said Dad.

"What else?" asked Rada.

"There are hills, and they are covered with soft green grass. You can roll down the hills," answered Mom.

"Dad, have you ever rolled down a hill?" asked Rada.

"ⓐYes, it's really amazing!" answered Dad.

Jonny was thirsty, so he opened a milk container and shook it. The milk floated in the air and formed balls. Jonny swallowed the balls.

ⓑ"Jonny, if you will drink milk that way on Earth, you'll get wet," said Mom.

04 위 글의 내용과 일치하도록 다음 빈칸 (A)~(D)에 알맞은 말을 쓰시오.

	in space	on Earth
wear your big heavy space suits	(A) _____	(A) need not
to jump	easy	(B)_____
how to have milk	swallow the milk (C)_____	drink milk

05 위 글의 밑줄 친 ⓐYes, 뒤에 생략된 말을 쓰시오. (2 단어)

➡ _____

06 위 글의 밑줄 친 ⓑ에서 어법상 틀린 부분을 찾아 고치시오.

_____ ➡ _____

[07~09] 다음 글을 읽고 물음에 답하시오.

The spaceship finally landed.

"Dad, it's difficult to walk on Earth," said Rada.

"I know. Earth is pulling you down," said Dad.

ⓐRada and Jonny couldn't float anymore. That was the first new thing.

"What's that sound?" asked Rada.

"A bird is singing," said Mom.

"(A)I've ( ) heard a bird sing," said Rada.

"And (B)I've ( ) felt the wind," said Jonny.

These were all new things.

Rada and Jonny ran up the nearest hill. At the top, they looked at each other and laughed. Then they lay down on the soft green grass and rolled down the hill. That was their secret!

07 위 글의 밑줄 친 (A)와 (B)가 각각 다음 문장과 같은 뜻이 되도록 빈칸에 공통으로 들어갈 알맞은 한 단어를 쓰시오.

> (A): This is the first time I've ever heard a bird sing.
> (B): This is the first time I've ever felt the wind.

➡ _____

08 위 글의 밑줄 친 ⓐ를 다음과 같이 바꿔 쓸 때 빈칸에 들어갈 알맞은 말을 쓰시오.

> Rada and Jonny could _____ float.

09 What was Rada and Jonny's secret? Fill in the blanks with the suitable words.

> It was that they _____ _____ on the soft green grass and _____ _____ the hill.

[10~12] 다음 글을 읽고 물음에 답하시오.

Rada lived on a little world, far out in space. She lived there with her father, mother, and brother Jonny. Rada's father and (A)[another / other] people worked on spaceships. Only Rada and Jonny were children, and they were born in space.

One day, Dad told Rada and Jonny, "We're going back to Earth tomorrow."

ⓐRada and Jonny looked at Dad in surprise and ran towards him.

Rada asked Dad, "(B)[How / What] is it like on Earth?"

"Everything is (C)[different / similar] ⓑthere. For example, the sky is blue," answered Dad.

"I've never seen a blue sky," said Jonny.

"The sky is always black ⓒhere," said Rada.

10 위 글의 괄호 (A)~(C)에서 문맥이나 어법상 알맞은 낱말을 골라 쓰시오.

(A) _____ (B) _____ (C) _____

11 위 글의 밑줄 친 ⓐ에서 흐름상 어색한 부분을 찾아 고치시오.

_____ ➡ _____

12 위 글의 밑줄 친 ⓑthere와 ⓒhere가 가리키는 것을 본문에서 찾아 쓰시오.

ⓑ _____ ⓒ _____

해석

새 책인 **Dave**의 모험에 관해 들어 봤니? 이 책은 **Dave**와 숲에서의 그의 모험에 관한 거야. 주인공은 **Dave**와 큰 곰이야. 이야기가 재미있어. 그 책에 관해 궁금하니? 그러면 그것을 꼭 읽어 봐야 해!

One Minute Speech

Did you hear about the new book, *Dave's Adventures*?
상대방이 알고 있는지 물어보는 표현이다
This book is about Dave and his adventures in the woods.
~에 관한 것이다
The main characters are Dave and a big bear. The story is fun.

Are you curious about the book?
be curious about ~: ~에 관해 궁금해하다
Then you should read it!

구문해설 · adventure 모험 · be about ~에 관한 것이다 · main character 주인공
· curious 궁금한, 호기심 있는

Read and Complete

1. Rada의 가족은 우주에서 살고 있었다. 어느 날, 그들은 지구로 돌아가기로 결정했다.
2. Rada의 가족은 지구의 생활에 대해 이야기했다. 그들은 파란 하늘과 초록색 잔디로 뒤덮인 언덕에 대해 이야기했다.
3. 다음날, Rada의 가족은 우주선에 올랐다. 그것은 지구로의 긴 여행이었다.
4. 그들이 지구에 도착했을 때, Rada와 Jonny는 가장 가까운 언덕으로 뛰어 올라가 아래로 굴러 내려갔다. 그것은 그들에게 최고의 새로운 것이었다.

1. Rada's family lived in space. One day, they decided to go back to Earth.
decide는 to부정사를 목적어로 취한다.
2. Rada's family talked about life on Earth. They talked about the blue sky and

hills which are covered with green grass.
주격 관계대명사+be동사: 생략 가능
3. The next day, Rada's family got on a spaceship. It was a long trip to Earth.
get on: 타다, 오르다, get off: 내리다
4. When they arrived on Earth, Rada and Jonny ran up the nearest hill and
arrive on: ~에 도착하다 형용사 near의 최상급
rolled down it. That was the best new thing to them.
the hill

구문해설 · in space: 우주에서 · decide: ~을 결정하다 · be covered with: ~으로 뒤덮여 있다
· roll down: 굴러 내려가다

Around the World

1. 러시아는 우주에 최초의 개를 보냈다. 그것은 작았고, 이름은 **Laika**였다.
2. **Yuri Gagarin**이 최초로 우주에 갔다.
3. 미국은 달에 최초의 인간을 보냈다. 그의 이름은 **Neil Armstrong**이었다.
4. 러시아가 최초의 우주 정거장을 건설하였다. 그것은 거의 3천 번 지구 주변을 돌았다.

1. Russia sent the first dog into space. It was small, and its name was Laika.
the+서수: 최초의 the dog's
2. Yuri Gagarin went into space for the first time.
처음으로, 최초로
3. The USA sent the first human to the moon. His name was Neil Armstrong.
~을 …로 보냈다
4. Russia built the first space station. It flew around the Earth almost 3,000
날아다녔다, 선회했다 지구
times.

구문해설 · space station: 우주 정거장 · almost: 거의 · times: ~ 번, ~ 배

Words & Expressions

01 다음 주어진 두 단어의 관계가 같도록 빈칸에 알맞은 단어를 쓰시오.

> excited : bored = take off : _____

02 다음 글의 빈칸 ⓐ와 ⓑ에 들어갈 단어로 바르게 짝지어진 것은?

> • You ⓐ_____ wear your big heavy space suits because there is air everywhere.
> • It's also hard to jump there because Earth ⓑ_____.

① have to – rolls you down
② must not – pulls down you
③ don't need to – pulls you up
④ don't have to – pulls you down
⑤ cannot – pulls down you

[03~04] 다음 영영풀이에 해당하는 것을 고르시오.

03

> to come out of a mother's body

① be curious about   ② roll down
③ be born   ④ swallow
⑤ get on

04

> to arrive on the ground or other surface after moving down through the air

① land   ② float
③ take off ④ get on
⑤ form

05 다음 빈칸에 공통으로 들어갈 말을 쓰시오.

> • That desk takes up too much _____.
> *take up: 차지하다
> • There are 90 parking _____s in this parking lot.
> • On June 18, China sent its first spacewoman into _____.
> *spacewoman: 여성 우주비행사

06 다음 밑줄 친 부분의 뜻이 잘못된 것은?

① This is a poster of the spaceship. (우주선)
② It's a type of ice cream. (종류)
③ Rada and Jonny looked at Dad in surprise. (놀라서)
④ They were born in space. (태어났다)
⑤ On sunny days, people go to parks and lie down on the grass. (구르다)

Conversation

07 다음 대화를 순서에 맞게 바르게 배열한 것은?

> (A) Yes, and here it is. It looks good.
> (B) Yes, I did. It's a type of ice cream.
> (C) Did you hear about the new space food?
> (D) I'm really curious about the taste.

① (A) – (B) – (D) – (C)
② (B) – (A) – (C) – (D)
③ (C) – (A) – (B) – (D)
④ (C) – (B) – (A) – (D)
⑤ (D) – (B) – (C) – (A)

[08~10] 다음 대화를 읽고 물음에 답하시오.

B: Subin, did you hear about the new movie, *Life on the Moon*?
G: No, I didn't.
B: I heard it's really good. (①)
G: I'm really curious about the movie. (②)
B: It's about a man who is trying to live on the moon. (③)
G: That sounds interesting.
B: Look. The movie is playing at the Space Theater here. (④)
G: What time is the movie?
B: It begins at 2:30. (⑤)
G: Let's eat lunch first and then see the movie.
B: OK. I'm hungry. Let's go!

08 주어진 문장이 들어갈 위치로 알맞은 것은?

What's it about?

①   ②   ③   ④   ⑤

09 다음 질문에 대한 답을 위 대화에서 찾아 쓰시오.

Q: What is the movie, *Life on the Moon*, about?

➡ _____

10 위 대화의 내용과 일치하지 <u>않는</u> 것은?

① Subin heard the new movie is really good.
② Subin has an interest in the new movie.
③ The new movie is playing now.
④ They are going to see the movie after eating lunch.
⑤ The movie is about a man trying to live on the moon.

11 다음 그림을 보고 제시된 〈조건〉에 맞게 아래 대화의 빈칸을 완성하시오.

┤ 조건 ├
(1) 'hear'를 사용할 것.
(2) 'really'와 'curious'를 사용하여 새로운 정보에 관심을 나타내는 표현을 쓸 것.
(3) 축약형을 사용하여 세 단어로 쓸 것

A: (1) _____ the new book, *The Best New Thing*?
B: No, I didn't.
A: I heard it's really interesting.
B: (2) _____
   (3) _____
A: It's about a family who lives in space.
B: That sounds interesting.

12 다음 대화의 밑줄 친 부분에 대한 설명으로 적절하지 <u>않은</u> 것은?

G: ⓐDid you hear about the new book, *Living in a Foreign Country*?
B: No, I didn't.
G: Look. It's ⓑright here. ⓒIt's about living in New York.
B: Great. ⓓI'm really curious about this book.
G: ⓔMe, too.

① ⓐ: 상대방이 어떤 정보를 알고 있는지를 묻는 말이다.
② ⓑ: 형용사로 '올바른'의 의미다.
③ ⓒ: 새 책의 내용에 관해 설명하는 말이다.
④ ⓓ: 새로운 정보에 대해 궁금증을 표현하는 말이다.
⑤ ⓔ: 상대방의 말에 자신도 그렇다고 동의하는 표현이다.

Grammar

13 다음 빈칸에 들어갈 말이 나머지와 <u>다른</u> 하나는?

① It was easy _____ me to find his new house.

② It was foolish _____ you to believe him.

③ It's difficult _____ me to play the piano well.

④ It was exciting _____ him to play soccer with his friends.

⑤ It can be dangerous _____ her to drive fast.

14 다음 빈칸에 들어갈 표현이 순서대로 바르게 짝지어진 것을 고르시오.

> I _____ him since I _____ a child.

① have known – was

② have known – has been

③ have known – had been

④ knew – was

⑤ knew – has been

15 다음 밑줄 친 부분의 쓰임이 나머지 넷과 <u>다른</u> 것은?

① I <u>have eaten</u> French food before.

② Jane <u>has been</u> to Jeju-do many times.

③ She <u>has never met</u> a movie star.

④ <u>Have</u> you ever <u>tried</u> to protect the environment?

⑤ My English <u>has improved</u> since I moved to Australia.

16 다음 문장을 주어진 말로 시작하여 다시 쓰시오.

(1) Tony must hand in his report by tomorrow.

→ It is necessary _____

_____.

(2) You should be careful when you cross the street.

→ It is necessary _____

_____.

17 다음 ⓐ~ⓗ 중 옳은 것을 <u>모두</u> 고르면?

> ⓐ Has Daniel found his wallet yesterday?
>
> ⓑ I have lost my backpack.
>
> ⓒ I've never gone to Egypt before.
>
> ⓓ How long has Mr. Williams worked for this company?
>
> ⓔ I have taught English since 10 years.
>
> ⓕ It's important follows the rules.
>
> ⓖ That is a pity that you cannot come to my party.
>
> ⓗ It's fun to ride a horse.

① ⓐ, ⓒ   ② ⓑ, ⓒ, ⓓ

③ ⓑ, ⓓ, ⓗ   ④ ⓓ, ⓔ, ⓗ

⑤ ⓓ, ⓔ, ⓖ

18 다음 밑줄 친 부분의 쓰임이 <u>다른</u> 하나는?

① It's hard <u>to fix</u> a bike.

② It's nice <u>to take</u> a walk in the park.

③ It's necessary <u>to learn</u> English.

④ He has gone never <u>to return</u>.

⑤ It is exciting <u>to cook</u>.

19 다음 중 어법상 어색한 문장은?

① It is bad for your teeth to drink too much soda.

② It was exciting to watch the baseball game.

③ It is important for you to be careful all the time.

④ James has eaten too much and he is sick now.

⑤ Peter, have you finished your project yesterday?

Reading

[20~22] 다음 글을 읽고 물음에 답하시오.

One day, Dad told Rada and Jonny, "We ⓐ are going back to Earth tomorrow."

Rada and Jonny looked at Dad in surprise and floated towards him.

Rada asked Dad, "ⓑ지구는 어떤 곳인가요?"

"Everything is different there. ___(A)___, the sky is blue," answered Dad.

"I've never seen a blue sky," said Jonny.

"The sky is always black here," said Rada.

20 위 글의 빈칸 (A)에 들어갈 알맞은 말을 고르시오.

① However   ② Therefore
③ In addition   ④ For example
⑤ That is

21 위 글의 밑줄 친 ⓐare going과 문법적 쓰임이 같은 것을 모두 고르시오.

① He is studying English in his room.

② What is she doing now?

③ She is leaving Seoul tonight.

④ Who is singing a song there?

⑤ He is coming here next week.

22 위 글의 밑줄 친 ⓑ의 우리말에 맞게 5 단어로 영작하시오.

➡ _____

[23~24] 다음 글을 읽고 물음에 답하시오.

"You don't have to wear your big heavy space suits (A)[because / though] there is air everywhere. It's also hard to jump there because Earth pulls you down," said Dad.

"(B)[How / What] else?" asked Rada.

"There are hills, and they are covered with soft green grass. You can roll down the hills," answered Mom.

"Dad, have you ever rolled down a hill?" asked Rada.

"Yes, it's really amazing!" answered Dad.

Jonny was thirsty, so he opened a milk container and shook it. The milk floated in the air and formed balls. Jonny swallowed the balls.

"Jonny, (C)[if / unless] you drink milk that way on Earth, you'll get wet," said Mom.

23 위 글의 괄호 (A)~(C)에서 문맥상 알맞은 낱말을 골라 쓰시오.

(A) _____   (B) _____   (C) _____

24 위 글의 내용과 일치하지 않는 것은?

① 지구에서는 크고 무거운 우주복을 입을 필요가 없다.

② 지구에서는 점프하는 것이 어렵다.

③ 지구에서는 언덕을 굴러 내려갈 수도 있다.

④ 아빠는 언덕을 굴러 내려가 본 적이 있다.

⑤ Jonny는 목이 말라서 우유 용기를 열고 그것을 마셨다.

[25~27] 다음 글을 읽고 물음에 답하시오.

Later that night, Rada and Jonny talked a long time about Earth. It was exciting ⓐto think about all the new things they were going to see and do. ⓑThere was one new thing Rada and Jonny really wanted to do. They thought about it all night and didn't tell Mom and Dad about it. It was their secret.

The next day, Rada's family got on a spaceship.

"It's going to be a long trip," said Mom.

"ⓒThat's alright. I'm so excited!" said Rada.

25 위 글의 밑줄 친 ⓐto think와 to부정사의 용법이 다른 것을 모두 고르시오.

① He opened the door, only to find the room empty.
② It is difficult to know oneself.
③ He has many children to look after.
④ She was very happy to get the birthday present.
⑤ To see is to believe.

26 위 글의 밑줄 친 문장 ⓑ에 생략된 한 단어를 넣어 문장을 다시 쓰시오.

➡ _____

_____

27 위 글의 밑줄 친 ⓒThat이 가리키는 것을 본문에서 찾아 쓰시오.

➡ _____

[28~30] 다음 글을 읽고 물음에 답하시오.

The spaceship finally landed.

"Dad, it's difficult to walk on Earth," said Rada.

"I know. Earth is pulling you down," said Dad.

Rada and Jonny couldn't float anymore. That was the first new thing.

"What's that sound?" asked Rada.

"A bird is singing," said Mom.

"I've never heard a bird sing," said Rada.

"And I've never felt the wind," said Jonny. (①) Rada and Jonny ran up the nearest hill. (②) At the top, they looked at each other and laughed. (③) Then they lay down on the soft green grass and rolled down the hill. (④) That was their secret! (⑤)

"This is the best new thing of all!" shouted Rada and Jonny.

And they ran up to the top of the hill again.

28 위 글의 흐름으로 보아, 주어진 문장이 들어가기에 가장 적절한 곳은?

These were all new things.

①   ②   ③   ④   ⑤

29 다음 문장에서 위 글의 내용과 다른 부분을 찾아서 고치시오.

Rada has ever heard a bird sing and Jonny has ever felt the wind.

_____ ➡ _____

_____ ➡ _____

30 본문의 내용과 일치하도록 다음 빈칸에 알맞은 단어를 쓰시오.

To Rada and Jonny, the _____ _____ _____ of all was to lie down on the soft green grass and roll down the hill.

01 출제율 95%

다음 짝지어진 단어의 관계가 같도록 빈칸에 알맞은 말을 쓰시오.

> intelligent : stupid = rough : _____

02 출제율 90%

다음 영영 풀이에 해당하는 단어는?

> in the direction of, or closer to someone or something

① along   ② out   ③ towards

④ into   ⑤ across

03 출제율 85%

다음 대화의 밑줄 친 (A)와 같은 의미의 문장을 주어진 단어를 활용하여 쓰시오.

> G: Did you hear about the space marathon?
> B: No, I didn't.
> G: It's a marathon on a space station. Look at this video.
> B: OK. (A)I'm really curious about it.

➡ _____ (interest)

04 출제율 95%

다음 대화의 밑줄 친 부분 중 어법상 어색한 것은?

> G: ⓐDid you hear about the new book, *Living in a Foreign Country*?
> B: ⓑNo, I didn't.
> G: Look. It's right here. It's about ⓒto live in New York.
> B: Great. ⓓI'm really curious about this book.
> G: ⓔMe, too.

① ⓐ   ② ⓑ   ③ ⓒ   ④ ⓓ   ⑤ ⓔ

05 출제율 100%

다음 글의 밑줄 친 (A)~(E)의 해석으로 틀린 것은?

> Later that night, Rada and Jonny (A)talked a long time about Earth. It was (B)exciting to think about all the new things they were going to see and do. There was one new thing Rada and Jonny really wanted to do. They thought about it (C)all night and didn't tell Mom and Dad about it. It was their (D)secret. The next day, Rada's family (E)got on a spaceship.

① (A) 오랜 시간 이야기했다
② (B) 흥미진진한
③ (C) 밤새
④ (D) 비밀
⑤ (E) 우주선에서 내렸다

[06~07] 다음 대화를 읽고 물음에 답하시오.

> B: (A)너는 우주로 간 첫 번째 우주선에 대해 들어봤니?
> G: No, I didn't. I'm curious about it.
> B: This is a poster of the spaceship.
> G: Really? _____ (B)

06 출제율 85%

위 대화의 밑줄 친 (A)의 우리말에 맞게 주어진 문장의 빈칸을 채우시오.

> Did you _____ _____ the first spaceship _____ went _____ space?

07 출제율 95%

위 대화의 (B)에 들어갈 말로 알맞은 것을 고르시오.

① What about you?
② I want to buy it.
③ I'm sorry to hear that.
④ I haven't heard about it.
⑤ I'm very interested in fashion.

[08~10] 다음 대화를 읽고 물음에 답하시오.

B: Subin, (A)did you hear about the new movie, *Life on the Moon*?

G: No, I didn't.

B: I heard it's really good.

G: (B)그 영화가 정말 궁금해. What's it about?

B: It's about a man _____ ⓐ _____

G: That sounds interesting.

B: Look. The movie is playing at the Space Theater here.

G: What time is the movie?

B: It begins at 2:30.

G: Let's eat lunch first and then see the movie.

B: OK. I'm hungry. Let's go!

출제율 95%

08 위 대화의 빈칸 ⓐ에 들어갈 말을 주어진 단어를 배열하여 의미가 통하도록 문장을 완성하시오.

is / to / live / the / trying / who / on / moon

➡ _____

출제율 90%

09 위 대화의 밑줄 친 (A)와 같은 의미가 되도록 '현재완료'를 사용하여 문장을 쓰시오.

➡ _____

출제율 85%

10 위 대화의 밑줄 친 (B)의 우리말에 맞게 주어진 어휘를 배열 하여 대화를 완성하시오.

really / about / I'm / curious / the / movie

➡ _____

출제율 100%

11 다음 빈칸에 알맞은 말이 순서대로 짝지어진 것은?

- I have known her _____ 10 years.
- I have known her _____ 2010.

① for – during
② during – for
③ for – since
④ since – for
⑤ as – for

출제율 90%

12 다음 우리말을 주어진 어휘를 이용하여 영작하시오.

(1) 그는 삼십 분째 잠들어 있다. (sleep)

➡ _____

(2) 그 유명 인사는 방금 공항에 도착했어.
(the celebrity, the airport, arrive)

➡ _____

(3) Sue는 전에 프랑스에 가 본 적이 없다.
(be, never, to)

➡ _____

(4) 나는 새로 온 그 학생의 이름을 잊어버렸다.
(그래서 지금 생각나지 않는다.)
(forget, the new student)

➡ _____

(5) 다양한 의견을 나누는 것이 중요해.
(share, various, important, to)

➡ _____

(6) 네가 내 생일을 기억해 줘서 고마워.
(nice, remember, to)

➡ _____

출제율 95%

13 다음 중 어법상 적절한 문장은?

① It's great to is here.
② It's fun to playing with friends.
③ It is boring fish in the lake.
④ It's exciting for us having you here.
⑤ It is better to drink ice tea in summer.

14 다음 중 어법상 바르지 <u>않은</u> 것은?

① I have known him since I was young.
② Have you gone to London before?
③ It has been cold and cloudy for the last three days.
④ The banana has not turned brown yet.
⑤ How long have you known her?

15 다음 두 문장이 같도록 할 때 빈칸에 알맞은 것은?

> To predict the future is impossible.
> ➡ It is impossible _____ the future.

① predict
② predicts
③ to predicting
④ predicting
⑤ to predict

[16~17] 다음 글을 읽고 물음에 답하시오.

One day, Dad told Rada and Jonny, "We're going back ⓐ Earth tomorrow."
Rada and Jonny looked ⓑ Dad ⓒ surprise and floated ⓓ him.
Rada asked Dad, "What's it (A)like ⓔ Earth?"
"Everything is different there. For example, the sky is blue," answered Dad.
"I've never seen a blue sky," said Jonny.
"The sky is always black here," said Rada.

16 위 글의 빈칸 ⓐ~ⓔ에 알맞지 <u>않은</u> 전치사를 고르시오.

① to   ② at   ③ with
④ towards ⑤ on

17 위 글의 밑줄 친 (A)like와 같은 의미로 쓰인 것을 고르시오.

① Does he <u>like</u> to go there?
② She was <u>like</u> a daughter to me.
③ I <u>like</u> playing the piano.
④ There are many things of <u>like</u> shape.
⑤ How did you <u>like</u> it?

[18~20] 다음 글을 읽고 물음에 답하시오.

"You don't have to wear your big heavy space suits ____ⓐ____. ⓑIt's also hard to jump there because Earth pulls you down," said Dad.
"What else?" asked Rada.
"There are hills, and ⓒthey are covered with soft green grass. You can roll down the hills," answered Mom.
"Dad, have you ever rolled down a hill?" asked Rada.
"Yes, ⓓit's really amazing!" answered Dad.
Jonny was thirsty, so he opened a milk container and shook ⓔit. The milk floated in the air and formed balls. Jonny swallowed the balls.
"Jonny, if you drink milk that way on Earth, you'll get wet," said Mom.

18 위 글의 빈칸 ⓐ에 들어갈 알맞은 말을 고르시오.

① because they are so heavy
② so that you can jump easily
③ because there is air everywhere
④ because Earth pulls you down
⑤ so that you can roll down the hills

19 위 글의 밑줄 친 ⓑ와 바꿔 쓸 수 없는 말을 모두 고르시오.

① To jump there is also hard
② That's also hard jumping there
③ It's also hard for you to jump there
④ Jumping there is also hard
⑤ That's also hard to jump there

20 위 글의 밑줄 친 ⓒthey, ⓓit, ⓔit이 가리키는 것을 각각 영어로 쓰시오.

ⓒ _____
ⓓ _____
ⓔ _____

[21~23] 다음 글을 읽고 물음에 답하시오.

Later that night, Rada and Jonny talked a long time about Earth. ⓐIt was exciting to think about all the new things they were going to see and do. There was one new thing Rada and Jonny really wanted to do. They thought about it all night and didn't tell Mom and Dad about it. It was their secret.

The next day, Rada's family got on a spaceship.
"It's going to be a long trip," said Mom.
"That's alright. I'm so ___(A)___ !" said Rada.

21 위 글의 빈칸 (A)에 들어갈 알맞은 말을 고르시오.

① bored
② interesting
③ pleasant
④ excited
⑤ surprised

22 위 글의 밑줄 친 문장 ⓐ에서 all the new things와 they 사이에 들어갈 수 있는 말을 모두 고르시오.

① which
② who
③ that
④ what
⑤ whom

23 위 글의 내용과 일치하지 않는 것은?

① 밤 늦게, Rada와 Jonny는 지구에 대해서 오랜 시간 이야기했다.
② Rada와 Jonny는 지구에서 그들이 보고, 그리고 하게 될 모든 새로운 것들을 생각했다.
③ Rada와 Jonny는 정말로 하고 싶었던 한 가지 새로운 것이 있었다.
④ 부모님은 Rada와 Jonny가 정말로 하고 싶어 하는 한 가지 새로운 것에 대해 듣고서 흥미로워 하셨다.
⑤ "긴 여행이 될 거야."라고 엄마가 말했다.

[24~25] 다음 글을 읽고 물음에 답하시오.

The spaceship ⓐfinally landed.
"Dad, it's difficult to walk on Earth," said Rada.
"I know. Earth is pulling you down," said Dad.
Rada and Jonny couldn't float anymore. That was the first new thing.
"What's that sound?" asked Rada.
"A bird is singing," said Mom.
"I've never heard a bird sing," said Rada.
"And I've never felt the wind," said Jonny.
ⓑThese were all new things.

24 위 글의 밑줄 친 ⓐfinally와 바꿔 쓸 수 없는 말을 고르시오.

① at last
② consequently
③ after all
④ in the end
⑤ in the long run

25 위 글의 밑줄 친 ⓑThese가 가리키는 것 세 가지를 본문에서 찾아 우리말로 쓰시오.

(1) _____
(2) _____
(3) _____

다음 그림을 보고 아래 〈조건〉에 따라 대화를 완성하시오.

It tastes like Gimchi.

new snack

┤ 조건 ├

(A) new snack에 대한 정보를 알고 있는 지 묻는 말을 hear를 사용하여 쓸 것.

(B) 새로운 정보에 대하여 궁금증을 표현할 때 사용하는 표현을 전치사 about을 이용하여 쓸 것.

A: (A) _____

B: No, I didn't.

A: It tastes like Gimchi.

B: Oh, (B) _____

02 다음 대화의 밑줄 친 우리말을 주어진 어휘를 배열하여 완성하시오.

A: Did you hear about the new game, *MVP*?

B: No, I didn't, but I'm curious about it.

A: It's a baseball game. 네가 좋아하는 선수를 선택하고 경기할 수 있어.

you / a player / can / who / choose / you / and / like / play

➡ _____

03 다음 빈칸에 알맞은 단어를 〈보기〉에서 골라 쓰시오.

┤ 보기 ├

before   ago   since   for

(1) I caught a cold two weeks ago. I have caught a cold _____ two weeks.

(2) Yesterday I adopted a pet. I have never had a pet _____.

(3) Joe started to live in Seoul from 2010. Joe has lived in Seoul _____ 2010.

04 다음 대화를 읽고 아래 물음에 영어로 답하시오.

Andy: Subin, did you hear about the new movie, *Life on the Moon*?

Subin: No, I didn't.

Andy: I heard it's really good.

Subin: I'm really curious about the movie. What's it about?

Andy: It's about a man who is trying to live on the moon.

Subin: That sounds interesting.

Andy: Look. The movie is playing at the Space Theater here.

Subin: What time is the movie?

Andy: It begins at 2:30.

Subin: Let's eat lunch first and then see the movie.

Andy: OK. I'm hungry. Let's go!

(1) What are Subin and Andy talking about?

➡ _____

(2) What will Subin and Andy do before they see the movie? (4 단어로 쓸 것)

➡ _____

05 가주어 It을 사용하여 주어진 문장과 같은 의미가 되도록 쓰시오.

(1) To answer his questions was easy.

➡ _____

(2) Camping food is easy to cook.

➡ _____

(3) Seoul is safe and comfortable to live in.

➡ _____

(4) She was very wise to say so.

➡ _____

06 다음 두 문장의 의미가 같도록 문장의 빈칸을 완성하시오.

(1) He was born in Busan and he still lives in Busan.

➡ He _____ _____ in Busan _____ he was born.

(2) I read the book twice and I read it again today.

➡ I _____ _____ the book _____ _____.

(3) Somebody took my umbrella, so I don't have my umbrella now.

➡ Somebody _____ _____ my umbrella.

[07~09] 다음 글을 읽고 물음에 답하시오.

"You (A)[have to / don't have to] wear your big heavy space suits because there is air everywhere. It's also (B)[easy / hard] to jump there ⓐbecause Earth pulls down you," said Dad.

"What else?" asked Rada.

"There are hills, and they are covered with soft green grass. You can roll down the hills," answered Mom.

"Dad, have you ever rolled down a hill?" asked Rada.

"Yes, it's really (C)[amazing / amazed]!" answered Dad.

Jonny was thirsty, so he opened a milk container and shook it. The milk floated in the air and formed balls. Jonny swallowed the balls.

ⓑ"Jonny, if you drink milk that way on Earth, you'll get wet," said Mom.

07 위 글의 괄호 (A)~(C)에서 문맥이나 어법상 알맞은 낱말을 골라 쓰시오.

(A) _____ (B) _____ (C) _____

08 위 글의 밑줄 친 ⓐ에서 어법상 틀린 부분을 찾아 고치시오.

_____ ➡ _____

09 다음 빈칸 (A)와 (B)에 알맞은 단어를 넣어 엄마가 밑줄 친 ⓑ처럼 말한 이유를 완성하시오.

> It's because milk will spill out of the container and make you (A)_____
> _____ if you open a milk container and (B)_____ it on Earth.
>
> *spill: (액체가) 흐르다, 쏟아지다; 쏟다

01 주어진 어휘와 가주어 It을 이용하여 3 문장 이상을 쓰시오.

> ┌─ 보기 ───┐
>
> learn a new language   see a doctor   exercise regularly
>
> learn Chinese   go to the beach   search information
>
> └──┘

(1) _____

(2) _____

(3) _____

(4) _____

(5) _____

02 다음 내용을 바탕으로 Rada와 Jonny가 지구에 도착한 다음 날 했을 새로운 경험에 대한 글을 쓰시오.

> The next morning, Rada's family went to a park.
> Dad, I've never ridden a bike before.
> OK. Let's ride bikes.
> In the afternoon, they went to the beach.
> Mom, I've never swum before.
> Let's swim, then.
> At night, Rada and Jonny talked about living on Earth.
> It's wonderful to live on Earth.
> Yes. It's great to be here.

> The next morning, Rada's family went to a park. Rada said to Dad, "Dad, I've never (A)_____ before." "Let's ride bikes, then," said Dad. They then (B)_____ together. The weather was great, and it was so fun.
> In the afternoon, Rada's family went to the beach. Jonny said to Mom, "I've never (C)_____." "Let's swim, then," said Mom. It was great (D)_____ in the cool blue sea.
> At night, Rada and Jonny talked about (E)_____. "It's wonderful to live on Earth," Rada said to Jonny. "Yes. It's great to be here," Jonny said.

단원별 모의고사

01 다음 단어에 대한 영어 설명이 <u>어색한</u> 것은?

① in surprise: feeling or showing surprise because of something unexpected
② container: something that you keep things in
③ lie: to be or to get into a position with your body flat on something
④ roll down: to move something down, using your hands
⑤ thrilling: exciting and interesting

02 다음 짝지어진 단어의 관계가 같도록 빈칸에 알맞은 말을 쓰시오.

different : same = _____ : depart

03 다음 영영풀이에 해당하는 단어를 고르시오.

to stay on the surface of a liquid and not sink

① float   ② swallow   ③ lie
④ roll   ⑤ arrive

04 다음 중 짝지어진 대화가 <u>어색한</u> 것은?

① A: Did you hear about the new running shoes, *Speed*?
　 B: No, I didn't. What about them?
② A: Did you hear about the new restaurant, *Rose*?
　 B: Yes, I did. It has good service.
③ A: The new snack tastes like Gimchi.
　 B: Oh, I'm curious about it.
④ A: Did you hear about the new song, *Loving You*?
　 B: No, I didn't. It's a Korean pop song.
⑤ A: Did you hear about the new TV show?
　 B: No, I didn't.

[05~06] 다음 대화의 빈칸에 들어갈 말로 알맞은 것을 고르시오.

05

G: _____
B: No, I didn't. I'm really curious about Mars.
G: Look. It's right here. It's about Mars and its moons.
B: Great. I think I'll buy the book.

① Have you ever been to Mars?
② Did you know Mars has its moons?
③ Did you hear about the new book about Mars?
④ Do you want to know about Mars?
⑤ Did you buy the book about Mars?

06

G: Tony, did you hear about the movie, *My Hero*?
B: No, I didn't.
G: Well, I heard it's really good.
B: I'm really curious about the movie.

_____
G: It's about a father who saves his son.

① What about you?
② What is going on?
③ Is it good?
④ Look at this video.
⑤ What's the movie about?

[07~09] 다음 대화를 읽고 물음에 답하시오.

Andy: Subin, did you hear about the new movie, *Life on the Moon*?

Subin: No, I didn't.

Andy: I heard it's really good.

Subin: _____(A)_____ What's it about?

Andy: It's about a man who is trying to live on the moon.

Subin: That sounds interesting.

Andy: Look. The movie is playing at the Space Theater here.

Subin: What time is the movie?

Andy: It begins at 2:30.

Subin: Let's eat lunch first and then see the movie.

Andy: OK. I'm hungry. Let's go!

07 위 대화의 빈칸 (A)에 들어갈 말로 알맞은 것은?

① I want to know more about the man.

② I'm really curious about the movie.

③ I'm not interested in the movie.

④ What do you want to know about the movie?

⑤ I'm not really curious about it.

08 What are they going to do after this dialogue? (6 단어로 답할 것)

➡ _____

09 위 대화를 요약한 글이다. 빈칸에 들어갈 알맞은 말을 쓰시오.

Andy and Subin are talking about the movie, *Life on the Moon*. It is _____ a man _____ is trying to live on the moon.

10 다음 대화의 내용과 일치하면 T, 일치하지 않으면 F에 표시하시오.

Girl: Did you hear about the new book, *Living in a Foreign Country*?

Boy: No, I didn't.

Girl: Look. It's right here. It's about living in New York.

Boy: Great. I'm really curious about this book.

Girl: Me, too.

(1) They are talking about living in New York. (T / F)

(2) The boy is interested in the new book. (T / F)

11 다음 대화의 빈칸에 들어갈 말은?

G: Tony, did you hear about the movie, *My Hero*?

B: No, I didn't.

G: _____

B: I'm really curious about the movie. What's it about?

G: It's about a father who saves his son.

① I don't know about the movie, either.

② I want to know what the movie is about.

③ Why don't we see the movie?

④ What time does the movie begin?

⑤ Well, I heard it's really good.

12 다음 대화의 마지막 말 앞에 올 순서가 바르게 배열된 것은?

> (A) No, I didn't.
> (B) Great. I'm really curious about this book.
> (C) Look. It's right here. It's about living in New York.
> (D) Did you hear about the new book, *Living in a Foreign Country*?

> G: Me, too.

① (A) – (C) – (B) – (D)
② (B) – (C) – (D) – (A)
③ (C) – (D) – (A) – (B)
④ (D) – (A) – (C) – (B)
⑤ (D) – (B) – (A) – (C)

13 다음 중 어법상 어색한 것을 고르시오.

① I've never swum before.
② When have you visited Italy?
③ She has lost her notebook in the classroom.
④ I have just finished my project.
⑤ Have you ever been to Spain before?

14 다음 주어진 문장의 밑줄 친 부분과 쓰임이 같은 것은?

> It was interesting to watch sci-fi movies.

① How long does it take to go to the station?
② It was Mike that we visited yesterday.
③ It was difficult for me to answer the question.
④ Start a new file and put this letter in it.
⑤ It will take time to get to the new city hall.

15 다음 문장에서 어법상 어색한 것을 바르게 고치시오.

(1) Have you found your umbrella an hour ago?

⎯⎯⎯⎯⎯ ➡ ⎯⎯⎯⎯⎯

(2) I started to play the piano long time ago. And I still enjoy playing it. So, I played the piano since a long time.

⎯⎯⎯⎯⎯ ➡ ⎯⎯⎯⎯⎯

(3) I have never gone to London.

⎯⎯⎯⎯⎯ ➡ ⎯⎯⎯⎯⎯

(4) Search information using the Internet is easy.

⎯⎯⎯⎯⎯ ➡ ⎯⎯⎯⎯⎯

(5) It's necessary of you to wear a helmet.

⎯⎯⎯⎯⎯ ➡

16 다음 우리말을 주어진 어휘를 이용하여 영작하시오.

(1) 그는 10살 때부터 그녀를 알았다.
(know, since, ten years old)
➡ ⎯⎯⎯⎯⎯⎯⎯⎯⎯⎯

(2) 그는 아직 숙제를 끝마치지 못했다. (finish)
➡ ⎯⎯⎯⎯⎯⎯⎯⎯⎯⎯

(3) 그들은 그 영화를 네 번 보았다.
(see the movie)
➡ ⎯⎯⎯⎯⎯⎯⎯⎯⎯⎯

(4) 그녀는 파리로 가 버렸다. (현재 여기에 없다.)
(have)
➡ ⎯⎯⎯⎯⎯⎯⎯⎯⎯⎯

(5) 이 웹사이트를 방문한 것이 도움이 되었다.
(helpful, this web site)
➡ ⎯⎯⎯⎯⎯⎯⎯⎯⎯⎯

(6) 아이가 큰 개를 목욕시키기는 힘들다.
(a child, wash, hard, to)
➡ ⎯⎯⎯⎯⎯⎯⎯⎯⎯⎯

[17~18] 다음 글을 읽고 물음에 답하시오.

One day, Dad told Rada and Jonny, "We're going back to Earth tomorrow."

Rada and Jonny looked at Dad in surprise and floated towards him.

Rada asked Dad, "What's it like on Earth?"

"Everything is different there. For example, the sky is blue," answered Dad.

"ⓐI've never seen a blue sky," said Jonny.

"The sky is always black here," said Rada.

17 다음 빈칸 (A)와 (B)에 알맞은 단어를 넣어 지구와 우주의 하늘의 색깔에 대한 설명을 완성하시오.

On Earth, the color of the sky is (A)_____ from that in space. It's (B)_____, not black.

18 위 글의 밑줄 친 ⓐ의 현재완료와 용법이 다른 것을 모두 고르시오.

① How long <u>have</u> you <u>known</u> Mr. Green?
② I <u>have</u> just <u>finished</u> my work.
③ I <u>have visited</u> New York three times.
④ She <u>has been</u> ill for a week.
⑤ <u>Have</u> you ever <u>written</u> a letter in English?

[19~21] 다음 글을 읽고 물음에 답하시오.

"You don't have to wear your big heavy space suits because there is air everywhere. It's also hard to jump there because Earth pulls you down," said Dad.

"What ____ⓐ____?" asked Rada.

"There are hills, and they are covered with soft green grass. You can roll down the hills," answered Mom.

"Dad, ⓑ언덕을 굴러 내려가 본 적 있어요?" asked Rada.

"Yes, it's really amazing!" answered Dad.

Jonny was thirsty, so he opened a milk container and shook it. The milk floated in the air and formed balls. Jonny swallowed the balls.

"Jonny, if you drink milk that way on Earth, you'll get wet," said Mom.

19 주어진 영영풀이를 참고하여 빈칸 ⓐ에 철자 e로 시작하는 단어를 쓰시오.

in addition; besides

➡ e_____

20 위 글의 밑줄 친 ⓑ의 우리말에 맞게 한 단어를 보충하여, 주어진 어휘를 알맞게 배열하시오.

a hill / ever / you / rolled / have / ?

➡ _____

21 다음 중 위 글의 내용을 올바르게 이해하지 <u>못한</u> 사람을 고르시오.

혜수: It's not necessary for Rada and Jonny to wear their big heavy space suits on Earth.
정미: Unlike in space, there is air everywhere on Earth and there is gravity, too.
수민: It's not easy to jump on Earth because of gravity.
규식: It will be easy to jump on Earth if Rada and Jonny wear their space suits.
나윤: Rada and Jonny will be able to roll down the hills.

① 혜수   ② 정미   ③ 수민
④ 규식   ⑤ 나윤

Lesson 8

Pride of Korea

 의사소통 기능

- 허가 여부 묻기
  A: Is it OK to sit here?
  B: Sure. Go ahead. / I'm afraid not.

- 금지하기
  Sitting is not allowed here.

 언어 형식

- 간접의문문
  Please tell me **how you found them**.

- because of
  Many Koreans became interested in *Uigwe*
  because of your book.

Words & Expressions

Key Words

- **abroad**[əbrɔ́ːd] 부 해외에서, 해외로
- **allow**[əláu] 동 허락하다, 허용하다
- **army**[áːrmi] 명 군대, 육군
- **behind**[biháind] 전 ~ 뒤에, ~ 배후에
- **college**[kálidʒ] 명 대학
- **continue**[kəntínju] 동 계속하다
- **delicious**[dilíʃəs] 형 맛있는
- **dessert**[dizə́ːrt] 명 디저트, 후식
- **difficulty**[dífikʌlti] 명 어려움
- **display**[displéi] 명 전시
- **exhibition**[èksəbíʃən] 명 박람회, 전시회
- **fan dance** 부채춤
- **finally**[fáinəli] 부 마침내, 결국
- **find**[faind] 동 발견하다, 찾다 (–found–found)
- **fire**[faiər] 동 해고하다
- **fitting room** 탈의실
- **flash**[flæʃ] 명 (카메라) 플래시
- **government**[gʌ́vərnmənt] 명 정부
- **grass**[græs] 명 잔디, 풀
- **historian**[histɔ́ːriən] 명 역사학자
- **however**[hauévər] 부 하지만, 그러나
- **instrument**[ínstrəmənt] 명 악기
- **interesting**[íntərəstiŋ] 형 흥미로운
- **knee**[niː] 명 무릎
- **metal**[métl] 명 금속
- **movable metal type** 금속활자
- **million**[míljən] 명 100만, 수많은
- **museum**[mjuːzíːəm] 명 박물관
- **noise**[nɔiz] 명 소리, 소음
- **printing**[príntiŋ] 명 인쇄
- **pride**[praid] 명 자부심, 긍지
- **prove**[pruːv] 동 입증하다, 증명하다
- **publish**[pʌ́bliʃ] 동 출판하다, 발행하다
- **research**[risə́ːrtʃ] 명 연구, 조사
- **researcher**[risə́ːrtʃər] 명 연구가
- **result**[rizʌ́lt] 명 결과, 결실
- **return**[ritə́ːrn] 명 반환
- **royal**[rɔ́iəl] 형 왕실의
- **search**[səːrtʃ] 동 찾아보다
- **silver**[sílvər] 명 은, 은색
- **special**[spéʃəl] 형 특별한
- **spend**[spend] 동 (돈을) 쓰다, (시간을) 보내다 (–spent–spent)
- **spy**[spai] 명 스파이, 첩자
- **steal**[stiːl] 동 도둑질하다, 훔치다 (–stole–stolen)
- **storm**[stɔːrm] 명 폭풍
- **succeed**[səksíːd] 동 성공하다
- **thief**[θiːf] 명 도둑
- **traditional**[trədíʃənl] 형 전통적인
- **treasure**[tréʒər] 명 보물
- **value**[vǽljuː] 명 가치
- **wedding**[wédiŋ] 명 결혼식
- **while**[hwail] 접 ~하는 동안
- **whole**[houl] 형 전부의, 전체의

Key Expressions

- **as soon as**+주어+동사 ~하자마자
- **because**+주어+동사 ~ 때문에
- **because of**+명사 ~ 때문에
- **be full of** ~로 가득 차 있다
- **become interested in** ~에 관심을 가지다
- **give up** 포기하다
- **Is it OK to**+동사원형~? ~해도 되나요?
- **look at** ~을 보다
- **look for** ~을 찾다
- **right away** 바로, 즉시
- **spend**+시간+-ing ~하면서 시간을 보내다
- **take pictures** 사진을 찍다
- **thanks to** ~ 덕분에
- **try on** ~을 입어[신어] 보다
- **Why don't you**+동사원형 ~? ~하는 게 어때?
- **would like to**+동사원형 ~하고 싶다

Word Power

※ 동사와 명사의 뜻을 둘 다 가지는 어휘

☐ **display** (동) 전시하다 (명) 전시

☐ **return** (동) 돌려주다 (명) 반환

☐ **fire** (동) 해고하다 (명) 불, 화재

☐ **result** (동) 발생하다 (명) 결과

☐ **value** (동) 소중히 여기다 (명) 가치

☐ **flash** (동) 비추다 (명) 플래시 번쩍임

☐ **search** (동) 찾아보다 (명) 수색

☐ **research** (동) 조사하다 (명) 조사, 연구

※ 형태가 유사한 어휘

☐ **royal** (형) 왕실의 : **loyal** (형) 충실한

☐ **find** (동) 발견하다, 찾다 : **found** (동) 설립하다

☐ **dessert** (명) 디저트, 후식 : **desert** (명) 사막

☐ **abroad** (부) 해외에서 : **aboard** (부) 배를 타고, 승차하여

☐ **grass** (명) 잔디, 풀 : **glass** (명) 유리

☐ **metal** (명) 금속 : **mental** (형) 정신의

English Dictionary

☐ **abroad** 해외로, 해외에서
→ in or to a foreign country
외국에서 또는 외국으로

☐ **allow** 허락하다
→ to say that someone can do something
누군가가 무엇을 할 수 있다고 말하다

☐ **fitting room** 탈의실
→ a room in a clothes shop where you can put on clothes before you buy them
옷 가게에 있는 방으로 옷을 사기 전에 입을 수 있는 곳

☐ **flash** 플래시
→ a bright light on a camera that flashes as you take a photograph in order to provide enough light
사진을 찍을 때 충분한 빛을 제공하기 위해 번쩍이는 카메라의 밝은 빛

☐ **government** 정부
→ the group of people who are responsible for controlling a country or state
나라나 주를 통제하는 데 책임이 있는 사람들의 무리

☐ **pride** 자부심, 긍지
→ a feeling of satisfaction and pleasure in what you have done
당신이 한 일에 대한 만족감과 즐거움

☐ **prove** 입증하다
→ to show that something is true
어떤 일이 사실이라는 것을 보여주다

☐ **publish** 출판하다
→ to print a book, magazine, or newspaper for people to buy
사람들이 구입하도록 책이나 잡지, 신문을 인쇄하다

☐ **research** 조사
→ the work of finding out facts about something
어떤 것에 관한 사실을 알아내는 일

☐ **result** 결과
→ something that happens because of something else
다른 어떤 것 때문에 발생하는 것

☐ **royal** 왕실의
→ relating to or belonging to a king or queen
왕이나 여왕과 관련되거나 속해 있는

☐ **search** 찾아보다
→ to try to find someone or something by looking very carefully
주의 깊게 봄으로써 누군가나 무언가를 찾으려고 하다

☐ **silver** 은, 은빛
→ a shiny white metal that people use for making jewelry and other valuable things
보석이나 다른 귀중품을 만들기 위해 사용하는 반짝이는 흰 금속

☐ **spend** (시간을) 보내다
→ to use time doing something
어떤 일을 하면서 시간을 사용하다

☐ **steal** 훔치다
→ to take something that belongs to someone else
다른 누군가에게 속해 있는 물건을 가져가다

☐ **succeed** 성공하다
→ to do something that you tried or aimed to do
당신이 시도하거나 목표로 하는 일을 해내다

☐ **thanks to** ～ 덕분에
→ used for saying that someone or something is responsible for something good that happened
누군가나 무언가가 일어난 좋은 일에 책임이 있다고 말하는 데 사용되는

☐ **treasure** 보물
→ a group of valuable things, especially gold, silver, or jewels
금, 은, 또는 보석과 같은 귀중한 물건의 집합

중요

01 다음 빈칸에 들어갈 말이 알맞게 짝지어진 것은?

> • The box was full of _____ such as gold and silver.
> • The _____ of this painting is about one million dollars.

① trash – result   ② army – display
③ trash – value   ④ treasures – value
⑤ treasures – display

서답형

02 〈영어 설명〉을 읽고 빈칸에 알맞은 말을 쓰시오. (주어진 철자로 시작할 것)

> to keep doing something without stopping

> I studied history in college. I went to France to c_____ my studies in 1955.

[03~04] 다음 설명에 해당하는 단어를 고르시오.

03
> to say that someone can do something

① search   ② allow
③ spend   ④ publish
⑤ fire

 중요

04
> a feeling of satisfaction and pleasure in what you have done

① confidence   ② happiness
③ glory   ④ result
⑤ pride

서답형

05 다음 우리말에 맞게 빈칸에 알맞은 단어를 쓰시오.

> 1967년에 국립도서관의 연구원이 되자마자, 저는 "의궤"를 찾기 시작했어요.
> ➡ _____ _____ _____ I became a researcher at the National Library in 1967, I began to look for *Uigwe*.

06 다음 글의 흐름상 빈칸에 들어갈 말로 알맞은 것은?

> I thought that *Uigwe*, a collection of royal books, should be returned to Korea, but my bosses at the library didn't like that idea. They even thought that I was a Korean spy and _____ me.

① promoted   ② valued
③ fired   ④ missed
⑤ proved

서답형

07 다음 짝지어진 단어의 관계가 같도록 빈칸에 알맞은 말을 쓰시오.

> stop : continue – fail : _____

 중요

08 다음 빈칸에 들어갈 말이 알맞게 짝지어진 것은?

> I hope people will become more _____ our national treasures abroad and work for their _____.

① indifferent to – value
② indifferent to – return
③ interested in – government
④ interested in – return
⑤ interested in – value

01 다음 빈칸에 들어갈 말을 〈보기〉에서 찾아 쓰시오. (필요하면 변형하여 쓰시오.)

> ┤ 보기 ├
>
> abroad　allow　prove
> tradition　research

(1) I went to the library every day to finish my _____.

(2) That's a *haegeum*, a _____ Korean musical instrument.

(3) He is _____ now, but he will go back to his country soon.

(4) Sitting on the grass is not _____.

02 다음 우리말과 같은 표현이 되도록 문장의 빈칸을 채우시오.

(1) 박 박사님, 당신의 노고 덕분에 "직지"와 "의궤"가 발견되었고, 모든 한국인들이 그 점을 당신에게 감사하고 있어요.

➡ Dr. Park, _____ _____ your hard work, *Jikji* and *Uigwe* were _____, and all Koreans thank you for that.

(2) 1992년에 한국 정부는 프랑스 정부에 그것의 반환을 요청했다.

➡ In 1992, the Korean _____ asked the French _____ for its _____.

03 다음 빈칸에 공통으로 알맞은 단어를 주어진 철자로 시작하여 쓰시오.

(1) • Most animals are afraid of f_____.
　　• We had to f_____ him for dishonesty.

(2) • How do you s_____ your spare time?
　　• My parents s_____ a lot of money on books every month.

(3) • He has carried out r_____ into renewable energy sources.
　　• Many researchers r_____ into the matter thoroughly.

(4) • We have to work hard to s_____ in life.
　　• After many failures, the scientists finally s_____ed in proving their theory.

　　　　　　　　* renewable: 재생 가능한
　　　　　　　　* thoroughly: 철저히

04 다음 영영풀이에 해당하는 단어를 〈보기〉에서 찾아 첫 번째 칸에 쓰고, 두 번째 칸에는 우리말 뜻을 쓰시오.

> ┤ 보기 ├
>
> royal　steal　skip　prove　metal

(1) _____ : to show that something is true: _____

(2) _____ : to take something that belongs to someone else: _____

(3) _____ : relating to or belonging to a king or queen: _____

(4) _____ : a hard substance, such as iron, gold, or steel, that is good at conducting electricity and heat: _____

Conversation

교과서

① 허가 여부 묻기

> **A** Is it OK to sit here? 여기에 앉아도 되나요?
> **B** Sure. Go ahead. / I'm afraid not. 물론이죠. 그렇게 하세요. / 안 될 것 같아요.

- 'Is it OK to ~?'는 '~해도 될까요?'라는 의미로 허가 여부를 묻는 표현이다. 'to+동사원형' 대신 'if+주어+동사'를 써서 말할 수도 있다.

- 허가 여부를 묻는 표현
  - May[Can] I use your cellphone? / Is it okay if I use your cellphone? / Would it be all right if I use your cellphone? / Do you mind if I use your cellphone?

- 허락을 할 때
  - Sure. / Go ahead. / Yes, you can[may]. / Of course. 등으로 답한다.

- 허락을 하지 않을 때
  - I'm sorry, but you can't. / I'm afraid not./ You are not allowed to do that. / You can't do that.

※ 주의할 점
- 'Do you mind if I ~?'로 물을 때는 mind가 '꺼리다, 싫어하다'라는 뜻이기 때문에, 허락의 의미로 Of course not. / No, go ahead. / No, I don't. / Not at all. / No problem. 등 부정문을 사용하고, 허락을 하지 않을 때는 Yes, I do. / Of course. 등을 사용한다.
  - A: Is it OK to take a picture here? 여기서 사진을 찍어도 되나요?
    B: Yes, you can. 네. 찍어도 됩니다.

  - A: Is it okay if I turn on the TV? TV를 켜도 괜찮겠니?
    B: Sure. / I'm afraid not. I'm doing my homework. 물론이야. / 안 될 것 같아. 나는 숙제를 하는 중이야.

핵심 Check

1. 다음 대화의 빈칸에 들어갈 말로 <u>어색한</u> 것은?

A: _____ ride your bike?
B: Yes, it's OK.

① Can I ② May I
③ Is it OK to ④ Is it OK if I
⑤ Do you mind

② 금지하기

> **Sitting is not allowed here.** 여기에 앉는 것은 허용되지 않습니다.

- '~ is not allowed'는 '~하는 것이 허락되지 않는다'라는 뜻으로, 금지를 나타낼 때 쓰는 표현이다. 비슷한 표현으로는 'You must not ~'이 있다.

금지하는 표현

- You shouldn't ~. (~하면 안 돼요.)
- 명령문을 이용하여 'Don't ~. (~하지 마.)'라고 말하거나 허락의 의미를 나타내는 조동사 can을 이용하여 'You cannot ~. (~해서는 안 돼.)'라고 말할 수도 있다.
- 강력한 금지의 표현은 'You must not ~. (~하면 안 됩니다.)'을 사용한다.
- 경고의 의미가 섞인 'You'd better not ~. (~하지 않는 편이 나을 거예요.)'이라는 표현을 쓰기도 한다.

- A: Excuse me. You shouldn't use your cell phone here.
  실례합니다. 당신은 여기서 휴대전화를 사용하시면 안 됩니다.
  B: Oh, I'm sorry. 오, 미안합니다.

- A: You are not allowed to use your smartphone in class.
  수업 중에 휴대폰을 사용하는 것이 허락되어 있지 않아.
  B: I see. 알았습니다.

- A: Don't play the piano at night. 밤에 피아노를 치면 안 돼.
  B: Oh, I'm sorry. 아, 죄송해요.

핵심 Check

2. 다음 대화의 밑줄 친 부분과 바꿔 쓸 수 <u>없는</u> 것은?

A: <u>You must not park here.</u>

B: Oh, I'm sorry.

① You are not allowed to park here.

② Don't park here.

③ You'd better not park here.

④ You shouldn't park here.

⑤ You don't have to park here.

Listen and Talk A-1

> B: Excuse me. What's this? ❶I've never seen any food like this.
>
> W: Oh, ❷it's Tteok, a Korean dessert.
>
> B: ❸Is it OK to try some?
>
> W: ❹Sure. Go ahead. It's really delicious.

B: 실례합니다. 이것이 무엇인가요? 저는 이런 음식을 본 적이 없어요.

W: 오, 그것은 한국의 후식인 떡이에요.

B: 먹어 봐도 될까요?

W: 물론이죠. 그렇게 하세요. 정말 맛있답니다.

❶ 현재완료를 사용하여 이전에 한 일에 대한 경험을 표현하는 말이다.
❷ 동격의 콤마로 앞의 명사를 설명하는 역할을 한다.
❸ Is it OK to ~?는 '~해도 될까요?'라는 의미로 허가 여부를 묻는 표현이다.
❹ 허가를 묻는 표현에 대한 허락의 답으로 Sure. Go ahead. / Yes, you can[may]. / Of course. 등으로 답한다.

Check(√) True or False

(1) The boy hasn't eaten Tteok before. T ☐ F ☐

(2) The boy is allowed to eat Tteok. T ☐ F ☐

Listen and Talk A-2

> G: Excuse me. ❶Is it OK to sit over there?
>
> M: You mean, on the grass?
>
> G: Yes. Is it all right?
>
> M: ❷I'm sorry, but sitting on the grass is not allowed.
>
> G: OK, I understand.

G: 실례합니다. 저기에 앉아도 되나요?

M: 잔디 위를 말하는 건가요?

G: 네. 괜찮은가요?

M: 미안하지만, 잔디 위에 앉는 것은 허락되지 않습니다.

G: 알겠습니다. 이해합니다.

❶ 'Is it OK to ~?'는 '~해도 될까요?'라는 의미로 허가 여부를 묻는 표현이다. 'Is it OK if I sit over there?'로 바꾸어 쓸 수 있다.
❷ 'be not allowed'는 허가를 묻는 표현에 대해 허락을 하지 않을 때 사용하는 표현으로 'You can't do that.'으로 표현할 수 있다.

Check(√) True or False

(3) The girl wants to sit on the grass. T ☐ F ☐

(4) The girl is not allowed to sit on the grass. T ☐ F ☐

Listen and Talk A-3

B: Excuse me. What's this? It looks interesting.
W: Oh, that's a haegeum, a traditional Korean musical instrument.
B: ❶Is it OK to play it?
W: ❷I'm sorry, but it's only for display. Playing it is not allowed.
B: I see.

❶ Is it OK to ~?'는 '~해도 될까요?'라는 의미로 허가 여부를 묻는 표현이다. Is it OK if I play it?과 같은 표현이다.
❷ 허가를 묻는 표현에 대해 허락을 하지 않을 때 사용하는 표현이다.

Listen and Talk A-4

G: Excuse me. ❶Is it OK to take pictures here?
M: Yes, it's all right.
G: ❷How about using a flash? Can I use it, too?
M: I'm afraid not. ❸Using a flash is not allowed here.
G: Oh, I see. Thank you.

❶ 'Is it OK to ~?'는 '~해도 될까요?'라는 의미로 허가 여부를 묻는 표현이다.
❷ 'How about -ing?'는 '~는 어때요?'의 뜻이다.
❸ 'Using a flash'는 동명사 주어이고 'is not allowed'는 허락을 하지 않을 때 사용하는 표현이다.

Listen and Talk B

A: ❶Is it OK to sit here?
B: I'm afraid not. Sitting is not allowed here.
A: Oh, I see.

❶ 'Is it OK to ~?'는 '~해도 될까요?'라는 의미로 허가 여부를 묻는 표현이다. 'Is it OK if I sit here?'로 바꾸어 쓸 수 있다.

Listen and Talk C

G: Excuse me, but ❶is it OK to try on this hanbok?
M: Sure. The fitting room is over there.
G: Thanks. Wait a minute. ❷That's also very pretty.
M: Oh, the little hat over there?
G: Yes. What is it?
M: It's a jokduri, ❸a traditional Korean hat for women. It's usually worn on a wedding day.
G: Really? ❹Is it OK to try it on, too?
M: ❺I'm sorry, but it's only for display. Trying it on is not allowed.
G: Oh. Then, I'll just try on this hanbok.

❶ 'Is it OK to ~?'는 '~해도 될까요?'라는 의미로 허가 여부를 묻는 표현이다.
❷ That은 'the little hat over there'를 가리키는 지시대명사다.
❸ 콤마 뒤의 말은 앞의 명사 'jokduri'를 설명하는 동격어다.
❹ 'Is it OK to ~?'는 '~해도 될까요?'라는 의미로 허가 여부를 묻는 표현이고, 'try on'은 이어 동사다. 인칭대명사가 목적어일 때는 반드시 '동사+대명사+부사' 어순으로 사용한다.
❺ 허가를 묻는 표현에 대해 허락을 하지 않을 때 사용하는 표현이다.

Talk and Play

A: ❶Which place do you want to go first in the museum?
B: ❷Why don't you guess?
A: OK. ❸Is it OK to eat food there?
B: Yes. Eating food is allowed.
A: Is it OK to take pictures?
B: No. ❹Taking pictures is not allowed.
A: ❺I got it. You're thinking of going to the Video Room.
B: You're right.

❶ which는 '어떤, 무슨'의 의미의 의문형용사로 명사 place를 수식하는 역할을 한다.
❷ 'Why don't you+동사원형 ~?'은 '~하는 게 어때?'의 뜻이다.
❸ 'Is it OK to ~?'는 '~해도 될까요?'라는 의미로 허가 여부를 묻는 표현이다.
❹ 'Taking pictures'는 동명사 주어로 '사진을 찍는 것은'의 뜻이다. 'is not allowed'는 '허락되지 않는다'라는 뜻으로 허가를 묻는 말에 대한 부정의 답이다.
❺ 'I got it.'은 '알겠어.'라는 뜻이다.

Review 1

G: Excuse me. What's this? It looks interesting.
B: Oh, that's a janggu, a traditional Korean musical instrument.
G: Is it OK to play it?
B: I'm sorry, but ❶it's only for display. Playing it is not allowed.
G: I see.

❶ for display는 '전시를 위한'의 뜻으로, display는 명사로 사용되었다.

Review 2

G: Excuse me, but is it OK to take pictures here?
M: Yes. Go ahead.
G: Can I use a flash, too?
M: Yes. That's also OK.
G: I'm sorry, but I have one more question. Can I eat food here?
M: I'm sorry, but ❶that's not allowed.

❶ that은 'Eating food here'을 나타내는 대명사다.

● 다음 우리말과 일치하도록 빈칸에 알맞은 말을 쓰시오.

Listen and Talk A-1

B: Excuse me. What's this? _____ _____ _____ any food _____ this.

W: Oh, it's Tteok, a Korean _____.

B: _____ _____ _____ _____ try some?

W: Sure. Go _____. It's really _____.

Listen and Talk A-2

G: Excuse me. Is it OK _____ _____ over there?

M: You _____, on the grass?

G: Yes. Is it all right?

M: I'm sorry, but _____ on the grass _____ _____ _____.

G: OK, I understand.

Listen and Talk A-3

B: Excuse me. What's this? It _____ _____.

W: Oh, that's a haegeum, a _____ Korean musical _____.

B: _____ _____ _____ _____ _____ it?

W: _____ _____, but it's only _____ _____. Playing it is not _____.

B: I see.

Listen and Talk A-4

G: _____ me. _____ _____ _____ _____ _____ pictures here?

M: Yes, it's all right.

G: _____ _____ _____ a flash? Can I use it, too?

M: I'm _____ not. _____ a flash is _____ _____ here.

G: Oh, I see. Thank you.

Listen and Talk B

A: _____ _____ _____ _____ _____ _____ _____ ?

B: I'm _____ _____. _____ is _____ _____ here.

A: Oh, I see.

해석

B: 실례합니다. 이것이 무엇인가요? 저는 이런 음식을 본 적이 없어요.
W: 오, 그것은 한국의 후식인 떡이에요.
B: 먹어 봐도 될까요?
W: 물론이죠. 그렇게 하세요. 정말 맛있답니다.

G: 실례합니다. 저기에 앉아도 되나요?
M: 잔디 위를 말하는 건가요?
G: 네. 괜찮은가요?
M: 미안하지만, 잔디 위에 앉는 것은 허락되지 않습니다.
G: 알겠습니다. 이해합니다.

B: 실례합니다. 이것은 무엇인가요? 흥미롭게 생겼네요.
W: 오, 그것은 한국의 전통 악기인 해금이에요.
B: 연주를 해 봐도 될까요?
W: 미안하지만, 전시용입니다. 연주를 하는 것은 허락되지 않습니다.
B: 알겠습니다.

G: 실례합니다. 여기서 사진을 찍어도 되나요?
M: 네, 괜찮습니다.
G: 플래시를 사용하는 것은 어떤가요? 사용해도 되나요?
M: 안 될 것 같아요. 플래시를 사용하는 것은 여기서 허용되지 않습니다.
G: 오, 알겠어요. 감사합니다.

A: 여기 앉아도 될까요?
B: 안 될 것 같아요. 여기에 앉는 것은 허용되지 않습니다.
A: 오, 알겠습니다.

Talk and Play

A: _____ place do you want _____ _____ first in the museum?
B: _____ _____ _____ guess?
A: OK. _____ _____ _____ _____ _____ food there?
B: Yes. _____ food is _____ .
A: _____ _____ _____ _____ _____ pictures?
B: No. Taking pictures _____ _____ _____ .
A: I _____ _____ . You're thinking of going to the Video Room.
B: You're right.

Listen and Talk C

G: Excuse me, but _____ _____ _____ to try on this hanbok?
M: Sure. The _____ _____ is over there.
G: Thanks. Wait a minute. That's also very pretty.
M: Oh, the little hat _____ _____ ?
G: Yes. What is it?
M: It's a jokduri, a _____ Korean hat _____ women. It's usually _____ on a _____ day.
G: Really? _____ _____ _____ _____ _____ _____ _____ , too?
M: I'm sorry, but it's only _____ _____ . Trying it _____ is not _____ .
G: Oh. Then, I'll just _____ _____ this hanbok.

Review 1

G: Excuse me. What's this? It _____ _____ .
B: Oh, that's a janggu, a _____ Korean _____ _____ .
G: _____ _____ _____ play it?
B: I'm sorry, but it's only _____ _____ . Playing it is not _____ .
G: I see.

Review 2

G: Excuse me, but _____ _____ _____ to take pictures here?
M: Yes. Go _____ .
G: _____ _____ use a flash, too?
M: Yes. That's also OK.
G: I'm sorry, _____ I have _____ _____ question. Can I eat food here?
M: I'm sorry, but that's _____ _____ .

해석

A: 박물관에서 어떤 장소를 먼저 가고 싶니?
B: 알아맞혀 볼래?
A: 좋아. 거기에서 음식을 먹어도 되니?
B: 응. 음식을 먹는 것은 허용돼.
A: 사진을 찍어도 되니?
B: 아니. 사진을 찍는 것은 허용되지 않아.
A: 알겠다. 너는 Video Room에 갈 생각이구나.
B: 맞아.

G: 실례지만, 이 한복을 입어 봐도 될까요?
M: 물론이죠. 탈의실은 저쪽입니다.
G: 고마워요. 잠깐만요. 저것도 매우 예쁘네요.
M: 오, 저기 있는 작은 모자요?
G: 네. 그건 뭔가요?
M: 그것은 여자들이 쓰는 한국 전통 모자인 족두리예요. 주로 결혼식 날 쓰죠.
G: 정말요? 그것도 써 봐도 될까요?
M: 죄송하지만, 그것은 전시만 하는 거예요. 써 보시는 건 안 돼요.
G: 오. 그럼, 그냥 이 한복만 입어 볼게요.

G: 실례합니다. 이것은 무엇인가요? 흥미로워 보이네요.
B: 오, 저것은 한국의 전통 악기인 장구예요.
G: 연주해 봐도 되나요?
B: 미안하지만, 전시용이에요. 연주하는 것은 허용되지 않아요.
G: 알겠어요.

G: 실례합니다만, 여기서 사진을 찍어도 되나요?
M: 네. 그렇게 하세요.
G: 플래시를 사용해도 되나요?
M: 네. 그것도 괜찮습니다.
G: 죄송하지만, 질문이 하나 더 있어요. 여기서 음식을 먹어도 되나요?
M: 미안하지만, 그것은 허용되지 않습니다.

01 다음 우리말에 맞게 주어진 단어를 이용하여 빈칸에 알맞은 말을 쓰시오.

플래시를 사용하는 것은 여기서 허용되지 않습니다. (allow)
➡ _____ a flash _____ not _____ here.

[02~03] 다음 대화의 빈칸에 들어갈 말로 알맞은 것을 고르시오.

02
A: Is it OK _____ I use your pencil?
B: No problem.

① that   ② if   ③ whether
④ who   ⑤ why

03
A: Is it OK to sit here?
B: _____ Sitting is not allowed here.
A: Oh, I see.

① Sure.   ② No problem.   ③ Of course.
④ Yes. Go ahead.   ⑤ I'm afraid not.

04 다음 대화의 밑줄 친 부분과 바꿔 쓸 수 <u>없는</u> 것은?

A: <u>You are not allowed to smoke here.</u>
B: Oh, I'm sorry. I'll never do that again.

① You cannot smoke here.
② You don't have to smoke here.
③ You'd better not smoke here.
④ You shouldn't smoke here.
⑤ You must not smoke here.

05 다음 대화의 밑줄 친 부분의 의도로 알맞은 것은?

A: Is it OK to play it?
B: I'm sorry, but it's only for display. <u>Playing it is not allowed.</u>

① 금지하기   ② 좋아하는 것 묻기
③ 허가 여부 묻기   ④ 부탁하기
⑤ 예정된 것 말하기

[01~02] 다음 대화를 읽고 물음에 답하시오.

A: Excuse me. What's this? (a)<u>저는 이런 음식을 본 적이 없어요.</u>

B: Oh, it's Tteok, a Korean dessert.

A: _____ (A)

B: Sure. Go ahead. It's really delicious.

01 위 대화의 빈칸 (A)에 들어갈 말로 <u>어색한</u> 것은?

① Can I try some?

② Is it OK to try some?

③ May I try some?

④ Must I try some?

⑤ Is it OK if I try some?

02 위 대화의 밑줄 친 (a)의 우리말에 맞게 주어진 어구를 이용하여 영어로 쓰시오. (현재완료를 이용하여 쓸 것)

> never / see / any food / like

➡ _____

03 자연스러운 대화가 되도록 (A)~(D)를 바르게 배열한 것은?

> (A) I'm sorry, but sitting on the grass is not allowed.
> (B) You mean, on the grass?
> (C) Excuse me. Is it OK to sit over there?
> (D) Yes. Is it all right?

> OK, I understand.

① (A) – (B) – (C) – (D)

② (B) – (A) – (C) – (D)

③ (B) – (C) – (A) – (D)

④ (C) – (B) – (D) – (A)

⑤ (D) – (B) – (A) – (C)

04 밑줄 친 (A)의 우리말에 맞게 주어진 단어를 이용하여 영어로 쓰시오. (주어진 단어를 포함하여 다섯 단어로 쓸 것 / 어형 변화 필수)

> (sit / not / allow)

> A: Is it OK to sit here?
> B: I'm afraid not. (A)<u>여기에 앉는 것은 허용되지 않습니다.</u>
> A: Oh, I see.

➡ _____ here.

05 다음 대화의 빈칸에 들어갈 말로 <u>어색한</u> 것은?

> G: Excuse me. Is it OK to take pictures here?
> M: Yes, it's all right.
> G: How about using a flash? _____, too?
> M: I'm afraid not. Using a flash is not allowed here.
> G: Oh, I see. Thank you.

① Is it OK if I use it

② Can I use it

③ Should I use it

④ Would it be all right if I use it

⑤ May I use it

[06~07] 다음 대화를 읽고 물음에 답하시오.

B: Excuse me. What's this? It ⓐ<u>looks interesting</u>.

W: Oh, that's ⓑ<u>a haegeum, a traditional Korean musical instrument</u>.

B: Is it OK ⓒ<u>to play</u> it?

W: I'm sorry, but it's only ⓓ<u>for display</u>. Playing it ⓔ<u>is not allow</u>.

B: I see.

06 위 대화의 밑줄 친 ⓐ~ⓔ 중 어법상 어색한 것은?

① ⓐ ② ⓑ ③ ⓒ ④ ⓓ ⑤ ⓔ

서답형

07 다음 물음의 답을 위 대화에서 찾아 쓰시오.

> Q: What isn't allowed?

➡ _____

[08~09] 다음 대화를 읽고 물음에 답하시오.

G: Excuse me, but (A)여기서 사진을 찍어도 되나요?
M: Yes. Go ahead.
G: Can I use a flash, too?
M: Yes. That's also OK.
G: I'm sorry, but I have one more question. Can I eat food here?
M: I'm sorry, but _____(B)_____ .

서답형

08 위 대화의 밑줄 친 (A)의 우리말에 맞게 주어진 단어를 이용하여 영어로 쓰시오.

> it / OK / take pictures / here

➡ _____
➡ _____

09 위 대화의 빈칸 (B)에 들어갈 말로 알맞은 것은?

① it's possible ② that's not allowed
③ no problem ④ eat food here
⑤ that's allowed

[10~12] 다음 대화를 읽고 물음에 답하시오.

Kate: Excuse me, but ⓐis it OK to try on this hanbok?
Man: Sure. The fitting room is over there. (①)
Kate: Thanks. Wait a minute. That's also very pretty. (②)
Man: Oh, the little hat over there?
Kate: Yes. What is it? (③)
Man: It's a jokduri, ⓑa traditional Korean hat for women. (④)
Kate: Really? Is it OK to ⓒtry on it, too?
Man: I'm sorry, but it's only for display. (⑤) ⓓTrying it on is not allowed.
Kate: Oh. Then, I'll just ⓔtry on this hanbok.

10 위 대화의 (①)~(⑤) 중 다음 문장이 들어갈 위치로 알맞은 것은?

> It's usually worn on a wedding day.

① ② ③ ④ ⑤

11 위 대화의 밑줄 친 ⓐ~ⓔ 중 어법상 어색한 것은?

① ⓐ ② ⓑ ③ ⓒ ④ ⓓ ⑤ ⓔ

12 위 대화의 내용과 일치하지 <u>않는</u> 것은?

① Kate is going to try on the hanbok.
② A jokduri is a traditional Korean hat for women.
③ Kate is not allowed to wear a jokduri.
④ A jokduri is usually worn on a wedding day.
⑤ Both the hanbok and the jokduri are only for display.

01 다음 대화의 (A)와 (B)에 들어갈 표현을 주어진 조건에 맞게 영어로 쓰시오.

> A: Which place do you want to go first in the museum?
> B: Why don't you guess?
> A: OK. Is it OK to eat food there?
> B: Yes. _____(A)_____
> A: Is it OK to take pictures?
> B: No. _____(B)_____
> A: I got it. You're thinking of going to the Video Room.
> B: You're right.

⊣ 보기 ⊢
• (A)와 (B) 모두 동명사로 문장을 시작할 것.
• allow를 사용하여 (A)는 허락의 표현을, (B)는 금지의 표현을 사용할 것.

(A) _____
(B) _____

02 다음 대화의 밑줄 친 물음에 대한 답을 주어진 〈조건〉에 맞게 빈칸을 완성하시오.

> G: Excuse me. Is it OK to take pictures here?
> M: Yes, it's all right.
> G: How about using a flash? <u>Can I use it, too?</u>
> M: I'm afraid not. _____
> G: Oh, I see. Thank you.

⊣ 조건 ⊢
• 동명사를 주어로 쓸 것.
• allow를 사용할 것.
• here를 포함시킬 것.

➡ _____.

03 다음 대화의 빈칸에 들어갈 문장을 주어진 〈조건〉대로 완성하시오.

> G: Excuse me. What's this? It looks interesting.
> B: Oh, that's a janggu, a traditional Korean musical instrument.
> G: _____
> B: I'm sorry, but it's only for display. Playing it is not allowed.
> G: I see.

⊣ 조건 ⊢
• 장구를 연주해도 되는지 허가 여부를 묻는 표현을 쓸 것.
• OK와 it을 사용하고, 부정사를 이용할 것.

➡ _____.

04 다음 대화의 빈칸에 들어갈 알맞은 표현을 〈보기〉에서 찾아 쓰시오.

> G: Excuse me, but _____(A)_____
> M: Yes. Go ahead.
> G: _____(B)_____
> M: Yes. That's also OK.
> G: I'm sorry, but _____(C)_____ Can I eat food here?
> M: I'm sorry, but _____(D)_____

⊣ 보기 ⊢
• I have one more question.
• is it OK to take pictures here?
• Can I use a flash, too?
• that's not allowed.

(A) _____
(B) _____
(C) _____
(D) _____

Grammar

① 간접의문문

- **Please tell me how you found them.** 그것들을 어떻게 발견하셨는지 말씀해 주세요.

■ 의문문이 동사의 목적절 등과 같이 다른 문장의 일부로 쓰일 때 간접의문문이라고 하며, 직접의문문과 달리 주어와 동사의 도치 현상이 일어나지 않는다. 의문사가 있는 간접의문문의 경우 '의문사+주어+동사'의 어순이 된다. 다른 문장 안에서 주어, 목적어, 보어 역할을 하며 동사의 목적어로 주로 쓰인다. 명사처럼 쓰이므로 주로 '…가 ~하는지'로 해석한다.

- **When he left here** was unknown. 〈주어〉 그가 언제 이곳을 떠났는지는 알려지지 않았다.
- I want to know **what his name is.** 〈목적어〉 나는 그 사람의 이름이 무엇인지 알고 싶다.
- This was **when Gandhi stood up for his nation.** 〈보어〉 이때가 간디가 그의 국가를 지지한 때예요.

■ 의문사가 없는 경우에는 의문사 대신에 if나 whether를 쓴다.

- I don't know. + Does he have a brother or a sister?
  → I don't know **if[whether] he has a brother or a sister.** 나는 그에게 남자 형제나 여자 형제가 있는지 모른다.

■ 의문사가 주어인 경우에는 의문사가 주어 역할을 하므로 직접의문문처럼 '의문사+동사'의 어순임에 유의한다.

- Do you know **who is over there?** 저기 누가 있는지 아십니까?

■ 간접의문문으로 바꾸어 쓸 때에는 의문문에 쓰이는 조동사 do, does, did가 쓰이지 않는 대신, 조동사 do의 시제를 간접의문문의 동사에 반영해야 한다.

- He asked me. + When does the next bus come?
  → He asked me **when the next bus came.** 그는 내게 다음 버스가 언제 오는지 물었다.

■ believe, imagine, suppose, consider, think, guess 등과 같은 동사가 주절에 있을 경우 간접의문문의 의문사를 문장 맨 앞으로 배치한다.

- Do you think? + What did the thief steal?
  → Do you think **what the thief stole?** (×)
  → **What** do you think **the thief stole?** (○) 너는 도둑이 무엇을 훔쳤다고 생각하니?

핵심 Check

1. 다음 우리말과 일치하도록 빈칸에 알맞은 말을 쓰시오.

   (1) 네가 무슨 걱정을 하고 있는지 말해 줄 수 있니?

   ➡ Can you tell me _____ _____ _____ worried about?

   (2) 그는 내게 밖이 추운지 물었다.

   ➡ He asked me _____ _____ _____ cold outside.

2 because of

- Many Koreans became interested in *Uigwe* **because of** your book.
  많은 한국인들이 당신의 책 때문에 "의궤"에 관심을 갖게 되었어요.

- I couldn't sleep last night **because** I was so afraid. 간밤에 너무 무서워서 잠을 잘 수 없었다.

■ because와 because of는 둘 다 '~ 때문에'라는 뜻으로 뒤에 나오는 말이 원인을 나타낸다.

- I couldn't arrive on time **because** I missed the bus. 버스를 놓쳐서 정각에 올 수가 없었어.
- His absence from work was **because of** his illness. 그가 결근한 것은 아파서였다.

■ because는 이유를 나타내는 접속사이고, because of는 부사구이다. 접속사 because 뒤에는 주어와 동사가 있는 절이, 부사구 because of 뒤에는 명사 또는 명사구가 온다.

- They cancelled the game **because** there was a storm.
- They cancelled the game **because of** a storm. 그들은 폭풍 때문에 시합을 취소했다.

■ because는 '이유'를 나타내는 as, since 등의 접속사와 바꿔 쓸 수 있으며, because of는 on account of, due to, thanks to 등과 바꿔 쓸 수 있다.

- I came here a bit early **because** my watch gained time.
  = I came here a bit early **since[as]** my watch gained time. 내 시계가 빨라서 나는 이곳에 조금 일찍 왔다.

- **Because of** bad weather, the school outing was cancelled.
  = **On account of[Due to]** bad weather, the school outing was cancelled.
  악천후 때문에, 학교 소풍은 취소되었다.

핵심 Check

2. 다음 우리말과 일치하도록 빈칸에 알맞은 말을 쓰시오.
  (1) 그는 아파서 학교에 오지 않았다.
    ➡ He didn't come to school _____ he was sick.
  (2) 나는 교통 체증 때문에 늦었어.
    ➡ I was late _____ _____ the heavy traffic.

01 다음 두 문장을 한 문장으로 연결할 때 올바른 것은?

> Can you tell me? What time is it now?

① Can you tell me what time is it now?
② Can you tell me what time it is now?
③ Can you tell me it is what time now?
④ What can you tell me it is time now?
⑤ What can you tell me is it time now?

02 다음 빈칸에 알맞은 것을 고르시오.

> A: Do you know _____?
> B: She is my sister.

① if who is she   ② if who she is
③ that she is   ④ who is she
⑤ who she is

03 다음 빈칸 ⓐ와 ⓑ에 들어갈 말이 알맞게 짝지어진 것을 고르시오.

> • I didn't go to school ___ⓐ___ I had a bad cold.
> • I didn't go to school ___ⓑ___ a bad cold.

① because – because   ② because – because of
③ because of – because for ④ because of – because
⑤ because for – because

04 다음 주어진 단어를 바르게 배열하여 다음 우리말을 영어로 쓰시오. 필요하다면 단어를 추가하시오.

> 그는 건강상의 이유로 직장을 그만두었다.
> (he, his, the job, health, quit, because)

➡ _____

01 다음 빈칸에 들어갈 말로 가장 적절한 것은?

Can you tell me _____?

① you became a director why
② why did you become a director
③ did why you become a director
④ why you became a director
⑤ why became you a director

02 다음 중 어법상 바르지 <u>않은</u> 것은?

① I couldn't sleep last night because of the loud noise.
② I stayed home because of it snowed too much.
③ She didn't buy it because it looked too small for him.
④ I stayed home because of a bad cold.
⑤ Tom had to leave early because of a traffic jam.

03 다음 중 어법상 옳은 것은?

① Can you tell me where were you born?
② Minho doesn't know where does Kevin live.
③ I stayed home because of I had a high fever.
④ The picnic was canceled because the bad weather.
⑤ I don't remember what time it was.

04 다음 괄호 안에서 알맞은 말을 고르시오.

(1) I didn't sleep well (because / because of) the loud noise.
(2) Sujin studied hard (because / because of) the exam.
(3) She was fired from the National Library of France (because / because of) her bosses thought that she was a spy.
(4) I don't remember what (was his name / his name was).
(5) I want to know what (are you / you are) interested in.
(6) Tell me (that / if) you enjoyed the movie.

05 다음 중 밑줄 친 부분의 쓰임이 <u>다른</u> 하나는?

① <u>If</u> you're finished, may I use the phone?
② <u>If</u> my guess is right, he must be about forty.
③ I want to know <u>if</u> he saw the movie.
④ Do you mind <u>if</u> I speak frankly?
⑤ I can do the shopping for you <u>if</u> you're tired.

06 주어진 단어를 이용하여 영작하시오.

너는 언제 영화가 시작하는지 아니? (start)

➡ _____

07 다음 두 문장을 한 문장으로 연결할 때 빈칸에 알맞은 것은?

> She has a test tomorrow. So, she is studying.
> → She's studying _____ she has a test tomorrow.

① because   ② because of
③ so   ④ and
⑤ but

08 다음 우리말을 영어로 바르게 옮긴 것은?

> 그가 그 상점에서 무엇을 샀는지 내게 묻지 마.

① Don't ask me whether he bought at the store.
② Don't ask me he bought what at the store.
③ Don't ask me what did he buy at the store.
④ Don't ask me he bought at the store what.
⑤ Don't ask me what he bought at the store.

09 다음 중 빈칸에 들어갈 말이 나머지 넷과 다른 것은?

① I am nervous _____ I have an exam tomorrow.
② _____ I was hungry, I had a hamburger.
③ Minho was tired, _____ he went to bed early.
④ Kevin got upset _____ his young brother went out with his jacket on.
⑤ Jane didn't go for a walk _____ it was too cold.

10 다음 중 밑줄 친 부분의 어순이 올바르지 않은 것은?

① I want to know what your favorite subject is.
② How he solved the problem is unknown.
③ He wondered if something was wrong with him.
④ The man asked me if or not he could borrow some money.
⑤ The woman was not sure whether the thief was a man.

서답형
11 다음 두 문장을 because를 이용하여 한 문장으로 다시 쓰시오.

(1) It was getting dark. We had to hurry.
   ➡ _____

(2) Jim couldn't take a nap. His little sister cried a lot.
   ➡ _____
   _____

(3) We didn't go camping. It was because of the bad weather.
   ➡ _____

12 다음 중 어법상 바르지 않은 문장의 개수는?

> ⓐ I want to know where is she.
> ⓑ Jim couldn't take a nap because he had to study for the exam.
> ⓒ I wonder if is he at home.
> ⓓ Tell me when the guests will arrive.
> ⓔ We ran away because we were afraid.
> ⓕ Peter couldn't play soccer because the rain.

① 1개   ② 2개   ③ 3개
④ 4개   ⑤ 5개

서답형

13 다음 문장에서 어법상 어색한 것을 바르게 고쳐 다시 쓰시오.

(1) Can I ask you why did you decide to become a teacher?

➡ _____

(2) I want to know you were born where.

➡ _____

(3) Do you think who the girl is?

➡ _____

(4) He asked me that I am Simon's sister.

➡ _____

(5) I took some medicine because a bad cold.

➡ _____

(6) You can't watch the movie because of you're not old enough.

➡ _____
_____

14 다음 두 문장을 간접의문문으로 바르게 바꾼 것은?

> • Can you tell me?
> • When did you become a teacher?

① When you became a teacher can you tell me?

② When can you tell me did you become a teacher?

③ When can you tell me you became a teacher?

④ Can you tell me when did you become a teacher?

⑤ Can you tell me when you became a teacher?

15 다음 중 어법상 바르지 않은 것은?

> I ①missed the airplane ②to New York ③because ④a ⑤heavy traffic jam.

①   ②   ③   ④   ⑤

16 우리말과 의미가 같도록 빈칸에 들어갈 말로 알맞은 것을 고르시오.

> 나는 그녀가 내 선물을 좋아할지 잘 모르겠다.
> → I'm not sure _____.

① if she will like my present

② she will like my present

③ will she like my present

④ that she likes my present

⑤ whether she likes my present

[17~18] 다음 빈칸에 가장 알맞은 것을 고르시오.

17
> I want to go to Hawaii _____ it's warm and beautiful.

① and   ② but   ③ so
④ though   ⑤ because

18
> I forgot to ask you _____ you are hungry.

① because   ② because of
③ as   ④ that
⑤ if

서답형

19 다음 두 문장을 하나의 문장으로 바꿔 쓰시오.

> • Please tell me.
> • What did the thief steal?

➡ _____

 01 다음 두 문장을 하나의 문장으로 바꿔 쓰시오.

(1) I'd like to know. + What did you want to be when you were young?

  ➡ _____

    _____

(2) Can you tell me? + When and where were you born?

  ➡ _____

(3) I don't know. + Who borrowed your book?

  ➡ _____

(4) I wonder. + Does my child express himself well in English?

  ➡ _____

    _____

(5) Do you know? + Will it rain today?

  ➡ _____

(6) Do you believe? + What were you in a previous life?

  ➡ _____

02 because를 이용하여 주어진 문장과 같은 의미가 되도록 한 문장으로 쓰시오.

(1) It's snowing a lot. So, there is no school today.

  ➡ _____

    _____

    _____

(2) Jaemin didn't arrive. So, we couldn't start the meeting.

  ➡ _____

    _____

 03 다음 그림을 참고하여 주어진 대화의 빈칸을 완성하시오.

A: Please tell us (1)_____ 297 books of *Uigwe*?

B: Oh, I found them in 1977.

A: Could you tell us (2)_____?

B: I found them in the National Library of France.

04 다음 그림을 참고하여 다음 빈칸에 알맞은 말을 7 단어로 쓰시오.

A: Why can't I enter the zoo?

B: You can't enter the zoo _____

_____.

05 다음 문장은 두 개의 문장을 한 문장으로 쓴 것이다. 원래의 두 문장을 쓰시오.

(1) I'd like to know who your best friend is.

➡ _____

(2) She didn't tell me whom she met yesterday.

➡ _____

(3) He wondered if something was wrong with him.

➡ _____

(4) What do you think you will wear on Monday?

➡ _____

06 괄호 안에 주어진 어휘를 이용하여 다음 우리말을 영작하시오.

(1) Jessie한테 무슨 일이 생겼는지 내게 말해 줄 수 있니? (tell, happen, to, 8 단어)

➡ _____

(2) 그는 내게 돈이 좀 있는지 물었다.
(ask, have, any money, 8 단어)

➡ _____

(3) 나는 누가 이 책을 썼는지 알고 싶다.
(want, write, 8 단어)

➡ _____

(4) 건강의 비결이 뭐라고 생각하십니까?
(the secret, your health, think, 10 단어)

➡ _____

(5) 나는 감기 때문에 그의 생일 파티에 가지 않았다.
(a cold, because, 11 단어)

➡ _____

(6) 나는 어지러워서 앉았다.
(sit down, feeling dizzy, 8 단어)

➡ _____

(7) Michael과 Jane이 다투는 바람에 모두 일찍 떠났다.
(everyone, leave, have an argument, 10 단어)

➡ _____

_____

07 다음 문장을 어법에 맞게 고쳐 쓰시오.

(1) I don't remember what was the thief wearing.

➡ _____

(2) I don't know did who steal my camera.

➡ _____

(3) Can you tell me how did you become interested in *Uigwe*?

➡ _____

(4) I asked her that she was ready to go.

➡ _____

(5) Do you suppose what most American teenagers seek help for?

➡ _____

_____

(6) Jane woke up in the middle of the night because a bad dream.

➡ _____

_____

(7) Yesterday Mary went shopping because of she wanted to buy a gift for her dad.

➡ _____

_____

08 다음 빈칸에 알맞은 말을 쓰시오.

It snowed a lot. So I couldn't go outside.
➡ I couldn't go outside _____ it snowed a lot.

An Interview with Dr. Park Byeong-seon

On May 27, 2011, 297 books of *Uigwe*, a collection of royal books
날이나 요일 앞에 전치사 on   동격 관계
the French army took in 1866, came back to Korea. The person behind
books와 the French army 사이에 목적격 관계대명사 which 또는 that 생략
this return is Dr. Park Byeong-seon, a historian who spent her whole
          Dr. Park Byeong-seon과 a historian은 동격 관계   주격 관계대명사
life searching for Korean national treasures abroad.
spend+시간+-ing: ~하는 데 시간을 보내다

Q: Can you tell me how you became interested in *Uigwe*?
          의문문이 다른 문장의 일부로 쓰이면 '의문사＋주어＋동사' 어순의 간접의문이 된다.

Dr. Park: I studied history in college. I went to France to continue
                                      부사적 용법(목적)
my studies in 1955. As you know, the French army took many of
                    ~ 처럼
our national treasures in 1866. I wanted to find them while I was
                                      1866년에 프랑스군이 가져간 우리 문화재
studying there. *Uigwe* was one of them.

Q: You found 297 books of *Uigwe* in the National Library of France, in
Paris. Please tell me how you found them.
                  의문문이 다른 문장의 일부로 쓰이면 '의문사＋주어＋동사' 어순의 간접의문이 된다.

Dr. Park: As soon as I became a researcher at the National Library in
            ~하자마자
1967, I began to look for *Uigwe*. After 10 years, in 1977, I finally
            begin은 목적어로 to부정사와 동명사를 모두 취할 수 있다.
found the books. I think I looked at more than 30 million books.
                                      ~ 이상

Q: I'm sure you were very excited when you found the books.

Dr. Park: Yes, I was, but more difficulties were waiting for me. I thought
that the books should be returned to Korea, but my bosses at the
            조동사가 있는 문장의 수동태: 조동사＋be동사＋과거분사
library didn't like that idea. They even thought that I was a Korean
            '그 책들이 한국에 반환되어야 한다는 박병선 박사의 생각
spy and fired me.
            fire: 해고하다

royal 왕의, 왕실의
army 군대, 육군
spend (시간을) 보내다
search ~을 찾다
treasure 보물
abroad 해외에서
continue 계속하다
million 100만
research 연구
value 가치
result 결과
publish 출판하다, 발행하다
government 정부

확인문제

● 다음 문장이 본문의 내용과 일치하면 T, 일치하지 않으면 F를 쓰시오.

1 *Uigwe* is a collection of royal books the French army took in 1866. ☐

2 When Dr. Park became a researcher, she looked at *Uigwe*. ☐

3 Dr. Park thinks she looked at less than 30 million books. ☐

4 Dr. Park was very excited when she found *Uigwe*. ☐

After that, I had to go to the library as a visitor, so it was not easy to 도서관의 상사들이 박병선 박사를 해고한 것   '~로(서)'(자격)   가주어

do research on *Uigwe*. However, I didn't give up. For more than ten 진주어   포기하다

years, I went to the library every day to finish my research. I wanted to 목적을 나타내는 to부정사의 부사적 용법

show people the value of *Uigwe*. 3형식: show the value of *Uigwe* to people

Q: The results of your research were published as a book in Korea in 1990. 수동태   ~으로

Many Koreans became interested in *Uigwe* because of your book. '~에 관심을 갖게 되다'   because of+명사(구)

Dr. Park: Yes. In 1992, the Korean government asked the French ask A for B: A에게 B를 요청하다

government for its return and, finally, the 297 books are here now.

Q: Before I finish this interview, I'd like to ask you about *Jikji*, a book *Jikji*와 a book은 동격 관계

that changed the history of printing. 주격 관계대명사

Dr. Park: I found it in my first year at the library. I knew right away that it = *Jikji*   = immediately

was very special. I worked hard to prove its value and finally succeeded. 목적을 나타내는 to부정사의 부사적 용법

At a book exhibition in Paris in 1972, *Jikji* was displayed as the oldest be동사+과거분사: (수동태) '전시되었다'

book in the world that was printed with movable metal type. 주격 관계대명사   ~으로(도구)

Q: Dr. Park, thanks to your hard work, *Jikji* and *Uigwe* were found, and '~ 덕택에, ~ 덕분에'   수동태

all Koreans thank you for that. thank A for B: B에 대해 A에게 감사하다

Dr. Park: I hope people will become more interested in our national

treasures abroad and work for their return. 해외에 있는 우리의 문화재

---

visitor 손님, 방문객

prove 입증하다, 증명하다

succeed 성공하다

metal 금속

printing 인쇄

thanks to ~ 덕분에

📎 **확인문제**

● 다음 문장이 본문의 내용과 일치하면 T, 일치하지 않으면 F를 쓰시오.

1   It was not easy for Dr. Park to do research on *Uigwe*. ☐

2   The results of Dr. Park's research were published as a book in France in 1990. ☐

3   Many Koreans became interested in *Uigwe* because of Dr. Park's book. ☐

4   *Jikji* is a book that changed the history of printing. ☐

5   Dr. Park found *Jikji* in 1972. ☐

● 우리말을 참고하여 빈칸에 알맞은 말을 쓰시오.

1 An _____ _____ Dr. Park Byeong-seon

2 _____ May 27, 2011, 297 books of *Uigwe*, _____ _____ _____ royal books the French army took in 1866, _____ _____ _____ Korea.

3 The person _____ _____ _____ is Dr. Park Byeong-seon, a historian who spent her whole life _____ _____ Korean national treasures _____.

4 Q: Can you tell me _____ you _____ _____ _____ *Uigwe*?

5 Dr. Park: I _____ _____ in college.

6 I went to France _____ _____ my studies in 1955.

7 _____ _____ _____, the French army took many of our national treasures in 1866.

8 I wanted to find them _____ I was studying there.

9 *Uigwe* was _____ _____ _____.

10 Q: You found _____ _____ _____ _____ in the National Library of France, in Paris.

11 Please tell me _____ you found them.

12 Dr. Park: _____ _____ _____ I became a researcher at the National Library in 1967, I began to _____ _____ *Uigwe*.

13 After 10 years, in 1977, I _____ found the books.

14 I think I _____ _____ more than _____ _____ books.

15 Q: _____ _____ you were very excited when you found the books.

16 Dr. Park: Yes, I was, but _____ _____ _____ were waiting for me.

17 I thought that the books _____ _____ _____ Korea, but my bosses at the library didn't like _____ _____.

1 박병선 박사와의 인터뷰

2 2011년 5월 27일에 프랑스군이 1866년에 가져갔던 왕실 서적인 "의궤" 297권이 한국으로 돌아왔다.

3 이 반환 뒤에 있는 인물이 해외에 있는 한국의 문화재를 찾기 위해 전 생애를 바친 역사학자 박병선 박사이다.

4 Q: "의궤"에 어떻게 관심을 갖게 되셨는지 말씀해 주시겠어요?

5 Dr. Park: 저는 대학에서 역사를 공부했어요.

6 저는 1955년에 학업을 계속하기 위해 프랑스에 갔습니다.

7 아시다시피, 프랑스군은 1866년에 우리 문화재를 많이 가져갔어요.

8 저는 그곳에서 공부하는 동안 그것들을 찾고 싶었어요.

9 "의궤"는 그것들 중의 하나였어요.

10 Q: 당신은 파리에 있는 프랑스 국립도서관에서 297권의 "의궤"를 발견하셨어요.

11 그것들을 어떻게 발견하셨는지 말씀해 주세요.

12 Dr. Park: 1967년에 국립도서관의 연구원이 되자마자, 저는 "의궤"를 찾기 시작했어요.

13 10년 후인 1977년에 마침내 그 책들을 발견했죠.

14 제 생각에 3천만 권 이상의 책을 본 것 같아요.

15 Q: 그 책들을 발견했을 때 무척 흥분하셨겠어요.

16 Dr. Park: 네, 하지만 더 큰 어려움이 저를 기다리고 있었어요.

17 저는 그 책들이 한국에 반환되어야 한다고 생각했지만, 도서관의 제 상사들은 그 생각을 좋아하지 않았어요.

18 They _____ _____ that I was a Korean spy and _____ me.

19 After that, I had to go to the library _____ _____ _____, so it was not easy to _____ _____ _____ Uigwe.

20 _____, I didn't give up.

21 _____ _____ _____ ten years, I went to the library every day to finish my research.

22 I wanted to show people _____ _____ _____ _____.

23 Q: The results of your research _____ _____ _____ a book in Korea in 1990.

24 Many Koreans became interested in Uigwe _____ your book.

25 Dr. Park: Yes. In 1992, the Korean government _____ the French government _____ its return and, finally, the 297 books _____ _____ _____.

26 Q: Before I finish this interview, _____ _____ _____ _____ you about Jikji, a book that changed the history of _____.

27 Dr. Park: I found it _____ _____ _____ _____ at the library.

28 I knew _____ _____ that it was very special.

29 I worked hard _____ _____ _____ _____ and finally succeeded.

30 At a book exhibition in Paris in 1972, Jikji _____ _____ _____ the oldest book in the world that was printed with _____ _____ _____.

31 Q: Dr. Park, _____ _____ your hard work, Jikji and Uigwe were found, and all Koreans _____ you _____ that.

32 Dr. Park: I hope people will become more interested in _____ _____ _____ _____ and work for their _____.

18 그들은 심지어 제가 한국의 스파이라고 생각했고 저를 해고했죠.

19 그 후에, 저는 방문객으로 도서관에 가야만 했고, 그래서 "의궤"를 연구하는 것이 쉽지 않았어요.

20 하지만 저는 포기하지 않았죠.

21 10년 넘게, 연구를 끝마치기 위해 매일 도서관에 갔어요.

22 저는 사람들에게 "의궤"의 가치를 보여 주고 싶었어요.

23 Q: 당신의 연구 결과가 1990년 한국에서 책으로 출판되었죠.

24 많은 한국인들이 당신의 책 때문에 "의궤"에 관심을 갖게 되었어요.

25 Dr. Park: 네. 1992년에 한국 정부는 프랑스 정부에 그것의 반환을 요청했고, 마침내 297권의 책이 지금 여기 있게 된 거죠.

26 Q: 인터뷰를 마치기 전에, 인쇄의 역사를 바꾼 책인 "직지"에 대해 여쭙고 싶어요.

27 Dr. Park: 저는 도서관에서 근무한 첫해에 그것을 발견했어요.

28 그것이 아주 특별하다는 것을 바로 알았어요.

29 저는 그것의 가치를 증명하기 위해 열심히 연구했고 마침내 성공했죠.

30 1972년에 파리 도서 박람회에서 "직지"는 금속 활자로 인쇄된 세계에서 가장 오래된 책으로 전시되었죠.

31 Q: 박 박사님, 당신의 노고 덕분에 "직지"와 "의궤"가 발견되었고, 모든 한국인들이 그 점을 당신에게 감사하고 있어요.

32 Dr. Park: 저는 사람들이 해외에 있는 우리의 문화재에 더 많은 관심을 갖고 그것의 반환을 위해 애써 주시기를 바랍니다.

● 우리말을 참고하여 본문을 영작하시오.

1 박병선 박사와의 인터뷰

➡ _____

2 2011년 5월 27일에 프랑스군이 1866년에 가져갔던 왕실 서적인 "의궤" 297권이 한국으로 돌아왔다.

➡ _____

3 이 반환 뒤에 있는 인물이 해외에 있는 한국의 문화재를 찾기 위해 전 생애를 바친 역사학자 박병선 박사이다.

➡ _____

4 Q: "의궤"에 어떻게 관심을 갖게 되셨는지 말씀해 주시겠어요?

➡ _____

5 Dr. Park: 저는 대학에서 역사를 공부했어요.

➡ _____

6 저는 1955년에 학업을 계속하기 위해 프랑스에 갔습니다.

➡ _____

7 아시다시피, 프랑스군은 1866년에 우리 문화재를 많이 가져갔어요.

➡ _____

8 저는 그곳에서 공부하는 동안 그것들을 찾고 싶었어요.

➡ _____

9 "의궤"는 그것들 중의 하나였어요.

➡ _____

10 Q: 당신은 파리에 있는 프랑스 국립도서관에서 297권의 "의궤"를 발견하셨어요.

➡ _____

11 그것들을 어떻게 발견하셨는지 말씀해 주세요.

➡ _____

12 Dr. Park: 1967년에 국립도서관의 연구원이 되자마자, 저는 "의궤"를 찾기 시작했어요.

➡ _____

13 10년 후인 1977년에 마침내 그 책들을 발견했죠.

➡ _____

14 제 생각에 3천만 권 이상의 책을 본 것 같아요.

➡ _____

15 Q: 그 책들을 발견했을 때 무척 흥분하셨겠어요.

➡ _____

16 Dr. Park: 네, 하지만 더 큰 어려움이 저를 기다리고 있었어요.

➡ _____

17 저는 그 책들이 한국에 반환되어야 한다고 생각했지만, 도서관의 제 상사들은 그 생각을 좋아하지 않았어요.

➡ _____

_____

18 그들은 심지어 제가 한국의 스파이라고 생각했고 저를 해고했죠.

➡ _____

19 그 후에, 저는 방문객으로 도서관에 가야만 했고, 그래서 "의궤"를 연구하는 것이 쉽지 않았어요.

➡ _____

20 하지만 저는 포기하지 않았죠.

➡ _____

21 10년 넘게, 연구를 끝마치기 위해 매일 도서관에 갔어요.

➡ _____

22 저는 사람들에게 "의궤"의 가치를 보여 주고 싶었어요.

➡ _____

23 Q: 당신의 연구 결과가 1990년 한국에서 책으로 출판되었죠.

➡ _____

24 많은 한국인들이 당신의 책 때문에 "의궤"에 관심을 갖게 되었어요.

➡ _____

25 Dr. Park: 네. 1992년에 한국 정부는 프랑스 정부에 그것의 반환을 요청했고, 마침내 297권의 책이 지금 여기 있게 된 거죠.

➡ _____
_____

26 Q: 인터뷰를 마치기 전에, 인쇄의 역사를 바꾼 책인 "직지"에 대해 여쭙고 싶어요.

➡ _____
_____

27 Dr. Park: 저는 도서관에서 근무한 첫해에 그것을 발견했어요.

➡ _____

28 그것이 아주 특별하다는 것을 바로 알았어요.

➡ _____

29 저는 그것의 가치를 증명하기 위해 열심히 연구했고 마침내 성공했죠.

➡ _____

30 1972년에 파리 도서 박람회에서 "직지"는 금속 활자로 인쇄된 세계에서 가장 오래된 책으로 전시되었죠.

➡ _____
_____

31 Q: 박 박사님, 당신의 노고 덕분에 "직지"와 "의궤"가 발견되었고, 모든 한국인들이 그 점을 당신에게 감사하고 있어요.

➡ _____
_____

32 Dr. Park: 저는 사람들이 해외에 있는 우리의 문화재에 더 많은 관심을 갖고 그것의 반환을 위해 애써 주시기를 바랍니다.

➡ _____
_____

[01~03] 다음 글을 읽고 물음에 답하시오.

①In May 27, 2011, 297 books ②of *Uigwe*, a collection of royal books the French army took ③in 1866, came back to Korea. The person behind this return is Dr. Park Byeong-seon, a historian who spent her whole life searching ④for Korean national treasures abroad.

Q: Can you tell me how you became interested ⑤in *Uigwe*?

Dr. Park: I studied history in college. I went to France to continue my studies in 1955. ⓐ 아시다시피, the French army took many of our national treasures in 1866. I wanted to find them while I was studying there. *Uigwe* was one of them.

서답형

01 위 글의 밑줄 친 전치사 ①~⑤ 중에서 옳지 않은 것을 찾아 고치시오.

_____ ➡ _____

서답형

02 위 글의 밑줄 친 ⓐ의 우리말을 세 단어로 쓰시오.

➡ _____

중요

03 위 글의 내용과 일치하지 않는 것은?

① In 2011, *Uigwe* came back to Korea.

② The French army took *Uigwe* from Korea in 1866.

③ Dr. Park spent her whole life searching for Korean national treasures abroad.

④ In 1955, Dr. Park went to France to continue her studies.

⑤ Dr. Park wanted to introduce *Uigwe* while she was studying in France.

[04~07] 다음 글을 읽고 물음에 답하시오.

Q: You found 297 books of *Uigwe* in the National Library of France, in Paris.
_____ⓐ_____

Dr. Park: As soon as I became a researcher at the National Library in 1967, I began to look for *Uigwe*. After 10 years, in 1977, I ⓑfinally found the books. I think I looked at more than 30 million books.

Q: I'm sure you were very excited when you found the books.

Dr. Park: Yes, I was, but more difficulties were waiting for me. I thought that the books should be returned to Korea, but my bosses at the library didn't like that idea. They even thought that I was a Korean spy and fired me. After that, I had to go to the library as a visitor, so it was not easy to do research on *Uigwe*. However, I didn't give up. For more than ten years, I went to the library every day to finish my research. I wanted to show people the value of *Uigwe*.

서답형

04 다음 두 문장을 합쳐서 위 글의 빈칸 ⓐ에 알맞은 형태로 쓰시오.

• Please tell me.
• How did you find them?

➡ _____

05 위 글의 밑줄 친 ⓑfinally와 바꿔 쓸 수 없는 말을 모두 고르시오.

① at least   ② in the end

③ lastly   ④ at last

⑤ in the long run

서답형

06 Why was Dr. Park fired? Fill in the blanks with the suitable words.

> Because her bosses at the library didn't like _____ _____ and they even thought that she was _____ _____ _____.

중요

07 위 글의 마지막 부분에서 알 수 있는 Dr. Park의 성격으로 가장 알맞은 것을 고르시오.

① friendly   ② strong-willed
③ polite   ④ creative
⑤ curious

[08~11] 다음 글을 읽고 물음에 답하시오.

Q: Before I finish this interview, I'd like to ask you about *Jikji*, a book ⓐthat changed the history of printing.

Dr. Park: I found it in my first year at the library. I knew right away that it was very special. I worked hard to prove its value and finally succeeded. At a book exhibition in Paris in 1972, *Jikji* was displayed as the oldest book in the world that was printed with movable ⓑ금속 활자.

Q: ⓒDr. Park, in spite of your hard work, *Jikji* and *Uigwe* were found, and all Koreans thank you for that.

Dr. Park: I hope people will become more interested in our national treasures abroad and work for their return.

08 위 글의 밑줄 친 ⓐthat과 문법적 쓰임이 같은 것을 모두 고르시오.

① Look at the boy and the dog that are running there.
② I can't walk that far.
③ She said that the story was true.
④ Which would you prefer, this or that?
⑤ It's the best novel that I've ever read.

서답형

09 위 글의 밑줄 친 ⓑ의 우리말을 두 단어로 쓰시오.

➡ _____

서답형

10 위 글의 밑줄 친 ⓒ에서 흐름상 어색한 부분을 찾아 고치시오.

_____ ➡ _____

11 위 글의 제목으로 알맞은 것을 고르시오.

① Let Me Ask You a Final Question
② What Is *Jikji*?
③ Dr. Park Proved the Value of *Jikji*
④ *Jikji* Was Displayed at a Book Exhibition
⑤ Our National Treasures Abroad Must Be Returned

[12~14] 다음 글을 읽고 물음에 답하시오.

On May 27, 2011, ⓐ297 books of *Uigwe*, a collection of royal books the French army took in 1866, came back to Korea. The person behind this return is Dr. Park Byeong-seon, a historian who spent her whole life searching for Korean national treasures abroad.

Q: Can you tell me how you became interested in *Uigwe*?

Dr. Park: I studied history in college. I went to France to continue my studies in 1955. ⓑ As you know, the French army took many of our national treasures in 1866. I wanted to find them while I was studying there. *Uigwe* was one of them.

12 위 글의 밑줄 친 ⓐ에서 royal books와 the French army 사이에 생략된 말로 옳은 것을 <u>모두</u> 고르시오.

① that   ② who   ③ whom
④ which   ⑤ what

13 위 글의 밑줄 친 ⓑAs와 같은 의미로 쓰인 것을 고르시오.

① He came up to me <u>as</u> I was speaking.
② <u>As</u> you see, he is a genius.
③ <u>As</u> I was tired, I soon fell asleep.
④ He treats me <u>as</u> a child.
⑤ <u>As</u> we go up, the air grows colder.

14 위 글을 읽고 "의궤"에 대해 대답할 수 <u>없는</u> 것을 고르시오.

① What is *Uigwe*?
② How many books does it have in all?
③ Who made it and what is recorded in it?
④ Who took it from Korea?
⑤ When did it come back to Korea?

[15~18] 다음 글을 읽고 물음에 답하시오.

Q: You found 297 books of *Uigwe* in the National Library of France, in Paris. Please tell me how you found ①them.

Dr. Park: As soon as I became a researcher at the National Library in 1967, I began to look for *Uigwe*. After 10 years, in 1977, I finally found ②the books. I think I looked at ③more than 30 million books.

Q: I'm sure you were very excited when you found ④the books.

Dr. Park: Yes, I was, but more difficulties were waiting for me. I thought that ⑤ the books should be returned to Korea, but my bosses at the library didn't like that idea. They even thought that I was a Korean spy and fired me. After that, I had to go to the library as a visitor, so it was not easy to do research on *Uigwe*.   ⓐ   , I didn't give up. For more than ten years, I went to the library every day to finish my research. I wanted to show people the value of *Uigwe*.

15 위 글의 빈칸 ⓐ에 들어갈 알맞은 말을 고르시오.

① Therefore   ② For example

③ Besides   ④ However

⑤ In other words

16 밑줄 친 ①~⑤ 중에서 가리키는 대상이 나머지 넷과 <u>다른</u> 것은?

①   ②   ③   ④   ⑤

17 위 글의 내용과 어울리는 속담을 고르시오. (두 개)

① A stitch in time saves nine.

② Where there is a will, there is a way.

③ It never rains but it pours.

④ Better late than never.

⑤ Many drops make a shower.

18 위 글을 읽고 대답할 수 <u>없는</u> 질문은?

① When did Dr. Park begin to look for *Uigwe*?

② How long did it take for Dr. Park to find *Uigwe*?

③ How many books did she look at before finding *Uigwe*?

④ What did she think when she found *Uigwe*?

⑤ What's the value of *Uigwe*?

[19~20] 다음 글을 읽고 물음에 답하시오.

Q: Before I finish this interview, I'd like to ask you about *Jikji*, a book ___①___ changed the history of printing.

Dr. Park: I found it in my first year at the library. I knew right away ___②___ it was very special. I worked hard to prove its value and finally succeeded. At a book exhibition in Paris in 1972, *Jikji* was displayed ___③___ the oldest book in the world ___④___ was printed with movable metal type.

Q: Dr. Park, thanks to your hard work, *Jikji* and *Uigwe* were found, and all Koreans thank you for ___⑤___.

Dr. Park: I hope people will become more interested in our national treasures abroad and work for their return.

19 위 글의 빈칸 ①~⑤에 들어갈 말이 나머지 넷과 <u>다른</u> 것은?

①   ②   ③   ④   ⑤

20 위 글의 내용과 일치하지 <u>않는</u> 것은?

① The last question was about *Jikji*.

② *Jikji* changed the history of printing.

③ Dr. Park succeeded in proving the value of *Jikji*.

④ In 1972, Gutenberg Bible was proved as the oldest book in the world.

⑤ Thanks to Dr. Park's hard work, *Jikji* and *Uigwe* were found.

[21~23] 다음 글을 읽고 물음에 답하시오.

> Q: I'm sure you were very excited when you found the books.
>
> Dr. Park: Yes, I was, but more difficulties were waiting for me. (①) They even thought that I was a Korean spy and ⓐ<u>fired</u> me. (②) After that, I had to go to the library as a visitor, so it was not easy to do research on *Uigwe*. (③) However, I didn't give up. (④) For more than ten years, I went to the library every day ⓑ<u>to finish my research</u>. (⑤) I wanted to show people the value of *Uigwe*.

21 위 글의 흐름으로 보아, 주어진 문장이 들어가기에 가장 적절한 곳은?

> I thought that the books should be returned to Korea, but my bosses at the library didn't like that idea.

①   ②   ③   ④   ⑤

22 위 글의 밑줄 친 ⓐ<u>fired</u>와 같은 의미로 쓰인 것을 고르시오.

① She <u>fired</u> an arrow at the target.

② They <u>fired</u> questions at him.

③ He was <u>fired</u> because he was lazy.

④ The book <u>fired</u> his imagination.

⑤ He <u>fired</u> the gun into the air.

서답형

23 위 글의 밑줄 친 ⓑ를 다음과 같이 바꿔 쓸 때 빈칸에 들어갈 알맞은 말을 쓰시오.

(1) _____ _____ _____ my research

(2) _____ _____ _____ my research

(3) _____ _____ I _____ my research

(4) _____ _____ I _____ finish my research

[24~26] 다음 글을 읽고 물음에 답하시오.

> Q: Before I finish this interview, I'd like to ask you about *Jikji*, a book that changed the history of printing.
>
> Dr. Park: I found it in my first year at the library. I knew right away that it was very (A)[common / special]. I worked hard to prove its value and finally succeeded. At a book (B)[exhibition / explanation] in Paris in 1972, *Jikji* (C)[displayed / was displayed] as the oldest book in the world that was printed with movable metal type.
>
> Q: Dr. Park, thanks to your hard work, *Jikji* and *Uigwe* were found, and all Koreans thank you for ⓐ<u>that</u>.
>
> Dr. Park: I hope people will become more interested in our national treasures abroad and work for ⓑ<u>their return</u>.

24 위 글의 괄호 (A)~(C)에서 문맥이나 어법상 알맞은 낱말을 골라 쓰시오.

(A) _____ (B) _____ (C) _____

25 위 글의 밑줄 친 ⓐthat과 ⓑtheir가 가리키는 내용을 우리말로 쓰시오.

ⓐ _____

ⓑ _____

26 위 글의 두 사람의 관계로 알맞은 것을 고르시오.

① employer – employee

② interviewer – applicant

③ trainer – trainee

④ interviewer – interviewee

⑤ manager – candidate

[27~28] 다음 인터뷰 기사를 읽고 물음에 답하시오.

An Interview with Kim Yubin

The following is the interview I had with Kim Yubin, a local police officer.

Q: Can you tell me ⓐwhen and where were you born?

A: I was born in Seoul on March 11, 1980.

Q: I'd like (A)[to know / knowing] what your goal in life is.

A: My goal in life is (B)[to make / making] a better world.

Q: Can you tell me ⓑwhat do you like about your job?

A: I like (C)[to help / helping] people.

I think that Kim Yubin is a great police officer.

27 위 글의 밑줄 친 ⓐ와 ⓑ를 어법상 바르게 고쳐 쓰시오.

ⓐ _____

ⓑ _____

28 위 글의 괄호 (A)~(C)에서 어법상 알맞은 낱말을 골라 쓰시오. (둘 다 가능한 경우에는 둘 다 쓰시오.)

ⓐ _____

ⓑ _____

ⓒ _____

[01~03] 다음 글을 읽고 물음에 답하시오.

On May 27, 2011, 297 books of *Uigwe*, a (A)[collection / correction] of royal books the French army took in 1866, came back to Korea. The person (B)[behind / in front of] ⓐthis return is Dr. Park Byeong-seon, a historian who spent her whole life searching for Korean national treasures (C)[aboard / abroad].

Q: Can you tell me ⓑ"의궤"에 어떻게 관심을 갖게 되셨는지?

Dr. Park: I studied history in college. I went to France to continue my studies in 1955. As you know, the French army took many of our national treasures in 1866. I wanted to find them while I was studying there. *Uigwe* was one of them.

01 위 글의 괄호 (A)~(C)에서 문맥상 알맞은 낱말을 골라 쓰시오.

(A) _____ (B) _____ (C) _____

02 다음 빈칸 (A)와 (B)에 알맞은 단어를 넣어 ⓐthis return에 대한 설명을 완성하시오.

the return of *Uigwe* from (A)_____ to (B)_____

03 위 글의 밑줄 친 ⓑ의 우리말에 맞게 주어진 어휘를 이용하여 6 단어로 영작하시오.

how, became

➡ _____

[04~07] 다음 글을 읽고 물음에 답하시오.

Q: You found 297 books of *Uigwe* in the National Library of France, in Paris. Please tell me how you found them.

Dr. Park: As soon as I became a researcher at the National Library in 1967, ⓐI began to look for *Uigwe*. After 10 years, in 1977, I finally found the books. I think I looked at more than 30 million books.

Q: I'm sure you were very excited when you found the books.

Dr. Park: Yes, I was, but more difficulties were waiting for me. ⓑ저는 그 책들이 한국에 반환되어야 한다고 생각했어요, but my bosses at the library didn't like that idea. ⓒThey even thought that I was a Korean spy and hired me. After that, I had to go to the library as a visitor, so it was not easy to do research on *Uigwe*. However, I didn't give up. For more than ten years, I went to the library every day to finish my research. I wanted to show people the value of *Uigwe*.

04 위 글의 밑줄 친 ⓐ를 다음과 같이 바꿔 쓸 때 빈칸에 들어갈 알맞은 말을 쓰시오.

I began _____ for *Uigwe*.

05 위 글의 밑줄 친 ⓑ의 우리말에 맞게 주어진 어휘를 이용하여 10 단어로 영작하시오.

that, should, return to

➡ _____

06 위 글의 밑줄 친 ⓒ에서 흐름상 어색한 부분을 찾아 고치시오.

_____ ➡ _____

07 위 글의 내용과 일치하도록 다음 빈칸 (A)~(C)에 알맞은 단어를 쓰시오.

> (A)_____ _____ _____ Dr. Park became a researcher at the National Library in 1967, she began to look for *Uigwe*. In spite of many (B)_____, she didn't give up because she wanted to show people the (C)_____ of *Uigwe*, and after 10 years, she found the books.

[08~09] 다음 글을 읽고 물음에 답하시오.

Q: Before I finish this interview, I'd like to ask you about *Jikji*, a book that changed the history of printing.

Dr. Park: I found it in my first year at the library. I knew right away that it was very special. I worked hard to prove its value and finally ⓐsucceeded. At a book exhibition in Paris in 1972, *Jikji* was displayed as the oldest book in the world that was printed with movable metal type.

Q: Dr. Park, thanks to your hard work, *Jikji* and *Uigwe* were found, and all Koreans thank you for that.

Dr. Park: I hope people will become more interested in our national treasures abroad and work for their return.

08 위 글의 밑줄 친 ⓐsucceeded 뒤에 생략된 말을 쓰시오.
(전치사 in을 포함하여 4 단어)

➡ _____

09 다음 빈칸 (A)~(C)에 알맞은 단어를 넣어 *Jikji*에 대한 소개를 완성하시오.

> *Jikji* is a book that changed the history of (A)_____ because it turned out that *Jikji* was the (B)_____ book in the world that was printed with (C)_____ _____ _____.

[10~12] 다음 글을 읽고 물음에 답하시오.

On May 27, 2011, 297 books of *Uigwe*, a collection of royal books the French army took in 1866, came back to Korea. ⓐThe person (___) this return is Dr. Park Byeong-seon, a historian who spent her whole life searching for Korean national treasures abroad.

Q: Can you tell me how you became interested in *Uigwe*?

Dr. Park: I studied history in college. I went to France to continue my studies in 1955. As you know, the French army took many of our national treasures in 1866. I wanted to find ⓑthem while I was studying there. *Uigwe* was one of them.

10 다음과 같은 뜻이 되도록 위 글의 밑줄 친 ⓐ의 빈칸에 들어갈 알맞은 한 단어를 쓰시오.

> The person who made this return possible

➡ _____

11 위 글의 밑줄 친 ⓑthem이 가리키는 것을 영어로 쓰시오.

➡ _____
_____

12 다음 빈칸 (A)~(C)에 알맞은 단어를 넣어 *Uigwe*에 대한 소개를 완성하시오.

> It is a collection of (A)_____ _____ of Korea which the French army took in 1866. Thanks to the effort of (B)_____ _____ _____ _____, however, it came back to Korea from France on May 27, 2011.

After You Read C Think and Talk

A: What do you think about Dr. Park?
<u>How(x)</u>

B: I think she had a strong will. She had many difficulties, but she didn't give
   think와 she 사이에 접속사 that 생략
   up.

C: I think she had a great passion for her work. As a historian, she was very
                                    ~에 대한   ~으로서(역할, 자격)
   passionate about finding Korean national treasures abroad.
   전치사 다음에 동명사를 쓴다.   해외에 있는 한국의 문화재

구문해설 • will: 의지 • give up: 포기하다 • passion: 열정 • passionate: 열정적인

해석

A: 박 박사에 대해 어떻게 생각하니?

B: 그녀는 강한 의지를 가졌다고 생각해. 그녀는 많은 어려움을 겪었지만 포기하지 않았어.

C: 그녀는 자신의 일에 대해 강한 열정을 가졌다고 생각해. 역사학자로서, 그녀는 해외에 있는 한국의 문화재를 찾는 것에 대해 매우 열정적이었어.

Think and Write Step 2

An Interview with Kim Yubin

The following is the interview I had with Kim Yubin, a local police officer.
다음은   Kim Yubin을 설명하는 동격어구다.

Q: Can you tell me when and where you were born?
   tell의 직접목적어로 '의문사+주어+동사' 어순의 간접의문문

A: I was born in Seoul on March 11, 1980.
   태어났다

Q: I'd like to know what your goal in life is.
   '~하고 싶다'(= want to) know의 목적어로 '의문사+주어+동사' 어순의 간접의문문

A: My goal in life is to make a better world.
                   보어 자리에 사용된 부정사의 명사적 용법

Q: Can you tell me what you like about your job?
   tell의 직접목적어로 '의문사+주어+동사' 어순의 간접의문문

A: I like helping people.

I think that Kim Yubin is a great police officer.
       명사절을 이끄는 접속사

구문해설 • interview: 인터뷰 • be born: 태어나다 • would like to+동사원형: ~하고 싶다
         • goal: 목표

김유빈 씨와의 인터뷰
다음은 제가 지역 경찰관 김유빈 씨와 한 인터뷰입니다.
Q: 당신은 언제, 어디서 태어나셨는지 말씀해 주시겠어요?
A: 저는 1980년 3월 11일에 서울에서 태어났어요.
Q: 당신의 인생의 목표가 무엇인지 알고 싶어요.
A: 저의 인생의 목표는 더 나은 세상을 만드는 것입니다.
Q: 당신의 직업에 관해 당신이 좋아하는 것이 무엇인지 말씀해 주시겠어요?
A: 저는 사람들을 돕는 것이 좋아요.
저는 김유빈 씨가 대단한 경찰관이라고 생각합니다.

Team Project Create

Jikji, South Korea's National Treasure No. 1132

Jikji was printed at Heungdeoksa in 1377. It is now in the National Library of
      수동태
France, in Paris. It is the world's oldest book that was printed with movable
                              최상급   수동태   금속활자
metal type.

구문해설 • treasure: 보물 • National Library: 국립도서관 • movable: 움직일 수 있는, 이동할 수
         있는 • metal: 금속

직지, 한국의 국보 1132번
직지는 1377년 흥덕사에서 인쇄되었다. 현재는 파리의 프랑스 국립도서관에 있다. 직지는 금속활자로 인쇄된 세계에서 가장 오래된 책이다.

01 다음 단어 중 나머지 넷과 성격이 다른 하나는?

① fire   ② allow   ③ return
④ display   ⑤ flash

02 다음 빈칸 ⓐ와 ⓑ에 들어갈 단어가 바르게 짝지어진 것은?

- As you know, the French army took many of our national   ⓐ   in 1866.
- At a book exhibition in Paris in 1972, *Jikji* was   ⓑ   as the oldest book in the world.

① values – displayed
② value – fired
③ treasures – spent
④ treasures – displayed
⑤ treasures – returned

[03~04] 다음 영영 풀이에 해당하는 것을 고르시오.

03

used for saying that someone or something is responsible for something good that happened

① at last   ② look for
③ thanks to   ④ right away
⑤ give up

04

the work of finding out facts about something

① research   ② silver
③ result   ④ government
⑤ flash

05 다음 문장의 빈칸에 공통으로 들어갈 알맞은 말을 쓰시오.

- It wasn't easy for him, but he didn't _____ _____.
- They don't _____ _____ easily even though they fail many times.

06 다음 중 밑줄 친 부분의 뜻이 잘못된 것은?

① They even thought that I was a Korean spy and <u>fired</u> me. (해고했다)
② I went to the library every day to finish my <u>research</u>. (연구)
③ The results of your research were <u>published</u> as a book in Korea in 1990. (입증되었다)
④ I knew <u>right away</u> that it was very special. (바로)
⑤ <u>As soon as</u> I became a researcher at the National Library in 1967, I began to look for *Uigwe*. (~하자마자)

07 다음 대화의 밑줄 친 ⓐ의 의도로 알맞은 것은?

W: Excuse me, but ⓐ<u>is it OK if I park my car here?</u>
M: Did you come to Star Theater?
W: No. I came to Tim's Restaurant.
M: I'm sorry, but this parking lot is only for the customers of the theater.
W: Oh. I didn't know that.

① 금지하기   ② 좋아하는 것 묻기
③ 허락 구하기   ④ 부탁하기
⑤ 예정된 것 말하기

[08~10] 다음 대화를 읽고 물음에 답하시오.

G: Excuse me, but is it OK to try on this hanbok? (①)

M: Sure. The fitting room is over there.

G: Thanks. Wait a minute. (②)

M: Oh, the little hat over there? (③)

G: Yes. What is it?

M: It's a jokduri, a traditional Korean hat for women. (④) It's usually worn on a wedding day.

G: Really? Is it OK to try it on, too? (⑤)

M: I'm sorry, but (A)그것은 전시만 하는 거예요. Trying it on is not allowed.

G: Oh. Then, I'll just try on this hanbok.

08 다음 주어진 문장이 들어갈 위치로 알맞은 것은?

That's also very pretty.

①   ②   ③   ④   ⑤

09 다음 질문에 대한 답을 위 대화에서 찾아 쓰시오.

Q: What two things does the girl want to try on?

➡ She _____.

10 위 대화의 밑줄 친 (A)의 우리말에 맞게 주어진 단어를 이용하여 영어로 쓰시오. (four words)

only / display

➡ _____

11 다음 대화의 밑줄 친 (A)~(E) 중 어법상 어색한 것은?

A: (A)Which place do you want to go to first in the museum?

B: (B)Why don't you guess?

A: OK. (C)Is it OK to use smartphones there?

B: Yes. (D)Using smartphones are allowed.

A: Is it OK to take pictures?

B: No. Taking pictures is not allowed.

A: I got it. You're thinking of (E)going to the Gift Shop.

B: You're right.

① (A)   ② (B)   ③ (C)   ④ (D)   ⑤ (E)

12 우리말에 맞게 영어로 바르게 표현하지 <u>않은</u> 것은?

① 알아맞혀 볼래?

   → Why don't you guess?

② 저는 이런 음식을 한번도 본 적이 없어요.

   → I've never seen any food like this.

③ 저기에 앉아도 되나요?

   → Is it OK to sit over there?

④ 그것은 여자들이 쓰는 한국 전통 모자인 족두리예요.

   → It's a jokduri, a traditional Korean hat for women.

⑤ 헬스장은 저쪽입니다.

   → The fitting room is over there.

13 다음에 제시된 단어와 〈조건〉에 맞게 아래 대화의 빈칸을 완성하시오.

┌─── 조건 ───┐

(A) • 앉아도 되는지 허가 여부를 묻는 표현을 쓸 것.
　　• to sit / over there
(B) • (A)의 물음에 대한 금지의 답을 쓸 것.
　　• 동명사를 이용할 것.
　　• allow를 이용할 것.

A: Excuse me. _____ (A)
B: You mean, on the grass?
A: Yes. Is it all right?
B: I'm sorry, but ____ (B) ____.
A: OK, I understand.

(A) _____

(B) _____

14 다음 대화를 읽고 아래 물음에 영어로 답하시오.

G: Excuse me, but is it OK to try on this hanbok?
M: Sure. The fitting room is over there.
G: Thanks. Wait a minute. That's also very pretty.
M: Oh, the little hat over there?
G: Yes. What is it?
M: It's a jokduri, a traditional Korean hat for women. It's usually worn on a wedding day.
G: Really? Is it OK to try it on, too?
M: I'm sorry, but it's only for display. Trying it on is not allowed.
G: Oh. Then, I'll just try on this hanbok.

Q: Is trying on a jokduri allowed?
➡ _____, _____ _____. The jokduri is only _____.

15 다음 문장의 빈칸에 공통으로 들어갈 알맞은 말을 쓰시오.

• The game was cancelled _____ of the storm.
• I had to stay home all day _____ I had a bad cold.

16 다음 중 어법상 바르지 <u>않은</u> 것은?

① I'd like to know what color the thief's hair was.
② Can you tell me what you like about your job?
③ I wonder who you danced with at the party.
④ Do you have any idea what is going to happen?
⑤ However, she is not sure she will return in the future.

17 다음 문장을 두 문장으로 나누어 쓰시오.

(1) I'm not sure if my grandfather will like my present.
　➡ _____

(2) Can you tell me where the bathroom is?
　➡ _____

(3) I'd like to know who you met at the party.
　➡ _____

(4) Did you know who was in the classroom?
　➡ _____

(5) What do you think Jane's secret is?
　➡ _____

(6) I'm curious if you can lend me the book.
　➡ _____

18 다음 밑줄 친 ㎃[if]의 쓰임이 나머지 넷과 다른 하나를 고르시오.

① She is not sure *if* it's a great idea.

② I asked her *if* she knew French.

③ I can't hear you *if* you don't speak loudly.

④ Please tell me *if* there's anything I can do to help you.

⑤ We have no idea *if* they like it or not.

19 다음 우리말을 영어로 바르게 옮긴 것은?

> 얼마나 오래 여기 머물지 내게 말해 줄 수 있니?

① How long can you tell me you will stay here?

② How long will you stay here can you tell me?

③ Can you tell me how long will you stay here?

④ Can you tell me how long you will stay here?

⑤ Can you tell me how you will stay here long?

Reading

[20~22] 다음 글을 읽고 물음에 답하시오.

ⓐOn May 27, 2011, 297 books of *Uigwe*, a collection of royal books the French army took them in 1866, came back to Korea. The person behind this return is Dr. Park Byeong-seon, a historian who spent her whole life searching for Korean national treasures abroad.

Q: Can you tell me how you became interested in *Uigwe*?

Dr. Park: I studied history in college. I went to France to continue my studies in 1955. As you know, the French army took many of our national treasures in 1866. I wanted to find them ⓑwhile I was studying there. *Uigwe* was one of them.

20 위 글의 밑줄 친 ⓐ에서 어법상 틀린 부분을 찾아 고치시오.

＿＿＿＿＿ ➡ ＿＿＿＿＿

21 위 글의 밑줄 친 ⓑ를 다음과 같이 바꿔 쓸 때 빈칸에 들어갈 알맞은 말을 쓰시오.

> ＿＿＿＿ my stay there for study

22 위 글을 읽고 대답할 수 <u>없는</u> 질문은?

① When was *Uigwe* returned to Korea?

② What did Dr. Park study in college?

③ When did the French army take *Uigwe*?

④ How long did it take for Dr. Park to find *Uigwe*?

⑤ When did Dr. Park want to find our national treasures abroad?

[23~26] 다음 글을 읽고 물음에 답하시오.

Q: I'm sure you were very excited when you found the books.

Dr. Park: Yes, I was, but more difficulties were waiting for me. I thought that the books should be returned to Korea, but my bosses at the library didn't like that idea. They even thought that I was a Korean spy and fired me. After that, I had to go to the library ⓐas a visitor, so it was not easy to do research on *Uigwe*. However, I didn't give up. For more than ten years, I went to the library every day to finish my research. ⓑI wanted to show people the value of *Uigwe*.

23 위 글의 밑줄 친 @as와 같은 의미로 쓰인 것을 고르시오.

① As the door was open, I walked in.
② Her anger grew as she talked.
③ My sister runs as fast as you.
④ She came up as I was speaking.
⑤ He was famous as a poet.

24 Why did Dr. Park have to go to the library as a visitor? Fill in the blanks with the suitable words.

> Because her _____ at the library thought that she was a Korean spy and _____ her.

25 위 글의 밑줄 친 ⓑ와 같은 뜻이 되도록 빈칸에 알맞을 말을 쓰시오.

> I wanted to show the value of *Uigwe* _____ people.

26 위 글의 내용과 일치하지 않는 것은?

① Dr. Park was very excited when she found the books.
② More difficulties were awaiting her after Dr. Park found the books.
③ Dr. Park's bosses at the library thought that the books should be returned to Korea.
④ It was hard for Dr. Park to do research on *Uigwe*.
⑤ For over ten years, Dr. Park went to the library every day in order that she could finish her research.

[27~29] 다음 글을 읽고 물음에 답하시오.

Q: Before I finish this interview, I'd like to ask you about *Jikji*, ①a book that changed the history of printing.

Dr. Park: I found ②it in my first year at the library. I knew @right away that ③it was very special. I worked hard to prove its value and finally succeeded. At ④a book exhibition in Paris in 1972, *Jikji* was displayed as ⑤the oldest book in the world that was printed with movable metal type.

Q: Dr. Park, thanks to your hard work, *Jikji* and *Uigwe* were found, and all Koreans thank you for that.

Dr. Park: I hope people will become more interested in our national treasures abroad and work for their return.

27 위 글의 밑줄 친 ①~⑤ 중에서 가리키는 대상이 나머지 넷과 다른 것은?

①   ②   ③   ④   ⑤

28 위 글의 밑줄 친 @right away와 바꿔 쓸 수 있는 한 단어를 쓰시오. (i로 시작할 것.)

➡ _____

29 위 글의 주제로 알맞은 것을 고르시오.

① Learn how to finish the interview well.
② Thanks to Dr. Park, the value of *Jikji* was found.
③ Dr. Park found *Jikji* in her first year at the library.
④ Koreans thank Dr. Park for her hard work.
⑤ Dr. Park hopes for the return of our national treasures abroad.

출제율 95%

01 다음 글의 괄호 안에서 알맞은 단어를 선택하시오.

> On May 27, 2011, 297 books of *Uigwe*, a collection of [loyal / royal] books the French army took in 1866, came back to Korea.

출제율 90%

02 다음 영영 풀이에 해당하는 단어는?

> a bright light on a camera that flashes as you take a photograph in order to provide enough light

① silver　　② result　　③ flash
④ success　　⑤ pride

출제율 90%

03 다음 글의 괄호 (A)~(C)에서 알맞은 단어를 고르시오.

> I thought that the books should be (A)[stolen / returned] to Korea, but my bosses at the library didn't like that idea. They even thought that I was a Korean spy and fired me. After that, I had to go to the library as (B)[a visitor / an employee], so it was not easy to do research on *Uigwe*. However, I didn't give up. For more than ten years, I went to the library every day to finish my research. I wanted to show people the (C)[return / value] of *Uigwe*.

① stolen – a visitor – return
② stolen – an employee – value
③ returned – a visitor – return
④ returned – an employee – return
⑤ returned – a visitor – value

출제율 100%

04 다음 대화의 밑줄 친 부분 중 어법상 어색한 것은?

> G: Excuse me. ⓐIs it OK to take pictures here?
> M: Yes, it's all right.
> G: ⓑHow about to use a flash? ⓒCan I use it, too?
> M: ⓓI'm afraid not. ⓔUsing a flash is not allowed here.
> G: Oh, I see. Thank you.

① ⓐ　　② ⓑ　　③ ⓒ　　④ ⓓ　　⑤ ⓔ

출제율 95%

05 다음 글의 밑줄 친 (A)~(E)의 해석으로 틀린 것은?

> Before I (A)finish this interview, I'd like to ask you about *Jikji*, a book that changed the history of (B)printing.
> Dr. Park: I found it in my first year at the library. I knew right away that it was very special. I worked hard to (C)prove its value and finally succeeded. At a book (D)exhibition in Paris in 1972, *Jikji* was displayed as the oldest book in the world that was printed with (E)movable metal type.

① (A) 끝내다　　② (B) 인쇄
③ (C) 발견하다　　④ (D) 박람회
⑤ (E) 금속활자

[06~07] 다음 대화를 읽고 물음에 답하시오.

> A: Which place do you want to go first in the museum?
> B: Why don't you guess?
> A: OK. ＿＿＿＿＿＿(A)＿＿＿＿＿＿
> B: Yes. Eating food is allowed.
> A: Is it OK to take pictures?
> B: No. (B)사진을 찍는 것은 허용되지 않아.
> A: I got it. You're thinking of going to the Video Room.
> B: You're right.

06 위 대화의 (A)에 들어갈 말로 알맞은 것을 고르시오.

① Is it OK to sit over there?

② Is it OK to eat food there?

③ Can I play it?

④ Is it OK to take pictures here?

⑤ Do you mind if I eat food there?

출제율 85%

07 위 대화의 밑줄 친 (B)의 우리말에 맞게 다음 문장의 빈칸을 채우시오. (allow를 이용할 것.)

_____ pictures _____ not _____.

[08~09] 다음 대화를 읽고 물음에 답하시오.

G: Excuse me, but is it OK ____ⓐ____ this hanbok?

M: Sure. The fitting room is over there.

G: Thanks. Wait a minute. (A)That is also very pretty.

M: Oh, the little hat over there?

G: Yes. What is it?

M: It's a jokduri, a ____ⓑ____ Korean hat for women. It's usually worn on a wedding day.

G: Really? Is it OK to try it on, too?

M: I'm sorry, but it's only for ____ⓒ____. Trying it on is not allowed.

G: Oh. Then, I'll just try on this hanbok.

출제율 90%

08 위 대화의 ⓐ~ⓒ에 들어갈 말로 알맞은 것은?

① if you – traditional – display

② if you – modern – women

③ to try on– traditional – display

④ to try on – modern – display

⑤ to try on – traditional – women

출제율 95%

09 위 대화의 밑줄 친 (A)가 가리키는 말을 본문에서 찾아 세 단어로 쓰시오.

➡ _____

출제율 9%

10 다음 대화의 빈칸 ⓐ, ⓑ에 'allow'를 알맞은 형태로 바꾸어 쓰시오.

A: Which place do you want to go to first in the museum?
B: Why don't you guess?
A: OK. Is it OK to use smartphones there?
B: Yes. Using smartphones ⓐ_____ _____.
A: Is it OK to eat food?
B: OK. Eating food ⓑ_____ _____.
A: I got it. You're thinking of going to the Restaurant.
B: You're right.

출제율 100%

11 다음 중 어법상 옳은 것은?

① I want to know how did you spend your vacation.

② Please tell me where the book is.

③ I wonder if or not she got angry at me.

④ We didn't win the game because my mistake.

⑤ You can't watch the movie because of you're not old enough.

출제율 90%

12 다음 두 문장을 한 문장으로 쓰시오.

(1) Do you think? What is the best way to encourage kids to study more?

➡ _____

_____

(2) Can you tell me? Who is your favorite actor?

➡ _____

(3) The car accident happened. The road was slippery.

➡ _____

_____

(4) Tina ran into the house. It started to rain.

➡ _____

_____

출제율 100%

13 다음 그림을 보고 주어진 어휘를 이용하여 빈칸에 알맞은 말을 쓰시오.

A: Can you tell me _____
_____? (in your free time, like doing, what)?
B: I like riding a horse a lot.
A: Why do you like riding a horse?
B: I enjoy riding a horse _____
_____. (it, fun, really)

출제율 95%

14 because와 because of를 이용하여 두 문장을 한 문장으로 각각 연결하시오.

(1) I went to the school health room.
I had a headache.

➡ _____

_____

(2) He got food poisoning.
He ate undercooked chicken.

➡ _____

_____

_____

[15~18] 다음 글을 읽고 물음에 답하시오.

On May 27, 2011, 297 books of *Uigwe*, a collection of (A)[loyal / royal] books the French army took in 1866, came back to Korea. The person behind this return is Dr. Park Byeong-seon, ⓐ해외에 있는 한국의 문화재를 찾기 위해 전 생애를 바친 역사학자.

Q: Can you tell me how you became (B) [interesting / interested] in *Uigwe*?

Dr. Park: I studied history in college. I went to France ⓑto continue my studies in 1955. As you know, the French army took many of our national treasures in 1866. I wanted to find them (C)[during / while] I was studying there. *Uigwe* was one of them.

출제율 90%

15 위 글의 괄호 (A)~(C)에서 문맥이나 어법상 알맞은 낱말을 골라 쓰시오.

(A) _____ (B) _____ (C) _____

출제율 85%

16 위 글의 밑줄 친 ⓐ의 우리말에 맞게 주어진 어휘를 이용하여 13 단어로 영작하시오.

> who, searching, Korean national treasures abroad

➡ _____

_____

출제율 90%

17 위 글의 밑줄 친 ⓑto continue와 to부정사의 용법이 다른 것을 고르시오. (2개)

① Was it possible to continue her studies in France?

② She left for France to continue her studies.

③ She was happy to continue her studies in France.

④ Did she want to continue her studies?

⑤ She must be a woman of strong will to continue her studies abroad.

출제율 100%

18 위 글을 읽고 박병선 박사에 대해 알 수 없는 것을 고르시오.

① What did Dr. Park Byeong-seon do throughout her lifetime?

② What subject did she study in college?

③ How old was she when she went to France?

④ Why did she go to France?

⑤ What did she want to find while she was studying in France?

[19~22] 다음 글을 읽고 물음에 답하시오.

Q: You found 297 books of *Uigwe* in the National Library of France, in Paris. Please tell me how you found them.

Dr. Park: ⓐAs soon as I became a researcher at the National Library in 1967, I began to look ___(A)___ *Uigwe*. After 10 years, in 1977, I finally found the books. I think I looked ___(B)___ ⓑmore than 30 millions books.

출제율 95%

19 위 글의 빈칸 (A)와 (B)에 들어갈 전치사가 바르게 짝지어진 것은?

① for – after   ② at – for

③ for – at   ④ at – after

⑤ with – for

출제율 90%

20 위 글의 밑줄 친 ⓐAs soon as와 바꿔 쓸 수 없는 말을 고르시오.

① Directly   ② Exactly

③ The moment   ④ The instant

⑤ Immediately

출제율 90%

21 위 글의 밑줄 친 ⓑ에서 어법상 틀린 부분을 찾아 고치시오.

_____ ➡ _____

출제율 95%

22 다음 문장에서 위 글의 내용과 다른 부분을 찾아서 고치시오.

> In 1967, Dr. Park became a researcher at the National Library of France, in Paris, and in 1977, she tried to find 297 books of *Uigwe*.

_____ ➡ _____

01 아래 〈조건〉에 맞게 주어진 단어를 이용하여 빈칸에 알맞은 말을 쓰시오.

> B: Excuse me. What's this? It looks interesting.
> W: Oh, that's a haegeum, a traditional Korean musical instrument.
> B: (A) _____
> W: I'm sorry, but it's only for display.
> (B) _____
> B: I see.

> ┤ 조건 ├
> (A) • 해금을 연주해도 되는지 허가 여부를 묻는 표현을 쓸 것.
> • if절을 쓸 것.
> • OK, it을 이용할 것.
> (B) • 금지하는 표현을 5 단어로 쓸 것.
> • must를 이용할 것.

02 다음 그림을 보고 '허락과 금지'의 표현을 사용하여 대화의 빈칸을 완성하시오.

> ┤ 조건 ├
> • 동명사 주어로 시작할 것.
> • allow를 이용할 것.

> A: Which place do you want to go to first in the museum?
> B: Why don't you guess?
> A: OK. Is it OK to use smartphones there?
> B: Yes. (A) _____.
> A: Is it OK to take pictures?
> B: No. (B) _____.
> A: I got it. You're thinking of going to the Gift Shop.
> B: You're right.

03 두 문장을 한 문장으로 만들었을 때, 나머지 한 문장을 쓰시오.

(1) • I want to ask you.
• _____
➡ I want to ask you what you like to do.

(2) • I'm not sure.
• _____
➡ I'm not sure if my boss will accept my idea.

(3) • I was very tired.
• _____
➡ I was very tired because I worked all day yesterday.

04 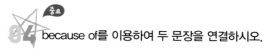 because of를 이용하여 두 문장을 연결하시오.

(1) There was a heavy rain. I stayed home.
➡ _____

(2) I had a high fever. I couldn't sleep last night.
➡ _____

05 괄호 안에 주어진 어휘를 이용하여 다음 우리말을 영작하시오.

(1) 그녀는 불편한 신발 때문에 달릴 수 없었다. (her uncomfortable shoes)
➡ _____
_____

(2) Mark는 일을 해야 해서 우리와 함께 하지 않았다. (us, join, work, have to)
➡ _____

(3) 너는 그녀가 어디에 갔는지 알고 있니? (know)
➡ _____

(4) 그녀는 자기가 그 영화를 보았는지 기억할 수 없었다. (remember, watch)
➡ _____
_____

[06~08] 다음 글을 읽고 물음에 답하시오.

On May 27, 2011, 297 books of *Uigwe*, a collection of royal books the French army took in 1866, ⓐcame back to Korea. The person behind this return is Dr. Park Byeong-seon, ⓑa historian who spent her whole life to search for Korean national treasures abroad.

Q: Can you tell me how you became interested in *Uigwe*?

Dr. Park: I studied history in college. I went to France to continue my studies in 1955. As you know, the French army took many of our national treasures in 1866. I wanted to find them while I was studying there. *Uigwe* was one of them.

06 How did Dr. Park Byeong-seon become interested in *Uigwe*? Fill in the blanks with the suitable words.

> She went to France to continue to study history (A)_____ _____. While she was studying there, she wanted to find many of our (B)_____ _____ that the French army took (C)_____ _____ and *Uigwe* was one of them.

07 위 글의 밑줄 친 ⓐ를 다음과 같이 바꿔 쓸 때 빈칸에 들어갈 알맞은 말을 본문의 한 단어를 변형하여 쓰시오.

> _____ _____ to Korea

08 위 글의 밑줄 친 ⓑ에서 어법상 틀린 부분을 찾아 고치시오.

_____ ➡ _____

[09~11] 다음 글을 읽고 물음에 답하시오.

Q: I'm sure you were very excited when you (A)[found / founded] the books.

Dr. Park: Yes, I (B)[am / was], but ⓐmore difficulties were waiting for me. I thought that ⓑthe books should be returned to Korea, but my bosses at the library didn't like that idea. They even thought that I was a Korean spy and fired me. After that, I had to go to the library as a (C)[librarian / visitor], so it was not easy to do research on *Uigwe*. However, I didn't give up. For more than ten years, I went to the library every day to finish my research. I wanted to show people the value of *Uigwe*.

09 위 글의 괄호 (A)~(C)에서 문맥이나 어법상 알맞은 낱말을 골라 쓰시오.

(A) _____ (B) _____ (C) _____

10 위 글의 ⓐmore difficulties에 해당하는 것 세 가지를 우리말로 쓰시오.

(1) _____

_____

(2) _____

_____

(3) _____

11 위 글의 밑줄 친 ⓑ를 they로 시작하여 능동태로 고치시오.

➡ _____

01 다음 주어진 정보를 이용하여 대화의 빈칸을 완성하시오.

> allowed: set up a tent / not allowed: fish in the lake

> G: Excuse me. _____?
> M: Yes, it's all right.
> G: _____ fishing in the lake? Can I fish in the lake, too?
> M: I'm _____. Fishing in the lake _____.
> G: Oh, I see. Thank you.

02 주어진 어구를 이용하여 자신의 경우를 생각하여 쓰시오.

> ─ 보기 ─
> because … / because of … / I don't know …

(1) _____

(2) _____

(3) _____

03 다음 내용을 바탕으로 박병선 박사에 관한 미니북을 만드시오.

> In 1955: • studied history in college • went to France to continue to study history
> In 1967: • became a researcher at the National Library • began to look for *Uigwe*
> In 1972: • found *Jikji* • worked hard to prove value of *Jikji* • finally, displayed at a book exhibition
> In 1977: • she looked at more than 30 million books • she finally found *Uigwe*
> In 1990: • result of research on *Uigwe* published as a book in Korea
> In 2011: • *Uigwe* came back to Korea • spent whole life for Korean treasure

> Dr. Park Byeong-seon
> In 1955, she studied history and went to France (A)_____ to study histoy.
> In 1967, she became (B)_____ at the National Library and began to look for (C)_____.
> In 1972, she found (D)_____ and worked hard to prove the value of *Jikji*. Finally, *Jikji* was displayed at a book exhibition.
> In 1977, after she looked at (E)_____, she finally found *Uigwe*.
> In 1990, the results of her research on *Uigwe* (F)_____ as a book in Korea.
> In 2011, *Uigwe* came back to Korea. She spent her whole life for Korean national treasures abroad.

단원별 모의고사

01 다음 단어에 대한 영어 설명이 <u>어색한</u> 것은?

① fitting room: a room in a clothes shop where you can put on clothes before you buy them

② silver: a shiny white metal that people use for making jewelry and other valuable things

③ succeed: to do something that you tried or aimed to do

④ government: the group of people who are responsible for controlling a country or state

⑤ aboard: in or to a foreign country

02 다음 글의 빈칸에 공통으로 들어갈 말을 주어진 철자로 쓰시오.

• To get the best r_____, you have to do your best.

• Disease can often r_____ from poverty.

03 다음 영영풀이에 해당하는 단어를 고르시오.

to try to find someone or something by looking very carefully

① search   ② allow

③ spend   ④ prove

⑤ publish

[04~05] 다음 대화의 빈칸에 들어갈 말로 알맞은 것을 고르시오.

04

B: Excuse me. What's this? It looks interesting.

W: Oh, that's a haegeum, a traditional Korean musical instrument.

B: Is it OK to play it?

W: I'm sorry, but it's only for display.

_____

B: I see.

① Playing it is allowed.

② How about playing the haegeum?

③ You can play it.

④ Playing it is not allowed.

⑤ I play it well.

05

A: Which place do you want to go first in the museum?

B: Why don't you guess?

A: OK. _____

B: Yes. Eating food is allowed.

A: Is it OK to take pictures?

B: No. Taking pictures is not allowed.

① Do I have to eat food there?

② Is it OK to eat food there?

③ Where can we eat food?

④ Do you mind if I eat food there?

⑤ When did you eat food there?

06 다음 중 짝지어진 대화가 <u>어색한</u> 것은?

① A: Excuse me, but is it OK to take pictures here?
B: Yes. Go ahead.

② A: What's this? It looks interesting.
B: Oh, that's a janggu, a traditional Korean musical instrument.

③ A: Excuse me. Is it OK to sit over there?
B: I'm sorry, but sitting on the grass is allowed.

④ A: Excuse me, but is it OK if I try on this jacket?
B: Sure. The fitting room is over there.

⑤ A: Is it OK to take pictures?
B: No. Taking pictures is not allowed.

[07~09] 다음 대화를 읽고 물음에 답하시오.

Kate: Excuse me, but _____(A)_____
Man: Sure. The fitting room is over there.
Kate: Thanks. Wait a minute. That's also very pretty.
Man: Oh, the little hat over there?
Kate: Yes. What is it?
Man: It's a jokduri, a traditional Korean hat for women. It's usually worn on a wedding day.
Kate: Really? Is it OK to try it on, too?
Man: I'm sorry, but it's only for display. Trying it on is not allowed.
Kate: Oh. Then, I'll just try on this hanbok.

07 위 대화의 빈칸 (A)에 들어갈 말로 알맞은 것은?

① is it OK to take pictures here?
② is it OK to eat food there?
③ is it OK to sit here?
④ is it OK to try on this hanbok?
⑤ is it OK to play it?

08 What is Kate going to do?

➡ She is _____.

09 위 대화를 읽고 Kate가 쓴 글을 완성하시오.

Today, I tried on a hanbok. I also wanted to try on a jokduri, a _____ Korean hat for _____, but I could not. It was only for _____, so trying it on was not _____. A jokduri is usually worn on a _____ _____.

10 다음 대화의 빈칸에 들어갈 말은?

G: Excuse me, but is it OK to take pictures here?
M: _____
G: Can I use a flash, too?
M: Yes. That's also OK.
G: I'm sorry, but I have one more question. Can I eat food here?
M: I'm sorry, but that's not allowed.

① I'm sorry, but you can't.
② I'm afraid not.
③ You are not allowed to do that.
④ Yes. Go ahead.
⑤ You can't do that.

11 다음 대화의 빈칸에 들어갈 말은?

A: Which place do you want to go to first in the museum?
B: Why don't you guess?
A: OK. Is it OK to use smartphones there?
B: Yes. Using smartphones is allowed.
A: Is it OK to take pictures?
B: No. _____
A: I got it. You're thinking of going to the Gift Shop.
B: You're right.

① Taking pictures is allowed.
② Of course.
③ Taking pictures is not allowed.
④ You can take pictures.
⑤ That's also OK.

12 다음 중 빈칸에 들어갈 말이 나머지 넷과 다른 것은?

① Jim couldn't take a nap _____ the room was too hot.
② There was a heavy snow, _____ the road was closed.
③ The children were hungry _____ there was no food in the house.
④ Many Koreans became interested in *Jikji* _____ of her book .
⑤ Peter couldn't play soccer _____ it rained.

13 다음 밑줄 친 부분의 쓰임이 나머지 넷과 다른 것은?

① I'm not sure if we're going to find her.
② Mariel asked me if I would love her forever.
③ I wonder if the news is true.
④ You may fail if you are lazy.
⑤ Please see if the children are dressed for school.

14 다음 빈칸에 알맞은 표현을 모두 고르시오.

I was late this morning _____ there was heavy traffic.

① because of ② because ③ so
④ if ⑤ since

15 다음 두 문장을 간접의문문을 이용하여 한 문장으로 쓰시오.

(1) I don't know. + Who broke the window?
➡ _____
(2) Tell me. + How did you find the key?
➡ _____
(3) I have no idea. + Does he loves me or not?
➡ _____
(4) Do you think? + Who will be selected as the best player of the game?
➡ _____
_____

16 주어진 어휘를 이용하여 다음 우리말을 영작하시오. (because나 간접의문문을 이용하여 쓸 것.)

(1) 나는 조부모님이 멀리 사시기 때문에 자주 뵙지 못한다. (my grandparents, see, live, often, far away)
➡ _____
(2) 그들은 그녀의 일 때문에 일본으로 이사 갔다. (move, job)
➡ _____
(3) 그의 부주의 때문에 사고가 일어났다. (the accident, his carelessness, happen)
➡ _____
(4) Minho는 Kevin이 장래에 무엇이 되고 싶은지 알고 있다. (want, be, in the future)
➡ _____
(5) Daniel은 그가 전화를 어디에 두었는지 확신하지 못한다. (put, sure, his phone)
➡ _____
(6) 사장님이 지금 당신을 만나실 수 있는지 확인해 보겠습니다. (the president, check, meet)
➡ _____

[17~18] 다음 글을 읽고 물음에 답하시오.

On May 27, 2011, 297 books of *Uigwe*, a collection of royal books the French army took in 1866, came back to Korea. The person behind this return is Dr. Park Byeong-seon, a historian ___ⓐ___ spent her whole life searching for Korean national treasures abroad.

Q: Can you tell me how you became interested in *Uigwe*?

Dr. Park: I studied history in college. I went to France to continue my studies in 1955. As you know, the French army took many of our national treasures in 1866. I wanted to find them while I was studying there. *Uigwe* was one of them.

17 위 글의 빈칸 ⓐ에 들어갈 알맞은 말을 쓰시오.

➡ _____

18 다음 빈칸 (A)와 (B)에 알맞은 단어를 넣어 박병선 박사에 대한 소개를 완성하시오.

> Dr. Park Byeong-seon was (A)_____
> _____ who spent her whole life searching for Korean national treasures (B)_____.

[19~21] 다음 글을 읽고 물음에 답하시오.

Q: I'm sure you were very excited when you found the books.

Dr. Park: Yes, I was, but more difficulties were waiting for me. I thought that the books should be returned to Korea, but my bosses at the library didn't like ⓐthat idea. They even thought that I was a Korean spy and fired me. After that, I had to go to the library as a visitor, so it was not easy ⓑto do research on *Uigwe*. However, I didn't give up. For more than ten years, I went to the library every day to finish my research. I wanted to show people the value of *Uigwe*.

Q: The results of your research were published as a book in Korea in 1990. Many Koreans became interested in *Uigwe* ⓒbecause of your book.

Dr. Park: Yes. In 1992, the Korean government asked the French government for its return and, finally, the 297 books are here now.

19 위 글의 밑줄 친 ⓐthat idea가 가리키는 것을 본문에서 찾아 쓰시오.

➡ _____

20 아래 〈보기〉에서 위 글의 밑줄 친 ⓑto do와 to부정사의 용법이 같은 것의 개수를 고르시오.

> ┤ 보기 ├
> ① He stopped to listen to music.
> ② Do you have any questions to ask?
> ③ He didn't want to do it.
> ④ She came home early to help her mother.
> ⑤ My dream is to be a famous pianist.

① 1개   ② 2개   ③ 3개   ④ 4개   ⑤ 5개

21 위 글의 밑줄 친 ⓒbecause of와 바꿔 쓸 수 없는 말을 고르시오.

① thanks to   ② owing to

③ due to   ④ because

⑤ on account of

Special

Creative Ideas in Stories

Words & Expressions

Key Words

- **batter** [bǽtər] 명 반죽
- **before** [bifɔ́ːr] 전 ~ 전에
- **button** [bʌ́tən] 명 버튼, 단추
- **counter** [káuntər] 명 계산대
- **creative** [kriéitiv] 형 창의적인
- **delicious** [dilíʃəs] 형 맛있는
- **diamond** [dáiəmənd] 명 다이아몬드
- **doughnut** [dóunət] 명 도넛
- **drop** [drɑp] 동 떨어지다
- **enough** [inʌ́f] 형 충분한
- **find** [faind] 동 찾다 (-found-found)
- **fresh** [freʃ] 형 신선한
- **fun** [fʌn] 형 재미있는, 즐거운
- **happen** [hǽpən] 동 발생하다, 일어나다
- **idea** [aidíːə] 명 아이디어
- **inside** [ìnsáid] 전 ~ 안에
- **leave** [liːv] 동 떠나다, ~에 두다 (-left-left)
- **lose** [luːz] 동 잃어버리다 (-lost-lost)
- **machine** [məʃíːn] 명 기계
- **mix** [miks] 동 섞다
- **oil** [ɔil] 명 기름
- **own** [oun] 동 소유하다
- **pile** [pail] 동 쌓아 올리다, 쌓다
- **prize** [praiz] 명 상금
- **P.S.** 추신 (= postscript)
- **push** [puʃ] 동 누르다
- **ready** [rédi] 형 준비된
- **recipe** [résəpi] 명 요리법
- **remember** [rimémbər] 동 기억하다
- **ring** [riŋ] 명 반지
- **sell** [sel] 동 팔다 (-sold-sold)
- **should** [ʃud] 조 ~해야 한다
- **shout** [ʃaut] 동 외치다, 소리치다
- **sign** [sain] 명 표지판
- **start** [stɑːrt] 동 (기계를) 작동시키다
- **taste** [teist] 동 ~한 맛이 나다
- **try** [trai] 동 시도하다, 먹어보다
- **visit** [vízit] 동 방문하다
- **watch** [wɑtʃ] 동 보다, (잠깐 동안) 봐 주다
- **work** [wəːrk] 동 효과가 있다, 작동하다
- **wrong** [rɔːŋ] 형 잘못된, 이상이 있는

Key Expressions

- **a lot of** 많은
- **a piece of paper** 종이 한 장
- **all of a sudden** 갑자기
- **be full of** ~으로 가득 차다
- **break up** ~을 부수다, 쪼개다
- **drop into** ~ 속으로 떨어지다
- **fall into** ~로 떨어지다
- **for a while** 잠시
- **get ~ back** ~을 되찾다
- **give ~ back** ~을 돌려주다
- **give a reward** 포상금을 지급하다
- **have to+동사원형** ~해야 한다
- **in front of** ~ 앞에
- **in the end** 결국, 마침내
- **just then** 바로 그때
- **keep+-ing** 계속해서 ~하다
- **look for** ~을 찾다
- **need to+동사원형** ~할 필요가 있다
- **one day** 어느 날
- **one of 복수명사** ~ 중 하나
- **pile A on B** A를 B에 쌓아 올리다
- **put A in B** A를 B에 넣다
- **right away** 즉시, 지금 당장
- **step out** ~에서 나오다, 내리다
- **take off** ~을 벗다
- **thank ~ for -ing** ~에게 -에 대해 감사하다
- **turn on** ~을 켜다, 작동시키다
- **with excitement** 흥분하여

Word Power

※ 서로 반대되는 뜻을 가진 어휘

- □ **fun** (재미있는) ↔ **boring** (지루한)
- □ **inside** (~ 안에) ↔ **outside** (~ 밖에)
- □ **difficult** (어려운) ↔ **easy** (쉬운)
- □ **leave** (떠나다) ↔ **arrive** (도착하다)
- □ **push** (누르다) ↔ **pull** (당기다)

- □ **wrong** (잘못된) ↔ **right** (옳은)
- □ **sell** (팔다) ↔ **buy** (사다)
- □ **remember** (기억하다) ↔ **forget** (잊다)
- □ **take off** (벗다) ↔ **put on** (입다)
- □ **turn on** (켜다) ↔ **turn off** (끄다)

※ 서로 비슷한 뜻을 가진 어휘

- □ **a lot of** : **lots of** (많은)
- □ **batter** : **dough** (반죽)
- □ **creative** : **ingenious** (창의적인)
- □ **delicious** : **tasty** (맛있는)
- □ **shout** : **yell** (외치다)
- □ **own** : **have** (소유하다)

- □ **drop** : **fall** (떨어지다)
- □ **happen** : **take place** (발생하다, 일어나다)
- □ **mix** : **blend** (섞다)
- □ **right away** : **right now** (즉시, 지금 당장)
- □ **in the end** : **finally** (결국)
- □ **be full of** : **be filled with** (~으로 가득 차다)

English Dictionary

- □ **batter** 반죽
  - → a mixture of flour, eggs, milk, etc. used in cooking and for making bread, cakes, etc.

    요리를 하거나 빵이나 케이크를 만들기 위해 사용되는 밀가루, 달걀, 우유 등을 섞은 것

- □ **compare** 비교하다
  - → to think about how two or more things are different or the same

    둘 또는 그 이상의 것이 어떻게 다르거나 같은지에 관해 생각하다

- □ **counter** 계산대
  - → the place where you pay in a shop, bank, restaurant, etc.

    가게, 은행, 식당 등에서 돈을 지불하기 위한 장소

- □ **doughnut** 도넛
  - → a small round cake that usually has a hole in the middle

    보통 중간에 구멍이 있는 작고 둥근 케이크

- □ **excitement** 흥분
  - → the feeling you have when you are excited

    당신이 신날 때 갖는 느낌

- □ **give a reward** 포상금을 주다
  - → to give something to someone because he or she has done something good

    좋은 일을 했기 때문에 누군가에게 무언가를 주다

- □ **machine** 기계
  - → a piece of equipment that you use to do a job

    일을 할 때 사용하는 하나의 장비

- □ **remember** 기억하다
  - → to have an image in your mind of something that happened or was said in the past

    과거에 일어났거나 말하여진 어떤 것의 이미지를 마음속에 갖다

- □ **step out** ~에서 나오다
  - → to go out for a short time

    잠시 동안 밖으로 나가다

- □ **work** 효과가 있다
  - → to be effective or successful

    효과적이거나 성공하다

The Doughnuts

machine 기계

batter 반죽

step out 내리다

diamond 다이아몬드

Homer's uncle, Bob, had a doughnut shop. Uncle Bob liked machines, so the shop was full of cooking machines. One day, Homer visited Uncle Bob's shop.
결과를 나타내는 접속사. be full of: ~으로 가득 차다   동명사(of의 목적어)

Homer: Hello, Uncle Bob!

Bob: Hi, Homer. Nice to see you. Look at this new doughnut machine. Isn't it great? Homer, I need to go back home for a while. Can you watch the shop for me and make some doughnuts?
need to+동사원형: ~할 필요가 있다   잠시 동안
watch와 make가 등위접속사 and로 연결

Homer: OK, I'll try but ....

Bob: It's easy to do. First, make the doughnut batter and put it in the machine. Then just start the machine. Here's the recipe.
부사적 용법(형용사 수식)   명령문으로 make와 put이 and로 연결
여기 있다

Homer: I can do that. Don't worry.

After Uncle Bob left, a big car stopped in front of the shop, and a lady stepped out.
~ 앞에

Lady: Can I have some doughnuts and a coffee?

Homer: I'm sorry, but the doughnuts aren't ready.

Lady: Are you making the doughnut batter now?
현재진행형 의문문

Homer: Yes, but this is my first time.

The lady took off her coat and her big diamond ring. She started to mix the batter.
take off: ~을 벗다   start+to부정사: ~하기 시작하다
= start+-ing

📎 **확인문제**

- 다음 문장이 본문의 내용과 일치하면 T, 일치하지 않으면 F를 쓰시오.

1 Bob's doughnut shop was filled with cooking machines. ☐

2 Bob allowed Homer to eat some doughnuts. ☐

3 Homer has made doughnuts before. ☐

Lady: I can help you. I can make delicious doughnuts.

Homer: Uh, OK. This is a lot of batter.
많은 ~(뒤에 셀 수 있는 명사와 셀 수 없는 명사 모두 올 수 있다)

Lady: Just wait and see. The doughnuts will taste great.
~의 맛이 나다, 맛이 ~하다(감각동사). 뒤에 형용사가 보어로 온다.

Homer turned on the doughnut machine. Rings of batter started
= started

dropping into the hot oil.
to drop

Lady: You try the first doughnut. Here.
명령문이므로 You를 생략할 수 있다.

Homer: Wow! It's really delicious!

Lady: I have to go now. This was so much fun! Good-bye!
have to+동사원형: ~해야 한다 (의무)

Homer: Thank you for helping me. Good-bye!
thank A for B: A에게 B에 대해 감사하다

Homer had enough doughnuts, so he pushed the stop button, but
'충분한'이라는 뜻의 형용사로 명사 앞에 위치. enough는 부사로도 쓰일 수 있다.

nothing happened. The doughnuts kept coming out of the machine.
keep+-ing: 계속해서 ~하다

Homer: Hmm... What's wrong? I think I should call Uncle Bob.
= What's the matter?

The shop was now full of doughnuts. Homer piled the doughnuts on
~으로 가득 찼다

the counter.

Homer: Uncle Bob! Please come back right away. Something's wrong
즉시   = There is something wrong

with the doughnut machine.

Bob: Oh, no! How can we sell all these doughnuts?

Just then the lady came back to the shop.
~으로 돌아왔따

Lady: I lost my diamond ring. I think I left it on the counter.

Homer: Oh, I remember. You took it off before you started to mix the
목적어가 인칭대명사일 때는 동사와 부사 사이에 위치. it = your diamond ring

batter.

turn on ~을 켜다

drop into ~ 속으로 떨어지다

out of ~에서, ~으로 부터

counter 계산대

확인문제

● 다음 문장이 본문의 내용과 일치하면 T, 일치하지 <u>않으면</u> F를 쓰시오.

1 When Homer turned on the doughnut machine, rings of batter started dropping into the hot oil. ☐

2 Homer pushed the stop button, but the doughnuts kept coming out of the machine. ☐

3 Homer piled the doughnuts on the floor. ☐

Everyone looked for the diamond ring, but they couldn't find it.
~을 찾았다
Homer: I can't find it.
= the diamond ring

Lady: I'll give a reward of one hundred dollars to the person who finds
give+사물+to+사람: ~에게 …을 주다
that ring!
주격 관계대명사절의 동사는 관계대명사 앞에 오는 명사 person에 수를 일치시킨다.

Homer: I know! The ring fell into the batter. I'm sure it's inside one of
fall–fell–fallen
these doughnuts!
one of+복수 명사: ~ 중의 하나

Lady: You're right!

Bob: Oh, no! Now we have to break up all of these doughnuts to find
쪼개다, 나누다   찾기 위해서(목적) = in order to find
the ring.

Homer: Don't worry, Uncle. I have an idea.

Homer took a piece of paper and made a sign.
종이 한 장
He then put it in the shop's window.

Fresh Doughnuts

2 for 5 cents

$100 prize for finding a ring inside a doughnut
동명사(for의 목적어)
P.S. You have to give the ring back.
타동사+목적어(명사)+부사

Then many people began to buy the doughnuts.
= began buying
All of a sudden, a man shouted with excitement.
흥분해서

Man: I found it! I found the ring!

Homer: See, my idea worked!
(어떤 계획이) 효과가 있다, 잘 작동하다
Lady: Here's one hundred dollars!

In the end, everybody was happy. The man went home with one
결국, 마침내
hundred dollars. The lady got her diamond ring back, and Uncle Bob
sold lots of doughnuts. And, what about Homer? He was happy that his
= a lot of   감정을 나타내는 형용사 뒤에 이어지는 that절은 그 감정의 원인을 나타낸다.
idea worked so well!

📎 **확인문제**

- 다음 문장이 본문의 내용과 일치하면 T, 일치하지 않으면 F를 쓰시오.

1 They started to break up all the doughnuts to find the ring. ☐
2 A man found the ring inside a doughnut and received $100. ☐

give a reward 보상금을 주다
give ~ back ~을 돌려주다
all of a sudden 갑자기
get ~ back ~을 돌려받다

● 우리말을 참고하여 빈칸에 알맞은 말을 쓰시오.

1 The _____

2 Homer's uncle, Bob, _____ a doughnut shop.

3 Uncle Bob liked machines, _____ the shop _____ _____ _____ cooking machines.

4 One day, Homer _____ Uncle Bob's shop.

5 Homer: Hello, _____ Bob!

6 Bob: Hi, Homer. Nice to see you. Look at this new doughnut machine. _____ _____ _____?

7 Bob: Homer, I need to go back home _____ _____ _____.

8 Can you watch the shop _____ _____ and make some doughnuts?

9 Homer: OK, I'll try but ....

10 Bob: It's easy to do. First, make the _____ _____ and put it in the machine.

11 Then just start the machine. Here's the _____.

12 Homer: I can do that. _____ _____.

13 After Uncle Bob left, a big car stopped in _____ of the shop, and a lady _____ _____.

14 Lady: _____ _____ _____ some doughnuts and a coffee?

15 Homer: I'm sorry, but the doughnuts _____ _____.

16 Lady: _____ _____ _____ the doughnut batter now?

17 Homer: Yes, but this is _____ _____ _____.

18 The lady _____ _____ her coat and her big diamond ring.

19 She started _____ _____ the batter.

20 Lady: _____ _____ _____ _____. I can make delicious doughnuts.

1 도넛

2 Homer의 삼촌인 Bob은 도넛 가게를 가지고 있었다.

3 Bob 삼촌은 기계를 좋아해서, 가게는 요리 기계들로 가득 차 있었다.

4 어느 날, Homer가 Bob 삼촌의 가게를 방문했다.

5 Homer: 안녕하세요, Bob 삼촌!

6 Bob: 안녕, Homer. 만나서 반갑구나. 이 새 도넛 기계 좀 봐. 멋지지 않니?

7 Bob: Homer, 내가 잠시 집에 가 봐야 해.

8 나 대신 가게를 봐 주고 도넛을 좀 만들어 줄 수 있겠니?

9 Homer: 네, 해 볼게요. 그런데 …

10 Bob: 하기 쉬워. 먼저, 도넛 반죽을 만들고 그것을 기계에 넣으렴.

11 그런 다음에 기계를 작동하기만 하면 돼. 여기 요리법이 있어.

12 Homer: 그건 할 수 있어요. 걱정하지 마세요.

13 Bob 삼촌이 떠난 후, 큰 차 한 대가 가게 앞에 섰고, 한 귀부인이 내렸다.

14 Lady: 도넛과 커피 한 잔 주겠니?

15 Homer: 그건 죄송하지만, 도넛이 준비가 안 됐어요.

16 Lady: 지금 도넛 반죽을 만들고 있는 거니?

17 Homer: 네, 하지만 처음 만드는 거예요.

18 그 귀부인은 외투를 벗고 커다란 다이아몬드 반지를 뺐다.

19 그녀는 반죽을 섞기 시작했다.

20 Lady: 내가 도와줄게. 나는 맛있는 도넛을 만들 수 있단다.

21 Homer: Uh, OK.

22 Homer: This is _____ _____ _____ batter.

23 Lady: Just _____ _____ _____. The doughnuts will taste _____.

24 Homer _____ _____ the doughnut machine.

25 Rings of batter started _____ _____ the hot oil.

26 Lady: You try the _____ doughnut. Here.

27 Homer: Wow! It's really _____!

28 Lady: I have to go now. This was _____ _____ _____! Good-bye!

29 Homer: Thank you _____ _____ me. Good-bye!

30 Homer had _____ doughnuts, so he pushed the stop button, but _____ _____.

31 The doughnuts _____ _____ out of the machine.

32 Homer: Hmm... What's wrong? I think I _____ _____ Uncle Bob.

33 The shop _____ now _____ _____ doughnuts. Homer _____ the doughnuts on the counter.

34 Homer: Uncle Bob! Please come back _____ _____.

35 _____ _____ with the doughnut machine.

36 Bob: Oh, no! How can we sell _____ _____ doughnuts?

37 Just then the lady _____ _____ to the shop.

38 Lady: I lost my diamond ring. I think I _____ it on the counter.

39 Homer: Oh, I remember. You _____ _____ _____ before you started to mix the batter.

40 Everyone _____ _____ the diamond ring, but they couldn't find it.

21 Homer: 아, 좋아요.

22 Homer: 반죽이 많군요.

23 Lady: 좀 기다려 보렴. 도넛이 아주 맛있을 거야.

24 Homer는 도넛 기계를 작동했다.

25 링 모양의 반죽들이 뜨거운 기름 속으로 떨어지기 시작했다.

26 Lady: 첫 번째 도넛을 맛보렴. 여기 있어.

27 Homer: 와! 정말 맛있네요!

28 Lady: 난 이제 가 봐야 해. 정말 재미있었어! 잘 있으렴!

29 Homer: 도와주셔서 감사해요. 안녕히 가세요!

30 Homer는 도넛이 충분하게 있어서 정지 버튼을 눌렀지만, 아무 일도 일어나지 않았다.

31 도넛이 계속해서 기계에서 나오고 있었다.

32 Homer: 흐음 … 뭐가 잘못된 거지? Bob 삼촌에게 전화를 해야겠어.

33 가게는 이제 도넛으로 가득 찼다. Homer는 도넛들을 계산대 위로 쌓아 올렸다.

34 Homer: Bob 삼촌! 지금 당장 돌아와 주세요.

35 도넛 기계에 이상이 있어요.

36 Bob: 오, 이런! 이 도넛들을 모두 어떻게 팔지?

37 바로 그때 그 귀부인이 다시 가게로 돌아왔다.

38 Lady: 내 다이아몬드 반지를 잃어버렸어. 내 생각엔 계산대 위에 그것을 놓은 것 같은데.

39 Homer: 오, 기억나요. 반죽을 섞기 전에 그것을 뺐어요.

40 모두가 다이아몬드 반지를 찾았지만, 찾을 수 없었다.

41 Homer: I _____ _____ it.

42 Lady: I'll _____ _____ _____ of one hundred dollars to the person who finds that ring!

43 Homer: I know! The ring fell into the batter. _____ _____ it's inside one of these doughnuts!

44 Lady: You're _____!

45 Bob: Oh, no! Now we have to _____ _____ all of these doughnuts _____ _____ the ring.

46 Homer: _____ _____, Uncle. I have an idea.

47 Homer took a piece of paper and _____ _____ _____.

48 He then _____ _____ in the shop's window.

49 Fresh Doughnuts _____ _____ _____ _____

50 $100 prize _____ _____ a ring inside a doughnut

51 P.S. You have to _____ the ring _____.

52 Then many people began _____ _____ the doughnuts.

53 _____ _____ _____ _____, a man shouted with excitement.

54 Man: I _____ _____! I found the ring!

55 Homer: See, my idea _____!

56 Lady: _____ one hundred dollars!

57 _____ _____ _____, everybody was happy.

58 The man went home _____ one hundred dollars.

59 The lady _____ her diamond ring _____, and Uncle Bob sold _____ _____ doughnuts.

60 And, _____ _____ Homer?

61 He was happy that _____ _____ _____ so well!

---

41 Homer: 저는 못 찾겠어요.

42 Lady: 그 반지를 찾는 사람에게 100달러의 보상금을 드릴게요!

43 Homer: 알겠어요! 그 반지는 반죽 속으로 떨어졌어요. 반지는 이 도넛들 중 하나 안에 있다고 확신해요!

44 Lady: 네 말이 맞아!

45 Bob: 오, 안 돼! 이제 우리는 반지를 찾기 위해 이 도넛들을 모두 쪼개야 해요.

46 Homer: 걱정하지 마세요, 삼촌. 저에게 아이디어가 있어요.

47 Homer는 종이 한 장을 가져와 안내판을 만들었다.

48 그러고 나서 그것을 가게 창문에 걸었다.

49 신선한 도넛 2개에 5센트

50 도넛 안에 있는 반지를 찾으면 100달러의 상금을 드려요.

51 추신. 반지를 돌려주어야 합니다.

52 그러자, 많은 사람들이 도넛을 사기 시작했다.

53 갑자기, 한 남자가 흥분해서 소리쳤다.

54 Man: 찾았어요! 내가 반지를 찾았어요!

55 Homer: 보세요, 제 아이디어가 통했어요!

56 Lady: 여기 100달러예요!

57 결국 모두가 행복했다.

58 남자는 100달러를 갖고 집으로 갔다.

59 귀부인은 다이아몬드 반지를 다시 찾았고, Bob 삼촌은 도넛을 많이 팔았다.

60 그러면, Homer는 어떻게 됐을까?

61 그는 자신의 아이디어가 아주 잘 통해서 행복했다!

● 우리말을 참고하여 본문을 영작하시오.

1 도넛
➡ _____

2 Homer의 삼촌인 Bob은 도넛 가게를 가지고 있었다.
➡ _____

3 Bob 삼촌은 기계를 좋아해서, 가게는 요리 기계들로 가득 차 있었다.
➡ _____

4 어느 날, Homer가 Bob 삼촌의 가게를 방문했다.
➡ _____

5 Homer: 안녕하세요, Bob 삼촌!
➡ _____

6 Bob: 안녕, Homer. 만나서 반갑구나. 이 새 도넛 기계 좀 봐. 멋지지 않니?
➡ _____

7 Bob: Homer, 내가 잠시 집에 가 봐야 해.
➡ _____

8 나 대신 가게를 봐 주고 도넛을 좀 만들어 줄 수 있겠니?
➡ _____

9 Homer: 네, 해 볼게요, 그런데….
➡ _____

10 Bob: 하기 쉬워. 먼저, 도넛 반죽을 만들고 그것을 기계에 넣으렴.
➡ _____

11 그런 다음에 기계를 작동하기만 하면 돼. 여기 요리법이 있어.
➡ _____

12 Homer: 그건 할 수 있어요. 걱정하지 마세요.
➡ _____

13 Bob 삼촌이 떠난 후, 큰 차 한 대가 가게 앞에 섰고, 한 귀부인이 내렸다.
➡ _____

14 Lady: 도넛과 커피 한 잔 주겠니?
➡ _____

15 Homer: 죄송하지만, 도넛이 준비가 안 됐어요.
➡ _____

16 Lady: 지금 도넛 반죽을 만들고 있는 거니?
➡ _____

17 Homer: 네, 하지만 처음 만드는 거예요.
➡ _____

18 그 귀부인은 외투를 벗고 커다란 다이아몬드 반지를 뺐다.
➡ _____

19 그녀는 반죽을 섞기 시작했다.
➡ _____

20 Lady: 내가 도와줄게. 나는 맛있는 도넛을 만들 수 있단다.
➡ _____

21 Homer: 아, 좋아요.
➡ _____

22 Homer: 반죽이 많군요.
➡ _____

23 Lady: 좀 기다려 보렴. 도넛이 아주 맛있을 거야.
➡ _____

24 Homer는 도넛 기계를 작동했다.
➡ _____

25 링 모양의 반죽들이 뜨거운 기름 속으로 떨어지기 시작했다.
➡ _____

26 Lady: 첫 번째 도넛을 맛보렴. 여기 있어.
➡ _____

27 Homer: 와! 정말 맛있네요!
➡ _____

28 Lady: 난 이제 가 봐야 해. 정말 재미있었어! 잘 있으렴!
➡ _____

29 Homer: 도와주셔서 감사해요. 안녕히 가세요!
➡ _____

30 Homer는 도넛이 충분하게 있어서 정지 버튼을 눌렀지만, 아무 일도 일어나지 않았다.
➡ _____

31 도넛이 계속해서 기계에서 나오고 있었다.
➡ _____

32 Homer: 흐음 … 뭐가 잘못된 거지? Bob 삼촌에게 전화를 해야겠어.
➡ _____

33 가게는 이제 도넛으로 가득 찼다. Homer는 도넛들을 계산대 위로 쌓아 올렸다.
➡ _____

34 Homer: Bob 삼촌! 지금 당장 돌아와 주세요.
➡ _____

35 도넛 기계에 이상이 있어요.
➡ _____

36 Bob: 오, 이런! 이 도넛들을 모두 어떻게 팔지?
➡ _____

37 바로 그때 그 귀부인이 다시 가게로 돌아왔다.
➡ _____

38 Lady: 내 다이아몬드 반지를 잃어버렸어. 내 생각엔 계산대 위에 그것을 놓은 것 같은데.
➡ _____

39 Homer: 오, 기억나요. 반죽을 섞기 전에 그것을 뺐어요.
➡ _____

40 모두가 다이아몬드 반지를 찾았지만, 찾을 수 없었다.
➡ _____

41 Homer: 저는 못 찾겠어요.
➡ _____

42 Lady: 그 반지를 찾는 사람에게 100달러의 보상금을 드릴게요!
➡ _____

43 Homer: 알겠어요! 그 반지는 반죽 속으로 떨어졌어요. 반지는 이 도넛들 중 하나 안에 있다고 확신해요!
➡ _____

44 Lady: 네 말이 맞아!
➡ _____

45 Bob: 오, 안 돼! 이제 우리는 반지를 찾기 위해 이 도넛들을 모두 쪼개야 해요.
➡ _____

46 Homer: 걱정하지 마세요, 삼촌. 저에게 아이디어가 있어요.
➡ _____

47 Homer는 종이 한 장을 가져와 안내판을 만들었다.
➡ _____

48 그러고 나서 그것을 가게 창문에 걸었다.
➡ _____

49 신선한 도넛   2개에 5센트
➡ _____

50 도넛 안에 있는 반지를 찾으면 100달러의 상금을 드려요.
➡ _____

51 추신. 반지를 돌려주어야 합니다.
➡ _____

52 그러자, 많은 사람들이 도넛을 사기 시작했다.
➡ _____

53 갑자기, 한 남자가 흥분해서 소리쳤다.
➡ _____

54 Man: 찾았어요! 내가 반지를 찾았어요!
➡ _____

55 Homer: 보세요, 제 아이디어가 통했어요!
➡ _____

56 Lady: 여기 100달러예요!
➡ _____

57 결국 모두가 행복했다.
➡ _____

58 남자는 100달러를 갖고 집으로 갔다.
➡ _____

59 귀부인은 다이아몬드 반지를 다시 찾았고, Bob 삼촌은 도넛을 많이 팔았다.
➡ _____

60 그러면, Homer는 어떻게 됐을까?
➡ _____

61 그는 자신의 아이디어가 아주 잘 통해서 행복했다!
➡ _____

서술형 실전문제

01 다음 문장에 공통으로 들어갈 말을 쓰시오.

> (1) Can I _____ some doughnuts and a coffee?
>
> (2) I _____ to go now. This was so much fun! Good-bye!

02 다음 빈칸에 들어갈 말을 〈보기〉에서 찾아 쓰시오. (필요하면 변형하여 쓰시오.)

> ┌─── 보기 ───┐
>
> drop into   reward   batter   step out

(1) I'll give a _____ of one hundred dollars to the person who finds that ring!

(2) Rings of batter started _____ _____ the hot oil.

(3) After Uncle Bob left, a big car stopped in front of the shop, and a lady _____ _____.

03 다음 영영풀이에 해당하는 단어를 〈보기〉에서 찾아 첫 번째 칸에 쓰고, 두 번째 칸에는 우리말 뜻을 쓰시오.

> ┌─── 보기 ───┐
>
> compare   remember   batter
> excitement   machine   work

(1) _____ : to have an image in your mind of something that happened or was said in the past: _____

(2) _____ : to think about how two or more things are different or the same: _____

(3) _____ : the feeling you have when you are excited: _____

(4) _____ : to be effective or successful: _____

04 다음 우리말 해석과 같은 뜻이 되도록 주어진 철자로 시작하여 빈칸을 채우시오.

(1) Homer의 삼촌인 Bob은 도넛 가게를 갖고 있었다.

➡ Homer's uncle, Bob, o_____ a doughnut shop.

(2) 내가 잠시 집으로 되돌아가야 해.

➡ I need to go back home f_____ _____ _____.

(3) 그 귀부인은 외투를 벗고 커다란 다이아몬드 반지를 뺐다.

➡ The lady t_____ _____ her coat and her big diamond ring.

05 다음 문장에서 어법상 어색한 부분을 바르게 고쳐 다시 쓰시오.

(1) Bob liked books, because his room was full of books.

➡ _____

(2) That is easy to make doughnuts.

➡ _____

(3) Homer thinks that the doughnuts smell greatly.

➡ _____

(4) After Bob made doughnuts with the doughnut machine, he turned off it.

➡ _____
_____

(5) We ordered three piece of pizzas and two can of colas at the restaurant.

➡ _____
_____

06 다음 두 문장을 관계대명사를 이용하여 한 문장으로 연결하여 쓰시오.

(1) • Have you met the girl?
   • She is talking to Judy.

   ➡ _____
   _____

(2) • Yuna is good at figure skating.
   • Figure skating is hard to learn.

   ➡ _____
   _____

(3) • The hotel was clean and beautiful.
   • I stayed at the hotel.

   ➡ _____
   _____
   _____

[07~09] 다음 글을 읽고, 물음에 답하시오.

Homer's uncle, Bob, had a doughnut shop. Uncle Bob liked machines, so the shop was full of cooking machines. One day, Homer visited Uncle Bob's shop.

Homer: Hello, Uncle Bob!

Bob: Hi, Homer. Nice to see you. Look at this new doughnut machine. Isn't it great?

Bob: Homer, I need to go back home for a while. Can you watch the shop for me and make some doughnuts?

Homer: OK, I'll try but ....

Bob: It's easy to do. First, make the doughnut batter and put it in the machine. Then just start the machine. Here's the recipe.

Homer: I can do that. Don't worry.

After Uncle Bob left, a big car stopped in front of the shop, and a lady stepped out.

07 Why was Bob's doughnut shop filled with cooking machines? Answer in English. (4 words)

➡ _____

08 위 글에서 다음 영영풀이에 해당하는 단어를 찾아 쓰시오.

a mixture of flour, eggs, and milk that is used in cooking

➡ _____

중요

09 위 글에서 Bob 삼촌이 말하는 도넛 만드는 법을 우리말로 쓰시오.

(1) _____
(2) _____
(3) _____

[10~12] 다음 글을 읽고, 물음에 답하시오.

Just then the lady came back to the shop.

Lady: I lost my diamond ring. I think I left it on the counter.

Homer: Oh, I remember. ⓐ반죽을 섞기 전에 그것을 뺐어요.

Everyone looked for the diamond ring, but they couldn't find it.

Homer: I can't find it.

Lady: ⓑI'll give a reward of one hundred dollars to the person who finds that ring!

Homer: I know! The ring fell into the batter. I'm sure it's inside one of these doughnuts!

Lady: You're right!

Bob: Oh, no! Now we have to break up all of these doughnuts ⓒto find the ring.

10 위 글의 밑줄 친 ⓐ의 우리말에 맞게 한 단어를 보충하여, 주어진 어휘를 알맞게 배열하시오.

started / it / you / to mix / before / took / the batter / you

➡ _____

11 위 글의 밑줄 친 문장 ⓑ를 4형식 문장으로 고치시오.

➡ _____

_____

★**12** 위 글의 밑줄 친 ⓒ를 다음과 같이 바꿔 쓸 때 빈칸에 들어갈 알맞은 말을 쓰시오.

(1) _____ _____ _____ _____ the ring

(2) _____ _____ _____ _____ the ring

(3) _____ _____ _____ we can find the ring

(4) _____ _____ we _____ find the ring

[13~16] 다음 글을 읽고, 물음에 답하시오.

Homer: Don't worry, Uncle. I have an idea.

Homer took a piece of paper and made a sign.

He then put it in the shop's window.

Fresh Doughnuts

2 for 5 cents

$100 prize for finding a ring inside a doughnut

P.S. You have to give the ring back.

Then many people began to buy the doughnuts.

All of a sudden, a man shouted with excitement.

Man: I found it! I found the ring!

Homer: See, my idea worked!

Lady: Here's one hundred dollars!

In the end, everybody was happy. The man went home with one hundred dollars. The lady got her diamond ring back, and Uncle Bob sold lots of doughnuts. And, what about Homer? He was happy that his idea worked so well!

13 If a person buys 10 doughnuts, what's the price of them?

➡ _____

14 다음 빈칸에 들어갈 알맞은 단어를 본문에서 찾아 넣어 위 글의 요지를 완성하시오.

> The main idea of this text is how creative ideas can _____ in solving problems.

➡ _____

★**15** 위 글의 등장인물들 각자에게 어떤 일이 일어났는지 결말을 우리말로 쓰시오.

• Man: _____

• Lady: _____

• Uncle Bob: _____

• Homer: _____

16 위 글의 밑줄 친 worked와 같은 의미로 쓰인 것을 고르시오.

① He worked for a bank.

② She worked a farm.

③ The plan worked well.

④ This machine is worked by wind power.

⑤ They often worked very long hours.

단원별 예상문제

출제율 85%

01 다음 단어에 대한 영어 설명이 <u>어색한</u> 것은?

① doughnut: a small round cake that usually has a hole in the middle

② give a reward: to give something to someone because he or she has done something good

③ counter: the place where you pay in a shop, bank, restaurant, etc.

④ batter: a mixture of flour, eggs, milk, etc. used in cooking and for making bread, cakes, etc.

⑤ step out: to fall or to allow something to fall

출제율 95%

02 다음 짝지어진 단어의 관계가 같도록 빈칸에 알맞은 말을 쓰시오.

> mix : blend = fall : _____

출제율 90%

03 다음 영영풀이에 해당하는 단어를 고르시오.

> a set of instructions telling you how to prepare and cook food

① recipe　　② batter　　③ machine

④ counter　　⑤ cooker

출제율 95%

04 다음 그림에 맞게 대화의 빈칸에 들어갈 말을 쓰시오.

Lady: Are you making the doughnut _____ now?

Boy: Yes, but this is my first time.

출제율 95%

05 다음 문장의 밑줄 친 단어와 같은 말을 네 단어로 쓰시오.

> • <u>All at once</u> it became dark.
> • I <u>suddenly</u> remembered I had left something at home.

➡ _____

출제율 100%

06 다음 빈칸에 들어갈 말이 알맞게 짝지어진 것은?

> • Homer turned on the doughnut machine. Rings of batter started dropping _____ the hot oil.
> • The shop was now full _____ doughnuts.
> • Now we have to break _____ all of these doughnuts to find the ring.

① on – with – down　② into – of – up

③ by – of – up　　　④ into – with – down

⑤ by – of – down

출제율 90%

07 다음 중 짝지어진 단어의 관계가 <u>다른</u> 것은?

① easy : difficult　② sell : buy

③ push : pull　　　④ shout : yell

⑤ fun : boring

08 다음 문장의 빈칸에 공통으로 들어갈 말을 쓰시오.

> • Homer, I need to go _____ home for a while.
> • Uncle Bob! Please come _____ right away. Something's wrong with the doughnut machine.
> • You have to give the ring _____.
> • The lady got her diamond ring _____, and Uncle Bob sold lots of doughnuts.

09 다음 문장에서 어법상 어색한 부분을 바르게 고쳐 다시 쓰시오.

(1) Homer is the person which is very creative.

➡ _____

(2) Bob had to fix the machine making doughnuts.

➡ _____

(3) Homer found the lost ring with easy.

➡ _____

(4) Sean was happy what his idea was finally accepted.

➡ _____

10 다음 빈칸에 알맞은 말을 모두 고르시오.

> The food _____ really delicious.

① bought　② brought　③ asked
④ tasted　⑤ smelled

11 다음 중 〈보기〉의 밑줄 친 부분과 용법이 같은 것을 고르시오.

┤ 보기 ├
> We eat to live, not live to eat.

① It is very important for him to eat delicious food.
② We decided to eat pizza.
③ They had nothing to eat.
④ We went to the restaurant to eat lunch.
⑤ What I like is to eat delicious food.

12 우리말을 괄호 안에 주어진 어휘를 이용하여 영작하시오.

(1) Grace는 스커트를 하나 사서 그것을 입었다. (buy, and, put)

➡ _____

(2) Charlie Brown은 운이 없는 소년이다. (bad luck, a boy, have, who)

➡ _____

(3) 그 금속은 촉감이 매끄럽고 차가웠다. (metal, smooth, cold, feel)

➡ _____

(4) 그녀는 그녀의 손가락을 튼튼하게 하기 위하여 피아노를 치기 시작했다. (make, start, playing, strong, fingers)

➡ _____
_____

13 다음 중 어법상 옳지 <u>않은</u> 것은?

① The rock looks like a big battle ship.

② A teacher is a person whom teaches students at school.

③ Will you throw them away, please?

④ Her face turned red with excitement.

⑤ The hens are hungry, so I must feed them now.

[14~16] 다음 글을 읽고 물음에 답하시오.

Homer's uncle, Bob, had a doughnut shop. ⓐUncle Bob liked machines, so the shop was full of cooking machines. One day, Homer visited Uncle Bob's shop.

Homer: Hello, Uncle Bob!

Bob: Hi, Homer. Nice to see you. Look at this new doughnut machine. Isn't it great?

Bob: Homer, I need to go back home for a while. Can you watch the shop for me and make some doughnuts?

Homer: OK, I'll try but ....

Bob: It's easy to do. First, make the doughnut batter and put ⓑit in the machine. Then just start the machine. Here's the recipe.

Homer: I can do that. Don't worry.

After Uncle Bob left, a big car stopped in front of the shop, and a lady stepped out.

14 위 글의 밑줄 친 ⓐ를 다음과 같이 바꿔 쓸 때 빈칸에 들어갈 알맞은 단어를 고르시오.

_____ Uncle Bob liked machines, the shop was full of cooking machines.

① That ② If ③ As
④ While ⑤ Though

15 위 글의 밑줄 친 ⓑit이 가리키는 것을 본문에서 찾아 쓰시오.

➡ _____

16 위 글의 내용과 일치하도록 다음 빈칸 (A)와 (B)에 들어갈 알맞은 말을 쓰시오.

Uncle Bob wanted Homer to (A) _____ _____ _____ for him and (B)_____ _____ _____.

[17~19] 다음 글을 읽고, 물음에 답하시오.

Lady: Can I have some doughnuts and a coffee?

Homer: I'm sorry, but the doughnuts aren't ready.

Lady: Are you making the doughnut batter now?

Homer: Yes, but this is my first time.

The lady (A)[put on / took off] her coat and her big diamond ring.

She started to mix the batter.

Lady: I can help you. I can make delicious doughnuts.

Homer: Uh, OK.

Homer: This is a lot of batter.

Lady: Just wait and see. The doughnuts will taste (B)[great / greatly].

Homer (C)[turned on / turned off] the doughnut machine. Rings of batter started dropping into the hot oil.

Lady: You try the first doughnut. Here.

Homer: Wow! It's really delicious!

17 위 글의 괄호 (A)~(C)에서 문맥이나 어법상 알맞은 낱말을 골라 쓰시오.

(A) _____ (B) _____ (C) _____

18 위 글에서 알 수 있는 'Lady'의 성격으로 가장 알맞은 것을 고르시오.

① curious   ② polite
③ patient   ④ kind
⑤ creative

19 위 글의 내용과 일치하지 않는 것은?

① The lady asked Homer if she could have some doughnuts and a coffee.
② Homer said that the doughnuts weren't ready.
③ Homer was making the doughnut batter for the first time.
④ Homer made a lot of batter.
⑤ The lady gave Homer the first doughnut.

20 위 글의 흐름으로 보아, 주어진 문장이 들어가기에 가장 적절한 곳은?

> The doughnuts kept coming out of the machine.

①   ②   ③   ④   ⑤

21 위 글의 밑줄 친 ⓐfull of와 바꿔 쓸 수 있는 두 단어를 쓰시오.

➡ _____

22 위 글의 밑줄 친 ⓑ가 가리키는 내용을 본문에서 찾아 쓰시오.

➡ _____
_____

[20~22] 다음 글을 읽고 물음에 답하시오.

Lady: I have to go now. This was so much fun! Good-bye!

Homer: Thank you for helping me. Good-bye!

Homer had enough doughnuts, so he pushed the stop button, but nothing happened. (①)

Homer: Hmm... What's wrong? (②) I think I should call Uncle Bob. (③)

The shop was now ⓐ<u>full of</u> doughnuts. (④) Homer piled the doughnuts on the counter. (⑤)

Homer: Uncle Bob! Please come back right away. ⓑ<u>Something's wrong with the doughnut machine.</u>

Bob: Oh, no! How can we sell all these doughnuts?

[23~26] 다음 글을 읽고 물음에 답하시오.

Just then the lady came back to the shop.

Lady: I lost my diamond ring. I think I ___ⓐ___ it on the counter.

Homer: Oh, I remember. You took it off before you started to mix the batter.

Everyone looked for the diamond ring, but they couldn't find it.

Homer: I can't find it.

Lady: I'll give a reward of one hundred dollars to the person who finds that ring!

Homer: I know! The ring fell into the batter. I'm sure it's inside one of these doughnuts!

Lady: You're right!

Bob: Oh, no! Now we have to break up all of these doughnuts ⓑ<u>to find</u> the ring.

23 위 글의 빈칸 ⓐ에 들어갈 알맞은 말을 고르시오.

① lay　　② held　　③ gave

④ left　　⑤ found

24 아래 〈보기〉에서 위 글의 밑줄 친 ⓑto find와 to부정사의 용법이 같은 것의 개수를 고르시오.

① They went there to find the ring.

② It was not easy to find the ring.

③ Can you think of the way to find the ring?

④ I wanted to find the ring.

⑤ I wonder who will be the person to find the ring.

① 1개　② 2개　③ 3개　④ 4개　⑤ 5개

25 위 글의 마지막 부분에서 알 수 있는 'Uncle Bob'의 심경으로 가장 알맞은 것을 고르시오.

① embarrassed　　② excited

③ ashamed　　④ bored

⑤ relieved

26 위 글의 내용과 일치하지 <u>않는</u> 것은? (2개)

① The lady came back to the shop because she lost her diamond ring.

② Homer remembers that she took off her ring before she started to mix the batter.

③ Homer thinks that the lady lost the ring on the street.

④ The person who finds that ring will receive a reward from Homer.

⑤ Homer says that the ring fell into the batter.

[27~29] 다음 글을 읽고, 물음에 답하시오.

Homer: Don't worry, Uncle. I have an idea.
Homer took a piece of paper and made a sign. He then put it in the shop's window.

Fresh Doughnuts
2 for 5 cents
$100 prize for finding a ring inside a doughnut
P.S. You have to give the ring back.

Then many people began to buy the doughnuts. ⓐAll of a sudden, a man shouted with excitement.
Man: I found it! I found the ring!
Homer: See, my idea worked!
Lady: ⓑHere're one hundred dollars!
In the end, everybody was happy. The man went home with one hundred dollars. The lady got her diamond ring back, and Uncle Bob sold lots of doughnuts. And, what about Homer? He was happy that his idea worked so well!

27 위 글의 제목으로 알맞은 것을 고르시오.

① Homer Made a Sign!

② Put the Sign in the Shop's Window

③ $100 Prize for Finding a Ring

④ Uncle Bob Sold Lots of Doughnuts

⑤ Creative Idea Worked Well!

28 위 글의 밑줄 친 ⓐAll of a sudden과 바꿔 쓸 수 있는 말을 모두 고르시오.

① At one time　　② Suddenly

③ Actually　　④ All at once

⑤ Immediately

29 위 글의 밑줄 친 문장 ⓑ에서 어법상 틀린 부분을 찾아 고치시오.

_____ ➡ _____

중간 + 기말

plus

적중100

영어 기출문제집

영어 중 2

동아 | 윤정미

Best Collection

내용문의 중등영어발전소 적중100 편집부 TEL 070-7707-0457

INSIGHT
on the textbook

교과서 파헤치기

영어 기출 문제집

2학기 전과정

적중100 plus

영어 중 2

동아 | 윤정미

INSIGHT
on the textbook
교과서 파헤치기

※ 다음 영어를 우리말로 쓰시오.

01 advice _____

02 celebrity _____

03 during _____

04 unwise _____

05 sore _____

06 fever _____

07 simple _____

08 blink _____

09 thumb _____

10 prevent _____

11 throat _____

12 health _____

13 skin _____

14 nervous _____

15 various _____

16 hole _____

17 subject _____

18 dry _____

19 meal _____

20 medicine _____

21 regularly _____

22 intelligent _____

23 difficult _____

24 hurt _____

25 promise _____

26 accident _____

27 safety _____

28 example _____

29 increase _____

30 author _____

31 terrible _____

32 addiction _____

33 cause _____

34 pain _____

35 from now on _____

36 all over the world _____

37 fall asleep _____

38 instead of ~ _____

39 get into ~ _____

40 take a rest _____

41 have a sore throat _____

42 for example _____

43 look well _____

※ 다음 우리말을 영어로 쓰시오.

01 엄지손가락	22 건조한, 마른
02 구덩이, 구멍	23 똑똑한, 지적인
03 건강	24 목구멍
04 어려운	25 식사
05 약속	26 증가하다
06 규칙적으로	27 치과의사
07 단순한	28 현명한, 말쑥한
08 초조한, 불안한	29 운동
09 충고	30 중독
10 막다, 예방하다	31 ~ 없이
11 다치다	32 치통
12 ~ 동안	33 안전
13 피부	34 작가, 저자
14 눈을 깜박이다	35 ~ 대신에
15 다양한	36 몇몇의
16 유명인사, 유명인	37 요즈음
17 아픈, 쓰린	38 콧물이 흐르다
18 현명하지 않은	39 예를 들어
19 과목	40 휴식을 취하다, 쉬다
20 약	41 ~하려고 애쓰다[노력하다]
21 열, 열병	42 잠들다
	43 지금부터

※ 다음 영영풀이에 알맞은 단어를 <보기>에서 골라 쓴 후, 우리말 뜻을 쓰시오.

1 _____ : a time when you relax or sleep: _____

2 _____ : a thick piece of soft material: _____

3 _____ : to make something happen: _____

4 _____ : a hollow place in something solid or in the surface of something: _____

5 _____ : to open and close your eyes very quickly: _____

6 _____ : at the same time every day, every week, etc.: _____

7 _____ : the feeling you have when a part of your body hurts: _____

8 _____ : to send someone a written message using a cell phone: _____

9 _____ : the passage at the back of your mouth, where you swallow: _____

10 _____ : to become larger or greater in size, amount, number, etc.: _____

11 _____ : a pill or a liquid that you take when you are sick to help you get better: _____

12 _____ : to stop something from happening, or stop someone from doing: _____

13 _____ : the state of being safe and protected from danger or harm: _____

14 _____ : the short thick finger on your hand that helps you hold things: _____

15 _____ : physical activity that is done in order to become stronger and healthier: _____

16 _____ : the problem when someone cannot stop doing something, or does something too much: _____

보기			
throat	medicine	exercise	cause
prevent	addiction	rest	text
hole	thumb	blink	increase
pad	pain	regularly	safety

※ 다음 우리말과 일치하도록 빈칸에 알맞은 말을 쓰시오.

Listen and Talk A-1

W: You _____ _____. _____ _____, Inho?

B: I _____ _____ _____ _____. I _____ _____ _____, too.

W: I think you _____ _____ _____. _____ this _____ and _____ you _____ a good _____.

B: OK. _____ _____.

W: 너 아파 보인다. 무슨 일이니, 인호야?
B: 목이 아파요. 열도 나요.
W: 감기에 걸린 것 같구나. 이 약을 먹고 좀 쉬도록 하렴.
B: 알겠어요. 감사합니다.

Listen and Talk A-2

W: What's _____, Peter?

B: I don't know, Ms. Kim, but my _____ _____ _____ _____.

W: _____ a heating pad _____ it.

B: OK, _____ _____.

W: And _____ _____ you do some _____ _____.

W: 무슨 일이니, Peter?
B: 모르겠어요, 김 선생님, 등이 아파요.
W: 그곳에 찜질 패드를 올려놓으렴.
B: 네, 그럴게요.
W: 그리고 스트레칭 운동을 하렴.

Listen and Talk A-3

W: What's the _____, Chris?

B: I _____ _____ terrible _____.

W: _____ _____ some _____. _____ this.

B: Thank you.

W: And _____ _____ you go to the _____.

B: OK, _____ _____.

W: 무슨 일이니, Chris?
B: 저는 심한 치통이 있어요.
W: 여기 약이 있단다. 이것을 먹으렴.
B: 감사합니다.
W: 그리고 치과에 가도록 하렴.
B: 네, 알겠어요.

Listen and Talk A-4

W: What's _____ _____ your leg, Sam?

B: I _____ and _____ my foot _____ I was playing soccer.

W: _____ you _____?

B: Yes, but it _____ a lot.

W: _____ _____ _____ put some ice on it? And _____ _____ you _____ _____ soccer _____ next week.

W: 다리에 무슨 문제가 있니, Sam?
B: 축구를 하다가 넘어져서 발을 다쳤어요.
W: 걸을 수는 있겠니?
B: 네, 하지만 많이 아파요.
W: 얼음을 그 위에 올려놓는 게 어떠니? 그리고 다음 주까지는 축구를 하지 않도록 하렴.

Listen and Talk B

1. A: You _____ _____ _____. What's _____?
   B: I _____ _____ _____.
   A: _____ _____ _____. _____ _____ you _____ some medicine.
   B: OK, I _____.

2. A: You _____ _____ _____. What's _____?
   B: I _____ _____ _____.
   A: That's too bad. _____ _____ you go see a _____.
   B: OK, _____ _____.

Listen and Talk C

W: What's _____, Andy?
B: Hello, Ms. Kim. My right _____ _____.
W: Hmm. Do you _____ your smartphone _____ _____?
B: Yes, I _____ _____ _____. Why?
W: I think you _____ _____ _____.
B: Texting thumb? What's texting thumb?
W: It's _____ in _____ _____. You can _____ it _____ _____ too much.
B: Oh, I _____ _____ that.
W: _____ _____ _____ do some finger stretching exercises?
B: OK, I will.
W: And _____ _____ _____ _____ _____ too much.

Review 1

G: What's _____, Mike?
B: I _____ _____ _____ _____.
G: I think you _____ _____ _____ _____.
B: OK, _____ _____.

Review 2

M: What's _____ _____, Mina?
G: I _____ _____ _____ _____. I also _____ _____ _____ _____.
M: I think you have a _____. _____ _____ you _____ _____ _____.
G: OK, _____.

---

1. A: 너 몸이 안 좋아 보여. 무슨 일 있니?
   B: 머리가 아파.
   A: 안됐다. 약을 먹으렴.
   B: 응, 그럴게.

2. A: 너 몸이 안 좋아 보여. 무슨 일 있니?
   B: 감기에 걸렸어.
   A: 안됐다. 병원에 가도록 하렴.
   B: 응, 그럴게.

W: 무슨 일이니, Andy?
B: 안녕하세요, 김 선생님. 제 오른손 엄지손가락이 아파요.
W: 음. 너 스마트폰을 많이 사용하니?
B: 네, 저 문자를 많이 해요. 왜요?
W: 내 생각에 너는 texting thumb인 것 같아.
B: texting thumb이요? texting thumb이 뭐예요?
W: 엄지손가락에 통증이 있는 거야. 문자를 너무 많이 하면 생길 수 있어.
B: 오, 그건 몰랐네요.
W: 손가락 스트레칭 운동을 좀 하는 게 어떠니?
B: 네, 그럴게요.
W: 그리고 문자를 너무 많이 하지 않도록 하렴.

G: 무슨 일 있니, Mike?
B: 머리가 너무 아파.
G: 너는 약을 먹는 것이 좋겠다.
B: 알겠어, 그럴게.

M: 무슨 일 있니, 미나야?
G: 목이 아파요. 그리고 콧물도 나요.
M: 내 생각에 네가 감기에 걸린 것 같구나. 좀 쉬도록 하렴.
G: 네, 그럴게요.

※ 다음 우리말에 맞도록 대화를 영어로 쓰시오.

Listen and Talk A-1

W: _____

B: _____

W: _____

B: _____

W: 너 아파 보인다. 무슨 일이니, 인호야?
B: 목이 아파요. 열도 나요.
W: 감기에 걸린 것 같구나. 이 약을 먹고 좀 쉬도록 하렴.
B: 알겠어요. 감사합니다.

Listen and Talk A-2

W: _____

B: _____

W: _____

B: _____

W: _____

W: 무슨 일이니, Peter?
B: 모르겠어요, 김 선생님, 등이 아파요.
W: 그곳에 찜질 패드를 올려놓으렴.
B: 네, 그럴게요.
W: 그리고 스트레칭 운동을 하렴.

Listen and Talk A-3

W: _____

B: _____

W: _____

B: _____

W: _____

B: _____

W: 무슨 일이니, Chris?
B: 저는 심한 치통이 있어요.
W: 여기 약이 있단다. 이것을 먹으렴.
B: 감사합니다.
W: 그리고 치과에 가도록 하렴.
B: 네, 알겠어요.

Listen and Talk A-4

W: _____

B: _____

W: _____

B: _____

W: _____

W: 다리에 무슨 문제가 있니, Sam?
B: 축구를 하다가 넘어져서 발을 다쳤어요.
W: 걸을 수는 있겠니?
B: 네, 하지만 많이 아파요.
W: 얼음을 그 위에 올려놓는 게 어떠니? 그리고 다음 주까지는 축구를 하지 않도록 하렴.

Listen and Talk B

1. A: _____

   B: _____

   A: _____

   B: _____

2. A: _____

   B: _____

   A: _____

   B: _____

Listen and Talk C

W: _____

B: _____

W: _____

B: _____

W: _____

B: _____

W: _____

B: _____

W: _____

B: _____

W: _____

Review 1

G: _____

B: _____

G: _____

B: _____

Review 2

M: _____

G: _____

M: _____

G: _____

1. A: 너 몸이 안 좋아 보여. 무슨 일 있니?
   B: 머리가 아파.
   A: 안됐다. 약을 먹으렴.
   B: 응, 그럴게.

2. A: 너 몸이 안 좋아 보여. 무슨 일 있니?
   B: 감기에 걸렸어.
   A: 안됐다. 병원에 가도록 하렴.
   B: 응, 그럴게.

W: 무슨 일이니, Andy?
B: 안녕하세요, 김 선생님. 제 오른손 엄지손가락이 아파요.
W: 음. 너 스마트폰을 많이 사용하니?
B: 네, 저 문자를 많이 해요. 왜요?
W: 내 생각에 너는 texting thumb인 것 같아.
B: texting thumb이요? texting thumb이 뭐예요?
W: 엄지손가락에 통증이 있는 거야. 문자를 너무 많이 하면 생길 수 있어.
B: 오, 그건 몰랐네요.
W: 손가락 스트레칭 운동을 좀 하는 게 어떠니?
B: 네, 그럴게요.
W: 그리고 문자를 너무 많이 하지 않도록 하렴.

G: 무슨 일 있니, Mike?
B: 머리가 너무 아파.
G: 너는 약을 먹는 것이 좋겠다.
B: 알겠어, 그럴게.

M: 무슨 일 있니, 미나야?
G: 목이 아파요. 그리고 콧물도 나요.
M: 내 생각에 네가 감기에 걸린 것 같구나. 좀 쉬도록 하렴.
G: 네, 그럴게요.

※ 다음 우리말과 일치하도록 빈칸에 알맞은 것을 골라 쓰시오.

1 _____ _____ _____ Your Smartphones!

   A. with   B. Smart   C. Be

2 _____ _____ smartphones is _____ for many of us these _____.

   A. days   B. living   C. difficult   D. without

3 However, _____ or too much _____ of smartphones can _____ various problems.

   A. use   B. cause   C. unwise

4 _____ you a _____?

   A. smombie   B. are

5 All _____ the world, people are walking _____ zombies.

   A. like   B. over   C. around

6 Their heads are _____, and their _____ are _____ their smartphones.

   A. on   B. down   C. eyes

7 We _____ _____ _____ smombies, smartphone zombies.

   A. such   B. people   C. call

8 _____ you are a smombie, you can have _____ _____ problems.

   A. safety   B. if   C. various

9 You _____ not see a hole in the street, _____ you may _____ and get _____.

   A. so   B. hurt   C. may   D. fall

10 You may _____ _____ a car accident, _____.

   A. get   B. too   C. into

11 So _____ can you do _____ _____ these problems?

   A. to   B. what   C. prevent

12 _____ _____.

   A. simple   B. it's

13 Do not look _____ your smartphone _____ you are _____!

   A. while   B. at   C. walking

14 Do you have _____ eyes or _____ _____?

   A. text   B. dry   C. neck

15 Smartphones can _____ various _____ _____.

   A. health   B. cause   C. problems

16 One _____ is _____ _____.

   A. example   B. eyes   C. dry

---

1 스마트폰을 현명하게 사용하라!

2 스마트폰 없이 사는 것은 요즘 많은 사람들에게 어렵다.

3 하지만 스마트폰을 현명하지 않게 사용하거나 너무 과도하게 사용하는 것은 다양한 문제를 야기할 수 있다.

4 당신은 스몸비인가요?

5 전 세계적으로 사람들이 좀비처럼 걸어다니고 있다.

6 그들의 머리는 아래를 향하고, 그들의 눈은 스마트폰을 향하고 있다.

7 우리는 그런 사람들을 스몸비, 즉 스마트폰 좀비라고 부른다.

8 만약 당신이 스몸비라면, 당신은 다양한 안전 관련 문제들을 겪을 수 있다.

9 당신은 거리에 있는 구덩이를 보지 못할 수도 있고, 그래서 넘어져서 다칠지도 모른다.

10 당신은 또한 교통사고를 당할지도 모른다.

11 그렇다면 이런 문제들을 방지하기 위해 무엇을 할 수 있을까?

12 간단하다.

13 걷고 있는 동안에는 스마트폰을 보지 마라!

14 당신은 안구 건조증이나 거북목 증후군이 있나요?

15 스마트폰은 다양한 건강상의 문제를 일으킬 수 있다.

16 한 가지 예가 안구 건조증이다.

17 _____ you _____ _____ your smartphone, you do not _____ often.
    A. blink   B. look   C. when   D. at

18 Then _____ eyes will _____ _____.
    A. dry   B. feel   C. your

19 _____ problem you can _____ is neck _____.
    A. have   B. pain   C. another

20 When you look _____ _____ your smartphone, the stress _____ your neck _____.
    A. at   B. increases   C. on   D. down

21 Too much _____ of your smartphone, _____ example, too much _____, can _____ neck pain.
    A. texting   B. for   C. use   D. cause

22 We _____ this _____ neck.
    A. text   B. call

23 _____ are some _____ for these _____.
    A. tips   B. problems   C. here

24 For _____ eyes, _____ to _____ often.
    A. blink   B. try   C. dry

25 For text neck, _____ your smartphone _____ to your eye _____.
    A. level   B. up   C. move

26 You can _____ do some neck _____ _____.
    A. stretching   B. also   C. exercises

27 _____ do you _____ when you _____ have your smartphone with you?
    A. feel   B. how   C. don't

28 Do you _____ _____ when your smartphone is not _____?
    A. nervous   B. around   C. feel

29 Do you _____ _____ when you _____ your smartphone and there is no _____ message?
    A. sad   B. text   C. feel   D. check

30 If your _____ are "yes," you _____ have smartphone _____.
    A. may   B. answers   C. addiction

31 _____ are _____ things you can do to _____ this.
    A. prevent   B. there   C. various

32 For example, _____ your smartphone _____ meals or meetings.
    A. off   B. turn   C. during

33 You can talk to people _____ _____ _____ them.
    A. texting   B. instead   C. of

17 스마트폰을 볼 때, 당신은 눈을 자주 깜박거리지 않는다.

18 그러면 눈이 건조하다고 느낄 것이다.

19 일어날 수 있는 또 다른 문제는 목 통증이다.

20 스마트폰을 내려다볼 때, 목에 가해지는 압박이 증가한다.

21 스마트폰을 너무 많이 사용하는 것은, 예를 들어, 너무 많이 문자를 하는 것은 목 통증을 일으킬 수 있다.

22 이런 증상을 거북목 증후군이라고 부른다.

23 여기에 이런 문제들을 위한 몇 가지 조언이 있다.

24 안구 건조증에는, 눈을 자주 깜박이려고 노력해라.

25 거북목 증후군에는 당신의 눈높이까지 스마트폰을 위로 올려라.

26 목 스트레칭 운동 또한 할 수 있다.

27 스마트폰이 없을 때 어떤 기분이 드나요?

28 스마트폰이 주위에 없을 때 당신은 초조한 기분이 드는가?

29 스마트폰을 확인했을 때 아무런 문자 메시지가 없으면 슬픈 기분이 드는가?

30 만약 당신의 대답이 '그렇다'이면, 당신은 스마트폰 중독일지도 모른다.

31 이것을 방지하기 위해 할 수 있는 일은 여러 가지가 있다.

32 예를 들어, 식사나 회의 중에는 스마트폰을 꺼라.

33 문자를 보내는 대신에 사람들과 이야기를 할 수 있다.

※ 다음 우리말과 일치하도록 빈칸에 알맞은 말을 쓰시오.

1 _____ _____ _____ Your Smartphones!

2 _____ _____ _____ is difficult for many of us _____ _____.

3 However, _____ _____ _____ _____ _____ of smartphones _____ _____ various problems.

4 _____ you _____ _____?

5 _____ _____ _____ _____, people are _____ _____ _____ _____.

6 Their heads are _____, and their eyes are _____ _____ _____.

7 We _____ _____ _____ _____, smartphone zombies.

8 If you are a smombie, you can have _____ _____ _____.

9 You _____ _____ _____ a hole in the street, _____ you _____ _____ and _____ _____.

10 You _____ _____ _____ a car accident, _____.

11 So what can you do _____ _____ _____ _____?

12 It's _____.

13 _____ _____ _____ _____ your smartphone _____ you are _____!

14 Do you have _____ _____ or _____ _____?

15 Smartphones can cause _____ _____ _____.

16 _____ _____ is _____ _____.

1 스마트폰을 현명하게 사용하라!

2 스마트폰 없이 사는 것은 요즘 많은 사람들에게 어렵다.

3 하지만 스마트폰을 현명하지 않게 사용하거나 너무 과도하게 사용하는 것은 다양한 문제를 야기할 수 있다.

4 당신은 스몸비인가요?

5 전 세계적으로 사람들이 좀비처럼 걸어다니고 있다.

6 그들의 머리는 아래를 향하고, 그들의 눈은 스마트폰을 향하고 있다.

7 우리는 그런 사람들을 스몸비, 즉 스마트폰 좀비라고 부른다.

8 만약 당신이 스몸비라면, 당신은 다양한 안전 관련 문제들을 겪을 수 있다.

9 당신은 거리에 있는 구덩이를 보지 못할 수도 있고, 그래서 넘어져서 다칠지도 모른다.

10 당신은 또한 교통사고를 당할지도 모른다.

11 그렇다면 이런 문제들을 방지하기 위해 무엇을 할 수 있을까?

12 간단하다.

13 걷고 있는 동안에는 스마트폰을 보지 마라!

14 당신은 안구 건조증이나 거북목 증후군이 있나요?

15 스마트폰은 다양한 건강상의 문제를 일으킬 수 있다.

16 한 가지 예가 안구 건조증이다.

17 When you _____ _____ your smartphone, you do not _____ _____.

18 Then your eyes _____ _____ _____.

19 _____ _____ you can have _____ _____ _____.

20 When you _____ _____ _____ your smartphone, the _____ _____ your neck _____.

21 _____ _____ _____ of your smartphone, for example, _____ _____ _____, can cause _____ _____.

22 We _____ this _____ _____.

23 _____ _____ _____ _____ for these problems.

24 For _____ _____, _____ _____ _____ often.

25 For text neck, _____ your smartphone _____ _____ _____ _____ _____.

26 You _____ _____ do some _____ _____ _____.

27 _____ _____ _____ _____ when you don't have your smartphone with you?

28 Do you _____ _____ when your smartphone is not _____?

29 Do you _____ _____ when you check your smartphone and there is _____ _____ _____?

30 If your _____ are "yes," you may have _____ _____.

31 There are various things you can do _____ _____ _____.

32 _____ _____, _____ _____ your smartphone _____ meals or meetings.

33 You _____ talk to people _____ _____ _____ them.

17 스마트폰을 볼 때, 당신은 눈을 자주 깜박거리지 않는다.

18 그러면 눈이 건조하다고 느낄 것이다.

19 일어날 수 있는 또 다른 문제는 목 통증이다.

20 스마트폰을 내려다볼 때, 목에 가해지는 압박이 증가한다.

21 스마트폰을 너무 많이 사용하는 것은, 예를 들어, 너무 많이 문자를 하는 것은 목 통증을 일으킬 수 있다.

22 이런 증상을 거북목 증후군이라고 부른다.

23 여기에 이런 문제들을 위한 몇 가지 조언이 있다.

24 안구 건조증에는, 눈을 자주 깜박이려고 노력해라.

25 거북목 증후군에는 당신의 눈높이까지 스마트폰을 위로 올려라.

26 목 스트레칭 운동 또한 할 수 있다.

27 스마트폰이 없을 때 어떤 기분이 드나요?

28 스마트폰이 주위에 없을 때 당신은 초조한 기분이 드는가?

29 스마트폰을 확인했을 때 아무런 문자 메시지가 없으면 슬픈 기분이 드는가?

30 만약 당신의 대답이 '그렇다'이면, 당신은 스마트폰 중독일지도 모른다.

31 이것을 방지하기 위해 할 수 있는 일은 여러 가지가 있다.

32 예를 들어, 식사나 회의 중에는 스마트폰을 꺼라.

33 문자를 보내는 대신에 사람들과 이야기를 할 수 있다.

※ 다음 문장을 우리말로 쓰시오.

1   Be Smart with Your Smartphones!

➡ _____

2   Living without smartphones is difficult for many of us these days.

➡ _____

3   However, unwise or too much use of smartphones can cause various problems.

➡ _____

4   Are you a smombie?

➡ _____

5   All over the world, people are walking around like zombies.

➡ _____

6   Their heads are down, and their eyes are on their smartphones.

➡ _____

7   We call such people smombies, smartphone zombies.

➡ _____

8   If you are a smombie, you can have various safety problems.

➡ _____

9   You may not see a hole in the street, so you may fall and get hurt.

➡ _____

10   You may get into a car accident, too.

➡ _____

11   So what can you do to prevent these problems?

➡ _____

12   It's simple.

➡ _____

13   Do not look at your smartphone while you are walking!

➡ _____

14   Do you have dry eyes or text neck?

➡ _____

15   Smartphones can cause various health problems.

➡ _____

16   One example is dry eyes.

➡ _____

17 ▶ When you look at your smartphone, you do not blink often.

➡ _____

18 ▶ Then your eyes will feel dry.

➡ _____

19 ▶ Another problem you can have is neck pain.

➡ _____

20 ▶ When you look down at your smartphone, the stress on your neck increases.

➡ _____

21 ▶ Too much use of your smartphone, for example, too much texting, can cause neck pain.

➡ _____

22 ▶ We call this text neck.

➡ _____

23 ▶ Here are some tips for these problems.

➡ _____

24 ▶ For dry eyes, try to blink often.

➡ _____

25 ▶ For text neck, move your smartphone up to your eye level.

➡ _____

26 ▶ You can also do some neck stretching exercises.

➡ _____

27 ▶ How do you feel when you don't have your smartphone with you?

➡ _____

28 ▶ Do you feel nervous when your smartphone is not around?

➡ _____

29 ▶ Do you feel sad when you check your smartphone and there is no text message?

➡ _____

30 ▶ If your answers are "yes," you may have smartphone addiction.

➡ _____

31 ▶ There are various things you can do to prevent this.

➡ _____

32 ▶ For example, turn off your smartphone during meals or meetings.

➡ _____

33 ▶ You can talk to people instead of texting them.

➡ _____

※ 다음 괄호 안의 단어들을 우리말에 맞도록 바르게 배열하시오.

1 (Smart / Be / with / Smartphones! / Your)
➡ _____

2 (without / living / is / smartphones / for / difficult / of / many / us / days. / these)
➡ _____

3 (unwise / however, / or / much / too / of / use / can / smartphones / problems. / various / cause)
➡ _____

4 (you / are / smombie? / a)
➡ _____

5 (over / all / world, / the / are / people / around / walking / zombies. / like)
➡ _____

6 (heads / their / down, / are / and / eyes / their / are / smartphones. / their / on)
➡ _____

7 (call / we / people / such / smombies, / zombies. / smartphone)
➡ _____

8 (you / if / a / are / smombie, / can / you / various / have / problems. / safety)
➡ _____

9 (may / you / see / not / hole / a / the / in / street, / you / so / fall / may / hurt. / get / and)
➡ _____

10 (may / you / into / get / car / a / too. / accident,)
➡ _____

11 (what / so / you / can / to / do / problems? / these / prevent)
➡ _____

12 (simple. / it's)
➡ _____

13 (not / do / at / look / smartphone / your / you / while / walking! / are)
➡ _____

14 (you / do / dry / have / or / eyes / neck? / text)
➡ _____

15 (can / smartphones / cause / problems. / health / various)
➡ _____

16 (example / one / eyes. / dry / is)
➡ _____

---

1 스마트폰을 현명하게 사용하라!

2 스마트폰 없이 사는 것은 요즘 많은 사람들에게 어렵다.

3 하지만 스마트폰을 현명하지 않게 사용하거나 너무 과도하게 사용하는 것은 다양한 문제를 야기할 수 있다.

4 당신은 스몸비인가요?

5 전 세계적으로 사람들이 좀비처럼 걸어다니고 있다.

6 그들의 머리는 아래를 향하고, 그들의 눈은 스마트폰을 향하고 있다.

7 우리는 그런 사람들을 스몸비, 즉 스마트폰 좀비라고 부른다.

8 만약 당신이 스몸비라면, 당신은 다양한 안전 관련 문제들을 겪을 수 있다.

9 당신은 거리에 있는 구덩이를 보지 못할 수도 있고, 그래서 넘어져서 다칠지도 모른다.

10 당신은 또한 교통사고를 당할지도 모른다.

11 그렇다면 이런 문제들을 방지하기 위해 무엇을 할 수 있을까?

12 간단하다.

13 걷고 있는 동안에는 스마트폰을 보지 마라!

14 당신은 안구 건조증이나 거북목 증후군이 있나요?

15 스마트폰은 다양한 건강상의 문제를 일으킬 수 있다.

16 한 가지 예가 안구 건조증이다.

17 (you / when / at / look / smartphone, / your / do / you / not / often. / blink)
➡ _____

18 (your / then / will / eyes / dry. / feel)
➡ _____

19 (problem / another / can / you / is / have / pain. / neck)
➡ _____

20 (you / when / down / look / your / at / smartphone, / stress / the / on / increases. / neck / your)
➡ _____

21 (much / too / of / use / smartphone, / your / example,/ for / much / too / texting, / cause / can / pain. / neck)
➡ _____
_____

22 (call / we / neck. / text / this)
➡ _____

23 (are / here / tips / some / for / problems. / these)
➡ _____

24 (dry / for / eyes, / to / try / often. / blink)
➡ _____

25 (text / for / neck, / your / move / smartphone / to / up / level. / eye / your)
➡ _____

26 (can / you / do / also / neck / some / exercises. / stretching)
➡ _____

27 (do / how / feel / you / you / when / have / don't / smartphone / you? / with / your)
➡ _____

28 (you / do / nervous / feel / when / smartphone / your / around? / not / is)
➡ _____

29 (you / do / sad / feel / you / when / check / smartphone / your / and / is / there / text / message? / no)
➡ _____

30 (your / if / answers / "yes," / are / may / you / addiction. / smartphone / have)
➡ _____

31 (are / there / things / various / can / you / to / do / this. / prevent)
➡ _____

32 (example, / for / off / turn / smartphone / your / meals / meetings. / during / or)
➡ _____

33 (can / you / talk / people / to / of / instead / them. / texting)
➡ _____

17 스마트폰을 볼 때, 당신은 눈을 자주 깜박거리지 않는다.
18 그러면 눈이 건조하다고 느낄 것이다.
19 일어날 수 있는 또 다른 문제는 목 통증이다.
20 스마트폰을 내려다볼 때, 목에 가해지는 압박이 증가한다.
21 스마트폰을 너무 많이 사용하는 것은, 예를 들어, 너무 많이 문자를 하는 것은 목 통증을 일으킬 수 있다.
22 이런 증상을 거북목 증후군이라고 부른다.
23 여기에 이런 문제들을 위한 몇 가지 조언이 있다.
24 안구 건조증에는, 눈을 자주 깜박이려고 노력해라.
25 거북목 증후군에는 당신의 눈높이까지 스마트폰을 위로 올려라.
26 목 스트레칭 운동 또한 할 수 있다.
27 스마트폰이 없을 때 어떤 기분이 드나요?
28 스마트폰이 주위에 없을 때 당신은 초조한 기분이 드는가?
29 스마트폰을 확인했을 때 아무런 문자 메시지가 없으면 슬픈 기분이 드는가?
30 만약 당신의 대답이 '그렇다'이면, 당신은 스마트폰 중독일지도 모른다.
31 이것을 방지하기 위해 할 수 있는 일은 여러 가지가 있다.
32 예를 들어, 식사나 회의 중에는 스마트폰을 꺼라.
33 문자를 보내는 대신에 사람들과 이야기를 할 수 있다.

※ 다음 우리말을 영어로 쓰시오.

1 스마트폰을 현명하게 사용하라!

➡ _____

2 스마트폰 없이 사는 것은 요즘 많은 사람들에게 어렵다.

➡ _____

3 하지만 스마트폰을 현명하지 않게 사용하거나 너무 과도하게 사용하는 것은 다양한 문제를 야기할 수 있다.

➡ _____

4 당신은 스몸비인가요?

➡ _____

5 전 세계적으로 사람들이 좀비처럼 걸어다니고 있다.

➡ _____

6 그들의 머리는 아래를 향하고, 그들의 눈은 스마트폰을 향하고 있다.

➡ _____

7 우리는 그런 사람들을 스몸비, 즉 스마트폰 좀비라고 부른다.

➡ _____

8 만약 당신이 스몸비라면, 당신은 다양한 안전 관련 문제들을 겪을 수 있다.

➡ _____

9 당신은 거리에 있는 구덩이를 보지 못할 수도 있고, 그래서 넘어져서 다칠지도 모른다.

➡ _____

10 당신은 또한 교통사고를 당할지도 모른다.

➡ _____

11 그렇다면 이런 문제들을 방지하기 위해 무엇을 할 수 있을까?

➡ _____

12 간단하다.

➡ _____

13 걷고 있는 동안에는 스마트폰을 보지 마라!

➡ _____

14 당신은 안구 건조증이나 거북목 증후군이 있나요?

➡ _____

15 스마트폰은 다양한 건강상의 문제를 일으킬 수 있다.

➡ _____

16 한 가지 예가 안구 건조증이다.

➡ _____

17 스마트폰을 볼 때, 당신은 눈을 자주 깜박거리지 않는다.

➡ _____

18 그러면 눈이 건조하다고 느낄 것이다.

➡ _____

19 일어날 수 있는 또 다른 문제는 목 통증이다.

➡ _____

20 스마트폰을 내려다볼 때, 목에 가해지는 압박이 증가한다.

➡ _____

21 스마트폰을 너무 많이 사용하는 것은, 예를 들어, 너무 많이 문자를 하는 것은 목 통증을 일으킬 수 있다.

➡ _____

22 이런 증상을 거북목 증후군이라고 부른다.

➡ _____

23 여기에 이런 문제들을 위한 몇 가지 조언이 있다.

➡ _____

24 안구 건조증에는, 눈을 자주 깜박이려고 노력해라.

➡ _____

25 거북목 증후군에는 당신의 눈높이까지 스마트폰을 위로 올려라.

➡ _____

26 목 스트레칭 운동 또한 할 수 있다.

➡ _____

27 스마트폰이 없을 때 어떤 기분이 드나요?

➡ _____

28 스마트폰이 주위에 없을 때 당신은 초조한 기분이 드는가?

➡ _____

29 스마트폰을 확인했을 때 아무런 문자 메시지가 없으면 슬픈 기분이 드는가?

➡ _____

30 만약 당신의 대답이 '그렇다'이면, 당신은 스마트폰 중독일지도 모른다.

➡ _____

31 이것을 방지하기 위해 할 수 있는 일은 여러 가지가 있다.

➡ _____

32 예를 들어, 식사나 회의 중에는 스마트폰을 꺼라.

➡ _____

33 문자를 보내는 대신에 사람들과 이야기를 할 수 있다.

➡ _____

※ 다음 우리말과 일치하도록 빈칸에 알맞은 말을 쓰시오.

Talk and Play

1. A: What's _____?

2. B: I _____ _____ _____.

3. A: That's too bad. _____ _____ you get _____ _____.

4. B: OK, _____ _____.

1. A: 무슨 일이니?
2. B: 나는 열이 나.
3. A: 안됐다. 좀 쉬도록 하렴.
4. B: 응, 알겠어.

After You Read B

1. _____ _____ _____ Your Smartphones!

2. Minho: Yesterday, I _____ on the street and _____ _____.

3. I _____ _____ and I _____ _____ a hole.

4. Reply: _____ _____ use your smartphone _____ you _____ _____.

5. Emma: My eyes _____ _____ when I use my smartphone.

6. Reply: _____ _____ _____ often.

7. Suji: I have neck pain _____ I _____ _____ _____.

8. Reply: Move your smartphone _____ _____ your _____ _____ and do some neck _____ _____.

9. Eric: I think I _____ _____ _____.

10. Reply: _____ _____ your smartphone _____ meals or meetings and talk to people _____ _____ _____ them.

1. 스마트폰을 현명하게 사용하라!
2. 민호: 어제, 나는 길에서 넘어져서 다쳤다.
3. 나는 문자를 보내고 있었고 구덩이를 보지 못했다.
4. 대답: 걷는 동안에는 스마트폰을 사용하지 마라.
5. Emma: 나는 스마트폰을 사용할 때 눈이 건조하다고 느낀다.
6. 대답: 눈을 자주 깜박이도록 노력해라.
7. 수지: 나는 문자를 많이 보낼 때 목 통증이 있다.
8. 대답: 스마트폰을 눈높이까지 들고, 목 스트레칭 운동을 해라.
9. Eric: 나는 스마트폰 중독인 것 같다.
10. 대답: 식사나 회의 중에는 스마트폰을 끄고 문자를 보내는 대신에 사람들과 이야기해라.

Around the World

1. This sign says, "_____ _____ of _____ your smartphone _____ you are walking."

2. _____ _____ traffic lights on the ground, _____ people can see them _____ they _____ _____ their smartphones.

3. This sign on the ground _____, "This _____ of the street is for people _____ _____ _____."

1. 이 표지판은 "걷는 동안 스마트폰 사용을 주의하세요."라는 의미이다.
2. 바닥에 신호등이 있어서, 사람들이 스마트폰을 사용하는 동안에도 신호등을 볼 수 있다.
3. 바닥에 있는 이 표지판은 "길의 이쪽 편은 문자를 보내고 있는 사람들을 위한 곳입니다."라는 의미이다.

※ 다음 우리말을 영어로 쓰시오.

Talk and Play

1. A: 무슨 일이니?
➡️ _____

2. B: 나는 열이 나.
➡️ _____

3. A: 안됐다. 좀 쉬도록 하렴.
➡️ _____

4. B: 응, 알겠어.
➡️ _____

After You Read B

1. 스마트폰을 현명하게 사용하라!
➡️ _____

2. 민호: 어제, 나는 길에서 넘어져서 다쳤다.
➡️ _____

3. 나는 문자를 보내고 있었고 구덩이를 보지 못했다.
➡️ _____

4. 대답: 걷는 동안에는 스마트폰을 사용하지 마라.
➡️ _____

5. Emma: 나는 스마트폰을 사용할 때 눈이 건조하다고 느낀다.
➡️ _____

6. 대답: 눈을 자주 깜박이도록 노력해라.
➡️ _____

7. 수지: 나는 문자를 많이 보낼 때 목 통증이 있다.
➡️ _____

8. 대답: 스마트폰을 눈높이까지 들고, 목 스트레칭 운동을 해라.
➡️ _____

9. Eric: 나는 스마트폰 중독인 것 같다.
➡️ _____

10. 대답: 식사나 회의 중에는 스마트폰을 끄고 문자를 보내는 대신에 사람들과 이야기해라.
➡️ _____

Around the World

1. 이 표지판은 "걷는 동안 스마트폰 사용을 주의하세요."라는 의미이다.
➡️ _____

2. 바닥에 신호등이 있어서, 사람들이 스마트폰을 사용하는 동안에도 신호등을 볼 수 있다.
➡️ _____

3. 바닥에 있는 이 표지판은 "길의 이쪽 편은 문자를 보내고 있는 사람들을 위한 곳입니다."라는 의미이다.
➡️ _____

※ 다음 영어를 우리말로 쓰시오.

01	special
02	brave
03	creative
04	simple
05	detail
06	adventurous
07	whole
08	beauty
09	subject
10	warning
11	melt
12	dynamic
13	escape
14	flight
15	exhibition
16	romantic
17	difference
18	skip
19	forever
20	gather
21	glue

22	imaginative
23	feather
24	different
25	sentence
26	forget
27	inventor
28	example
29	foolish
30	outline
31	furthermore
32	ready
33	myth
34	warn
35	fall in love with ~
36	be interested in ~
37	deal with
38	in addition to
39	be proud of ~
40	in contrast
41	focus on ~
42	Why don't you+동사원형~?
43	try to+동사원형

※ 다음 우리말을 영어로 쓰시오.

01 주제		22 다른	
02 전부의, 전체의		23 어리석은	
03 역동적인		24 문장	
04 경고하다		25 영원히	
05 달아나다, 탈출하다		26 상상력이 풍부한	
06 전시회		27 잊어버리다, 잊다	
07 단순한		28 발명가	
08 신화		29 준비된	
09 아름다움, 미		30 게다가, 더욱이	
10 특별한		31 예, 사례	
11 모으다		32 세부 사항	
12 로맨틱한, 낭만적인		33 빼먹다, 거르다	
13 공상 과학 영화		34 경고, 주의	
14 모험심이 강한		35 ~을 다루다	
15 (새의) 털, 깃털		36 점점 더 높이	
16 차이		37 ~와 사랑에 빠지다	
17 용감한		38 ~ 앞에	
18 녹다		39 ~에 더하여	
19 창의적인		40 ~하려고 시도하다	
20 비행, 날기		41 ~에 관심이 있다	
21 윤곽, 외형		42 ~을 자랑스러워하다	
		43 ~에 초점을 맞추다	

※ 다음 영영풀이에 알맞은 단어를 <보기>에서 골라 쓴 후, 우리말 뜻을 쓰시오.

1 _____ : a public show of something: _____

2 _____ : to say something very loudly: _____

3 _____ : silly or not sensible: _____

4 _____ : the act of flying through the air: _____

5 _____ : showing a strong feeling of love: _____

6 _____ : to get away from a place or person: _____

7 _____ : to come together in a group: _____

8 _____ : a small fact, feature, or piece of information: _____

9 _____ : willing to try new or exciting things: _____

10 _____ : a line that shows the shape of something: _____

11 _____ : to avoid something or not to do something: _____

12 _____ : one of the light soft things that cover a bird's body: _____

13 _____ : one of the parts of bird's or insect's body that it uses to fly: _____

14 _____ : used when adding another piece of information: _____

15 _____ : an old story about gods, brave people, magical creatures, etc.: _____

16 _____ : to tell someone that something bad might happen, so that he or she can avoid it: _____

보기

warn	feather	gather	adventurous
exhibition	escape	myth	foolish
romantic	wing	flight	furthermore
skip	shout	detail	outline

※ 다음 우리말과 일치하도록 빈칸에 알맞은 말을 쓰시오.

Listen and Talk A-1

G: I'm _____ _____ _____ to a piano concert tomorrow. Do you want _____ _____ _____ me, Kevin?

B: Sure. _____ _____ _____ we _____?

G: The concert _____ _____ 7 o'clock, so _____ _____ at 6 at the bus stop.

B: OK. _____ you _____.

Listen and Talk A-2

G: I'm _____ _____ _____ _____ _____ Cats this Saturday. Do you _____ _____ _____ with me?

B: Sure. _____ _____ and _____ _____ we meet?

G: The musical starts _____ _____ _____. _____ _____ at 2 at Dream Art Hall.

B: Great. _____ you _____ _____.

Listen and Talk A-3

G: I'm _____ _____ _____ _____ a soccer game next Friday. _____ _____ _____ me, Jinho?

B: That _____ great. What time _____ _____ _____?

G: _____ _____ at 10:30 _____ _____ _____ Green Stadium.

B: OK. See you then.

Listen and Talk A-4

B: _____ are you _____ _____ _____ this Sunday?

G: I'm _____ _____ _____ to Dream Amusement Park with my brother. You can go with us _____ you _____ _____.

B: I'd _____ _____. _____ _____ we meet?

G: I want to go early, so _____ _____ at 9 at the subway station.

B: _____ good. I'll see you then.

Listen and Talk B

A: I'm _____ _____ _____ a movie this Saturday. Do you _____ _____ go with me?

B: Sure. _____ _____ and _____ should we _____?

A: _____ about _____ at 2:30 in front of Star Movie Theater?

B: OK. _____ _____ _____.

해석

G: 나는 내일 피아노 콘서트에 갈 예정이야. 나랑 같이 갈래, Kevin?
B: 물론이지. 몇 시에 만날까?
G: 콘서트는 7시에 시작하니까 6시에 버스 정류장에서 만나자.
B: 좋아. 그때 보자.

G: 나는 이번 주 토요일에 'Cats'를 보러 갈 계획이야. 나랑 같이 갈래?
B: 좋아. 몇 시에 어디서 만날까?
G: 뮤지컬은 3시에 시작해. 2시에 Dream 아트 홀에서 만나자.
B: 좋아. 토요일에 만나자.

G: 나는 다음 주 금요일에 축구 경기를 보러 갈 계획이야. 나랑 같이 가는 게 어떠니, 진호야?
B: 좋은 생각이다. 몇 시에 만날까?
G: Green 경기장 앞에서 10시 30분에 만나자.
B: 좋아. 그때 보자.

B: 이번 주 일요일에 무엇을 할 계획이니?
G: 나는 내 남동생과 Dream 놀이동산에 갈 예정이야. 만약 네가 원한다면 우리와 함께 가도 돼.
B: 그러고 싶어. 언제 만날까?
G: 나는 일찍 가고 싶어, 그래서 9시에 지하철역에서 만나자.
B: 좋아. 그때 보자.

A: 나는 이번 주 토요일에 영화를 볼 계획이야. 나랑 같이 갈래?
B: 물론이지. 몇 시에 어디에서 만날까?
A: Star 영화관 앞에서 2시 30분에 만나는 게 어때?
B: 좋아. 그때 보자.

Listen and Talk C

(*Smartphone rings.*)

B: Hi, Kate. What's _____?

G: Hi, Minho. What are you _____ _____ _____ this Saturday?

B: _____ _____. Why?

G: I'm _____ _____ _____ to the Van Gogh exhibition at the National Art Museum. Do you _____ _____ _____ with me?

B: I'd _____ _____! He's my favorite painter. _____ _____ _____ we _____?

G: _____ _____ _____ at 11?

B: OK. _____ _____ we meet?

G: _____ meet _____ _____ _____ the ticket office.

B: Sounds good. I'll _____ _____ _____ at 11.

Review 1

G: I'm _____ _____ go to a piano concert this Friday. _____ _____ _____ _____ me, Kevin?

B: Sure. What time _____ _____ _____?

G: _____ _____ at 10:30 _____ _____ _____ _____.

B: OK. See you _____.

Review 2

B: I'm _____ _____ _____ to a soccer game tomorrow. _____ _____ _____ to go with me, Susan?

G: Sure. _____ _____ _____ we _____?

B: The game begins at 7, so _____ _____ at 6 _____ _____ _____ Dream Stadium.

G: OK. See you then.

Review 3

B: Sumi, _____ _____ _____ _____ _____ with Jenny this Saturday. Will you _____ us?

G: Sounds great. _____ time should we _____?

B: How _____ _____ at 12:30?

G: OK. _____ _____ we _____?

B: Let's _____ _____ _____ the shopping mall.

(스마트폰이 울린다.)

B: 안녕, Kate. 무슨 일이야?

G: 안녕, 민호야. 이번 토요일에 뭐 할 거야?

B: 특별한 일은 없어. 왜?

G: 나는 국립 미술관에서 하는 반 고흐 전시회에 갈 계획이야. 나와 함께 갈래?

B: 그러고 싶어! 그는 내가 가장 좋아하는 화가거든. 몇 시에 만날까?

G: 11시에 만나는 게 어때?

B: 좋아. 어디에서 만날까?

G: 매표소 앞에서 만나자.

B: 좋아. 11시에 거기에서 봐.

G: 나는 이번 주 금요일에 피아노 콘서트에 갈 계획이야. 나랑 같이 가는 게 어때, Kevin?

B: 물론이지. 몇 시에 만날까?

G: 10시 30분에 버스 정류장에서 만나자.

B: 좋아. 그때 보자.

B: 나는 내일 축구 경기에 갈 계획이야. 나랑 같이 갈래, Susan?

G: 물론이지. 몇 시에 만날까?

B: 경기는 7시에 시작하니까, Dream 경기장 앞에서 6시에 만나자.

G: 좋아. 그때 보자.

B: 수미야, 나 이번 주 토요일에 Jenny와 쇼핑을 갈 계획이야. 너도 같이 갈래?

G: 좋은 생각이야. 몇 시에 만날까?

B: 12시 30분에 만나는 게 어때?

G: 좋아. 어디서 만날까?

B: 쇼핑몰 앞에서 만나자.

※ 다음 우리말에 맞도록 대화를 영어로 쓰시오.

Listen and Talk A-1

G: _____

_____

B: _____

G: _____

B: _____

G: 나는 내일 피아노 콘서트에 갈 예정이야. 나랑 같이 갈래, Kevin?
B: 물론이지. 몇 시에 만날까?
G: 콘서트는 7시에 시작하니까 6시에 버스 정류장에서 만나자.
B: 좋아. 그때 보자.

Listen and Talk A-2

G: _____

B: _____

G: _____

B: _____

G: 나는 이번 주 토요일에 'Cats'를 보러 갈 계획이야. 나랑 같이 갈래?
B: 좋아. 몇 시에 어디서 만날까?
G: 뮤지컬은 3시에 시작해. 2시에 Dream 아트 홀에서 만나자.
B: 좋아. 토요일에 만나자.

Listen and Talk A-3

G: _____

_____

B: _____

G: _____

B: _____

G: 나는 다음 주 금요일에 축구 경기를 보러 갈 계획이야. 나랑 같이 가는 게 어떠니, 진호야?
B: 좋은 생각이다. 몇 시에 만날까?
G: Green 경기장 앞에서 10시 30분에 만나자.
B: 좋아. 그때 보자.

Listen and Talk A-4

B: _____

G: _____

_____

B: _____

G: _____

B: _____

B: 이번 주 일요일에 무엇을 할 계획이니?
G: 나는 내 남동생과 Dream 놀이동산에 갈 예정이야. 만약 네가 원한다면 우리와 함께 가도 돼.
B: 그러고 싶어. 언제 만날까?
G: 나는 일찍 가고 싶어, 그래서 9시에 지하철역에서 만나자.
B: 좋아. 그때 보자.

Listen and Talk B

A: _____

B: _____

A: _____

B: _____

A: 나는 이번 주 토요일에 영화를 볼 계획이야. 나랑 같이 갈래?
B: 물론이지. 몇 시에 어디에서 만날까?
A: Star 영화관 앞에서 2시 30분에 만나는 게 어때?
B: 좋아. 그때 보자.

Listen and Talk C

(*Smartphone rings.*)

B: _____

G: _____

B: _____

G: _____

_____

B: _____

G: _____

B: _____

G: _____

B: _____

(스마트폰이 울린다.)

B: 안녕, Kate. 무슨 일이야?

G: 안녕, 민호야. 이번 토요일에 뭐 할 거야?

B: 특별한 일은 없어. 왜?

G: 나는 국립 미술관에서 하는 반 고흐 전시회에 갈 계획이야. 나와 함께 갈래?

B: 그러고 싶어! 그는 내가 가장 좋아하는 화가거든. 몇 시에 만날까?

G: 11시에 만나는 게 어때?

B: 좋아. 어디에서 만날까?

G: 매표소 앞에서 만나자.

B: 좋아. 11시에 거기에서 봐.

Review 1

G: _____

_____

B: _____

G: _____

B: _____

G: 나는 이번 주 금요일에 피아노 콘서트에 갈 계획이야. 나랑 같이 가는 게 어때, Kevin?

B: 물론이지. 몇 시에 만날까?

G: 10시 30분에 버스 정류장에서 만나자.

B: 좋아. 그때 보자.

Review 2

B: _____

_____

G: _____

B: _____

G: _____

B: 나는 내일 축구 경기에 갈 계획이야. 나랑 같이 갈래, Susan?

G: 물론이지. 몇 시에 만날까?

B: 경기는 7시에 시작하니까, Dream 경기장 앞에서 6시에 만나자.

G: 좋아. 그때 보자.

Review 3

B: _____

G: _____

B: _____

G: _____

B: _____

B: 수미야, 나 이번 주 토요일에 Jenny와 쇼핑을 갈 계획이야. 너도 같이 갈래?

G: 좋은 생각이야. 몇 시에 만날까?

B: 12시 30분에 만나는 게 어때?

G: 좋아. 어디서 만날까?

B: 쇼핑몰 앞에서 만나자.

※ 다음 우리말과 일치하도록 빈칸에 알맞은 것을 골라 쓰시오.

1 _____ Story, _____ Paintings
A. Different   B. Same

2 We often find _____ _____ with the _____ _____.
A. subject   B. paintings   C. same   D. different

3 An _____ is *The Flight of Icarus* by Henri Matisse _____ *The Fall of Icarus* _____ Marc Chagall.
A. by   B. and   C. example

4 They are _____ about the _____ Greek _____.
A. both   B. myth   C. same

5 The _____ _____ of Icarus
A. Myth   B. Greek

6 Daedalus was _____ _____ _____.
A. great   B. a   C. inventor

7 King Minos liked Daedalus' work _____ much _____ he wanted to _____ Daedalus with him _____.
A. that   B. keep   C. forever   D. so

8 Daedalus, _____, _____ to leave, _____ the King _____ him and his son, Icarus, in a tall tower.
A. so   B. however   C. kept   D. tried

9 Daedalus _____ _____ _____.
A. to   B. escape   C. wanted

10 _____ day, Daedalus _____ birds _____.
A. saw   B. one   C. flying

11 "Wings! I _____ _____!" he _____.
A. shouted   B. need   C. wings

12 Daedalus then _____ bird _____ and _____ them together with _____.
A. wax   B. feathers   C. gathered   D. glued

13 When the wings were _____, he _____ his son, "_____ fly too _____ to the sun.
A. warned   B. close   C. don't   D ready

14 The _____ will _____."
A. melt   B. wax

15 Daedalus and Icarus _____ _____ _____.
A. to   B. began   C. fly

16 Icarus was _____ excited _____ he _____ his father's _____.
A. warning   B. that   C. forgot   D. so

17 He _____ higher and _____, and the wax began to _____.
A. melt   B. flew   C. higher

18 "Oh, no! I'm _____," Icarus _____ _____.
A. cried   B. falling   C. out

19 Icarus _____ _____ the sea and _____.
A. into   B. died   C. fell

20 Two _____ _____

A. Paintings   B. Different

21 Matisse and Chagall both _____ _____ the same _____ in their paintings, but they are _____ .

A. with   B. different   C. subject   D. deal

22 First, in Matisse's _____ , you can _____ Icarus _____ , but in Chagall's painting, the boy is _____ .

A. painting   B. flying   C. falling   D. see

23 This difference _____ _____ the _____ _____ that the two painters had.

A. different   B. from   C. comes   D. ideas

24 Matisse _____ that Icarus was _____ and _____ .

A. adventurous   B. thought   C. brave

25 In _____ , Chagall _____ that Icarus was _____ .

A. contrast   B. foolish   C. thought

26 Second, Matisse's painting is very _____ , _____ Chagall's painting has many _____ .

A. but   B. details   C. simple

27 In Matisse's painting, _____ are _____ Icarus and _____ _____ .

A. only   B. stars   C. there   D. some

28 _____ , Icarus' body has _____ a simple _____ .

A. outline   B. furthermore   C. just

29 _____ _____ , Chagall painted many people and houses in _____ _____ Icarus.

A. addition   B. contrast   C. to   D. in

30 This _____ comes from the _____ painting _____ of the two painters.

A. styles   B. different   C. difference

31 _____ _____ do you like _____ ?

A. more   B. painting   C. whose

32 People will have different answers _____ they may see the _____ thing in _____ _____ .

A. because   B. different   C. same   D. ways

20 다른 두 그림

21 Matisse와 Chagall 둘 다 그들의 그림에서 같은 주제를 다루지만, 그것들은 다르다.

22 첫째, Matisse의 그림에서, 여러분은 Icarus가 날고 있는 것을 볼 수 있지만, Chagall의 그림에서는 그 소년이 추락하고 있다.

23 이러한 차이는 두 화가들이 갖고 있던 서로 다른 생각에서 기인한다.

24 Matisse는 Icarus가 용감하고 모험심이 강하다고 생각했다.

25 반면에 Chagall은 Icarus가 어리석다고 생각했다.

26 둘째, Matisse의 그림은 매우 단순하지만, Chagall의 그림에는 세부적인 것들이 많다.

27 Matisse의 그림에는 Icarus와 몇 개의 별들만 있다.

28 게다가 Icarus의 몸은 단지 단순한 윤곽만으로 되어 있다.

29 반면에 Chagall은 Icarus뿐만 아니라 많은 사람들과 집들을 그렸다.

30 이러한 차이는 두 화가의 서로 다른 화풍에서 기인한다.

31 여러분은 누구의 그림이 더 좋은가?

32 사람들은 같은 것을 다른 방식들로 볼 수도 있기 때문에 서로 다른 대답을 할 것이다.

※ 다음 우리말과 일치하도록 빈칸에 알맞은 말을 쓰시오.

1 _____ Story, _____ _____

2 We often find _____ _____ with _____ _____ _____.

3 An _____ is *The Flight of Icarus* _____ Henri Matisse and *The Fall of Icarus* _____ Marc Chagall.

4 They are _____ about _____ _____ _____ _____.

5 The _____ _____ of Icarus

6 Daedalus was _____ _____ _____.

7 King Minos liked Daedalus' _____ _____ much _____ he _____ _____ _____ Daedalus with him _____.

8 Daedalus, _____, _____ _____ _____, _____ the King _____ him and his son, Icarus, in a tall tower.

9 Daedalus _____ _____ _____.

10 One day, Daedalus _____ _____ _____.

11 "Wings! _____ _____ _____!" he _____.

12 Daedalus then _____ bird feathers and _____ _____ _____ _____ _____.

13 When the wings were _____, he _____ his son, "_____ _____ _____ _____ to the sun.

14 The wax _____ _____."

15 Daedalus and Icarus _____ _____ _____.

16 Icarus was _____ excited _____ he forgot his father's _____.

17 He flew _____ _____ _____, and the wax began to melt.

18 "Oh, no! I'm _____," Icarus _____ _____.

19 Icarus _____ _____ the sea and _____.

1 같은 이야기, 다른 그림

2 우리는 종종 같은 주제의 다른 그림들을 발견한다.

3 한 예가 Henri Matisse가 그린 "The Flight of Icarus(이카로스의 비행)"와 Marc Chagall이 그린 "The Fall of Icarus(이카로스의 추락)"이다.

4 그것들은 둘 다 같은 그리스 신화에 관한 것이다.

5 Icarus에 관한 그리스 신화

6 Daedalus는 훌륭한 발명가였다.

7 Minos왕은 Daedalus의 작품을 매우 좋아해서 Daedalus를 그의 곁에 영원히 두고 싶어 했다.

8 그러나 Daedalus는 떠나려고 했고, 그러자 왕은 그와 그의 아들인 Icarus를 높은 탑에 가두었다.

9 Daedalus는 탈출하고 싶었다.

10 어느 날, Daedalus는 새가 날고 있는 것을 보았다.

11 "날개! 날개가 필요해!" 그가 외쳤다.

12 그 다음에 Daedalus는 새의 깃털을 모아 그것들을 밀랍으로 붙였다.

13 날개가 준비되었을 때, 그는 아들에게 경고했다. "태양에 너무 가까이 날지 마라.

14 밀랍이 녹을 거야."

15 Daedalus와 Icarus는 날기 시작했다.

16 Icarus는 매우 흥분해서 아버지의 경고를 잊었다.

17 그는 점점 더 높이 날았고, 밀랍은 녹기 시작했다.

18 "오, 안 돼! 추락하고 있어." Icarus는 비명을 질렀다.

19 Icarus는 바다로 떨어져서 죽었다.

20 Two _____ _____

21 Matisse and Chagall _____ _____ _____ the _____ _____ in their paintings, but they are _____.

22 First, in Matisse's painting, you can _____ _____ _____ , but in Chagall's painting, the boy is _____.

23 This difference _____ _____ the _____ _____ that the two painters had.

24 Matisse _____ that Icarus was _____ and _____.

25 _____ _____, Chagall thought that Icarus was _____.

26 Second, Matisse's painting is _____ _____, but Chagall's painting has _____ _____.

27 In Matisse's painting, there are _____ _____ and _____ _____.

28 _____, Icarus' body has just a _____ _____.

29 _____ _____, Chagall painted many people and houses _____ _____ _____ Icarus.

30 This _____ _____ _____ the _____ _____ _____ of the two painters.

31 _____ _____ do you _____ _____?

32 People will have different answers _____ they may see the _____ _____ _____ _____ _____.

20 다른 두 그림

21 Matisse와 Chagall 둘 다 그들의 그림에서 같은 주제를 다루지만, 그것들은 다르다.

22 첫째, Matisse의 그림에서, 여러분은 Icarus가 날고 있는 것을 볼 수 있지만, Chagall의 그림에서는 그 소년이 추락하고 있다.

23 이러한 차이는 두 화가들이 갖고 있던 서로 다른 생각에서 기인한다.

24 Matisse는 Icarus가 용감하고 모험심이 강하다고 생각했다.

25 반면에 Chagall은 Icarus가 어리석다고 생각했다.

26 둘째, Matisse의 그림은 매우 단순하지만, Chagall의 그림에는 세부적인 것들이 많다.

27 Matisse의 그림에는 Icarus와 몇 개의 별들만 있다.

28 게다가 Icarus의 몸은 단지 단순한 윤곽만으로 되어 있다.

29 반면에 Chagall은 Icarus뿐만 아니라 많은 사람들과 집들을 그렸다.

30 이러한 차이는 두 화가의 서로 다른 화풍에서 기인한다.

31 여러분은 누구의 그림이 더 좋은가?

32 사람들은 같은 것을 다른 방식들로 볼 수도 있기 때문에 서로 다른 대답을 할 것이다.

※ 다음 문장을 우리말로 쓰시오.

1 ▸ Same Story, Different Paintings
➡ _____

2 ▸ We often find different paintings with the same subject.
➡ _____

3 ▸ An example is *The Flight of Icarus* by Henri Matisse and *The Fall of Icarus* by Marc Chagall.
➡ _____
_____

4 ▸ They are both about the same Greek myth.
➡ _____

5 ▸ The Greek Myth of Icarus
➡ _____

6 ▸ Daedalus was a great inventor.
➡ _____

7 ▸ King Minos liked Daedalus' work so much that he wanted to keep Daedalus with him forever.
➡ _____

8 ▸ Daedalus, however, tried to leave, so the King kept him and his son, Icarus, in a tall tower.
➡ _____

9 ▸ Daedalus wanted to escape.
➡ _____

10 ▸ One day, Daedalus saw birds flying.
➡ _____

11 ▸ "Wings! I need wings!" he shouted.
➡ _____

12 ▸ Daedalus then gathered bird feathers and glued them together with wax.
➡ _____

13 ▸ When the wings were ready, he warned his son, "Don't fly too close to the sun.
➡ _____

14 ▸ The wax will melt."
➡ _____

15 ▸ Daedalus and Icarus began to fly.
➡ _____

16 ▸ Icarus was so excited that he forgot his father's warning.
➡ _____

17 ▸ He flew higher and higher, and the wax began to melt.
➡ _____

18 ▸ "Oh, no! I'm falling," Icarus cried out.
➡ _____

19 ▸ Icarus fell into the sea and died.
➡ _____

20 Two Different Paintings

➡ _____

21 Matisse and Chagall both deal with the same subject in their paintings, but they are different.

➡ _____

22 First, in Matisse's painting, you can see Icarus flying, but in Chagall's painting, the boy is falling.

➡ _____

_____

23 This difference comes from the different ideas that the two painters had.

➡ _____

24 Matisse thought that Icarus was brave and adventurous.

➡ _____

25 In contrast, Chagall thought that Icarus was foolish.

➡ _____

26 Second, Matisse's painting is very simple, but Chagall's painting has many details.

➡ _____

27 In Matisse's painting, there are only Icarus and some stars.

➡ _____

28 Furthermore, Icarus' body has just a simple outline.

➡ _____

29 In contrast, Chagall painted many people and houses in addition to Icarus.

➡ _____

30 This difference comes from the different painting styles of the two painters.

➡ _____

31 Whose painting do you like more?

➡ _____

32 People will have different answers because they may see the same thing in different ways.

➡ _____

※ 다음 괄호 안의 단어들을 우리말에 맞도록 바르게 배열하시오.

1 (Story, / Paintings / Same / Different)
➡ _____

2 (often / we / different / find / with / paintings / same / subject. / the)
➡ _____

3 (example / an / is *Icarus* / *of* / *Flight* / *The* / Henri / by / Matisse / and / *of* / *The* / *Icarus* / *Fall* / Marc / by / Chagall.)
➡ _____

4 (are / they / about / both / the / Greek / same / myth.)
➡ _____

5 (Greek / The / Icarus / of / Myth)
➡ _____

6 (was / Daedalus / a / inventor. / great)
➡ _____

7 (Minos / King / Daedalus' / liked / so / work / much / that / wanted / he / keep / to / Daedalus / forever. / him / with)
➡ _____
_____

8 (however, / Daedalus, / to / tried / leave, / the / so / King / him / kept / and / son, / his / Icarus, / a / in / tower. / tall)
➡ _____
_____

9 (wanted / Daedalus / escape. / to)
➡ _____

10 (day, / one / saw / Daedalus / flying. / birds)
➡ _____

11 ("wings! / need / I / wings!" / shouted. / he)
➡ _____

12 (then / Daedalus / gathered / feathers / bird / and / them / glued / wax. / with / together)
➡ _____

13 (the / when / wings / ready, / were / warned / he / son, / his / "don't / too / fly / close / sun. / the / to)
➡ _____
_____

14 (wax / the / melt." / will)
➡ _____

15 (Icarus / and / Daedalus / began / fly. / to)
➡ _____

16 (was / Icarus / excited / so / that / forgot / he / warning. / father's / his)
➡ _____

17 (flew / he / higher, / and / higher / and / wax / the / melt. / to / began)
➡ _____

18 ("oh, / I'm / no! / falling," / cried / Icarus / out.)
➡ _____

19 (fell / Icarus / into / sea / the / died. / and)
➡ _____

1 같은 이야기, 다른 그림

2 우리는 종종 같은 주제의 다른 그림들을 발견한다.

3 한 예가 Henri Matisse가 그린 "The Flight of Icarus(이카로스의 비행)"와 Marc Chagall이 그린 "The Fall of Icarus(이카로스의 추락)"이다.

4 그것들은 둘 다 같은 그리스 신화에 관한 것이다.

5 Icarus에 관한 그리스 신화

6 Daedalus는 훌륭한 발명가였다.

7 Minos왕은 Daedalus의 작품을 매우 좋아해서 Daedalus를 그의 곁에 영원히 두고 싶어 했다.

8 그러나 Daedalus는 떠나려고 했고, 그러자 왕은 그와 그의 아들인 Icarus를 높은 탑에 가두었다.

9 Daedalus는 탈출하고 싶었다.

10 어느 날, Daedalus는 새가 날고 있는 것을 보았다.

11 "날개! 날개가 필요해!" 그가 외쳤다.

12 그 다음에 Daedalus는 새의 깃털을 모아 그것들을 밀랍으로 붙였다.

13 날개가 준비되었을 때, 그는 아들에게 경고했다. "태양에 너무 가까이 날지 마라.

14 밀랍이 녹을 거야."

15 Daedalus와 Icarus는 날기 시작했다.

16 Icarus는 매우 흥분해서 아버지의 경고를 잊었다.

17 그는 점점 더 높이 날았고, 밀랍은 녹기 시작했다.

18 "오, 안 돼! 추락하고 있어." Icarus는 비명을 질렀다.

19 Icarus는 바다로 떨어져서 죽었다.

20 (Different / Two / Paintings)

➡ _____

21 (Chagall / and / Matisse / deal / both / with / same / the / subject / their / in / paintings, / they / but / different. / are)

➡ _____

22 (in / first, / painting, / Matisse's / can / you / see / flying, / Icarus / in / but / painting, / Chagall's / boy / falling. / is / the)

➡ _____

23 (difference / this / from / comes / different / the / ideas / that / two / the / had. / painters)

➡ _____

24 (thought / Matisse / that / was / Icarus / adventurous. / and / brave)

➡ _____

25 (contrast, / in / thought / Chagall / Icarus / that / foolish. / was)

➡ _____

26 (Matisse's / second, / is / painting / simple, / very / Chagall's / but / has / painting / details. / many)

➡ _____

27 (Matisse's / in / painting, / are / there / Icarus / only / and / stars. / some)

➡ _____

28 (Icarus' / furthermore, / body / just / has / a / outline. / simple)

➡ _____

29 (contrast, / in / painted / Chagall / people / many / and / houses / addition / in / Icarus. / to)

➡ _____

30 (difference / this / from / comes / different / the / styles / painting / the / of / painters. / two)

➡ _____

31 (painting / whose / like / you / more? / do)

➡ _____

32 (will / people / different / have / because / answers / they / see / may / same / the / in / thing / ways. / different)

➡ _____

20 다른 두 그림

21 Matisse와 Chagall 둘 다 그들의 그림에서 같은 주제를 다루지만, 그것들은 다르다.

22 첫째, Matisse의 그림에서, 여러분은 Icarus가 날고 있는 것을 볼 수 있지만, Chagall의 그림에서는 그 소년이 추락하고 있다.

23 이러한 차이는 두 화가들이 갖고 있던 서로 다른 생각에서 기인한다.

24 Matisse는 Icarus가 용감하고 모험심이 강하다고 생각했다.

25 반면에 Chagall은 Icarus가 어리석다고 생각했다.

26 둘째, Matisse의 그림은 매우 단순하지만, Chagall의 그림에는 세부적인 것들이 많다.

27 Matisse의 그림에는 Icarus와 몇 개의 별들만 있다.

28 게다가 Icarus의 몸은 단지 단순한 윤곽만으로 되어 있다.

29 반면에 Chagall은 Icarus뿐만 아니라 많은 사람들과 집들을 그렸다.

30 이러한 차이는 두 화가의 서로 다른 화풍에서 기인한다.

31 여러분은 누구의 그림이 더 좋은가?

32 사람들은 같은 것을 다른 방식들로 볼 수도 있기 때문에 서로 다른 대답을 할 것이다.

※ 다음 우리말을 영어로 쓰시오.

1 같은 이야기, 다른 그림
➡ _____

2 우리는 종종 같은 주제의 다른 그림들을 발견한다.
➡ _____

3 한 예가 Henri Matisse가 그린 "*The Flight of Icarus*(이카로스의 비행)"와 Marc Chagall이 그린 "*The Fall of Icarus*(이카로스의 추락)"이다.
➡ _____

4 그것들은 둘 다 모두 같은 그리스 신화에 관한 것이다.
➡ _____

5 Icarus에 관한 그리스 신화
➡ _____

6 Daedalus는 훌륭한 발명가였다.
➡ _____

7 Minos왕은 Daedalus의 작품을 매우 좋아해서 Daedalus를 그의 곁에 영원히 두고 싶어 했다.
➡ _____

8 그러나 Daedalus는 떠나려고 했고, 그러자 왕은 그와 그의 아들인 Icarus를 높은 탑에 가두었다.
➡ _____

9 Daedalus는 탈출하고 싶었다.
➡ _____

10 어느 날, Daedalus는 새가 날고 있는 것을 보았다.
➡ _____

11 "날개! 날개가 필요해!" 그가 외쳤다.
➡ _____

12 그 다음에 Daedalus는 새의 깃털을 모아 그것들을 밀랍으로 붙였다.
➡ _____

13 날개가 준비되었을 때, 그는 아들에게 경고했다. "태양에 너무 가까이 날지 마라.
➡ _____

14 밀랍이 녹을 거야."
➡ _____

15 Daedalus와 Icarus는 날기 시작했다.
➡ _____

16 Icarus는 매우 흥분해서 아버지의 경고를 잊었다.
➡ _____

17 그는 점점 더 높이 날았고, 밀랍은 녹기 시작했다.
➡ _____

18 "오, 안 돼! 추락하고 있어." Icarus는 비명을 질렀다.
➡ _____

19 Icarus는 바다로 떨어져서 죽었다.
➡ _____

20 다른 두 그림

➡ _____

21 Matisse와 Chagall 둘 다 그들의 그림에서 같은 주제를 다루지만, 그것들은 다르다.

➡ _____

22 첫째, Matisse의 그림에서, 여러분은 Icarus가 날고 있는 것을 볼 수 있지만, Chagall의 그림에서는 그 소년이 추락하고 있다.

➡ _____

23 이러한 차이는 두 화가들이 갖고 있던 서로 다른 생각에서 기인한다.

➡ _____

24 Matisse는 Icarus가 용감하고 모험심이 강하다고 생각했다.

➡ _____

25 반면에 Chagall은 Icarus가 어리석다고 생각했다.

➡ _____

26 둘째, Matisse의 그림은 매우 단순하지만, Chagall의 그림에는 세부적인 것들이 많다.

➡ _____

27 Matisse의 그림에는 Icarus와 몇 개의 별들만 있다.

➡ _____

28 게다가 Icarus의 몸은 단지 단순한 윤곽만으로 되어 있다.

➡ _____

29 반면에 Chagall은 Icarus뿐만 아니라 많은 사람들과 집들을 그렸다.

➡ _____

30 이러한 차이는 두 화가의 서로 다른 화풍에서 기인한다.

➡ _____

31 여러분은 누구의 그림이 더 좋은가?

➡ _____

32 사람들은 같은 것을 다른 방식들로 볼 수도 있기 때문에 서로 다른 대답을 할 것이다.

➡ _____

※ 다음 우리말과 일치하도록 빈칸에 알맞은 말을 쓰시오.

Talk and Play

1. A: _____ _____ _____ go to the library this Monday. Do you _____ _____ _____ me, Jiho?

2. B: Sure. _____ _____ should we _____?

3. A: _____ _____ _____ at 5:30?

4. B: OK. _____ should we _____?

5. A: _____ _____ _____ _____ the library.

6. B: _____ good. _____ you _____.

Around the World

1. Narcissus: Narcissus _____ _____ _____ his beauty.

2. _____ _____, he saw his face in the water and _____ _____ _____ _____.

3. Pandora: There was a box _____ had _____ _____ _____ in the world inside.

4. Pandora opened it, and _____ _____ _____ _____.

5. Orpheus: Orpheus was _____ _____.

6. When his wife died, he _____ Hades and told him, "Please _____ _____ _____ to me."

After You Read D Reading Project

1. _____: *The Flight of Icarus*

2. _____: Henri Matisse

3. _____ Matisse's _____, Icarus _____ _____.

4. He _____ Icarus was _____ and _____.

5. His painting is very _____. He _____ _____ Icarus and _____ _____.

6. _____: *The Fall of Icarus*

7. _____: Marc Chagall

8. In Chagall's painting, Icarus _____ _____. He _____ Icarus _____ _____.

9. His painting has _____ _____. He painted many people and houses _____ _____ _____ Icarus.

1. A: 나는 이번 주 월요일에 도서관에 갈 예정이야. 나랑 같이 갈래, 지호야?
2. B: 물론이지. 몇 시에 만날까?
3. A: 5시 30분에 만나는 게 어때?
4. B: 좋아. 어디서 만날까?
5. A: 도서관 앞에서 만나자.
6. B: 좋은 생각이야. 그때 보자.

1. Narcissus: Narcissus는 그의 아름다움을 자랑스러워했다.
2. 어느 날, 그는 물에 비친 그의 얼굴을 봤고 자신과 사랑에 빠졌다.
3. 판도라: 세상의 온갖 나쁜 것들이 들어 있는 상자가 하나 있었다.
4. 판도라는 그 상자를 열었고, 그것들이 모두 밖으로 나왔다.
5. 오르페우스: 오르페우스는 훌륭한 음악가였다.
6. 그는 아내가 죽었을 때 하데스를 만나, "제발 제 아내를 제게 돌려보내 주세요."라고 말했다.

1. 제목: The Flight of Icarus(이카로스의 비행)
2. 화가: Henri Matisse
3. Matisse의 그림에서, Icarus는 날고 있다.
4. 그는 Icarus가 용감하고 모험심이 강하다고 생각했다.
5. 그의 그림은 매우 단순하다. 그는 Icarus와 몇 개의 별들만 그렸다.
6. 제목: The Fall of Icarus(이카로스의 추락)
7. 화가: Marc Chagall
8. Chagall의 그림에서, Icarus는 추락하고 있다. 그는 Icarus가 어리석다고 생각했다.
9. 그의 그림에는 세부적인 것들이 많다. 그는 Icarus뿐만 아니라 많은 사람들과 집들을 그렸다.

※ 다음 우리말을 영어로 쓰시오.

Talk and Play

1. A: 나는 이번 주 월요일에 도서관에 갈 예정이야. 나랑 같이 갈래, 지호야?
➡ _____

2. B: 물론이지. 몇 시에 만날까?
➡ _____

3. A: 5시 30분에 만나는 게 어때?
➡ _____

4. B: 좋아. 어디서 만날까?
➡ _____

5. A: 도서관 앞에서 만나자.
➡ _____

6. B: 좋은 생각이야. 그때 보자.
➡ _____

Around the World

1. Narcissus: Narcissus는 그의 아름다움을 자랑스러워했다.
➡ _____

2. 어느 날, 그는 물에 비친 그의 얼굴을 봤고 자신과 사랑에 빠졌다.
➡ _____

3. 판도라: 세상의 온갖 나쁜 것들이 들어 있는 상자가 하나 있었다.
➡ _____

4. 판도라는 그 상자를 열었고, 그것들이 모두 밖으로 나왔다.
➡ _____

5. 오르페우스: 오르페우스는 훌륭한 음악가였다.
➡ _____

6. 그는 아내가 죽었을 때 하데스를 만나, "제발 제 아내를 제게 돌려보내 주세요."라고 말했다.
➡ _____

After You Read D Reading Project

1. 제목: 이카로스의 비행
➡ _____

2. 화가: Henri Matisse
➡ _____

3. Matisse의 그림에서, Icarus는 날고 있다.
➡ _____

4. 그는 Icarus가 용감하고 모험심이 강하다고 생각했다.
➡ _____

5. 그의 그림은 매우 단순하다. 그는 Icarus와 몇 개의 별들만 그렸다.
➡ _____

6. 제목: 이카로스의 추락
➡ _____

7. 화가: Marc Chagall
➡ _____

8 Chagall의 그림에서, Icarus는 추락하고 있다. 그는 Icarus가 어리석다고 생각했다.
➡ _____

9. 그의 그림에는 세부적인 것들이 많다. 그는 Icarus뿐만 아니라 많은 사람들과 집들을 그렸다.
➡ _____

Step1

※ 다음 영어를 우리말로 쓰시오.

01	arrive		22	shake	
02	adventure		23	towards	
03	taste		24	spaceship	
04	amazing		25	fix	
05	difficult		26	wet	
06	float		27	laugh	
07	shout		28	save	
08	balloon		29	recently	
09	container		30	space suit	
10	different		31	form	
11	curious		32	secret	
12	thirsty		33	soft	
13	everywhere		34	thrilling	
14	space station		35	don't have to+동사원형	
15	exploration		36	each other	
16	finally		37	be covered with	
17	since		38	pull down	
18	foreign		39	lie down	
19	excited		40	for example	
20	lie		41	be curious about ~	
21	swallow		42	run up to ~	
			43	not ~ anymore	

※ 다음 우리말을 영어로 쓰시오.

01	모험	
02	풍선	
03	어려운	
04	떠가다	
05	신난, 흥분한	
06	다른	
07	탐험, 탐사	
08	부드러운	
09	놀라운	
10	마침내	
11	~한 이래로	
12	고치다	
13	외국의	
14	우주선	
15	비밀, 기밀	
16	모든 곳에	
17	바람	
18	외치다	
19	흔들다	
20	궁금한, 호기심이 많은	
21	~쪽으로, ~을 향하여	

22	우주복	
23	목마른	
24	그릇, 용기	
25	삼키다	
26	언덕	
27	눕다	
28	아주 신나는	
29	웃다	
30	젖은	
31	풀, 잔디	
32	최근에	
33	구하다	
34	맛	
35	~에 관해 궁금해 하다	
36	~하려고 시도하다	
37	놀라서	
38	더 이상 ~ 않다	
39	~으로 뒤덮이다	
40	~에 타다	
41	예를 들어	
42	(둘 사이의) 서로	
43	굴러 내려가다	

※ 다음 영영풀이에 알맞은 단어를 <보기>에서 골라 쓴 후, 우리말 뜻을 쓰시오.

1 _____ : extremely surprising: _____

2 _____ : to stay on the surface of a liquid and not sink: _____

3 _____ : a vehicle used for travel in space: _____

4 _____ : to make something into a particular shape: _____

5 _____ : to reach a place, especially at the end of a journey: _____

6 _____ : to keep someone or something safe from death, harm, loss, etc.:
_____

7 _____ : interested in learning about people or things around you: _____

8 _____ : covered with or containing liquid, especially water: _____

9 _____ : the activity of searching and finding out about something: _____

10 _____ : belonging or connected to a country that is not your own: _____

11 _____ : in the direction of, or closer to someone or something: _____

12 _____ : a place or vehicle in space where people can stay: _____

13 _____ : an unusual, exciting, and possibly dangerous activity, such as a trip:
_____

14 _____ : to cause food, drink, pills, etc. to move from your mouth into your
stomach by using the muscles of your throat: _____

15 _____ : to arrive on the ground or other surface after moving down through the
air: _____

16 _____ : a piece of information that is only known by one person or a few people
and should not be told to others: _____

보기			
land	foreign	amazing	spaceship
form	arrive	towards	secret
adventure	float	wet	save
swallow	space station	curious	exploration

※ 다음 우리말과 일치하도록 빈칸에 알맞은 말을 쓰시오.

Listen and Talk A-1

B: Did you _____ _____ the first spaceship _____ _____ _____ _____ ?

G: No, I didn't. I'm _____ _____ it.

B: This is a poster of the _____ .

G: Really? I _____ _____ _____ it.

B: 너는 우주에 간 첫 번째 우주선에 대해 들어 봤니?
G: 아니, 못 들어 봤어. 궁금하다.
B: 이것이 그 우주선 포스터야.
G: 정말? 그것을 사고 싶다.

Listen and Talk A-2

G: _____ you _____ _____ the new book about Mars?

B: No, I didn't. _____ _____ _____ _____ _____ Mars.

G: Look. It's _____ _____ . It's _____ Mars and its moons.

B: Great. I think I'll _____ the book.

G: 너는 화성에 관한 새로운 책에 관해 들어 봤니?
B: 아니, 못 들어 봤어. 나는 화성에 관해 정말 궁금해.
G: 봐, 바로 여기 있어. 그것은 화성과 그것의 위성들에 관한 내용이야.
B: 멋지다. 이 책을 사야겠어.

Listen and Talk A-3

G: _____ _____ _____ _____ _____ the space marathon?

B: No, _____ _____ .

G: It's a marathon on a _____ _____ . _____ _____ this video.

B: OK. _____ _____ _____ _____ it.

G: 너는 우주 마라톤에 대해 들어 봤니?
B: 아니, 못 들어 봤어.
G: 그것은 우주 정거장에서 하는 마라톤이야. 이 비디오를 봐.
B: 알겠어. 정말 궁금하다.

Listen and Talk A-4

G: Did you hear _____ the new _____ _____ ?

B: Yes, I did. It's _____ _____ _____ ice cream.

G: Yes, and _____ _____ _____ . It _____ _____ .

B: I'm really _____ _____ _____ _____ .

G: 너는 새로운 우주 음식에 대해 들어 봤니?
B: 응, 들어 봤어. 그건 일종의 아이스크림이야.
G: 응, 여기 있어. 맛있어 보인다.
B: 그 맛이 참 궁금하다.

Listen and Talk B

1. A: Look at this. Did you hear _____ the new musical?

   B: Yes, I did. I _____ it has great songs.

   A: Oh, I'm really _____ _____ it.

2. A: _____ _____ this. Did you _____ _____ the new musical?

   B: _____ , I _____ .

   A: I heard _____ _____ _____ _____ .

   B: Oh, I'm _____ _____ _____ it.

1. A: 이것 봐. 새 뮤지컬에 대해 들어 봤니?
   B: 응, 들어 봤어. 좋은 노래들이 나온다고 들었어.
   A: 오, 정말 궁금하다.

2. A: 이것 봐. 새 뮤지컬에 대해 들어 봤니?
   B: 아니, 못 들어 봤어.
   A: 좋은 노래들이 나온다고 들었어.
   B: 오, 정말 궁금하다.

Listen and Talk C

B: Subin, did you _____ _____ the new movie, *Life on the Moon*?

G: No, I _____.

B: I _____ it's really _____.

G: I'm really _____ _____ the movie. What's it _____?

B: It's _____ a man _____ is _____ _____ _____ on the moon.

G: That _____ _____.

B: Look. The movie _____ _____ at the Space Theater here.

G: _____ _____ is the movie?

B: It _____ _____ 2:30.

G: _____ _____ _____ first _____ _____ see the movie.

B: OK. I'm _____. _____ _____!

B: 수빈아, "달에서의 생활"이라는 새 영화에 대해서 들어 봤니?
G: 아니.
B: 굉장히 좋다고 들었거든.
G: 그 영화가 정말 궁금하네. 뭐에 관한 거야?
B: 달에서 살기 위해 노력하는 한 남자에 관한 영화래.
G: 그거 재미있겠다.
B: 봐. 그 영화가 여기 우주 극장에서 상영되고 있어.
G: 영화가 몇 시에 상영되는데?
B: 2시 30분에 시작해.
G: 우선 점심부터 먹고 영화를 보자.
B: 좋아. 나 배고파. 가자!

Review 1

G: Tony, _____ _____ _____ _____ the movie, *My Hero*?

B: _____, I _____.

G: Well, I _____ it's really good.

B: I'm really _____ _____ the movie. What's it _____?

G: It's _____ a father _____ _____ _____ _____.

G: Tony, 영화 My Hero에 대해 들어 봤니?
B: 아니, 못 들어 봤어.
G: 음, 정말 좋다고 들었어.
B: 그 영화에 대해 정말 궁금하다. 무엇에 대한 것이니?
G: 그것은 아들을 구하는 아빠에 관한 거야.

Review 2

G: _____ you _____ _____ the new book, *Living in a Foreign Country*?

B: No, I didn't.

G: Look. It's _____ here. It's _____ _____ in New York.

B: Great. I'm _____ _____ _____ this book.

G: _____, _____.

G: 새 책인 "Living in a Foreign Country"에 대해 들어 봤니?
B: 아니, 못 들어 봤어.
G: 봐. 바로 여기 있어. 그것은 뉴욕에서의 삶에 관한 거야.
B: 멋지다. 이 책이 정말 궁금해.
G: 나도 그래.

※ 다음 우리말에 맞도록 대화를 영어로 쓰시오.

Listen and Talk A-1

B: _____

G: _____

B: _____

G: _____

Listen and Talk A-2

G: _____

B: _____

G: _____

B: _____

Listen and Talk A-3

G: _____

B: _____

G: _____

B: _____

Listen and Talk A-4

G: _____

B: _____

G: _____

B: _____

Listen and Talk B

1. A: _____

   B: _____

   A: _____

2. A: _____

   B: _____

   A: _____

   B: _____

B: 너는 우주에 간 첫 번째 우주선에 대해 들어 봤니?
G: 아니, 못 들어 봤어. 궁금하다.
B: 이것이 그 우주선 포스터야.
G: 정말? 그것을 사고 싶다.

G: 너는 화성에 관한 새로운 책에 관해 들어 봤니?
B: 아니, 못 들어 봤어. 나는 화성에 관해 정말 궁금해.
G: 봐. 바로 여기 있어. 그것은 화성과 그것의 위성들에 관한 내용이야.
B: 멋지다. 이 책을 사야겠어.

G: 너는 우주 마라톤에 대해 들어 봤니?
B: 아니, 못 들어 봤어.
G: 그것은 우주 정거장에서 하는 마라톤이야. 이 비디오를 봐.
B: 알겠어. 정말 궁금하다.

G: 너는 새로운 우주 음식에 대해 들어 봤니?
B: 응, 들어 봤어. 그건 일종의 아이스크림이야.
G: 응, 여기 있어. 맛있어 보인다.
B: 그 맛이 참 궁금하다.

1. A: 이것 봐. 새 뮤지컬에 대해 들어 봤니?
   B: 응, 들어 봤어. 좋은 노래들이 나온다고 들었어.
   A: 오, 정말 궁금하다.

2. A: 이것 봐. 새 뮤지컬에 대해 들어 봤니?
   B: 아니, 못 들어 봤어.
   A: 좋은 노래들이 나온다고 들었어.
   B: 오, 정말 궁금하다.

Listen and Talk C

B: _____

G: _____

B: _____

G: _____

B: _____

G: _____

B: _____

G: _____

B: _____

G: _____

B: _____

B: 수빈아, "달에서의 생활"이라는 새 영화에 대해서 들어 봤니?

G: 아니.

B: 굉장히 좋다고 들었거든.

G: 그 영화가 정말 궁금하네. 뭐에 관한 거야?

B: 달에서 살기 위해 노력하는 한 남자에 관한 영화래.

G: 그거 재미있겠다.

B: 봐. 그 영화가 여기 우주 극장에서 상영되고 있어.

G: 영화가 몇 시에 상영되는데?

B: 2시 30분에 시작해.

G: 우선 점심부터 먹고 영화를 보자.

B: 좋아. 나 배고파. 가자!

Review 1

G: _____

B: _____

G: _____

B: _____

G: _____

G: Tony, 영화 My Hero에 대해 들어 봤니?

B: 아니, 못 들어 봤어.

G: 음, 정말 좋다고 들었어.

B: 그 영화에 대해 정말 궁금하다. 무엇에 대한 것이니?

G: 그것은 아들을 구하는 아빠에 관한 거야.

Review 2

G: _____

B: _____

G: _____

B: _____

G: _____

G: 새 책인 "Living in a Foreign Country"에 대해 들어 봤니?

B: 아니, 못 들어 봤어.

G: 봐. 바로 여기 있어. 그것은 뉴욕에서의 삶에 관한 거야.

B: 멋지다. 이 책이 정말 궁금해.

G: 나도 그래.

※ 다음 우리말과 일치하도록 빈칸에 알맞은 것을 골라 쓰시오.

1 The _____ New _____
A. Thing　　　　B. Best

2 Rada lived on a _____ world, _____ _____ in space.
A. out　　　　B. little　　　　C. far

3 She _____ _____ her father, mother, and brother Jonny.
A. with　　　　B. there　　　　C. lived

4 Rada's father and _____ people _____ _____ spaceships.
A. on　　　　B. other　　　　C. worked

5 _____ Rada and Jonny were children, and they _____ _____ in space.
A. were　　　　B. only　　　　C. born

6 _____ day, Dad told Rada and Jonny, "We're _____ _____ to Earth tomorrow."
A. going　　　　B. one　　　　C. back

7 Rada and Jonny looked at Dad _____ _____ and _____ _____ him.
A. towards　　　　B. in　　　　C. floated　　　　D. surprise

8 Rada asked Dad, "_____ _____ _____ on Earth?"
A. it　　　　B. what's　　　　C. like

9 "_____ is _____ there.
A. different　　　　B. everything

10 _____ _____ , the sky is blue," _____ Dad.
A. answered　　　　B. example　　　　C. for

11 "I've _____ _____ a blue sky," _____ Jonny.
A. seen　　　　B. never　　　　C. said

12 "The sky _____ _____ _____ here," said Rada.
A. always　　　　B. is　　　　C. black

13 "You _____ _____ to wear your big heavy space _____ because _____ is air everywhere.
A. have　　　　B. there　　　　C. don't　　　　D. suits

14 It's also _____ to jump there _____ Earth _____ you _____ ," said Dad.
A. pulls　　　　B. hard　　　　C. down　　　　D. because

15 "_____ _____ ?" asked Rada.
A. else　　　　B. what

16 "There are hills, and they are _____ _____ soft green _____ .
A. with　　　　B. grass　　　　C. covered

---

1 최고의 새로운 것

2 Rada는 먼 우주의 작은 세계에 살고 있었다.

3 그녀는 아빠, 엄마 그리고 남동생 Jonny와 함께 그곳에서 살고 있었다.

4 Rada의 아빠와 다른 사람들은 우주선에서 일했다.

5 Rada와 Jonny만이 아이들이었고, 그들은 우주에서 태어났다.

6 어느 날, 아빠가 Rada와 Jonny에게, "우리는 내일 지구로 돌아갈 거야."라고 말했다.

7 Rada와 Jonny는 깜짝 놀라 아빠를 바라보았고, 그에게 둥둥 떠서 갔다.

8 Rada가 아빠에게, "지구는 어떤 곳인가요?"라고 물었다.

9 "그곳에선 모든 것이 다르단다.

10 예를 들어, 하늘은 파란색이지."라고 아빠가 대답했다.

11 "전 한 번도 파란 하늘을 본 적이 없어요."라고 Jonny가 말했다.

12 "여기는 하늘이 항상 검은색이잖아요."라고 Rada가 말했다.

13 "그곳에는 모든 곳에 공기가 있기 때문에 크고 무거운 우주복을 입을 필요가 없단다.

14 또한 지구가 너희들을 끌어당기기 때문에 거기에서는 점프하는 것도 어렵단다." 아빠가 말했다.

15 "그 밖에 또 뭐가 있어요?" Rada가 물었다.

16 "언덕들이 있는데 그것들은 부드러운 초록색의 잔디로 뒤덮여 있단다.

17 You can _____ _____ the hills," _____ Mom.

    A. down   B. roll   C. answered

18 "Dad, _____ you _____ _____ _____ a hill?" asked Rada.

    A. ever   B. down   C. have   D. rolled

19 "Yes, it's really _____!" _____ Dad.

    A. answered   B. amazing

20 Jonny was _____, so he _____ a milk container and _____ it.

    A. shook   B. thirsty   C. opened

21 The milk _____ in the _____ and _____ balls.

    A. formed   B. floated   C. air

22 Jonny _____ the _____.

    A. balls   B. swallowed

23 "Jonny, _____ you drink milk that _____ on Earth, you'll _____ _____," said Mom.

    A. way   B. wet   C. get   D. if

24 _____ that night, Rada and Jonny _____ a _____ time about Earth.

    A. long   B. talked   C. later

25 It was _____ to think about _____ the new _____ they were _____ to see and do.

    A. things   B. exciting   C. all   D. going

26 There was _____ _____ _____ Rada and Jonny really wanted to do.

    A. new   B. thing   C. one

27 They _____ about it _____ _____ and didn't tell Mom and Dad _____ it.

    A. night   B. thought   C. all   D. about

28 It was _____ _____.

    A. secret   B. their

29 The _____ day, Rada's family _____ _____ a spaceship.

    A. got   B. next   C. on

30 "It's _____ to _____ a long _____," said Mom.

    A. trip   B. going   C. be

31 "That's _____. I'm _____ _____!" said Rada.

    A. so   B. alright   C. excited

32 The spaceship _____ _____.

    A. landed   B. finally

---

17 언덕을 굴러 내려갈 수도 있어." 엄마가 대답했다.

18 "아빠, 언덕을 굴러 내려가 본 적 있어요?" Rada가 물었다.

19 "그럼, 정말 놀라워!" 아빠가 대답했다.

20 Jonny는 목이 말라서 우유 용기를 열어 그것을 흔들었다.

21 우유가 공기 중으로 떠서 방울을 형성했다.

22 Jonny는 그 우유 방울을 삼켰다.

23 "Jonny, 만약 네가 지구에서 그런 식으로 우유를 마신다면, 다 젖을 거야." 엄마가 말했다.

24 그날 밤 늦게, Rada와 Jonny는 지구에 대해서 오랜 시간 이야기했다.

25 그들이 보고, 하게 될 모든 새로운 것들을 생각하는 것은 흥미로웠다.

26 Rada와 Jonny가 정말로 하고 싶었던 한 가지 새로운 것이 있었다.

27 그들은 밤새 그것에 대해서 생각했고 엄마와 아빠에게는 그것을 말하지 않았다.

28 그것은 그들의 비밀이었다.

29 다음날, Rada의 가족은 우주선에 올랐다.

30 "긴 여행이 될 거야." 엄마가 말했다.

31 "괜찮아요. 정말 신나요!" Rada가 말했다.

32 우주선이 마침내 착륙했다.

33 "Dad, it's _____ _____ _____ on Earth," said Rada.

    A. walk   B. to   C. difficult

34 "I know. Earth is _____ _____ _____," said Dad.

    A. down   B. you   C. pulling

35 Rada and Jonny _____ _____ _____.

    A. float   B. couldn't   C. anymore

36 That was the _____ _____ _____.

    A. new   B. first   C. thing

37 "_____ that _____?" asked Rada.

    A. sound   B. what's

38 "A _____ is _____," said Mom.

    A. singing   B. bird

39 "I've _____ _____ a bird _____," said Rada.

    A. heard   B. sing   C. never

40 "And I've _____ _____ the _____," said Jonny.

    A. felt   B. wind   C. never

41 _____ were _____ _____ things.

    A. new   B. these   C. all

42 Rada and Jonny _____ _____ _____ _____ hill.

    A. ran   B. nearest   C. up   D. the

43 At the _____, they looked at _____ _____ and _____.

    A. other   B. top   C. laughed   D. each

44 Then they _____ _____ on the _____ green grass and _____ down the hill.

    A. rolled   B. down   C. lay   D. soft

45 That was _____ _____!

    A. secret   B. their

46 "This is the _____ _____ thing of all!" _____ Rada and Jonny.

    A. shouted   B. new   C. best

47 And they _____ _____ _____ the _____ of the hill again.

    A. top   B. up   C. ran   D. to

---

33 "아빠, 지구에서는 걷는 것이 어려워요." Rada가 말했다.

34 "그래. 지구가 너를 끌어당기고 있거든." 아빠가 말했다.

35 Rada와 Jonny는 더 이상 떠다닐 수 없었다.

36 그것이 첫 번째 새로운 것이었다.

37 "저건 무슨 소리죠?"라고 Rada가 물었다.

38 "새가 노래하는 거야." 엄마가 말했다.

39 "새가 노래하는 것을 들어 본 적이 없어요."라고 Rada가 말했다.

40 "그리고 저는 바람을 느껴 본 적도 없어요."라고 Jonny가 말했다.

41 이러한 것들이 모두 새로운 것들이었다.

42 Rada와 Jonny는 가장 가까운 언덕으로 뛰어 올라갔다.

43 꼭대기에서, 그들은 서로를 쳐다보고 웃었다.

44 그리고 나서 그들은 부드러운 초록 잔디에 누워서 언덕 아래로 굴러 내려갔다.

45 그것이 그들의 비밀이었다!

46 "이것이 모든 것들 중에서 최고의 새로운 것이에요!" Rada와 Jonny는 외쳤다.

47 그리고 그들은 언덕 꼭대기로 다시 뛰어 올라갔다.

※ 다음 우리말과 일치하도록 빈칸에 알맞은 말을 쓰시오.

1 The _____ New _____

2 Rada lived on a little world, _____ _____ _____ _____.

3 She _____ _____ _____ her father, mother, and _____ Jonny.

4 Rada's father and _____ people _____ _____ spaceships.

5 _____ Rada and Jonny were children, and they _____ _____ _____ _____.

6 _____ _____, Dad told Rada and Jonny, "We're _____ _____ _____ Earth tomorrow."

7 Rada and Jonny looked at Dad _____ _____ and _____ _____ him.

8 Rada asked Dad, "_____ _____ _____ on Earth?"

9 "_____ _____ _____ there.

10 _____ _____, the sky is blue," answered Dad.

11 "_____ _____ _____ a blue sky," said Jonny.

12 "The sky _____ _____ _____ here," said Rada.

13 "You _____ _____ _____ wear your big heavy space suits _____ _____ _____ _____ everywhere.

14 It's also hard to _____ there because Earth _____ _____ _____," said Dad.

15 "_____ _____?" asked Rada.

16 "There are hills, and they _____ _____ _____ soft green grass.

17 You can _____ _____ the hills," answered Mom.

18 "Dad, _____ _____ _____ _____ _____ a hill?" asked Rada.

19 "Yes, it's _____ _____!" answered Dad.

20 Jonny was _____, _____ he _____ a milk container and _____ it.

21 The milk _____ in the air and _____ balls.

22 Jonny _____ the balls.

23 "Jonny, _____ you drink milk _____ _____ on Earth, you'll _____ _____," said Mom.

---

1 최고의 새로운 것

2 Rada는 먼 우주의 작은 세계에 살고 있었다.

3 그녀는 아빠, 엄마 그리고 남동생 Jonny와 함께 그곳에서 살고 있었다.

4 Rada의 아빠와 다른 사람들은 우주선에서 일했다.

5 Rada와 Jonny만이 아이들이었고, 그들은 우주에서 태어났다.

6 어느 날, 아빠가 Rada와 Jonny에게, "우리는 내일 지구로 돌아갈 거야."라고 말했다.

7 Rada와 Jonny는 깜짝 놀라 아빠를 바라보았고, 그에게 둥둥 떠서 갔다.

8 Rada가 아빠에게, "지구는 어떤 곳인가요?"라고 물었다.

9 "그곳에선 모든 것이 다르단다.

10 예를 들어, 하늘은 파란색이지."라고 아빠가 대답했다.

11 "전 한 번도 파란 하늘을 본 적이 없어요."라고 Jonny가 말했다.

12 "여기는 하늘이 항상 검은색이잖아요."라고 Rada가 말했다.

13 "그곳에는 모든 곳에 공기가 있기 때문에 크고 무거운 우주복을 입을 필요가 없단다.

14 또한 지구가 너희들을 끌어당기기 때문에 거기에서는 점프하는 것도 어렵단다." 아빠가 말했다.

15 "그 밖에 또 뭐가 있어요?" Rada가 물었다.

16 "언덕들이 있는데 그것들은 부드러운 초록색의 잔디로 뒤덮여 있단다.

17 언덕을 굴러 내려갈 수도 있어." 엄마가 대답했다.

18 "아빠, 언덕을 굴러 내려가 본 적 있어요?" Rada가 물었다.

19 "그럼, 정말 놀라워!" 아빠가 대답했다.

20 Jonny는 목이 말라서 우유 용기를 열어 그것을 흔들었다.

21 우유가 공기 중으로 떠서 방울을 형성했다.

22 Jonny는 그 우유 방울을 삼켰다.

23 "Jonny, 만약 네가 지구에서 그런 식으로 우유를 마신다면, 다 젖을 거야." 엄마가 말했다.

24 _____ _____ _____, Rada and Jonny talked _____ _____ _____ about Earth.

25 It was _____ to _____ about _____ _____ they were _____ _____ see and do.

26 There was _____ _____ _____ Rada and Jonny really _____ _____ _____.

27 They thought about it _____ _____ and didn't tell Mom and Dad about it.

28 It was _____ _____.

29 The next day, Rada's family _____ _____ a spaceship.

30 "_____ _____ _____ _____ a long trip," said Mom.

31 "That's _____. I'm _____ _____!" said Rada.

32 The spaceship _____ _____.

33 "Dad, it's difficult _____ _____ on Earth," said Rada.

34 "I know. Earth is _____ _____ _____," said Dad.

35 Rada and Jonny _____ _____ _____ _____.

36 That was _____ _____ _____ _____ _____.

37 "_____ that _____?" asked Rada.

38 "A bird _____ _____," said Mom.

39 "_____ _____ _____ a bird _____," said Rada.

40 "And _____ _____ _____ the wind," said Jonny.

41 _____ were _____ _____ _____ _____.

42 Rada and Jonny _____ _____ _____ _____ _____ hill.

43 At the top, they looked at _____ _____ and _____.

44 Then they _____ _____ on the soft green grass and _____ _____ the hill.

45 That was _____ _____!

46 "This is the _____ _____ _____ of all!" shouted Rada and Jonny.

47 And they ran _____ _____ _____ _____ of the hill again.

24 그날 밤 늦게, Rada와 Jonny는 지구에 대해서 오랜 시간 이야기했다.

25 그들이 보고, 하게 될 모든 새로운 것들을 생각하는 것은 흥미로웠다.

26 Rada와 Jonny가 정말로 하고 싶었던 한 가지 새로운 것이 있었다.

27 그들은 밤새 그것에 대해서 생각했고 엄마와 아빠에게는 그것을 말하지 않았다.

28 그것은 그들의 비밀이었다.

29 다음날, Rada의 가족은 우주선에 올랐다.

30 "긴 여행이 될 거야." 엄마가 말했다.

31 "괜찮아요. 정말 신나요!" Rada가 말했다.

32 우주선이 마침내 착륙했다.

33 "아빠, 지구에서는 걷는 것이 어려워요." Rada가 말했다.

34 "그래. 지구가 너를 끌어당기고 있거든." 아빠가 말했다.

35 Rada와 Jonny는 더 이상 떠다닐 수 없었다.

36 그것이 첫 번째 새로운 것이었다.

37 "저건 무슨 소리죠?"라고 Rada가 물었다.

38 "새가 노래하는 거야." 엄마가 말했다.

39 "새가 노래하는 것을 들어 본 적이 없어요."라고 Rada가 말했다.

40 "그리고 저는 바람을 느껴 본 적도 없어요."라고 Jonny가 말했다.

41 이러한 것들이 모두 새로운 것들이었다.

42 Rada와 Jonny는 가장 가까운 언덕으로 뛰어 올라갔다.

43 꼭대기에서, 그들은 서로를 쳐다보고 웃었다.

44 그러고 나서 그들은 부드러운 초록 잔디에 누워서 언덕 아래로 굴러 내려갔다.

45 그것이 그들의 비밀이었다!

46 "이것이 모든 것들 중에서 최고의 새로운 것이에요!" Rada와 Jonny는 외쳤다.

47 그리고 그들은 언덕 꼭대기로 다시 뛰어 올라갔다.

※ 다음 문장을 우리말로 쓰시오.

1 The Best New Thing
➡ _____

2 Rada lived on a little world, far out in space.
➡ _____

3 She lived there with her father, mother, and brother Jonny.
➡ _____

4 Rada's father and other people worked on spaceships.
➡ _____

5 Only Rada and Jonny were children, and they were born in space.
➡ _____

6 One day, Dad told Rada and Jonny, "We're going back to Earth tomorrow."
➡ _____

7 Rada and Jonny looked at Dad in surprise and floated towards him.
➡ _____

8 Rada asked Dad, "What's it like on Earth?"
➡ _____

9 "Everything is different there.
➡ _____

10 For example, the sky is blue," answered Dad.
➡ _____

11 "I've never seen a blue sky," said Jonny.
➡ _____

12 "The sky is always black here," said Rada.
➡ _____

13 "You don't have to wear your big heavy space suits because there is air everywhere.
➡ _____

14 It's also hard to jump there because Earth pulls you down," said Dad.
➡ _____

15 "What else?" asked Rada.
➡ _____

16 "There are hills, and they are covered with soft green grass.
➡ _____

17 You can roll down the hills," answered Mom.
➡ _____

18 "Dad, have you ever rolled down a hill?" asked Rada.
➡ _____

19 "Yes, it's really amazing!" answered Dad.
➡ _____

20 Jonny was thirsty, so he opened a milk container and shook it.
➡ _____

21 The milk floated in the air and formed balls.
➡ _____

22 Jonny swallowed the balls.
➡ _____

23 "Jonny, if you drink milk that way on Earth, you'll get wet," said Mom.
➡ _____

24 Later that night, Rada and Jonny talked a long time about Earth.
➡ _____

25 It was exciting to think about all the new things they were going to see and do.
➡ _____

26 There was one new thing Rada and Jonny really wanted to do.
➡ _____

27 They thought about it all night and didn't tell Mom and Dad about it.
➡ _____

28 It was their secret.
➡ _____

29 The next day, Rada's family got on a spaceship.
➡ _____

30 "It's going to be a long trip," said Mom.
➡ _____

31 That's alright. I'm so excited!" said Rada.
➡ _____

32 The spaceship finally landed.
➡ _____

33 "Dad, it's difficult to walk on Earth," said Rada.
➡ _____

34 "I know. Earth is pulling you down," said Dad.
➡ _____

35 Rada and Jonny couldn't float anymore.
➡ _____

36 That was the first new thing.
➡ _____

37 "What's that sound?" asked Rada.
➡ _____

38 "A bird is singing," said Mom.
➡ _____

39 "I've never heard a bird sing," said Rada.
➡ _____

40 "And I've never felt the wind," said Jonny.
➡ _____

41 These were all new things.
➡ _____

42 Rada and Jonny ran up the nearest hill.
➡ _____

43 At the top, they looked at each other and laughed.
➡ _____

44 Then they lay down on the soft green grass and rolled down the hill.
➡ _____

45 That was their secret!
➡ _____

46 "This is the best new thing of all!" shouted Rada and Jonny.
➡ _____

47 And they ran up to the top of the hill again.
➡ _____

※ 다음 괄호 안의 단어들을 우리말에 맞도록 바르게 배열하시오.

1 (Best / Thing / New / The)
➡ _____

2 (lived / Rada / a / on / world, / little / out / far / space. / in)
➡ _____

3 (there / lived / she / with / father, / her / and / mother, / Jonny. / brother)
➡ _____

4 (father / Rada's / and / people / other / on / spaceships. / worked)
➡ _____

5 (Rada / only / and / were / Jonny / children, / and / were / they / space. / in / born)
➡ _____

6 (day, / one / told / Dad / Rada / Jonny, / and / "we're / back / going / to / tomorrow." / Earth)
➡ _____

7 (Jonny / and / Rada / at / looked / Dad / surprise / in / and / him. / towards / floated)
➡ _____

8 (asked / Rada / Dad, / it / "what's / on / Earth?" / like)
➡ _____

9 (is / "everything / there. / different)
➡ _____

10 (example, / for / sky / the / blue," / is / Dad. / answered)
➡ _____

11 (never / "I've / seen / a / sky," / blue / Jonny. / said)
➡ _____

12 (sky / "the / always / is / here," / black / Rada. / said)
➡ _____

13 (don't / "you / to / wear / have / big / your / heavy / suits / space / because / is / there / everywhere. / air)
➡ _____
_____

14 (also / it's / to / hard / jump / there / Earth / because / pulls / down," / you / Dad. / said)
➡ _____

15 (else?" / "what / Rada. / asked)
➡ _____

16 (are / "there / hills, / and / are / they / with / covered / soft / grass. / green)
➡ _____

1 최고의 새로운 것

2 Rada는 먼 우주의 작은 세계에 살고 있었다.

3 그녀는 아빠, 엄마 그리고 남동생 Jonny와 함께 그곳에서 살고 있었다.

4 Rada의 아빠와 다른 사람들은 우주선에서 일했다.

5 Rada와 Jonny만이 아이들이었고, 그들은 우주에서 태어났다.

6 어느 날, 아빠가 Rada와 Jonny에게, "우리는 내일 지구로 돌아갈 거야."라고 말했다.

7 Rada와 Jonny는 깜짝 놀라 아빠를 바라보았고, 그에게 둥둥 떠서 갔다.

8 Rada가 아빠에게, "지구는 어떤 곳인가요?"라고 물었다.

9 "그곳에선 모든 것이 다르단다.

10 예를 들어, 하늘은 파란색이지."라고 아빠가 대답했다.

11 "전 한 번도 파란 하늘을 본 적이 없어요."라고 Jonny가 말했다.

12 "여기는 하늘이 항상 검은색이잖아요."라고 Rada가 말했다.

13 "그곳에는 모든 곳에 공기가 있기 때문에 크고 무거운 우주복을 입을 필요가 없단다.

14 또한 지구가 너희들을 끌어당기기 때문에 거기에서는 점프하는 것도 어렵단다." 아빠가 말했다.

15 "그 밖에 또 뭐가 있어요?" Rada가 물었다.

16 "언덕들이 있는데 그것들은 부드러운 초록색의 잔디로 뒤덮여 있단다.

17 (you / roll / can / down / hills," / the / Mom. / answered)

➡ _____

18 (have / "Dad / ever / you / down / rolled / hill?" / a / Rada. / asked)

➡ _____

19 ("yes, / really / it's / amazing!" Dad. / answered)

➡ _____

20 (was / Jonny / thirsty, / he / so / opened / a / container / milk / and / it. / shook)

➡ _____

21 (milk / the / in / floated / the / air / and / balls. / formed)

➡ _____

22 (swallowed / Jonny / balls. / the)

➡ _____

23 ("Jonny, / you / if / milk / drink / way / that / Earth, / on / get / you'll / wet," / Mom. / said)

➡ _____

24 (that / later / night, / Jonny / and / Rada / talked / long / a / Earth. / about / time)

➡ _____

25 (was / it / exciting / think / to / all / about / new / the / things / were / they / going / see / do. / and / to)

➡ _____

26 (was / there / new / one / Rada / thing / and / really / Jonny / do. / to / wanted)

➡ _____

27 (thought / they / it / about / night / all / and / didn't / Mom / tell / and / it. / about / Dad)

➡ _____

28 (was / it / secret. / their)

➡ _____

29 (next / the / day, / family / Rada's / on / got / spaceship. / a)

➡ _____

30 (going / "it's / be / to / long / a / trip," / Mom. / said)

➡ _____

31 (alright. / "that's // so / I'm / excited!" Rada. / said)

➡ _____

32 (spaceship / the / landed. / finally)

➡ _____

17 언덕을 굴러 내려갈 수도 있어." 엄마가 대답했다.

18 "아빠, 언덕을 굴러 내려가 본 적 있어요?" Rada가 물었다.

19 "그럼, 정말 놀라워!" 아빠가 대답했다.

20 Jonny는 목이 말라서 우유 용기를 열어 그것을 흔들었다.

21 우유가 공기 중으로 떠서 방울을 형성했다.

22 Jonny는 그 우유 방울을 삼켰다.

23 "Jonny, 만약 네가 지구에서 그런 식으로 우유를 마신다면, 다 젖을 거야." 엄마가 말했다.

24 그날 밤 늦게, Rada와 Jonny는 지구에 대해서 오랜 시간 이야기했다.

25 그들이 보고, 하게 될 모든 새로운 것들을 생각하는 것은 흥미로웠다.

26 Rada와 Jonny가 정말로 하고 싶었던 한 가지 새로운 것이 있었다.

27 그들은 밤새 그것에 대해서 생각했고 엄마와 아빠에게는 그것을 말하지 않았다.

28 그것은 그들의 비밀이었다.

29 다음날, Rada의 가족은 우주선에 올랐다.

30 "긴 여행이 될 거야." 엄마가 말했다.

31 "괜찮아요. 정말 신나요!" Rada가 말했다.

32 우주선이 마침내 착륙했다.

33 ("Dad, / difficult / it's / walk / to / Eaeth," / on / Rada. / said)

➡ _____

34 (know. / "I / is / Earth / you / pulling / down," / Dad. / said)

➡ _____

35 (Jonny / and / Rada / couldn't / anymore. / float)

➡ _____

36 (was / that / first / the / thing. / new)

➡ _____

37 ("what's / sound?" / that / Rada. / asked)

➡ _____

38 (bird / "a / singing," / is / Mom. / said)

➡ _____

39 (never / "I've / heard / bird / a / sing," / Rada. / said)

➡ _____

40 ("and / never / I've / felt / wind," / the / Jonny. / said)

➡ _____

41 (were / these / new / things. / all)

➡ _____

42 (Jonny / and / Rada / up / ran / nearest / the / hill.)

➡ _____

43 (the / at / top, / looked / they / each / at / other / laughed. / and)

➡ _____

44 (they / then / down / lay / the / on / green / soft / grass / and / down / rolled / hill. / the)

➡ _____

45 (was / that / secret! / their)

➡ _____

46 (is / "this / best / the / thing / new / all!" / of / Rada / shouted / Jonny. / and)

➡ _____

47 (and / ran / they / up / the / to / top / of / hill / again. / the)

➡ _____

33 "아빠, 지구에서는 걷는 것이 어려워요." Rada가 말했다.

34 "그래. 지구가 너를 끌어당기고 있거든." 아빠가 말했다.

35 Rada와 Jonny는 더 이상 떠다닐 수 없었다.

36 그것이 첫 번째 새로운 것이었다.

37 "저건 무슨 소리죠?"라고 Rada가 물었다.

38 "새가 노래하는 거야." 엄마가 말했다.

39 "새가 노래하는 것을 들어 본 적이 없어요."라고 Rada가 말했다.

40 "그리고 저는 바람을 느껴 본 적도 없어요."라고 Jonny가 말했다.

41 이러한 것들이 모두 새로운 것들이었다.

42 Rada와 Jonny는 가장 가까운 언덕으로 뛰어 올라갔다.

43 꼭대기에서, 그들은 서로를 쳐다보고 웃었다.

44 그리고 나서 그들은 부드러운 초록 잔디에 누워서 언덕 아래로 굴러 내려갔다.

45 그것이 그들의 비밀이었다!

46 "이것이 모든 것들 중에서 최고의 새로운 것이에요!" Rada와 Jonny는 외쳤다.

47 그리고 그들은 언덕 꼭대기로 다시 뛰어 올라갔다.

※ **다음 우리말을 영어로 쓰시오.**

1 최고의 새로운 것
➡ _____

2 Rada는 먼 우주의 작은 세계에 살고 있었다.
➡ _____

3 그녀는 아빠, 엄마 그리고 남동생 Jonny와 함께 그곳에서 살고 있었다.
➡ _____

4 Rada의 아빠와 다른 사람들은 우주선에서 일했다.
➡ _____

5 Rada와 Jonny만이 아이들이었고, 그들은 우주에서 태어났다.
➡ _____

6 어느 날, 아빠가 Rada와 Jonny에게, "우리는 내일 지구로 돌아갈 거야."라고 말했다.
➡ _____

7 Rada와 Jonny는 깜짝 놀라 아빠를 바라보았고, 그에게 둥둥 떠서 갔다.
➡ _____

8 Rada가 아빠에게, "지구는 어떤 곳인가요?"라고 물었다.
➡ _____

9 "그곳에선 모든 것이 다르단다.
➡ _____

10 예를 들어, 하늘은 파란색이지."라고 아빠가 대답했다.
➡ _____

11 "전 한 번도 파란 하늘을 본 적이 없어요."라고 Jonny가 말했다.
➡ _____

12 "여기는 하늘이 항상 검은색이잖아요."라고 Rada가 말했다.
➡ _____

13 "그곳에는 모든 곳에 공기가 있기 때문에 크고 무거운 우주복을 입을 필요가 없단다.
➡ _____

14 또한 지구가 너희들을 끌어당기기 때문에 거기에서는 점프하는 것도 어렵단다." 아빠가 말했다.
➡ _____

15 "그 밖에 또 뭐가 있어요?" Rada가 물었다.
➡ _____

16 "언덕들이 있는데 그것들은 부드러운 초록색의 잔디로 뒤덮여 있단다.
➡ _____

17 언덕을 굴러 내려갈 수도 있어." 엄마가 대답했다.
➡ _____

18 "아빠, 언덕을 굴러 내려가 본 적 있어요?" Rada가 물었다.
➡ _____

19 "그럼, 정말 놀라워!" 아빠가 대답했다.
➡ _____

20 Jonny는 목이 말라서 우유 용기를 열어 그것을 흔들었다.
➡ _____

21 우유가 공기 중으로 떠서 방울을 형성했다.
➡ _____

22 Jonny는 그 우유 방울을 삼켰다.
➡ _____

23 "Jonny, 만약 네가 지구에서 그런 식으로 우유를 마신다면, 다 젖을 거야." 엄마가 말했다.
➡ _____

24 그날 밤 늦게, Rada와 Jonny는 지구에 대해서 오랜 시간 이야기했다.
➡ _____

25 그들이 보고, 하게 될 모든 새로운 것들을 생각하는 것은 흥미로웠다.
➡ _____

26 Rada와 Jonny가 정말로 하고 싶었던 한 가지 새로운 것이 있었다.
➡ _____

27 그들은 밤새 그것에 대해서 생각했고 엄마와 아빠에게는 그것을 말하지 않았다.
➡ _____

28 그것은 그들의 비밀이었다.
➡ _____

29 다음날, Rada의 가족은 우주선에 올랐다.
➡ _____

30 "긴 여행이 될 거야." 엄마가 말했다.
➡ _____

31 "괜찮아요. 정말 신나요!" Rada가 말했다.
➡ _____

32 우주선이 마침내 착륙했다.
➡ _____

33 "아빠, 지구에서는 걷는 것이 어려워요." Rada가 말했다.
➡ _____

34 "그래. 지구가 너를 끌어당기고 있거든." 아빠가 말했다.
➡ _____

35 Rada와 Jonny는 더 이상 떠다닐 수 없었다.
➡ _____

36 그것이 첫 번째 새로운 것이었다.
➡ _____

37 "저건 무슨 소리죠?"라고 Rada가 물었다.
➡ _____

38 "새가 노래하는 거야." 엄마가 말했다.
➡ _____

39 "새가 노래하는 것을 들어 본 적이 없어요."라고 Rada가 말했다.
➡ _____

40 "그리고 저는 바람을 느껴 본 적도 없어요."라고 Jonny가 말했다.
➡ _____

41 이러한 것들이 모두 새로운 것들이었다.
➡ _____

42 Rada와 Jonny는 가장 가까운 언덕으로 뛰어 올라갔다.
➡ _____

43 꼭대기에서, 그들은 서로를 쳐다보고 웃었다.
➡ _____

44 그러고 나서 그들은 부드러운 초록 잔디에 누워서 언덕 아래로 굴러 내려갔다.
➡ _____

45 그것이 그들의 비밀이었다!
➡ _____

46 "이것이 모든 것들 중에서 최고의 새로운 것이에요!" Rada와 Jonny는 외쳤다.
➡ _____

47 그리고 그들은 언덕 꼭대기로 다시 뛰어 올라갔다.
➡ _____

※ 다음 우리말과 일치하도록 빈칸에 알맞은 말을 쓰시오.

One Minute Speech

1. Did you _____ _____ the new book, *Dave's Adventures*?

2. This book _____ _____ Dave and his _____ in the _____.

3. The _____ _____ are Dave and a big bear. The story is fun.

4. _____ you _____ _____ the book?

5. Then you _____ _____ it!

1. 새 책인 Dave의 모험에 관해 들어 봤니?
2. 이 책은 Dave와 숲에서의 그의 모험에 관한 거야.
3. 주인공은 Dave와 큰 곰이야. 이야기가 재미있어.
4. 그 책에 관해 궁금하니?
5. 그러면 그것을 꼭 읽어 봐야 해!

Read and Complete

1. Rada's family lived in space. One day, they _____ _____ _____ _____ to Earth.

2. Rada's family talked about life on Earth. They talked about the blue sky and hills which _____ _____ _____ green grass.

3. The next day, Rada's family _____ _____ a spaceship. It was _____ _____ _____ to Earth.

4. When they _____ _____ Earth, Rada and Jonny _____ _____ the nearest hill and _____ _____ it. That was _____ _____ _____ _____ to them.

1. Rada의 가족은 우주에서 살고 있었다. 어느 날, 그들은 지구로 돌아가기로 결정했다.
2. Rada의 가족은 지구의 생활에 대해 이야기했다. 그들은 파란 하늘과 초록색 잔디로 뒤덮인 언덕에 대해 이야기했다.
3. 다음날, Rada의 가족은 우주선에 올랐다. 그것은 지구로의 긴 여행이었다.
4. 그들이 지구에 도착했을 때, Rada와 Jonny는 가장 가까운 언덕으로 뛰어 올라가 아래로 굴러 내려갔다. 그것은 그들에게 최고의 새로운 것이었다.

Around the World

1. Russia _____ the first dog _____ _____. It was small, and _____ _____ was Laika.

2. Yuri Gagarin _____ _____ space _____ _____ _____.

3. The USA _____ the _____ _____ _____ the moon. His name was Neil Armstrong.

4. Russia _____ the first space station. It _____ _____ the Earth _____ 3,000 times.

1. 러시아는 우주에 최초의 개를 보냈다. 그것은 작았고, 이름은 Laika였다.
2. Yuri Gagarin이 최초로 우주에 갔다.
3. 미국은 달에 최초의 인간을 보냈다. 그의 이름은 Neil Armstrong이었다.
4. 러시아가 최초의 우주정거장을 건설하였다. 그것은 거의 3천 번 지구 주변을 돌았다.

※ 다음 우리말을 영어로 쓰시오.

One Minute Speech

1. 새 책인 Dave의 모험에 관해 들어 봤니?

   ➡ _____

2. 이 책은 Dave와 숲에서의 그의 모험에 관한 거야.

   ➡ _____

3. 주인공은 Dave와 큰 곰이야. 이야기가 재미있어.

   ➡ _____

4. 그 책에 관해 궁금하니?

   ➡ _____

5. 그러면 그것을 꼭 읽어 봐야 해!

   ➡ _____

Read and Complete

1. Rada의 가족은 우주에서 살고 있었다. 어느 날, 그들은 지구로 돌아가기로 결정했다.

   ➡ _____

2. Rada의 가족은 지구의 생활에 대해 이야기했다. 그들은 파란 하늘과 초록색 잔디로 뒤덮인 언덕에 대해 이야기했다.

   ➡ _____

   _____

3. 다음날, Rada의 가족은 우주선에 올랐다. 그것은 지구로의 긴 여행이었다.

   ➡ _____

4. 그들이 지구에 도착했을 때, Rada와 Jonny는 가장 가까운 언덕으로 뛰어 올라가 아래로 굴러 내려갔다. 그것은 그들에게 최고의 새로운 것이었다.

   ➡ _____

   _____

Around the World

1. 러시아는 우주에 최초의 개를 보냈다. 그것은 작았고, 이름은 Laika였다.

   ➡ _____

2. Yuri Gagarin이 최초로 우주에 갔다.

   ➡ _____

3. 미국은 달에 최초의 인간을 보냈다. 그의 이름은 Neil Armstrong이었다.

   ➡ _____

4. 러시아가 최초의 우주정거장을 건설하였다. 그것은 거의 3천 번 지구 주변을 돌았다.

   ➡ _____

※ 다음 영어를 우리말로 쓰시오.

01 college

02 grass

03 display

04 exhibition

05 fan dance

06 continue

07 abroad

08 treasure

09 army

10 behind

11 research

12 wedding

13 storm

14 researcher

15 allow

16 traditional

17 museum

18 fitting room

19 government

20 result

21 historian

22 printing

23 instrument

24 succeed

25 value

26 royal

27 finally

28 pride

29 prove

30 delicious

31 steal

32 publish

33 difficulty

34 whole

35 because of+명사

36 give up

37 be full of

38 would like to+동사원형

39 as soon as+주어+동사

40 try on

41 right away

42 thanks to

43 spend+시간+ -ing

※ 다음 우리말을 영어로 쓰시오.

01	해외에서, 해외로	22	결과, 결실
02	자부심, 긍지	23	해고하다
03	정부	24	금속
04	대학	25	전통적인
05	맛있는	26	도둑질하다, 훔치다
06	성공하다	27	군대
07	허락하다, 허용하다	28	소리, 소음
08	반환	29	100만, 수많은
09	입증하다, 증명하다	30	결혼식
10	왕실의	31	출판하다, 발행하다
11	박람회, 전시회	32	연구, 조사
12	어려움	33	도둑
13	전시	34	가치
14	역사학자	35	~ 덕분에
15	보물	36	~하자마자
16	계속하다	37	바로, 즉시
17	악기	38	~을 입어 보다
18	폭풍	39	포기하다
19	마침내, 결국	40	~하면서 시간을 보내다
20	연구가	41	~ 때문에
21	탈의실	42	~로 가득 차 있다
		43	~을 찾다

※ 다음 영영풀이에 알맞은 단어를 <보기>에서 골라 쓴 후, 우리말 뜻을 쓰시오.

1 _____ : to use time doing something: _____

2 _____ : in or to a foreign country: _____

3 _____ : to show that something is true: _____

4 _____ : a feeling of satisfaction and pleasure in what you have done: _____

5 _____ : to say that someone can do something: _____

6 _____ : the work of finding out facts about something: _____

7 _____ : something that happens because of something else: _____

8 _____ : to do something that you tried or aimed to do: _____

9 _____ : relating to or belonging to a king or queen: _____

10 _____ : to take something that belongs to someone else: _____

11 _____ : to try to find someone or something by looking very carefully: _____

12 _____ : a group of valuable things, especially gold, silver, or jewels: _____

13 _____ : to print a book, magazine, or newspaper for people to buy: _____

14 _____ : the group of people who are responsible for controlling a country or state: _____

15 _____ : a bright light on a camera that flashes as you take a photograph in order to provide enough light: _____

16 _____ : a room in a clothes shop where you can put on clothes before you buy them: _____

보기

flash	abroad	allow	succeed
prove	fitting room	government	treasure
royal	pride	result	search
spend	steal	publish	research

※ 다음 우리말과 일치하도록 빈칸에 알맞은 말을 쓰시오.

Listen and Talk A-1

B: _____ me. What's this? _____ _____ _____ any food
_____ this.

W: Oh, it's Tteok, a Korean _____.

B: _____ _____ _____ _____ _____ some?

W: Sure. _____ _____. It's really _____.

B: 실례합니다. 이것이 무엇인가요? 저는 이런 음식을 본 적이 없어요.
W: 오, 그것은 한국의 후식인 떡이에요.
B: 먹어 봐도 될까요?
W: 물론이죠. 그렇게 하세요. 정말 맛있답니다.

Listen and Talk A-2

G: Excuse me. Is it OK _____ _____ _____ _____?

M: You _____, on the grass?

G: Yes. Is it _____ _____?

M: I'm sorry, but _____ on the grass _____ _____ _____.

G: OK, I _____.

G: 실례합니다. 저기에 앉아도 되나요?
M: 잔디 위를 말하는 건가요?
G: 네. 괜찮은가요?
M: 미안하지만, 잔디 위에 앉는 것은 허락되지 않습니다.
G: 알겠습니다, 이해합니다.

Listen and Talk A-3

B: Excuse me. What's this? It _____ _____.

W: Oh, that's a haegeum, a _____ Korean _____ _____.

B: _____ _____ _____ _____ _____ it?

W: _____ _____, but it's only _____ _____. _____ it is
not _____.

B: I see.

B: 실례합니다. 이것은 무엇인가요? 흥미롭게 생겼네요.
W: 오, 그것은 한국의 전통 악기인 해금이에요.
B: 연주를 해 봐도 될까요?
W: 미안하지만, 전시용입니다. 연주를 하는 것은 허락되지 않습니다.
B: 알겠습니다.

Listen and Talk A-4

G: _____ me. _____ _____ _____ _____ _____ pictures
here?

M: Yes, it's _____ _____.

G: _____ _____ _____ a flash? Can I use it, _____?

M: I'm _____ _____. _____ a flash is _____ _____ here.

G: Oh, I see. Thank you.

G: 실례합니다. 여기서 사진을 찍어도 되나요?
M: 네, 괜찮습니다.
G: 플래시를 사용하는 것은 어떤가요? 사용해도 되나요?
M: 안 될 것 같아요. 플래시를 사용하는 것은 여기서 허용되지 않습니다.
G: 오, 알겠어요. 감사합니다.

Listen and Talk B

A: _____ _____ _____ _____ _____ _____ _____?

B: I'm _____ _____. _____ is _____ _____ here.

A: Oh, I see.

A: 여기 앉아도 될까요?
B: 안 될 것 같아요. 여기에 앉는 것은 허용되지 않습니다.
A: 오, 알겠어요.

Talk and Play

A: _____ place do you want _____ _____ first in the museum?
B: _____ _____ _____ guess?
A: OK. _____ _____ _____ _____ _____ food there?
B: Yes. _____ _____ is _____.
A: _____ _____ _____ _____ _____ pictures?
B: No. Taking pictures _____ _____ _____
A: I _____ _____. You're _____ _____ _____ to the Video Room.
B: You're right.

A: 박물관에서 어떤 장소를 먼저 가고 싶니?
B: 알아맞혀 볼래?
A: 좋아. 거기에서 음식을 먹어도 되니?
B: 응. 음식을 먹는 것은 허용돼.
A: 사진을 찍어도 되니?
B: 아니. 사진을 찍는 것은 허용되지 않아.
A: 알겠다. 너는 Video Room에 갈 생각이구나.
B: 맞아.

Listen and Talk C

G: Excuse me, but _____ _____ _____ to try on this hanbok?
M: Sure. The _____ _____ is _____ _____.
G: Thanks. Wait a _____. That's also very pretty.
M: Oh, the little hat _____ _____?
G: Yes. What is it?
M: It's a jokduri, a _____ Korean hat _____ _____. It's usually _____ on a _____ day.
G: Really? _____ _____ _____ _____ _____ _____ _____, too?
M: I'm sorry, but it's only _____. Trying it _____ is _____ _____.
G: Oh. Then, I'll just _____ _____ this hanbok.

G: 실례지만, 이 한복을 입어 봐도 될까요?
M: 물론이죠. 탈의실은 저쪽입니다.
G: 고마워요. 잠깐만요. 저것도 매우 예쁘네요.
M: 오, 저기 있는 작은 모자요?
G: 네. 그건 뭔가요?
M: 그것은 여자들이 쓰는 한국 전통 모자인 족두리예요. 주로 결혼식 날 쓰죠.
G: 정말요? 그것도 써 봐도 될까요?
M: 죄송하지만, 그것은 전시만 하는 거예요. 써 보시는 건 안 돼요.
G: 오. 그럼, 그냥 이 한복만 입어 볼게요.

Review 1

G: _____ _____. What's this? It _____ _____.
B: Oh, that's a janggu, a _____ Korean _____.
G: _____ _____ _____ _____ play it?
B: I'm sorry, but it's only _____ _____. Playing it is not _____.
G: I see.

G: 실례합니다. 이것은 무엇인가요? 흥미로워 보이네요.
B: 오, 저것은 한국의 전통 악기인 장구예요.
G: 연주해 봐도 되나요?
B: 미안하지만, 전시용이에요. 연주하는 것은 허용되지 않아요.
G: 알겠어요.

Review 2

G: Excuse me, but _____ _____ _____ to take pictures here?
M: Yes. Go _____.
G: _____ _____ _____ a flash, _____?
M: Yes. That's _____ OK.
G: I'm sorry, _____ I have _____ _____ question. Can I eat food here?
M: I'm sorry, but that's _____ _____.

G: 실례합니다만, 여기서 사진을 찍어도 되나요?
M: 네. 그렇게 하세요.
G: 플래시를 사용해도 되나요?
M: 네. 그것도 괜찮습니다.
G: 죄송하지만, 질문이 하나 더 있어요. 여기서 음식을 먹어도 되나요?
M: 미안하지만, 그것은 허용되지 않습니다.

※ 다음 우리말에 맞도록 대화를 영어로 쓰시오.

Listen and Talk A-1

B: _____

W: _____

B: _____

W: _____

B: 실례합니다. 이것이 무엇인가요? 저는 이런 음식을 본 적이 없어요.
W: 오, 그것은 한국의 후식인 떡이에요.
B: 먹어 봐도 될까요?
W: 물론이죠. 그렇게 하세요. 정말 맛있답니다.

Listen and Talk A-2

G: _____

M: _____

G: _____

M: _____

G: _____

G: 실례합니다. 저기에 앉아도 되나요?
M: 잔디 위를 말하는 건가요?
G: 네. 괜찮은가요?
M: 미안하지만, 잔디 위에 앉는 것은 허락되지 않습니다.
G: 알겠습니다, 이해합니다.

Listen and Talk A-3

B: _____

W: _____

B: _____

W: _____

B: _____

B: 실례합니다. 이것은 무엇인가요? 흥미롭게 생겼네요.
W: 오, 그것은 한국의 전통 악기인 해금이에요.
B: 연주를 해 봐도 될까요?
W: 미안하지만, 전시용입니다. 연주를 하는 것은 허락되지 않습니다.
B: 알겠습니다.

Listen and Talk A-4

G: _____

M: _____

G: _____

M: _____

G: _____

G: 실례합니다. 여기서 사진을 찍어도 되나요?
M: 네, 괜찮습니다.
G: 플래시를 사용하는 것은 어떤가요? 사용해도 되나요?
M: 안 될 것 같아요. 플래시를 사용하는 것은 여기서 허용되지 않습니다.
G: 오, 알겠어요. 감사합니다.

Listen and Talk B

A: _____

B: _____

A: _____

A: 여기 앉아도 될까요?
B: 안 될 것 같아요. 여기에 앉는 것은 허용되지 않습니다.
A: 오, 알겠습니다.

Talk and Play

A: _____

B: _____

A: _____

B: _____

A: _____

B: _____

A: _____

B: _____

A: 박물관에서 어떤 장소를 먼저 가고 싶니?

B: 알아맞혀 볼래?

A: 좋아. 거기에서 음식을 먹어도 되니?

B: 응. 음식을 먹는 것은 허용돼.

A: 사진을 찍어도 되니?

B: 아니. 사진을 찍는 것은 허용되지 않아.

A: 알겠다. 너는 Video Room에 갈 생각이구나.

B: 맞아.

Listen and Talk C

G: _____

M: _____

G: _____

M: _____

G: _____

M: _____

G: _____

M: _____

G: _____

M: _____

G: _____

G: 실례지만, 이 한복을 입어 봐도 될까요?

M: 물론이죠. 탈의실은 저쪽입니다.

G: 고마워요. 잠깐만요. 저것도 매우 예쁘네요.

M: 오, 저기 있는 작은 모자요?

G: 네. 그건 뭔가요?

M: 그것은 여자들이 쓰는 한국 전통 모자인 족두리예요. 주로 결혼식 날 쓰죠.

G: 정말요? 그것도 써 봐도 될까요?

M: 죄송하지만, 그것은 전시만 하는 거예요. 써 보시는 건 안 돼요.

G: 오. 그럼, 그냥 이 한복만 입어 볼게요.

Review 1

G: _____

B: _____

G: _____

B: _____

G: _____

G: 실례합니다. 이것은 무엇인가요? 흥미로워 보이네요.

B: 오, 저것은 한국의 전통 악기인 장구예요.

G: 연주해 봐도 되나요?

B: 미안하지만, 전시용이에요. 연주하는 것은 허용되지 않아요.

G: 알겠어요.

Review 2

G: _____

M: _____

G: _____

M: _____

G: _____

M: _____

G: 실례합니다만, 여기서 사진을 찍어도 되나요?

M: 네. 그렇게 하세요.

G: 플래시를 사용해도 되나요?

M: 네. 그것도 괜찮습니다.

G: 죄송하지만, 질문이 하나 더 있어요. 여기서 음식을 먹어도 되나요?

M: 미안하지만, 그것은 허용되지 않습니다.

※ 다음 우리말과 일치하도록 빈칸에 알맞은 것을 골라 쓰시오.

1 An _____ _____ Dr. Park Byeong-seon
A. with   B. Interview

2 _____ May 27, 2011, 297 books of *Uigwe*, a _____ of royal books the French army _____ in 1866, came _____ to Korea.
A. back   B. on   C. collection   D. took

3 The person _____ this _____ is Dr. Park Byeong-seon, a historian who spent her whole life _____ for Korean national treasures _____.
A. return   B. abroad   C. behind   D. searching

4 Q: Can you tell me _____ you _____ _____ in *Uigwe*?
A. interested   B. how   C. became

5 Dr. Park: I _____ _____ in _____.
A. college   B. history   C. studied

6 I went to France _____ _____ my _____ in 1955.
A. continue   B. studies   C. to

7 _____ you know, the French _____ took many of our national _____ in 1866.
A. treasures   B. as   C. army

8 I wanted to _____ them _____ I was _____ there.
A. while   B. find   C. studying

9 *Uigwe* was _____ _____ _____.
A. them   B. one   C. of

10 Q: You _____ 297 _____ of *Uigwe* in the National Library of France, _____ Paris.
A. books   B. found   C. in

11 Please _____ me _____ you _____ them.
A. how   B. tell   C. found

12 Dr. Park: _____ _____ as I became a researcher at the National Library in 1967, I began to _____ _____ *Uigwe*.
A. for   B. soon   C. look   D. as

13 _____ 10 years, in 1977, I _____ _____ the books.
A. finally   B. after   C. found

14 I think I _____ _____ more _____ 30 _____ books.
A. million   B. than   C. at   D. looked

15 Q: I'm _____ you were very _____ when you _____ the books.
A. excited   B. found   C. sure

16 Dr. Park: Yes, I was, but _____ _____ were _____ _____ me.
A. for   B. difficulties   C. more   D. waiting

17 I _____ that the books _____ be _____ to Korea, _____ my bosses at the library didn't like that idea.
A. returned   B. thought   C. should   D. but

---

1 박병선 박사와의 인터뷰

2 2011년 5월 27일에 프랑스군이 1866년에 가져갔던 왕실 서적인 "의궤" 297권이 한국으로 돌아왔다.

3 이 반환 뒤에 있는 인물이 해외에 있는 한국의 문화재를 찾기 위해 전 생애를 바친 역사학자 박병선 박사이다.

4 Q: "의궤"에 어떻게 관심을 갖게 되셨는지 말씀해 주시겠어요?

5 Dr. Park: 저는 대학에서 역사를 공부했어요.

6 저는 1955년에 학업을 계속하기 위해 프랑스에 갔습니다.

7 아시다시피, 프랑스군은 1866년에 우리 문화재를 많이 가져갔어요.

8 저는 그곳에서 공부하는 동안 그것들을 찾고 싶었어요.

9 "의궤"는 그것들 중의 하나였어요.

10 Q: 당신은 파리에 있는 프랑스 국립도서관에서 297권의 "의궤"를 발견하셨어요.

11 그것들을 어떻게 발견하셨는지 말씀해 주세요.

12 Dr. Park: 1967년에 국립도서관의 연구원이 되자마자, 저는 "의궤"를 찾기 시작했어요.

13 10년 후인 1977년에 마침내 책들을 발견했죠.

14 제 생각에 3천만 권 이상의 책을 본 것 같아요.

15 Q: 그 책들을 발견했을 때 무척 흥분하셨겠어요.

16 Dr. Park: 네, 하지만 더 큰 어려움이 저를 기다리고 있었어요.

17 저는 그 책들이 한국에 반환되어야 한다고 생각했지만, 도서관의 제 상사들은 그 생각을 좋아하지 않았어요.

18 They _____ _____ that I was a Korean spy and _____ me.

    A. fired   B. thought   C. even

19 After that, I had to go to the library _____ a visitor, _____ it was not easy to _____ research _____ *Uigwe*.

    A. as   B. on   C. so   D. do

20 _____, I didn't _____ _____.

    A. give   B. however   C. up

21 For _____ than ten years, I went to the library _____ day _____ finish my _____.

    A. every   B. research   C. to   D. more

22 I _____ to _____ people the _____ of *Uigwe*.

    A. show   B. wanted   C. value

23 Q: The _____ of your _____ were _____ a book in Korea in 1990.

    A. as   B. results   C. published   D. research

24 Many Koreans became _____ _____ *Uigwe* _____ your book.

    A. because   B. interested   C. of   D. in

25 Dr. Park: Yes. In 1992, the Korean government _____ the French government _____ its _____ and, _____, the 297 books are here now.

    A. for   B. finally   C. asked   D. return

26 Q: Before I _____ this interview, I'd _____ to ask you about *Jikji*, a book that _____ the history of _____.

    A. printing   B. changed   C. like   D. finish

27 Dr. Park: I _____ it _____ my first _____ at the library.

    A. year   B. in   C. found

28 I knew _____ _____ that it was very _____.

    A. special   B. away   C. right

29 I worked _____ to _____ its _____ and finally _____.

    A. succeeded   B. value   C. prove   D. hard

30 At a book _____ in Paris in 1972, *Jikji* was _____ _____ the oldest book in the world that was printed with movable _____ type.

    A. displayed   B. metal   C. exhibition   D. as

31 Q: Dr. Park, _____ _____ your hard work, *Jikji* and *Uigwe* were found, and all Koreans _____ you _____ that.

    A. thank   B. to   C. for   D. thanks

32 Dr. Park: I hope people will become more _____ in our national _____ and work for their _____.

    A. treasures   B. return   C. interested   D. abroad

---

18 그들은 심지어 제가 한국의 스파이라고 생각했고 저를 해고했죠.

19 그 후에, 저는 방문객으로 도서관에 가야만 했고, 그래서 "의궤"를 연구하는 것이 쉽지 않았어요.

20 하지만 저는 포기하지 않았죠.

21 10년 넘게, 연구를 끝마치기 위해 매일 도서관에 갔어요.

22 저는 사람들에게 "의궤"의 가치를 보여 주고 싶었어요.

23 Q: 당신의 연구 결과가 1990년 한국에서 책으로 출판되었죠.

24 많은 한국인들이 당신의 책 때문에 "의궤"에 관심을 갖게 되었어요.

25 Dr. Park: 네. 1992년에 한국 정부는 프랑스 정부에 그것의 반환을 요청했고, 마침내 297권의 책이 지금 여기 있게 된 거죠.

26 Q: 인터뷰를 마치기 전에, 인쇄의 역사를 바꾼 책인 "직지"에 대해 여쭙고 싶어요.

27 Dr. Park: 저는 도서관에서 근무한 첫해에 그것을 발견했어요.

28 그것이 아주 특별하다는 것을 바로 알았어요.

29 저는 그것의 가치를 증명하기 위해 열심히 연구했고 마침내 성공했죠.

30 1972년에 파리 도서 박람회에서 "직지"는 금속 활자로 인쇄된 세계에서 가장 오래된 책으로 전시되었죠.

31 Q: 박 박사님, 당신의 노고 덕분에 "직지"와 "의궤"가 발견되었고, 모든 한국인들이 그 점을 당신에게 감사하고 있어요.

32 Dr. Park: 저는 사람들이 해외에 있는 우리의 문화재에 더 많은 관심을 갖고 그것의 반환을 위해 애써 주시기를 바랍니다.

※ 다음 우리말과 일치하도록 빈칸에 알맞은 말을 쓰시오.

1 An _____ _____ Dr. Park Byeong-seon

2 _____ May 27, 2011, 297 books of *Uigwe*, _____ _____ _____ _____ _____ the French army took in 1866, _____ _____ _____ Korea.

3 The person _____ _____ _____ is Dr. Park Byeong-seon, a historian who _____ her _____ _____ _____ _____ Korean national treasures _____.

4 Q: Can you tell me _____ you _____ _____ _____ *Uigwe*?

5 Dr. Park: I _____ _____ _____ _____ _____.

6 I went to France _____ _____ my studies in 1955.

7 _____ _____ _____ _____, the French army took many of our _____ _____ in 1866.

8 I wanted to find them _____ I _____ _____ there.

9 *Uigwe* was _____ _____ _____ _____.

10 Q: You found _____ _____ in the _____ _____ of France, in Paris.

11 Please _____ _____ _____ you _____ them.

12 Dr. Park: _____ _____ _____ I became a _____ at the National Library in 1967, I began to _____ _____ *Uigwe*.

13 _____ 10 years, in 1977, I _____ _____ the books.

14 I think I _____ _____ more than _____ _____ books.

15 Q: _____ _____ you were very _____ when you found the books.

16 Dr. Park: Yes, I was, but _____ _____ were _____ me.

17 I thought that the books _____ _____ _____ Korea, but my bosses at the library didn't like _____ _____.

1 박병선 박사와의 인터뷰

2 2011년 5월 27일에 프랑스군이 1866년에 가져갔던 왕실 서적인 "의궤" 297권이 한국으로 돌아왔다.

3 이 반환 뒤에 있는 인물이 해외에 있는 한국의 문화재를 찾기 위해 전 생애를 바친 역사학자 박병선 박사이다.

4 Q: "의궤"에 어떻게 관심을 갖게 되셨는지 말씀해 주시겠어요?

5 Dr. Park: 저는 대학에서 역사를 공부했어요.

6 저는 1955년에 학업을 계속하기 위해 프랑스에 갔습니다.

7 아시다시피, 프랑스군은 1866년에 우리 문화재를 많이 가져갔어요.

8 저는 그곳에서 공부하는 동안 그것들을 찾고 싶었어요.

9 "의궤"는 그것들 중의 하나였어요.

10 Q: 당신은 파리에 있는 프랑스 국립도서관에서 297권의 "의궤"를 발견하셨어요.

11 그것들을 어떻게 발견하셨는지 말씀해 주세요.

12 Dr. Park: 1967년에 국립도서관의 연구원이 되자마자, 저는 "의궤"를 찾기 시작했어요.

13 10년 후인 1977년에 마침내 그 책들을 발견했죠.

14 제 생각에 3천만 권 이상의 책을 본 것 같아요.

15 Q: 그 책들을 발견했을 때 무척 흥분하셨겠어요.

16 Dr. Park: 네, 하지만 더 큰 어려움이 저를 기다리고 있었어요.

17 저는 그 책들이 한국에 반환되어야 한다고 생각했지만, 도서관의 제 상사들은 그 생각을 좋아하지 않았어요.

18 They _____ _____ that I was a Korean spy and _____ me.

19 After that, I had to go to the library _____ _____ _____, _____ it was not easy _____ _____ _____ _____ *Uigwe*.

20 _____, I didn't give up.

21 _____ _____ _____ ten years, I went to the library every day _____ _____ _____ _____.

22 I wanted to show people _____ _____ _____ _____.

23 Q: The results of your research _____ _____ _____ a book in Korea in 1990.

24 Many Koreans _____ _____ _____ *Uigwe* _____ _____ your book.

25 Dr. Park: Yes. In 1992, the Korean government _____ the French government _____ _____ _____ and, finally, the 297 books _____ _____ _____.

26 Q: Before I finish this interview, _____ _____ _____ _____ you about *Jikji*, a book that _____ the history of _____.

27 Dr. Park: I found it _____ _____ _____ at the library.

28 I knew _____ _____ that it was _____ _____.

29 I worked hard _____ _____ _____ _____ and finally _____.

30 At a book exhibition in Paris in 1972, *Jikji* _____ _____ _____ the _____ _____ in the world that was printed with _____ _____ _____.

31 Q: Dr. Park, _____ _____ your hard work, *Jikji* and *Uigwe* were found, and all Koreans _____ you _____ that.

32 Dr. Park: I hope people will become more interested in _____ _____ _____ _____ and work for their _____.

18 그들은 심지어 제가 한국의 스파이라고 생각했고 저를 해고했죠.

19 그 후에, 저는 방문객으로 도서관에 가야만 했고, 그래서 "의궤"를 연구하는 것이 쉽지 않았어요.

20 하지만 저는 포기하지 않았죠.

21 10년 넘게, 연구를 끝마치기 위해 매일 도서관에 갔어요.

22 저는 사람들에게 "의궤"의 가치를 보여 주고 싶었어요.

23 Q: 당신의 연구 결과가 1990년 한국에서 책으로 출판되었죠.

24 많은 한국인들이 당신의 책 때문에 "의궤"에 관심을 갖게 되었어요.

25 Dr. Park: 네. 1992년에 한국 정부는 프랑스 정부에 그것의 반환을 요청했고, 마침내 297권의 책이 지금 여기에 있게 된 거죠.

26 Q: 인터뷰를 마치기 전에, 인쇄의 역사를 바꾼 책인 "직지"에 대해 여쭙고 싶어요.

27 Dr. Park: 저는 도서관에서 근무한 첫해에 그것을 발견했어요.

28 그것이 아주 특별하다는 것을 바로 알았어요.

29 저는 그것의 가치를 증명하기 위해 열심히 연구했고 마침내 성공했죠.

30 1972년에 파리 도서 박람회에서 "직지"는 금속 활자로 인쇄된 세계에서 가장 오래된 책으로 전시되었죠.

31 Q: 박 박사님, 당신의 노고 덕분에 "직지"와 "의궤"가 발견되었고, 모든 한국인들이 그 점을 당신에게 감사하고 있어요.

32 Dr. Park: 저는 사람들이 해외에 있는 우리의 문화재에 더 많은 관심을 갖고 그것의 반환을 위해 애써 주시기를 바랍니다.

※ 다음 문장을 우리말로 쓰시오.

1 An Interview with Dr. Park Byeong-seon

➡ _____

2 On May 27, 2011, 297 books of *Uigwe*, a collection of royal books the French army took in 1866, came back to Korea.

➡ _____

3 The person behind this return is Dr. Park Byeong-seon, a historian who spent her whole life searching for Korean national treasures abroad.

➡ _____

4 Q: Can you tell me how you became interested in *Uigwe*?

➡ _____

5 Dr. Park: I studied history in college.

➡ _____

6 I went to France to continue my studies in 1955.

➡ _____

7 As you know, the French army took many of our national treasures in 1866.

➡ _____

8 I wanted to find them while I was studying there.

➡ _____

9 *Uigwe* was one of them.

➡ _____

10 Q: You found 297 books of *Uigwe* in the National Library of France, in Paris.

➡ _____

11 Please tell me how you found them.

➡ _____

12 Dr. Park: As soon as I became a researcher at the National Library in 1967, I began to look for *Uigwe*.

➡ _____

13 After 10 years, in 1977, I finally found the books.

➡ _____

14 I think I looked at more than 30 million books.

➡ _____

15 Q: I'm sure you were very excited when you found the books.

➡ _____

16 Dr. Park: Yes, I was, but more difficulties were waiting for me.

➡ _____

17 I thought that the books should be returned to Korea, but my bosses at the library didn't like that idea.

➡ _____

18 ▸ They even thought that I was a Korean spy and fired me.

➡ _____

19 ▸ After that, I had to go to the library as a visitor, so it was not easy to do research on *Uigwe*.

➡ _____

20 ▸ However, I didn't give up.

➡ _____

21 ▸ For more than ten years, I went to the library every day to finish my research.

➡ _____

22 ▸ I wanted to show people the value of *Uigwe*.

➡ _____

23 ▸ Q: The results of your research were published as a book in Korea in 1990.

➡ _____

24 ▸ Many Koreans became interested in *Uigwe* because of your book.

➡ _____

25 ▸ Dr. Park: Yes. In 1992, the Korean government asked the French government for its return and, finally, the 297 books are here now.

➡ _____

_____

26 ▸ Q: Before I finish this interview, I'd like to ask you about *Jikji*, a book that changed the history of printing.

➡ _____

27 ▸ Dr. Park: I found it in my first year at the library.

➡ _____

28 ▸ I knew right away that it was very special.

➡ _____

29 ▸ I worked hard to prove its value and finally succeeded.

➡ _____

30 ▸ At a book exhibition in Paris in 1972, *Jikji* was displayed as the oldest book in the world that was printed with movable metal type.

➡ _____

31 ▸ Q: Dr. Park, thanks to your hard work, *Jikji* and *Uigwe* were found, and all Koreans thank you for that.

➡ _____

32 ▸ Dr. Park: I hope people will become more interested in our national treasures abroad and work for their return.

➡ _____

_____

※ 다음 괄호 안의 단어들을 우리말에 맞도록 바르게 배열하시오.

1 (Interview / An / Dr. / with / Byeong-seon / Park)
➡ _____

2 (May / on / 2011, / 27, / books / 297 / *Uigwe* / of / collection / a / royal / of / books / French / the / army / in / took / 1866, / back / came / Korea. / to)
➡ _____

3 (person / the / behind / return / this / Dr. / is / Park / a / Byeong-seon / historian / spent / who / whole / her / searching / life / for / national / Korean / abroad. / treasures)
➡ _____

4 (Q: / you / can / me / tell / you / how / interested / became / *Uigwe*? / in)
➡ _____

5 (Dr. Park: / I / history / studied / college. / in)
➡ _____

6 (went / I / France / to / continue / to / studies / 1955. / in / my)
➡ _____

7 (you / as / know, / French / the / took / army / of / many / our / treasures / 1866. / in / national)
➡ _____

8 (wanted / I / find / to / them / I / while / was / there. / studying)
➡ _____

9 (was / *Uigwe* / of / them. / one)
➡ _____

10 (Q: / found / you / books / 297 / *Uigwe* / of / the / in / Library / of / National / Paris. / in / France)
➡ _____

11 (tell / please / how / me / found / them. / you)
➡ _____

12 (Dr. Park: / soon / as / I / as / became / researcher / a / at / Library / the / National / 1976, / in / began / I / look / to / *Uigwe*. / for)
➡ _____

13 (10 / after / years, / 1977, / in / finally / I / books. / the / found)
➡ _____

14 (I / looked / I / think / more / at / 30 / than / books. / million)
➡ _____

15 (Q: / sure / I'm / were / you / excited / very / you / when / books. / the / found)
➡ _____

16 (Dr. Park: / I / yes, / was, / more / but / were / difficulties / waiting / me. / for)
➡ _____

17 (thought / I / that / books / the / be / should / to / returned / Korea, / my / but / bosses / at / library / didn't / the / idea. / that / like)
➡ _____

---

1 박병선 박사와의 인터뷰

2 2011년 5월 27일에 프랑스군이 1866년에 가져갔던 왕실 서적인 "의궤" 297권이 한국으로 돌아왔다.

3 이 반환 뒤에 있는 인물이 해외에 있는 한국의 문화재를 찾기 위해 전 생애를 바친 역사학자 박병선 박사이다.

4 Q: "의궤"에 어떻게 관심을 갖게 되셨는지 말씀해 주시겠어요?

5 Dr. Park: 저는 대학에서 역사를 공부했어요.

6 저는 1955년에 학업을 계속하기 위해 프랑스에 갔습니다.

7 아시다시피, 프랑스군은 1866년에 우리 문화재를 많이 가져갔어요.

8 저는 그곳에서 공부하는 동안 그것들을 찾고 싶었어요.

9 "의궤"는 그것들 중의 하나였어요.

10 Q: 당신은 파리에 있는 프랑스 국립도서관에서 297권의 "의궤"를 발견하셨어요.

11 그것들을 어떻게 발견하셨는지 말씀해 주세요.

12 Dr. Park: 1967년에 국립도서관의 연구원이 되자마자, 저는 "의궤"를 찾기 시작했어요.

13 10년 후인 1977년에 마침내 그 책들을 발견했죠.

14 제 생각에 3천만 권 이상의 책을 본 것 같아요.

15 Q: 그 책들을 발견했을 때 무척 흥분하셨겠어요.

16 Dr. Park: 네, 하지만 더 큰 어려움이 저를 기다리고 있었어요.

17 저는 그 책들이 한국에 반환되어야 한다고 생각했지만, 도서관의 제 상사들은 그 생각을 좋아하지 않았어요.

18 (even / they / thought / I / that / a / was / Korean / and / spy / me. / fired)

➡ _____

19 (that, / after / had / I / go / to / to / library / the / a / as / visitor, / it / so / was / easy / not / do / to / *Uigwe.* / on / research)

➡ _____

_____

20 (I / however, / didn't / up. / give)

➡ _____

21 (more / for / ten / than / years, / went / I / to / library / the / day / every / to / my / research. / finish)

➡ _____

_____

22 (wanted / I / to / people / show / value / the / *Uigwe.* / of)

➡ _____

23 (Q: / results / the / your / of / were / research / as / published / a / in / book / in / 1990. / Korea)

➡ _____

24 (Koreans / many / interested / became / in / because / *Uigwe* / of / book. / your)

➡ _____

25 (Dr. Park: / yes. // 1992, / in / Korean / the / government / asked / French / the / government / its / for / and, / return / finally, / 297 / the / are / now. / here / books)

➡ _____

_____

26 (Q: / I / before / this / finish / interview, / like / I'd / ask / to / about / you / *Jikji*, / book / a / changed / that / history / the / painting. / of)

➡ _____

_____

27 (Dr. Park: / found / I / it / my / in / year / first / at / library. / the)

➡ _____

28 (knew / I / away / right / that / was / it / special. / very)

➡ _____

29 (worked / I / to / hard / its / prove / value / succeeded. / finally / and)

➡ _____

30 (a / at / exhibition / book / Paris / in / 1972, / in / was / *Jikji* / as / displayed / the / book / oldest / the / in / world / was / that / with / printed / metal / movable / type.)

➡ _____

_____

31 (Q: / Park, / Dr. / to / thanks / your / work, / hard / *Uigwe* / and / *Jikji* / found, / were / and / Koreans / all / you / that. / for / thank)

➡ _____

32 (Dr. Park: / hope / I / will / people / become / interested / more / national / our / in / abroad / treasures / and / for / return. / their / work)

➡ _____

_____

---

18 그들은 심지어 제가 한국의 스파이라고 생각했고 저를 해고했죠.

19 그 후에, 저는 방문객으로 도서관에 가야만 했고, 그래서 "의궤"를 연구하는 것이 쉽지 않았어요.

20 하지만 저는 포기하지 않았죠.

21 10년 넘게, 연구를 끝마치기 위해 매일 도서관에 갔어요.

22 저는 사람들에게 "의궤"의 가치를 보여 주고 싶었어요.

23 Q: 당신의 연구 결과가 1990년 한국에서 책으로 출판되었죠.

24 많은 한국인들이 당신의 책 때문에 "의궤"에 관심을 갖게 되었어요.

25 Dr. Park: 네. 1992년에 한국 정부는 프랑스 정부에 그것의 반환을 요청했고, 마침내 297권의 책이 지금 여기 있게 된 거죠.

26 Q: 인터뷰를 마치기 전에, 인쇄의 역사를 바꾼 책인 "직지"에 대해 여쭙고 싶어요.

27 Dr. Park: 저는 도서관에서 근무한 첫해에 그것을 발견했어요.

28 그것이 아주 특별하다는 것을 바로 알았어요.

29 저는 그것의 가치를 증명하기 위해 열심히 연구했고 마침내 성공했죠.

30 1972년에 파리 도서 박람회에서 "직지"는 금속 활자로 인쇄된 세계에서 가장 오래된 책으로 전시되었죠.

31 Q: 박 박사님, 당신의 노고 덕분에 "직지"와 "의궤"가 발견되었고, 모든 한국인들이 그 점을 당신에게 감사하고 있어요.

32 Dr. Park: 저는 사람들이 해외에 있는 우리의 문화재에 더 많은 관심을 갖고 그것의 반환을 위해 애써 주시기를 바랍니다.

※ 다음 우리말을 영어로 쓰시오.

1 박병선 박사와의 인터뷰

➡ _____

2 2011년 5월 27일에 프랑스군이 1866년에 가져갔던 왕실 서적인 "의궤" 297권이 한국으로 돌아왔다.

➡ _____

3 이 반환 뒤에 있는 인물이 해외에 있는 한국의 문화재를 찾기 위해 전 생애를 바친 역사학자 박병선 박사이다.

➡ _____

4 Q: "의궤"에 어떻게 관심을 갖게 되셨는지 말씀해 주시겠어요?

➡ _____

5 Dr. Park: 저는 대학에서 역사를 공부했어요.

➡ _____

6 저는 1955년에 학업을 계속하기 위해 프랑스에 갔습니다.

➡ _____

7 아시다시피, 프랑스군은 1866년에 우리 문화재를 많이 가져갔어요.

➡ _____

8 저는 그곳에서 공부하는 동안 그것들을 찾고 싶었어요.

➡ _____

9 "의궤"는 그것들 중의 하나였어요.

➡ _____

10 Q: 당신은 파리에 있는 프랑스 국립도서관에서 297권의 "의궤"를 발견하셨어요.

➡ _____

11 그것들을 어떻게 발견하셨는지 말씀해 주세요.

➡ _____

12 Dr. Park: 1967년에 국립도서관의 연구원이 되자마자, 저는 "의궤"를 찾기 시작했어요.

➡ _____

_____

13 10년 후인 1977년에 마침내 그 책들을 발견했죠.

➡ _____

14 제 생각에 3천만 권 이상의 책을 본 것 같아요.

➡ _____

15 Q: 그 책들을 발견했을 때 무척 흥분하셨겠어요.

➡ _____

16 Dr. Park: 네, 하지만 더 큰 어려움이 저를 기다리고 있었어요.

➡ _____

17 저는 그 책들이 한국에 반환되어야 한다고 생각했지만, 도서관의 제 상사들은 그 생각을 좋아하지 않았어요.

➡ _____

_____

18 그들은 심지어 제가 한국의 스파이라고 생각했고 저를 해고했죠.

➡ _____

19 그 후에, 저는 방문객으로 도서관에 가야만 했고, 그래서 "의궤"를 연구하는 것이 쉽지 않았어요.

➡ _____

20 하지만 저는 포기하지 않았죠.

➡ _____

21 10년 넘게, 연구를 끝마치기 위해 매일 도서관에 갔어요.

➡ _____

22 저는 사람들에게 "의궤"의 가치를 보여 주고 싶었어요.

➡ _____

23 Q: 당신의 연구 결과가 1990년 한국에서 책으로 출판되었죠.

➡ _____

24 많은 한국인들이 당신의 책 때문에 "의궤"에 관심을 갖게 되었어요.

➡ _____

25 Dr. Park: 네. 1992년에 한국 정부는 프랑스 정부에 그것의 반환을 요청했고, 마침내 297권의 책이 지금 여기 있게 된 거죠.

➡ _____

_____

26 Q: 인터뷰를 마치기 전에, 인쇄의 역사를 바꾼 책인 "직지"에 대해 여쭙고 싶어요.

➡ _____

_____

27 Dr. Park: 저는 도서관에서 근무한 첫해에 그것을 발견했어요.

➡ _____

28 그것이 아주 특별하다는 것을 바로 알았어요.

➡ _____

29 저는 그것의 가치를 증명하기 위해 열심히 연구했고 마침내 성공했죠.

➡ _____

30 1972년에 파리 도서 박람회에서 "직지"는 금속 활자로 인쇄된 세계에서 가장 오래된 책으로 전시되었죠.

➡ _____   _____

31 Q: 박 박사님, 당신의 노고 덕분에 "직지"와 "의궤"가 발견되었고, 모든 한국인들이 그 점을 당신에게 감사하고 있어요.

➡ _____

_____

32 Dr. Park: 저는 사람들이 해외에 있는 우리의 문화재에 더 많은 관심을 갖고 그것의 반환을 위해 애써 주시기를 바랍니다.

➡ _____

_____

※ 다음 우리말과 일치하도록 빈칸에 알맞은 말을 쓰시오.

After You Read C Think and Talk

1. A: _____ do you _____ _____ Dr. Park?

2. B: I _____ she had a strong _____. She had many _____, but she didn't _____ _____.

3. C: I think she had a _____ _____ for her work.

4. _____ a historian, she was very _____ about _____ Korean national treasures _____.

1. A: 박 박사에 대해 어떻게 생각하니?
2. B: 그녀는 강한 의지를 가졌다고 생각해. 그녀는 많은 어려움을 겪었지만 포기하지 않았어.
3. C: 그녀는 자신의 일에 대해 강한 열정을 가졌다고 생각해.
4. 역사학자로서, 그녀는 해외에 있는 한국의 문화재를 찾는 것에 대해 매우 열정적이었어.

Think and Write Step 2

1. An _____ _____ Kim Yubin

2. The _____ is the interview I had with Kim Yubin, a _____ _____ _____.

3. Q: Can you tell me _____ _____ _____ _____ _____?

4. A: I _____ _____ in Seoul _____ March 11, 1980.

5. Q: I'd _____ _____ know _____ _____ _____ _____ _____.

6. A: _____ _____ in life is _____ _____ a better world.

7. Q: Can you tell me _____ _____ _____ about your job?

8. A: I _____ _____ people.

9. I think _____ Kim Yubin is a great _____ _____.

1. 김유빈 씨와의 인터뷰
2. 다음은 제가 지역 경찰관 김유빈 씨와 한 인터뷰입니다.
3. Q: 당신은 언제, 어디서 태어나셨는지 말씀해 주시겠어요?
4. A: 저는 1980년 3월 11일에 서울에서 태어났어요.
5. Q: 당신의 인생의 목표가 무엇인지 알고 싶어요.
6. A: 저의 인생의 목표는 더 나은 세상을 만드는 것입니다.
7. Q: 당신의 직업에 관해 당신이 좋아하는 것이 무엇인지 말씀해 주시겠어요?
8. A: 저는 사람들을 돕는 것이 좋아요.
9. 저는 김유빈 씨가 대단한 경찰관이라고 생각합니다.

Team Project Create

1. *Jikji*, _____ _____ _____ _____ No. 1132

2. *Jikji* _____ _____ at Heungdeoksa in 1377.

3. It is now in the _____ _____ of France, in Paris.

4. It is the _____ _____ _____ that was printed with movable _____ _____.

1. 직지, 한국의 국보 1132번
2. 직지는 1377년 흥덕사에서 인쇄되었다.
3. 현재는 파리의 프랑스 국립도서관에 있다.
4. 직지는 금속활자로 인쇄된 세계에서 가장 오래된 책이다.

※ 다음 우리말을 영어로 쓰시오.

After You Read C Think and Talk

1. A: 박 박사에 대해 어떻게 생각하니?
➡ _____

2. B: 그녀는 강한 의지를 가졌다고 생각해. 그녀는 많은 어려움을 겪었지만 포기하지 않았어.
➡ _____

3. C: 그녀는 자신의 일에 대해 강한 열정을 가졌다고 생각해.
➡ _____

4. 역사학자로서, 그녀는 해외에 있는 한국의 문화재를 찾는 것에 대해 매우 열정적이었어.
➡ _____

Think and Write Step 2

1. 김유빈 씨와의 인터뷰
➡ _____

2. 다음은 제가 지역 경찰관 김유빈 씨와 한 인터뷰입니다.
➡ _____

3. Q: 당신은 언제, 어디서 태어나셨는지 말씀해 주시겠어요?
➡ _____

4. A: 저는 1980년 3월 11일에 서울에서 태어났어요.
➡ _____

5. Q: 당신의 인생의 목표가 무엇인지 알고 싶어요.
➡ _____

6. A: 저의 인생의 목표는 더 나은 세상을 만드는 것입니다.
➡ _____

7. Q: 당신의 직업에 관해 당신이 좋아하는 것이 무엇인지 말씀해 주시겠어요?
➡ _____

8 A: 저는 사람들을 돕는 것이 좋아요.
➡ _____

9. 저는 김유빈 씨가 대단한 경찰관이라고 생각합니다.
➡ _____

Team Project Create

1. 직지, 한국의 국보 1132번
➡ _____

2. 직지는 1377년 흥덕사에서 인쇄되었다.
➡ _____

3. 현재는 파리의 프랑스 국립도서관에 있다.
➡ _____

4. 직지는 금속활자로 인쇄된 세계에서 가장 오래된 책이다.
➡ _____

※ 다음 영어를 우리말로 쓰시오.

01 button

02 fun

03 creative

04 delicious

05 enough

06 taste

07 work

08 pile

09 batter

10 own

11 counter

12 recipe

13 mix

14 drop

15 fresh

16 sell

17 inside

18 push

19 happen

20 prize

21 sign

22 machine

23 shout

24 P.S.(=postscript)

25 ready

26 try

27 lose

28 wrong

29 leave

30 remember

31 break up

32 all of a sudden

33 with excitement

34 for a while

35 in the end

36 be full of

37 drop into

38 pile A on B

39 give ~ back

40 right away

41 step out

42 give a reward

43 keep+-ing

※ 다음 우리말을 영어로 쓰시오.

01 도넛	
02 반죽	
03 쌓아 올리다, 쌓다	
04 창의적인	
05 표지판	
06 상금	
07 ~한 맛이 나다	
08 떨어지다	
09 잃어버리다	
10 외치다, 소리치다	
11 계산대	
12 발생하다, 일어나다	
13 ~ 전에	
14 시도하다, 먹어보다	
15 반지	
16 잘못된, 이상이 있는	
17 떠나다, ~에 두다	
18 섞다	
19 팔다	
20 요리법	
21 기계	

22 누르다	
23 효과가 있다, 작동하다	
24 준비된	
25 ~ 안에	
26 소유하다	
27 맛있는	
28 충분한	
29 신선한	
30 기억하다	
31 ~ 앞에	
32 잠시	
33 결국, 마침내	
34 ~으로 가득 차다	
35 ~에서 나오다, 내리다	
36 ~을 벗다	
37 ~을 부수다, 쪼개다	
38 갑자기	
39 어느 날	
40 종이 한 장	
41 ~로 떨어지다	
42 ~을 되찾다	
43 즉시, 지금 당장	

※ 다음 영영풀이에 알맞은 단어를 <보기>에서 골라 쓴 후, 우리말 뜻을 쓰시오.

1 _____ : to go out for a short time: _____

2 _____ : to be effective or successful: _____

3 _____ : a piece of jewelry that is worn usually on a finger: _____

4 _____ : the feeling you have when you are excited: _____

5 _____ : a set of instructions for making food: _____

6 _____ : to say something in a loud voice: _____

7 _____ : to give something to somebody in exchange for money: _____

8 _____ : to think about how two or more things are different or the same:
     _____

9 _____ : a small round cake that usually has a hole in the middle: _____

10 _____ : a piece of equipment that you use to do a job: _____

11 _____ : the place where you pay in a shop, bank, restaurant, etc.: _____

12 _____ : to give something to someone because he or she has done something
     good: _____

13 _____ : a mixture of flour, eggs, milk, etc. used in cooking and for making bread,
     cakes, etc.: _____

14 _____ : an award that is given to a person who wins a competition, race, etc. or
     who does very good work: _____

15 _____ : a piece of paper, wood, or metal that has writing or a picture on it that
     gives you information, instructions, a warning, etc.: _____

16 _____ : to have an image in your mind of a something that happened or was said
     in the past: _____

보기			
sign	remember	excitement	doughnut
shout	ring	counter	give a reward
batter	prize	compare	machine
work	sell	step out	recipe

※ 다음 우리말과 일치하도록 빈칸에 알맞은 것을 골라 쓰시오.

1 _____ _____
A. Doughnuts   B. The

2 Homer's _____, Bob, _____ a doughnut _____.
A. had   B. uncle   C. shop

3 Uncle Bob liked machines, _____ the shop was _____ _____ _____ machines.
A. full   B. so   C. cooking   D. of

4 _____ day, Homer _____ Uncle Bob's _____.
A. shop   B. one   C. visited

5 Homer: Hello, _____ _____!
A. Bob   B. Uncle

6 Bob: Hi, Homer. _____ to see you. Look _____ this new doughnut machine. _____ it great?
A. at   B. isn't   C. nice

7 Bob: Homer, I need to go _____ home _____ a _____.
A. while   B. back   C. for

8 Can you _____ the shop _____ me and _____ some doughnuts?
A. for   B. make   C. watch

9 Homer: OK, I'll _____ _____ ....
A. try   B. but

10 Bob: It's _____ to do. First, _____ the doughnut _____ and _____ it in the machine.
A. put   B. make   C. easy   D. batter

11 Then _____ start the _____. Here's the _____.
A. recipe   B. machine   C. just

12 Homer: I can _____ that. _____ _____.
A. do   B. worry   C. don't

13 After Uncle Bob left, a big car _____ in _____ of the shop, and a lady _____ _____.
A. front   B. out   C. stopped   D. stepped

14 Lady: _____ I _____ _____ doughnuts and a coffee?
A. some   B. have   C. can

15 Homer: I'm sorry, _____ the doughnuts _____ _____.
A. ready   B. but   C. aren't

16 Lady: Are you _____ the doughnut _____ now?
A. batter   B. making

17 Homer: Yes, but this is _____ _____ _____.
A. first   B. my   C. time

18 The lady _____ _____ her coat and _____ big diamond _____.
A. off   B. ring   C. took   D. her

19 She _____ _____ _____ the batter.
A. mix   B. to   C. started

20 Lady: I _____ you. I can make _____ doughnuts.
A. delicious   B. help   C. can

1 도넛

2 Homer의 삼촌인 Bob은 도넛 가게를 가지고 있었다.

3 Bob 삼촌은 기계를 좋아해서, 가게는 요리 기계들로 가득 차 있었다.

4 어느 날, Homer가 Bob 삼촌의 가게를 방문했다.

5 Homer: 안녕하세요, Bob 삼촌!

6 Bob: 안녕, Homer. 만나서 반갑구나. 이 새 도넛 기계 좀 봐. 멋지지 않니?

7 Bob: Homer, 내가 잠시 집에 가 봐야 해.

8 나 대신 가게를 봐 주고 도넛을 좀 만들어 줄 수 있겠니?

9 Homer: 네, 해 볼게요, 그런데 …

10 Bob: 하기 쉬워. 먼저, 도넛 반죽을 만들고 그것을 기계에 넣으렴.

11 그런 다음에 기계를 작동하기만 하면 돼. 여기 요리법이 있어.

12 Homer: 그건 할 수 있어요. 걱정하지 마세요.

13 Bob 삼촌이 떠난 후, 큰 차 한 대가 가게 앞에 섰고, 한 귀부인이 내렸다.

14 Lady: 도넛과 커피 한 잔 주겠니?

15 Homer: 그건 죄송하지만, 도넛이 준비가 안 됐어요.

16 Lady: 지금 도넛 반죽을 만들고 있는 거니?

17 Homer: 네, 하지만 처음 만드는 거예요.

18 그 귀부인은 외투를 벗고 커다란 다이아몬드 반지를 뺐다.

19 그녀는 반죽을 섞기 시작했다.

20 Lady: 내가 도와줄게. 나는 맛있는 도넛을 만들 수 있단다.

21 Homer: _____, _____.
  A. OK   B. uh

22 Homer: This is _____ _____ _____ batter.
  A. of   B. lot   C. a

23 Lady:Just _____ and see. The doughnuts will _____ _____.
  A. great   B. wait   C. taste

24 Homer _____ _____ the doughnut _____.
  A. machine   B. on   C. turned

25 _____ of batter started _____ _____ the hot oil.
  A. dropping   B. rings   C. into

26 Lady: You _____ the _____ doughnut. Here.
  A. first   B. try

27 Homer: Wow! It's _____ _____!
  A. delicious   B. really

28 Lady: I _____ _____ go now. This was _____ _____ fun! Good-bye!
  A. so   B. have   C. much   D. to

29 Homer: _____ you _____ _____ me. Good-bye!
  A. for   B. thank   C. helping

30 Homer had _____ doughnuts, so he _____ the stop button, but _____ _____.
  A. happened   B. enough   C. pushed   D. nothing

31 The doughnuts _____ _____ _____ of the machine.
  A. out   B. coming   C. kept

32 Homer: Hmm... What's _____? I think I _____ _____ Uncle Bob.
  A. call   B. wrong   C. should

33 The shop was now _____ _____ doughnuts. Homer _____ the doughnuts on the counter.
  A. piled   B. full   C. of

34 Homer: Uncle Bob! Please come _____ _____ _____.
  A. away   B. back   C. right

35 _____ _____ _____ the doughnut machine.
  A. wrong   B. with   C. something's

36 Bob: Oh, no! _____ can we sell _____ _____ doughnuts?
  A. these   B. all   C. how

37 _____ then the lady _____ _____ to the shop.
  A. back   B. just   C. came

38 Lady: I _____ my diamond _____. I think I _____ it on the _____.
  A. left   B. lost   C. counter   D. ring

39 Homer: Oh, I remember. You _____ it _____ before you started to _____ the batter.
  A. off   B. mix   C. took

40 Everyone _____ _____ the diamond ring, but they _____ find it.
  A. couldn't   B. for   C. looked

---

21 Homer: 아, 좋아요.

22 Homer: 반죽이 많군요.

23 Lady: 좀 기다려 보렴. 도넛이 아주 맛있을 거야.

24 Homer는 도넛 기계를 작동했다.

25 링 모양의 반죽들이 뜨거운 기름 속으로 떨어지기 시작했다.

26 Lady: 첫 번째 도넛을 맛보렴. 여기 있어.

27 Homer: 와! 정말 맛있네요!

28 Lady: 난 이제 가 봐야 해. 정말 재미있었어! 잘 있으렴!

29 Homer: 도와주셔서 감사해요. 안녕히 가세요!

30 Homer는 도넛이 충분하게 있어서 정지 버튼을 눌렀지만, 아무 일도 일어나지 않았다.

31 도넛이 계속해서 기계에서 나오고 있었다.

32 Homer: 흐음 … 뭐가 잘못된 거지? Bob 삼촌에게 전화를 해야겠어.

33 가게는 이제 도넛으로 가득 찼다. Homer는 도넛들을 계산대 위로 쌓아 올렸다.

34 Homer: Bob 삼촌! 지금 당장 돌아와 주세요.

35 도넛 기계에 이상이 있어요.

36 Bob: 오, 이런! 이 도넛들을 모두 어떻게 팔지?

37 바로 그때 그 귀부인이 다시 가게로 돌아왔다.

38 Lady: 내 다이아몬드 반지를 잃어버렸어. 내 생각엔 계산대 위에 그것을 놓은 것 같은데.

39 Homer: 오, 기억나요. 반죽을 섞기 전에 그것을 뺐어요.

40 모두가 다이아몬드 반지를 찾았지만, 찾을 수 없었다.

41 Homer: I _____ _____ it.
A. find　　　　　　　B. can't

42 Lady: I'll _____ a _____ of one hundred dollars to the person _____ _____ that ring!
A. reward　　　　B. finds　　　　C. give　　　　D. who

43 Homer: I know! The ring _____ _____ the batter. I'm sure it's _____ one of these doughnuts!
A. inside　　　　B. fell　　　　C. into

44 Lady: _____ _____!
A. right　　　　B. you're

45 Bob: Oh, no! Now we have to _____ _____ all of these doughnuts _____ the ring.
A. up　　　　B. to　　　　C. break　　　　D. find

46 Homer: _____ _____, Uncle. I _____ an idea.
A. have　　　　B. worry　　　　C. don't

47 Homer _____ a _____ of paper and _____ a _____.
A. made　　　　B. took　　　　C. sign　　　　D. piece

48 He then _____ it _____ the _____ window.
A. in　　　　B. put　　　　C. shop's

49 Fresh Doughnuts　2 _____ 5 _____
A. cents　　　　B. for

50 $100 prize _____ _____ a ring _____ a doughnut
A. finding　　　　B. inside　　　　C. for

51 P.S. You _____ to _____ the ring _____.
A. back　　　　B. have　　　　C. give

52 Then _____ people began _____ _____ the doughnuts.
A. buy　　　　B. many　　　　C. to

53 _____ of a _____, a man shouted _____ _____.
A. with　　　　B. sudden　　　　C. excitement　　　　D. all

54 Man: I _____ it! I found the _____!
A. ring　　　　B. found

55 Homer: See, my _____ _____!
A. idea　　　　B. worked

56 Lady: _____ one _____ dollars!
A. hundred　　　　B. here's

57 _____ the _____, everybody _____ happy.
A. end　　　　B. was　　　　C. in

58 The man _____ home _____ one _____ dollars.
A. went　　　　B. hundred　　　　C. with

59 The lady _____ her diamond ring _____, and Uncle Bob _____ _____ of doughnuts.
A. back　　　　B. sold　　　　C. lots　　　　D. got

60 And, _____ _____ Homer?
A. about　　　　B. what

61 He was happy _____ his idea _____ so _____!
A. worked　　　　B. well　　　　C. that

---

41 Homer: 저는 못 찾겠어요.

42 Lady: 그 반지를 찾는 사람에게 100달러의 보상금을 드릴게요!

43 Homer: 알겠어요! 그 반지는 반죽 속으로 떨어졌어요. 반지는 이 도넛들 중 하나 안에 있다고 확신해요!

44 Lady: 네 말이 맞아!

45 Bob: 오, 안 돼! 이제 우리는 반지를 찾기 위해 이 도넛들을 모두 쪼개야 해요.

46 Homer: 걱정하지 마세요, 삼촌. 저에게 아이디어가 있어요.

47 Homer는 종이 한 장을 가져와 안내판을 만들었다.

48 그러고 나서 그것을 가게 창문에 걸었다.

49 신선한 도넛　2개에 5센트

50 도넛 안에 있는 반지를 찾으면 100달러의 상금을 드려요.

51 추신. 반지를 돌려주어야 합니다.

52 그러자, 많은 사람들이 도넛을 사기 시작했다.

53 갑자기, 한 남자가 흥분해서 소리쳤다.

54 Man: 찾았어요! 내가 반지를 찾았어요!

55 Homer: 보세요. 제 아이디어가 통했어요!

56 Lady: 여기 100달러예요!

57 결국 모두가 행복했다.

58 남자는 100달러를 갖고 집으로 갔다.

59 귀부인은 다이아몬드 반지를 다시 찾았고, Bob 삼촌은 도넛을 많이 팔았다.

60 그러면, Homer는 어떻게 됐을까?

61 그는 자신의 아이디어가 아주 잘 통해서 행복했다!

※ 다음 우리말과 일치하도록 빈칸에 알맞은 말을 쓰시오.

1 The _____

2 Homer's _____, Bob, _____ a doughnut shop.

3 Uncle Bob liked machines, _____ the shop _____ _____ _____ _____ _____.

4 _____ _____, Homer _____ Uncle Bob's shop.

5 Homer: Hello, _____ Bob!

6 Bob: Hi, Homer. Nice to see you. _____ _____ this new doughnut machine. _____ _____ _____?

7 Bob: Homer, I need to go back home _____ _____.

8 Can you watch the shop _____ _____ and make some doughnuts?

9 Homer: OK, I'll _____ but ....

10 Bob: It's _____ _____ _____. First, make the _____ _____ and _____ it _____ the machine.

11 Then just start the _____. Here's the _____.

12 Homer: I _____ that. _____ _____.

13 After Uncle Bob left, a big car stopped _____ _____ the shop, and a lady _____ _____.

14 Lady: _____ _____ some doughnuts and a coffee?

15 Homer: I'm sorry, but the doughnuts _____ _____.

16 Lady: _____ _____ the doughnut _____ now?

17 Homer: Yes, but this is _____ _____.

18 The lady _____ her coat and her big diamond _____.

19 She _____ _____ the batter.

20 Lady: _____ _____. I can _____ doughnuts.

1 도넛

2 Homer의 삼촌인 Bob은 도넛 가게를 가지고 있었다.

3 Bob 삼촌은 기계를 좋아해서, 가게는 요리 기계들로 가득 차 있었다.

4 어느 날, Homer가 Bob 삼촌의 가게를 방문했다.

5 Homer: 안녕하세요, Bob 삼촌!

6 Bob: 안녕, Homer. 만나서 반갑구나. 이 새 도넛 기계 좀 봐. 멋지지 않니?

7 Bob: Homer, 내가 잠시 집에 가 봐야 해.

8 나 대신 가게를 봐 주고 도넛을 좀 만들어 줄 수 있겠니?

9 Homer: 네, 해 볼게요, 그런데 …

10 Bob: 하기 쉬워. 먼저, 도넛 반죽을 만들고 그것을 기계에 넣으렴.

11 그런 다음에 기계를 작동하기만 하면 돼. 여기 요리법이 있어.

12 Homer: 그건 할 수 있어요. 걱정하지 마세요.

13 Bob 삼촌이 떠난 후, 큰 차 한 대가 가게 앞에 섰고, 한 귀부인이 내렸다.

14 Lady: 도넛과 커피 한 잔 주겠니?

15 Homer: 그건 죄송하지만, 도넛이 준비가 안 됐어요.

16 Lady: 지금 도넛 반죽을 만들고 있는 거니?

17 Homer: 네, 하지만 처음 만드는 거예요.

18 그 귀부인은 외투를 벗고 커다란 다이아몬드 반지를 뺐다.

19 그녀는 반죽을 섞기 시작했다.

20 Lady: 내가 도와줄게. 나는 맛있는 도넛을 만들 수 있단다.

21 Homer: Uh, _____.

22 Homer: This is _____ _____ _____ batter.

23 Lady: Just _____ _____ _____. The doughnuts _____ _____ _____.

24 Homer _____ _____ the doughnut machine.

25 Rings of batter started _____ _____ the _____ _____.

26 Lady: You _____ the _____ doughnut. Here.

27 Homer: Wow! It's really _____!

28 Lady: I _____ _____ _____ now. This was _____ _____ _____! Good-bye!

29 Homer: Thank you _____ _____ me. Good-bye!

30 Homer had _____ doughnuts, so he pushed the stop button, but _____ _____.

31 The doughnuts _____ _____ _____ _____ the machine.

32 Homer: Hmm... What's _____? I think I _____ _____ Uncle Bob.

33 The shop _____ now _____ _____ doughnuts. Homer _____ the doughnuts _____ _____ _____.

34 Homer: Uncle Bob! Please come _____ _____ _____.

35 _____ _____ _____ _____ the doughnut machine.

36 Bob: Oh, no! How can we sell _____ _____ doughnuts?

37 Just then the lady _____ _____ _____ the shop.

38 Lady: I _____ my diamond ring. I think I _____ it on the counter.

39 Homer: Oh, I remember. You _____ _____ _____ before you started to _____ _____ _____.

40 Everyone _____ _____ the diamond ring, but they _____ _____ it.

---

21 Homer: 아, 좋아요.

22 Homer: 반죽이 많군요.

23 Lady: 좀 기다려 보렴. 도넛이 아주 맛있을 거야.

24 Homer는 도넛 기계를 작동했다.

25 링 모양의 반죽들이 뜨거운 기름 속으로 떨어지기 시작했다.

26 Lady: 첫 번째 도넛을 맛보렴. 여기 있어.

27 Homer: 와! 정말 맛있네요!

28 Lady: 난 이제 가 봐야 해. 정말 재미있었어! 잘 있으렴!

29 Homer: 도와주셔서 감사해요. 안녕히 가세요!

30 Homer는 도넛이 충분하게 있어서 정지 버튼을 눌렀지만, 아무 일도 일어나지 않았다.

31 도넛이 계속해서 기계에서 나오고 있었다.

32 Homer: 흐음 … 뭐가 잘못된 거지? Bob 삼촌에게 전화를 해야겠어.

33 가게는 이제 도넛으로 가득 찼다. Homer는 도넛들을 계산대 위로 쌓아 올렸다.

34 Homer: Bob 삼촌! 지금 당장 돌아와 주세요.

35 도넛 기계에 이상이 있어요.

36 Bob: 오, 이런! 이 도넛들을 모두 어떻게 팔지?

37 바로 그때 그 귀부인이 다시 가게로 돌아왔다.

38 Lady: 내 다이아몬드 반지를 잃어버렸어. 내 생각엔 계산대 위에 그것을 놓은 것 같은데.

39 Homer: 오, 기억나요. 반죽을 섞기 전에 그것을 뺐어요.

40 모두가 다이아몬드 반지를 찾았지만, 찾을 수 없었다.

41 Homer: I _____ _____ it.

42 Lady: I'll _____ _____ _____ of one hundred dollars to the person _____ _____ that ring!

43 Homer: I know! The ring _____ _____ the batter. _____ _____ it's _____ one of these doughnuts!

44 Lady: You're _____!

45 Bob: Oh, no! Now we _____ _____ _____ _____ all of these doughnuts _____ _____ the ring.

46 Homer: _____ _____, Uncle. I have an idea.

47 Homer took a _____ of paper and _____ _____ _____.

48 He then _____ _____ in the shop's window.

49 Fresh Doughnuts _____ _____ _____ _____

50 $100 prize _____ _____ a ring _____ a doughnut

51 P.S. You _____ _____ _____ the ring _____.

52 Then many people began _____ _____ the doughnuts.

53 _____ _____ _____ _____ _____, a man shouted with excitement.

54 Man: I _____ _____! I found the ring!

55 Homer: See, my idea _____!

56 Lady: _____ one _____ dollars!

57 _____ _____ _____, everybody _____ happy.

58 The man went home _____ one hundred dollars.

59 The lady _____ her diamond ring _____, and Uncle Bob sold _____ _____ doughnuts.

60 And, _____ _____ Homer?

61 He was happy that _____ _____ _____ so well!

---

41 Homer: 저는 못 찾겠어요.

42 Lady: 그 반지를 찾는 사람에게 100달러의 보상금을 드릴게요!

43 Homer: 알겠어요! 그 반지는 반죽 속으로 떨어졌어요. 반지는 이 도넛들 중 하나 안에 있다고 확신해요!

44 Lady: 네 말이 맞아!

45 Bob: 오, 안 돼! 이제 우리는 반지를 찾기 위해 이 도넛들을 모두 쪼개야 해요.

46 Homer: 걱정하지 마세요, 삼촌. 저에게 아이디어가 있어요.

47 Homer는 종이 한 장을 가져와 안내판을 만들었다.

48 그러고 나서 그것을 가게 창문에 걸었다.

49 신선한 도넛   2개에 5센트

50 도넛 안에 있는 반지를 찾으면 100달러의 상금을 드려요.

51 추신. 반지를 돌려주어야 합니다.

52 그러자, 많은 사람들이 도넛을 사기 시작했다.

53 갑자기, 한 남자가 흥분해서 소리쳤다.

54 Man: 찾았어요! 내가 반지를 찾았어요!

55 Homer: 보세요, 제 아이디어가 통했어요!

56 Lady: 여기 100달러예요!

57 결국 모두가 행복했다.

58 남자는 100달러를 갖고 집으로 갔다.

59 귀부인은 다이아몬드 반지를 다시 찾았고, Bob 삼촌은 도넛을 많이 팔았다.

60 그러면, Homer는 어떻게 됐을까?

61 그는 자신의 아이디어가 아주 잘 통해서 행복했다!

※ 다음 문장을 우리말로 쓰시오.

1 The Doughnuts
➡ _____

2 Homer's uncle, Bob, had a doughnut shop.
➡ _____

3 Uncle Bob liked machines, so the shop was full of cooking machines.
➡ _____

4 One day, Homer visited Uncle Bob's shop.
➡ _____

5 Homer: Hello, Uncle Bob!
➡ _____

6 Bob: Hi, Homer. Nice to see you. Look at this new doughnut machine. Isn't it great?
➡ _____

7 Bob: Homer, I need to go back home for a while.
➡ _____

8 Can you watch the shop for me and make some doughnuts?
➡ _____

9 Homer: OK, I'll try but ....
➡ _____

10 Bob: It's easy to do. First, make the doughnut batter and put it in the machine.
➡ _____

11 Then just start the machine. Here's the recipe.
➡ _____

12 Homer: I can do that. Don't worry.
➡ _____

13 After Uncle Bob left, a big car stopped in front of the shop, and a lady stepped out.
➡ _____

14 Lady: Can I have some doughnuts and a coffee?
➡ _____

15 Homer: I'm sorry, but the doughnuts aren't ready.
➡ _____

16 Lady: Are you making the doughnut batter now?
➡ _____

17 Homer: Yes, but this is my first time.
➡ _____

18 The lady took off her coat and her big diamond ring.
➡ _____

19 She started to mix the batter.
➡ _____

20 Lady: I can help you. I can make delicious doughnuts.
➡ _____

21 ▸ Homer: Uh, OK.
➡ _____

22 ▸ Homer: This is a lot of batter.
➡ _____

23 ▸ Lady: Just wait and see. The doughnuts will taste great.
➡ _____

24 ▸ Homer turned on the doughnut machine.
➡ _____

25 ▸ Rings of batter started dropping into the hot oil.
➡ _____

26 ▸ Lady: You try the first doughnut. Here.
➡ _____

27 ▸ Homer: Wow! It's really delicious!
➡ _____

28 ▸ Lady: I have to go now. This was so much fun! Good-bye!
➡ _____

29 ▸ Homer: Thank you for helping me. Good-bye!
➡ _____

30 ▸ Homer had enough doughnuts, so he pushed the stop button, but nothing happened.
➡ _____

31 ▸ The doughnuts kept coming out of the machine.
➡ _____

32 ▸ Homer: Hmm... What's wrong? I think I should call Uncle Bob.
➡ _____

33 ▸ The shop was now full of doughnuts. Homer piled the doughnuts on the counter.
➡ _____

34 ▸ Homer: Uncle Bob! Please come back right away.
➡ _____

35 ▸ Something's wrong with the doughnut machine.
➡ _____

36 ▸ Bob: Oh, no! How can we sell all these doughnuts?
➡ _____

37 ▸ Just then the lady came back to the shop.
➡ _____

38 ▸ Lady: I lost my diamond ring. I think I left it on the counter.
➡ _____

39 ▸ Homer: Oh, I remember. You took it off before you started to mix the batter.
➡ _____

40 ▸ Everyone looked for the diamond ring, but they couldn't find it.
➡ _____

41 Homer: I can't find it.
➡ _____

42 Lady: I'll give a reward of one hundred dollars to the person who finds that ring!
➡ _____

43 Homer: I know! The ring fell into the batter. I'm sure it's inside one of these doughnuts!
➡ _____

44 Lady: You're right!
➡ _____

45 Bob: Oh, no! Now we have to break up all of these doughnuts to find the ring.
➡ _____

46 Homer: Don't worry, Uncle. I have an idea.
➡ _____

47 Homer took a piece of paper and made a sign.
➡ _____

48 He then put it in the shop's window.
➡ _____

49 Fresh Doughnuts   2 for 5 cents
➡ _____

50 $100 prize for finding a ring inside a doughnut
➡ _____

51 P.S. You have to give the ring back.
➡ _____

52 Then many people began to buy the doughnuts.
➡ _____

53 All of a sudden, a man shouted with excitement.
➡ _____

54 Man: I found it! I found the ring!
➡ _____

55 Homer: See, my idea worked!
➡ _____

56 Lady: Here's one hundred dollars!
➡ _____

57 In the end, everybody was happy.
➡ _____

58 The man went home with one hundred dollars.
➡ _____

59 The lady got her diamond ring back, and Uncle Bob sold lots of doughnuts.
➡ _____

60 And, what about Homer?
➡ _____

61 He was happy that his idea worked so well!
➡ _____

※ 다음 괄호 안의 단어들을 우리말에 맞도록 바르게 배열하시오.

1 (Doughnuts / The)
➡ _____

2 (uncle, / Homer's / Bob, / a / had / shop. / doughnut)
➡ _____

3 (Bob / Uncle / machines, / liked / so / shop / the / was / of / full / machines. / cooking)
➡ _____

4 (day, / one / visited / Homer / Uncle / shop. / Bob's)
➡ _____

5 (Homer: / Bob! / Uncle / Hello,)
➡ _____

6 (Bob: / Homer. / hi, // to / nice / you. / see // at / look / new / this / machine / doughnut // isn't / great? / it)
➡ _____

7 (Bob: / Homer, / need / I / go / to / back / for / while. / home / a)
➡ _____

8 (you / can / watch / shop / the / me / for / and / make / doughnuts? / some)
➡ _____

9 (Homer: / OK, / try / but / I'll / ....)
➡ _____

10 (Bob: / easy / it's / do. / to // first, / the / make / batter / doughnut / and / it / put / the / machine. / in)
➡ _____

11 (then / start / just / machine. / the // recipe. / the / here's)
➡ _____

12 (Homer: / can / I / that. / do // worry. / don't)
➡ _____

13 (Uncle / left, / after / Bob / big / a / car / stopped / front / of / in / shop, / the / and / lady / a / out. / stepped)
➡ _____

14 (Lady: / I / can / have / doughnuts / some / and / coffee? / a)
➡ _____

15 (Homer: / sorry, / I'm / but / doughnuts / the / ready. / aren't)
➡ _____

16 (Lady: / you / are / making / doughnut / the / now? / batter)
➡ _____

17 (Homer: / yes, / this / but / is / my / time. / first)
➡ _____

18 (lady / the / off / took / coat / her / and / her / diamond / ring. / big)
➡ _____

19 (started / she / mix / to / batter. / the)
➡ _____

20 (Lady: / can / I / you. / help // can / I / make / doughnuts. / delicious)
➡ _____

1 도넛

2 Homer의 삼촌인 Bob은 도넛 가게를 가지고 있었다.

3 Bob 삼촌은 기계를 좋아해서, 가게는 요리 기계들로 가득 차 있었다.

4 어느 날, Homer가 Bob 삼촌의 가게를 방문했다.

5 Homer: 안녕하세요, Bob 삼촌!

6 Bob: 안녕, Homer. 만나서 반갑 구나. 이 새 도넛 기계 좀 봐. 멋 지지 않니?

7 Bob: Homer, 내가 잠시 집에 가 봐야 해.

8 나 대신 가게를 봐 주고 도넛을 좀 만들어 줄 수 있겠니?

9 Homer: 네, 해 볼게요, 그런데 …

10 Bob: 하기 쉬워. 먼저, 도넛 반 죽을 만들고 그것을 기계에 넣 으렴.

11 그런 다음에 기계를 작동하기만 하면 돼. 여기 요리법이 있어.

12 Homer: 그건 할 수 있어요. 걱 정하지 마세요.

13 Bob 삼촌이 떠난 후, 큰 차 한 대가 가게 앞에 섰고, 한 귀부인 이 내렸다.

14 Lady: 도넛과 커피 한 잔 주겠 니?

15 Homer: 그건 죄송하지만, 도넛 이 준비가 안 됐어요.

16 Lady: 지금 도넛 반죽을 만들고 있는 거니?

17 Homer: 네, 하지만 처음 만드는 거예요.

18 그 귀부인은 외투를 벗고 커다 란 다이아몬드 반지를 뺐다.

19 그녀는 반죽을 섞기 시작했다.

20 Lady: 내가 도와줄게. 나는 맛 있는 도넛을 만들 수 있단다.

21 (Homer: / OK. / uh,)
➡ _____

22 (Homer: / is / this / a / batter. / of / lot)
➡ _____

23 (Lady: / wait / just / see. / and // doughnuts / the / great. / taste / will)
➡ _____

24 (turned / Homer / the / on / machine. / doughnut)
➡ _____

25 (batter / of / rings / started / into / dropping / the / oil. / hot)
➡ _____

26 (Lady: / try / you / first / doughnut. / the // here.)
➡ _____

27 (Homer: / wow! // really / it's / delicious!)
➡ _____

28 (Lady: / have / I / go / to / now. // was / this / much / so / fun! // good-bye!)
➡ _____

29 (Homer: / you / thank / helping / for / me. // good-bye!)
➡ _____

30 (Homer / enough / had / doughnuts, / so / pushed / he / stop / the / button, / but / happened. / nothing)
➡ _____

31 (doughnuts / the / coming / kept / of / out / machine. / the)
➡ _____

32 (Homer: / hmm... // wrong? / what's // think / I / should / I / Bob. / call / Uncle)
➡ _____

33 (shop / the / was / full / now / doughnuts. / of // Homer / the / piled / doughnuts / the / counter. / on)
➡ _____

34 (Homer: / Bob! / Uncle // come / please / right / back / away.)
➡ _____

35 (wrong / something's / with / the / machine. / doughnut)
➡ _____

36 (Bob: / no! / oh, // can / how / sell / we / all / doughnuts? / these)
➡ _____

37 (then / just / lady / the / back / came / shop. / tne / to)
➡ _____

38 (Lady: / lost / I / ring. / diamond / my // I / left / I / think / it / counter. / the / on)
➡ _____

39 (Homer: / oh, / remember. / I // took / you / off / it / before / started / you / mix / batter. / the / to)
➡ _____
➡ _____

40 (looked / everyone / the / for / ring, / diamond / but / they / find / it. / couldn't)
➡ _____

---

21 Homer: 아, 좋아요.

22 Homer: 반죽이 많군요.

23 Lady: 좀 기다려 보렴. 도넛이 아주 맛있을 거야.

24 Homer는 도넛 기계를 작동했다.

25 링 모양의 반죽들이 뜨거운 기름 속으로 떨어지기 시작했다.

26 Lady: 첫 번째 도넛을 맛보렴. 여기 있어.

27 Homer: 와! 정말 맛있네요!

28 Lady: 난 이제 가 봐야 해. 정말 재미있었어! 잘 있으렴!

29 Homer: 도와주셔서 감사해요. 안녕히 가세요!

30 Homer는 도넛이 충분하게 있어서 정지 버튼을 눌렀지만, 아무 일도 일어나지 않았다.

31 도넛이 계속해서 기계에서 나오고 있었다.

32 Homer: 흐음 … 뭐가 잘못된 거지? Bob 삼촌에게 전화를 해야겠어.

33 가게는 이제 도넛으로 가득 찼다. Homer는 도넛들을 계산대 위로 쌓아 올렸다.

34 Homer: Bob 삼촌! 지금 당장 돌아와 주세요.

35 도넛 기계에 이상이 있어요.

36 Bob: 오, 이런! 이 도넛들을 모두 어떻게 팔지?

37 바로 그때 그 귀부인이 다시 가게로 돌아왔다.

38 Lady: 내 다이아몬드 반지를 잃어버렸어. 내 생각엔 계산대 위에 그것을 놓은 것 같은데.

39 Homer: 오, 기억나요. 반죽을 섞기 전에 그것을 뺐어요.

40 모두가 다이아몬드 반지를 찾았지만, 찾을 수 없었다.

41 (Homer: / I / find / it. / can't)
➡ _____

42 (Lady: / give / I'll / reward / a / one / of / dollars / hundred / the / to / person / finds / who / ring! / that)
➡ _____

43 (Homer: / know! / I // ring / the / into / fell / batter. / the // I'm / it's / sure / one / inside / of / doughnuts! / these)
➡ _____

44 (Lady: / right! / you're)
➡ _____

45 (Bob: / no! / oh, // we / now / to / have / break / all / up / these / of / to / doughnuts / ring. / the / find)
➡ _____

46 (Homer: / worry, / don't / Uncle. // have / I / idea. / an)
➡ _____

47 (took / Homer / piece / a / paper / of / and / sign. / a / made)
➡ _____

48 (then / he / it / put / in / shop's / the / window.)
➡ _____

49 (Doughnuts / Fresh // for / 2 / cents / 5)
➡ _____

50 (prize / $100 / finding / for / ring / a / inside / doughnut / a)
➡ _____

51 (P.S. / have / you / give / to / back. / ring / the)
➡ _____

52 (many / then / began / people / buy / to / doughnuts / the)
➡ _____

53 (of / all / sudden, / a / man / a / with / shouted / excitement.)
➡ _____

54 (Man: / found / I / it! // the / I / ring! / found)
➡ _____

55 (Homer: / my / see, / worked! / idea)
➡ _____

56 (Lady: / one / here's / dallars! / hundred)
➡ _____

57 (the / in / end, / was / happy. / everybody)
➡ _____

58 (man / the / home / went / with / hundred / dollars. / one)
➡ _____

59 (lady / the / her / got / ring / diamond / back, / and / Bob / Uncle / lots / sold / doughnuts. / of)
➡ _____

60 (and, / Homer? / about / what)
➡ _____

61 (was / he / happy / that / idea / his / well! / so / worked)
➡ _____

41 Homer: 저는 못 찾겠어요.

42 Lady: 그 반지를 찾는 사람에게 100달러의 보상금을 드릴게요!

43 Homer: 알겠어요! 그 반지는 반죽 속으로 떨어졌어요. 반지는 이 도넛들 중 하나 안에 있다고 확신해요!

44 Lady: 네 말이 맞아!

45 Bob: 오, 안 돼! 이제 우리는 반지를 찾기 위해 이 도넛들을 모두 쪼개야 해요.

46 Homer: 걱정하지 마세요, 삼촌. 저에게 아이디어가 있어요.

47 Homer는 종이 한 장을 가져와 안내판을 만들었다.

48 그러고 나서 그것을 가게 창문에 걸었다.

49 신선한 도넛 2개에 5센트

50 도넛 안에 있는 반지를 찾으면 100달러의 상금을 드려요.

51 추신. 반지를 돌려주어야 합니다.

52 그러자, 많은 사람들이 도넛을 사기 시작했다.

53 갑자기, 한 남자가 흥분해서 소리쳤다.

54 Man: 찾았어요! 내가 반지를 찾았어요!

55 Homer: 보세요, 제 아이디어가 통했어요!

56 Lady: 여기 100달러예요!

57 결국 모두가 행복했다.

58 남자는 100달러를 갖고 집으로 갔다.

59 귀부인은 다이아몬드 반지를 다시 찾았고, Bob 삼촌은 도넛을 많이 팔았다.

60 그러면, Homer는 어떻게 됐을까?

61 그는 자신의 아이디어가 아주 잘 통해서 행복했다!

※ 다음 우리말을 영어로 쓰시오.

1 도넛
➡ _____

2 Homer의 삼촌인 Bob은 도넛 가게를 가지고 있었다.
➡ _____

3 Bob 삼촌은 기계를 좋아해서, 가게는 요리 기계들로 가득 차 있었다.
➡ _____

4 어느 날, Homer가 Bob 삼촌의 가게를 방문했다.
➡ _____

5 Homer: 안녕하세요, Bob 삼촌!
➡ _____

6 Bob: 안녕, Homer. 만나서 반갑구나. 이 새 도넛 기계 좀 봐. 멋지지 않니?
➡ _____

7 Bob: Homer, 내가 잠시 집에 가 봐야 해.
➡ _____

8 나 대신 가게를 봐 주고 도넛을 좀 만들어 줄 수 있겠니?
➡ _____

9 Homer: 네, 해 볼게요, 그런데….
➡ _____

10 Bob: 하기 쉬워. 먼저, 도넛 반죽을 만들고 그것을 기계에 넣으렴.
➡ _____

11 그런 다음에 기계를 작동하기만 하면 돼. 여기 요리법이 있어.
➡ _____

12 Homer: 그건 할 수 있어요. 걱정하지 마세요.
➡ _____

13 Bob 삼촌이 떠난 후, 큰 차 한 대가 가게 앞에 섰고, 한 귀부인이 내렸다.
➡ _____

14 Lady: 도넛과 커피 한 잔 주겠니?
➡ _____

15 Homer: 죄송하지만, 도넛이 준비가 안 됐어요.
➡ _____

16 Lady: 지금 도넛 반죽을 만들고 있는 거니?
➡ _____

17 Homer: 네, 하지만 처음 만드는 거예요.
➡ _____

18 그 귀부인은 외투를 벗고 커다란 다이아몬드 반지를 뺐다.
➡ _____

19 그녀는 반죽을 섞기 시작했다.
➡ _____

20 Lady: 내가 도와줄게. 나는 맛있는 도넛을 만들 수 있단다.
➡ _____

21 Homer: 아, 좋아요.
➡ _____

22 Homer: 반죽이 많군요.
➡ _____

23 Lady: 좀 기다려 보렴. 도넛이 아주 맛있을 거야.
➡ _____

24 Homer는 도넛 기계를 작동했다.
➡ _____

25 링 모양의 반죽들이 뜨거운 기름 속으로 떨어지기 시작했다.
➡ _____

26 Lady: 첫 번째 도넛을 맛보렴. 여기 있어.
➡ _____

27 Homer: 와! 정말 맛있네요!
➡ _____

28 Lady: 난 이제 가 봐야 해. 정말 재미있었어! 잘 있으렴!
➡ _____

29 Homer: 도와주셔서 감사해요. 안녕히 가세요!
➡ _____

30 Homer는 도넛이 충분하게 있어서 정지 버튼을 눌렀지만, 아무 일도 일어나지 않았다.
➡ _____

31 도넛이 계속해서 기계에서 나오고 있었다.
➡ _____

32 Homer: 흐음 … 뭐가 잘못된 거지? Bob 삼촌에게 전화를 해야겠어.
➡ _____

33 가게는 이제 도넛으로 가득 찼다. Homer는 도넛들을 계산대 위로 쌓아 올렸다.
➡ _____

34 Homer: Bob 삼촌! 지금 당장 돌아와 주세요.
➡ _____

35 도넛 기계에 이상이 있어요.
➡ _____

36 Bob: 오, 이런! 이 도넛들을 모두 어떻게 팔지?
➡ _____

37 바로 그때 그 귀부인이 다시 가게로 돌아왔다.
➡ _____

38 Lady: 내 다이아몬드 반지를 잃어버렸어. 내 생각엔 계산대 위에 그것을 놓은 것 같은데.
➡ _____

39 Homer: 오, 기억나요. 반죽을 섞기 전에 그것을 뺐어요.
➡ _____

40 모두가 다이아몬드 반지를 찾았지만, 찾을 수 없었다.
➡ _____

41 Homer: 저는 못 찾겠어요.

➡ _____

42 Lady: 그 반지를 찾는 사람에게 100달러의 보상금을 드릴게요!

➡ _____

43 Homer: 알겠어요! 그 반지는 반죽 속으로 떨어졌어요. 반지는 이 도넛들 중 하나 안에 있다고 확신해요!

➡ _____

44 Lady: 네 말이 맞아!

➡ _____

45 Bob: 오, 안 돼! 이제 우리는 반지를 찾기 위해 이 도넛들을 모두 쪼개야 해요.

➡ _____

46 Homer: 걱정하지 마세요, 삼촌. 저에게 아이디어가 있어요.

➡ _____

47 Homer는 종이 한 장을 가져와 안내판을 만들었다.

➡ _____

48 그러고 나서 그것을 가게 창문에 걸었다.

➡ _____

49 신선한 도넛   2개에 5센트

➡ _____

50 도넛 안에 있는 반지를 찾으면 100달러의 상금을 드려요.

➡ _____

51 추신. 반지를 돌려주어야 합니다.

➡ _____

52 그러자, 많은 사람들이 도넛을 사기 시작했다.

➡ _____

53 갑자기, 한 남자가 흥분해서 소리쳤다.

➡ _____

54 Man: 찾았어요! 내가 반지를 찾았어요!

➡ _____

55 Homer: 보세요, 제 아이디어가 통했어요!

➡ _____

56 Lady: 여기 100달러예요!

➡ _____

57 결국 모두가 행복했다.

➡ _____

58 남자는 100달러를 갖고 집으로 갔다.

➡ _____

59 귀부인은 다이아몬드 반지를 다시 찾았고, Bob 삼촌은 도넛을 많이 팔았다.

➡ _____

60 그러면, Homer는 어떻게 됐을까?

➡ _____

61 그는 자신의 아이디어가 아주 잘 통해서 행복했다!

➡ _____

MEMO

MEMO

MEMO

적중100 plus

2학기 전과정

영어 기출 문제집

영어 기출 문제집

적중100 plus
2학기 전과정

2학기

정답 및 해설

동아 | 윤정미

중 2

Lesson
5

Living Healthily and Safely

시험대비 실력평가

01 instead of　02 ①　　03 blink　　04 ③
05 ③　　　06 ⑤　　07 nervous　08 ④

01 한 가지가 또 다른 것을 대체하거나 다른 것을 할 때 사용하는. 식사나 회의 중에는 스마트폰을 꺼라. 문자를 보내는 대신에 사람들과 직접 대화를 나눌 수 있다.

02 take medicine: '약을 복용하다', take a rest: '휴식을 취하다'

04 스마트폰을 확인했을 때 아무런 문자 메시지가 없다면 슬픈 기분이 드는가? 만약 당신의 대답이 '그렇다'이면, 당신은 스마트폰 중독일지 모른다.

05 신체의 일부가 아플 때 가지는 느낌 – 고통

05 매일, 매주 등의 같은 시간에 – 규칙적으로

07 유의어 관계이다. 건강한 = 초조한, 불안한

08 '스마트폰을 현명하지 않게 또는 과도하게 사용하면 다양한 문제가 일어날 수 있다.', '스마트폰을 내려다볼 때, 목에 가해지는 압박이 증가한다.'

서술형 시험대비　p.09

01 (1) has　(2) well　(3) smombie　(4) nervous
02 (1) prevent, 방지하다, 막다　(2) medicine, 약, 약물
(3) addiction, 중독　　03 (t)ext / (c)ause
04 (1) without　(2) such　(3) From now on　(4) fall
asleep　　05 (1) addiction　(2) regularly
(3) various　(4) texting

01 (1) '머리가 아프다'는 표현으로 동사 have를 사용한다. (2) '건강해 보이다'는 look well을 사용한다. (3) 글의 흐름상 단어 '스몸비'가 적절하다. (4) 나는 스마트폰이 곁에 없을 때 초조해진다.

03 • 많은 사람들은 전화를 하기 보다는 문자 메시지를 보내기를 좋아한다. • 스마트폰을 과도하게 사용하면 눈이 건조해질 수 있다.

04 (1) without: ~ 없이 (2) such: 그러한 (3) from now on: 지금부터 (4) fall asleep: 잠들다

05 (1) 스마트폰 중독의 의미로 동사 addict를 명사 addiction으로 바꾸어야 한다. (2) 빈칸에는 동사 exercise를 수식하는 부

사가 적절하므로 regularly가 적절하다. (3) 명사 problems를 수식하는 형용사 형태가 적절하므로 동사 vary를 various로 고친다. (4) 문자를 보내다는 의미로 동사 text를 현재분사인 texting으로 바꾸는 것이 적절하다.

Conversation 교과서

핵심 Check　p.10~11

1 What's wrong　　2 anything wrong
3 ⑤

교과서 대화문 익히기

Check(√) True or False　p.12

1 T　2 T　3 T　4 F

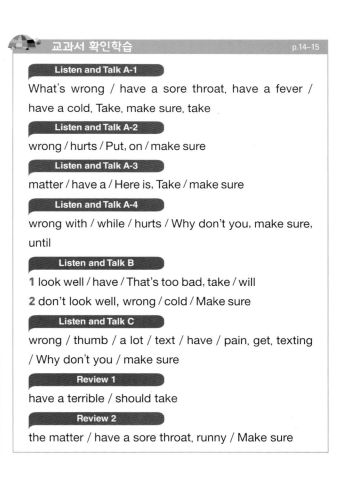

교과서 확인학습　p.14~15

Listen and Talk A-1
What's wrong / have a sore throat, have a fever / have a cold. Take, make sure, take

Listen and Talk A-2
wrong / hurts / Put, on / make sure

Listen and Talk A-3
matter / have a / Here is, Take / make sure

Listen and Talk A-4
wrong with / while / hurts / Why don't you, make sure, until

Listen and Talk B
1 look well / have / That's too bad, take / will
2 don't look well, wrong / cold / Make sure

Listen and Talk C
wrong / thumb / a lot / text / have / pain, get, texting / Why don't you / make sure

Review 1
have a terrible / should take

Review 2
the matter / have a sore throat, runny / Make sure

시험대비 기본평가   p.16

01 Make sure   02 ④   03 ③   04 have a

01 상대방에게 당부하는 표현으로 '반드시 ~하도록 해라, ~을 확실
   히 해라'라는 의미의 'make sure ~'를 사용한다.

02 빈칸에는 상대방이 어딘가 아파 보일 때 묻는 말이 적절하다..

03 감기에 걸린 것 같다는 말 다음에 이어질 말로 치과에 가라는 말
   은 어색하다.

04 '~가 아프다'는 표현은 'have a/an+명사' 형태로 쓴다. 명사 자
   리에 아픈 증상이나 병명을 써서 어디가 아픈지 표현한다.

시험대비 실력평가   p.17~18

01 ④   02 ⑤   03 ④   04 ⑤
05 the matter[problem], happened   06 ⑤
07 ④   08 pain   09 Here is   10 ③
11 What's the matter with you   12 ④
13 ⑤   14 ④

01 B의 대답으로 보아 빈칸에는 문제점이나 증상을 묻는 말이 오는
   것이 적절하다.

02 빈칸 뒤의 this는 medicine을 가리키므로 '약을 먹다'는 표현으
   로 동사 take를 사용한다.

03 (D) 상대방의 증상을 묻는 표현 → (A) 증상 말하기 → (B) 상
   대방에게 당부하는 표현 말하기 → (C) 알았다고 대답하기

04 '~가 아프다'는 표현은 'have a/an+명사' 형태로 쓴다.

06 (B)는 상대방에게 당부하는 표현이다.

07 '반드시 ~하도록 하다, ~을 확실히 하다'라는 의미의 'make
   sure ~'는 상대방에게 당부할 때 사용하는 표현이다.

08 toothache는 '치통'이기 때문에 '아픔, 통증'을 나타내는 pain
   이 적절하다.

09 '여기에 ~가 있다'는 표현으로 'Here is+단수 명사'를 사용한다.

10 이가 아프다고 했기 때문에 치과에 가라는 충고가 적절하다.

11 문제점이나 증상을 묻는 표현이다.

12 It은 texting thumb을 가리키는 대명사로 'What's texting
   thumb?'에 대한 대답으로 ④에 들어가는 것이 적절하다.

13 Ms. Kim이 문자 메시지를 많이 보내지 않는다는 것은 본문에
   언급되어 있지 않다.

14 ④번은 '몸이 안 좋아 보여. 무슨 일 있니?'라는 물음에 '아무 문
   제없다.'는 대답 다음에 머리가 아프다고 말하는 것은 어색하다.

서술형 시험대비   p.19

01 ⓐ wrong ⓑ have ⓒ have

02 Take this medicine and make sure you take a
   good rest.

03 (A) What's wrong with your leg
   (B) while I was playing soccer
   (C) make sure you don't play socce
04 pain, thumb   05 make sure, don't text
06 I get tired easily.

01 ⓐ 아파 보인다는 말 다음에 상대방의 증상을 묻는 표현이 적절
   하다. ⓑ와 ⓒ는 '~가 아프다'는 의미로 동사 have를 사용한다.

02 '이 약을 먹어'라는 명령문으로 동사 Take로 문장을 시작한다.
   그리고 '꼭 ~하도록 해라'는 당부의 표현으로 'make sure+주
   어+동사' 어순이 적절하다.

03 (B)의 while은 접속사로 '~하는 동안'의 의미를 가지고 뒤에는
   '주어+동사'가 와야 한다. be동사와 함께 사용이 되어 축구를 하
   다는 표현은 진행형으로 나타내는 것이 적절하다. (C)는 상대방
   에게 당부하는 표현으로 'make sure+주어+동사'의 어순이 적
   절하다.

04 Andy가 엄지손가락이 아프다는 말을 한 것으로 보아 texting
   thumb은 엄지손가락에 있는 통증을 말한다는 것을 알 수 있다.

05 texting thumb은 문자 메시지를 너무 많이 보내서 생기는 통증
   이므로 Ms. Kim의 충고는 '문자 메시지를 너무 많이 보내지 말
   라'는 것이 적절하다.

06 get+형용사: ~하게 되다 / tire를 tired로 바꾸어 '피로한, 피곤
   하게 된'을 의미하도록 한다.

교과서
Grammar

핵심 Check   p.20~21

1 (1) who/whom/that (2) which/that
2 (1) call, text neck (2) made, rich man

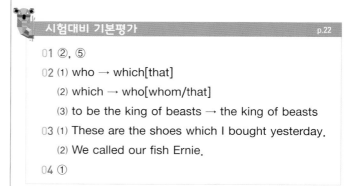

시험대비 기본평가   p.22

01 ②, ⑤
02 (1) who → which[that]
   (2) which → who[whom/that]
   (3) to be the king of beasts → the king of beasts
03 (1) These are the shoes which I bought yesterday.
   (2) We called our fish Ernie.
04 ①

01 선행사가 The friend로 사람이며 met의 목적어 역할을 할 수
   있는 목적격 관계대명사 who나 whom 또는 that이 적절하다.

02 (1) 선행사가 사물이므로 who를 which나 that으로 고쳐야 한

3

다. (2) 선행사가 사람이므로 which를 who나 whom 또는 that으로 고쳐야 한다. (3) call은 목적격 보어로 to부정사를 취하지 않는다.

03 (1) which는 관계대명사 목적격이다. (2) 'call+목적어+목적격 보어'의 어순을 취한다.

04 call A B: A를 B라고 부르다 the arrow on the screen: 화면의 화살표

시험대비 실력평가
p.23~25

01 ②　　　　02 ④　　　　03 ⑤
04 (1) that　(2) which　(3) which　(4) which
(5) consider　05 I still remember the stories
(which[that]) my grandfather told me.　06 ⑤
07 ④　　　　08 ①　　　　09 ③
10 (1) that　(2) whom　(3) who is　　11 ⑤
12 ②
13 (1) New York is a big city which[that] many people
　　visit every year.
　(2) My favorite subject is math which[that] I'm
　　good at.
　(3) The man who[whom/that] I saw at the mall was
　　my math teacher.
　(4) She is a famous movie star who[whom/that]
　　many people like.
　(5) I was surprised at the speed with which he
　　learned to speak. 또는 I was surprised at the
　　speed which[that] he learned to speak with.
　(6) Do you know the girl to whom Anne is
　　talking? 또는 Do you know the girl who[whom/
　　that] Anne is talking to?
14 ①　　　　15 ④
16 (1) We call Shakespeare England's national poet.
　(2) I consider him to be a coward.
17 ②, ④

01 <보기>와 나머지는 목적격 관계대명사이지만, ②번은 주격 관계대명사이다.

02 모두 주격이나 목적격으로 사용된 관계대명사 that이 들어갈 수 있지만 ④번은 소유격 관계대명사 whose가 들어가야 한다.

03 take는 보통 to부정사나 as와 함께 쓰이며 take A(명사) B(명사)의 형태로 쓰이지 않는다.

04 (1) 선행사가 사람이므로 that, (2) 선행사가 사물이므로 which, (3) 전치사 in이 있으므로 that은 쓸 수 없다. (4) 선행사가 사물이므로 which, (5) to부정사를 목적격 보어로 쓸 수 있는 것은 consider이다.

05 '이야기들을 아직 기억한다'에서 목적격 관계대명사를 이용하여

'이야기들'을 '할아버지께서 내게 해 주신'이 수식하는 구조로 만들어 준다.

06 call은 동사 다음에 두 개의 명사(구)가 목적어, 목적격 보어로 쓰이므로 'as hip hop'이 아니라 as 없이 'hip hop'이 되어야 한다.

07 관계대명사의 선행사가 사람이면 who, whom이나 that을 쓰고 사물이면 which나 that을 쓴다. ③ This is the house which she lives in.

08 ①번은 접속사이지만 나머지는 모두 관계대명사이다.

09 ③번은 4형식이지만 <보기>와 나머지는 모두 목적어와 목적격 보어가 있는 5형식이다. call A B는 목적격 보어 자리에 to부정사나 형용사를 쓰지 않지만 to부정사나 형용사를 목적격 보어로 취하는 많은 동사들이 있다.

10 목적격 관계대명사와 '주격 관계대명사+be 동사'는 생략할 수 있다.

11 선행사가 사람이므로 who, whom이나 that을 이용하고 목적격이므로 목적어로 쓰인 him은 쓰지 말아야 한다.

12 call은 동사 다음에 두 개의 명사(구)가 목적어와 목적격 보어로 쓰인다. 형용사나 to부정사가 목적격 보어로 올 수 없다. call A B: A를 B라고 부르다

13 목적격 관계대명사는 수식하는 선행사가 사람이면 who나 whom, that을, 사람이 아니면 which나 that을 쓴다. 일반적으로 목적격 관계대명사는 생략될 수 있다. 목적격 관계대명사가 전치사의 목적어인 경우 전치사는 관계대명사절의 끝에 오거나 관계대명사 앞에 올 수 있다. 전치사가 관계대명사절의 끝에 올 경우에는 관계대명사를 생략할 수 있다. 전치사가 관계대명사 앞에 올 경우에는 관계대명사 that을 쓸 수 없으며, 관계대명사를 생략하지 않는다.

14 call은 동사 다음에 두 개의 명사(구)가 목적어와 목적격 보어로 쓰인다. regard가 'A를 B로 여기다'의 뜻으로 쓰이는 경우 보통 'regard A as B'의 형태를 취한다.

15 ④ 관계대명사 that은 전치사 다음에는 쓸 수 없다. that → whom

16 call A B: A를 B라고 부르다 (2) consider는 call과는 다르게 목적격 보어로 to부정사를 취할 수 있다.

17 주어진 문장과 ②, ④번은 목적격 관계대명사이다. ① 동격절을 이끄는 접속사, ③번은 의문사, ⑤번은 주격 관계대명사이다. swallow: 제비

서술형 시험대비
p.26~27

01 (1) I bought the snack which[that] everyone likes.
　(2) Romeo and Juliet is the movie which[that]
　　Helen saw.
　(3) The person who[whom/that] I love the most is
　　my sister.
　(4) The author who[whom/that] I like the most is
　　C.S. Lewis.

(5) Look at the boy to whom Mary is talking. 또는 Look at the boy who[whom/that] Mary is talking to.

(6) Look at Chris and his dog that Bella is playing with.

02 (1) People call New York City the Big Apple.

(2) Some people may not consider him as a hero.

(3) They named her the Boxer of the Year.

(4) His ability made him a famous person.

(5) We elected him to be a leader.

(6) His followers believed him to be a genius.

(7) They regard Mike as a fool.

03 call the rooftop garden the park in the sky

04 (1) Andy is the boy (who/whom/that) Hajun met in Canada.

(2) The table (which/that) my dad made for me is sturdy.

(3) Hemingway is the author whom I like the most.

(4) The book which he wrote is fun.

(5) Can I borrow the book (which/that) you told me about? 또는 Can I borrow the book about which you told me?

05 (1) My grandmother made the chocolate cake.

(2) We met the people on the plane.

(3) He wants to rent a car.

(4) Do you have a friend?

06 (1) They called him Mr. Long.

(2) They regarded him as their leader.

07 (1) We call Chicago the Windy City because it is very windy there.

(2) I like the cookies (which/that) my mother made for me.

(3) The country (which/that) I want to visit the most is France.

(4) Harry was the partner that I worked with last year.

---

01 (1), (2) 선행사가 사물이므로 관계대명사 which나 that, (3), (4) 선행사가 사람이므로 관계대명사 who, whom이나 that, (5) 목적격 관계대명사가 전치사의 목적어인 경우 전치사는 관계대명사절의 끝에 오거나 관계대명사 앞에 올 수 있으며 전치사가 관계대명사절의 끝에 올 경우에는 관계대명사를 생략할 수 있다. 전치사가 관계대명사 앞에 올 경우에는 관계대명사 that을 쓸 수 없다. (6) 선행사가 '사람+동물'이므로 관계대명사 that을 써야 한다. 목적격 관계대명사는 생략될 수 있다.

02 (1) call A B: A를 B라고 부르다 (2) consider는 consider A as B의 형태로도 쓰인다. (3) name A B: A를 B라고 이름 짓다 (4) make A B: A를 B로 만들다 (5) elect는 to부정사를

목적격 보어로 취할 수 있다. (6) believe는 to부정사를 목적격 보어로 취한다. (7) regard A as B: A를 B로 여기다

03 call A B: A를 B라고 부르다 rooftop: 지붕[옥상] / 우리는 옥상 정원을 하늘의 공원이라고 부른다.

04 (1) 선행사가 사람이므로 who, whom이나 that, (2) 선행사가 사물이므로 which나 that, (3) 관계대명사가 접속사와 대명사의 역할을 하므로 him을 삭제해야 한다. (4) 관계대명사가 접속사와 대명사의 역할을 하므로 it을 삭제해야 한다. (5) 전치사가 관계대명사 앞에 올 경우에는 관계대명사 that을 쓸 수 없으며, 관계대명사를 생략하지 않는다. sturdy: 억센, 튼튼한

05 목적격 관계대명사는 선행사가 사람이면 who나 whom, that, 사물이나 동물이면 which나 that을 쓰고 관계대명사절에서 목적어 역할을 한다. 목적격 관계대명사절에는 동사 뒤에 목적어가 없다는 것에 주의한다.

06 (1) call A B는 목적격 보어 자리에 to부정사나 형용사를 쓰지 않는다. (2) regard는 'regard A as B(A를 B로 여기다)' 형태로 쓰인다.

07 선행사가 사물이면 which나 that, 사람이면 who, whom이나 that을 쓴다. (4) 함께 일한 파트너이므로 전치사 with를 빠뜨리면 안 된다. 또한 that을 사용해야 하므로 전치사 with를 관계대명사절의 마지막에 위치시켜야 한다.

교과서
Reading

확인문제   p.28

1 T   2 F   3 F   4 T

확인문제   p.29

1 F   2 F   3 T   4 T   5 F   6 T

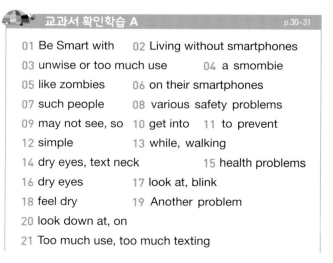

교과서 확인학습 A   p.30~31

01 Be Smart with   02 Living without smartphones

03 unwise or too much use   04 a smombie

05 like zombies   06 on their smartphones

07 such people   08 various safety problems

09 may not see, so   10 get into   11 to prevent

12 simple   13 while, walking

14 dry eyes, text neck   15 health problems

16 dry eyes   17 look at, blink

18 feel dry   19 Another problem

20 look down at, on

21 Too much use, too much texting

22 text neck   23 some tips
24 try to blink   25 up to your eye level
26 neck stretching exercises
27 How do you feel   28 feel nervous, around
29 feel sad, no text message
30 smartphone addiction   31 to prevent this
32 turn off, during   33 instead of texting

1 Be Smart with Your Smartphones!
2 Living without smartphones is difficult for many of us these days.
3 However, unwise or too much use of smartphones can cause various problems.
4 Are you a smombie?
5 All over the world, people are walking around like zombies.
6 Their heads are down, and their eyes are on their smartphones.
7 We call such people smombies, smartphone zombies.
8 If you are a smombie, you can have various safety problems.
9 You may not see a hole in the street, so you may fall and get hurt.
10 You may get into a car accident, too.
11 So what can you do to prevent these problems?
12 It's simple.
13 Do not look at your smartphone while you are walking!
14 Do you have dry eyes or text neck?
15 Smartphones can cause various health problems.
16 One example is dry eyes.
17 When you look at your smartphone, you do not blink often.
18 Then your eyes will feel dry.
19 Another problem you can have is neck pain.
20 When you look down at your smartphone, the stress on your neck increases.
21 Too much use of your smartphone, for example, too much texting, can cause neck pain.
22 We call this text neck.
23 Here are some tips for these problems.
24 For dry eyes, try to blink often.
25 For text neck, move your smartphone up to your eye level.
26 You can also do some neck stretching exercises.

27 How do you feel when you don't have your smartphone with you?
28 Do you feel nervous when your smartphone is not around?
29 Do you feel sad when you check your smartphone and there is no text message?
30 If your answers are "yes," you may have smartphone addiction.
31 There are various things you can do to prevent this.
32 For example, turn off your smartphone during meals or meetings.
33 You can talk to people instead of texting them.

01 ②   02 ①, ④   03 ⑤   04 ③
05 Other → Another   06 ④   07 ②
08 (A) nervous   (B) sad   (C) to prevent   09
addiction   10 people   11 ③, ④   12 ②
13 (A) smartphone   (B) safety   14 ⑤
15 ②   16 Another problem that[which] you
can have is neck pain.   17 ③
18 is around → is not around
19 smartphone addiction
20 (1) I can turn off my smartphone during meals or
   meetings.
   (2) I can talk to people instead of texting them.
21 ④   22 he was texting and (he) didn't see a
hole   23 ①, ③   24 ④   25 ③
26 ①   27 (A) addiction   (B) off   (C) instead of
28 ④   29 ③   30 ⑤

01 ② 앞에 나오는 내용과 상반되는 내용이 뒤에 이어지므로
   However가 가장 적절하다. ① 그러므로, ③ 게다가, ⑤ 즉,
   다시 말해
02 ⓑ와 ①, ④번은 5형식, call A B는 'A를 B라고 부르다'라는
   의미이며, smombies와 smartphone zombies는 동격이다.
   call A B와 유사하게 목적격 보어 자리에 명사가 올 수 있는 동
   사로는 make, name, elect, consider 등이 있다. ② 3형식,
   ③, ⑤ 4형식
03 안전 관련 문제들을 예방하는 것은 '간단하다.'
04 주어진 문장의 these problems에 주목한다. ③번 앞 문장의
   내용들을 받고 있으므로 ③번이 적절하다.
05 other 뒤에는 복수명사, another 뒤에는 단수명사가 온다.
06 ② 부사적 용법(목적), ⓑ와 나머지는 명사적 용법

07 ② 위 글은 '스마트폰으로 인한 건강상의 문제들과 이런 문제들을 방지하기 위한 몇 가지 조언'에 관한 글이다.

08 (A) feel은 감각동사로 '형용사'를 보어로 써야 하므로 nervous가 적절하다. (B) feel은 감각동사로 '형용사'를 보어로 써야 하므로 sad가 적절하다. (C) 이것을 '예방하기 위해' 할 수 있는 일이라고 해야 하므로 to prevent가 적절하다.

09 addiction: 중독, 1. 해로운 약을 복용하거나 그것의 복용을 중단할 수 없는 상태, 2. 어떤 것에 대한 매우 강한 소망이나 그것에 대한 욕구

10 '사람들'을 가리킨다.

11 ⓐ와 ③, ④번은 동명사, 나머지는 모두 현재분사

12 위 글은 스몸비들이 스마트폰을 보며 걷다가 일어날 수 있는 안전 관련 문제들에 관한 글이므로, '당신은 스몸비인가요?'가 적절하다. ⑤ troublemaker: 말썽꾸러기

13 다양한 '안전' 관련 문제들을 예방하기 위해 걷고 있는 동안에는 '스마트폰'을 보지 말아야 한다.

14 ⑤ 스몸비들이 가질 수 있는 가장 위험한 문제가 무엇인지는 대답할 수 없다. ① No. ② Yes. ③ It means a smartphone zombie. ④ They can have various safety problems.

15 ⓐ look at: ~을 보다, look down at: ~을 내려다보다 ⓑ For dry eyes[text neck]: 안구 건조증[거북목 증후군]에는

16 목적격 관계대명사 'that'이나 'which'가 생략되어 있다.

17 ⓓ와 ③번: (특정한 수·정도)까지, up to your eye level: 당신의 눈높이까지, ① (육체적·정신적으로) ~할 수 있는, ② ~에게 달려 있는, ~의 의무[책임]인, ④ (특히 나쁜 짓을) 하고 있는, ⑤ look up to: ~을 우러러보다, 존경하다

18 스마트폰이 주위에 '없을' 때 당신은 초조한 기분이 드는가?라고 하는 것이 흐름상 적절하다.

19 '스마트폰 중독'을 가리킨다.

20 (1) 식사나 회의 중에는 스마트폰을 끌 수 있다. (2) 문자를 보내는 대신에 사람들과 이야기를 할 수 있다.

21 이 글은 '스마트폰 중독과 예방'에 관한 글이다.

22 '문자를 보내고 있었고 구덩이를 보지 못했기 때문'이다.

23 ⓐ와 ①, ③번은 접속사(때), ②, ④, ⑤번은 의문부사(언제)

24 ④ 스마트폰을 눈높이까지 들고, 목 스트레칭 운동을 해야 하는 사람은 '수지'이다.

25 주어진 문장의 this에 주목한다. ③번 앞 문장의 smartphone addiction을 받고 있으므로 ③번이 적절하다.

26 앞의 내용의 예가 나오고 있으므로 For example이 가장 적절하다. ② 그러므로, ③ 게다가, 더욱이, ④ 그러나, ⑤ 다른 한편으로는, 반면에

27 (A) 스마트폰 '중독'이라고 해야 하므로 addiction이 적절하다. addition: 덧셈, 추가(된 것), (B) 식사나 회의 중에는 스마트폰을 '끄라'고 해야 하므로 off가 적절하다. turn on: 켜다, (C) 문자를 보내는 '대신에'라고 해야 하므로 instead of가 적절하다.

28 빈칸 뒤에 이어지는 예들(거리에 있는 구덩이를 보지 못해서 넘어져서 다칠지도 모르고, 또한 교통사고를 당할지도 모르는 것)은 다양한 '안전' 관련 문제들에 해당한다. ② 정신적인, ③ 경제적인, ⑤ 신체적인

29 ⓐ와 ①, ④: 현재분사, ②, ③, ⑤: 동명사

30 이 글은 '현명하지 않은 스마트폰 사용으로 인한 다양한 안전 관련 문제들'에 관한 글이다.

01 (A) is   (B) like   (C) It's
02 (A) zombies   (B) heads   (C) eyes
03 (1) 당신은 거리에 있는 구덩이를 보지 못할 수도 있고, 그래서 넘어져서 다칠지도 모른다.
   (2) 당신은 또한 교통사고를 당할지도 모른다.
04 blink
05 When you look down at your smartphone, the stress on your neck increases.
06 (A) too much use   (B) texting
07 머리는 아래를 향하고 눈은 스마트폰을 향한 채로 스마트폰을 보며 걷는 것
08 We call such people smombies, smartphone zombies.   09 As[Because]
10 원인: 스마트폰을 볼 때, 눈을 자주 깜박거리지 않기 때문이다.
   원인: 눈을 자주 깜박이려고 노력해라.
11 for instance

01 (A) 동명사 'Living'이 주어이므로 is가 적절하다. (B) 좀비'처럼'이라고 해야 하므로 like가 적절하다. alike는 명사 앞에는 쓸 수 없다. (C) '주어+동사'가 와야 하므로 소유격 Its가 아니라 It's가 적절하다.

02 그들은 '머리'를 숙이고, 그들의 '눈'은 스마트폰을 향한 채로 '좀비'처럼 걸어다니고 있는 사람들이다. walk with one's head hanging down: 머리를 숙이고 걷다

03 스마트폰을 보며 걷다가 일어날 수 있는 안전 관련 문제들이 ⓐ번 뒤에 설명되어 있다.

04 blink: 눈을[눈이] 깜박이다, 눈을 감고 아주 빨리 다시 눈을 뜨다

05 'on'을 보충하면 된다.

06 너무 많이 '문자'를 하는 것과 같이 스마트폰을 '너무 많이 사용하는 것'으로 인해 생기는 목 통증을 의미한다.

07 스몸비의 모습이 스마트폰을 현명하지 않게 사용하거나 너무 과도하게 사용하는 것의 예에 해당한다.

08 smombies와 smartphone zombies는 동격이므로 사이에 콤마를 찍는 것이 적절하다.

09 'so' 대신에, 이유를 나타내는 접속사 'As'나 'Because'를 맨 앞에 쓰는 것이 적절하다.

7

10 '스마트폰을 볼 때, 당신은 눈을 자주 깜박거리지 않기 때문에' 눈이 건조하다고 느낄 것이라고 했다. 안구 건조증에는, '눈을 자주 깜박이려고 노력하라'는 조언을 하고 있다.

11 for example = for instance: 예를 들어

01 (i)ntelligent	02 ④	03 ③
04 ①	05 cause	06 ③	07 ④
08 ③	09 문자를 너무 많이 하면 texting thumb	

09 문자를 너무 많이 하면 texting thumb 이 생길 수 있다는 것   10 ⑤   11 ⑤

12 ④   13 ③   14 ⑤   15 ③

16 ④   17 ①   18 ④

19 (1) *Jane Eyre* is the book (which) Yumi read yesterday.
  (2) The jacket (which) I'm wearing is a present from my grandmother.
  (3) People call such food fajitas.
  (4) The festival made the city a popular place to visit.

20 ①   21 ③   22 ②, ⑤   23 ④

24 ②   25 (A) Another (B) increases (C) tips

26 Do you feel nervous when your smartphone is not around?   27 while → during

28 ④   29 Emma / feel dry

30 (1) 스마트폰이 주위에 없을 때 초조한 기분이 드는 경우
  (2) 스마트폰을 확인했을 때 아무런 문자 메시지가 없으면 슬픈 기분이 드는 경우

31 texting

01 반의어 관계이다. 비싼 : 싼 = 어리석은 : 똑똑한

02 스마트폰 없이 사는 것은 요즘 많은 사람들에게 어려울 수 있다. 하지만 스마트폰을 현명하지 않게 또는 과도하게 사용하면 다양한 문제를 야기할 수 있다.

03 팔, 다리, 몸을 가능한 멀리 펴라. '뻗다, 기지개를 켜다'

04 잠이 든; 자고 있는

05 • 그 사고의 원인은 분명하지 않다. 경찰은 여전히 그것을 조사 중이다. • 스마트폰을 과도하게 사용하는 것은 건조한 눈을 야기할 수 있다. look into: 조사하다

06 blink는 '눈을 깜박거리다'는 뜻이다.

07 상대방의 증상을 묻는 표현이 아닌 것을 찾는다.

08 texting thumb이 무엇이냐는 물음에 'It's pain in your thumb.'이라고 답하는 것이 적절하다.

09 that은 앞의 문장을 가리키는 대명사로 사용되었다.

10 Texting thumb은 문자를 너무 많이 해서 생길 수 있는 아픔이기 때문에 마지막 문장은 'you don't text too much'가 되어야 적절하다.

11 make sure는 뒤에 '주어+동사'가 나와야 한다. 그래서 'make sure you don't play soccer'로 바꾸는 것이 적절하다.

12 ④ A의 '축구하다 넘어져 다쳤다'는 말에 B가 '그거 좋겠다'고 답하는 것은 적절하지 않다.

13 ©의 take는 '먹다, 복용하다'는 의미로 사용되었다.   this는 'some medicine'을 가리킨다.

14 call A B는 목적격 보어 자리에 to부정사나 형용사를 쓰지 않는다.

15 ③ The card (which/that) I bought yesterday was sent to Sue.

16 ④번은 주격 관계대명사이고 나머지는 모두 목적격 관계대명사이다.

17 call을 제외하고 모두 to be를 목적격 보어로 받을 수 있는 동사들이다. call은 동사 다음에 두 개의 명사(구)가 목적어와 목적격 보어로 쓰인다.

18 ④번은 목적격 관계대명사로 생략할 수 있다. ① 주격 관계대명사, ② 지시형용사, ③ 접속사, ⑤ 지시대명사이다.

19 (1) Jane Eyre는 책이름으로 사물이므로 which를 사용한다. (2) '입고 있는'은 진행형으로 나타내는 것이 적절하다. (3) call A B: A를 B라고 부르다 (4) The festival made the city to visit이 a popular place를 수식하도록 만든다.

20 주어진 문장의 various safety problems에 주목한다. ①번 뒤 문장에서 안전 관련 문제들의 예가 나오고 있으므로 ①번이 적절하다.

21 ⓐ their eyes are on their smartphones: 그들의 눈은 스마트폰을 향하고 있다, ⓑ get into a car accident: 교통사고를 당하다

22 ©와 ①, ③, ④는 부사적 용법, ② 형용사적 용법, ⑤ 명사적 용법

23 위 글은 스마트폰이 일으킬 수 있는 건강상의 문제들 중에서 안구 건조증과 목 통증에 대해 설명하는 글이므로, '당신은 안구 건조증이나 거북목 증후군이 있나요?'가 적절하다.

24 앞의 내용의 예가 나오고 있으므로 for example이 가장 적절하다. ① 게다가, ④ 사실은, ⑤ 그 결과

25 (A) various health problems 중에서 일어날 수 있는 '또 다른 문제'이므로 Another가 적절하다. another: 셋 이상 중에서 두 번째, the other: 둘 중에서 나머지 하나, (B) 스마트폰을 내려다볼 때, 목에 가해지는 압박이 '증가한다'고 해야 하므로 increases가 적절하다. decrease: 줄다[감소하다], (C) advice는 셀 수 없는 명사이므로 복수 형태로 쓸 수 없다. some pieces of advice로 쓸 수 있다.

26 when 이하는 시간의 부사절로 '~할 때'라는 의미이다. around는 부사로 쓰였다.

27 during+특정한 때를 나타내는 명사, while+주어+동사

28 식사나 회의 중에는 스마트폰을 끄고 '문자를 보내는 대신에' 사람들과 이야기하라고 하는 것이 적절하다.

29 Q1: 'Emma'가 눈을 자주 깜박이도록 노력해야 한다. Q2: 스마트폰을 사용할 때 눈이 '건조하다고 느끼기' 때문이다.

30 본문 앞부분의 질문에 대한 대답이 '그렇다'이면, 당신은 스마트폰 중독일지도 모른다고 했다.

31 전치사 다음에 명사로 쓰는 것이 적절하다.

단원별 예상문제
p.48~51

01 various   02 ③   03 (A) Here are
(B) (n)ervous   04 look well   05 ②, ④   06 ④
07 ④   08 (A) What's wrong   (B) It's pain in
your thumb   (C) make sure you don't text too much
09 Why don't you do some finger stretching
exercises?   10 ③
11 (1) The pizza (which/that) my dad made was really
delicious.
(2) I know the girl (whom/who/that) you are talking
about.
(3) We elected Chris class president.
(4) The game that we saw was very boring.
(5) He called me Queen.
12 ①, ③, ⑤   13 ④
14 (1) We call such a dance Salsa.
(2) Nobody liked the spaghetti which Nicole made.
(3) We elected Alex president of our club.
(4) She is the singer who[whom] I like most.
15 ②   16 ③
17 various safety problems   18 ⑤
19 ③   20 healthier
21 (1) 운동을 많이 하지 않는다.
→ 매일 30분 동안 걸으려고 노력할 것이다.
(2) 너무 많은 패스트푸드를 먹는다.
→ 일주일에 한 번만 패스트푸드를 먹을 것이다.
(3) 종종 밤에 먹는다.
→ 10시 이후에 먹지 않을 것이다.
22 ②

01 유의어 관계이다. 아픈 = 다양한

02 유명한 사람: 유명 인사

03 '여기에 ~가 있다'는 표현은 Here is[are] ~를 사용한다. some tips라는 복수명사가 있으므로 Here are가 적절하다.

04 'look+형용사'를 이용하여 '~처럼 보이다'를 쓰고, well은 형용사로 '건강한'의 의미를 가지고 있다.

05 머리가 아프다는 말에 '안 됐구나'라는 표현이 적절하다.

06 스마트폰이 야기할 수 있는 여러 문제를 언급하고 있기 때문에 (A)는 various가 적절하고, (B)는 눈을 자주 깜박거리지 않기 때문에 눈이 건조해진다는 dry가 적절하고, (C)는 목에 가해지는 압박이 증가한다는 increases가 적절하다.

07 ⓓ 'have + a/an+병명/증상' 형태로 '어디가 아프다'는 표현이다. have cold → have a cold

08 (A)는 상대방의 증상을 묻는 표현이 적절하다. (B)는 texting thumb이 무엇이냐는 물음에 대한 답으로 적절한 것을 고르면 된다. (C)는 texting thumb을 예방하기 위한 조언으로 적절한 표현을 찾는다.

09 'Why don't you+동사원형 ~?' 형태를 이용하여 영작한다.

10 등이 아프다는 증상에 대해 스트레칭 운동을 하라는 조언이 적절하다.

11 (1) 선행사가 사물이므로 which나 that, (2) 선행사가 사람이므로 who, whom이나 that, (3) '목적어+목적격 보어'의 어순이 되어야 한다. (4) 관계대명사가 접속사와 대명사의 역할을 하므로 it을 삭제해야 한다. (5) call은 동사 다음에 두 개의 명사(구)가 목적어와 목적격 보어로 쓰인다. as를 삭제해야 한다.

12 선행사가 사람이므로 목적격 관계대명사로 who나 whom 또는 that을 써야 한다.

13 ④ They called the ship Titanic. call은 동사 다음에 두 개의 명사(구)가 목적어와 목적격 보어로 쓰인다. 목적격 보어 자리에 to부정사나 형용사를 쓰지 않는다는 것에 주의한다.

14 (1) call A B: A를 B라고 부르다 (2) 선행사가 사물이므로 목적격 관계대명사로 which를 쓴다. (3) elect A B: A를 B로 선출하다 (4) 선행사가 사람이므로 목적격 관계대명사로 who나 whom을 쓴다.

15 these problems는 스마트폰을 보며 '걷다가' 일어날 수 있는 안전 관련 문제들이므로, '걷고 있는' 동안에는 스마트폰을 보지 마라고 하는 것이 적절하다.

16 ③번: 비슷한(형용사), ⓐ와 나머지: ~와 같이[마찬가지로], ~처럼(전치사)

17 these problems는 'various safety problems'를 가리킨다.

18 글의 흐름으로 보아 '건강' 문제가 알맞다.

19 스마트폰을 내려다볼 때, 목에 가해지는 압박이 '증가한다'.

20 healthy-healthier-healthiest

21 First, Second, Third 다음의 내용을 쓰면 된다.

22 ⓑ는 부사적 용법(목적), ① 부사적 용법(형용사 수식), ④ 부사적 용법(원인), ⑤ 부사적 용법(이유), ② 형용사적 용법, ③ 명사적 용법(진목적어), persuade: 설득하다

서술형 실전문제
p.52~53

01 wrong / have a, headache / should take / will

02 texting thumb, pain / (1) finger stretching
exercises   (2) tex

03 (A) What's the matter   (B) have a sore throat
(C) Make sure you get some rest

04 (1) The book which/that I'm reading is about
nature.

9

(2) Kenya is the country which/that John wants to visit.

(3) J. K. Rowling is a famous novelist who/whom/that many people like.

(4) I want to know the name of the girl who/whom/that I met at the party.

(5) Start by identifying the people with whom you want to work. 또는 Start by identifying the people that/who/whom you want to work with.

(6) The rate at which hair grows can be very slow. 또는 The rate which/that hair grows at can be very slow.

05 (A) without (B) hole (C) prevent

06 Their heads are down, and their eyes are on their smartphones.

07 (A) smartphones (B) hole

08 (A) dry eyes (B) neck pain 09 up → down

10 원인: 스마트폰을 너무 많이 사용하는 것, 예를 들어 너무 많이 문자를 하는 것

조언: (1) 당신의 눈높이까지 스마트폰을 위로 올려라.
(2) 목 스트레칭 운동을 할 수 있다.

01 그림으로 보아 Mike는 두통이 심하다.

03 (A)는 B의 대답으로 보아 어디가 아파 보일 때 증상을 묻는 표현이 적절하다. (B)는 아픈 증상을 이야기하는 표현으로 동사 have를 이용한다. (C)는 Mina에게 당부를 하는 표현으로 'make sure+주어+동사'의 어순을 이용한다.

04 목적격 관계대명사는 선행사가 사람이면 who나 whom, that을, 사람이 아니면 which나 that을 쓴다. 보통 목적격 관계대명사는 생략할 수 있다. 목적격 관계대명사가 전치사의 목적어일 때 전치사는 관계사절의 끝에 오거나 관계대명사 앞에 올 수 있다. 전치사가 관계사절의 끝에 올 경우에는 관계대명사를 생략할 수 있다. 전치사가 관계대명사 앞에 올 경우에는 관계대명사 that을 쓸 수 없으며, 관계대명사를 생략하지 않는다.

05 (A) 글의 흐름상 스마트폰 '없이' 사는 것이 어렵다고 하는 것이 적절하다. (B) 거리에 있는 '구덩이'를 보지 못할 수도 있다고 해야 하므로 hole이 적절하다. whole: 전체[전부]의, (C) 이런 문제들을 '예방하기' 위해라고 해야 하므로 prevent가 적절하다. protect: 보호하다

06 'down'을 보충하면 된다.

07 그들은 걷고 있는 동안에 '스마트폰'을 보고 거리에 있는 '구덩이'를 보지 못할 수도 있기 때문이다.

08 스마트폰이 일으킬 수 있는 건강상의 문제들 중의 하나는 '안구 건조증'이고 또 다른 문제는 '목 통증'이다.

09 거북목 증후군에는 당신의 눈높이까지 스마트폰을 위로 올리라고 조언하고 있기 때문에 스마트폰을 '내려다'볼 때, 목에 가해지는 압박이 증가한다고 하는 것이 적절하다.

10 스마트폰을 내려다볼 때, 목에 가해지는 압박이 증가하므로 '스마트폰을 너무 많이 사용하는 것'이 목 통증을 일으킬 수 있다. text neck에는 '당신의 눈높이까지 스마트폰을 위로 올리고 목 스트레칭 운동 또한 할 수 있다'는 조언을 하고 있다.

창의사고력 서술형 문제 p.54

|모범답안|

01 (1) A: You don't look well. What's wrong? B: I have a toothache.
A: That's too bad. Make sure you go to the dentist. B: OK, I will.

(2) A: You don't look well. What's wrong? B: I have a sore throat.
A: That's too bad. Make sure you drink a lot of water. B: OK, I will.

02 call the clock tower Big Ben

03 (A) to change (B) From now on
(C) once a week (D) after (E) my best

02 call A B: A를 B라고 부르다 the clock tower: 시계탑

단원별 모의고사 p.55~58

01 ③	02 pain	03 ①	04 ⑤
05 ④	06 ②	07 ⑤	
08 your back		09 ①	10 ④
11 ②		12 texting thumb	

13 (1) Cameron is the director (who/whom/that) Gillian likes best.

(2) We liked the story Jason told us.

(3) His business made him a millionaire.

(4) We call Bali the island of gods.

14 ②

15 (1) Every student respects him.

(2) You can do various things to prevent this.

16 ⑤

17 (1) He is a gentleman (who/whom/that) I built a good trust on.

(2) These are the pants (which/that) I bought yesterday.

(3) She doesn't consider him an artist.

(4) This is the issue about which we need to express our opinion. 또는 This is the issue (which/that) we need to express our opinion about.

(5) Ella received some flowers that her boy friend had sent to her.

(6) They call it 'Non La.'

눈이 건조하다고 느낄 것이라고 했기 때문에 눈을 자주 깜박거리는 것은 스마트폰으로 인한 다양한 건강상의 문제에 해당하지 않는다.

21 목적격 관계대명사 which 또는 that이 생략되어 있다.

22 ③ 스마트폰 중독을 예방하기 위해 할 수 있는 일은 '여러 가지가 있다.'

01 ③의 prevent는 '예방하다, 막다'는 의미로 'to stop something from happening, or stop someone from doing'이 되어야 한다.

02 유의어 관계이다. 건강한 = 고통

03 빨리 배우고 이해할 수 있는: 똑똑한

04 빈칸에는 모두 아픈 증상을 나타내는 표현으로 'have a+증상/병명' 형태가 적절하다.

05 (D)의 증상을 묻는 질문에 (A)의 답이 적절하고, 이어서 (C)의 걸을 수 있는지에 대한 물음에 (B)가 적절하다.

06 ② A의 몸이 안 좋아 보인다는 말에 노래 경연대회에서 일등을 했다는 말은 어색하다.

07 ⑤ 문제점을 묻는 질문에 대해 상대에게 당부하는 표현은 자연스럽지 않다.

08 Peter의 등이 아픈 것에 대해 처방을 해주는 문장으로 it은 Peter의 등을 가리킨다.

10 ④ 콧물이 난다는 말에 치과에 가라는 말은 어색하다.

11 ② Andy가 Ms. Kim을 찾아간 이유는 오른손 엄지손가락이 아파서이다.

13 선행사가 사람이면 who나 whom, that을 쓰고, 사물이나 동물이면 which나 that을 쓴다. 보통 목적격 관계대명사는 생략될 수 있다. call A B: A를 B라고 부르다 make A B: A를 B로 만들다

14 목적격 보어로 명사와 동사원형을 취할 수 있는 동사로는 make가 적절하다.

15 선행사가 사람이면 who나 that을 쓰고, 사물이나 동물이면 which나 that을 쓴다.

16 call은 동사 다음에 두 개의 명사(구)가 목적어, 목적격 보어로 쓰이므로 'as Cookie Eater'가 아니라 as 없이 'Cookie Eater'가 되어야 한다.

17 (1) 선행사가 사람이므로 who, whom이나 that, (2) 선행사가 사물이므로 which나 that, (3) '목적어+목적격 보어'의 어순이 되어야 한다. (4) 전치사가 관계대명사 앞에 올 경우에는 관계대명사 that을 쓸 수 없으며, 관계대명사를 생략하지 않는다. (5) 관계대명사가 접속사와 대명사의 역할을 하므로 them을 삭제해야 한다. (6) call은 동사 다음에 두 개의 명사(구)가 목적어와 목적격 보어로 쓰인다. as를 삭제해야 한다.

18 (A) feel은 감각동사로 '형용사'를 보어로 써야 하므로 dry가 적절하다. (B) Another problem이 주어이므로 is가 적절하다. (C) '목 스트레칭' 운동 또한 할 수 있다고 해야 하므로 stretching이 적절하다.

19 ②번과 ⑤번은 4형식, ③번은 3형식, ⓐ와 ①, ④번은 5형식이다.

20 스마트폰을 볼 때, 당신은 눈을 자주 '깜박거리지 않기' 때문에

Different People, Different Views

시험대비 실력평가   p.62

01 ④   02 myth   03 ③   04 ⑤
05 deal with 06 ②   07 gather   08 ④

01 '한 예가 Henri Matisse가 그린 "The Flight of Icarus (이
   카로스의 비행)"와 Marc Chagall이 그린 "The Fall of
   Icarus(이카로스의 추락)"이다'고 했으므로, 같은 (same) 주제
   를 가진 다른 그림이라는 것을 알 수 있다.

02 '신이나 용감한 사람들, 마법의 생물 등에 관한 오래된 이야기'로
   신화(myth)가 적절하다.

03 '새의 몸을 덮고 있는 가볍고 부드러운 것 중 하나'는 '깃털' 이다.

04 '매우 크게 무언가를 말하다'는 '외치다'이다.

05 deal with ~: ~을 다루다

06 in contrast는 '그에 반해서, 반면에'라는 뜻으로, 앞 문장 과 대
   조의 관계를 나타낼 때 쓰는 연결어구이다.

07 유의어 관계이다. 소리치다 : 모으다

08 • 접속사 but이 있기 때문에 앞 문장과 대조를 이루는 내용이 적
   절하다. 'Matisse의 그림은 매우 단순하지만, Chagall의 그림
   에는 세부적인 것들이 많다. • 태양에 너무 가까이 날지 마라. 밀
   랍이 녹을 거야(melt).

🦉 서술형 시험대비   p.63

01 (1) warned   (2) gathered, wax
   (3) simple   (4) adventurous

02 (1) foolish, 어리석은   (2) skip, 빼먹다, 거르다
   (3) adventurous, 모험심이 강한   (4) glue, 붙이다

03 (1) details   (2) Furthermore
   (3) outline   (4) in addition to

04 (1) escape   (2) warning

01 (1) 날개가 준비되었을 때, 그는 아들에게 경고했다. "태양에 너
   무 가까이 날지 마라." (2) 그 다음에 Daedalus는 새의 깃털을
   모아 그것들을 밀랍으로 붙였다. (3) Matisse의 그림은 매우 단
   순하다. 그의 그림에서, Icarus의 몸은 단 지 단순한 윤곽만으로
   되어 있다. (4) Matisse는 Icarus가 용감하고 모험심이 강하다
   고 생각했다. 반면에 Chagall은 Icarus가 어리석다고 생각했다.

02 (1) 어리석거나 현명하지 않은 (2) 무언가를 피하거나 하지 않

다 (3) 새롭고 흥미로운 일을 기꺼이 시도하려고 하는 (4) 풀을
사용하여 물건을 결합하다

03 (1) Matisse의 그림이 단순하다고 했으므로 but 뒤에는 대
   조되는 단어가 적절하다. many 뒤에는 복수 명사가 와야 한
   다. (2) Matisse의 그림에 대한 추가적인 설명이 오기 때문에
   furthermore가 적절하다. (3) Matisse의 그림을 보면 Icarus의
   몸은 윤곽만으로 되어 있다. (4) Chagall의 그림은 Icarus 이외
   에도(in addition to) 사람들과 집을 그렸다.

교과서
Conversation

핵심 Check   p.64~65

1 ③   2 ⑤

교과서 대화문 익히기

Check(√) True or False   p.66

1 T   2 F   3 T   4 T

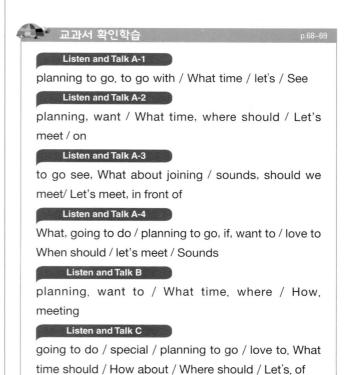

🐦 교과서 확인학습   p.68~69

Listen and Talk A-1
planning to go, to go with / What time / let's / See

Listen and Talk A-2
planning, want / What time, where should / Let's
meet / on

Listen and Talk A-3
to go see, What about joining / sounds, should we
meet/ Let's meet, in front of

Listen and Talk A-4
What, going to do / planning to go, if, want to / love to
When should / let's meet / Sounds

Listen and Talk B
planning, want to / What time, where / How,
meeting

Listen and Talk C
going to do / special / planning to go / love to, What
time should / How about / Where should / Let's, of

Review 1

Why don't you / should we meet / Let's meet / then

Review 2

Do you want / should / let's, front

Review 3

I'm planning to, join / meeting / Where / in front of

시험대비 기본평가 p.70

01 planning to see   02 ④   03 ⑤
04 ③

01 'be planning to+동사원형'은 '~할 계획이다'라는 의미로 미래의 계획을 말할 때 쓴다.

02 (A)에는 B의 대답으로 보아 A가 몇 시에 만날지 시간 약속을 정하고 있고, (B)는 B가 '도서관 앞에서 만나자'고 했기 때문에 어디서 만날지 약속 장소를 정하는 것을 알 수 있다.

03 B의 대답으로 보아 미래의 계획에 대해 물어보는 말이 적절하다.

04 대화에서 A의 대답으로 보아 시간 약속을 정하고 있다는 것을 알 수 있다.

시험대비 실력평가 p.71~72

01 ②   02 What time should we meet?
03 (B)–(C)–(A)–(D)
04 I'm planning to go hiking this Sunday.   05 ⑤
06 ①   07 to meet at 9 at the subway station
08 How about meeting at 2:30 in front of Star Movie Theater?
09 ③   10 ⑤   11 ③
12 What time should we meet?
13 don't we meet in front of the library /
we meet in front of the library

01 Jenny가 Kevin에게 피아노 콘서트에 함께 하자고 제안하는 말이다. ②는 '2시경에 만날까?'라는 시간 약속을 정하는 말이다.

03 함께 가자는 제안에 (B)가 승낙하고, 시간 약속을 묻는 말에 (C) 10시 30분에 만나자고 제안하고, (A)의 찬성하는 말과 약속 장소를 정하는 질문에 (D)의 버스 정류장에서 만나자는 말이 적절하다.

04 'be planning to+동사원형(~할 계획이다)'이라는 표현을 이용한다. '하이킹을 가다'는 go hiking을 사용한다.

05 'be planning to+동사원형'은 '~할 계획이다'라는 의미로 계획을 말할 때 사용한다.

06 여자의 마지막 말에 9시에 만나자고 했기 때문에 약속 시간을 묻는 When이 적절하다.

---

07 여자의 마지막 말에 지하철역에서 9시에 만나자고 했다.

08 '~하는 게 어때?'는 How about+-ing ~? 형태를 이용한다. '~ 앞에서'는 in front of를 쓴다.

09 'I'd love to!'는 '그러고 싶다!'라는 의미로 '함께 갈래?'라는 제안에 대한 답으로 적절하다.

10 Kate가 전시회에 가자고 Minho를 초대했으나, 그 이유는 대화에 언급되어 있지 않다.

11 전치사 about 뒤에는 동명사 meeting이 적절하다.

12 약속 시간을 정하는 표현으로 의문사 what을 이용한 'What time should we meet?'이 적절하다.

13 제안을 할 때 'Let's+동사원형, Why don't we+동사원형?, Shall we+동사원형?' 등을 사용한다.

서술형 시험대비 p.73

01 I'm planning to go to a piano concert this Friday.
02 Do you want to go with me /
Where should we meet?
03 (A) What are you going to do this Sunday?
(B) You can go with us if you want to.
(C) When should we meet?
04 What time and where should we meet?

01 'be planning to+동사원형(~할 계획이다)'이라는 표현을 이용한다.

02 (A) 함께 하자고 제안하는 표현은 'Do you want to go with ~?'를 사용한다. (B) 약속 장소를 정하는 표현은 의문사 Where와 조동사 should를 이용하여 'Where should we meet?'으로 쓴다.

04 밑줄 친 문장에서 Dream 아트 홀에서 2시에 만나자고 했기 때문에 만날 시간과 장소를 묻는 말이 적절하다.

교과서

Grammar

핵심 Check p.74~75

1 (1) saw, do[doing]   (2) heard, do[doing]   (3) cleaned

2 (1) Emma was so bored that she started singing by herself.

(2) Our team practiced hard so that we could win the game.

(3) I was so tired that I couldn't work.

01 (1) sang → sing(또는 singing)
   (2) to fly → fly(또는 flying)
   (3) very → so
   (4) what → that
02 (1) cry(또는 crying)   (2) thrown
   (3) burn(또는 burning)   (4) fall(또는 falling)
03 ④
04 He arrived so late that he missed his plane.

01 (1), (2) 지각동사의 목적격보어는 목적어와의 관계가 능동일 경우 원형부정사나 현재분사가 쓰인 다. (3), (4) 'so+형용사[부사]+that+주어+동사'의 형태로 '매우 ~해서 …하다'라는 의미를 나타 낸다.

02 (1) 지각동사의 목적격보어는 목적어와의 관계가 능동일 경우 원형부정사나 현재분사가 쓰인다. (2) 지각동사의 목적격보어 는 목적어와의 관계가 수동일 경우 과거분사가 쓰인다. (3) 집이 타는 것이므로 burnt가 아닌 burn 또는 burning이 적절하다. (4) 비가 떨어지는 것이므로 능동의 의 미를 나타내는 fall 또는 falling이 적절하다.

03 'so+형용사[부사]+that+주어+동사'의 형태로 '너무 ~해서 … 하다'

04 so를 추가하여 'so+형용사[부사]+that+주어+동사(매우 ~해 서 …하다)' 구문으로 쓴다.

01 ⑤   02 ②   03 ①
04 The fish is so fast that I can't catch it. 05 ④
06 (1) touching   (2) sing   (3) repeated   (4) clean
   (5) so   (6) that   (7) too
07 ③   08 thirsty so that → so thirsty that
09 ③, ④   10 ③, ⑤
11 her open[opening] the window   12 ②, ⑤
13 ③   14 ②   15 ③
16 (1) My sister was so tired that she went to bed early.
   (2) It rained so hard that we had to stay at home.
17 (1) When I was reading a book in the garden, I heard a rabbit talk[talking] to himself.
   (2) I could feel him pull[pulling] my hair.
   (3) Somin saw Minji ride[riding] a bike.
   (4) She walked so slowly that everybody passed by her.
   (5) I'm so full that I can't eat anymore.
18 (1) to download → download(또는 downloading)
   (2) very → so
   (3) surprised enough → too surprised

01 목적어와의 관계가 능동이므로 지각동사의 목적격보어로 원형부정사 혹은 현재분사가 적절하고 원인과 결과를 나타내는 'so+형용사[부사]+that+주어+동사' 구문이 적절하다.

02 hear는 지각동사이므로 목적격보어로 원형부정사 혹은 현재분사, 과거분사를 취한다. someone이 내 이름을 부르는 주체가 되므로 call 또는 calling이 적절하다.

03 원인과 결과를 나타내는 'so ~ that ...' 구문이 적절하다.

04 원인과 결과를 나타내는 'so ~ that ...' 구문이 적절하다.

05 지각동사 watch의 목적격보어로 원형부정사 혹은 현재분사가 적절하다. I watched him sing[singing] in his first performance.

06 (1) 지각동사 see의 목적격보어로 현재분사가 적절하다. (2) 지각동사 hear의 목적격보어로 원형부정사가 적절하다. (3) 노래가 반복되는 것이므로 목적격보어로 수동의 의미를 갖는 과거분사가 적절하다 (4) make는 사역동사이므로 목적격보어로 원형부정사가 적절하다. (5), (6) 'so+형용사[부사]+that+주어+동사' 구문이다. (7) 'so+형용사[부 사]+that+주어+can't ~'는 'too+형용사[부사]+to 동사원형'으로 바꿔 쓸 수 있다.

07 이웃에 의해 내 이름이 불린 것이므로 지각동사 heard의 목적격보어로 과거분사 called를 쓰는 것이 적절하다.

08 'so+형용사[부사]+that+주어+동사'는 원인과 결과를 나타내지만 'so that+주어+동사'는 목적을 나타낸다.

09 목적어와의 관계가 능동이므로 지각동사의 목적격보어로 원형부정사 혹은 현재분사가 적절하다.

10 'so+형용사[부사]+that+주어+can ~'은 '형용사[부사]+enough+to 동사원형'으로 바꿔 쓸 수 있다.

11 Mina가 창문을 여는 소리를 들었다는 의미이다. 목적어와 목적격보어의 관계가 능동이므로 원형부정사 또는 현재분사로 써야 한다.

12 ① I heard Somi talking[talk] with Yubin. ③ He was so busy that he skipped lunch. ④ It was such a nice day that we went on a picnic.

13 (A) 지각동사의 목적어와 목적격보어의 관계가 능동이므로 현재분사가 적절하다. (B) 지각동사의 목적어와 목적격보어의 관계가 능동이므로 원형부정사가 적절하다. (C) 지각동사의 목적어와 목적격보어의 관계가 수동이므로 과거분사가 적절하다.

14 'so that+주어+동사'는 목적을 나타내어 '~하기 위해서' 또는 '~하도록'이라는 의미로 to부정사의 부사적 용법의 '목적'과 바꿔 쓸 수 있다. 원인과 결과를 나타내는 'so ~ that ...' 과 혼동하지 않도록 유의한다.

15 주어진 문장과 ③번은 목적격보어로 쓰인 현재분사이다. ① 분사구문 ② 진행형을 만드는 현재분사 ④, ⑤ 동명사

16 (1) 결과를 나타내는 so와 (2) 이유를 나타내는 because절 이므로 'so+형용사[부사]+that+주어+동사' 구문으로 원인과 결과를 나타낼 수 있다.

17 (1)~(3) 지각동사의 목적격보어로 원형부정사나 현재분사를 이용한다. (4), (5) 'so+형용사[부사]+that+주어+동사'의 형태로 '매우 ~해서 …하다'라는 의미를 나타낸다.

18 (1) 지각동사의 목적격보어로 원형부정사나 현재분사가 적절하다. (2) 'so+형용사[부사]+that+주어+동사(너무 ~해서 …하다)' 구문으로 원인과 결과를 나타낸다. (3) 내용상 '너무 ~해서 …할 수 없다'는 'too+형용사[부사]+to 동사원형' 구문이 적절하다. so+형용사[부사]+that+주어+can … = 형용사[부사]+enough+to 동사원형, so+형용사[부사]+that+주어+can't … = too+형용사[부사]+to 동사원형

서술형 시험대비   p.80~81

01 (1) Eric heard Mina play[playing] the guitar.

(2) I saw Mike swim[swimming] in the lake.

(3) She felt her heart beat[beating] fast.

(4) Simpson won the Trophy in 2008 but saw it stolen 10 years ago.

(5) She got up so late that she had to run all the way to school.

(6) She speaks too quietly for me to understand.

(7) I left early enough to arrive on time.

02 I heard Maryline singing a song at the concert.

03 (1) Dad was too busy to play with us.

(2) The dog was small enough to go through the hole.

(3) The coffee is too hot for her to drink.

(4) The math problem was easy enough for Laura to solve.

04 Pandora was so foolish that she opened the box which Zeus had given to her.

05 (1) It rained so hard that he couldn't play soccer.

(2) Last night I was so tired that I went to bed early.

(3) The box was so heavy that I couldn't carry it.

(4) There were so many people that we didn't get into the sea.

(5) It rained so heavily that they had to cancel the game.

06 (1) to carry   (2) arrested

(3) open[opening]   (4) take

07 (1) It was so dark that we couldn't see anything.

(2) I want to live so long that I can see you rise in the world.

08 (1) He looked at the violinist dancing.

(2) The teacher heard Somin playing the piano.

09 (1) fall(또는 falling)

---

01 (1)~(3) 지각동사의 목적어와 목적격보어의 관계가 능동이므로 목적격보어로 원형부정사 혹은 현재분사가 적절하다 (4) 지각동사의 목적어와 목적격보어의 관계가 수동이므로 과거 분사가 적절하다. (5) 'so+형용사[부사]+that+주어+동사 (너무 ~해서 …하다)' 구문으로 원인과 결과를 나타낸다. (6) so+형용사[부사]+that+주어+can't … = too+형용사[부사]+to 동사원형 (7) so+형용사[부사]+that+주어+can … = 형용사[부사]+enough+to 동사원형

02 진행형의 문장이므로 목적격보어로 현재분사가 적절하다.

03 (1) so ~ that 주어 can't … = too ~ to … (2) so ~ that 주어 can … = ~ enough to … (3), (4) 'so ~ that …' 구문에서 주절의 주어와 that절의 주어가 서로 다를 경우 'too ~ to …'나 '~ enough to …'로 바꿔 쓸 때 'for+ 목적격'으로 주어를 나타낸다. drink와 solve의 목적어가 문장의 주어와 같으므로 목적어를 쓰지 않음에 주의한다.

04 '매우 ~해서 …하다'라는 의미를 나타내는 'so+형용사[부사]+that+주어+동사' 구문을 이용한다.

05 'so+형용사[부사]+that+주어+동사'의 형태로 '매우 ~해서 …하다'라는 의미를 나타낸다. so 뒤의 형용사[부사]는 원인을, that 뒤에 나오는 내용은 그에 따른 결과를 나타낸다.

06 (1) want는 to부정사를 목적격보어로 받는다. (2) 지각동사의 목적어와 목적격보어의 관계가 수동일 때 목적격보어로 과거분사가 적절하다. (3) 목적어와 목적격보어의 관계가 능동일 때 목적격보어로 원형부정사나 현재분사가 적절하다. (4) 사역동사 make는 원형부정사를 목적격보어로 받는다.

07 (1) too ~ to … = so ~ that 주어 can't … (2) ~ enough to … = so ~ that 주어 can …, rise in the world: 출세하다

08 지각동사의 목적어와 목적격보어의 관계가 능동이며, 진행형으로 쓰이고 있으므로 현재분사를 이용한다.

09 지각동사 see의 목적어 Icarus와 목적격보어의 관계가 능동이므로 목적격보어로 원형부정사나 현재분사가 적절하다.

교과서
Reading

확인문제   p.82

1 T   2 F   3 F   4 T   5 T   6 F

확인문제   p.83

1 T   2 F   3 F   4 T   5 T   6 F

01 Same, Different

02 different paintings, the same subject

03 example, by, by

04 the same Greek myth   05 Greek Myth

06 a great inventor

07 so, that, keep, forever

08 however, to leave, kept

09 to escape   10 flying   11 I need wings

12 glued them together

13 Don't fly too close   14 melt

15 to fly   16 so, that, warning

17 higher and higher   18 cried out

19 fell into   20 Different

21 deal with, same subject, different

22 flying, falling   23 comes from, different ideas

24 brave, adventurous   25 In contrast

26 very simple, many details

27 only Icarus, some stars

28 Furthermore, outline

29 In contrast, in addition to

30 difference, different painting styles

31 Whose painting

32 same thing in different ways

1 Same Story, Different Paintings

2 We often find different paintings with the same subject.

3 An example is The Flight of Icarus by Henri Matisse and The Fall of Icarus by Marc Chagall.

4 They are both about the same Greek myth.

5 The Greek Myth of Icarus

6 Daedalus was a great inventor.

7 King Minos liked Daedalus' work so much that he wanted to keep Daedalus with him forever.

8 Daedalus, however, tried to leave, so the King kept him and his son, Icarus, in a tall tower.

9 Daedalus wanted to escape.

10 One day, Daedalus saw birds flying.

11 "Wings! I need wings!" he shouted.

12 Daedalus then gathered bird feathers and glued them together with wax.

13 When the wings were ready, he warned his son, "Don't fly too close to the sun.

14 The wax will melt."

15 Daedalus and Icarus began to fly.

16 Icarus was so excited that he forgot his father's warning.

17 He flew higher and higher, and the wax began to melt.

18 "Oh, no! I'm falling," Icarus cried out.

19 Icarus fell into the sea and died.

20 Two Different Paintings

21 Matisse and Chagall both deal with the same subject in their paintings, but they are different.

22 First, in Matisse's painting, you can see Icarus flying, but in Chagall's painting, the boy is falling.

23 This difference comes from the different ideas that the two painters had.

24 Matisse thought that Icarus was brave and adventurous.

25 In contrast, Chagall thought that Icarus was foolish.

26 Second, Matisse's painting is very simple, but Chagall's painting has many details.

27 In Matisse's painting, there are only Icarus and some stars.

28 Furthermore, Icarus' body has just a simple outline.

29 In contrast, Chagall painted many people and houses in addition to Icarus.

30 This difference comes from the different painting styles of the two painters.

31 Whose painting do you like more?

32 People will have different answers because they may see the same thing in different ways.

01 ②   02 ②, ⑤   03 ③   04 ③

05 their paintings   06 wise → foolish 또는 stupid   07 ②   08 ④

09 the different subject → the same subject
the same ways → different ways

10 ④   11 ⑤   12 ③

13 difference 14 ④   15 ⓐ ③, ⑤   ⓑ ①, ②, ④

16 (A) simple   (B) the same   (C) different 17 ②

18 ③

19 (A) playing 또는 play   (B) dancing 또는 dance
(C) standing 또는 stand

20 (1) Chagall의 그림에서는 바이올린 연주자의 얼굴을 볼 수 있지만 Matisse의 그림에서는 바이올린 연주자의 얼굴을 볼 수 없다.

(2) Chagall의 그림에서 바이올린 연주자가 춤추고 있는 것을 볼 수 있지만, Matisse의 그림에서는 그가 가만히 서 있는 것을 볼 수 있다.

(3) Chagall의 그림은 더 역동적이다.   21 ①

22 than Matisse's   23 Matisse의 그림에는 Icarus와 몇 개의 별들만 있고, 게다가 Icarus의 몸은 단지 단순한 윤곽만으로 되어 있기 때문이다.   24 outline

25 (A) simple   (B) many details

26 (A) flying   (B) falling   27 ③   28 ④

29 ⑤   30 ②

31 (A) different painting styles   (B) subject

32 1. ④ 2. ⑤ 3. ⑦ 4. ② 5. ① 6. ③ 7. ⑥

01 바로 뒤에 같은 그리스 신화에 관한 두 화가의 다른 그림에 대한 설명이 이어지고 있으므로, '같은' 주제의 '다른' 그림 들을 발견한다고 하는 것이 적절하다. ① usual: 흔히 하는[있는], 평상시의, 보통의, unusual: 특이한, 흔치 않은, 드문, ③ equal: 동일한[같은], unequal: 불공평한

02 ⓒ와 ②, ⑤번: 신화, legend: 전설, ①, ③, ④: (근거 없는) 이야기, 사회적 통념[미신]

03 ③ 'Icarus'가 아니라 'Daedalus'가 새의 깃털을 모아 그 것들을 밀랍으로 붙였다.

04 위 글은 '화가들이 갖고 있던 서로 다른 생각들이 같은 주제를 다르게 그리도록 만드는 것'에 관한 글이다.

05 'Matisse와 Chagall의 그림'을 가리킨다.

06 Chagall의 그림에서 Icarus가 추락하고 있는 것은 Chagall이 Icarus를 '어리석다'고 생각했기 때문이라고 하는 것이 적절하다.

07 ② 십인십색(十人十色), 취향도 가지가지다, 사람들은 같은 것을 다른 방식들로 볼 수 있기 때문에, 누구의 그림이 더 좋은가에 대해 서로 다른 대답을 할 것이라고 했으므로 어울리는 속담으로는 '십인십색'이 적절하다.

08 A in addition to B = A besides B = not only A but also B = B as well as A: A뿐만 아니라 B도, not A but B: A가 아니라 B

09 화풍이 달랐기 '때문에' Matisse와 Chagall은 '같은' 주제를 '다른' 방법으로 그렸다.

10 ⓐ 같은 주제를 '가진' 다른 그림들이라고 하는 것이 적절하다. ⓑ 저자 이름 앞의 'by': …가 그린[쓴/만든]

11 글의 도입부에서 '우리는 종종 같은 주제의 다른 그림들을 발견한다.'고 말한 뒤에 같은 주제의 예로 Icarus에 관한 그리스 신화를 설명하는 내용의 글이므로, 제목으로는 'Icarus에 관한 그리스 신화'가 적절하다.

12 주어진 문장의 gathered bird feathers에 주목한다. ③ 번 앞 문장에서 필요하다고 말한 날개를 만들기 위해서 새의 깃털을 모은 것이므로 ③번이 적절하다.

13 주어 자리이므로 different의 명사형인 'difference'를 쓰는 것이 적절하다.

14 앞에 나오는 내용과 상반되는 내용이 뒤에 이어지므로 In contrast가 가장 적절하다. in contrast: 그에 반해서, 반면에, ① 그러므로, ② 즉, 다시 말해, ③ 게다가, ⑤ 게다가, 더욱이

15 ⓐthat: 목적격 관계대명사, ⓑthat: 접속사

16 (A) Matisse의 그림은 매우 '단순하다'고 해야 하므로 simple 이 적절하다. complex: 복잡한, (B), (C) 사람들은 '같은' 것을 '다른' 방식들로 볼 수 있다고 해야 하므로 (B)는 the same이, (C)는 different가 적절하다.

17 위 글은 '비교와 대조'의 방식으로 쓰인 글이다.

18 왜 Matisse와 Chagall이 Icarus를 그렸는지는 대답할 수 없다. ① Matisse's. ② We can see only Icarus and some stars. ④ We can see many people and houses. ⑤ Because their painting styles were different.

19 지각동사 see의 목적격보어 자리이므로 동사원형이나 현재분사로 쓰는 것이 적절하다.

20 뒤에 나오는 문장들을 쓰는 것이 적절하다.

21 (B)와 ①번: 가만히 있는, ②, ⑤: 아직(도) (계속해서), ③ (비교급을 강조하여) 훨씬[더욱], ④ 그런데도, 그럼에도 불구하고

22 Chagall의 그림은 'Matisse의 그림(Matisse의 것)보다' 더 역동적이다.

23 바로 다음 문장의 내용을 쓰는 것이 적절하다.

24 outline: 윤곽 / 세부가 없는 사물의 주된 형태나 가장자리

25 Matisse는 매우 '단순하게' 그렸지만, Chagall은 그의 그림에 '많은 세부적인 것들'을 그렸다.

26 Matisse의 그림에서 Icarus는 '날고' 있지만, Chagall의 그림에서 그는 '추락하고'있다.

27 in contrast: 그에 반해서

28 Matisse가 왜 Icarus를 용감하고 모험심이 강하다고 생각 했는지는 대답할 수 없다. ① Yes. ② He is flying. ③ He is falling. ⑤ No.=

29 but 이하의 has many details와 대조되는 simple이 적절하다.

30 ⓑ: 앞에 나오는 내용에 추가하는 내용이 뒤에 이어지므로 Furthermore가 가장 적절하다. ⓒ: 앞에 나오는 내용과 상반되는 내용이 뒤에 이어지므로 In contrast가 가장 적 절하다. ① Therefore: 그러므로, On the other hand: 한편, 반면에, ③ Likewise: 마찬가지로, ④ In other words: 즉, 다시 말해, ⑤ Moreover = In addition: 게 다가, 더욱이

31 화풍이 달랐기' 때문에 Matisse와 Chagall은 같은 '주제'를 다른 방법으로 그렸다.

32 Matisse: ④ 용감하고 모험심이 강한, ⑤ 매우 단순한, ⑦ 날고 있다, 주제: ② Icarus, Chagall: ① 많은 세부적인 것들, ③ 추락하고 있다, ⑥ 어리석은

01 warning

02 ⓐ The Flight of Icarus by Henri Matisse and The Fall of Icarus by Marc Chagall

ⓑ bird feathers

03 (A) subject (B) forever (C) excited

04 Icarus

05 painters had them → painters had

06 (A) brave and adventurous (B) flying

(C) foolish(또는 stupid) (D) falling

07 has many details → is very simple / is very simple → has many details 또는 Matisse's painting → Chagall's painting / Chagall's painting → Matisse's painting

08 because they may see the same thing in different ways

09 (A) Icarus (B) some stars

(C) a simple outline (D) Icarus

10 (A) so (B) that

11 to fly → flying 또는 fly

12 different subject → same subject

01 Icarus는 "태양에 너무 가까이 날지 마라. 밀랍이 녹을 거야."라 는 아버지의 '경고'를 잊은 것이다. warn의 명사형인 'warning' 이 적절하다.

02 ⓐ Henri Matisse가 그린 "The Flight of Icarus"와 Marc Chagall이 그린 "The Fall of Icarus", ⓑ '새의 깃털'을 가리 킨다.

03 (A) 같은 '주제'의 다른 그림들이라고 해야 하므로 subject 가 적절하다. object: 물건, 목적, subject: (논의 등의) 주제 [대 상/화제], (그림·사진 등의) 대상[소재], (B) Minos왕은 Daedalus 의 작품을 매우 좋아해서 Daedalus를 그의 곁에 '영원히' 두고 싶어 했다고 해야 하므로 forever가 적절하다. temporarily: 일시적으로, 임시로, (C) 감정을 나타내는 동사 는 수식받는 명사가 감정을 느끼게 되는 경우에 과거분사를 써 야 하므로 excited가 적절하다.

04 Matisse와 Chagall의 그림에서 같은 주제는 'Icarus'이 다.

05 that이 목적격 관계대명사이므로, 맨 끝의 목적어 them을 삭제 하는 것이 적절하다.

06 Matisse는 Icarus가 '용감하고 모험심이 강하다'고 생각했 기 때문 에 그의 그림에서 Icarus가 '날고 있지만', Chagall은 Icarus가 '어리석 다'고 생각했기 때문에 그의 그림에서 여러분 은 Icarus가 '추락하고 있는 것'을 볼 수 있다.

07 Matisse의 그림은 '매우 단순하지만', Chagall의 그림은 '세부 적인 것들이 많다'로 고치는 것이 적절하다.

08 in different ways: 다른 방식들로

09 Matisse의 그림에서 여러분들은 'Icarus'와 '몇 개의 별들'

만 볼 수 있다. 게다가 Icarus의 몸은 단지 '단순한 윤곽'만으 로 되어 있다. 반면 에 Chagall의 그림에서 여러분들은 단지 'Icarus'뿐만 아니라 많은 사람 들과 집들도 볼 수 있다.

10 so＋형용사/부사＋that＋주어＋동사: 매우 ~해서 …하다

11 지각동사 saw의 목적격보어이므로 현재분사나 원형부정사로 고치는 것이 적절하다.

12 The Flight of Icarus 와 The Fall of Icarus 는 다른 그 림 들이지만 '같은' 주제를 가지고 있다.

01 (f)urthermore 02 ④ 03 ③

04 ① 05 deal with 06 ⑤

07 (C)–(B)–(A)–(D) 08 ⑤

09 They are going to go to the Van Gogh exhibition.

10 ② 11 (1) I'm planning to go swimming

(2) How about meeting (3) Where should we meet?

12 ⑤ 13 ⑤ 14 (1) play(또는 playing)

(2) carry(또는 carrying) (3) paint(또는 painting)

15 ② 16 ④

17 (1) I heard someone repeat[repeating] my name.

(2) A girl saw a boy feed[feeding] fish.

(3) Did you listen to him tell[telling] the news?

(4) He was so hungry that he ate three pieces of pizza.

(5) The food was so awful that we didn't eat it.

(6) This box is too heavy for me to carry.

18 ⓐ Flight ⓑ flying 또는 fly ⓒ fly

ⓓ to fly 또는 flying ⓔ flew

19 ② 20 ⑤ 21 ③ 22 ②, ⑤

23 Matisse의 그림에서, 여러분은 Icarus가 날고 있는 것을 볼 수 있지만, Chagall의 그림에서는 그가 추락하고 있다.

24 ③ 25 ⑤ 26 ④ 27 ④

01 유의어 관계이다. 녹다 : 게다가

02 ⓐ furthermore는 '게다가, 더욱이'라는 뜻으로 앞 문장에 또 다른 정보를 덧붙여 제시할 때 쓰는 연결어이다. ⓑ in contrast 는 '그에 반해서, 반면에'라는 뜻으로, 앞 문장과 대조 관계를 나 타낼 때 쓰는 연결어구이다.

03 말린 잎에 끓는 물을 부어 만든 뜨거운 음료

04 공중을 나는 행위, 즉 '비행'을 나타낸다.

05 • 이번 주에, 여러분의 분노를 어떻게 다뤄야 하는지에 대해 배 워 보 도록 합시다. • 그 책은 사랑이라는 주제를 다루고 있다. • A: 이 상황을 혼자 다룰 수 있니? B: 물론, 할 수 있어. 어떤 도 움 없이 그것을 다룰 수 있어.

06 in addition to는 '~에 더하여, ~ 이외에도'의 뜻이고, '게다가' 는 furthermore, in addition이다.

07 (C) 계획을 말하고 함께 하자고 제안함 → (B) 승낙의 답과 함께 만 날 시간을 제안한다. → (A) 약속 시간과 장소를 정하고 → (D) 마지 막으로 그때 보자는 말로 대화를 마친다.

08 만날 장소를 물어보는 말은 Kate의 마지막 말(Let's meet in front of the ticket office.) 앞에 오는 것이 적절하다.

09 그들은 Van Gogh 전시회에 갈 예정이다.

10 ② Minho는 이번 주 토요일에 특별한 일이 없다고 했기 때문에 바쁘지 않다는 것을 알 수 있다.

12 ⑤의 'Do you want to go with me?'는 함께 가자고 제안하는 표현이다.

13 첫 문장의 smell은 목적격 보어로 현재분사가 나와야 한다. 두 번째 문장 에서 see는 목적격보어로 동사원형이나 현재분사가 나와야 한다. (엄마가 만드 는 것이므로 능동)

14 (1)~(3) 지각동사의 목적어가 목적격보어의 행위의 주체가 될 경우 목적격보어로 원형부정사나 현재분사를 쓴다.

15 ② I was so hungry that I ate a whole pizza.

16 the man이 개를 산책시키는 것이므로(능동) walk나 walking 이 적절하다.

17 (1)~(3) 지각동사의 목적어와 목적격보어의 관계가 능동일 경우 목적격보어로 동사원형이나 현재분사가 적절하다. (4)~(6) 'so+형용사[부사]+that+주어+동사(너무 ~해서 …하다)' 구문으로 원인과 결과를 나타낸다. so+형용사[부사]+that+주어 +can't … = too+형용사[부사]+to 동사원형

18 ⓐ 이카로스의 '비행'이라고 해야 하므로 Flight 가 적절하다. ⓑ 지각동사 saw의 목적격보어이므로 현재분사나 원형부정사가 적절하다. ⓒ 부정명령문이므로 동사원형이 적절하다. ⓓ begin은 목적어로 to부정사와 동명사를 둘 다 쓸 수 있다. ⓔ 과거시제로 쓰는 것이 적절하다.

19 새의 깃털을 모아 그것들을 밀랍으로 붙였기 때문에, 태양에 너무 가 까이 날면 '밀랍이 녹을 것'이라고 하는 것이 적절하다.

20 (A)와 ⑤: (그림·사진 등의) 주제[소재], ① 학과, 과목, ② 지 배를 받는, 복종하는(형용사), ③ 연구[실험] 대상, 피험자, ④ 주어

21 Icarus는 매우 흥분해서 아버지의 경고를 잊고 점점 더 높이 날 아 밀랍이 녹아 바다로 떨어져서 죽었기 때문에, '부주 의한' 성격이라고 하는 것이 적절하다. ② patient: 인내심 있는, ③ careless: 부주의한, ④ reasonable: 사리를 아 는, 합리적인, ⑤ 호기심 많은

22 ⓐ와 ②, ⑤: (주제·소재로) ~을 다루다, ① 제어하다, 통제하 다, ③ 거래하다, ④ 준비하다

23 they는 Matisse와 Chagall의 그림을 가리키므로, 두 그 림의 차이를 설명하는 것이 적절하다.

24 두 그림의 차이는 '두 화가들이 갖고 있던 서로 다른 생각'에 서 기인한다.

25 주어진 문장의 This difference에 주목한다. ⑤번 앞 문장 의 내용을 받고 있으므로 ⑤번이 적절하다.

26 '둘째'라고 하면서 Matisse와 Chagall이 Icarus를 다르게 그 린 것에 대한 설명을 하고 있으므로, 앞에는 '두 화가가 같은 주 제(Icarus)를 다르게 다룬 것에 대한 첫 번째 설명'이 나왔을 것이라고 하는 것이 적절하다.

27 ④ Matisse와 Chagall은 서로 '다른' 화풍을 가지고 있어서, '같은' 주제를 '다르게' 그렸다.

단원별 예상문제   p.102~105

01 (f)oolish   02 ③   03 ⑤   04 ⑤
05 ③   06 planning to go to   07 ②
08 ③   09 What are you going to do this Saturday?   10 I'd love to go with you!   11 ②
12 ①, ⑤   13 ③, ④   14 ④   15 ②
16 ①, ④   17 ④   18 Matisse and Chagall both deal with the same subject in their paintings, but they are different.   19 falling → flying / flying → falling   20 ③, ⑤   21 Matisse는 Icarus가 용감하고 모험심이 강하다고 생각 했다. 반면에 Chagall은 Icarus가 어리석다고 생각했다.   22 different   23 ③
24 (A) a simple outline   (B) many details

01 유의어 관계이다. 소리치다 : 어리석은

02 '그 혹은 그녀가 그것을 피할 수 있도록 누군가에게 나쁜일 이 일어날 수 있다고 말하다'라는 의미로 '경고하다'가 적절 하다.

03 (A) Daedalus는 달아나기를 원했기 때문에 날개가 필요하다고 '외쳤다'가 적절하다. (B) 새 깃털을 '모아서' 왁스로 붙 였다가 적절하다. (C) 태양에 너무 가까이 가면 '밀랍'이 녹는다가 적절 하다.

04 let's는 뒤에 동사원형을 취한다.

05 (C)의 in contrast는 '반면에'란 뜻이다.

06 '~할 계획이다'는 'be planning to+동사원형'을 쓴다.

07 G의 마지막 말에 10시 30분에 만나자고 했기 때문에 약속 시간 을 정하는 말이 적절하다.

08 ⓐ에는 시간을 정하는 When이나 What time이 적절하고, ⓑ 에는 '~하는 게 어때?'라는 How about ~?이나 What about ~?가 적절하다. ⓒ는 장소를 정하는 표현으로 의문 사 Where 가 적절하다.

09 의문사 what으로 문장을 시작하고 'be going to+동사원형' 구 문을 이용한다.

10 '너와 함께 가고 싶다'는 의미로 중복되는 말인 'go with you'가 생략되어 있다.

11 첫 번째 문장에서는 지각동사의 목적격보어로 원형부정사나 현재 분사가 적절하다. 두 번째 문장에서는 '형용사[부사]+enough+to 동사원형 (= so+형용사[부사]+that+주어+can ...)' 구문이 적절 하다.

12 ② The teacher saw Hoyeong dance[dancing]. ③ I felt

19

somebody watch[watching] me. ④ He was looking at the monkey eat[eating] bananas.

13 ① It was so sad that I cried a lot ② The cake was so delicious that I ate it all. ⑤ The man is so rich that he can buy anything he wants.

14 ⓑ We heard her play[playing] the piano. ⓓ Jocelyn felt him hold[holding] her hand. ⓕ The dog ran too quickly for me to catch. catch의 목적어와 문장의 주어 가 같으므로 it을 쓰지 않는 것이 적절하다. ⓖ The sky was clear enough to see stars very well.

15 앞에 나오는 내용과 상반되는 내용이 뒤에 이어지므로 however 가 가장 적절하다. ① 그러므로, ③ 게다가, ⑤ 그 결과

16 ⓑ와 ②, ③, ⑤: 명사적 용법, ① 형용사적 용법, ④ 부사적 용법

17 Daedalus가 새의 깃털을 어떻게 모았는지는 대답할 수 없다. ① No. ② It's the Greek Myth of Icarus. ③ Because Daedalus tried to leave. ⑤ Because he was so excited that he forgot his father's warning.

18 with를 보충하면 된다. deal with: (주제·소재로) ~을 다루다

19 Matisse는 Icarus가 용감하고 모험심이 강하다고 생각했 던 반면에 Chagall은 Icarus가 어리석다고 생각했기 때문에, Matisse의 그림에서, 여러분은 Icarus가 '날고 있는 것'을 볼 수 있지만, Chagall의 그림에서는 그 소년이 '추락하고 있다'고 하는 것이 적절하다.

20 ⓒ와 ①, ②, ④: ~에서 기인하다, ③ is caused by로 고 치는 것 이 적절하다. ⑤ 원인 results in 결과

21 Matisse는 Icarus가 날고 있는 것을 그렸고 Chagall은 그 소 년이 추락하고 있는 것을 그린 원인을 설명하면 된다.

22 'difference'의 형용사형인 'different'를 쓰는 것이 적절하다.

23 furthermore = additionally = moreover = in addition = besides: 게다가, 더욱이, ③ beside: ~ 옆에

24 Matisse는 몸이 단지 '단순한 윤곽'만으로 되어 있는 Icarus와 몇 개의 별들만 그렸지만, Chagall은 Icarus뿐 만 아니라 많은 사람들과 집들과 같은 '많은 세부적인 것들' 도 그렸다.

---

(2) Did you hear Sophia open[opening] the window?

(3) Did you feel your mom touch[touching] you on the shoulder?

06 Orpheus was such a great musician that Hades returned his wife to him.

07 We often find different paintings with the same subject.

08 ⓑ The Greek Myth of Icarus
ⓓ Don't fly too close to the sun. The wax will melt.

09 because

02 함께 가자고 제안하는 표현으로 Do you ~로 시작하는 일반동 사 의문문을 이용한다.

03 (1) 이번 주 월요일에 도서관에 갈 계획이다. (2) 5시 30분에 만나기로 했다.

04 'so+형용사[부사]+that+주어+can't ...' = 'too+형용사 [부 사]+to동사원형', 'so+형용사[부사]+that+주어+can ...' = '형 용사[부사]+enough+to 동사원형' 의미상의 주어 for us와 for me를 빠뜨리지 않도록 주의한다. 의미상의 주어 for anyone은 일반인을 말하므로 생략할 수 있다. 또 한 that절의 목적어와 문 장의 주어가 같으므로 her나 it을 쓰지 않는 것이 적절하다.

05 (1)~(3) 지각동사의 목적어와 목적격보어의 관계가 능동이므로 목적격보어로 원형부정사나 현재분사가 적절하다.

06 'so ... that' 구문에서 that 앞에 형용사나 부사 대신 명사가 오면 so 대신 such를 쓴다.

07 빈도부사 'often'을 일반동사 앞에 쓰는 것이 적절하다.

08 ⓑ 'Icarus에 관한 그리스 신화'를 가리킨다. ⓓ '태양에 너무 가 까이 날지 마라. 밀랍이 녹을 거야.'를 가리킨다.

09 so + 부사 + that + 주어 + 동사: '매우 ~해서 …하다'라는 의미이 므 로, because, as, since 등의 이유를 나타내는 접속사를 사용 하 여 고치는 것이 적절하다.

---

01 (A) You can go with us if you want to.
(B) let's meet at 9 at the subway station

02 Do you want to go with me

03 (1) They are going to go to the library.
(2) They are going to meet at 5:30.

04 (1) The room was too noisy for us to hear him speak.
(2) She speaks too fast for me to understand.
(3) The math problem is easy enough to solve.

05 (1) Did you see Minsu play[playing] soccer?

|모범답안|

01 I'm planning to go / What time should we meet / about meeting

02 (1) Tom was so nervous that he couldn't play well.
(2) I was so happy that I danced.
(3) The boy was so tired that he fell asleep on the floor.
(4) The movie was so sad that everybody cried.

03 (A) a violinist (B) can see (C) dancing
(D) standing still (E) more dynamic

01 ④   02 simple   03 ③   04 ⑤

05 ①   06 ⑤   07 ②

08 They are going to meet in front of the ticket office.

09 plan, in front of, ticket office

10 (1) F   (2) T   11 ③   12 (C) → (B) → (A) → (D)

13 (1) I heard my uncle play[playing] the guitar.

  (2) I saw them wear[wearing] their sneakers in the house.

  (3) I saw a queen smell[smelling] a rose.

  (4) The movie was so good that they watched it twice.

  (5) The weather was so bad that they stayed home.

  (6) John is too sick to go to school.

14 (1) This problem is so easy that everybody can solve it.

  (2) The meal was so good that we decided to have dinner at the restaurant once again.

15 ①   16 ②

17 (1) ran → run[running]   (2) to beat → beat[beating]

  (3) burns → burning   (4) too → so

  (5) slippery so that → so slippery that

  (6) carry it → carry

18 ③   19 ⑤

20 (A) same subject   (B) warning

21 He flew higher and higher, and the wax began to melt.

---

01 ④번은 'escape'에 대한 설명이다. skip은 'to avoid something or not to do something(무언가를 피하거 나 하지 않다)'가 적절하다.

02 반의어 관계이다. 다른 : 같은 = 복잡한 : 단순한

03 약속 시간을 정하는 물음에 대한 답은 ③이 적절하다.

04 G의 대답으로 보아 약속 시간을 정하는 표현이 적절하다.

05 '사소한 사실, 특징 또는 정보'는 detail(세부 사항)을 의미 한다.

06 '언제 어디서 만날까?'라는 물음에 '좋아. 그때 보자.'라는 말은 자 연스럽지 못하다.

07 Kate가 '11시에 만나는 게 어때?'라고 말하는 것으로 보아 약속 시간을 정하는 말이 적절하다.

09 Kate는 Minho와 이번 주 토요일에 대한 계획을 말하고 있고, 11시 국립미술관 매표소 앞에서 만나기로 했다.

10 (1) Minho는 Jenny와 함께 쇼핑을 갈 계획이다. (2) Minho 와 Sumi는 12시 30분에 쇼핑몰 앞에서 만나기로 했 다.

11 대화의 마지막 말에 그때 보자고 했기 때문에 시간을 정하는 말 이 오는 것이 적절하다.

12 (C) 이번 주 토요일의 계획을 말하며, 함께 가자고 제안한 다음 → (B)에서 승낙의 표현과 함께 만날 시간과 장소를 정하는 질문

을 하고 → (A) 2시에 Dream 아트 홀에서 만나자는 말이 오고 → 마지막으로 (D) 토요일에 보자는 말이 자연 스럽다.

13 (1)~(3) 지각동사의 목적어와 목적격보어가 능동의 관계일 경 우 목적격보어로 원형부정사나 현재분사를 쓴다. (4), (5) 'so+ 형용사[부사]+that+주어+동사' 구문을 이용하여 원인과 결과 를 나타낸다. (6) so+형용사[부사]+that+주어 +can't ... = too+형용사[부사]+to 동사원형

14 (1), (2) 'so+형용사[부사]+that+주어+동사' 구문을 이용하 여 원인과 결과를 나타낸다.

15 지각동사의 목적어와 목적격보어가 능동의 관계일 경우 목적격 보어로 원형부정사나 현재분사를 쓴다.

16 ② 첫 번째 문장은 'so+형용사[부사]+that+주어+동사' 구문 으로 원인과 결과를 나타내지만, 두 번째 문장은 'so that+주어 +동사' 구문으로 목적을 나타낸다.

17 (1)~(2) 지각동사의 목적어와 목적격보어가 능동의 관계에 있을 경우 목적격보어로 원형부정사나 현재분사를 쓴다. (3) smell은 목적격보어로 현재분사를 취한다. (4) 'so+형용사[부 사]+that+주어+동사(너무 ~해서 …하다)' 구문으로 원인과 결 과를 나타낸다. (5) 'so+형용사[부사]+that+ 주어+동사'는 원 인과 결과를 나타내지만 'so that+주어+동사'는 목적을 나타낸 다. (6) 'so+형용사[부사]+that+주어+can ...' 구문을 '형용사 [부사]+enough+to 동사원형' 구문으로 바꿀 때, that절 내의 동사의 목적어 와 문장의 주어가 같으면 목적어를 쓰지 않는 것 이 적절하다.

18 (A)와 ①, ②, ④: 현재분사, ③, ⑤: 동명사

19 ⓐ: King Minos, ⓑ와 ⓒ: Daedalus, ⓓ와 ⓔ: Icarus 를 가리킨다.

20 Matisse와 Chagall은 'Icarus에 관한 그리스 신화'라는 '같은 주제'의 다른 그림들을 그렸는데, Icarus는 아버지의 '경고'를 잊었기 때문에 바다로 떨어져서 죽었다.

21 higher and higher(비교급＋and＋비교급): 점점 더 ~하 게

Life in Space

시험대비 실력평가　　　　　　　　p.116

01 secret　　02 ①　　03 ④　　04 ⑤
05 are covered with　　06 ③　　07 recently
08 ④

01 한 사람이나 몇 사람만 알고 다른 사람에게는 말하지 말아야 하는 정보: secret(비밀)

02 Jonny가 우유 용기를 열고는 흔들었다. 우유가 공기 중으로 떠서 공 모양이 되었다.

03 손을 이용하여 무언가를 아래로 옮기다: pull down(아래로 끌어내리다)

04 물이나 다른 액체로 덮여 있거나 가득 차 있는: wet(젖은)

05 be covered with: ~로 덮여 있다

06 동사로 '삼키다'라는 의미와 명사로 '제비'의 뜻을 가지고 있는 swallow가 적절하다. 두 번째 문장은 '제비 한 마리가 왔다고 해서 여름이 온 것은 아니다.'라는 뜻으로 작은 조짐 하나를 너무 확대 해석하지 말라는 의미이다.

07 유의어 관계이다. 놀라운 = 최근에

08 • 그들은 서로(each other)를 쳐다보고 웃었다. • Rada 와 Jonny는 부드러운 초록색의 잔디 위에 누워서(lay down) 언덕 아래로 굴러갔다.

서술형 시험대비　　　　　　　　p.117

01 (1) pulls　(2) covered　(3) exciting　(4) curious
02 (1) shaking　(2) rolling down　(3) landing
03 (1) (f)orm　(2) (l)and
04 (1) were born　(2) surprise
　(3) don't have to, space suit, everywhere
05 (1) air: 공기　(2) secret: 비밀　(3) space suit: 우주복

01 (1) 또한 그곳에서는 지구가 끌어당기고 있기 때문에 뛰어오르는 것이 어렵지. (2) 언덕들은 초록색의 잔디로 덮여 있지. (3) 그들이 보고, 그리고 하게 될 새로운 모든 것들에 대해서 생각하는 것은 흥미로웠다. (4) 나는 우주 마라톤에 대해 정말 궁금하다.

02 be동사와 함께 현재진행형(be+동사-ing) 형태를 사용한다.

03 (1) form: 양식; 형성하다, 만들다 (2) land: 육지; 착륙하다

04 (1) be born: 태어나다 (2) in surprise: 놀라서 (3) space suit: 우주복

---

05 (1) 당신이 숨을 쉬는 당신 주위에 있는 기체 (2) 한 사람 또는 몇몇 사람 들에 의해서만 알려진, 그리고 다른 사람들에게 말해져서는 안 되는 정보 (3) 우주비행사들이 우주에서 입는 특별한 옷

교과서 Conversation

핵심 Check　　　　　　　　p.118~119

1 ③　2 Have, heard about　3 ⑤　4 ①, ②, ⑤

교과서 대화문 익히기

Check(√) True or False　　　　　　　　p.120

1 T　2 T　3 F　4 T

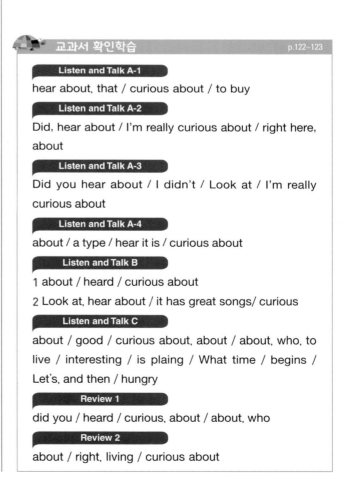

교과서 확인학습　　　　　　　　p.122~123

Listen and Talk A-1
hear about, that / curious about / to buy

Listen and Talk A-2
Did, hear about / I'm really curious about / right here, about

Listen and Talk A-3
Did you hear about / I didn't / Look at / I'm really curious about

Listen and Talk A-4
about / a type / hear it is / curious about

Listen and Talk B
1 about / heard / curious about
2 Look at, hear about / it has great songs/ curious

Listen and Talk C
about / good / curious about, about / about, who, to live / interesting / is plaing / What time / begins / Let's, and then / hungry

Review 1
did you / heard / curious, about / about, who

Review 2
about / right, living / curious about

01 curious about   02 ④   03 ①, ③

04 hear about

01 궁금증을 표현하거나 보다 많은 정보를 알고 싶을 때 사용하는 표현으로 be curious about을 쓴다.

02 B의 No, I didn't.와 어울리는 질문은 ④번이 적절하다. ④번은 새로운 정보를 알고 있는지 물어 보는 말이다.

03 새로운 정보에 대하여 궁금증을 표현하는 것으로 'I want to know ~. I'd like to know ~, I'm curious about ~' 등을 사용할 수 있다.

04 '~에 대해서 들어 봤니?'라는 표현으로 'Did you hear about ~?'을 사용한다.

시험대비 실력평가   p.125~126

01 ④   02 ④, ⑤   03 ⑤   04 ②

05 here it is   06 ④

07 It's about a father who saves his son.   08 ①

09 ③   10 ⑤   11 ②

12 (c)urious

01 G가 No, I didn't.로 과거시제로 답하고 있기 때문에 과거 시제 의문문이 적절하다. 그리고 G의 마지막 말에 I want to buy it.이라고 관심을 가지고 있다는 것을 알 수 있으므로 ⑤는 적절하지 않다.

02 새로운 정보에 대해 궁금증을 나타내는 표현이 적절하다.

03 (D) 우주 마라톤에 대해 들어 봤니?'에 대한 답으로 (C) 부정의 답이 오고 → (B) 우주 마라톤에 대한 설명과 비디오를 보라는 말에 → (A) 동의의 답과 함께 궁금증을 나타내는 표현이 적절하다.

04 '~에 관해 듣다'는 hear about, '~이 궁금하다'는 be curious about을 사용한다.

06 ④ 새로운 뮤지컬에 대해 들어본 적이 없다고 답하고 나서 좋은 노래들이 나온다고 들었다고 말하는 것은 어색하다.

07 '~에 관한 것이다'는 be about이고, a father를 수식하는 관계대명사절을 이용한다. 선행사가 단수 명사 a father이므로 save는 단수 형태 saves로 쓴다.

08 Did you hear about ~?은 상대방이 어떤 정보를 알고 있는지 묻는 표현이다.

09 선행사가 단수 명사 a man이므로 주격 관계대명사 뒤의 동사도 단수인 is가 적절하다.

10 영화를 본 후에 그들이 무엇을 할 것인지는 대화에서 언급되어 있지 않다.

11 '그건 일종의 아이스크림이야'라고 말하고 있으므로 알고 있다는 것을 알 수 있다.

12 어떤 것을 알고 싶거나 세상에 대해 배우고 싶어 하는: 궁금한, 호기심 많은

서술형 시험대비   p.127

01 Did you hear about the new book, Living in a Foreign Country?

02 I'm really curious about this book.

03 (A) Did you hear about the new running shoes, Speed?

    (B) What about them?

    (C) I'm curious about them.

04 about a father who[that] saves his son

05 That sounds interesting.

01 '~에 관해 들어 봤니?'라는 표현은 Did you hear about ~?으로 시작한다. 그리고 the new book과 Living in a Foreign Country는 동격 관계로 동격의 comma를 사용한다.

02 형용사 curious는 be curious about 형태로 '~에 관해 궁금해 하다'는 의미다.

04 '~에 관한 것이다'는 be about을 사용하고, 사람을 선행사로 하는 관계대명사 who나 that을 사용한다. 주격 관계대명사의 동사는 단수 동사인 saves를 쓴다.

05 (B) 새로운 영화에 대해 알고 있는지 묻고 → (F) 알지 못한다는 대답을 하고 → (A) 정말 좋다고 들었다고 이야기 해주고 → (C) 정말로 궁금해진다는 말로 관심을 표현하고 무엇에 관한 내용인지 묻는다. → (D) 영화 내용을 말해준다 → (E) 마지막으로 그거 재미있겠다는 문장이 오는 것이 자연스 럽다.

교과서

Grammar

핵심 Check   p.128~129

1 (1) has studied   (2) heard   (3) Have, met

2 (1) is it important to   (2) It, to

    (3) for me to play

시험대비 기본평가   p.130

01 ①   02 ③

03 (1) return → returned

    (2) has eaten → ate

    (3) do you have been → have you been

    (4) for → since

    (5) That → It

    (6) reads → to read

01 it을 가주어로 하고 to부정사를 진주어로 쓸 수 있는 ①번이 적절하다.

02 ③ 'have gone to'는 '~에 가고 없다'는 결과를 나타내는 것으로 3인칭만 주어로 쓸 수 있다. I have been to Hong Kong.으로 고쳐야 한다.

03 (1) 현재완료는 'have[has]+과거분사'의 형태이다. (2) 현재완료는 과거를 나타내는 어구와 함께 쓸 수 없다. (3) 현재완료의 의문문은 have 동사를 주어 앞으로 보낸다. (4) 현재완료에서 'since+시간 명사', 'for+기간 명사'를 쓴다. (5) 가주어로는 That이 아니라 It을 쓴다. (6) 진주어로 to부정사가 적절하다.

시험대비 실력평가   p.131~133

01 ④	02 ⑤	03 ③	04 ①
05 ③	06 (1) has (2) haven't (3) gone		
(4) went (5) to sleep (6) for			07 ④
08 ②	09 ①	10 It is necessary to	

take a break regularly.   **11** ⑤   **12** ②

13 ①

14 (1) It is difficult for me to guess the ending of story.

(2) It is boring to read a science book.

(3) It is important to read for an hour every day.

(4) I worked in the hospital snack bar then.

(5) Jim has had a cat for three years.

(6) Garry has gone to New York on business and he stays there now.

15 (1) Josh has lost his smartphone.

(2) Sophia has lived in Georgia for five years.

16 ⑤   **17** ③   **18** ②, ④

01 ④ 언제 영화를 봤는지 묻는 문장으로 특정한 과거의 한 시점을 묻는 것이므로 현재완료가 아니라 과거시제가 되어야 한다. when은 현재완료와 쓰이지 않는다.

02 '가주어(It) ~ 진주어(to부정사) …' 구문이 적절하다. ②번은 It is so kind of you to lend me the book.이 적절하다.

03 현재완료의 의문문은 'Have[Has]+주어+과거분사 ~?'이다. It이 나와 있으므로 It을 가주어로 하고 빈칸에는 진주어로 이용할 수 있는 to부정사가 나와야 한다. 그러므로 ③번이 적절하다.

04 가주어로 It이 적절하다.

05 부정문이므로 yet이 적절하다.

06 (1) 주어가 3인칭 단수이므로 has가 적절하다. (2) 현재완료의 부정문은 'have[has]+not[never]+과거분사'로 나타낸다. (3) have[has] gone to는 '~에 가고 없다'는 결과를 나타낸다. (4) 현재완료는 과거를 나타내는 어구와 함께 쓸 수 없다. (5) 진주어로 to부정사가 적절하다. (6) to부정사의 의미상 주어는 to부정사

바로 앞에 'for+명사의 목적격'의 형태로 쓴다.

07 ① Angie bought a new smartphone yesterday. ② Has she told you the good news yet? ③ I have been to England once. ⑤ I've been learning English for ten years.

08 ②번은 인칭대명사로 '그것'이라고 해석 가능하지만 나머지는 모두 가주어로 쓰인 it이다.

09 현재완료형의 질문에 대한 답은 have[has]를 이용하여 답한다.

10 '규칙적으로 휴식을 취하는 것(to take a break regularly)'을 진주어로 하고 가주어 It을 이용하여 'It ~ to …' 형식으로 쓴다.

11 현재완료의 결과적 용법(…해서 (그 결과) 지금 ~하다)을 이용하여 과거에 집으로 가서 지금 여기에 없다는 결과를 나타내도록 한다.

12 가주어로 it을 쓰고 진주어로 to부정사를 쓰는 것이 적절하다.

13 ①과 <보기>는 계속 용법이다. ②, ⑤ 결과 용법 ③ 경험 용법 ④ 완료 용법

14 (1) 진주어로 to guess를 쓴다. (2) 가주어로는 This가 아니라 It을 쓴다. (3) 진주어로 to부정사를 쓴다. (4) 현재완료 는 과거를 나타내는 어구와 함께 쓸 수 없다. then은 '그때, 그 당시'라는 뜻으로 과거를 나타내는 말이다. (5) 현재완료 에서 'since+시간 명사', 'for+기간 명사' (6) have[has] been to는 '~에 가 본 적이 있다'는 경험을 나타내고, have[has] gone to는 '~에 가고 없다'는 결과를 나타내므로 have gone to로 고쳐야 한다.

15 (1) 스마트폰을 잃어버려서 지금 가지고 있지 않으므로 현재완료의 '결과' 용법으로 나타낸다. (2) 5년 전에 살기 시작해서 아직도 살고 있으므로 현재완료의 '계속' 용법으로 나타 낸다.

16 현재완료는 과거를 나타내는 어구와 함께 쓸 수 없으며, 현재완료 에서는 'since+시간 명사', 'for+기간 명사'를 쓴다.

17 '가주어(It) ~ 진주어(to부정사: to hang out with my friends after finals) …' 구문으로 쓴 ③번이 적절하다.

18 문장에 쓰인 형용사가 사람의 성향, 성격을 나타내는 말일 때는 to부정사의 의미상의 주어로 'of+목적격'을 쓴다. 현재완료는 과거의 특정 시점을 나타내는 의문사 when과는 함께 쓰이지 않는다.

서술형 시험대비   p.134~135

01 (1) Kelly has lived in LA since she was 10 years old.

(2) The government has become more interested in education.

(3) He has heard about the rumor.

(4) It is wonderful to travel to other countries.

(5) Is it possible for him to get tickets for the game?

02 (1) To drive at night is dangerous.

(2) It is dangerous to drive at night.

(1) To steal things is wrong.

(2) It's wrong to steal things.

03 (1) |모범답안| I have eaten nacho several times.

I have never eaten nacho.

(2) |모범답안| I have never been to Jeju-do before.

I have been to Jeju-do two times.

04 (1) Sonya has visited New York three times.

(2) I have eaten dinner.

05 (1) It was exciting to think about all the new things.

(2) It was great to swim in the cool blue sea.

(3) It's good to eat a lot of vegetables.

(4) It is true that the pen is mightier than the sword.

06 (1) I have never seen a sunrise.

(2) He has taught English for 20 years.

(3) Is it safe to drink this water?

(4) It's lucky for me to play soccer on the team.

(5) It is important to brush your teeth every day.

07 (1) When did you hear from Susan?

(2) Mr. Brown has lived in Jeju-do since 2010.

(3) Have you been to Canada before?

(4) To use a ticket machine in the theater is easy.

또는 It is easy to use a ticket machine in the theater.

(5) It's important for her to understand him.

08 They haven't finished their project yet. /
Have they finished their project yet?

09 (1) has rained since[has been raining since]

(2) has gone

01 (1)~(3) 현재완료를 이용하여 배열한다. (4)~(5) '가주어(it) ~ 진주어(to부정사) …' 구문을 이용한다. (5)번에서 to부정사의 의미상의 주어로 for him을 써야 하는 것에 주의한다.

02 to부정사가 문장의 주어로 쓰일 때 주어 자리에 가주어 It을 두고 to부정사 부분(진주어)을 문장 뒤로 보낸다.

03 현재완료의 '경험' 용법을 이용하여 쓴다.

04 (1) 현재완료의 '경험' 용법을 이용한다. (2) 현재완료의 '결과' 용법을 이용한다.

05 (1)~(3) 문장의 주어로 쓰인 to부정사를 뒤로 보내고 대신 주어 자리에 가주어 it을 쓴다. (4) 주어로 쓰인 that절의 경우에도 긴 that절을 뒤로 보내고 주어 자리에 가주어 it을 쓴다.

06 (1) 현재완료의 '경험' 용법을 이용한다. (2) 현재완료의 '계속' 용법을 이용한다. (3)~(5) '가주어(It) ~ 진주어(to부정사) …' 구문을 이용한다. (4) 내가 축구를 하는 것이므로 의미상의 주어 for me를 써 주어야 한다.

07 (1) 현재완료는 과거의 특정 시점을 나타내는 어구와 함께 쓸 수 없다. (2) 현재완료에서 'since+시간 명사', 'for+기간 명사' (3) have[has] been to는 '~에 가 본 적이 있다'는 경험을 나타

내고, have[has] gone to는 '~에 가고 없 다'는 결과를 나타내므로 3인칭만 주어가 될 수 있다. 주어 가 you이므로 been to 로 고쳐야 한다. (4) to부정사를 주 어로 하거나 전체 문장을 '가주어(It) ~ 진주어(to부정사) …' 구문으로 고쳐 쓴다. (5) for her가 to understand의 의 미상의 주어가 되도록 고쳐야 한다.

08 현재완료의 부정문은 'have[has]+not[never]+과거분사' 로, 의문문은 'Have[Has]+주어+과거분사 ~?'로 나타낸다. already는 부정문이나 의문문에서 yet이 되어야 함에 주의한다.

09 (1) 현재완료의 '계속' 용법을 이용한다. (2) 현재완료의 '결과' 용법을 이용한다.

Reading

확인문제	p.136

1 T 2 T 3 F 4 T

확인문제	p.137

1 T 2 F 3 F 4 T

교과서 확인학습 A
p.138~139

01 Best   02 far out in space

03 lived there with   04 worked on

05 Only, were born   06 going back to

07 in surprise   08 What's it like   09 is different

10 For example   11 I've never seen

12 is always black

13 don't have to, there is air   14 pulls you down

15 What else   16 are covered with

17 roll down   18 have you ever rolled down

19 amazing   20 opened, shook

21 floated, formed   22 swallowed

23 get wet   24 Later that night

25 exciting, all the new things   26 one new thing

27 all night   28 their secret   29 got on

30 It's going to be   31 so excited

32 finally   33 to walk

34 pulling you down

35 couldn't float anymore

36 the first new thing   37 What's

38 is singing   39 I've never heard

40 I've never felt 41 These   42 the nearest

43 each other   44 lay down, rolled down

45 their secret 46 best new thing
47 up to the top

1 The Best New Thing

2 Rada lived on a little world, far out in space.

3 She lived there with her father, mother, and brother Jonny.

4 Rada's father and other people worked on spaceships

5 Only Rada and Jonny were children, and they were born in space.

6 One day, Dad told Rada and Jonny, "We're going back to Earth tomorrow."

7 Rada and Jonny looked at Dad in surprise and floated towards him.

8 Rada asked Dad, "What's it like on Earth?"

9 "Everything is different there.

10 For example, the sky is blue," answered Dad.

11 "I've never seen a blue sky," said Jonny.

12 "The sky is always black here," said Rada.

13 "You don't have to wear your big heavy space suits because there is air everywhere.

14 It's also hard to jump there because Earth pulls you down," said Dad.

15 "What else?" asked Rada.

16 "There are hills, and they are covered with soft green grass.

17 You can roll down the hills," answered Mom.

18 "Dad, have you ever rolled down a hill?" asked Rada.

19 "Yes, it's really amazing!" answered Dad.

20 Jonny was thirsty, so he opened a milk container and shook it.

21 The milk floated in the air and formed balls.

22 Jonny swallowed the balls.

23 "Jonny, if you drink milk that way on Earth, you'll get wet," said Mom.

24 Later that night, Rada and Jonny talked a long time about Earth.

25 It was exciting to think about all the new things they were going to see and do.

26 There was one new thing Rada and Jonny really wanted to do.

27 They thought about it all night and didn't tell Mom and Dad about it.

28 It was their secret.

29 The next day, Rada's family got on a spaceship.

30 "It's going to be a long trip," said Mom.

31 That's alright. I'm so excited!" said Rada.

32 The spaceship finally landed.

33 "Dad, it's difficult to walk on Earth," said Rada.

34 "I know. Earth is pulling you down," said Dad.

35 Rada and Jonny couldn't float anymore.

36 That was the first new thing.

37 "What's that sound?" asked Rada.

38 "A bird is singing," said Mom.

39 "I've never heard a bird sing," said Rada.

40 "And I've never felt the wind," said Jonny.

41 These were all new things.

42 Rada and Jonny ran up the nearest hill.

43 At the top, they looked at each other and laughed.

44 Then they lay down on the soft green grass and rolled down the hill.

45 That was their secret!

46 "This is the best new thing of all!" shouted Rada and Jonny.

47 And they ran up to the top of the hill again.

01 ③   02 ②, ⑤   03 ⑤   04 ③
05 shook   06 ②   07 if you drink milk that way on Earth, you'll get wet 08 ②
09 (A) to think about all the new things they were going to see and do
  (B) one new thing Rada and Jonny really wanted to do
  (C) one new thing Rada and Jonny really wanted to do
10 (A) exciting (B) night (C) on   11 ⑤
12 (A) landed (B) pulling (C) new
13 lie → lay   14 ④   15 ③   16 ②
17 (A) shake (B) balls (C) swallow   18 ④
19 Rada and Jonny couldn't float anymore
20 familiar → new   21 they lay down on the soft green grass and rolled down the hill.
22 ⓐ ridden ⓑ ride ⓒ rode
23 오전: 공원에서 자전거를 탔다.
  오후: 해변으로 가서 수영을 했다.
  밤: 지구에서 사는 것에 대해 Rada와 Jonny가 이야기를 했다.
24 Rada thought it was wonderful to live on Earth and Jonny thought it was great to be on Earth.

25 ②	26 do them → do	27 one
new thing they really wanted to do		28 ②
29 to sing → sing 또는 singing		30 ⑤

01 ⓐ in space: 우주에서, ⓑ on Earth: 지구(상)에서

02 (A)와 ②, ⑤번: 막연한 상황을 나타내는 비인칭 주어, As it happened: 공교롭게도, ① 가목적어, ③ It is[was] ... that의 구문으로 문장의 어떤 부분을 강조할 때 씀, ④ 가주어

03 위 글은 '공상 과학 소설(SF)'이다. ① 독후감, ② (신문, 잡지의) 글, 기사, ③ 전기, ④ 수필

04 ③ 'space'를 'Earth'로 고치는 것이 적절하다.

05 opened와 병렬구문을 이루도록 shook이라고 쓰는 것이 적절하다.

06 ⓑ와 ②, ⑤: 경험 용법, ① 결과 용법 ③ 계속 용법 ④ 완료 용법

07 조건의 부사절에서는 현재시제가 미래를 대신하므로, 'if you drink'라고 하는 것이 적절하다.

08 지구에서는 점프하는 것이 '어렵다'고 했다.

09 ⓐ It은 가주어로서 진주어인 to think about all the new things they were going to see and do를 대신 한다. ⓑ와 ⓒ: Rada와 Jonny가 정말로 하고 싶었던 한 가지 새로운 것을 가리킨다.

10 (A) 모든 새로운 것들을 생각하는 것이 '흥미로웠던' 것이므로 exciting이 적절하다. (감정을 나타내는 동사는 감정을 유발할 때 현재분사를 쓰는 것이 적절하다.) (B) all+단수 명사는 그 기간 내내 어떤 일이 계속 됨을 나타내므로 night가 적절하다. (C) 우주선에 '오르는' 것이므로 on이 적절하다. get on: 타다, 오르다, get off: 내리다

11 ⑤ (특히 좋거나 신나는 일을) 기대하는, Rada와 Jonny는 지구 여행을 기대하고 있다. ① 속상한, ② 혼란스러워 하는, ③ 걱정[우려]하는, ④ 실망한

12 (A) 우주선이 마침내 '착륙했다'고 해야 하므로 landed가 적절하다. take off: 이륙하다, (B) 지구가 너를 '끌어당기고' 있다고 해야 하므로 pulling이 적절하다. push: 밀다, (C) 지구에서 겪 는 모든 새로운 것들에 대해 이야기하고 있으므로 new를 써서 최고의 '새로운 것'이라고 하는 것이 적절하다. familiar: 친숙한

13 과거시제로 써야 하므로 lay로 고치는 것이 적절하다. lie-lay-lain: 눕다

14 이 글은 지구에서 겪는 모든 새로운 것들에 대해 이야기하는 글이므로, 제목으로는 '그들이 지구에서 겪은 새로운 것들'이 적절하다.

15 Rada는 새가 노래하는 것을 들어 본 적이 '없다'.

16 주어진 문장의 else에 주목한다. ②번 앞 문장에서 우주 와 지구의 다른 점을 설명한 것 외에 "그 밖에 또 뭐가 있어요?"라고 묻는 것이므로 ②번이 적절하다.

17 우주에서는 지구에서 사람들이 하는 방식으로 우유를 마실 수

없다. 먼저, 당신은 우유 용기를 열어 그것을 '흔든다'. 그 다음, 우유가 공기 중으로 떠서 '방울'을 형성한다. 마지막으로 그 우유 방울을 '삼킨다.'

18 아빠가 언제 언덕을 굴러 내려갔는지는 대답할 수 없다. ① Because there is air everywhere. ② Because Earth pulls you down. ③ You can roll down the hills. ⑤ He swallowed the balls of milk.

19 'Rada와 Jonny가 더 이상 떠다닐 수 없었던 것'이 첫 번째 새로운 것이었다.

20 These가 앞에서 말한 새로운 것들을 받은 것이기 때문에, 이러한 것들이 모두 '새로운' 것들이었다라고 고치는 것이 적절하다. familiar: 익숙한

21 'lie'의 과거 'lay'를 사용하여 영작하는 것이 적절하다.

22 ⓐ 현재완료 시제이므로 과거분사로 쓰는 것이 적절하다. ⓑ Let's 다음에 동사원형으로 쓰는 것이 적절하다. ⓒ 과거에 일어난 일이므로 과거시제로 쓰는 것이 적절하다.

23 오전에는 자전거를 탔고, 오후에는 수영을 했고, 밤에는 지구에서 사는 것에 대해 Rada와 Jonny가 이야기를 했다.

24 Rada와 Jonny는 지구에서 사는 것이 '멋있다'고 생각했다.

25 ⓐ와 ②, ④: 가주어, ① 비인칭주어, ③ 인칭대명사, 그것(앞에 이미 언급되었거나 현재 이야기되고 있는 사물·동물을 가리킴), ⑤ 가목적어

26 all the new things와 they 사이에 see and do의 목적어에 해당하는 목적격 관계대명사 which/that이 생략되어 있는데, 목적어 them을 또 쓰는 것은 옳지 않다.

27 Rada와 Jonny의 비밀은 '그들이 정말로 하고 싶었던 한 가지 새로운 것'이다.

28 이 글은 Rada와 Jonny가 지구에서 겪는 새로운 것들에 대해 이야기하는 글이다.

29 hear는 지각동사로서 'hear+목적어+동사원형/-ing'의 형태로 쓰인다.

30 Rada와 Jonny가 언덕 꼭대기로 몇 번 뛰어올라갈지는 대답할 수 없다. ① Because Earth is pulling you down. ② No. ③ No. ④ They lay down on the soft green grass and rolled down the hill.

🦉 서술형 시험대비
p.148~149

01 (A) children (B) who[that]

02 Rada and Jonny looked at Dad in surprise and floated towards him.

03 color

04 (A) must(또는 have to) (B) hard(또는 difficult)
   (C) balls

05 I have

06 will drink → drink

07 never

08 no more

09 lay down, rolled down

10 (A) other   (B) What   (C) different

11 ran → floated

12 ⓑ on Earth   ⓒ in space

01 우주에는 그곳에서 태어난 Rada와 Jonny를 제외하고는 '아이들'이 없었다. (B)에는 주격 관계대명사 who[that]를 쓰는 것이 적절하다.

02 'in'을 보충하면 된다.

03 지구의 하늘은 파란색이고, 우주의 하늘은 항상 검은색이라고 했으므로 하늘의 '색깔'이 서로 다르다.

04 (A) 우주에서는 크고 무거운 우주복을 입을 '필요가 있다.' have to = must (B) 지구에서는 점프하는 것이 '어렵다.' (C) 우주에서는 '우유 '방울'을 삼킨다.

05 현재완료로 물었기 때문에 Yes, I 'do'가 아니라 Yes, I 'have'로 답하는 것이 적절하다.

06 조건의 부사절에서는 현재시제가 미래를 대신하므로, 'if you drink'라고 하는 것이 적절하다.

07 (A) 이번이 새가 노래하는 것을 처음 들어 본 때이다. = 나는 새가 노래하는 것을 들어 본 적이 없다. (B) 이번이 내가 바람을 처음 느껴 본 때이다. = 나는 바람을 느껴 본 적이 없다.

08 not ~ anymore = no more: 더 이상 … 아닌[하지 않는], no longer도 가능하다.

09 부드러운 초록 잔디에 '누워서' 언덕 '아래로 굴러 내려간' 것이 그들의 비밀이었다.

10 (A) 뒤에 복수명사가 나오므로 other가 적절하다. another+단수 명사, (B) is like의 목적어가 와야 하므로 What이 적절하다. (C) 바로 뒤에 하늘의 색이 다른 예가 나오고 있으므로, 그곳에선 모든 것이 '다르다'고 하는 것이 적절하다. similar: 비슷한, 유사한

11 우주에서 일어나고 있는 일이므로, 그에게 '달려서' 가는 것이 아니라 '둥둥 떠서 갔다'로 고치는 것이 적절하다.

12 ⓑ는 '지구(상)에서', ⓒ는 '우주에서'를 가리킨다.

영역별 핵심문제   p.151~155

01 land   02 ④   03 ③   04 ①

05 space   06 ⑤   07 ④   08 ②

09 It's about a man who is trying to live on the moon.

10 ①   11 (1) Did you hear about (2) I'm really curious about it. (3) What's it about?   12 ②

13 ②   14 ①   15 ⑤

16 (1) for Tony to hand in his report by tomorrow

(2) for you to be careful when you cross the street

17 ③   18 ④   19 ⑤   20 ④

---

21 ③, ⑤   22 What's it like on Earth?

23 (A) because   (B) What   (C) if   24 ⑤

25 ①, ③, ④   26 There was one new thing which(또는 that) Rada and Jonny really wanted to do.

27 It's going to be a long trip   28 ①

29 has ever heard → has never heard

has ever felt → has never felt

30 best new thing

01 반의어 관계이다. 신난 : 지루한 = 이륙하다 : 착륙하다

02 모든 곳에 공기가 있기 때문에 크고 무거운 우주복을 입을 필요가 없다(don't have[need] to). 또한 그곳에서는 지구가 너희를 끌어당기고 있기(pulls you down) 때문에 뛰어 오르는 것이 어렵다. pull down은 이어 동사(동사+부사)로 대명사 you는 동사와 부사 사이에 위치한다.

03 엄마의 몸에서 나오다: 태어나다(be born)

04 공중에서 아래로 이동한 후 땅이나 다른 표면에 도착하다

05 • 저 책상은 너무 많은 공간을 차지한다. • 이 주차장에는 90대의 주차 공간이 있다. • 6월 18일, 중국은 첫 여성우주 비행사를 우주로 보냈다.

06 lie down은 '눕다'라는 뜻이다

07 (C) 새로운 우주 음식에 대해 들어 봤는지 묻고 → (B) 긍정의 답과 함께 우주 음식이 일종의 아이스크림이라고 말한다. → (A) 그 말에 동의하고 그 음식을 가리키며 맛있어 보인다고 말한다. → (D) 마지막으로 맛이 궁금하다고 말한다.

08 영화 내용을 설명하는 말 앞인 ②가 적절하다.

09 영화 'Life on the Moon'은 무엇에 관한 것인가?

10 ① 새 영화가 정말로 좋다는 말을 들은 사람은 Subin이 아니라 B다.

12 ⓑ의 'right'은 부사로 '바로'의 의미이다.

13 ②에는 사람의 성격이나 성질을 나타내는 형용사(foolish)가 왔으므로 의미상의 주어 앞에 of가 들어가야 한다. 나머지는 모두 for가 들어간다.

14 since(~한 이래로)는 보통 현재완료와 함께 많이 쓰인다. 이때 since절에는 과거 시제가 많이 쓰인다.

15 ⑤번은 '계속' 용법이지만 나머지는 '경험' 용법이다.

16 '~해야 한다'는 의미를 가주어 it을 이용하여 '~할 필요가 있다'라고 쓰려면 진주어로 to부정사를 이용한다. 이때 의미상의 주어를 빠뜨리지 않도록 주의한다.

17 ⓐ Has Daniel found → Did Daniel find ⓒ gone → been ⓔ since → for ⓕ follows → to follow ⓖ That → It

18 ④번은 to부정사의 부사적 용법이지만 나머지는 모두 진주어로 쓰인 명사적 용법으로 쓰였다.

19 ⑤ 현재완료는 과거를 나타내는 어구와 함께 쓸 수 없다.

20 앞의 내용의 예가 나오고 있으므로 For example이 가장 적절하

다. ① 그러나, ② 그러므로, ③ 게다가, ⑤ 즉

21 ⓐ와 ③, ⑤번: 미래를 나타내는 부사(구)와 함께 쓰여 현재진 행되는 의미가 아니라 가까운 미래를 나타낸다. 나머지는 다 현재 진행되는 의미를 나타낸다.

22 be like: ~와 같다

23 (A) 크고 무거운 우주복을 입을 필요가 없는 이유를 말해야 하므로 because가 적절하다. though: 비록 ~이지만(양보), (B) 그 밖에 또 '뭐가' 있냐고 물어야 하므로 What이 적절하다. (C) '만약' 그런 식으로라고 해야 하므로 if가 적절하다. unless = if ~ not

24 Jonny는 우유 용기를 열어 흔들었을 때 우유가 공기 중으로 떠서 형성된 '우유 방울을 삼켰다.'

25 ⓐ와 ②, ⑤: 명사적 용법, ①, ④ 부사적 용법, ③ 형용사적 용법

26 'ne new thing과 Rada and Jonny 사이에 do의 목적어에 해당하는 목적격 관계대명사 which/that이 생략되어 있다.

27 "긴 여행이 될 거야."라는 엄마의 말을 가리킨다.

28 주어진 문장의 These에 주목한다. ①번 앞 문장의 내용들을 받고 있으므로 ①번이 적절하다.

29 Rada는 새가 노래하는 것을 들어 본 적이 '없고', Jonny는 바람을 느껴 본 적이 '없다.'

30 Rada와 Jonny에게 모든 것들 중에서 '최고의 새로운 것'은 부드러운 초록 잔디에 누워서 언덕 아래로 굴러 내려간 것이었다.

단원별 예상문제
p.156~159

01 smooth   02 ③   03 I'm interested in it.
04 ③   05 ⑤   06 hear about, that, into
07 ②   08 who is trying to live on the moon
09 have you heard about the new movie
10 I'm really curious about the movie.   11 ③
12 (1) He has slept for thirty minutes.
   (2) The celebrity has just arrived at the airport.
   (3) Sue has never been to France before.
   (4) I have forgotten the new student's name.
   (5) It is important to share various opinions.
   (6) It is nice of you to remember my birthday.
13 ⑤   14 ②   15 ⑤   16 ③
17 ②   18 ③   19 ②, ⑤
20 ⓒ the hills   ⓓ to roll[rolling] down the hills
   ⓔ the milk container
21 ④   22 ①, ③   23 ④   24 ②
25 (1) Rada와 Jonny가 더 이상 떠다닐 수 없었던 것.
   (2) Rada가 새가 노래하는 것을 들어 본 것.
   (3) Jonny가 바람을 느껴 본 것.

01 반의어 관계이다. 똑똑한 : 어리석은 = 거친 : 부드러운

02 누군가나 어떤 것의 방향으로 또는 더 가까이: '~을 향해'

03 새로운 정보에 관심이 있다는 표현으로 be curious about, be

04 전치사 about 뒤에 있는 부정사 to live를 동명사 living으로 바꾸는 것이 적절하다.

05 get on은 '~을 타다, 탑승하다'라는 의미로 '우주선에 올랐다'가 맞다.

06 'hear about ~'은 '~에 관해 듣다'는 뜻이고, 선행사에 the first(서수)가 있을 때는 보통 관계대명사 that을 사용하는 것이 적절하다.

07 G의 첫 번째 말에 우주선에 대해 궁금하다고 했으므로 빈칸에는 긍정의 대답이 오는 것이 적절하다. ⑤번은 대화와 관련이 없는 말이다.

08 관계대명사 who 뒤에 동사 is를 사용하고 be동사 뒤에 현재분사 trying이 오는 것이 적절하다. 그 다음 'trying to+ 동사원형' 형태가 온다.

09 현재완료를 사용해 'Have you heard about ~?'이라고 들어 본 적이 있는지 물을 수 있다.

10 부사 really는 be동사 뒤에 오고 be curious about을 사용하여 문장을 완성한다.

11 현재완료에서 'since+시간 명사', 'for+기간 명사'

12 (1) 현재완료의 '계속' 용법을 이용한다. (2) 현재완료의 '완료' 용법을 이용한다. (3) 'have[has] been to'는 '~에 가본 적이 있다'는 경험을 나타낸다. (4) 현재완료의 '결과' 용법을 이용한다. (5) '가주어(it) ~ 진주어(to부정사) …' 구문을 이용한다. (6) 문장에 쓰인 형용사가 사람의 성향, 성격을 나타내는 말일 때는 to부정사의 의미상의 주어로 'of+목적격'을 쓴다.

13 ① It's great to be here. ② It's fun to play with friends. ③ It is boring to fish in the lake. ④ It's exciting for us to have you here

14 ② Have you been to London before?

15 가주어 it을 이용하여 바꿔 쓰는 것으로 원래 문장의 to부정사를 진주어로 쓴다.

16 ⓒ in

17 (A)와 ②번: (외관·내용 등이) …을 닮아, 유사하여; …일 것 같아, …과 다름없이(전치사), be like: ~와 같다, ①, ③, ⑤: ~을 좋아하다(동사), ④ [외관·형태·성질 등이] 같은 (same) (형용사)

18 '그곳에는 모든 곳에 공기가 있기 때문에' 크고 무거운 우주복을 입을 필요가 없다고 하는 것이 적절하다.

19 It은 가주어로서 진주어인 to jump there를 대신한 것이므로 to jump there나 jumping there를 가주어 It 자리에 쓸 수 있고, 의미상의 주어인 for you를 써도 된다.

20 ⓒ 언덕들, ⓓ 언덕을 굴러 내려가는 것, ⓔ 우유 용기를 가리킨다.

21 Rada는 지구 여행을 기대하고 있으므로 "괜찮아요. 정말 신나요!"라고 하는 것이 적절하다. ② 감정을 나타내는 동사는 사람을 수식할 때 보통 과거분사를 써야 하므로 interested가 적절하다. ③ pleasant는 '상냥한'이라는 뜻일 때를 제외하고는 사

람을 주어로 해서 쓸 수 없다. pleased로 쓰는 것이 적절하다.

22 all the new things와 they 사이에 see and do의 목적어에 해당하는 목적격 관계대명사 which/that이 생략되어 있다.

23 Rada와 Jonny는 정말로 하고 싶었던 한 가지 새로운 것에 대해서 엄마와 아빠에게 말하지 않았다.

24 consequently: 그 결과, 따라서, finally와 나머지는 다 '마침내'

25 앞의 세 문장들의 내용을 가리킨다.

서술형 실전문제
p.160~161

01 (A) Did you hear about the new snack?
   (B) I'm curious about it.

02 You can choose a player who you like and play.

03 (1) for (2) before (3) since

04 (1) They are talking about the new movie.
   (2) They will eat[have] lunch.

05 (1) It was easy to answer his questions.
   (2) It is easy to cook camping food.
   (3) It is safe and comfortable to live in Seoul.
   (4) It was very wise of her to say so.

06 (1) has live, since (2) have read, three times
   (3) has taken

07 (A) don't have to (B) hard (C) amazing

08 pulls down you → pulls you down

09 (A) get wet (B) shake

---

02 조동사 can 뒤에 동사원형 choose를 쓰고 관계대명사절 'who you like'가 선행사인 목적어 'a player'를 꾸며주고 and 뒤에 play가 choose와 병렬구조로 문장을 완성한다.

03 (1), (3) 현재완료에서 'since+시간 명사', 'for+ 기간 명사'
   (2) ago는 현재완료와 함께 사용할 수 없으나 before는 사용할 수 있다.

04 (1) Subin과 Andy는 새 영화에 관해 이야기하고 있다. (2) 영화를 보기 전에 점심을 먹을 것이다.

05 (1) It을 가주어로 하고 to부정사를 진주어로 쓴다. (2) It을 가주어로 하고 진주어 to cook의 목적어로 camping food를 쓴다. (3) 전치사 in의 목적어로 Seoul을 쓴다. (4) to say의 주어가 she이므로 of her로 의미상의 주어를 나타내야 한다.

06 (1) 현재완료의 '계속' 용법을 이용한다. (2) 현재완료의 '경험' 용법을 이용한다. (3) 현재완료의 '결과' 용법을 이용한다.

07 (A) 그곳에는 모든 곳에 공기가 있기 때문에 크고 무거운 우주복을 입을 '필요가 없다'고 해야 하므로 don't have to가 적절하다. (B) 지구가 너희들을 끌어당기기 때문에 거기에서는 점프하는 것도 '어렵다'고 해야 하므로 hard가 적절하다. (C) 언덕을 굴러 내려가는 것이 '놀라운' 것이므로 amazing이 적절하다. (감정을 나타내는 동사는 감정을 일으킬 때 현재분사를 쓰는 것이 적

절하다.)

08 목적어가 인칭대명사일 때는 타동사와 부사 사이에 목적어를 쓰는 것이 적절하다.

09 지구에서 우유 용기를 열어 그것을 '흔들면' 우유가 용기에서 쏟아져 나와서 당신을 '젖게' 만들 것이기 때문이다.

창의사고력 서술형 문제
p.162

|모범답안|

01 (1) It is exciting to learn a new language.
   (2) It's necessary for me to see a doctor.
   (3) It is important to exercise regularly.
   (4) It's difficult to learn Chinese.
   (5) It's fun to go to the beach.

02 (A) ridden a bike (B) rode bikes
   (C) swum before (D) to swim (E) living on Earth

단원별 모의고사
p.163~166

01 ④   02 arrive / reach   03 ①
04 ④   05 ③   06 ⑤   07 ②
08 They are going to eat lunch.
09 about, who   10 (1) F (2) T 11 ⑤
12 ④   13 ②   14 ③
15 (1) Have you found → Did you find
   (2) played the piano since → have played the piano for
   (3) gone → been
   (4) Search → To search[Searching] 또는 Search information using the Internet is easy. → It is easy to search information using the Internet.
   (5) of → for
16 (1) He has known her since he was ten years old.
   (2) He hasn't finished his homework yet.
   (3) They have seen the movie four times.
   (4) She has gone to Paris.
   (5) It was helpful to visit this web site.
   (6) It is hard for a child to wash a big dog.
17 (A) different (B) blue 18 ①, ②, ④ 19 (e)lse
20 have you ever rolled down a hill?   21 ④

---

01 ④번은 'pull down'에 대한 설명이다. roll down은 'to move downward by turning over and over(반복해서 돌면서 아래로 내려오다)'가 적절하다.

02 반의어 관계이다. 다른 : 같은 = 도착하다 : 출발하다

03 '액체의 표면에 머무르고 가라앉지 않다'는 float '뜨다'가 적절하다.

04 '새 노래에 대해 들어 봤느냐'는 A의 물음에 '아니, 못 들어 봤다'

고 말하고는 새 노래에 대한 설명을 하는 건 자연스럽지 않다.

05 대화는 화성에 관한 책에 대한 이야기다.

06 G의 답으로 보아 영화의 내용을 묻는 말이 적절하다.

07 빈칸 다음의 말이 영화의 내용이 무엇인지 묻고 있으므로 그 영화에 관심이 있다는 것을 알 수 있다.

10 (1) 두 사람은 새로운 책에 대해 이야기 중이다. (2) 소년은 새 책에 대해 궁금해 하기 때문에 관심이 있다는 것을 알 수 있다.

11 B가 그 영화가 정말 궁금하다고 말하는 것으로 보아 G는 영화에 대해 좋은 평가를 내리고 있다고 추측할 수 있다.

12 (D)에서 새 책에 대한 정보를 알고 있는지 묻고, (A)에서 부정의 답이 오고 이어서 (C)에서 책에 관한 내용을 이야기해 주고 나서 (B)에서 이 책이 궁금하다고 말하는 것이 자연스럽다.

13 현재완료는 과거의 특정 시점을 나타내는 의문사 when과 함께 쓸 수 없다. When did you visit Italy?

14 주어진 문장과 ③번은 가주어로 쓰이고 있다. ①, ⑤ 비인칭 주어 ② It ~ that 강조구문 ④ 인칭대명사

15 (1) 현재완료는 과거를 나타내는 ~ ago와는 함께 쓰이지 않는다. (2) 오래전에 시작해서 아직도 즐기고 있다고 했으므로 현재완료의 '계속' 용법으로 나타내는 것이 적절하다. 'since+시간 명사', 'for+ 기간 명사'임에 유의한다. (3) have[has] been to는 '~에 가 본 적이 있다'는 경험을 나타내고, have[has] gone to 는 '~에 가고 없다'는 결과를 나타내므로 have been to로 고쳐야 한다. (4) to부정사나 동명사가 주어가 되도록 하거나 가주어 it을 사용하고 진주어로 to부정사를 쓴다. (5) to부정사의 의미상 주어는 to부정사 바로 앞에 'for+명사의 목적격'의 형태로 쓴다.

16 (1) 현재완료의 '계속' 용법을 이용한다. (2) 현재완료의 '완료' 용법 을 이용한다. 부정문이므로 yet을 쓰는 것에 주의한다. (3) 현재완료의 '경험' 용법을 이용한다. (4) 현재완료의 '결과' 용법을 이용한다. have[has] been to는 '~에 가 본 적이 있다'는 경험을 나타내고, have[has] gone to 는 '~에 가고 없다'는 결과를 나타낸다. (5) '가주어(it) ~ 진주어(to부정사) …' 구문을 이용한다. (6) '가주어(it) ~ 진주어(to부정사) …' 구문을 이용하고 to 부정사의 의미상의 주어로 'for+목적격'을 쓴다

17 지구에서 하늘의 색깔은 우주의 그것과는 다르다. 그것은 검은 색이 아니라 '파란색'이다.

18 @와 ③, ⑤번: 경험 용법, ①, ④: 계속 용법, ② 완료 용법

19 else: 그 밖에

20 'down'을 보충하면 된다. roll down: 굴러 내려가다

21 지구가 끌어당기기 때문에 지구에서 점프하는 것이 어려운 것이므로, 우주복을 입는 것과 점프하는 것은 상관이 없다.

Lesson 8

Pride of Korea

01 • 상자가 금과 은과 같은 보물로 가득 차 있었다. • 이 그림의 가치는 약 백만 달러이다.

02 '멈추지 않고서 어떤 일을 계속하다'

03 '누군가가 무엇을 할 수 있다고 말하다'는 allow(허락하다)가 적절하다.

04 '당신이 한 일에 대한 만족감과 즐거움'은 pride(긍지, 자부심)가 적절하다.

05 as soon as는 접속사로 '~하자마자'라는 뜻이다.

06 글의 흐름상 도서관 상사들이 심지어 필자를 한국의 스파이라고 생각했기 때문에 '해고했다'가 적절하다.

07 반의어 관계이다. 멈추다: 계속하다 - 실패하다 : 성공하다

08 해외에 있는 우리의 문화재에 더 많은 관심을 갖고 그것의 반환을 위해 애써 주기를 바란다는 내용이 적절하다.

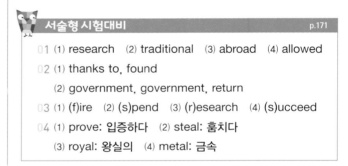

01 (1) 조사를 끝내기 위해 매일 도서관에 갔다는 뜻으로 research 가 적절하다. (2) 해금에 관한 내용이다. 전통적인 한국 악기라는 뜻으로 주어진 단어 'tradition'을 형용사 형태로 바꾸어 준다. (3) but 뒤에 그가 곧 그의 나라로 돌아 갈 것이라고 했기 때문에 그가 지금 'abroad(해외에)' 있다는 것을 알 수 있다. (4) 잔디에 앉는 것이 금지되어 있다는 수동의 의미로 주어진 단어 allow를 과거분사 allowed로 바꾸어 주어야 한다.

02 (1) '~ 덕분에'란 뜻으로 thanks to를 사용하고, 발견되었다는 수동의 의미로 were found가 적절하다. (2) 이 문장에서 'return'은 명사로 사용이 되었다.

03 (1) • 대부분의 동물들은 불을 두려워한다. • 우리는 그가 정직

31

하지 못해서 해고해야 했다. (2) • 여가 시간은 어떻게 보내세요? • 나의 부모님은 매달 책을 사는 데 많은 돈을 쓰신다. (3) • 그는 재생 가능한 에너지원에 대한 연구 조사를 수행해 왔다. • 많은 연구원들이 그 문제를 철저히 조사한다. (4) • 우리는 인생에서 성공하기 위해 열심히 일해야 한다. • 많은 실패 후에, 과학자들은 마침내 그들의 이론을 증명하는데 성공했다.

04 (1) 어떤 것이 사실이라는 것을 보여주다 (2) 다른 누군가에게 속해 있는 물건을 가져가다 (3) 왕이나 여왕과 관련되거나 속해 있는 (4) 전기와 열을 잘 전달하는 철, 금 또는 철강과 같은 단단한 물질 conduct: (열, 전기를) 전달[전도]하다

교과서
Conversation

핵심 Check   p.172~173

1 ⑤   2 ⑤

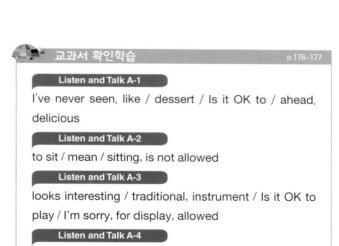

교과서 대화문 익히기

Check(√) True or False   p.174

1 T   2 T   3 T   4 T

교과서 확인학습   p.176~177

Listen and Talk A-1
I've never seen, like / dessert / Is it OK to / ahead, delicious

Listen and Talk A-2
to sit / mean / sitting, is not allowed

Listen and Talk A-3
looks interesting / traditional, instrument / Is it OK to play / I'm sorry, for display, allowed

Listen and Talk A-4
Excuse, Is it OK to take / How about using / afraid, Using, not allowed

Listen and Talk B
Is it OK to sit here / afraid not, Sitting, not allowed

Talk and Play
Which, to go / Why don't you / Is it OK to eat / Eating, allowed / Is it OK to take / is not allowed / got it

Listen and Talk C
Is it OK / fitting room / over there / traditional, for, worn, wedding / Is it OK to try it on / for display, on, allowed / try on

Review 1
looks interesting / traditional, musical instrument / Is it OK to / for display, allowed

Review 2
is it OK / ahead / Can I / but, one more / not allowed

시험대비 기본평가   p.178

01 Using, is, allowed   02 ②   03 ⑤
04 ②   05 ①

01 동명사 주어 using을 사용하고, 'be not allowed'가 '허용되지 않다'라는 뜻이다.

02 Is it OK if I ~?'는 '~해도 될까요?'라는 뜻으로 'Is it OK to+동사원형 ~?'과 같은 표현이다.

03 '여기에 앉는 것이 허용되지 않는다'고 했으므로 허락을 하지 않는 부정의 답이 적절하다.

04 금지를 나타내는 표현이 아닌 것은 don't have to(~할 필요가 없다)이다.

시험대비 실력평가   p.179~180

01 ④   02 I've never seen any food like this.
03 ④   04 Sitting is not allowed   05 ③
06 ⑤   07 Playing the haegeum is not allowed.   08 is it OK to take pictures here? → is it OK if I take pictures here?   09 ②
10 ④   11 ③   12 ⑤

01 허가 여부를 묻는 표현으로 ④는 어색하다.

02 현재완료 부정문 형태는 'have never+과거분사'이다. like는 전치사로 '~와 같은'의 의미다.

03 (C) 저기에 앉아도 되는지 허가 여부를 묻고 (B) 저기가 잔디 위를 말하는 건지 확인하는 말이 오고 (D)의 긍정의 답이 온다. 마지막으로 (A)의 앉으면 안 된다는 금지의 말이 오는 것이 적절하다.

04 동사 sit을 동명사 sitting으로 바꾸어 주어로 쓴다. '~이 허용되지 않는다.'는 수동태 be not allowed로 쓴다.

05 'Should I use it ~?'은 상대방에게 허가를 묻는 표현으로는 자연스럽지 않다.

06 ⓔ be동사 뒤에 일반동사 allow를 또 사용할 수 없다. be동사

뒤에 과거분사 형태로 수동태(is not allowed)가 적절하다.

07 해금을 연주하는 것이 허락되지 않는다.

08 '~해도 될까요?'라는 의미로 허가 여부를 묻는 표현으로 'Is it OK to+동사원형 ~?', 'Is it OK if+주어+동사 ~?'의 형태가 가능하다.

09 'Can I eat food here?'에 대한 답으로 'I'm sorry'라고 말하고 있으므로 먹을 수 없다는 부정의 답이 온다는 것을 알 수 있다.

10 제시문은 '그것은 보통 결혼식 날 착용된다.'는 의미로 It은 'jokduri'를 나타내므로 ④에 들어가는 것이 적절하다.

11 ⓒ의 try on은 '동사+부사' 형태의 이어동사로 대명사 it은 반드시 '동사와 부사' 사이에 위치해야 한다.

12 족두리만 전시용이다.

서술형 시험대비   p.181

01 (A) Eating food is allowed.
　 (B) Taking pictures is not allowed.
02 Using a flash is not allowed here.
03 Is it OK to play it?
04 (A) is it OK to take pictures here?
　 (B) Can I use a flash, too?
　 (C) I have one more question.
　 (D) that's not allowed.

01 (A) 음식을 먹어도 되는지에 대한 허락의 표현으로 동명사 Eating food로 문장을 시작하고, 음식을 먹는 것이 허락된다. 수동의 의미로 is allowed를 쓴다. (B) 사진을 찍는 것에 대한 금지의 표현으로 동명사 Taking pictures로 문장을 시작하고 부정문 수동태로 is not allowed를 쓰면 된다.

02 허가 여부를 묻는 'Can I ~?'의 질문에 'I'm afraid not.'이라는 부정의 답을 하고 있기 때문에, 금지의 표현인 'is not allowed'를 이용하는 것이 적절하다. 주어는 동명사 'Using a flash'를 쓴다.

03 허가 여부를 묻는 표현으로 'Is it OK ~?' 구문을 이용한다. 조건에 맞게 장구(a janggu)는 대명사 it을 사용한다.

교과서
Grammar

핵심 Check   p.182~183

1 (1) what you are (2) if[whether] it was
2 (1) because[as, since] (2) because of

시험대비 기본평가   p.184

01 ②　　　02 ⑤　　　03 ②
04 He quit the job because of his health.

01 의문사가 있는 간접의문문은 '의문사+주어+동사'의 형태로 다른 문장 안에서 주어, 목적어, 보어 역할을 한다.

02 간접의문문은 '의문사+주어+동사'의 어순이다.

03 because는 접속사이므로 뒤에는 주어와 동사가 있는 절이 나오고, because of는 부사구이므로 뒤에는 명사 또는 명사구가 나온다.

04 동사가 하나뿐이므로 접속사가 아닌 부사구 because of를 써야 하므로 of를 추가하여 문장을 배열한다.

시험대비 실력평가   p.185~187

01 ④　　　02 ②　　　03 ⑤
04 (1) because of (2) because of (3) because
　 (4) his name was (5) you are (6) if
05 ③　　　06 Do you know when the movie starts?
07 ①　　　08 ⑤　　　09 ③　　　10 ④
11 (1) Because it was getting dark, we had to hurry.
　 (2) Jim couldn't take a nap because his little sister cried a lot.
　 (3) We didn't go camping because of the bad weather.
12 ③
13 (1) Can I ask you why you decided to become a teacher?
　 (2) I want to know where you were born.
　 (3) Who do you think the girl is?
　 (4) He asked me if[whether] I am Simon's sister.
　 (5) I took some medicine because of a bad cold.
　 (6) You can't watch the movie because you're not old enough.
14 ⑤　　　15 ③　　　16 ①　　　17 ⑤
18 ⑤　　　19 Please tell me what the thief stole.

01 간접의문문의 어순은 '의문사+주어+동사'의 형태임에 유의한다.

02 because는 접속사이므로 뒤에는 주어와 동사가 있는 절이 나오고, because of는 부사구이므로 뒤에는 명사 또는 명사구가 나온다.

03 ① Can you tell me where you were born? ② Minho doesn't know where Kevin lives. ③ I stayed home because I had a high fever. ④ The picnic was canceled because of the bad weather.

04 (1), (2) because of는 부사구이므로 뒤에는 명사 또는 명사구

33

가 나온다. (3) because는 접속사이므로 뒤에는 주어와 동사가 있는 절이 나온다. (4), (5) 간접의문문의 어순은 '의문사+주어+동사'이다. (6) 간접의문문에서 의문사가 없는 경우에는 의문사 대신에 if나 whether를 쓴다.

05 ③번은 간접의문문에 쓰인 것이지만 나머지는 모두 조건의 부사절을 이끌고 있다.

06 간접의문문의 어순은 '의문사+주어+동사'이다.

07 because 다음에는 '이유'가 나오고, so 다음에는 '결과'가 나온다.

08 간접의문문의 어순은 '의문사+주어+동사'의 형태임에 유의한다.

09 ③은 뒤에 '결과'가 이어지고 있으므로 so가 들어가야 하고, 나머지는 모두 이유를 이끌고 있는 because가 들어가야 한다.

10 의문사가 없는 간접의문문의 어순은 'if[whether]+주어+동사'이며 if는 or not과 붙여 쓰지 않는다.

11 because+절(주어+동사 ~), because of+명사 또는 명사구

12 ⓐ I want to know where she is. ⓒ I wonder if he is at home. ⓕ Peter couldn't play soccer because of the rain.

13 (1), (2) 간접의문문의 어순은 '의문사+주어+동사'이다. (3) do you think가 있을 때에는 의문사가 문장 앞에 위치한다. (4) 의문사가 없는 간접의문문의 어순은 'if[whether]+ 주어+동사'로 쓴다. (5) 뒤에 명사구가 나오므로 because of가 적절하다. (6) 뒤에 절이 나오므로 because가 적절하다.

14 간접의문문의 어순은 '의문사+주어+동사'이다. 의문문에 쓰인 조동사 did를 안 쓰는 대신, did의 시제를 간접의문문의 동사에 반영한다.

15 뒤에 명사구가 나오므로 because of가 적절하다.

16 간접의문문의 어순은 '의문사+주어+동사'이며 의문사가 없는 경우는 'if[whether]+주어+동사'로 쓴다.

17 뒤에 '이유'가 이어지고 있으므로 because가 들어가야 한다.

18 의문사가 없는 간접의문문은 'if[whether]+주어+동사'로 쓴다.

19 간접의문문의 어순은 '의문사+주어+동사'이다. 의문문에 쓰인 조동사 did의 시제를 간접의문문의 동사에 반영한다.

서술형 시험대비
p.188~189

01 (1) I'd like to know what you wanted to be when you were young.
   (2) Can you tell me when and where you were born?
   (3) I don't know who borrowed your book.
   (4) I wonder if[whether] my child expresses himself well in English.
   (5) Do you know if[whether] it will rain today?
   (6) What do you believe you were in a previous life?

02 (1) There is no school today because it's snowing a lot. 또는 Because it's snowing a lot, there is no school today.

(2) We couldn't start the meeting because Jaemin didn't arrive. 또는 Because Jaemin didn't arrive, we couldn't start the meeting.

03 (1) when you found   (2) where you found them

04 because riding a bike is not allowed

05 (1) I'd like to know. Who is your best friend?
   (2) She didn't tell me. Whom did she meet yesterday?
   (3) He wondered. Was something wrong with him?
   (4) Do you think? What will you wear on Monday?

06 (1) Can you tell me what happened to Jessie?
   (2) He asked me if[whether] I had any money.
   (3) I want to know who wrote this book.
   (4) What do you think the secret of your health is?
   (5) I didn't go to his birthday party because of a cold.
   (6) I sat down because I was feeling dizzy.
   (7) Everyone left early because Michael and Jane had an argument.

07 (1) I don't remember what the thief was wearing.
   (2) I don't know who stole my camera.
   (3) Can you tell me how you became interested in Uigwe?
   (4) I asked her if[whether] she was ready to go.
   (5) What do you suppose most American teenagers seek help for?
   (6) Jane woke up in the middle of the night because of a bad dream.
   (7) Yesterday Mary went shopping because she wanted to buy a gift for her dad.

08 because[as, since]

01 간접의문문의 어순은 '의문사+주어+동사'이며 의문사가 없는 경우는 'if[whether]+주어+동사'로 쓰며 의문사가 주어인 경우에는 의문사가 주어 역할을 동시에 하므로 직접의문문처럼 '의문사+동사'의 어순임에 유의한다. believe 동사가 주절에 있을 경우 간접의문문의 의문사를 문장 맨 앞으로 배치한다. 또한 의문문에 쓰인 조동사 do를 안 쓰는 대신, do의 시제를 간접의문문의 동사에 반영한다.

02 'so+결과'를 'because+이유'로 바꿔 쓸 수 있다.

03 간접의문문의 어순은 '의문사+주어+동사'이며 (1)에는 언제 발견했는지를 묻는 표현이, (2)에는 어디서 발견했는지를 묻는 표현이 들어가는 것이 적절하다.

04 why로 묻고 있으므로 'because+주어+동사'로 '이유'를 답하면 된다.

05 간접의문문의 어순은 '의문사+주어+동사'이며 의문사가 없는 경우는 'if[whether]+주어+동사'로 쓴다. think 동사가 주절에 있을 경우 간접의문문의 의문사를 문장 맨 앞으로 배치한다.

또한 의문문에 쓰인 조동사 do를 안 쓰는 대신, do의 시제를 간접의문문의 동사에 반영한다.

06 간접의문문과 because를 이용하여 영작한다.

07 (1)~(5) 간접의문문의 어순은 '의문사+주어+동사'이며 의문사가 없는 경우는 'if[whether]+주어+동사'로 쓴다. 의문사가 주어인 경우에는 의문사가 주어 역할을 동시에 하므로 '의문사+동사'의 어순으로 쓴다. suppose 동사가 주절에 있을 경우 간접의문문의 의문사를 문장 맨 앞으로 배치한다. 또한 의문문에 쓰인 조동사 do를 안 쓰는 대신, do의 시제를 간접의문문의 동사에 반영한다. (6) 뒤에 명사구가 나오므로 because of가 적절하다. (7) 뒤에 절이 나오므로 because가 적절하다.

08 'so+결과'를 'because[as, since]+이유'로 바꿔 쓸 수 있다.

교과서 Reading

확인문제 p.190

1 T 2 F 3 F 4 T

확인문제 p.191

1 T 2 F 3 T 4 T 5 F

교과서 확인학습 A p.192~193

01 Interview with
02 On, a collection of, came back to
03 behind this return, searching for, abroad
04 how, became interested in   05 studied history
06 to continue   07 As you know   08 while
09 one of them   10 297 books of *Uigwe*
11 how   12 As soon as, look for
13 finally   14 looked at, 30 million
15 I'm sure   16 more difficulties
17 should be returned to, that idea
18 even thought, fired
19 as a visitor, do research on   20 However
21 For more than 22 the value of *Uigwe*
23 were published as   24 because of
25 asked, for, are here now
26 I'd like to ask, printing
27 in my first year   28 right away
29 to prove its value
30 was displayed as, movable metal type
31 thanks to, thank, for
32 our national treasures abroad, return

교과서 확인학습 B p.194~195

1 An Interview with Dr. Park Byeong-seon

2 On May 27, 2011, 297 books of Uigwe, a collection of royal books the French army took in 1866, came back to Korea.

3 the person behind this return is Dr. Park Byeong-seon, a historian who spent her whole life searching for Korean national treasures abroad.

4 Q: Can you tell me how you became interested in *Uigwe*?

5 Dr. Park: I studied history in college.

6 I went to France to continue my studies in 1955.

7 As you know, the French army took many of our national treasures in 1866.

8 I wanted to find them while I was studying there.

9 *Uigwe* was one of them.

10 Q: You found 297 books of *Uigwe* in the National Library of France, in Paris.

11 Please tell me how you found them.

12 Dr. Park: As soon as I became a researcher at the National Library in 1967, I began to look for *Uigwe*.

13 After 10 years, in 1977, I finally found the books.

14 I think I looked at more than 30 million books.

15 Q: I'm sure you were very excited when you found the books.

16 Dr. Park: Yes, I was, but more difficulties were waiting for me.

17 I thought that the books should be returned to Korea, but my bosses at the library didn't like that idea.

18 They even thought that I was a Korean spy and fired me.

19 After that, I had to go to the library as a visitor, so it was not easy to do research on *Uigwe*.

20 However, I didn't give up.

21 For more than ten years, I went to the library every day to finish my research.

22 I wanted to show people the value of *Uigwe*.

23 Q: The results of your research were published as a book in Korea in 1990.

24 Many Koreans became interested in *Uigwe* because of your book.

25 Dr. Park: Yes. In 1992, the Korean government asked the French government for its return and, finally, the 297 books are here now.

26 Q: Before I finish this interview, I'd like to ask you about *Jikji*, a book that changed the history of

printing.

27 Dr. Park: I found it in my first year at the library.

28 I knew right away that it was very special.

29 I worked hard to prove its value and finally succeeded.

30 At a book exhibition in Paris in 1972, *Jikji* was displayed as the oldest book in the world that was printed with movable metal type.

31 Q: Dr. Park, thanks to your hard work, *Jikji* and Uigwe were found, and all Koreans thank you for that.

32 Dr. Park: I hope people will become more interested in our national treasures abroad and work for their return.

시험대비 실력평가
p.196~201

01 ①번 In → On 02 As you know 03 ⑤
04 Please tell me how you found them. 05 ①, ③
06 her idea, a Korean spy 07 ② 08 ①, ⑤
09 metal type 10 in spite of → thanks to 11 ③
12 ①, ④ 13 ② 14 ③ 15 ④
16 ③ 17 ②, ⑤ 18 ⑤ 19 ③
20 ④ 21 ① 22 ③
23 (1) in order to finish (2) so as to finish
    (3) in order that, could[might] finish
    (4) so that, could[might] finish
24 (A) special (B) exhibition (C) was displayed
25 ⓐ 박 박사님의 노고 덕분에 "직지"와 "의궤"가 발견된 것
    ⓑ 해외에 있는 우리의 문화재
26 ④
27 ⓐ when and where you were born
    ⓑ what you like about your job
28 ⓐ to know
    ⓑ to make와 making
    ⓒ to help와 helping

01 ① 특정한 날 앞에는 전치사 on을 쓴다. ② 297 books of Uigwe: "의궤" 297권, [동격 관계] …의, …라고 하는, …인, e.g.: the five of us(우리 다섯 사람), ③ 연도 앞에는 in을 쓴다. ④ search for: ~을 찾다, ⑤ become interested in: ~에 관심을 갖게 되다

02 as: -하다시피[~이듯이](접속사)

03 Dr. Park은 프랑스에서 공부하는 동안, 프랑스군이 1866년에 가져 간 우리 문화재를 '찾고' 싶었고 "의궤"는 그것들 중의 하나였다.

04 의문문이 다른 문장의 일부로 쓰이면 '의문사＋주어＋동사' 어

순의 간접의문문이 된다. Please tell me에 맞춰 부호는 마침표를 찍는 것이 적절하다.

05 ① 적어도, ③ 마지막으로, 끝으로(무엇을 열거하면서 마지막 요소 앞에 붙이는 말), ⓐ와 나머지는 다 '마침내'

06 도서관의 그녀의 상사들이 '그녀의 생각'을 좋아하지 않았고, 그들은 심지어 그녀가 '한국의 스파이'라고 생각했기 때문이다.

07 ② 의지가 강한[확고한], ① 다정한, ③ 공손한, ④ 창의적인, ⑤ 호기심 많은

08 ⓐ와 ①, ⑤번: 관계대명사, ② 지시부사(그렇게), ③ 접속사, ④ 지시대명사

09 metal type: 금속 활자, movable: 이동시킬 수 있는, 움직이는

10 당신의 노고 '덕분에'라고 해야 하므로, 'thanks to'로 고치는 것이 적절하다. in spite of: ~에도 불구하고

11 이 글은 "직지"의 가치를 증명하기 위해 열심히 연구한 Dr. Park에 대한 인터뷰 내용이므로, 제목으로는 'Dr. Park이 직지의 가치를 증명했다'가 적절하다.

12 the French army took in 1866는 앞에 있는 선행사 a collection of royal books를 수식하는 관계대명사절이며 목적격 관계대명사 which 또는 that이 생략되었다.

13 ⓑ와 ②번: ~이다시피[~이듯이](접속사), As you see: 보다 시피, ① 때, ③ 이유, ④ ~처럼(전치사), ⑤ ~함에 따라, ~할수록

14 누가 그것을 만들었는지 그리고 무엇이 그 안에 기록되어 있는지는 알 수 없다. ① It's a collection of royal books. ② It has 297 books. in all: 총, ④ The French army did. ⑤ It came back on May 27, 2011.

15 앞에 나오는 내용과 상반되는 내용이 뒤에 이어지므로 However가 가장 적절하다. ① 그러므로, ② 예를 들어, ③ 게다가, ⑤ 즉, 다시 말해

16 ③은 Dr. Park이 "의궤"를 찾기 시작한 뒤부터 그 책들을 발견할 때까지 본 책들을 가리키고, 나머지는 다 "의궤"를 가리킨다.

17 ② 뜻이 있는 곳에 길이 있다. ⑤ 낙숫물이 바위를 뚫는다. (성실하게 꾸준

18 위 글만으로는 "의궤"의 가치가 무엇인지를 대답할 수 없다. ① As soon as she became a researcher at the National Library in 1967. ② It took 10 years. ③ More than 30 million books. ④ She thought that the books should be returned to Korea.

19 ③ as the oldest book: 가장 오래된 책으로, 나머지 빈칸들은 모두 that을 쓰는 것이 적절하다. ①과 ④ 주격관계 대명사, ② 접속사, ⑤ 지시대명사

20 1972년에 구텐베르크 성경(Gutenberg Bible)이 세계에서 가장 오래된 책으로 증명된 것이 아니라, "직지"가 금속 활자로 인쇄된 세계에서 가장 오래된 책으로 전시되었다.

21 ①번 다음 문장의 They에 주목한다. 주어진 문장의 my bosses at the library를 받고 있으므로 ①번이 적절하다.

22 ⓐ와 ③번: 해고하다, ① (화살을) 쏘다, ② (질문·비난 등을)

퍼붓다, ④ (감정·정열 따위를) 타오르게 하다, (사람을) 흥분[감격]하게 하다(up), ⑤ 사격[발사/발포]하다

23 in order to 동사원형 = so as to 동사원형 = in order that 주어 can[may] = so that 주어 can[may]: ~하기 위하여(목적)

24 (A) 그것이 아주 '특별하다'는 것을 바로 알았다고 해야 하므로 special이 적절하다. common: 흔한, 보통의, 평범한, (B) 도서 '박람회'라고 해야 하므로 exhibition이 적절하다. explanation: 설명, (C) 가장 오래된 책으로 '전시되었다'고 해야 하므로 was displayed가 적절하다.

25 ⓐ 'thanks to Dr. Park's hard work, Jikji and Uigwe were found' ⓑ 'our national treasures abroad'를 가리킨다.

26 두 사람은 '인터뷰 진행자'와 '인터뷰 받는 사람, 인터뷰 대상자'의 관계이다. ① employer: 고용주, employee: 종업원, ② applicant: 지원자, ③ trainer: 교육시키는 사람, 트레이너, trainee: 교육을 받는 사람, 수습 (직원), ⑤ manager: 경영자, candidate: (선거의) 입후보자[출마자], (일자리의) 후보자

27 의문문이 다른 문장의 일부로 쓰이면 '의문사＋주어＋동사' 어순의 간접의문문이 된다.

28 (A) would like는 목적어로 to부정사만 쓸 수 있다. (B) 보어 자리에는 to부정사와 동명사를 둘 다 쓸 수 있다. (C) like는 목적어로 to부정사와 동명사를 둘 다 쓸 수 있다.

서술형 시험대비
p.202~203

01 (A) collection (B) behind (C) abroad
02 (A) France (B) Korea
03 how you became interested in *Uigwe*
04 looking
05 I thought that the books should be returned to Korea
06 hired → fired
07 (A) As soon as (B) difficulties (C) value
08 in proving its value
09 (A) printing (B) oldest (C) movable metal type
10 behind
11 many of our national treasures (that/which) the French army took in 1866
12 (A) royal books (B) Dr. Park Byeong Seon

01 (A) 왕실 서적인 "의궤" 297권이라고 해야 하므로, '소장품'이라는 의미의 collection이 적절하다. correction: 정정[수정], (B) 이 반환 '뒤에 있는' 인물이라고 해야 하므로 behind가 적절하다. in front of: ~의 앞쪽에[앞에], (C) '해외에 있는' 한국의 문화재라고 해야 하므로 abroad가 적절하다. abroad: 해외에서, aboard: (배·기차·비행기 등에) 탄, 탑승[승선]한

02 '프랑스'로부터 '한국'으로의 "의궤"의 반환을 가리킨다.

03 의문문이 다른 문장의 일부로 쓰이면 '의문사＋주어＋동사' 어

04 begin은 목적어로 to부정사와 동명사를 모두 취할 수 있다.

05 return(돌려주다, 반납하다)을 수동태로 쓰면 된다.

06 그들이 저를 '해고했다'고 해야 하므로 'fired'로 고치는 것이 적절하다. hire: 고용하다

07 Dr. Park은 1967년에 국립도서관의 연구원이 '되자마자', "의궤"를 찾기 시작했다. 그녀는 사람들에게 "의궤"의 '가치'를 보여 주고 싶었기 때문에 많은 '어려움'에도 불구하고 포기하지 않았고, 10년 후, 마침내 그 책들을 발견했다.

08 succeed in ~ing: ~하는 데 성공하다

09 "직지"는 '금속 활자'로 인쇄된 세계에서 '가장 오래된' 책 으로 드러났기 때문에, '인쇄'의 역사를 바꾼 책이다. turn out: ~인 것으로 드러나다[밝혀지다]

10 이 반환 '뒤에 있는' 인물 = 이 반환을 가능하게 만든 인물, behind: ~ 뒤에 (숨은), ~의 배후에

11 '1866년에 프랑스군이 가져간 우리 문화재'를 가리킨다.

12 그것은 프랑스군이 1866년에 가져갔던 한국 '왕실 서적'이다. 하지만, '박병선 박사'의 노력 덕분에 2011년 5월 27일에 그것은 프랑스로부터 한국으로 돌아왔다.

영역별 핵심문제
p.205~209

01 ②　　02 ④　　03 ③　　04 ①
05 give up　06 ③　　07 ③　　08 ②
09 wants to try on the hanbok and the jokduri
10 it's only for display.　11 ④　　12 ⑤
13 (A) Is it OK to sit over there?
　　(B) sitting on the grass is not allowed
14 No, it isn't / for display　15 because
16 ⑤
17 (1) I'm not sure. Will my grandfather like my present?
　　(2) Can you tell me? Where is the bathroom?
　　(3) I'd like to know. Who did you meet at the party?
　　(4) Did you know? Who was in the classroom?
　　(5) Do you think? What is Jane's secret?
　　(6) I'm curious. Can you lend me the book?
18 ③　　　19 ④　　　20 took them → took
21 during　22 ④　　23 ⑤　　24 bosses, fired　25 to　　26 ③　　27 ④
28 immediately　　29 ②

01 나머지는 모두 동사와 명사의 뜻을 가지는 단어이지만, allow는 동사로만 사용된다.

02 ⓐ 프랑스 정부가 우리의 문화재(national treasures)를 가져갔다는 뜻이다. ⓑ 책 박람회에서 '직지'가 전시되었다 (displayed)는 의미가 적절하다.

37

03 '누군가나 무언가가 일어난 좋은 일에 책임이 있다고 말하는 데 사용되는'의 의미로 'thanks to(~ 덕분에)'가 적절하다.

04 어떤 것에 관한 사실들을 알아내는 일

05 • 그에게는 쉽지 않은 일이었지만, 그는 포기하지 않았습니다.
• 그들은 여러 번 실패할지라도 쉽게 포기하지 않습니다.

06 publish는 '출판하다'라는 의미이고, prove가 '입증하다'라는 의미이다.

08 제시문의 That은 그 다음에 나오는 the little hat을 가리키므로 ②가 적절하다.

09 소녀가 입고 싶어 하는 두 가지는 무엇인가?

10 'for display'는 '전시를 위한'의 의미이다.

11 Using smartphones는 동명사 주어로 단수 취급을 하므로 are를 is로 바꾸어야 한다.

12 헬스장은 fitness room이다. fitting room은 탈의실이다.

14 족두리를 써 보는 것은 허락되지 않는다. 족두리는 단지 전시만 하는 것이다.

15 뒤에 '이유'가 이어지고 있으므로 because가 들어가야 한다.

16 의문사가 없는 간접의문문의 어순은 'if[whether]+주어+동사'이다. However, she is not sure if[whether] she will return in the future.

17 간접의문문의 어순은 '의문사+주어+동사'이며 의문사가 없는 경우는 'if[whether]+주어+동사'로 쓴다. think 동사가 주절에 있을 경우 간접의문문의 의문사를 문장 맨 앞으로 배치한다.

18 ③번은 조건의 부사절에 쓰인 것이지만 나머지는 모두 간접 의문문을 이끌고 있다.

19 간접의문문의 어순은 '의문사+주어+동사'이다. how long 은 의문사 how가 long을 수식하는 부사로 쓰여 how long을 함께 의문사 취급을 한다.

20 the French army took in 1866는 앞에 있는 선행사 a collection of royal books를 수식하는 관계대명사절이며 took 의 목적어인 them은 목적격 관계대명사 which 또는 that으로 바꾼 다음에 생략되었는데 또 them을 쓰는 것은 적절하지 않다.

21 while+주어+동사, during+기간을 나타내는 명사, for study: 공부를 위하여

22 Dr. Park이 "의궤"를 찾는 데 얼마나 오래 걸렸는지는 대답할 수 없다. ① On May 27, 2011. ② History. ③ In 1866. ⑤ While she was studying in France.

23 ⓐ와 ⑤번: (역할·자격 따위를 나타내어) ~으로서, ① ~ 때문에, ② ~함에 따라서, ③ ~와 같을 만큼(지시부사, 보통 as ~ as …로 형용사·부사 앞에서), ④ ~할 때

24 도서관의 '상사들'이 그녀를 한국의 스파이라고 생각해서 그녀를 '해고했기' 때문이다.

25 show는 간접목적어를 직접목적어 뒤로 보낼 때 'to'를 붙인다.

26 그 책들이 한국에 반환되어야 한다고 생각한 것은 '도서관의 상사들'이 아니라 'Dr. Park'이었다.

27 ④는 일반적인 '도서'를 가리키고, 나머지는 다 '직지'를 가리 킨다.

28 right away = immediately: 즉시

29 위 글은 직지의 가치를 증명하기 위해 열심히 연구한 Dr. Park 에 관한 인터뷰 내용이므로, 주제로는 'Dr. Park 덕분에 직지의 가치가 발견되었다'가 적절하다.

단원별 예상문제
p.210~213

01 royal   02 ③   03 ⑤   04 ②

05 ③   06 ②   07 Taking, is, allowed

08 ③   09 the little hat

10 ⓐ is allowed   ⓑ is allowed   11 ②

12 (1) What do you think the best way to encourage kids to study more is?
(2) Can you tell me who your favorite actor is?
(3) The car accident happened because[as, since] the road was slippery.
(4) Tina ran into the house because[as, since] it started to rain.

13 what you like doing in your free time / because[as, since] it is really fun

14 (1) I went to the school health room because I had a headache. I went to the school health room because of a headache.
(2) He got food poisoning because he ate undercooked chicken. He got food poisoning because of undercooked chicken.

15 (A) royal   (B) interested   (C) while

16 a historian who spent her whole life searching for Korean national treasures abroad

17 ①, ④   18 ③   19 ③   20 ②

21 millions → million   22 tried to find → found

01 '왕실의 책'이란 의미로 royal이 적절하다. loyal은 '충실한 의미이다.

02 사진을 찍을 때 충분한 빛을 제공하기 위해 번쩍이는 카메라의 밝은 빛

03 (A) 그 책이 한국으로 반환되어야 한다고 생각했다. (B) 도서관의 상사들이 필자를 해고시켰기 때문에 그 후에는 방문객으로 방문했다가 적절하다 (C) 의궤의 가치를 사람들에게 보여주기를 원했다가 적절하다.

04 about은 전치사이므로 뒤에 동명사(-ing)가 와야 한다.

05 (C)의 prove는 '입증하다, 증명하다'라는 의미이다. 발견하다는 find이다.

06 빈칸 다음의 말이 'Eating food is allowed.'이므로 음식을 먹어도 되는지 여부를 묻는 말이 적절하다. ⑤번의 'Do you mind if I ~?' 표현도 허가 여부를 묻는 말이지만, B의 답이 'Yes'이기 때문에 허락하지 않는다는 뜻이 되어 어색하다.

08 ⓐ에는 '~을 입어 보다'라는 의미로 try on이 적절하다. ⓑ에는 족두 리에 대해 설명을 하는 말로, 전통적인(traditional) 한국 모자가 적절하다. ⓒ에는 써 봐도 되는지 묻는 말에 미안하다고 했기 때문에 써 볼 수 없다는 것을 알 수 있다.

09 저쪽에 있는 작은 모자를 가리킨다는 것을 알 수 있다.

10 ⓐ, ⓑ 모두 허락 여부를 묻는 말에 대해 Yes와 OK로 답하고 있기 때문에 모두 허락을 해주는 표현이 오는 것이 적절 하다.

11 ① I want to know how you spent your vacation. ③ I wonder if she got angry at me. ④ We didn't win the game because of my mistake. ⑤ You can't watch the movie because you're not old enough.

12 (접의문의 어순은 '의문사+주어+동사'이며 think 동사가 주절에 있을 경우 간접의문문의 의문사를 문장 맨 앞 에 써야 함에 유의한다. 두 개의 문장을 연결하는 것이므로 because를 이용하여 because 뒤에 이유에 해당하는 것을 쓴다. So를 이용하여 두 문장의 순서를 바꾸어 써도 좋다.

13 첫 번째 빈칸에는 간접의문문을 이용하여 '의문사+주어+동사'의 어순으 로 쓰고 두 번째 빈칸에는 'really fun'이라는 이유에 해당하는 말이 있으므로 because[as, since]를 이용하여 답한다.'

14 because+절(주어+동사 ~), because of+명사 또는 명사구

15 (A) '왕실' 서적이라고 해야 하므로 royal이 적절하다. loyal: 충실한, 충성스러운, (B) 감정을 나타내는 동사는 수식받는 명사가 감정을 느끼게 되는 경우에 과거분사를 써야 하므로 interested 가 적절하다. (C) while+주어+동사, during+기간을 나타내는 명사

16 spend+시간+~ing: ~하는 데 시간을 보내다, search for: ~을 찾다

17 ⓑ와 ②, ③, ⑤는 부사적 용법, strong will: 강한 의지, ①, ④ 명사적 용법

18 프랑스에 갔을 때 그녀가 몇 살이었는지는 알 수 없다. ① She searched for Korean national treasures abroad throughout her lifetime.(She spent her whole life searching for Korean national treasures abroad.) ② History. ④ To continue her studies. ⑤ Many of our national treasures the French army took in 1866.

19 (A) look for: ~을 찾다, (B) look at: ~을 보다, ① look after: ~을 돌보다

20 as soon as = the moment = the instant= immediately = directly: ~하자마자, ② exactly: 정확 히, 꼭, 틀림없이

21 more than 30 million books: 3천만 권 이상의 책, million 은 구체적인 숫자와 함께 쓰일 때 단수로 쓴다.

22 1977년에 그 책들을 '찾으려고 노력한 것'이 아니라, 마침내 그 책들을 '발견했다.'

01 (A) Is it OK if I play it?
   (B) You must not play it.

02 (A) Using smartphones is allowed
   (B) Taking pictures is not allowed.

03 (1) What do you like to do?
   (2) Will my boss accept my idea?
   (3) I worked all day yesterday.

04 (1) I stayed home because of a heavy rain.
   (2) Because of a high fever, I couldn't sleep last night.

05 (1) She couldn't run because of her uncomfortable shoes.
   (2) Mark didn't join us because he had to work.
   (3) Do you know where she went?
   (4) She could not remember if[whether) she watched the movie.

06 (A) in 1955　(B) national treasures　(C) in 1866

07 were returned

08 to search → searching

09 (A) found　(B) was　(C) visitor

10 (1) 그 책들이 한국에 반환되어야 한다는 Dr. Park의 생각을 도서관의 상사들이 좋아하지 않았다.
   (2) 도서관의 상사들이 Dr. Park을 한국의 스파이라고 생각했고 그녀를 해고했다.
   (3) 해고당한 뒤 방문객으로 도서관에 가야만 해서 "의궤" 를 연구하는 것이 쉽지 않았다.

11 they should return the books to Korea

03 (1), (2) 간접의문문의 어순은 '의문사+주어+동사'이며 의문사가 없는 경우는 'if[whether]+주어+동사'로 쓴다. (3) because를 이용하여 '이유'를 밝히고 있다. 이것을 따로 써주면 된다.

04 'because of' 다음에는 명사 또는 명사구가 나온다. 'because of'는 문장의 앞이나 뒤 모두에 올 수 있다.

05 (1), (2) because+절(주어+동사 ~), because of+명사 또는 명사구 (3), (4) 간접의문문의 어순은 '의문사+주 어+동사'이다. 의문사가 없는 경우에는 의문사 대신에 if나 whether를 쓴다.

06 그녀는 '1955년에' 역사를 계속 공부하기 위해 프랑스에 갔다. 그녀는 그곳에서 공부하는 동안 프랑스군이 '1866년에' 가져갔던 많은 우리 '문화재'를 찾고 싶었고 "의궤"는 그것들 중의 하나였다.

07 return(돌려주다, 반납하다)을 수동태로 쓰면 된다.

08 spend+시간+-ing: ~하는 데 시간을 보내다

09 (A) 그 책들을 '발견했을' 때 무척 흥분한 것이므로 found가 적절 하다. find-found-found: ~을 찾다, found-founded-founded: ~ 을 설립하다, (B) 그 책들을 발견했을 때 무척 '흥분

39

했다'고 하는 것이므로 was가 적절하다. (C) 도서관에서 해고당한 뒤 '방문객'으로 도서관에 가야 만 했다고 해야 하므로 visitor가 적절하다. librarian: 사서

10 뒤에 이어지는 내용을 쓰는 것이 적절하다.

11 조동사가 있는 문장의 능동태는 '조동사＋동사원형'의 형태로 쓰인다.

창의사고력 서술형 문제
p.216

|모범답안|

01 Is it OK to set up a tent / How about / afraid not / is no allowed

02 (1) I got up late this morning because I stayed up late last night.
   (2) I couldn't go out today because of a bad cold.
   (3) I don't know what my friend wants me to do.

03 (A) to continue (B) a researcher (C) *Uigwe*
   (D) *Jikji* (E) more than 30 million books
   (F) were published

단원별 모의고사
p.217~220

01 ⑤   02 (r)esult   03 ①   04 ④
05 ②   06 ③   07 ④

08 going to try on a hanbok

09 traditional, women, display, allowed, wedding day

10 ④   11 ③   12 ②   13 ④

14 ②, ⑤

15 (1) I don't know who broke the window.
   (2) Tell me how you found the key.
   (3) I have no idea if[whether] he loves me or not.
   (4) Who do you think will be selected as the best player of the game?

16 (1) I don't see my grandparents often because they live far away.
   (2) They moved to Japan because of her job.
   (3) The accident happened because of his carelessness.
   (4) Minho knows what Kevin wants to be in the future.
   (5) Daniel is not sure where he put his phone.
   (6) I will check if the president can meet you now.

17 who 또는 that

18 (A) a historian (B) abroad

19 the books should be returned to Korea

20 ②   21 ④

---

01 ⑤번의 'aboard'는 '(비행기에, 배에) 탄, 탑승하여'의 의미로 'on or onto a ship, aircraft, bus, or train'이 적절한 설명이

다. 'in or to a foreign country'는 abroad(해외로, 해외에서)에 대한 설명이다.

02 • 최고의 결과를 얻기 위해, 당신은 최선을 다해야 한다. • 질병은 종종 가난으로부터 발생할 수 있다.

03 '주의 깊게 봄으로써 누군가나 무언가를 찾으려고 하다'라는 뜻으로 '찾아보다'는 search가 적절하다.

04 해금은 전시를 위한 것이라고 했으므로, 연주하는 것이 허락되지 않는다는 대답이 적절하다.

05 B가 'Yes'라는 긍정의 답을 하고 있기 때문에 ④번의 'Do you mind if I ~?'는 적절하지 않다.

06 ③번은 저기에 앉아도 되는지 물어보는 말에 B가 미안하지만 앉는 것이 허락되지 않는다고 말하는 것이 자연스럽다. is allowed를 is not allowed로 바꾸어야 한다.

07 남자가 탈의실은 저기에 있다고 말하는 것으로 보아 옷을 입어봐도 되는지 물어보는 것이 적절하다.

08 Kate는 한복을 입어 볼 것이다.

09 Kate는 여자들을 위한 한국 전통 모자인 족두리를 써보려고 했지만 전시용이었기 때문에 써 볼 수가 없었다. 족두리는 주로 결혼식 날 쓴다.

10 빈칸 다음에 G가 '플래시도 사용할 수 있나요?'라고 묻고 있기 때문에 사진을 찍는 것이 가능하다는 것을 알 수 있다. 그래서 긍정의 답이 적절하다.

11 사진을 찍어도 되는지 묻는 말에 No라고 답하고 있으므로 사진을 찍는 것은 허락되지 않는다는 것을 알 수 있다.

12 ②번은 의미상 결과를 나타내는 so가 적절하다. 나머지는 다 because가 적절하다.

13 ④번은 조건절에 쓰인 if이지만 나머지는 모두 간접의문문을 이끌고 있다.

14 빈칸 뒤에 '이유'에 해당하는 내용이 나오며 절이 왔으므로 접속사 because나 since가 알맞다.

15 간접의문문의 어순은 '의문사＋주어＋동사'이며 의문사가 없는 경우에는 'if[whether]＋주어＋동사'로 쓴다. think 동사가 주절에 있을 경우 간접의문문의 의문사를 문장 맨 앞으로 배치한다.

16 (1)~(3) 뒤에 '이유'를 이끄는 because나 because of를 이용하여 쓴다. (4)~(6) 간접의문문을 이용하여 쓴다. 어순이 '의문사＋주어＋동사'이며 의문사가 없는 경우는 'if[whether]＋주어＋동사'로 쓰는 것에 유의한다.

17 주격 관계대명사 who 또는 that이 적절하다.

18 박병선 박사는 '해외에 있는' 한국의 문화재를 찾기 위해 전생애를 바친 '역사학자'였다.

19 '그 책들이 한국에 반환되어야 한다'는 것을 가리킨다.

20 ⓑ와 ③, ⑤: 명사적 용법, ①, ④ 부사적 용법, ② 형용사적 용법

21 because of+명사(구), because+절, because of = thanks to = owing to = due to = on account of: ~ 때문에

Creative Ideas in Stories

교과서 **Reading**

확인문제   p.224

1 T   2 F   3 F

확인문제   p.225

1 T   2 T   3 F

확인문제   p.226

1 F   2 T

교과서 확인학습 A   p.227~229

01 Doughnuts	02 had	03 so, was full of
04 visited	05 Uncle	06 Isn't it great
07 for a while	08 for me	
10 doughnut batter		11 recipe
12 Don't worry	13 front, stepped out	
14 Can I have	15 aren't ready	
16 Are you making		17 my first time
18 took off	19 to mix	20 I can help you
22 a lot of	23 wait and see, great	
24 turned on	25 dropping into	26 first
27 delicious	28 so much fun !	29 for helping
30 enough, nothing happened		31 kept coming
32 should call	33 was, full of, piled	
34 right away	35 Something's wrong	
36 all these	37 came back	38 left
39 took it off	40 looked for	41 can't find
42 give a reward	43 I'm sure	44 right
45 break up, to find		46 Don't worry
47 made a sign	48 put it	49 2 for 5 cents
50 for finding	51 give, back	52 to buy
53 All of a sudden		54 found it
55 worked	56 Here's	57 In the end
58 with	59 got, back, lots of	

교과서 확인학습 B   p.230~232

1 The Doughnuts

2 Homer's uncle, Bob, had a doughnut shop.

3 Uncle Bob liked machines, so the shop was full of cooking machines.

4 One day, Homer visited Uncle Bob's shop.

5 Homer: Hello, Uncle Bob!

6 Bob: Hi, Homer. Nice to see you. Look at this new doughnut machine. Isn't it great?

7 Bob: Homer, I need to go back home for a while.

8 Can you watch the shop for me and make some doughnuts?

9 Homer: OK, I'll try but ....

10 Bob: It's easy to do. First, make the doughnut batter and put it in the machine.

11 Then just start the machine. Here's the recipe.

12 Homer: I can do that. Don't worry.

13 After Uncle Bob left, a big car stopped in front of the shop, and a lady stepped out.

14 Lady: Can I have some doughnuts and a coffee?

15 Homer: I'm sorry, but the doughnuts aren't ready.

16 Lady: Are you making the doughnut batter now?

17 Homer: Yes, but this is my first time.

18 The lady took off her coat and her big diamond ring.

19 She started to mix the batter.

20 Lady: I can help you. I can make delicious doughnuts.

21 Homer: Uh, OK.

22 Homer: This is a lot of batter.

23 Lady: Just wait and see. The doughnuts will taste great.

24 Homer turned on the doughnut machine.

25 Rings of batter started dropping into the hot oil.

26 Lady: You try the first doughnut. Here.

27 Homer: Wow! It's really delicious!

28 Lady: I have to go now. This was so much fun! Good-bye!

29 Homer: Thank you for helping me. Good-bye!

30 Homer had enough doughnuts, so he pushed the stop button, but nothing happened.

31 The doughnuts kept coming out of the machine.

32 Homer: Hmm... What's wrong? I think I should call Uncle Bob.

33 The shop was now full of doughnuts. Homer

piled the doughnuts on the counter.

34 Homer: Uncle Bob! Please come back right away.

35 Something's wrong with the doughnut machine.

36 Bob: Oh, no! How can we sell all these doughnuts?

37 Just then the lady came back to the shop.

38 Lady: I lost my diamond ring. I think I left it on the counter.

39 Homer: Oh, I remember. You took it off before you started to mix the batter.

40 Everyone looked for the diamond ring, but they couldn't find it.

41 Homer: I can't find it.

42 Lady: I'll give a reward of one hundred dollars to the person who finds that ring!

43 Homer: I know! The ring fell into the batter. I'm sure it's inside one of these doughnuts!

44 Lady: You're right!

45 Bob: Oh, no! Now we have to break up all of these doughnuts to find the ring.

46 Homer: Don't worry, Uncle. I have an idea.

47 Homer took a piece of paper and made a sign.

48 He then put it in the shop's window.

49 Fresh Doughnuts   2 for 5 cents

50 $100 prize for finding a ring inside a doughnut

51 P.S. You have to give the ring back.

52 Then many people began to buy the doughnuts.

53 All of a sudden, a man shouted with excitement.

54 Man: I found it! I found the ring!

55 Homer: See, my idea worked!

56 Lady: Here's one hundred dollars!

57 In the end, everybody was happy.

58 The man went home with one hundred dollars.

59 The lady got her diamond ring back, and Uncle Bob sold lots of doughnuts.

60 And, what about Homer?

61 He was happy that his idea worked so well!

🦉 서술형 실전문제
p.233~235

01 have

02 (1) reward   (2) dropping[to drop] into
  (3) stepped out

03 (1) remember: 기억하다   (2) compare: 비교하다
  (3) excitement: 흥분   (4) work: 효과가 있다

04 (1) (o)wned   (2) (f)or a while   (3) (t)ook off

05 (1) Bob liked books, so his room was full of books.
  (2) It is easy to make doughnuts.

---

(3) Homer thinks that the doughnuts smell great.

(4) After Bob made doughnuts with the doughnut machine, he turned it off.

(5) We ordered three pieces of pizza and two cans of cola at the restaurant.

06 (1) Have you met the girl who[that] is talking to Judy?

(2) Yuna is good at figure skating which[that] is hard to learn.

(3) The hotel (which/that) I stayed at was clean and beautiful. 또는 The hotel at which I stayed was clean and beautiful.

07 Because he liked machines.

08 batter

09 (1) 먼저, 도넛 반죽을 만든다.
  (2) 그 반죽을 기계에 넣는다.
  (3) 그런 다음에 기계를 작동시킨다.

10 You took it off before you started to mix the batter.

11 I'll give the person who finds that ring a reward of one hundred dollars!

12 (1) in order to find   (2) so as to find
  (3) in order that   (4) so that, can[may]

13 25 cents   14 work

15 100달러를 갖고 집으로 갔다. / 다이아몬드 반지를 다시 찾았다. / 도넛을 많이 팔았다. / 자신의 아이디어가 아주 잘 통해서 행복했다.

16 ③

---

01 (1) 해석: 도넛과 커피 한 잔 주겠니?, 이 문장에서 have는 '먹다'와 '마시다'의 의미로 사용된다. (2) 해석: 난 이제 가 봐야 해. 정말 재미있었어. 잘 있으렴. 'have to+동사원형'은 '~해야 한다'는 의미다.

02 (1) 그 반지를 찾는 사람에게 100달러의 보상을 드릴게요. (2) 링 모양의 반죽들이 뜨거운 기름 속으로 떨어지기 시작했다. start는 뒤에 동명사나 to부정사를 취한다. (3) Bob 삼촌이 떠난 후, 큰 차 한 대가 가게 앞에 섰고, 한 귀부인이 내렸다. 시제가 과거이므로 step의 과거형 stepped를 써야 한다.

03 (1) 과거에 일어났거나 말하여진 어떤 것의 이미지를 마음속에 갖다 (2) 둘 또는 그 이상의 것이 어떻게 다르거나 같은지에 관해 생각하다 (3) 당신이 신날 때 갖는 느낌 (4) 효과적이거나 성공하다

05 (1) so는 결과를 이끌고 because는 이유를 이끈다. (2) 가주어로 It이 적절하다. (3) 감각동사+형용사 (4) turn off는 '동사+부사'의 형태로, 목적어가 인칭대명사일 때 목적어를 동사와 부사 사이에 써야 한다. (5) 물질명사를 셀 때는 세는 단위를 복수로 표시한다.

06 (1) 선행사가 사람이고 is의 주어 역할을 해야 하므로 관계대명사 who나 that을 써야 한다. (2) 선행사가 사물이고 is의 주어 역할을 해야 하므로 관계대명사 which나 that을 써야 한다. (3) 선행사가 사물이고 at의 목적어 역할을 해야 하므로 관계대명사 which나 that을 써야 한다. 목적격이므로 생략할 수도 있다. 또한 that은 전치사 다음에는 쓸 수 없음에 유의한다.

07 Bob은 '기계를 좋아해서', 그의 도넛 가게는 요리 기계들로 가득 차 있었다.

08 batter: 반죽(요리에서 사용되는 밀가루, 달걀, 우유의 혼합 물)

09 먼저, 도넛 반죽을 만들고 그것을 기계에 넣은 다음에 기계 를 작동하기만 하면 된다고 했다.

10 'off'를 보충하면 된다. take ~ off(~을 벗다, ~을 빼다)는 '동사+부사'의 형태로 목적어가 인칭대명사일 때는 동사와 부사 사이에 쓰는 것이 적절하다

11 전치사 'to'를 빼고 '간접목적어+직접목적어'의 어순으로 바꾼다.

12 in order to 동사원형 = so as to 동사원형 = in order that ~ can[may] = so that ~ can[may]: ~하기 위하여(목적)

13 2개에 5센트이므로 10개를 사면 가격은 '25센트'이다.

14 이 글의 요지는 문제를 해결할 때 창의적인 아이디어가 어떻게 '잘 되어 갈 수 있는가'이다. text: 본문, 지문, work: (계 획 등이) 잘 되어 가다

15 남자는 100달러를 갖고 집으로 갔다. 귀부인은 다이아몬드 반지를 다시 찾았다. Bob 삼촌은 도넛을 많이 팔았다. Homer는 자신의 아이디어가 아주 잘 통해서 행복했다.

16 ⓒ와 ③번: (계획 등이) 잘 되어 가다, ①, ⑤ 일하다, ② (광산·농장· 사업 등을) 경영하다, ④ (기계 등을) 작동시키다(타동사)
123서술형

단원별 예상문제

01 ⑤   02 drop   03 ①   04 batter
05 All of a sudden   06 ②   07 ④
08 back
09 (1) Homer is the person who[that] is very creative.
　(2) Bob had to fix the machine to make doughnuts.
　(3) Homer found the lost ring with ease.
　(4) Sean was happy that his idea was finally accepted.
10 ④, ⑤   11 ④
12 (1) Grace bought a skirt and put it on.
　(2) Charlie Brown is a boy who has bad luck.
　(3) The metal felt smooth and cold.
　(4) She started playing the piano to make her fingers strong.
13 ②   14 ③   15 the doughnut batter
16 (A) watch the shop   (B) make some doughnuts
17 (A) took off   (B) great   (C) turned on   18 ④

19 ④   20 ①   21 filled with
22 He pushed the stop button, but nothing happened. The doughnuts kept coming out of the machine.
23 ④   24 ①   25 ①   26 ③, ④
27 ⑤   28 ②, ④   29 Here're → Here's

01 ⑤번은 'drop'에 대한 설명이다. 'step out'은 'to go out for a short time(잠시 밖으로 나가다)'이 적절하다.

02 유의어 관계이다. 섞다 : 떨어지다

03 '음식을 준비하거나 요리하는 방법을 말해주는 일련의 설명서'

04 그림은 소년이 밀가루 반죽을 만들고 있는 모습이다.

05 • 갑자기 어두워졌다. • 나는 집에 물건을 두고 온 것이 갑자기 생각났다.

06 • drop into: ~속으로 떨어지다. drop by: 잠시 들리다 • be full of: ~으로 가득 차다(= be filled with) • break up: 쪼개다, break down: 고장나다, 분해하다

07 모두 반의어 관계이고, ④번은 '외치다'라는 유의어 관계이다.

08 • go back: 돌아가다 • come back: 돌아오다 • give 목적어 back: ~을 돌려주다 • get 목적어 back: ~을 돌 려받다

09 (1) 선행사가 사람이므로 주격 관계대명사 who나 that이 적절하다. (2) 부사적 용법으로 '목적'을 나타내는 to부정사가 적절하다. (3) 'with+추상명사'로 부사의 의미를 나타낸다. with ease = easily (4) 감정의 원인을 나타내는 부사절을 이끄는 that이 적절하다. (because로 써도 좋다.)

10 뒤에 형용사 delicious가 보어로 나오고 있으므로 감각동사가 적절하다. buy나 bring, ask 등은 형용사를 보어로 쓰지 않는다.

11 <보기>와 ④ 부사적 용법의 '목적' ① 명사적 용법(진주어) ② 명사적 용법(목적어) ③ 형용사적 용법 ⑤ 명사적 용법(보어)

12 (1) put on은 '동사+부사'의 형태로, 목적어가 인칭대명사 일 때 목적어를 동사와 부사 사이에 써야 한다. (2) 선행사가 사람이므로 주격 관계대명사 who나 that을 이용하여 쓴다. (3) 감각 동사의 보어로 형용사가 적절하다. (4) to부정사의 부사적 용법의 '목적'을 이용하여 쓴다.

13 a person을 선행사로 하고 있고 teaches의 주어 역할을 해야 하므로 who나 that이 적절하다. whom을 대신해서 who를 쓸 수는 있지만 who를 대신해서 whom을 쓸 수는 없다.

14 이유를 나타내는 접속사 As를 쓰는 것이 적절하다.

15 '도넛 반죽'을 가리킨다.

16 Bob 삼촌은 Homer가 자기 대신 '가게를 봐 주고' '도넛을 좀 만들어 주기'를 원했다.

17 (A) 외투를 '벗고' 커다란 다이아몬드 반지를 '뺐다'고 해야 하므로 took off가 적절하다. put on: ~을 입다, (B) 감각동사의 보어로 형용사를 써야 하므로 great이 적절하다. (C) 도넛 기계를 '작동시키자' 링 모양의 반죽들이 뜨거운 기름 속으로 떨어지기 시작한 것이므로 turned on이 적절하다. turn off: (전기·가스·수도 등을) 끄다

18 귀부인은 자발적으로 Homer가 도넛 반죽을 만들고 있는 것을 도와주었으므로, '친절한[다정한]' 성격이라고 하는 것이 적절하다. ① 호기심 많은, ② 공손한, ③ 끈기 있는, ⑤ 창의적인

19 Homer가 반죽을 만든 것이 아니라 '귀부인'이 반죽을 만들었다.

20 주어진 문장은 ①번 앞 문장의 내용을 부연 설명하는 것이므로 ①번이 적절하다.

21 be full of = be filled with: ~로 가득 차 있다

22 정지 버튼을 눌렀지만, 아무 일도 일어나지 않고, 도넛이 계속해서 기계에서 나오고 있었던 것을 가리킨다.

23 leave: ~에 두다, 놓다, ① lie-lay-lain: 눕다, 놓여 있다, lay-laid-laid: 놓다[두다], 과거시제를 써야 하므로 laid로 쓰는 것이 적절하다.

24 ⓑ와 ①: 부사적 용법(목적), ②, ④ 명사적 용법. ③, ⑤: 형용사적 용법

25 반지를 찾기 위해 도넛을 모두 쪼개야 했기 때문에 '당황스러운' 심경이라고 하는 것이 적절하다. ① 당황스러운, ② 흥분한, ③ 부끄러운, ④ 지루한, ⑤ 안도하는

27 이 글은 Homer의 창의적인 아이디어 덕분에 문제를 해결하는 내용의 글이므로, 제목으로는 '창의적인 아이디어가 잘 통했다!'가 적절하다.

28 all of a sudden = suddenly = all at once: 갑자기, ① 한꺼번에, 동시에, ③ 실제로, 정말로, ⑤ 즉시, 즉각

29 금액은 단수 취급한다.

교과서 파헤치기

단어 TEST Step 1   p.02

01 충고	02 유명인사, 유명인	03 ~ 동안
04 현명하지 않은	05 아픈, 쓰린	06 열, 열병
07 단순한	08 눈을 깜박이다	09 엄지손가락
10 막다, 예방하다	11 목구멍	12 건강
13 피부	14 초조한, 불안한	15 다양한
16 구덩이, 구멍	17 과목	18 건조한, 마른
19 식사	20 약	21 규칙적으로
22 똑똑한, 지적인	23 어려운	24 다치다
25 약속	26 사고	27 안전
28 예, 사례	29 증가하다	30 작가, 저자
31 끔찍한, 무서운	32 중독	33 야기하다
34 아픔, 고통	35 지금부터	36 전 세계적으로
37 잠들다	38 ~ 대신에	39 (~한 상태에) 처하다
40 휴식을 취하다, 쉬다		41 목이 아프다
42 예를 들어	43 건강해 보이다	

단어 TEST Step 2   p.03

01 thumb	02 hole	03 health
04 difficult	05 promise	06 regularly
07 simple	08 nervous	09 advice
10 prevent	11 hurt	12 during
13 skin	14 blink	15 various
16 celebrity	17 sore	18 unwise
19 subject	20 medicine	21 fever
22 dry	23 intelligent	24 throat
25 meal	26 increase	27 dentist
28 smart	29 exercise	30 addiction
31 without	32 toothache	33 safety
34 author	35 instead of ~	36 a few
37 these days	38 have a runny nose	
39 for example	40 take a rest	41 try to+동사원형
42 fall asleep	43 from now on	

단어 TEST Step 3   p.04

1 rest, 휴식   2 pad, 패드   3 cause, 야기하다
4 hole, 구덩이   5 blink, 눈을 깜박이다
6 regularly, 규칙적으로   7 pain, 고통
8 text, 문자를 보내다 9 throat, 목구멍

---

10 increase, 증가하다   11 medicine, 약, 약물
12 prevent, 막다, 예방하다   13 safety, 안전
14 thumb, 엄지손가락   15 exercise, 운동
16 addiction, 중독

대화문 TEST Step 1   p.05~06

Listen and Talk A-1

look sick, What's wrong / have a sore throat, have a fever / have a cold, Take, medicine, make sure, take, rest / Thank you

Listen and Talk A-2

wrong / back hurts a lot / Put, on / I will / make sure, stretching exercises

Listen and Talk A-3

matter / have a, toothache / Here is, medicine, Take / make sure, dentist / I will

Listen and Talk A-4

wrong with / fell, hurt, while / Can, walk / hurts / Why don't you, make sure, don't play, until

Listen and Talk B

1 don't look well, wrong / have a headache / That's too bad, Make sure, take / will

2 don't look well, wrong / have a cold / Make sure, doctor / I will

Listen and Talk C

wrong / thumb hurts / use, a lot / text a lot / have texting thumb / pain, your thumb, get, from texting / didn't know / Why don't you / make sure you don't text

Review 1

wrong / have a terrible headache / should take some medicine / I will

Review 2

the matter / have a sore throat, have a runny nose / cold, Make sure, get some rest / I will

대화문 TEST Step 2   p.07~08

Listen and Talk A-1

W: You look sick. What's wrong, Inho?
B: I have a sore throat. I have a fever, too.
W: I think you have a cold. Take this medicine and make sure you take a good rest.
B: OK. Thank you.

Listen and Talk A-2

W: What's wrong, Peter?

B: I don't know, Ms. Kim, but my back hurts a lot.

W: Put a heating pad on it.

B: OK, I will.

W: And make sure you do some stretching exercises.

Listen and Talk A-3

W: What's the matter, Chris?

B: I have a terrible toothache.

W: Here is some medicine. Take this.

B: Thank you.

W: And make sure you go to the dentist. B: OK, I will.

Listen and Talk A-4

W: What's wrong with your leg, Sam?

B: I fell and hurt my foot while I was playing soccer.

W: Can you walk?

B: Yes, but it hurts a lot.

W: Why don't you put some ice on it? And make sure you don't play soccer until next week.

Listen and Talk B

1 A: You don't look well. What's wrong?

B: I have a headache.

A: That's too bad. Make sure you take some medicine.

B: OK, I will.

2 A: You don't look well. What's wrong?

B: I have a cold.

A: That's too bad. Make sure you go see a doctor.

B: OK, I will.

Listen and Talk C

W: What's wrong, Andy?

B: Hello, Ms. Kim. My right thumb hurts.

W: Hmm. Do you use your smartphone a lot?

B: Yes, I text a lot. Why?

W: I think you have texting thumb.

B: Texting thumb? What's texting thumb?

W: It's pain in your thumb. You can get it from texting too much.

B: Oh, I didn't know that.

W: Why don't you do some finger stretching exercises?

B: OK, I will. W: And make sure you don't text too much.

Review 1

G: What's wrong, Mike?

B: I have a terrible headache.

G: I think you should take some medicine.

B: OK, I will.

Review 2

M: What's the matter, Mina?

G: I have a sore throat. I also have a runny nose.

M: I think you have a cold. Make sure you get some rest.

G: OK, I will.

본문 TEST Step 1 p.09~10

01 Be Smart with 02 Living without, difficult, days
03 unwise, use, cause 04 Are, smombie
05 over, around like 06 down, eyes, on
07 call such people
08 If, various safety
09 may, so, fall, hurt 10 get into, too
11 what, to prevent 12 It's simple
13 at, while, walking 14 dry, text neck
15 cause, health problems
16 example, dry eyes
17 When, look at, blink 18 your, feel dry
19 Another, have, pain
20 down at, on, increases
21 use, for, texting, cause
22 call, text 23 Here, tips, problems
24 dry, try, blink 25 move, up, level
26 also, stretching exercises
27 How, feel, don't
28 feel nervous, around
29 feel sad, check, text
30 answers, may, addiction
31 There, various, prevent 32 turn off, during
33 instead of texting

본문 TEST Step 2 p.11~12

01 Be Smart with
02 Living without smartphones, these days
03 unwise or too much use, can cause
04 Are, a smombie
05 All over the world, walking around like zombies
06 down, on their smartphones
07 call such people smombies
08 various safety problems
09 may not see, so, may fall, get hurt
10 may get into, too
11 to prevent these problems 12 simple

46 정답 및 해설

13 Do not look at, while, walking

14 dry eyes, text neck

15 various health problems

16 One example, dry eyes

17 look at, blink often   18 will feel dry

19 Another problem, is neck pain

20 look down at, stress on, increases

21 Too much use, too much texting, neck pain

22 call, text neck   23 Here are some tips

24 dry eyes, try to blink

25 move, up to, your eye level

26 can also, neck stretching exercises

27 How do you feel

28 feel nervous, around

29 feel sad, no text message

30 answers, smartphone addiction 31 to prevent this

32 For example, turn off, during

33 can, instead of texting

---

1 스마트폰을 현명하게 사용하라!

2 스마트폰 없이 사는 것은 요즘 많은 사람들에게 어렵다.

3 하지만 스마트폰을 현명하지 않게 사용하거나 너무 과도하게 사용하는 것은 다양한 문제를 야기할 수 있다.

4 당신은 스몸비인가요?

5 전 세계적으로 사람들이 좀비처럼 걸어다니고 있다.

6 그들의 머리는 아래를 향하고, 그들의 눈은 스마트폰을 향하고 있다.

7 우리는 그런 사람들을 스몸비, 즉 스마트폰 좀비라고 부른다.

8 만약 당신이 스몸비라면, 당신은 다양한 안전 관련 문제들을 겪을 수 있다.

9 당신은 거리에 있는 구덩이를 보지 못할 수도 있고, 그래서 넘어져서 다칠지도 모른다.

10 당신은 또한 교통사고를 당할지도 모른다.

11 그렇다면 이런 문제들을 방지하기 위해 무엇을 할 수 있을까?

12 간단하다.

13 걷고 있는 동안에는 스마트폰을 보지 마라!

14 당신은 안구 건조증이나 거북목 증후군이 있나요?

15 스마트폰은 다양한 건강상의 문제를 일으킬 수 있다.

16 한 가지 예가 안구 건조증이다.

17 스마트폰을 볼 때, 당신은 눈을 자주 깜박거리지 않는다.

18 그러면 눈이 건조하다고 느낄 것이다.

19 일어날 수 있는 또 다른 문제는 목 통증이다.

20 스마트폰을 내려다볼 때, 목에 가해지는 압박이 증가한다.

21 스마트폰을 너무 많이 사용하는 것은, 예를 들어, 너무 많이 문자를 하는 것은 목 통증을 일으킬 수 있다.

---

22 이런 증상을 거북목 증후군이라고 부른다.

23 여기에 이런 문제들을 위한 몇 가지 조언이 있다.

24 안구 건조증에는, 눈을 자주 깜박이려고 노력해라.

25 거북목 증후군에는 당신의 눈높이까지 스마트폰을 위로 올려라.

26 목 스트레칭 운동 또한 할 수 있다.

27 스마트폰이 없을 때 어떤 기분이 드나요?

28 스마트폰이 주위에 없을 때 당신은 초조한 기분이 드는가?

29 스마트폰을 확인했을 때 아무런 문자 메시지가 없으면 슬픈 기분이 드는가?

30 만약 당신의 대답이 '그렇다'이면, 당신은 스마트폰 중독일지도 모른다.

31 이것을 방지하기 위해 할 수 있는 일은 여러 가지가 있다.

32 예를 들어, 식사나 회의 중에는 스마트폰을 꺼라.

33 문자를 보내는 대신에 사람들과 이야기를 할 수 있다.

---

1 Be Smart with Your Smartphones!

2 Living without smartphones is difficult for many of us these days.

3 However, unwise or too much use of smartphones can cause various problems.

4 Are you a smombie?

5 All over the world, people are walking around like zombies.

6 Their heads are down, and their eyes are on their smartphones.

7 We call such people smombies, smartphone zombies.

8 If you are a smombie, you can have various safety problems.

9 You may not see a hole in the street, so you may fall and get hurt.

10 You may get into a car accident, too.

11 So what can you do to prevent these problems?

12 It's simple.

13 Do not look at your smartphone while you are walking!

14 Do you have dry eyes or text neck?

15 Smartphones can cause various health problems.

16 One example is dry eyes.

17 When you look at your smartphone, you do not blink often.

18 Then your eyes will feel dry.

19 Another problem you can have is neck pain.

20 When you look down at your smartphone, the

stress on your neck increases.

21 Too much use of your smartphone, for example, too much texting, can cause neck pain.

22 We call this text neck.

23 Here are some tips for these problems.

24 For dry eyes, try to blink often.

25 For text neck, move your smartphone up to your eye level.

26 You can also do some neck stretching exercises.

27 How do you feel when you don't have your smartphone with you?

28 Do you feel nervous when your smartphone is not around?

29 Do you feel sad when you check your smartphone and there is no text message?

30 If your answers are "yes," you may have smartphone addiction.

31 There are various things you can do to prevent this.

32 For example, turn off your smartphone during meals or meetings.

33 You can talk to people instead of texting them.

Talk and Play

1. wrong

2. have a fever

3. Make sure, some rest

4. I will

After You Read B

1. Be Smart with

2. fell, got hurt

3. was texting, didn't see

4. Do not, while, are walking

5. feel dry

6. Try to blink

7. when, text a lot

8. up to, eye level, stretching exercises

9. have smartphone addiction

10. Turn off, during, instead of texting

Around the World

1. Be careful, using, while

2. There are, so, while, are using

3. means, side, who are texting

Talk and Play

1. A: What's wrong?

2. B: I have a fever.

3. A: That's too bad. Make sure you get some rest.

4. B: OK, I will.

After You Read B

1. Be Smart with Your Smartphones!

2. Minho: Yesterday, I fell on the street and got hurt.

3. I was texting and I didn't see a hole.

4. Reply: Do not use your smartphone while you are walking.

5. Emma: My eyes feel dry when I use my smartphone.

6. Reply: Try to blink often.

7. Suji: I have neck pain when I text a lot.

8. Reply: Move your smartphone up to your eye level and do some neck stretching exercises .

9. Eric: I think I have smartphone addiction.

10. Reply: Turn off your smartphone during meals or meetings and talk to people instead of texting them.

Around the World

1. This sign says, "Be careful of using your smartphone while you are walking."

2. There are traffic lights on the ground, so people can see them while they are using their smartphones.

3. This sign on the ground means, "This side of the street is for people who are texting."

Lesson 6

9 adventurous, 모험심이 강한　10 outline, 윤곽, 외형

11 skip, 빼먹다, 거르다　12 feather, 깃털

13 wing, 날개　14 furthermore, 게다가

15 myth, 신화　16 warn, 경고하다

단어 TEST Step 1　　　　　　　　　　　　p.21

01 특별한　02 용감한　03 창의적인

04 단순한　05 세부 사항　06 모험심이 강한

07 전부의, 전체의　08 아름다움, 미　09 주제

10 경고, 주의　11 녹다　12 역동적인

13 달아나다, 탈출하다　14 비행, 날기

15 전시회　16 로맨틱한, 낭만적인

17 차이　18 빼먹다, 거르다　19 영원히

20 모으다　21 붙이다　22 상상력이 풍부한

23 (새의) 털, 깃털　24 다른　25 문장

26 잊어버리다, 잊다　27 발명가　28 예, 사례

29 어리석은　30 윤곽, 외형　31 게다가, 더욱이

32 준비된　33 신화　34 경고하다

35 ~와 사랑에 빠지다　36 ~에 관심이 있다

37 ~을 다루다　38 ~에 더하여, ~일 뿐 아니라

39 ~을 자랑스러워하다　40 그에 반해서

41 ~에 초점을 맞추다　42 ~하는 게 어때?

43 ~하려고 시도하다

단어 TEST Step 2　　　　　　　　　　　　p.22

01 subject　02 whole　03 dynamic

04 warn　05 escape　06 exhibition

07 simple　08 myth　09 beauty

10 special　11 gather　12 romantic

13 sci-fi movie　14 adventurous　15 feather

16 difference　17 brave　18 melt

19 creative　20 flight　21 outline

22 different　23 foolish　24 sentence

25 forever　26 imaginative　27 forget

28 inventor　29 ready　30 furthermore

31 example　32 detail　33 skip

34 warning　35 deal with

36 higher and higher　37 fall in love with ~

38 in front of ~　39 in addition to　40 try to+동사원형

41 be interested in ~　42 be proud of ~

43 focus on ~

단어 TEST Step 3　　　　　　　　　　　　p.23

1 exhibition, 전시회　2 shout, 소리치다

3 foolish, 어리석은　4 flight, 비행　5 romantic, 낭만적인

6 escape, 달아나다　7 gather, 모으다　8 detail, 세부 사항

대화문 TEST Step 1　　　　　　　　　　　p.24~25

Listen and Talk A-1

planning to go, to go with / What time should, meet / begins at, let's meet / See, then

Listen and Talk A-2

planning to go see, want to go / What time, where should / at 3 o'clock, Let's meet / See, on Saturday

Listen and Talk A-3

planning to go see, What about joining / sounds, should we meet / Let's meet, in front of

Listen and Talk A-4

What, going to do / planning to go, if, want to / love to When should / let's meet / Sounds

Listen and Talk B

planning to see, want to / What time, where, meet / How, meeting / See you then

Listen and Talk C

up / going to do / Nothing special / planning to go, want to go / love to, What time should, meet / How about meeting / Where should / Let's, in front of / see you there

Review 1

planning to, Why don't you join / should we meet / Let's meet, at the bus stop / then

Review 2

planning to go, Do you want / What time should, meet / let's meet, in front of

Review 3

I'm planning to go shopping, join / What, meet / about meeting / Where should, meet / meet in front of

대화문 TEST Step 2　　　　　　　　　　　p.26~27

Listen and Talk A-1

G: I'm planning to go to a piano concert tomorrow. Do you want to go with me, Kevin?

B: Sure. What time should we meet?

G: The concert begins at 7 o'clock, so let's meet at 6 at the bus stop.

B: OK. See you then.

49

G: I'm planning to go see Cats this Saturday. Do you want to go with me?

B: Sure. What time and where should we meet?

G: The musical starts at 3 o'clock. Let's meet at 2 at Dream Art Hall.

B: Great. See you on Saturday.

Listen and Talk A-3

G: I'm planning to go see a soccer game next Friday. What about joining me, Jinho?

B: That sounds great. What time should we meet?

G: Let's meet at 10:30 in front of Green Stadium.

B: OK. See you then.

Listen and Talk A-4

B: What are you going to do this Sunday?

G: I'm planning to go to Dream Amusement Park with my brother. You can go with us if you want to.

B: I'd love to. When should we meet?

G: I want to go early, so let's meet at 9 at the subway station.

B: Sounds good. I'll see you then.

Listen and Talk B

A: I'm planning to see a movie this Saturday. Do you want to go with me?

B: Sure. What time and where should we meet?

A: How about meeting at 2:30 in front of Star Movie Theater?

B: OK. See you then.

Listen and Talk C

B: Hi, Kate. What's up?

G: Hi, Minho. What are you going to do this Saturday?

B: Nothing special. Why?

G: I'm planning to go to the Van Gogh exhibition at the National Art Museum. Do you want to go with me?

B: I'd love to! He's my favorite painter. What time should we meet?

G: How about meeting at 11?

B: OK. Where should we meet?

G: Let's meet in front of the ticket office.

B: Sounds good. I'll see you there at 11.

Review 1

G: I'm planning to go to a piano concert this Friday. Why don't you join me, Kevin?

B: Sure. What time should we meet?

G: Let's meet at 10:30 at the bus stop.

B: OK. See you then.

Review 2

B: I'm planning to go to a soccer game tomorrow. Do you want to go with me, Susan?

G: Sure. What time should we meet?

B: The game begins at 7, so let's meet at 6 in front of Dream Stadium.

G: OK. See you then.

Review 3

B: Sumi, I'm planning to go shopping with Jenny this Saturday. Will you join us?

G: Sounds great. What time should we meet?

B: How about meeting at 12:30?

G: OK. Where should we meet?

B: Let's meet in front of the shopping mall.

본문 TEST Step 1   p.28~29

01 Same, Different

02 different paintings, same subject

03 example, and, by

04 both, same, myth   05 Greek Myth

06 a great inventor

07 so, that, keep, forever

08 however, tired, so, kept

09 wanted to escape

10 One, saw, flying

11 need wings, shouted

12 gathered, feathers, glued, wax

13 ready, warned, Don't, close   14 wax, melt

15 began to fly   16 so, that, forgot, warning

17 flew, higher, melt

18 falling, cried out   19 fell into, died

20 Different Paintings

21 deal with, subject, different

22 painting, see, flying, falling

23 comes from, different ideas

24 thought, brave, adventurous

25 contrast, thought, foolish

26 simple, but, details

27 there, only, some stars

28 Furthermore, just, outline

29 In contrast, addition to

30 difference, different, styles

31 Whose painting, more

32 because, same, different ways

본문 TEST Step 2   p.30~31

01 Same, Different Paintings

02 different paintings, the same subject

03 example, by, by

04 both, the same Greek myth   05 Greek Myth

06 a great inventor

07 work so, that, wanted to keep, forever

08 however, tired to leave, so, kept

09 wanted to escape

10 saw birds flying

11 I need wings, shouted

12 gathered, glued them together with wax

13 ready, warned, Don't fly too close

14 will melt   15 began to fly

16 so, that, warning

17 higher and higher

18 falling, cried out   19 fell into, died

20 Different Paintings

21 both deal with, same subject, different

22 see Icarus flying, falling

23 comes from, different ideas

24 thought, brave, adventurous

25 In contrast, foolish

26 very simple, many details

27 only Icarus, some stars

28 Furthermore, simple outline

29 In contrast, in addition to

30 difference comes from, different painting styles

31 Whose painting, like more

32 because, same thing in different ways

가까이 날지 마라.

14 밀랍이 녹을 거야."

15 Daedalus와 Icarus는 날기 시작했다.

16 Icarus는 매우 흥분해서 아버지의 경고를 잊었다.

17 그는 점점 더 높이 날았고, 밀랍은 녹기 시작했다.

18 "오, 안 돼! 추락하고 있어." Icarus는 비명을 질렀다.

19 Icarus는 바다로 떨어져서 죽었다.

20 다른 두 그림

21 Matisse와 Chagall 둘 다 그들의 그림에서 같은 주제를 다루지만, 그것들은 다르다.

22 첫째, Matisse의 그림에서, 여러분은 Icarus가 날고 있는 것을 볼 수 있지만, Chagall의 그림에서는 그 소년이 추락하고 있다.

23 이러한 차이는 두 화가들이 갖고 있던 서로 다른 생각에서 기인한다.

24 Matisse는 Icarus가 용감하고 모험심이 강하다고 생각했다.

25 반면에 Chagall은 Icarus가 어리석다고 생각했다.

26 둘째, Matisse의 그림은 매우 단순하지만, Chagall의 그림에는 세부적인 것들이 많다.

27 Matisse의 그림에는 Icarus와 몇 개의 별들만 있다.

28 게다가 Icarus의 몸은 단지 단순한 윤곽만으로 되어 있다.

29 반면에 Chagall은 Icarus뿐만 아니라 많은 사람들과 집들을 그렸다.

30 이러한 차이는 두 화가의 서로 다른 화풍에서 기인한다.

31 여러분은 누구의 그림이 더 좋은가?

32 사람들은 같은 것을 다른 방식들로 볼 수도 있기 때문에 서로 다른 대답을 할 것이다.

---

1 같은 이야기, 다른 그림

2 우리는 종종 같은 주제의 다른 그림들을 발견한다.

3 한 예가 Henri Matisse가 그린 "The Flight of Icarus (이카로스의 비행)"와 Marc Chagall이 그린 "The Fall of Icarus (이카로스의 추락)"이다.

4 그것들은 둘 다 모두 같은 그리스 신화에 관한 것이다.

5 Icarus에 관한 그리스 신화

6 Daedalus는 훌륭한 발명가였다.

7 Minos왕은 Daedalus의 작품을 매우 좋아해서 Daedalus를 그의 곁에 영원히 두고 싶어 했다.

8 그러나 Daedalus는 떠나려고 했고, 그러자 왕은 그와 그의 아들인 Icarus를 높은 탑에 가두었다.

9 Daedalus는 탈출하고 싶었다.

10 어느 날, Daedalus는 새가 날고 있는 것을 보았다.

11 "날개! 날개가 필요해!" 그가 외쳤다.

12 그 다음에 Daedalus는 새의 깃털을 모아 그것들을 밀랍으로 붙였다.

13 날개가 준비되었을 때, 그는 아들에게 경고했다. "태양에 너무

---

1 Same Story, Different Paintings

2 We often find different paintings with the same subject.

3 An example is The Flight of Icarus by Henri Matisse and The Fall of Icarus by Marc Chagall.

4 They are both about the same Greek myth.

5 The Greek Myth of Icarus

6 Daedalus was a great inventor.

7 King Minos liked Daedalus' work so much that he wanted to keep Daedalus with him forever.

8 Daedalus, however, tried to leave, so the King kept him and his son, Icarus, in a tall tower.

9 Daedalus wanted to escape.

10 One day, Daedalus saw birds flying.

11 "Wings! I need wings!" he shouted.

12 Daedalus then gathered bird feathers and glued them together with wax.

13 When the wings were ready, he warned his son,

"Don't fly too close to the sun.

14 The wax will melt."

15 Daedalus and Icarus began to fly.

16 Icarus was so excited that he forgot his father's warning.

17 He flew higher and higher, and the wax began to melt.

18 "Oh, no! I'm falling," Icarus cried out.

19 Icarus fell into the sea and died.

20 Two Different Paintings

21 Matisse and Chagall both deal with the same subject in their paintings, but they are different.

22 First, in Matisse's painting, you can see Icarus flying, but in Chagall's painting, the boy is falling.

23 This difference comes from the different ideas that the two painters had.

24 Matisse thought that Icarus was brave and adventurous.

25 In contrast, Chagall thought that Icarus was foolish.

26 Second, Matisse's painting is very simple, but Chagall's painting has many details.

27 In Matisse's painting, there are only Icarus and some stars.

28 Furthermore, Icarus' body has just a simple outline.

29 In contrast, Chagall painted many people and houses in addition to Icarus.

30 This difference comes from the different painting styles of the two painters.

31 Whose painting do you like more?

32 People will have different answers because they may see the same thing in different ways.

구석구석지문 TEST Step 1   p.38

Talk and Play

1. I'm planning to, want to go with
2. What time, meet
3. How about meeting
4. Where, meet
5. Let's meet in front of
6. Sounds, See, than

Around the World

1. was proud of
2. One day, fell in love with himself
3. that, all the bad things
4. they all came out
5. a great musician

6. met, return my wife

After You Read D Reading Project

1. Title
2. Painter
3. In, painting, is flying
4. thought, brave, adventurous
5. simple, drew only, some stars
6. Title
7. Painter
8. is falling, thought, was foolish
9. many details, in addition to

구석구석지문 TEST Step 2   p.39

Talk and Play

1. A: I'm planning to go to the library this Monday. Do you want to go with me, Jiho?
2. B: Sure. What time should we meet?
3. A: How about meeting at 5:30?
4. B: OK. Where should we meet?
5. A: Let's meet in front of the library.
6. B: Sounds good. See you then.

Around the World

1. Narcissus: Narcissus was proud of his beauty.
2. One day , he saw his face in the water and fell in love with himself.
3. Pandora: There was a box that had all the bad things in the world inside.
4. Pandora opened it, and they all came out.
5. Orpheus: Orpheus was a great musician.
6. When his wife died, he met Hades and told him, "Please return my wife to me."

After You Read D Reading Project

1. Title : The Flight of Icarus
2. Painter : Henri Matisse
3. In Matisse's painting , Icarus is flying .
4. He thought Icarus was brave and adventurous.
5. His painting is very simple . He drew only Icarus and some stars .
6. Title : The Fall of Icarus
7. Painter : Marc Chagall
8. In Chagall's painting, Icarus is falling . He thought Icarus was foolish .
9. His painting has many details . He painted many people and houses in addition to Icarus.

11 towards, ~을 향해   12 space station, 우주 정거장
13 adventure, 모험   14 swallow, 삼키다
15 land, 착륙하다   16 secret, 비밀

단어 TEST Step 1   p.40

01 도착하다	02 모험	03 맛
04 놀라운	05 어려운	06 뜨다, 떠가다
07 외치다	08 풍선	09 그릇, 용기
10 다른	11 궁금한, 호기심이 많은	
12 목마른	13 모든 곳에	14 우주 정거장
15 탐험, 탐사	16 마침내	17 ~한 이래로
18 외국의	19 신난, 흥분한	20 눕다
21 삼키다	22 흔들다	
23 ~쪽으로, ~을 향하여		24 우주선
25 고치다	26 젖은	27 웃다
28 구하다	29 최근에	30 우주복
31 형성하다, 만들어 내다		32 비밀, 기밀
33 부드러운	34 아주 신나는	35 ~할 필요 없다
36 (둘 사이의) 서로	37 ~으로 뒤덮이다	38 아래로 끌어내리다
39 눕다	40 예를 들어	
41 ~에 관해 궁금해 하다		42 ~으로 달려가다
43 더 이상 ~ 않다		

단어 TEST Step 2   p.41

01 dventure	02 balloon	03 difficult
04 float	05 excited	06 different
07 exploration	08 soft	09 amazing
10 finally	11 since	12 fix
13 foreign	14 spaceship	15 secret
16 everywhere	17 wind	18 shout
19 shake	20 curious	21 towards
22 space suit	23 thirsty	24 container
25 swallow	26 hill	27 lie
28 thrilling	29 laugh	30 wet
31 grass	32 recently	33 save
34 taste	35 be curious about ~	
36 try to+동사원형	37 in surprise	38 not ~ anymore
39 be covered with		40 get on
41 for example	42 each other	43 roll down

단어 TEST Step 3   p.42

1 amazing, 놀라운   2 float, 뜨다   3 spaceship, 우주선
4 form, 형성하다, 만들다   5 arrive , 도착하다
6 save, 구하다   7 curious, 호기심 많은   8 wet, 젖은
9 exploration, 탐험, 탐사   10 foreign, 외국의

대화문 TEST Step 1   p.43~44

Listen and Talk A-1
hear about, that went into space / curious about / spaceship / want to buy

Listen and Talk A-2
Did, hear about / I'm really curious about / right here, about / buy

Listen and Talk A-3
Did you hear about / I didn't / space station, Look at / I'm really curious about

Listen and Talk A-4
about, space food / a type of / hear it is, looks good / curious about the taste

Listen and Talk B
1 about / heard / curious about
2 Look at, hear about / No, didn't / it has great songs/ realy curious about

Listen and Talk C
hear about / didn't / heard good / curious about, about / about, who, trying to live / sounds interesting / is playing / What time / begins at / Let's eat lunch, and then / hungry, Let's go

Review 1
did you hear about / No, didn't / heard / curious about, about / about, who saves his son

Review 2
Did, hear about / right, about living / really curious about / Me, too

대화문 TEST Step 2   p.45~46

Listen and Talk A-1
B: Did you hear about the first spaceship that went into space?
G: No, I didn't. I'm curious about it.
B: This is a poster of the spaceship.
G: Really? I want to buy it.

Listen and Talk A-2
G: Did you hear about the new book about Mars?
B: No, I didn't. I'm really curious about Mars.
G: Look. It's right here. It's about Mars and its moons.
B: Great. I think I'll buy the book.

53

Listen and Talk A-3

G: Did you hear about the space marathon?

B: No, I didn't.

G: It's a marathon on a space station. Look at this video.

B: OK. I'm really curious about it.

Listen and Talk A-4

G: Did you hear about the new space food?

B: Yes, I did. It's a type of ice cream.

G: Yes, and here it is. It looks good.

B: I'm really curious about the taste.

Listen and Talk B

1 A: Look at this. Did you hear about the new musical?

 B: Yes, I did. I heard it has great songs.

 A: Oh, I'm really curious about it.

2 A: Look at this. Did you hear about the new musical?

 B: No, I didn't.

 A: I heard it has great songs.

 B: Oh, I'm really curious about it.

Listen and Talk C

B: Subin, did you hear about the new movie, Life on the Moon?

G: No, I didn't.

B: I heard it's really good.

G: I'm really curious about the movie. What's it about?

B: It's about a man who is trying to live on the moon.

G: That sounds interesting.

B: Look. The movie is playing at the Space Theater here.

G: What time is the movie?

B: It begins at 2:30.

G: Let's eat lunch first and then see the movie.

B: OK. I'm hungry. Let's go!

Review 1

G: Tony, did you hear about the movie, My Hero ?

B: No, I didn't.

G: Well, I heard it's really good.

B: I'm really curious about the movie. What's it about ?

G: It's about a father who saves his son.

Review 2

G: Did you hear about the new book, Living in a Foreign Country ?

B: No, I didn't.

G: Look. It's right here. It's about living in New York. B: Great. I'm really curious about this book.

G: Me, too.

01 Best, Thing   02 like, far out   03 lived there with

04 other, worked on   05 Only, were born

06 One, going back

07 in surprise, floated towards   08 What's it like

09 Everything, different

10 For example, answered

11 never seen, said

12 is always black

13 don't have, suits, there

14 hard, because, pulls, down

15 What else   16 covered with, grass

17 roll down, answered

18 have, ever rolled down

19 amazing, answered

20 thirsty, opened, shook

21 floated, air, formed

22 swallowed, balls

23 if, way, get wet

24 Later, talked, long

25 exciting, all, things, going   26 one new thing

27 thought, all night, about   28 their secret

29 next, got on   30 going, be, trip

31 alright, so excited   32 finally landed

33 difficult to walk

34 pulling you down

35 couldn't float anymore   36 first new thing

37 What's, sound   38 bird singing

39 never heard, sing

40 never felt, wind   41 These, all new

42 ran up the nearest

43 top, each other, laughed

44 lay down, soft, rolled   45 their secret

46 best new, shouted   47 ran up to, top

01 Best, Thing   02 far out in space

03 lived there with, brother

04 other, worked on

05 Only, were born in space

06 One day, going back to

07 in surprise, floated towards   08 What's it like

09 Everything is different   10 For example

11 I've never seen   12 is always black

13 don't have to, because there is air

14 jump, pulls you down   15 What else

16 are covered with
17 roll down   18 have you ever rolled down
19 really amazing 20 thirsty, so, opened, shook
21 floated, formed   22 swallowed
23 if, that way, get wet
24 Later that night, a long time
25 exciting, think, all the new things, going to
26 one new thing, wanted to do
27 all night   28 their secret   29 got on
30 It's going to be
31 alright, so excited
32 finally landed 33 to walk
34 pulling you down
35 couldn't float anymore
36 the first new thing   37 What's, sound
38 is singing   39 I've never heard, sing
40 I've never felt 41 These, all new things
42 ran up the nearest
43 each other, laughed
44 lay down, rolled down
45 their secret   46 best new thing
47 up to the top

1 최고의 새로운 것

2 Rada는 먼 우주의 작은 세계에 살고 있었다.

3 그녀는 아빠, 엄마 그리고 남동생 Jonny와 함께 그곳에서 살고 있었다.

4 Rada의 아빠와 다른 사람들은 우주선에서 일했다.

5 Rada와 Jonny만이 아이들이었고, 그들은 우주에서 태어났다.

6 어느 날, 아빠가 Rada와 Jonny에게, "우리는 내일 지구로 돌아갈 거야."라고 말했다.

7 Rada와 Jonny는 깜짝 놀라 아빠를 바라보았고, 그에게 둥둥 떠서 갔다.

8 Rada가 아빠에게, "지구는 어떤 곳인가요?"라고 물었다.

9 "그곳에선 모든 것이 다르단다.

10 예를 들어, 하늘은 파란색이지."라고 아빠가 대답했다.

11 "전 한 번도 파란 하늘을 본 적이 없어요."라고 Jonny가 말했다.

12 "여기는 하늘이 항상 검은색이잖아요."라고 Rada가 말했다.

13 "그곳에는 모든 곳에 공기가 있기 때문에 크고 무거운 우주복을 입을 필요가 없단다.

14 또한 지구가 너희들을 끌어당기기 때문에 거기에서는 점프하는 것도 어렵단다." 아빠가 말했다.

15 "그 밖에 또 뭐가 있어요?" Rada가 물었다.

16 "언덕들이 있는데 그것들은 부드러운 초록색의 잔디로 뒤덮여 있단다.

17 언덕을 굴러 내려갈 수도 있어." 엄마가 대답했다.

18 "아빠, 언덕을 굴러 내려가 본 적 있어요?" Rada가 물었다.

19 "그럼, 정말 놀라워!" 아빠가 대답했다.

20 Jonny는 목이 말라서 우유 용기를 열어 그것을 흔들었다.

21 우유가 공기 중으로 떠서 방울을 형성했다.

22 Jonny는 그 우유 방울을 삼켰다.

23 "Jonny, 만약 네가 지구에서 그런 식으로 우유를 마신다면, 다 젖을 거야." 엄마가 말했다.

24 그날 밤 늦게, Rada와 Jonny는 지구에 대해서 오랜 시간 이야기했다.

25 그들이 보고, 하게 될 모든 새로운 것들을 생각하는 것은 흥미로웠다.

26 Rada와 Jonny가 정말로 하고 싶었던 한 가지 새로운 것이 있었다.

27 그들은 밤새 그것에 대해서 생각했고 엄마와 아빠에게는 그것을 말하지 않았다.

28 그것은 그들의 비밀이었다.

29 다음날, Rada의 가족은 우주선에 올랐다.

30 "긴 여행이 될 거야." 엄마가 말했다.

31 "괜찮아요. 정말 신나요!" Rada가 말했다.

32 우주선이 마침내 착륙했다.

33 "아빠, 지구에서는 걷는 것이 어려워요." Rada가 말했다.

34 "그래. 지구가 너를 끌어당기고 있거든." 아빠가 말했다.

35 Rada와 Jonny는 더 이상 떠다닐 수 없었다.

36 그것이 첫 번째 새로운 것이었다.

37 "저건 무슨 소리죠?"라고 Rada가 물었다.

38 "새가 노래하는 거야." 엄마가 말했다.

39 "새가 노래하는 것을 들어 본 적이 없어요."라고 Rada가 말했다.

40 "그리고 저는 바람을 느껴 본 적도 없어요."라고 Jonny가 말했다.

41 이러한 것들이 모두 새로운 것이었다.

42 Rada와 Jonny는 가장 가까운 언덕으로 뛰어 올라갔다.

43 꼭대기에서, 그들은 서로를 쳐다보고 웃었다.

44 그러고 나서 그들은 부드러운 초록 잔디에 누워서 언덕 아래로 굴러 내려갔다.

45 그것이 그들의 비밀이었다!

46 "이것이 모든 것들 중에서 최고의 새로운 것이에요!" Rada와 Jonny는 외쳤다.

47 그리고 그들은 언덕 꼭대기로 다시 뛰어 올라갔다.

1 The Best New Thing

2 Rada lived on a little world, far out in space.

3 She lived there with her father, mother, and brother Jonny.

4 Rada's father and other people worked on spaceships

5 Only Rada and Jonny were children, and they were born in space.

6 One day, Dad told Rada and Jonny, "We're going back to Earth tomorrow."

7 Rada and Jonny looked at Dad in surprise and floated towards him.

8 Rada asked Dad, "What's it like on Earth?"

9 "Everything is different there.

10 For example, the sky is blue," answered Dad.

11 "I've never seen a blue sky," said Jonny.

12 "The sky is always black here," said Rada.

13 "You don't have to wear your big heavy space suits because there is air everywhere.

14 It's also hard to jump there because Earth pulls you down," said Dad.

15 "What else?" asked Rada.

16 "There are hills, and they are covered with soft green grass.

17 You can roll down the hills," answered Mom.

18 "Dad, have you ever rolled down a hill?" asked Rada.

19 "Yes, it's really amazing!" answered Dad.

20 Jonny was thirsty, so he opened a milk container and shook it.

21 The milk floated in the air and formed balls.

22 Jonny swallowed the balls.

23 "Jonny, if you drink milk that way on Earth, you'll get wet," said Mom.

24 Later that night, Rada and Jonny talked a long time about Earth.

25 It was exciting to think about all the new things they were going to see and do.

26 There was one new thing Rada and Jonny really wanted to do.

27 They thought about it all night and didn't tell Mom and Dad about it.

28 It was their secret.

29 The next day, Rada's family got on a spaceship.

30 "It's going to be a long trip," said Mom.

31 That's alright. I'm so excited!" said Rada.

32 The spaceship finally landed.

33 "Dad, it's difficult to walk on Earth," said Rada.

34 "I know. Earth is pulling you down," said Dad.

35 Rada and Jonny couldn't float anymore.

36 That was the first new thing.

37 "What's that sound?" asked Rada.

38 "A bird is singing," said Mom.

39 "I've never heard a bird sing," said Rada.

40 "And I've never felt the wind," said Jonny.

41 These were all new things.

42 Rada and Jonny ran up the nearest hill.

43 At the top, they looked at each other and laughed.

44 Then they lay down on the soft green grass and rolled down the hill.

45 That was their secret!

46 "This is the best new thing of all!" shouted Rada and Jonny.

47 And they ran up to the top of the hill again.

One Minute Speech

1. hear about
2. is about, adventures, woods
3. main characters
4. Are, curious about
5. should read

Read and Complete

1. decided to go back
2. are covered with
3. got on, a long trip
4. arrived on, ran up, rolled down, the best new thing

Around the World

1. sent, into space, its name
2. went into, for the first time
3. sent, first human to
4. built, flew around, almost

One Minute Speech

1. Did you hear about the new book, Dave's Adventures?
2. This book is about Dave and his adventures in the woods .
3. The main characters are Dave and a big bear. The story is fun.
4. Are you curious about the book? 5. Then you should read it!

Read and Complete

1. Rada's family lived in space. One day, they decided to go back to Earth.
2. Rada's family talked about life on Earth. They talked about the blue sky and hills which are covered with green grass.
3. The next day, Rada's family got on a spaceship. It was a long trip to Earth.
4. When they arrived on Earth, Rada and Jonny ran up the nearest hill and rolled down it. That was the best new thing to them.

Around the World

1. Russia sent the first dog into space . It was small, and its name was Laika.
2. Yuri Gagarin went into space for the first time .
3. The USA sent the first human to the moon. His name was Neil Armstrong.
4. Russia built the first space station. It flew around the Earth almost 3,000 times.

단어 TEST Step 1   p.61

01 대학	02 잔디, 풀	03 전시
04 박람회, 전시회	05 부채춤	06 계속하다
07 해외에서, 해외로	08 보물	09 군대, 육군
10 ~ 뒤에, ~ 배후에	11 연구, 조사	12 결혼식
13 폭풍	14 연구가	15 허락하다, 허용하다
16 전통적인	17 박물관	18 탈의실
19 정부	20 결과, 결실	21 역사학자
22 인쇄	23 악기	24 성공하다
25 가치	26 왕실의	27 마침내, 결국
28 자부심, 긍지	29 입증하다, 증명하다	
30 맛있는	31 도둑질하다, 훔치다	
32 출판하다, 발행하다		33 어려움
34 전부의, 전체의	35 ~ 때문에	36 포기하다
37 ~로 가득 차 있다	38 ~하고 싶다	39 ~하자마자
40 ~을 입어 보다	41 바로, 즉시	42 ~ 덕분에
43 ~하면서 시간을 보내다		

단어 TEST Step 2   p.62

01 abroad	02 pride	03 government
04 college	05 delicious	06 succeed
07 allow	08 return	09 prove
10 royal	11 exhibition	12 difficulty
13 display	14 historian	15 treasure
16 continue	17 instrument	18 storm
19 finally	20 researcher	21 fitting room
22 result	23 fire	24 metal
25 traditional	26 steal	27 army
28 noise	29 million	30 wedding
31 publish	32 research	33 thief
34 value	35 thanks to	
36 as soon as+주어+동사		37 right away
38 try on	39 give up	40 spend+시간+ -ing
40 because+주어+동사, because of+명사		
41 be full of	42 look for	

단어 TEST Step 3   p.63

1 spend, (시간을) 보내다   2 abroad, 해외로, 해외에서
3 prove, 입증하다   4 pride, 자부심, 긍지
5 allow , 허락하다   6 research, 조사   7 result, 결과
8 succeed, 성공하다   9 royal, 왕실의   10 steal, 훔치다

11 search, 찾아보다   12 treasure, 보물
13 publish, 출판하다   14 government, 정부
15 flash, 플래시   16 fitting room, 탈의실

대화문 TEST Step 1
p.64~65

Listen and Talk A-1

Excuse, I've never seen, like / dessert / Is it OK to try / Go ahead, delicious

Listen and Talk A-2

to sit over there / mean / all right / sitting, is not allowed / understand

Listen and Talk A-3

looks interesting / traditional, musical instrument / Is it OK to play / I'm sorry, for display, Playing, allowed

Listen and Talk A-4

Excuse, Is it OK to take / all right / How about using, too / afraid not, Using, not allowed

Listen and Talk B

Is it OK to sit here / afraid not, Sitting, not allowed

Talk and Play

Which, to go / Why don't you / Is it OK to eat / Eating food, allowed / Is it OK to take / is not allowed / got it, thinking of going

Listen and Talk C

Is it OK / fitting room, over there / minute / over there / traditional, for women, worn, wedding / Is it OK to try it on / for display, on, not allowed / try on

Review 1

Excuse me, looks interesting / traditional, musical instrument / Is it OK to / for display, allowed

Review 2

is it OK / ahead / Can I use, too / also / but, one more / not allowed

대화문 TEST Step 2
p.66~67

Listen and Talk A-1

B: Excuse me. What's this? I've never seen any food like this.

W: Oh, it's Tteok, a Korean dessert.

B: Is it OK to try some?

W: Sure. Go ahead. It's really delicious.

Listen and Talk A-2

G: Excuse me. Is it OK to sit over there?

M: You mean, on the grass?

G: Yes. Is it all right?

M: I'm sorry, but sitting on the grass is not allowed.

G: OK, I understand.

Listen and Talk A-3

B: Excuse me. What's this? It looks interesting.

W: Oh, that's a haegeum, a traditional Korean musical instrument.

B: Is it OK to play it?

W: I'm sorry, but it's only for display. Playing it is not allowed.

B: I see.

Listen and Talk A-4

G: Excuse me. Is it OK to take pictures here?

M: Yes, it's all right.

G: How about using a flash? Can I use it, too?

M: I'm afraid not. Using a flash is not allowed here.

G: Oh, I see. Thank you.

Listen and Talk B

A: Is it OK to sit here?

B: I'm afraid not. Sitting is not allowed here.

A: Oh, I see.

Talk and Play

A: Which place do you want to go first in the museum?

B: Why don't you guess?

A: OK. Is it OK to eat food there?

B: Yes. Eating food is allowed.

A: Is it OK to take pictures?

B: No. Taking pictures is not allowed.

A: I got it. You're thinking of going to the Video Room.

B: You're right.

Listen and Talk C

G: Excuse me, but is it OK to try on this hanbok?

M: Sure. The fitting room is over there.

G: Thanks. Wait a minute. That's also very pretty.

M: Oh, the little hat over there?

G: Yes. What is it?

M: It's a jokduri, a traditional Korean hat for women. It's usually worn on a wedding day.

G: Really? Is it OK to try it on, too?

M: I'm sorry, but it's only for display. Trying it on is not allowed.

G: Oh. Then, I'll just try on this hanbok.

Review 1

G: Excuse me. What's this? It looks interesting.

B: Oh, that's a janggu, a traditional Korean musical instrument.

G: Is it OK to play it?

B: I'm sorry, but it's only for display. Playing it is not allowed.

G: I see.

Review 2

G: Excuse me, but is it OK to take pictures here?

M: Yes. Go ahead.

G: Can I use a flash, too?

M: Yes. That's also OK.

G: I'm sorry, but I have one more question. Can I eat food here?

M: I'm sorry, but that's not allowed.

본문 TEST Step 1   p.68~69

01 Interview with

02 On, collection, took, back

03 behind, return, searching, abroad

04 how, became interested

05 studied history, college

06 to continue, studies

07 As, army, treasures

08 find, while, studying   09 one of them

10 found, books, in

11 tell, how, found

12 As soon, look for

13 After, finally found

14 looked at, than, million

15 sure, excited, found

16 more difficulties, waiting for

17 thought, should, returned, but

18 even thought, fired

19 as, so, do, on 20 However, give up

21 more, every, to, research

22 wanted, show, value

23 results, research, published as

24 interested in, because of

25 asked, for, return, finally

26 finish, like, changed, printing

27 found, in, year

28 right away, special

29 hard, prove, value, succeeded

30 exhibition, displayed as, metal

31 thanks to, thank, for

32 interested, treasures abroad, return

본문 TEST Step 2   p.70~71

01 Interview with

02 On, a collection of royal books, came back to

03 behind this return, spent, whole life searching for, abroad

04 how, became interested in

05 studied history in colleage

06 to continue   07 As you know, national treasures

08 while, was studying   09 one of them

10 297 books of *Uigwe*, National Library

11 tell me how, found

12 As soon as, researcher, look for

13 After, finally found

14 looked at, 30 million

15 I'm sure, excited

16 more difficulties, waiting for

17 should be returned to, that idea

18 even thought, fired

19 as a visitor so, do research on   20 However

21 For more than, to finish my research

22 the value of *Uigwe*

23 were published as

24 became interested in, because of

25 asked, for its return, are here now

26 I'd like to ask, changed, printing

27 in my first year

28 right away, very special

29 to prove its value, succeeded

30 was displayed as, oldest book, movable metal type

31 thanks to, thank, for

32 our national treasures abroad, return

본문 TEST Step 3   p.72~73

1 박영선 박사와의 인터뷰

2 2011년 5월 27일에 프랑스군이 1866년에 가져갔던 왕실 서적인 "의궤" 297권이 한국으로 돌아왔다.

3 이 반환 뒤에 있는 인물이 해외에 있는 한국의 문화재를 찾기 위해 전 생애를 바친 역사학자 박병선 박사이다..

4 Q: "의궤"에 어떻게 관심을 갖게 되셨는지 말씀해 주시겠어요?

5 Dr. Park: 저는 대학에서 역사를 공부했어요.

6 저는 1955년에 학업을 계속하기 위해 프랑스에 갔습니다.

7 아시다시피, 프랑스군은 1866년에 우리 문화재를 많이 가져갔어요.

8 저는 그곳에서 공부하는 동안 그것들을 찾고 싶었어요.

9 "의궤"는 그것들 중의 하나였어요.

10 Q: 당신은 파리에 있는 프랑스 국립도서관에서 297권의 "의궤" 를 발견하셨어요.

11 그것들을 어떻게 발견하셨는지 말씀해 주세요.

12 Dr. Park: 1967년에 국립도서관의 연구원이 되자마자, 저는 "

의궤"를 찾기 시작했어요.

13 10년 후인 1977년에 마침내 그 책들을 발견했죠.

14 제 생각에 3천만 권 이상의 책을 본 것 같아요.

15 Q: 그 책들을 발견했을 때 무척 흥분하셨겠어요.

16 Dr. Park: 네, 하지만 더 큰 어려움이 저를 기다리고 있었어요.

17 저는 그 책들이 한국에 반환되어야 한다고 생각했지만, 도서관의 제 상사들은 그 생각을 좋아하지 않았어요.

18 그들은 심지어 제가 한국의 스파이라고 생각했고 저를 해고했죠.

19 그 후에, 저는 방문객으로 도서관에 가야만 했고, 그래서 "의궤"를 연구하는 것이 쉽지 않았어요.

20 하지만 저는 포기하지 않았죠.

21 10년 넘게, 연구를 끝마치기 위해 매일 도서관에 갔어요.

22 저는 사람들에게 "의궤"의 가치를 보여 주고 싶었어요.

23 Q: 당신의 연구 결과가 1990년 한국에서 책으로 출판되었죠.

24 많은 한국인이 당신의 책 때문에 "의궤"에 관심을 갖게 되었어요.

25 Dr. Park: 네. 1992년에 한국 정부는 프랑스 정부에 그것의 반환을 요청했고, 마침내 297권의 책이 지금 여기 있게 된 거죠.

26 Q: 인터뷰를 마치기 전에, 인쇄의 역사를 바꾼 책인 "직지"에 대해 여쭙고 싶어요.

27 Dr. Park: 저는 도서관에서 근무한 첫해에 그것을 발견했어요.

28 그것이 아주 특별하다는 것을 바로 알았어요.

29 저는 그것의 가치를 증명하기 위해 열심히 연구했고 마침내 성공했죠.

30 1972년에 파리 도서 박람회에서 "직지"는 금속 활자로 인쇄된 세계에서 가장 오래된 책으로 전시되었죠.

31 Q: 박 박사님, 당신의 노고 덕분에 "직지"와 "의궤"가 발견되었고, 모든 한국인이 그 점을 당신에게 감사하고 있어요.

32 Dr. Park: 저는 사람들이 해외에 있는 우리의 문화재에 더 많은 관심을 갖고 그것의 반환을 위해 애써 주시기를 바랍니다.

1 An Interview with Dr. Park Byeong-seon

2 On May 27, 2011, 297 books of Uigwe , a collection of royal books the French army took in 1866, came back to Korea.

3 The person behind this return is Dr. Park Byeong-seon, a historian who spent her whole life searching for Korean national treasures abroad.

4 Q: Can you tell me how you became interested in Uigwe ?

5 Dr. Park: I studied history in college.

6 I went to France to continue my studies in 1955.

7 As you know, the French army took many of our national treasures in 1866.

8 I wanted to find them while I was studying there.

9 Uigwe was one of them.

10 Q: You found 297 books of Uigwe in the National Library of France, in Paris.

11 Please tell me how you found them.

12 Dr. Park: As soon as I became a researcher at the National Library in 1967, I began to look for Uigwe.

13 After 10 years, in 1977, I finally found the books.

14 I think I looked at more than 30 million books.

15 Q: I'm sure you were very excited when you found the books.

16 Dr. Park: Yes, I was, but more difficulties were waiting for me.

17 I thought that the books should be returned to Korea, but my bosses at the library didn't like that idea.

18 They even thought that I was a Korean spy and fired me.

19 After that, I had to go to the library as a visitor, so it was not easy to do research on Uigwe .

20 However, I didn't give up.

21 For more than ten years, I went to the library every day to finish my research.

22 I wanted to show people the value of Uigwe .

23 Q: The results of your research were published as a book in Korea in 1990.

24 Many Koreans became interested in Uigwe because of your book.

25 Dr. Park: Yes. In 1992, the Korean government asked the French government for its return and, finally, the 297 books are here now.

26 Q: Before I finish this interview, I'd like to ask you about Jikji, a book that changed the history of printing.

27 Dr. Park: I found it in my first year at the library.

28 I knew right away that it was very special.

29 I worked hard to prove its value and finally succeeded.

30 At a book exhibition in Paris in 1972, Jikji was displayed as the oldest book in the world that was printed with movable metal type.

31 Q: Dr. Park, thanks to your hard work, Jikji and Uigwe were found, and all Koreans thank you for that.

32 Dr. Park: I hope people will become more interested in our national treasures abroad and work for their return.

구석구석지문 TEST Step 1   p.78

After You Read C Think and Talk

1. What, think about
2. think, will, difficulties, give up
3. great passion
4. As, passionate, finding, abroad

Think and Write Step 2

1. Interview with
2. following, local police officer
3. when and where you were born
4. was born, on
5. like to, what your goal in life is
6. My goal, to make
7. what you like
8. like helping
9. that, police officer

Team Project Create

1. South Korea's National Treasure
2. was printed
3. National Library
4. world's oldest book, metal type

구석구석지문 TEST Step 2   p.79

After You Read C Think and Talk

1. A: What do you think about Dr. Park?
2. B: I think she had a strong will. She had many difficulties, but she didn't give up.
3. C: I think she had a great passion for her work.
4. As a historian, she was very passionate about finding Korean national treasures abroad.

Think and Write Step 2

1. An Interview with Kim Yubin
2. The following is the interview I had with Kim Yubin, a local police officer .
3. Q: Can you tell me when and where you were born ?
4. A: I was born in Seoul on March 11, 1980.
5. Q: I'd like to know what your goal in life is .
6. A: My goal in life is to make a better world.
7. Q: Can you tell me what you like about your job?
8. A: I like helping people.
9. I think that Kim Yubin is a great police officer .

Team Project Create

1. Jikji, South Korea's National Treasure No. 1132
2. Jikji was printed at Heungdeoksa in 1377.
3. It is now in the National Library of France, in Paris.
4. It is the world's oldest book that was printed with movable metal type .

단어 TEST Step 1   p.80

01 버튼, 단추	02 재미있는, 즐거운	03 창의적인
04 맛있는	05 충분한	06 ~한 맛이 나다
07 효과가 있다, 작동하다		08 쌓아 올리다. 쌓다
09 반죽	10 소유하다	11 계산대
12 요리법	13 섞다	14 떨어지다
15 신선한	16 팔다	17 ~ 안에
18 누르다	19 발생하다, 일어나다	
20 상금	21 표지판	22 기계
23 외치다, 소리치다	24 추신	25 준비된
26 시도하다, 먹어보다		27 잃어버리다
28 잘못된, 이상이 있는		29 떠나다, ~에 두다
30 기억하다	31 ~을 부수다, 쪼개다	
32 갑자기	33 흥분하여	34 잠시
35 결국, 마침내	36 ~ 으로 가득 차다	37 ~ 속으로 떨어지다
38 A를 B에 쌓아 올리다		39 ~을 돌려주다
40 즉시, 지금 당장	41 ~에서 나오다. 내리다	
42 포상금을 지급하다		43 계속해서 ~하다

단어 TEST Step 2   p.81

01 doughnut	02 batter	03 pile
04 creative	05 sign	06 prize
07 taste	08 drop	09 lose
10 shout	11 counter	12 happen
13 before	14 try	15 ring
16 wrong	17 leave	18 mix
19 sell	20 recipe	21 machine
22 push	23 work	24 ready
25 inside	26 own	27 delicious
28 enough	29 fresh	30 remember
31 in front of	32 for a while	33 in the end
34 be full of	35 step out	36 take off
37 break up	38 all of a sudden	
39 one day	40 a piece of paper	
41 fall into	42 get ~ back	43 right away

단어 TEST Step 3   p.82

1 step out, ~에서 나오다   2 work, 효과가 있다
3 ring, 반지   4 excitement, 흥분   5 recipe, 요리법
6 shout, 외치다, 소리치다   7 sell, 팔다
8 compare, 비교하다   9 doughnut, 도넛

10 machine, 기계　11 counter, 계산대
12 give a reward, 포상금을 주다　13 batter, 반죽
14 prize, 상금　15 sign, 표지판　16 remember, 기억하다

01 The Doughnuts
02 uncle, had, shop
03 so, full of cooking
04 One, visited, shop　　05 Uncle Bob
06 Nice, at, Isn't
07 back, for, while
08 watch, for, make　　09 try but
10 easy, make, batter, put
11 just, machine, recipe
12 do, Don't worry
13 stopped, front, stepped out
14 Can, have some
15 but, aren't ready　　16 making, batter
17 my first time　18 took off, her, ring
19 started to mix　20 can help, delicious
21 Uh, OK　　22 a lot of
23 wait, taste great
24 turned on, machine
25 Rigs, dropping into　　26 try, first
27 really delicious
28 have to, so much
29 Thank, for helping
30 enough, pushed, nothing happened
31 kept coming out
32 wrong, should call　　33 full of, piled
34 back right away
35 Something's wrong with　　36 How, all these
37 Just, came back
38 lost, ring, left, counter　　39 took, off, mix
40 looked for, couldn't　　41 can't find
42 give, reward, who finds　　43 fell into, inside
44 You're right　45 break up, to find
46 Don't worry, have
47 took, piece, made, sign　　48 put, it, shop's
49 for, cents　　50 for finding, inside
51 have, give, back　　52 many, to buy
53 All, sudden, with excitement　　54 found, ring
55 idea worked　56 Here's, hundred
57 In, end, was　58 went, with, hundred
59 got, back, sold lots
60 what about　　61 that, worked, well

01 Doughnuts　　02 uncle, had
03 so, was full of cooking machines
04 One day, visited　　05 Uncle
06 Look at, Isn't it great
07 for a while　08 for me　　09 try
10 easy to do, doughnut batter, put, in
11 machine, recipe
12 can do, Don't worry
13 in front of, stepped out　　14 Can I have
15 aren't ready
16 Are you making, batter　　17 my first time
18 took off, ring　19 started to mix
20 I can help you, make delicious　21 OK
22 a lot of　　23 wait and see, will taste great
24 turned on　　25 dropping into, hot oil
26 try, first　　27 delicious
28 have to go, so much fun　　29 for helping
30 enough, nothing happened
31 kept coming out of
32 wrong, should call
33 was, full of, piled, on the counter
34 back right away
35 Something's wrong with
36 all these　　37 came back to　38 lost, left
39 took it off, mix the batter
40 looked for, couldn't find　　41 can't find
42 give a reward, who finds
43 fell into, I'm sure, inside　　44 right
45 have to break up, to find　　46 Don't worry
47 piece, made a sign　　48 put it
49 2 for 5 cents　50 for finding
51 have to give, back　　52 to buy
53 All of a sudden　　54 found it
55 worked　56 Here's, hundred
57 In the end, was　　58 with
59 got, back, lots of
60 what about　61 his idea worked

1 도넛
2 Homer의 삼촌인 Bob은 도넛 가게를 가지고 있었다.
3 Bob 삼촌은 기계를 좋아해서, 가게는 요리 기계들로 가득 차 있었다.
4 어느 날, Homer가 Bob 삼촌의 가게를 방문했다.
5 Homer: 안녕하세요, Bob 삼촌!

6 Bob: 안녕, Homer. 만나서 반갑구나. 이 새 도넛 기계 좀 봐. 멋지지 않니?

7 Bob: Homer, 내가 잠시 집에 가 봐야 해.

8 나 대신 가게를 봐 주고 도넛을 좀 만들어 줄 수 있겠니?

9 Homer: 네, 해 볼게요, 그런데….

10 Bob: 하기 쉬워. 먼저, 도넛 반죽을 만들고 그것을 기계에 넣으렴.

11 그런 다음에 기계를 작동하기만 하면 돼. 여기 요리법이 있어.

12 Homer: 그건 할 수 있어요. 걱정하지 마세요.

13 Bob 삼촌이 떠난 후, 큰 차 한 대가 가게 앞에 섰고, 한 귀부인이 내렸다.

14 Lady: 도넛과 커피 한 잔 주겠니?

15 Homer: 죄송하지만, 도넛이 준비가 안 됐어요.

16 Lady: 지금 도넛 반죽을 만들고 있는 거니?

17 Homer: 네, 하지만 처음 만드는 거예요.

18 그 귀부인은 외투를 벗고 커다란 다이아몬드 반지를 뺐다.

19 그녀는 반죽을 섞기 시작했다.

20 Lady: 내가 도와줄게. 나는 맛있는 도넛을 만들 수 있단다.

21 Homer: 아, 좋아요.

22 Homer: 반죽이 많군요.

23 Lady: 좀 기다려 보렴. 도넛이 아주 맛있을 거야.

24 Homer는 도넛 기계를 작동했다.

25 링 모양의 반죽들이 뜨거운 기름 속으로 떨어지기 시작했다.

26 Lady: 첫 번째 도넛을 맛보렴. 여기 있어.

27 Homer: 와! 정말 맛있네요!

28 Lady: 난 이제 가 봐야 해. 정말 재미있었어! 잘 있으렴!

29 Homer: 도와주셔서 감사해요. 안녕히 가세요!

30 Homer는 도넛이 충분하게 있어서 정지 버튼을 눌렀지만, 아무 일도 일어나지 않았다.

31 도넛이 계속해서 기계에서 나오고 있었다.

32 Homer: 흐음 … 뭐가 잘못된 거지? Bob 삼촌에게 전화를 해야겠어.

33 가게는 이제 도넛으로 가득 찼다. Homer는 도넛들을 계산대 위로 쌓아 올렸다.

34 Homer: Bob 삼촌! 지금 당장 돌아와 주세요.

35 도넛 기계에 이상이 있어요.

36 Bob: 오, 이런! 이 도넛들을 모두 어떻게 팔지?

37 바로 그때 그 귀부인이 다시 가게로 돌아왔다.

38 Lady: 내 다이아몬드 반지를 잃어버렸어. 내 생각엔 계산대 위에 그것을 놓은 것 같은데.

39 Homer: 오, 기억나요. 반죽을 섞기 전에 그것을 뺐어요.

40 모두가 다이아몬드 반지를 찾았지만, 찾을 수 없었다.

41 Homer: 저는 못 찾겠어요.

42 Lady: 그 반지를 찾는 사람에게 100달러의 보상금을 드릴게요!

43 Homer: 알겠어요! 그 반지는 반죽 속으로 떨어졌어요. 반지는 이 도넛들 중 하나 안에 있다고 확신해요!

44 Lady: 네 말이 맞아!

45 Bob: 오, 안 돼! 이제 우리는 반지를 찾기 위해 이 도넛들을 모두 쪼개야 해요.

46 Homer: 걱정하지 마세요, 삼촌. 저에게 아이디어가 있어요.

47 Homer는 종이 한 장을 가져와 안내판을 만들었다.

48 그러고 나서 그것을 가게 창문에 걸었다.

49 신선한 도넛   2개에 5센트

50 도넛 안에 있는 반지를 찾으면 100달러의 상금을 드려요.

51 추신. 반지를 돌려주어야 합니다.

52 그러자, 많은 사람들이 도넛을 사기 시작했다.

53 갑자기, 한 남자가 흥분해서 소리쳤다.

54 Man: 찾았어요! 내가 반지를 찾았어요!

55 Homer: 보세요, 제 아이디어가 통했어요!

56 Lady: 여기 100달러예요!

57 결국 모두가 행복했다.

58 남자는 100달러를 갖고 집으로 갔다.

59 귀부인은 다이아몬드 반지를 다시 찾았고, Bob 삼촌은 도넛을 많이 팔았다.

60 그러면, Homer는 어떻게 됐을까?

61 그는 자신의 아이디어가 아주 잘 통해서 행복했다!

1 The Doughnuts

2 Homer's uncle, Bob, had a doughnut shop.

3 Uncle Bob liked machines, so the shop was full of cooking machines.

4 One day, Homer visited Uncle Bob's shop.

5 Homer: Hello, Uncle Bob!

6 Bob: Hi, Homer. Nice to see you. Look at this new doughnut machine. Isn't it great?

7 Bob: Homer, I need to go back home for a while.

8 Can you watch the shop for me and make some doughnuts?

9 Homer: OK, I'll try but ....

10 Bob: It's easy to do. First, make the doughnut batter and put it in the machine.

11 Then just start the machine. Here's the recipe.

12 Homer: I can do that. Don't worry.

13 After Uncle Bob left, a big car stopped in front of the shop, and a lady stepped out.

14 Lady: Can I have some doughnuts and a coffee?

15 Homer: I'm sorry, but the doughnuts aren't ready.

16 Lady: Are you making the doughnut batter now?

17 Homer: Yes, but this is my first time.

18 The lady took off her coat and her big diamond ring.

19 She started to mix the batter.

20 Lady: I can help you. I can make delicious doughnuts.

21 Homer: Uh, OK.

22 Homer: This is a lot of batter.

23 Lady: Just wait and see. The doughnuts will taste great.

24 Homer turned on the doughnut machine.

25 Rings of batter started dropping into the hot oil.

26 Lady: You try the first doughnut. Here.

27 Homer: Wow! It's really delicious!

28 Lady: I have to go now. This was so much fun! Good-bye!

29 Homer: Thank you for helping me. Good-bye!

30 Homer had enough doughnuts, so he pushed the stop button, but nothing happened.

31 The doughnuts kept coming out of the machine.

32 Homer: Hmm... What's wrong? I think I should call Uncle Bob.

33 The shop was now full of doughnuts. Homer piled the doughnuts on the counter.

34 Homer: Uncle Bob! Please come back right away.

35 Something's wrong with the doughnut machine.

36 Bob: Oh, no! How can we sell all these doughnuts?

37 Just then the lady came back to the shop.

38 Lady: I lost my diamond ring. I think I left it on the counter.

39 Homer: Oh, I remember. You took it off before you started to mix the batter.

40 Everyone looked for the diamond ring, but they couldn't find it.

41 Homer: I can't find it.

42 Lady: I'll give a reward of one hundred dollars to the person who finds that ring!

43 Homer: I know! The ring fell into the batter. I'm sure it's inside one of these doughnuts!

44 Lady: You're right!

45 Bob: Oh, no! Now we have to break up all of these doughnuts to find the ring.

46 Homer: Don't worry, Uncle. I have an idea.

47 Homer took a piece of paper and made a sign.

48 He then put it in the shop's window.

49 Fresh Doughnuts   2 for 5 cents

50 $100 prize for finding a ring inside a doughnut

51 P.S. You have to give the ring back.

52 Then many people began to buy the doughnuts.

53 All of a sudden, a man shouted with excitement.

54 Man: I found it! I found the ring!

55 Homer: See, my idea worked!

56 Lady: Here's one hundred dollars!

57 In the end, everybody was happy.

58 The man went home with one hundred dollars.

59 The lady got her diamond ring back, and Uncle Bob sold lots of doughnuts.

60 And, what about Homer?

61 He was happy that his idea worked so well!

적중 1◦◦ + 특별부록

Plan B

우리학교 최신기출

동아 · 윤정미 교과서를 배우는

학교 시험문제 분석 · 모음 · 해설집

전국단위 학교 시험문제 수집 및 분석
출제 빈도가 높은 문제 위주로 선별
문제 풀이에 필요한 상세한 해설

중2-2
영어

동아 · 윤정미

◎ 선택형 문항의 답안은 컴퓨터용 수정 싸인펜을 사용하여 OMR 답안지에 바르게 표기하시오.

◎ 서술형 문제는 답을 답안지에 반드시 검정 볼펜으로 쓰시오.

◎ 총 29문항 100점 만점입니다. 문항별 배점은 각 문항에 표시되어 있습니다.

[용산구 ○○중]

01 다음 빈칸에 들어갈 알맞은 말을 〈보기〉에서 골라 기호로 쓰시오. (4점)

보기
ⓐ creative   ⓑ protection
ⓒ thumb   ⓓ floss   ⓔ cause
ⓕ experiment   ⓖ sore

(1) Children have to wear helmets for _____ when they ride bikes.

(2) The scientists did a new _____ to learn more about monkeys.

(3) I think _____ people see things from different points of view.

(4) The _____ of the fire is not clear. The police are still looking into it.

[경북 ○○중]

02 다음 대화에서 말하는 증상에 대한 당부의 말이 <u>어색한</u> 것은? (3점)

① B: I have a runny nose.
　 G: Make sure you get some rest.
② B: I have a headache.
　 G: Make sure you take some medicine.
③ B: My back hurts a lot.
　 G: Make sure you put a heating pad on it.
④ B: I have a bad cold.
　 G: Make sure you share food with your friends.
⑤ B: I fell and hurt my foot while I was playing soccer.
　 G: Make sure you don't play soccer until next week.

[강북구 ○○중]

[3~4] 다음 대화를 읽고 물음에 답하시오.

K: What's wrong, Andy?
A: Hello, Ms. Kim. My right thumb hurts.
K: Hmm. Do you use your smartphone a lot?
A: Yes, I text a lot. Why?
K: I think you have texting thumb.
A: Texting thumb? What's texting thumb?
K: It's pain in your thumb. You can get it from texting too much.
A: Oh, I didn't know that.
K: (A)_____
A: OK, I will.
K: And make sure you don't text too much.
*A: Andy, K: Ms. Kim

03 Which of the following is the best for (A)? (3점)

① What's wrong with your thumb?
② Make sure you wake up early.
③ Why don't you do some finger stretching exercises?
④ Which thumb has more pain?
⑤ Why don't you use your smartphone more often?

04 According to the conversation, Andy has 'texting thumb' because ... (4점)

① he texts too much.
② he uses his both hands when he texts.
③ he hurt his thumb while he was playing tennis.
④ his smartphone was broken.
⑤ he didn't take any cold medicine.

[5~7] 다음 대화를 읽고, 각 질문에 답하시오.

(In the school)
Ms. Kim: Andy, (A)_____
Andy: Hello, Ms. Kim. My right thumb hurts.
Ms. Kim: Hmm. Do you use your smartphone a lot?
Andy: Yes, I text a lot. Why?
Ms. Kim: I think you have texting thumb.
Andy: Texting thumb? What's texting thumb?
Ms. Kim: It's pain in your thumb. You can get it (B)_____ texting too much.
Andy: Oh, I didn't know that.

05 위 대화의 빈칸 (A)에 적합하지 <u>않은</u> 것은? (3점)

① is anything wrong?
② is there any problem?
③ what's wrong with you?
④ what is right in this situation?
⑤ what is the matter with your finger?

06 위 대화의 빈칸 (B)에 들어갈 말로 적절한 것을 <u>모두</u> 고르면? (2점)

① from   ② in
③ without   ④ because of
⑤ as a result of

07 위 대화의 내용과 일치하는 것은? (3점)

① Ms. Kim is a doctor in the hospital.
② Andy feels pain in his right index finger.
③ Texting too much can cause texting thumb.
④ Andy already knows what texting thumb is.
⑤ Ms. Kim asks Andy how to text by her cell phone.

08 다음 대화의 빈칸에 알맞은 말은? (3점)

A: What's wrong?
B: I have a sore throat and runny nose.
A: That's too bad. _____
B: OK, I will.

① Why don't you take some medicine?
② I couldn't sleep last night. I'm so tired.
③ Don't forget to put some ice on your leg.
④ Make sure you go to the dentist after school.
⑤ You should put a heating pad on your back.

09 다음 중 짝지어진 대화가 <u>어색한</u> 것은? (3점)

① A: I have a runny nose. I have a fever, too.
   B: Why don't you bring your umbrella?
② A: What are you going to do this Saturday?
   B: I'm planning to see a movie.
③ A: You look sick. What's wrong?
   B: I have a sore throat.
④ A: What time and where should we meet?
   B: How about meeting at 9 at the bus stop?
⑤ A: Don't forget to see a doctor.
   B: I don't have much time, but OK. I won't.

10 우리말과 같도록 주어진 단어를 순서대로 배열할 때 (E)에 들어갈 알맞은 단어는? (3점)

• 사람들은 그 시계탑을 Big Ben이라고 부른다.
= (A)_____ (B)_____ (C)_____
(D)_____ (E)_____

① people   ② Big Ben   ③ tower
④ call   ⑤ the clock

11 다음 대화의 순서를 바르게 나열한 것은? (3점)

(A) I fell and hurt my foot while I was playing soccer.
(B) What's wrong with your leg, Sam?
(C) Why don't you put some ice on it? And make sure you don't play soccer until next week.
(D) Yes, but it hurts a lot.
(E) Can you walk?

① (A)-(B)-(C)-(D)-(E) ② (B)-(A)-(E)-(D)-(C)
③ (B)-(A)-(C)-(D)-(E) ④ (A)-(B)-(C)-(E)-(D)
⑤ (B)-(E)-(D)-(A)-(C)

12 다음 대화문의 내용과 일치하지 않는 것은? (3점)

A: What's wrong, Andy?
B: Hello, Ms. Kim. My right thumb hurts.
A: Hmm. Do you use your smartphone a lot?
B: Yes, I text a lot. Why?
A: I think you have texting thumb.
B: Texting thumb? What's texting thumb?
A: It's pain in your thumb. You can get it from texting too much.
B: Oh, I didn't know that.
A: Why don't you do some finger stretching exercises?
B: OK, I will.
A: And make sure you don't text too much.

① Andy's right thumb hurts.
② Andy uses his smartphone a lot.
③ Ms. Kim thinks she has texting thumb.
④ Andy asks Ms. Kim what texting thumb is.
⑤ Ms. Kim tells Andy to do finger stretching exercises.

13 다음 중 어법에 맞는 문장의 개수는? (4점)

(A) They called the baby Mark.
(B) I'll be here at 6 unless the bus is late.
(C) Jane is the girl that I talked yesterday.
(D) This is the skirt which I bought in Paris.
(E) Mike knows the boys whom are interested in cars.
(F) If you will stay up late, you will be tired tomorrow.
(G) Look at the boy and his dog which are running over there.

① 2개 ② 3개 ③ 4개 ④ 5개 ⑤ 6개

14 밑줄 친 부분을 생략할 수 없는 것은? (3점)

① Jane Eyre is the book <u>that</u> I read twice.
② Paris is the city <u>which</u> I want to visit most.
③ The cookies <u>which</u> she made were very delicious.
④ The boy band <u>that</u> you like is going to have a concert tomorrow.
⑤ Hemingway is one of the greatest authors <u>that</u> wrote many interesting stories.

15 다음 두 문장을 〈보기〉와 같이 한 문장으로 바꿔 쓰시오. (5점)

보기
• These are the books.
• I will read them this summer.
→ These are the books which I will read this summer.

• The soup was too salty.
• I had the soup for lunch.

→ _____

[16~20] 다음 글을 읽고 물음에 답하시오.

Are you a smombie?

All over the world, people are walking around like zombies. Their heads are down, and their eyes are on their smartphones. (A)우리는 그런 사람들을 스몸비라고 부른다(call, smombies, such people, we). If you are a smombie, you can have various safety problems. You may not see a hole in the street, so you may fall and get hurt. You may get into a car accident, too. So what can you do to prevent these problems? It's simple. Do not look at your smartphone while you are walking!

Do you have dry eyes or text neck?
ⓐSmartphones can cause various health problems. ⓑLiving without smartphones is difficult for many of us these days. ⓒOne example is dry eyes. When you look at your smartphone, you do not blink often. Then your eyes will feel dry. (B)당신이 겪을 수 있는 또 다른 문제는 목 통증이다. When you look down at your smartphone, the stress on your neck increases. Too much use of your smartphone, for example, too much texting, can cause neck pain. We call this text neck. ⓓHere are some tips for these problems. For dry eyes, try to blink often. For text neck, move your smartphone up to your eye level. ⓔYou can also do some neck stretching exercises.

How do you feel when you don't have your smartphone with you?
Do you feel nervous when your smartphone is not around? Do you feel sad when you check your smartphone and there is no text message? If your answers are "yes," you may have smartphone addiction. There are various things you can do to prevent (C)this. For example, turn off your smartphone during meals or meetings. You can talk to people instead of texting them.

16 위 글의 내용과 일치하는 것은? (3점)

① Smombies can have some safety problems.
② Your eyes can get dry if you blink your eyes a lot.
③ Too much texting can prevent neck pain.
④ When you look down at your smartphone, the stress in your neck decreases.
⑤ If you have smartphone addiction, you may feel excited when your smartphone is not around.

17 위 글의 밑줄 친 (A)의 우리말에 맞도록 주어진 단어들을 바르게 배열하시오. (4점)

→ _____

18 위 글의 (B)를 영어로 바르게 바꿔 쓴 것은? (3점)

① Another problem that can have is neck pain.
② Another problem who you can have is neck pain.
③ Another problem that you can have is neck pain.
④ Another problem whom you can have is neck pain.
⑤ Another problem which you can have a problem is neck pain.

19 위 글의 ⓐ~ⓔ 중 글의 흐름상 어색한 문장은? (4점)

① ⓐ   ② ⓑ   ③ ⓒ   ④ ⓓ   ⑤ ⓔ

20 위 글을 읽고 smartphone addiction을 예방하기 위한 방법 두 가지를 우리말로 쓰시오. (4점)

→ (1) _____

    (2) _____

[용산구 ○○중]

21 다음 글의 내용을 아래 대화 형식으로 바꾸었을 때 빈칸에 들어갈 말을 영어로 쓰시오. (6점)

> Do you feel nervous when your smartphone is not around? Do you feel sad when you check your smartphone and there is no text message? If your answers are "yes," you may have smartphone addiction. There are various things you can do to prevent this. For example, turn off your smartphone during meals or meetings. You can talk to people instead of texting them.

> Eric: I think I have smartphone addiction.
> Suji: Why do you think so?
> Eric: It is because I feel (A)_____ when my smartphone is not around.
> Suji: And, do you feel (B)_____ when you check your smartphone and there is no text message?
> Eirc: That's right. What can I do to fix this problem?
> Suji: It's simple. Don't (C)_____ your smartphone during meals or meetings and try to talk to people instead of texting them.
> *fix = solve: 해결하다, 고치다

(A)_____, (B)_____
(C)_____

[경북 ○○중]

[22~23] 다음 글을 읽고, 물음에 답하시오.

> Living without smartphones (A)[is / are] difficult for many of us these days. ⓐ_____, unwise or too much use of smartphones can cause various problems.
>
> Are you a smombie?
> All over the world, people are walking around like zombies. Their heads are down, and their eyes are on their smartphones. We call such people smombies, smartphone zombies. (B)[If / Unless] you are a smombie, you can have various safety problems. You may not see a hole in the street, ⓑ_____ you may fall and (C)[get / getting] hurt. You may get into a car accident, too. So what can you do to prevent these problems? It's simple. Do not look at your smartphone while you are walking!

22 위 글의 빈칸 ⓐ, ⓑ에 들어갈 말이 순서대로 바르게 짝지어진 것은? (4점)

	ⓐ	ⓑ
①	However	so
②	Furthermore	as
③	Likewise	but
④	Therefore	but
⑤	For example	however

23 위 글의 괄호 (A), (B), (C)에 주어진 말 중 어법상 올바른 것끼리 짝지어진 것은? (3점)

	(A)	(B)	(C)
①	is	Unless	get
②	is	If	get
③	are	Unless	get
④	are	If	getting
⑤	is	If	getting

[24~27] 다음 글을 읽고 물음에 답하시오.

Be Smart with Your Smartphones!
Living without smartphones ⓐare difficult for many of us these days. However, unwise or too much ⓑuse of smartphones can cause various problems.
Are you a smombie?
All over the world, people are walking around ⓒlike zombies. (A) Their heads are ⓓdown, and their eyes are on their smartphones. (B) (가)call, such, we, people, sombies, smartphone zombies. (C) If you are a smombie, you can have various safety problems. (D) You ⓔmay get into a car accident, too. So what can you do to prevent these problems? It's simple. Do not look at your smartphone while you are walking! (E)

24 위 글의 흐름상 주어진 문장이 들어가기에 가장 알맞은 곳은?
(3점)

You may not see a hole in the street, so you may fall and get hurt.

① (A)   ② (B)   ③ (C)   ④ (D)   ⑤ (E)

25 위 글의 밑줄 친 ⓐ~ⓔ 중 그 쓰임이 알맞지 <u>않은</u> 것은? (3점)

① ⓐ   ② ⓑ   ③ ⓒ   ④ ⓓ   ⑤ ⓔ

26 위 글의 (가)call, such, we, people, sombies를 문맥에 알맞게 배열하여 쓰시오.
(3점)

→ _____

27 위 글의 내용과 일치하지 <u>않는</u> 것은?
(3점)

① 요즘 스마트폰 없이 생활하는 것은 어렵다.
② 현명하지 않은 스마트폰 사용은 많은 문제를 일으킬 수 있다.
③ 스몸비는 스마트폰 좀비를 뜻한다.
④ 스몸비는 안전과 관련된 여러 문제를 가질 수 있다.
⑤ 걸을 때 스마트폰을 보지 않으면 위험하다.

[28~29] 다음 글을 읽고 물음에 답하시오.

Texting thumb is the thumb pain that comes with hours of texting on a smartphone. The best way to prevent texting thumb, of course, is to stop texting, but this is not easy. So here are some (A)_____ tips if you have texting thumb. First, ice the thumb. Keep the ice on your thumb for 20 minutes at a time, several times a day. Second, do many finger stretching exercises regularly. Third, text slowly. Fast texting makes the pain worse, so try to text slowly. Finally, using other fingers (B)_____ the thumb can also help. It not only (C)_____ the pressure on the thumb, but it also makes you slow down a little.

28 위 글의 제목으로 가장 적절한 것은?
(4점)

① The Effect of Icing a Thumb
② The Importance of Stretching Fingers
③ Useful Tips for Slow Texting
④ The Secret of Finger Exercises
⑤ Various Ways of Preventing Texting Thumb

29 위 글의 괄호 (A), (B), (C) 안에 들어갈 표현으로 알맞은 것은?
(4점)

	(A)	(B)	(C)
①	useful	cause	increases
②	awful	cause	lessens
③	useful	instead of	lessens
④	useful	instead of	increases
⑤	nice	for example	lessens

◎ 선택형 문항의 답안은 컴퓨터용 수정 싸인펜을 사용하여 OMR 답안지에 바르게 표기하시오.
◎ 서술형 문제는 답을 답안지에 반드시 검정 볼펜으로 쓰시오.
◎ 총 31문항 100점 만점입니다. 문항별 배점은 각 문항에 표시되어 있습니다.

[강북구 ○○중]
01 다음 빈칸 ⓐ~ⓓ에 들어갈 단어가 <u>아닌</u> 것은? (3점)

- Is there ⓐ_____ I can do to help you?
- My skin feels ⓑ_____ during the winter.
- This position puts ⓒ_____ on your back.
- The number of students won't ⓓ_____ next year.

① dry ② author ③ stress
④ increase ⑤ anything

[종로구 ○○중]
02 In the following dialogues, please choose the answer that is <u>unnatural</u>. (3점)

① A: Angela, you don't look too well. What's wrong?
   B: I hurt my arm while playing basketball.
② A: What's the matter, Chanseong?
   B: I don't know. I think I just miss my girlfriend.
③ A: Are you OK, Seho? You look worried.
   B: I won the first place in the English speaking contest.
④ A: I've got a sore throat and blocked nose. I think I caught a cold.
   B: Oh, you should see a doctor and get some medicine.
⑤ A: Is anything wrong? You don't look too well.
   B: I'm so tired. I didn't sleep well last night.

[대구 ○○중]
03 다음 밑줄 친 ⓐ~ⓔ 중 충고의 말에 해당하는 것은? (3점)

A: ⓐWhat's wrong, Andy?
B: Hello, Ms. Kim. ⓑMy right thumb hurts.
A: Hmm. Do you use your smartphone a lot?
B: ⓒYes, I text a lot. Why?
A: I think you have texting thumb. ⓓIt's pain in your thumb. You can get it from texting too much.
B: Oh, I didn't know that.
A: Why don't you do some finger stretching exercises? ⓔAlso, make sure you don't text too much.
B: Okay, I will.

① ⓐ ② ⓑ ③ ⓒ ④ ⓓ ⑤ ⓔ

[경북 ○○중]
04 다음 (A), (B)의 의사소통 기능으로 바르게 연결된 것은? (3점)

(A)
W: You look sick. What's wrong, Inho?
B: I have a sore throat. I have a fever, too.
(B)
B: What are you going to do this Sunday?
W: I'm planning to go to Dream Amusement Park.

	(A)	(B)
①	물건 사기	정보 묻기
②	외모 묘사하기	당부하기
③	약속 정하기	궁금증 표현하기
④	여가 활동 묻기	길 묻고 답하기
⑤	증상을 묻고 답하기	계획 말하기

Lesson 5 Living Healthily and Safely **7**

[5~6] 다음 대화문을 읽고 물음에 답하시오.

W: What's wrong, Andy?
B: Hello, Ms. Kim. My right thumb hurts. (A)
W: Hmm. Do you use your smartphone a lot?
B: (B) Yes, I text a lot. Why?
W: I think you have texting thumb.
B: Texting thumb? What's texting thumb?
W: (C) And you can get it from texting too much.
B: Oh, I didn't know that. (D)
W: Why don't you do some finger stretching exercises?
B: OK, I will.
W: And make sure you don't text too much. (E)

*texting thumb: 엄지손가락 증후군

05 위 대화의 흐름상 주어진 문장이 들어가기에 가장 알맞은 곳은? (3점)

It's pain in your thumb.

① (A)　② (B)　③ (C)　④ (D)　⑤ (E)

06 위 대화의 내용과 일치하지 <u>않는</u> 것은? (3점)

① Andy는 오른쪽 엄지손가락이 아프다.
② Andy는 스마트폰을 자주 사용한다.
③ Andy는 엄지손가락 증후군이 무엇인지 잘 모르고 있었다.
④ 엄지손가락 증후군은 문자 메시지를 자주 보내는 사람에게 생길 수 있다.
⑤ 손가락 스트레칭 운동은 엄지손가락 증후군에 별로 도움이 되지 않는다.

[7~8] 다음 대화를 읽고 물음에 답하시오.

Ms. Lee: (A)<u>What's wrong?</u>
Sangjin: I have a sore throat.
Ms. Lee: How about taking some medicine? Here it is!
Sangjin: Thank you.
Ms. Lee: And (B)<u>물 많이 마시는 것을 명심해.</u>
Sangjin: OK. I will.

07 위 대화의 (A)와 바꾸어 쓸 수 있는 문장을 한 개 쓰시오. (3점)

→ _____

08 위 대화의 (B)의 우리말과 의미가 일치하도록 문장을 완성하시오. (4점)

make _____

09 다음 중 짝지어진 대화가 <u>어색한</u> 것은? (3점)

① A: You look sick. What's wrong, Inho?
　 B: I have a sore throat. I have a fever, too.
② A: My back hurts a lot.
　 B: That's too bad. Put a heating pad on it.
③ A: What's wrong, Peter?
　 B: I fell and hurt my foot while I was playing soccer.
④ A: I have a headache.
　 B: Why don't you go see a doctor?
⑤ A: Here is some medicine. Take this.
　 B: That's too bad. Make sure you drink a lot of water.

10 다음 중 어법상 <u>어색한</u> 문장은? (3점)

① She named her daughter April.
② They made him a great doctor.
③ This is the girl whom rescued the cat.
④ I bought the book which I wanted to read.
⑤ He showed me the photos he had taken in Spain.

[11~12] 다음 대화를 읽고 물음에 답하시오.

> Ms. Kim: ⓐWhat's wrong, Andy?
>
> Andy: Hello, Ms. Kim. My right thumb hurts.
>
> Ms. Kim: Hmm. Do you use your smartphone a lot?
>
> Andy: Yes, I text a lot. Why?
>
> Ms. Kim: I think you have texting thumb.
>
> (A) Oh, I didn't know that.
>
> (B) Texting thumb? What's texting thumb?
>
> (C) Why don't you do some finger stretching exercises?
>
> (D) It's pain in your thumb. You can get it from texting too much.
>
> Andy: OK, I will.
>
> Ms. Kim: And make sure you don't text too much.

11 위 대화의 중간에 이어질 (A)~(D)의 순서를 가장 바르게 배열한 것은? (3점)

① (A)-(B)-(C)-(D)
② (B)-(D)-(A)-(C)
③ (B)-(D)-(C)-(A)
④ (C)-(D)-(A)-(B)
⑤ (D)-(B)-(A)-(C)

12 위 대화의 ⓐ와 바꾸어 쓸 수 없는 것은? (2점)

① What's the point, Andy?
② What's the matter, Andy?
③ What's wrong with you, Andy?
④ Is anything wrong, Andy?
⑤ What's the problem, Andy?

13 다음 중 대화에서 〈보기〉 문장들을 사용하는 목적으로 가장 적절한 것은? (3점)

> **보기**
>
> • Make sure you get some rest.
> • Why don't you do some back stretching exercises?

① to share a story
② to give an advice
③ to get an agreement
④ to ask information
⑤ to introduce a stranger

14 다음 중 어법상 옳은 문장은? (4점)

① The dish I can cook well is pasta.
② *Jane Eyre* is the book who I read yesterday.
③ Anna is the person Peter met her in the park.
④ The cookie which she made it was very good.
⑤ Kenya is the country whom John wants to visit.

15 다음 중 우리말과 의미가 같지 <u>않은</u> 문장은? (3점)

① 우리는 그런 사람들을 유명 인사라고 부른다.
→ We call celebrities such people.
② 사람들은 뉴욕시를 the Big Apple이라고 부른다.
→ People call New York City the Big Apple.
③ 영국 사람들은 그 시계탑을 Big Ben이라고 부른다.
→ British people call the clock tower Big Ben.
④ 그녀의 프랑스 팬들은 그녀를 춤의 여왕이라고 불렀다.
→ Her French fans called her Dancing Queen.
⑤ Andy는 아주 똑똑해서 우리는 모두 그를 Einstein이라고 불렀다.
→ Andy was very intelligent, so we all called him Einstein.

[16~18] 다음 글을 읽고 물음에 답하시오.

ⓐLiving without smartphones are difficult for many of us these days. ⓑHowever, unwise or to much use of smartphones can cause various problems.

Are you a smombie?
ⓒAll over the world, people are walking around alike zombies. ⓓTheir heads are down, and their eyes are on their smartphones. ⓔWe call such people smombies, smartphone zombies. ㉠_____ you are a smombie, you can have various safety problems. You may not see a hole in the street, so you may fall and get hurt. You may get ㉡_____ a car accident, too. ㉢_____ what can you do to prevent these problems? It's simple. Do not look at your smartphone ㉣_____ you are walking!

16 위 글을 읽고 답할 수 <u>없는</u> 질문은?　(3점)

① What do we call smartphone zombies?
② What can you do to prevent a car accident?
③ What can you use instead of a smartphone?
④ What are the safety problems smombies may have?
⑤ What will happen if you do not see a hole in the street?

17 위 글의 밑줄 친 ⓐ~ⓔ 중 어법상 옳은 것은? (2개)　(4점)

① ⓐ　② ⓑ　③ ⓒ　④ ⓓ　⑤ ⓔ

18 위 글의 빈칸 ㉠~㉣에 들어갈 수 <u>없는</u> 단어는? (대·소문자 무시)　(3점)

① off　② if　③ so
④ into　⑤ while

[19~21] 다음 글을 읽고 물음에 답하시오.

Do you feel nervous (A)when your smartphone is not around? Do you feel sad when you check ⓐit and (B)there is no text message? If your answers are "ⓑyes," (C)you may had smartphone addiction. (D)There are ⓒ(various things) you can do to prevent ⓓthis. For example, (E)turn off your smartphone during meals or meetings. You can talk to ⓔpeople instead of texting them.

19 위의 밑줄 친 (A)~(E) 중 어법상 <u>어색한</u> 것은?　(3점)

① (A)　② (B)　③ (C)　④ (D)　⑤ (E)

20 위의 밑줄 친 ⓐ~ⓔ가 지칭하는 것으로 <u>어색한</u> 것은?　(3점)

① ⓐ your smartphone
② ⓑ When my smartphone is not around and there is no text message, I'm not feeling good.
③ ⓒ lots of messages
④ ⓓ smartphone addiction
⑤ ⓔ people around you during meals or meetings

21 위 글을 다음과 같이 요약할 때 빈칸에 들어갈 단어의 영영풀이로 알맞은 것은?　(4점)

> • We should make efforts to prevent smartphone _____.

① being unable to stop doing something
② having positive results
③ finishing something
④ having something lucky and good
⑤ not feeling good from something

Living without smartphones is difficult for many of us these days. However, unwise or too much use of smartphones can cause various problems. All ⓐover the world, people are walking ⓑaround like zombies. Their heads are ⓒup, and their eyes are ⓓon their smartphones. (우리는 그런 사람들을 스몸비, 즉 스마트폰 좀비라고 부른다.) If you are a smombie, you can have various safety problems. You may not see a hole in the street, so you may fall and get hurt. You may get ⓔinto a car accident, too. So what can you do to prevent these problems? It's simple. Do not look at your smartphone while you are walking!

22 위 글의 첫 번째 문장의 밑줄 친 부분 Living과 동사의 쓰임이 같은 문장은? (3점)

① Minho is eating fast food on the bench.

② The girl dancing on the stage is Cathy.

③ Exercising too much can cause various diseases.

④ I'm looking for my bicycle which was lost yesterday.

⑤ Look at those musicians who are singing on the street.

23 위 글의 주어진 우리말을 〈조건〉에 맞게 완전한 문장으로 영작하시오. (4점)

> ┌─ 조건 ─────────────────────────
> • 반드시 총 7 단어만 사용하여 문장을 완성하시오.
> • 동격을 나타내는 콤마(,)를 반드시 1회 사용하시오.
> └──────────────────────────────

Answer: _____

24 위 글의 흐름상 밑줄 친 ⓐ~ⓔ 중 단어의 쓰임이 적절하지 않은 것은? (2점)

① ⓐ   ② ⓑ   ③ ⓒ   ④ ⓓ   ⑤ ⓔ

25 위 글의 내용상 밑줄 친 various safety problems에 해당되는 경우는? (4점)

① Amy fell into the hole and broke her leg.

② Mike picked up some money on the street.

③ Sam dropped his smartphone into the hole and got a new one.

④ Nick helped the old lady send a text message with her smartphone on his way to school.

⑤ Jenny crossed the street at a crosswalk after checking the green light on the traffic light.

26 다음 글의 흐름으로 보아 마지막 문장 다음에 올 수 있는 것은? (3점)

> Do you feel nervous when your smartphone is not around? Do you feel sad when you check your smartphone and there is no text message? If your answers are "yes," you may have smartphone addiction. There are various things you can do to prevent this. For example, turn off your smartphone during meals or meetings.

① Then you can text people.

② Then you cannot eat well.

③ Then you can talk to people.

④ Then you cannot see people.

⑤ Then you can see traffic lights.

[27~30] 다음 글을 읽고 물음에 답하시오.

(A)_____

Smartphones can cause various health problems. One example is dry eyes. When you look at your smartphone, you do not blink often. Then your eyes will feel dry.

(B)[is / can have / you / neck pain / another problem]. When you look down at your smartphone, the stress on your neck increases. Too much use of your smartphone, for example, too much texting, can cause neck pain. We call this text neck.

Here are some tips for these problems. For dry eyes, try to blink often. For text neck, move your smartphone up to your eye level. You can also do some neck stretching exercises.

27 위 글의 (A)에 들어갈 제목으로 가장 적절한 것은? (4점)

① Do you think you are a smombie?
② Do you have dry eyes or text neck?
③ What will happen if you do not blink often?
④ Have you done stretching exercises regularly?
⑤ How do you feel when you don't have your smartphone with you?

28 위 글을 읽고 질문에 대한 답으로 적절한 것을 <u>모두</u> 고르면? (정답 2개) (3점)

> • What can you do to prevent text neck?

① The stress on your neck increases.
② Too much texting can cause text neck.
③ Neck stretching exercises will prevent it.
④ I can move my smartphone up to my eye level.
⑤ Smartphones can cause various health problems such as dry eyes.

29 위 글의 내용과 일치하는 것은? (3점)

① Get some sleep when your eyes feel dry.
② Too much texting makes you feel nervous.
③ Smartphones can solve your health problems.
④ Regular exercises will prevent smartphone addiction.
⑤ Text neck means a pain in your neck caused by too much use of your smartphone.

30 위 글의 (B)를 배열한 순서가 올바른 것을 <u>모두</u> 고르면? (정답 2개) (4점)

① Another problem you can have is neck pain.
② Another problem is you neck pain can have.
③ You can have another problem is neck pain.
④ Neck pain can have you is another problem.
⑤ Neck pain is another problem you can have.

31 다음 사나가 쓴 다짐하는 글을 읽고 가장 <u>잘못</u> 이해한 사람은? (4점)

> There are a few things I need to change to have a healthier life. First, I don't exercise much. From now on, I will try to walk for 30 minutes every day. Second, I think I eat too much fast food. I will eat fast food only once a week. Third, I often eat at night. I will not eat after 10 o'clock. I will try my best to keep these promises.

① 채영: 사나는 지금 어디가 아픈가 봐.
② 지효: 사나는 평소에 운동을 많이 안 하나 봐.
③ 나연: 맞아. 패스트푸드를 많이 먹는 건 몸에 해롭지.
④ 정연: 사나는 밤 9시에 먹는 건 건강에 크게 문제없다고 생각하나 봐.
⑤ 다현: 저기 있는 세 약속만 잘 지켜도 건강해지겠다.

◎ 선택형 문항의 답안은 컴퓨터용 수정 싸인펜을 사용하여 OMR 답안지에 바르게 표기하시오.
◎ 서술형 문제는 답을 답안지에 반드시 검정 볼펜으로 쓰시오.
◎ 총 27문항 100점 만점입니다. 문항별 배점은 각 문항에 표시되어 있습니다.

[경북 ○○중]

01 다음 단어의 영영풀이가 알맞지 <u>않은</u> 것은? (4점)

① myth: showing a strong feeling of love
② hole: a space dug in the surface of the ground
③ blink: to open and close your eyes very quickly
④ skip: to avoid something or not to do something
⑤ adventurous: willing to try new or exciting things

[노원구 ○○중]

02 다음 빈칸에 공통으로 들어갈 가장 알맞은 말은? (4점)

> • The _____ of people living in this city increased.
> • Please enter your secret code _____.

① number　　② percent　　③ celebrity
④ degree　　⑤ name

[부산 ○○중]

03 다음 대화의 흐름상 빈칸에 들어갈 말로 가장 적절한 것은? (4점)

> B: What are you going to do this Saturday?
> G: I'm planning to go to Dream Amusement Park with my brother. _____
> B: I'd love to. When should we meet?
> G: I want to go early, so let's meet at 9 at the subway station.
> B: Sounds good. I'll see you then.

① I'll see you then.
② Can you do me a favor?
③ What would you like to do today?
④ You can go with us if you want to.
⑤ He is very busy doing his homework.

[경북 ○○중]

[4~5] 다음 대화를 읽고, 물음에 답하시오.

> A: Hi, Kate. What's up?
> B: Hi, Minho. What are you going to do this Saturday?
> A: Nothing special. Why?
> B: I'm planning to go to the Van Gogh exhibition at the National Art Museum. Do you want to go with me?
> A: I'd love to! He's my favorite painter. What time should we meet?
> B: How about meeting at 11?
> A: OK. (A)_____
> B: Let's meet in front of the ticket office.
> A: Sounds good. I'll see you there at 11.

04 위 대화의 빈칸 (A)에 들어갈 말로 가장 적절한 것은? (3점)

① Where is the museum?
② Where should we meet?
③ How much is the ticket?
④ Have you ever been to Paris?
⑤ What time does the museum open?

05 위 대화에서 민호의 주말 계획과 관련하여 알 수 <u>없는</u> 것은? (3점)

① 할 일　　　　② 같이 가는 사람
③ 가는 방법　　④ 약속 장소
⑤ 약속 시간

[6~7] 다음 대화를 읽고 물음에 답하시오.

> S1: Hi. What's up?
> S2: Hi. What are you going to do this Saturday?
> S1: Nothing special. Why?
> S2: I'm going to the Van Gogh (A)_____ at National Art Museum. Do you want to go with me?
> S1: I'd love to! He's my favorite painter. What time should we meet?
> S2: How about meeting at 11?
> S1: OK. Where should we meet?
> S2: Let's meet in front of the ticket office.
> S1: Sounds good. I'll see you there at 11.
>
> S1 = Student 1, S2 = Student 2

06 위 대화의 빈칸 (A)에 들어갈 단어로 가장 적절한 것은? (3점)

① excuse
② exercise
③ excitement
④ exhibition
⑤ examination

07 위 대화를 읽고 아래 빈칸에 들어갈 표현으로 가장 적절한 것은? (4점)

> • S1 and S2 are talking about _____ _____.

① where the ticket office is
② how to make an appointment
③ their favorite Art Museum and painter
④ their plans and how to make a reservation
⑤ how to change their plans and appointment

08 다음 짝지어진 대화가 <u>어색한</u> 것은? (4점)

① A: What are you going to do this Sunday?
 B: I'm thinking of going to a piano concert.

② A: Let's meet at 10:30 in front of Green Stadium.
 B: OK. See you then.

③ A: What time and where should we meet?
 B: The musical starts at 3 o'clock. Let's meet at 2 at Dream Art Hall.

④ A: I'm planning to go see Cats this Saturday. Do you want to go with me, Kevin?
 B: I'm sorry, but I have other plans.

⑤ A: I'm planning to go to Dream Amusement Park with my brother. Can you make it at 5?
 B: I'd love to. When should we meet?

09 다음 문장이 자연스러운 대화가 되도록 (A)~(E)를 바르게 연결한 것은? (4점)

> (A) No, my book club meets today in the library.
> (B) I'm going to play basketball after school. Would you like to join us?
> (C) Sorry, I can't. I'm planning to go to the library.
> (D) Do you have a lot of homework?
> (E) I see.

① (B) - (A) - (D) - (C) - (E)
② (B) - (C) - (A) - (D) - (E)
③ (B) - (C) - (D) - (A) - (E)
④ (D) - (C) - (B) - (A) - (E)
⑤ (C) - (D) - (A) - (B) - (E)

10 다음 중 어법상 바르게 쓰인 것은? (3점)

① They made the great king to him.

② What made her the Queen of Jazz?

③ She let her brother to carry the box.

④ He tried to make the child soccer players.

⑤ Mom calls sometimes me by my brother's name.

11 다음 〈보기〉와 의미가 같고 문법적으로 올바른 문장을 고르면? (3점)

보기

• Rachel was too sick to go to school.

---

① Rachel was so sick she could go to school.

② Rachel was so sick because she didn't go to school.

③ Rachel was very sick that she can go to school.

④ Because Rachel was too sick, she couldn't go to school.

⑤ Rachel is very sick that she can't go to school.

12 다음 두 문장을 같은 의미의 한 문장으로 옮겼을 때 가장 옳은 것은? (4점)

① He saw his brother. He was washing the dishes.

→ He saw his brother to wash the dishes.

② The people were rappers. I saw the people in the park.

→ The people I saw in the park were rappers.

③ The dog was very small. It could go through the hole.

→ The dog was too small to go through the hole.

④ The book sold out in one day. I told about the book.

→ The book that I told sold out in one day.

⑤ The coffee is very hot. She can't drink it.

→ The coffee is hot so that she can't drink.

13 다음 그림에 알맞은 말을 조건에 맞게 완성하시오. (6점)

(1) I'm _____.
  (tired / take a nap)

(2) I'm _____.
  (full / eat anymore)

조건

• 주어진 단어를 반드시 활용하시오. (단어 추가 가능)

• so ~ that 구문을 활용하여 완성하시오.

• 주어, 동사가 있는 완전한 문장으로 쓰시오.

---

(1) _____

(2) _____

[14~15] 다음 글을 읽고 물음에 답하시오.

Same Story, Different Paintings
We often find different paintings with the same subject. An example is *The Flight of Icarus* by Henri Matisse and *The Fall of Icarus* by Marc Chagall. ⓐThey are both about the same Greek myth.

The Greek Myth of Icarus
Daedalus was a great inventor. King Minos liked Daedalus' ⓑwork so much that he wanted to keep Daedalus with him forever. Daedalus, ⓒ_____, tried to leave, so the King kept him and his son, Icarus, in a tall tower. Daedalus wanted to escape. One day, Daedalus saw birds ⓓfly. "Wings! I need wings!" he shouted. Daedalus then gathered bird feathers and glued them together with was. When the wings were ready, he warned his son, "Don't fly too close to the sun. The wax will melt."
Daedalus and Icarus began to fly. Icarus was very excited, so he forgot his father's warning. He flew higher and higher, and the wax began to melt. "Oh, no! I'm falling." Icarus cried out. Icarus fell into the sea and died.

14 위 글을 읽고 답할 수 없는 질문은? (4점)

① Why did King Minos want to keep Daedalus with him?
② What did Daedalus and Icarus need to make wings?
③ What warning did Daedalus give to Icarus?
④ How long did Daedalus and Icarus fly?
⑤ How did Daedalus make wings?

15 위 글의 ⓐ~ⓓ에 대해 바르게 설명한 사람을 있는 대로 고른 것은? (3점)

Joy: ⓐThey는 Henri Matisse와 Marc Chagall 을 의미해.
Tom: ⓑwork는 '작품'이라는 뜻으로 해석해야 해.
Sumi: ⓒ에 들어갈 알맞은 말은 however야.
Sam: ⓓfly 대신에 to fly로 써야 해.

① Joy, Tom
② Tom, Sumi
③ Joy, Sam
④ Joy, Tom, Sumi
⑤ Tom, Sumi, Sam

[16~17] 다음 글을 읽고 물음에 답하시오.

Matisse and Chagall both deal (A)_____ the same subject in their paintings, but they are different.
The Flight of Icarus by Henri Matisse / *The Fall of Icarus* by Marc Chagall.
In Matisse's painting, you can see Icarus (B)_____, but in Chagall's painting, the boy is falling. This difference comes from the different ideas that the two painters had. Matisse thought that Icarus was brave and adventurous. (C)_____, Chagall thought that Icarus was foolish.

16 위 글의 제목은? (3점)

① The Icarus Story of Greek Myths
② The Two Painters' Favorite Painting
③ The Adventure of Matisse and Chagall
④ The Friendship Between the Two Painters
⑤ Two Different Paintings with the Same Story

17 위 글의 빈칸 (A)~(C)에 들어갈 말이 알맞은 것은? (4점)

	(A)	(B)	(C)
①	with	flying	In contrast
②	of	flying	In contrast
③	with	to fly	In addition to
④	of	flying	For example
⑤	in	fly	For example

[18~19] 다음 글을 읽고 물음에 답하시오.

Second, Matisse's painting is very simple, but Chagall's painting has many details. (A) In Matisse's painting, there are only Icarus and some stars. (B) However, Chagall painted many people and houses in addition to Icarus. (C) This difference comes from the different painting styles of the two painters. (D) Whose painting do you like more? (E) People will have different answers because they may see the ⓐ_____ thing in ⓑ _____ ways.

18 위 글의 흐름으로 보아, 주어진 문장이 들어가기에 가장 적절한 곳은? (3점)

Furthermore, Icarus' body has just a simple outline.

① (A)   ② (B)   ③ (C)   ④ (D)   ⑤ (E)

19 위 글의 문맥상 빈칸 ⓐ와 ⓑ에 들어갈 말로 가장 적절한 것을 바르게 짝지은 것은? (4점)

	ⓐ	ⓑ
①	same	different
②	same	same
③	usual	usual
④	different	same
⑤	different	different

[20~22] 다음 글을 읽고 물음에 답하시오.

The most famous story about Orpheus is that of ⓐhim and his wife Eurydice. Eurydice was taking a walk when a Satyr attacked her. Orpheus found ⓑhis wife's dead body and began to sing. (A)그의 노래들이 너무 슬퍼서 신들은 모두 울기 시작했다. They then told him to go to the Underworld and bring his wife back. Orpheus followed their advice. ⓒHe went to the Underworld and met Hades, the god of the Underworld. Orpheus asked Hades to return his wife to him and Hades said "yes" after listening to Orpheus' beautiful songs. However, ⓓhe told Orpheus not to look back until ⓔhe and his wife got to the surface. Orpheus agreed, but when he and his wife almost reached the surface, he looked back. Eurydice was behind him and he wanted to see her. All of a sudden, Eurydice disappeared back into the Underworld forever.

*Satyr: 사티로스 (그리스 신화에 나오는 숲의 신으로 남자의 얼굴에 염소의 다리와 뿔을 가지고 있음)

20 위 글을 읽고 답할 수 있는 질문을 모두 고르면? (4점)

ⓐ Who attacked Eurydice?
ⓑ How far was the Underworld to the surface?
ⓒ Where did Orpheus go to bring his wife back?
ⓓ How could Orpheus find his wife's dead body?
ⓔ What happened after Orpheus looked back at Eurydice?
ⓕ What did Orpheus do after finding his wife's dead body?

① ⓐ, ⓑ, ⓓ   ② ⓐ, ⓑ, ⓔ, ⓕ
③ ⓐ, ⓒ, ⓓ, ⓕ   ④ ⓐ, ⓒ, ⓔ, ⓕ
⑤ ⓐ, ⓑ, ⓒ, ⓔ, ⓕ

21 위 글의 밑줄 친 ⓐ~ⓔ 중 의미하는 것이 다른 하나는? (3점)

① ⓐ   ② ⓑ   ③ ⓒ   ④ ⓓ   ⑤ ⓔ

22 위 글의 밑줄 친 (A)의 우리말을 so ~ that을 사용하여 한 문장의 영어로 쓰시오. (4점)

→ _____.

[23~27] 다음을 읽고 물음에 답하시오.

Same Story, Different Paintings
We often find ⓐ_____ paintings with the same subject. An example is The Flight of Icarus by Henri Matisse and The Fall of Icarus by Marc Chagall. They are both about the ⓑ_____ Greek myth.

The Greek Myth of Icarus
Daedalus was a great inventor. King Minos liked Daedalus' ⓒwork so much that he wanted to keep Daedalus with him forever. Daedalus, however, tried to leave, so the King kept him and his son, Icarus, in a tall tower. Daedalus wanted to escape. One day, Daedalus saw birds ⓓflying. "Wings! I need wings!" he shouted. Daedalus then gathered bird feathers and glued them together with wax. When the wings were ready, he warned his son, "Don't fly too ⓔclose to the sun. The wax will melt."
Daedalus and Icarus began to ⓕfly. Icarus was so ⓖexciting that he forgot his father's warning. He flew ⓗhigher and higher, and the wax began to melt. "Oh, no! I'm falling," Icarus cried out. Icarus fell into the sea and died.

23 위 글의 내용상 빈칸 ⓐ, ⓑ에 들어갈 말이 순서대로 바르게 된 것은? (4점)

	ⓐ	ⓑ
①	same	simple
②	same	different
③	simple	different
④	different	simple
⑤	different	same

24 위 글의 밑줄 친 ⓒwork와 같은 의미로 쓰인 것은? (3점)

① People came from all over the world to view his work.
② My father has a lot of work to do this Friday.
③ She doesn't have to work on weekends.
④ I'm so tired because I work all the time.
⑤ They work nine to five.

25 위 글의 밑줄 친 ⓓ~ⓗ 중 어법상 적절하지 않은 것은? (4점)

① ⓓ　　② ⓔ　　③ ⓕ　　④ ⓖ　　⑤ ⓗ

26 위 글을 읽고 대답할 수 없는 질문은? (4점)

① What did Daedalus tell his son when the wax melted?
② Why did King Minos want to keep Daedalus?
③ What was Icarus's father's warning?
④ Why did Icarus fall into the sea?
⑤ How did Daedalus make wings?

27 위 글의 내용과 가장 일치하는 것은? (4점)

① Henri Matisse and Marc Chagall liked to read the Greek myth.
② Daedalus was a great painter as well as an inventor.
③ Daedalus gathered bird feathers because King Minos wanted them.
④ Daedalus decided to be with King Minos forever.
⑤ Icarus fell into the sea because he forgot his father's warning.

◎ 선택형 문항의 답안은 컴퓨터용 수정 싸인펜을 사용하여 OMR 답안지에 바르게 표기하시오.
◎ 서술형 문제는 답을 답안지에 반드시 검정 볼펜으로 쓰시오.
◎ 총 29문항 100점 만점입니다. 문항별 배점은 각 문항에 표시되어 있습니다.

[종로구 ○○중]

01 밑줄 친 단어 중 적절히 쓰이지 <u>않은</u> 것은? (3점)

① We went to see the Picasso <u>exhibition</u>.
② There are lots of <u>adventurous</u> about heroes.
③ Her poems often <u>deal with</u> the subject of love.
④ We spent the <u>whole</u> day at the beach.
⑤ The police tried to catch the robbers, but they <u>escaped</u>.

[대구 ○○중]

02 빈칸 ⓐ에 들어갈 말로 가장 적절한 것은? (3점)

We often find different paintings with the same ⓐ＿＿＿＿＿. An example is *The Flight of Icarus* by Henri Matisse and *The Fall of Icarus* by Marc Chagall. They are both about the same Greek myth.

① sketchbook ② music ③ subject
④ painter ⑤ invention

[종로구 ○○중]

03 다음 대화 중 <u>어색한</u> 것은? (3점)

① A: You don't look well.
  B: Yeah, I feel so energetic today.
② A: How about meeting at 12:30?
  B: Sounds wonderful! I'll see you soon.
③ A: I have a sore throat. I have a fever, too.
  B: That's too bad. You need to drink a lot of water.
④ A: I'm going to go to a piano concert. Do you want to go with me?
  B: I'm sorry, but I have other plans.
⑤ A: I fell and hurt my knee while I was playing soccer.
  B: I'm so sorry for you. Try to put some ice on it.

[경북 ○○중]

04 다음 (A)~(C)를 자연스러운 대화가 되도록 바르게 배열한 것은? (4점)

A: I'm planning to go see a soccer game this Friday. What about joining me, Jinho?
(A) OK. See you then.
(B) That sounds great. What time should we meet?
(C) Let's meet at 10:30 in front of Green Stadium.

① (A)-(B)-(C) ② (B)-(A)-(C)
③ (B)-(C)-(A) ④ (C)-(A)-(B)
⑤ (C)-(B)-(A)

[광진구 ○○중]

05 다음 대화의 흐름에 맞도록 빈칸에 들어갈 문장으로 가장 적합한 것은? (3점)

Boy: What are you going to do this Sunday?
Girl: I'm planning to go to Dream Amusement Park with my brother. ＿＿＿＿
＿＿＿＿＿＿＿＿＿＿＿＿＿＿＿
Boy: I'd love to. When should we meet?
Girl: I want to go early, so let's meet at 9 at the subway station.
Boy: Sounds good. I'll see you then.

① Can you make it?
② How about going at 9?
③ Where should we meet?
④ What time should we meet?
⑤ You can go with us if you want to.

[6~7] 다음 대화를 읽고, 물음에 답하시오.

Minho: Hi, Kate. What's up?
Kate: Hi, Minho. What are you going to do this Saturday?
Minho: Nothing special. Why?
Kate: I'm planning to go to the Van Gogh exhibition at the National Art Museum. Do you want to go with me?
Minho: I'd love to! He's my favorite painter. What time should we meet?
Kate: How about meeting at 11?
Minho: OK. Where should we meet?
Kate: Let's meet in front of the ticket office.
Minho: Sounds good. I'll see you there at 11.

06 위 대화를 읽고 답할 수 <u>없는</u> 질문은? (3점)

① Who is Kate's favorite painter?
② When will Kate and Minho meet?
③ What are Kate and Minho talking about?
④ Where are Kate and Minho going to meet?
⑤ What exhibition is Kate planning to go to this Saturday?

07 According to the passage, complete Kate's text message. (4점)

> • Minho, don't (A)_____ our plan for this Saturday. I'll see you at 11 in front of the ticket office. I can't (B)_____ to see the exhibition with you. See you then.

	(A)	(B)
①	forgive	imagine
②	join	prevent
③	say	think
④	remember	plan
⑤	forget	wait

[8~9] 다음 대화를 읽고 물음에 답하시오.

Stacie: ⓐ<u>내일 라이언 킹을 보러 갈 계획이야.</u> Do you want to join me?
John: Sure. Where should we meet?
Stacie: Let's meet at Star Movie Theater. The movie starts at 3. ⓑ<u>How about 2?</u>
John: That sounds good. See you then.

08 위 대화의 ⓐ를 영작하시오.(9 words) (4점)

→ _____

09 위 대화의 ⓑ와 바꿔 쓸 수 있는 표현을 2개 쓰시오. (6점)

→ _____

_____

10 다음 대화의 내용과 일치하지 <u>않는</u> 것은? (3점)

B: Hi, Kate. What's up?
G: Hi, Minho. What are you going to do this Saturday?
B: Nothing special. Why?
G: I'm planning to go to the Van Gogh exhibition at the National Art Museum. Do you want to go with me?
B: I'd love to! He's my favorite painter. What time should we meet?
G: How about meeting at 11?
B: OK. Where should we meet?
G: Let's meet in front of the ticket office.
B: Sounds good. I'll see you there at 11.

① 민호는 Kate를 전시회에 초대했다.
② Kate는 반 고흐 전시회에 갈 계획이다.
③ 민호도 반 고흐 전시회에 가고 싶어 한다.
④ 민호가 가장 좋아하는 화가는 반 고흐이다.
⑤ Kate가 11시에 만날 것을 제안하였다.

11 다음 두 문장을 so, that이 들어가는 하나의 문장으로 만드시오. (4점)

[부산 ○○중]

> • Emma was very bored.
> • She started singing to herself.

→ _____

[종로구 ○○중]

12 다음 두 문장을 유사한 의미를 가지는 한 문장으로 바꿀 때 어법상 옳지 않은 것은? (4점)

> • I saw my brother.
> • He was swimming in the river.
> → _____

① I saw my brother swim in the river.
② I saw my brother swimming in the river.
③ I saw my brother to swim in the river.
④ I saw my brother who was swimming in the river.
⑤ I saw my brother that was swimming in the river.

[경기 ○○중]

13 다음 글의 ⓐ~ⓔ 중 어법상 알맞은 것은? (3점)

> Today was a strange day. When I was ⓐread a book in the garden, I heard a rabbit ⓑtalking to himself. I followed him and found a ⓒsurprise world. There I saw a queen ⓓto smell a rose. I also saw a cat ⓔsmiled in a tree.

① ⓐ ② ⓑ ③ ⓒ ④ ⓓ ⑤ ⓔ

[경기 ○○중]

14 다음 우리말을 주어진 모든 영어 단어를 배열하여 영작할 때, 어법상 옳게 만들어지는 것을 〈보기〉에서 고른 것은? (4점)

보기

(A) 비가 너무 세차게 와서 그들은 경기를 취소해야 했다.
← it / cancel / that / they / heavily / rained / very / the game / had to /.
(B) 나는 그가 뱀을 만지고 있는 것을 보고 놀랐다.
← surprised / touching / see / he / was / I / to / the snake /.
(C) 나는 그들이 집안에서 운동화를 신고 있는 것을 보았다.
← them / the house / saw / in / sneakers / their / I / wearing /.
(D) 나는 누군가가 내 이름을 반복해서 부르는 것을 들었다.
← heard / someone / repeat / my / I / name /.

① (A), (C)   ② (A), (D)   ③ (B), (C)
④ (B), (D)   ⑤ (C), (D)

[강북구 ○○중]

15 Which of the followings are matched with the given Korean translation? (정답 2개) (3점)

> • 존은 너무 아파서, 학교에 갈 수가 없다.
> = 존은 학교에 가기에는 지나치게 아프다.

① John is so sick that he can't go to school.
② John isn't sick so that he goes to school.
③ John is too sick for his brother to take him to school.
④ John is too sick to go to school.
⑤ John isn't sick enough not to go to school.

[16~19] 다음 글을 읽고 물음에 답하시오.

Same Story, Different Paintings
We often find different paintings with the same subject. An example is *The Flight of Icarus* by Henri Matisse and *The Fall of Icarus* by Marc Chagall. They are both about the same Greek myth.

The Greek Myth of Icarus
Daedalus was a great inventor. King Minos liked Daedalus' work (A)_____ much (B)_____ he wanted to keep Daedalus with ⓐhim forever. Daedalus, however, tried to leave, so ⓑthe King kept ⓒhim and ⓓhis son, Icarus, in a tall tower. Daedalus wanted to escape. One day, Daedalus saw birds flying. "Wings! I need wings!" ⓔhe shouted. Daedalus then gathered bird feathers and glued them together with wax. When the wings were ready, ⓕhe warned his son, "Don't fly too close to the sun. The wax will melt."
Daedalus and Icarus began to fly. Icarus was (A)_____ excited (B)_____ he forgot his father's warning. ⓖHe flew higher and higher, and the wax began to melt. "Oh, no! ⓗI'm falling," Icarus cried out. Icarus fell into the sea and died.

17 위 글의 빈칸 (A), (B)에 들어갈 말을 알맞게 짝지은 것은? (3점)

	(A)	(B)
①	so	that
②	so	this
③	very	what
④	very	this
⑤	too	that

18 위 글의 밑줄 친 ⓐ~ⓗ가 가리키는 대상이 알맞게 짝지어진 것은? (4점)

	다이달로스	이카루스
①	ⓐ, ⓒ, ⓔ	ⓓ, ⓖ
②	ⓒ, ⓔ, ⓕ	ⓓ, ⓖ, ⓗ
③	ⓒ, ⓓ, ⓔ	ⓕ, ⓖ
④	ⓒ, ⓔ, ⓕ	ⓑ, ⓓ, ⓖ
⑤	ⓔ, ⓕ	ⓐ, ⓑ, ⓒ

16 위 글의 내용과 일치하지 <u>않는</u> 것은? (3점)

① 앙리 마티스와 마르크 샤갈이 같은 주제로 그린 그림이 있다.
② 그리스 신화 속 이카루스는 다이달로스의 아들이다.
③ 미노스 왕은 이카루스의 작품을 매우 좋아했다.
④ 다이달로스는 새가 나는 것을 보고 탈출할 방법에 대한 아이디어를 얻었다.
⑤ 이카루스는 결국 죽게 되었다.

19 위 글의 내용으로 미루어 볼 때 미노스 왕이 할 수 있는 말로 가장 알맞은 것은? (3점)

① I should make wings.
② Father! We're flying.
③ Don't go too close to the sun!
④ I'm going to keep you and your son in the tower!
⑤ Oh my god! I'm falling!

[20~24] 다음 글을 읽고 물음에 답하시오.

Daedalus was a great inventor. King Minos liked Daedalus' work (가)[to keep / much / so / he / that / wanted] Daedalus with him forever. Daedalus, however, tried to leave, so the King kept him and his son, Icarus, in a tall tower, Daedalus wanted to escape.

One day, Daedalus saw birds ⓐ_____. "Wings! I need wings!" he shouted. Daedalus then gathered bird feathers and glued them together with wax. When the wings were ready, he warned his son. "Don't ⓑ_____ too close to the sun. The wax will melt."

Daedalus and Icarus began ⓒ_____. (A)He flew higher and higher, and the wax started to melt. (B)Icarus was so excited that he forgot his father's warning. (C)Icarus fell into the sea and died. (D)"Oh, no! I'm falling," Icarus cried out.

20 위 글의 밑줄 친 부분 (가)의 주어진 단어를 순서대로 배열하여 문장을 완성하시오. (3점)

→ _____

21 위 글의 내용과 일치하는 것은? (3점)

① Daedalus는 훌륭한 화가였다.
② Daedalus의 아들은 아버지의 경고를 잘 따랐다.
③ Minos 왕은 Daedalus와 그의 아들을 섬에 가두었다.
④ Daedalus는 새의 깃털을 모아 날개를 만들었다.
⑤ 어느 날 Daedalus의 아들은 새들이 날아가는 것을 보았다.

22 위 글의 빈칸 ⓐ~ⓒ에 들어갈 알맞은 말이 바르게 짝지어진 것은? (4점)

	ⓐ	ⓑ	ⓒ
①	fly	flying	fly
②	fly	flying	flying
③	to fly	fly	flying
④	flying	fly	to fly
⑤	flying	to fly	to fly

23 위 글의 (A)~(D)를 순서대로 나열한 것은? (3점)

① (A)-(B)-(C)-(D)   ② (A)-(C)-(D)-(B)
③ (B)-(A)-(C)-(D)   ④ (B)-(D)-(C)-(A)
⑤ (B)-(A)-(D)-(C)

24 위 글의 내용과 다음 글에서 밑줄 친 부분이 다른 것은? (4점)

ⓐDaedalus tried to think of ways to stay. ⓑOne day, Daedalus watched birds flying. It gave him an idea. 'Every birds has this.', said Daedalus. He needed wings. ⓒDaedalus started to gather all the bird feathers. ⓓHe glued them together with wax. When two pairs of wings were ready, ⓔhe warned his young son not to fly too close to the sun or the wax would melt.

① ⓐ   ② ⓑ   ③ ⓒ   ④ ⓓ   ⑤ ⓔ

[25~29] 다음 글을 읽고 물음에 답하시오.

Two Different Paintings

Matisse and Chagall ⓐboth deal with ⓑthe same subject in their paintings, but ⓒthey are different.

First, in Matisse's painting, Icarus is flying, but in Chagall's painting, the boy is falling. This difference comes from the different ideas ⓓthat the two painters had. Matisse thought ⓔthat Icarus was brave and adventurous. But Chagall thought that Icarus was foolish.

Second, Matisse's painting is very simple, but Chagall's painting has many details. In Matisse's painting, there are only Icarus and some stars. (A)_____, Icarus' body has just a simple outline. (B)_____, Chagall painted many people and houses (C)_____ Icarus. This difference comes from the different painting styles of the two painters.

Whose painting do you like more? People will have different answers because they may see the same thing in different ways.

25 위 글을 읽고 답할 수 없는 질문은? (3점)

① What is Icarus doing in Chagall's painting?
② Who thought that Icarus was foolish?
③ What can you see in Matisse's painting?
④ Which picture is more popular in the world?
⑤ How is Matisse's painting different from Chagall's?

26 위 글의 ⓐ~ⓔ에 대한 설명으로 가장 옳은 것은? (3점)

① ⓐ의 both는 the paintings of Matisse and Chagall을 의미한다.
② ⓑ는 미술 과목을 의미한다.
③ ⓒ는 Matisse and Chagall을 의미한다.
④ ⓓ는 생략 가능하다.
⑤ ⓔ는 생략할 수 없다.

27 위 글의 빈칸 (A)~(C)에 알맞은 표현으로 가장 잘 짝지어진 것은? (3점)

    (A)   (B)   (C)

① In contrast - Furthermore - in addition to
② In contrast - In addition to - furthermore
③ Furthermore - In contrast - in addition to
④ Furthermore - in addition to - in contrast
⑤ In addition to - Furthermore - in contrast

28 위 글의 두 화가가 그린 그림의 내용을 비교, 대조하는 표이다. 빈칸에 들어갈 표현이 옳은 것은? (4점)

Matisse	Chagall
• He focused on Icarus' flying	• He focused on Icarus' falling.
• He looked at the (A)_____ of Icarus.	• He thought that Icarus was (B)_____.
• His painting is (C)_____.	• His painting has (D)_____.
• He drew only Icarus and (E)_____.	• There are many people and houses in his painting.

① (A) bright side   ② (B) careful
③ (C) many details   ④ (D) simple
⑤ (E) the sun

29 What is the main idea of the reading above? (3점)

① 화가는 상상력과 창의성이 풍부해야 한다.
② 사고의 다양성을 이해하고 인정해야 한다.
③ 화가는 사물을 정확하게 표현해야 한다.
④ 시대의 흐름에 따라 그림의 스타일을 변한다.
⑤ 그림을 감상하려면 역사적 지식이 있어야 한다.

2학년 영어 2학기 기말고사(7과) 1회

문항수 : 선택형(26문항)   서술형(2문항) | 20 . . .

◎ 선택형 문항의 답안은 컴퓨터용 수정 싸인펜을 사용하여 OMR 답안지에 바르게 표기하시오.

◎ 서술형 문제는 답을 답안지에 반드시 검정 볼펜으로 쓰시오.

◎ 총 28문항 100점 만점입니다. 문항별 배점은 각 문항에 표시되어 있습니다.

[경북 ○○중]

01 다음 빈칸에 들어갈 수 있는 단어가 <u>아닌</u> 것은?   (4점)

- The box was full of _____ such as gold and silver.
- My grandfather was in the _____ and he fought in the war.
- The _____ of this painting is about one million dollars.
- A _____ is a person who studies history.

① trash   ② treasures   ③ value
④ army   ⑤ historian

[세종 ○○중]

02 다음 중 밑줄 친 단어의 우리말 의미가 알맞지 <u>않은</u> 것은? (3점)

① The school <u>recently</u> built new buildings.
   (최근에)
② Grace is walking <u>towards</u> the bus stop.
   (~을 향하여)
③ The boys looked at <u>each other</u>. (서로)
④ I've known Joanna <u>since</u> she was born.
   (~한 이래로)
⑤ You can <u>lie</u> down if you're not feeling well.
   (거짓말하다)

[서대문구 ○○중]

03 다음 대화의 밑줄 친 부분의 의도로 알맞은 것은?   (3점)

A: <u>Did you hear about the new space food?</u>
B: Yes, I did. It's a type of ice cream.

① 의견 묻기   ② 상상한 내용 묻기
③ 관심에 대해 묻기   ④ 확인 요청하기
⑤ 알고 있는지 묻기

[전북 ○○중]

[4~5] 다음 대화를 읽고 물음에 답하시오.

A: Subin, did you hear about the new movie, *Life on the Moon*?
B: No, I didn't.
A: I heard it's really good.
B: I'm really curious about the movie.
_____
A: It's about a man who is trying to live on the moon.
B: That sounds interesting.
A: Look. The movie is playing at the Space Theater here.
B: What time is the movie?
A: It begins at 2:30.
B: Let's eat lunch first and then see the movie.
A: OK. I'm hungry. Let's go!

04 위 대화의 빈칸에 들어갈 말로 알맞은 것은?   (4점)

① Why are you curious about the movie?
② Where can you see the man?
③ What's it about?
④ What movie do you want to watch?
⑤ I want to know about a man who lives on the moon.

05 위 대화의 내용과 가장 일치하는 것은?   (3점)

① Subin heard about the new movie.
② The movie is about a man who got lost on the space.
③ The movie will finish at 2:30.
④ A doesn't know where the movie is playing.
⑤ After A and B eat lunch, they will see the movie.

[6~7] 다음 대화를 읽고 물음에 답하시오.

B: Subin, (A)_____,
Life on the Moon?
G: No, I didn't.
B: I heard it's really good.

(A) That sounds interesting.
(B) It's about a man who is trying to live on the moon.
(C) I'm really curious about the movie. What's it about?
(D) What time is the movie?
(E) Look. The movie is playing at the Space Theater here.

B: It begins at 2:30.
G: Let's eat lunch first and then see the movie.
B: OK. I'm hungry. Let's go!

06 위 대화의 빈칸 (A)에 들어갈 말로 어법상 가장 적절한 것은?

(3점)

① are you aware of the new movie
② do you know about the new movie
③ did you hear about the new movie
④ have you heard about the new movie
⑤ do you know the new movie was released

07 위 대화가 자연스럽게 이어지도록 (A)~(E)를 바르게 배열한 것은?

(4점)

① (C) - (B) - (A) - (E) - (D)
② (C) - (E) - (B) - (A) - (D)
③ (C) - (E) - (A) - (B) - (D)
④ (E) - (B) - (A) - (C) - (D)
⑤ (E) - (B) - (C) - (A) - (D)

08 Which of the following is the correct translation of (A)?

(3점)

B: Did you hear about the first spaceship that went into space?
G: No, I didn't. (A)나는 그것에 대해 궁금해.
B: This is a poster of the spaceship.
G: Really? I want to buy it.

※ B: Boy, G: Girl

① I already know about it.
② It's about Mars and its moons.
③ I'm curious about it.
④ I heard the spaceship was great.
⑤ It's a show about space travel.

09 다음 대화 중 어색한 것은?

(4점)

① A: What's wrong with you? You look sick.
B: I have had a cold for a week.
② A: Have you heard about Jane's car accident?
B: Yes, I have.
③ A: Are you still doing your homework?
B: No. I have already finished my homework.
④ A: What is the most delicious food you have eaten?
B: I've never tried tacos.
⑤ A: When did you first meet him?
B: Five years ago. Since then, we have been best friends.

[10~11] 다음 대화를 읽고 물음에 답하시오.

> B: Subin, did you hear about the new movie, *Life on the Moon*?
> G: No, I didn't.
> B: I heard it's really good.
> G: I'm really curious about the movie. What's it about?
> B: It's about a man who is trying to live on the moon.
> G: (A)_____
> B: Look. The movie is playing at the Space Theater here.
> G: What time is the movie?
> B: It begins at 2:30.
> G: Let's eat lunch first and then see the movie.
> B: OK. I'm hungry. Let's go!

10 위 대화의 빈칸 (A)에 들어갈 말로 가장 적절한 것은? (3점)

① That's a good price.

② That sounds interesting.

③ I lost it near the theater.

④ Here is some advice for you.

⑤ Make sure you get some rest.

11 위 대화를 읽고 답할 수 <u>없는</u> 질문은? (3점)

① What is the movie about?

② What time does the movie Subin is going to see begin?

③ Where do the speakers usually play?

④ What are the speakers talking about?

⑤ What will the speakers do before the movie?

12 다음 두 문장이 같도록 할 때 빈칸에 알맞은 것은? (4점)

> To follow the rules is important.
> → It is important _____ the rules.

① follow

② follows

③ following

④ to follow

⑤ to following

13 다음 주어진 우리말 뜻에 맞게, 빈칸에 알맞은 세 단어를 써서 문장을 완성하시오. (6점)

> • I _____ just _____ _____ my homework. (나는 방금 내 숙제를 끝마쳤다.)

→ _____ _____ _____

14 다음 빈칸 (A)~(C)에 들어갈 말로 바르게 나열한 것은? (4점)

> • A: How long has she lived in Ulsan?
>   B: She has lived in Ulsan (A)_____ 3 months.
> • A: Have you finished your project, Peter?
>   B: Yes. I have (B)_____ finished my project.
> • A: How long has Mr. Williams worked for this company?
>   B: He has worked (C)_____ he was 20 years old.

	(A)	(B)	(C)
①	for	just	for
②	since	just	for
③	for	just	since
④	since	already	since
⑤	for	since	since

[15~18] 다음 글을 읽고 물음에 답하시오.

(A) Later that night, Rada and Jonny talked a long time about Earth. It was exciting to think about all the new things they were going to see and do. There was ⓐone new thing Rada and Jonny really wanted to do. They thought about ⓑit all night and didn't tell Mom and Dad about it. It was their secret.

(B) Rada and Jonny ran up the nearest hill. At the top, they looked at each other and laughed. Then they lay down on the soft green grass and rolled down the hill. ⓒThat was their secret!
"ⓓThis is the best new thing of all!" shouted Rada and Jonny. And they ran up to the top of the hill again.

(C) The next day, Rada's family got on a spaceship. "It's going to be a long trip," said Mom. "That's alright. I'm so excited!" said Rada.

(D) The spaceship finally landed.
"Dad, it's difficult to walk on Earth," said Rada. "I know. Earth is pulling you down," said Dad.
Rada and Jonny couldn't float anymore. ⓔThat was the first new thing.
"What's the sound?" asked Rada.
"A bird is singing," said Mom.
"I've never heard a bird sing," said Rada.
"I've never felt the wind," said Jonny.
These were all new things.

15 위 글의 주어진 글 (A)에 이어질 내용을 순서에 맞게 배열한 것으로 가장 적절한 것은? (4점)

① (B) - (D) - (C) ② (C) - (B) - (D)
③ (C) - (D) - (B) ④ (D) - (B) - (C)
⑤ (D) - (C) - (B)

16 위 글의 제목으로 가장 적절한 것은? (4점)

① The Best New Thing
② The Power of a Secret
③ How to Land on Earth
④ The First Day on the Spaceship
⑤ Rolling down the Hill: Dangerous Secret

17 위 글의 밑줄 친 ⓐ~ⓔ 중에서 가리키는 대상이 나머지 넷과 다른 것은? (3점)

① ⓐ ② ⓑ ③ ⓒ ④ ⓓ ⑤ ⓔ

18 위 글의 내용과 일치하는 것은? (3점)

① Rada는 지구로 여행을 갈 생각에 신났다.
② Rada와 Jonny는 가장 높은 언덕으로 뛰어 올라갔다.
③ Rada는 부모님과 지구에 관해 이야기를 나누었다.
④ Rada는 지구에서 걷는 것이 어렵지 않다고 느꼈다.
⑤ Jonny는 바람을 맞을 때의 느낌을 알고 있었다.

19 다음 글의 밑줄 친 ⓐ~ⓔ 중 문법적으로 옳은 것은? (4점)

The next morning, Rada's family went to a park. Rada said to Dad, "Dad, I've never ⓐ ridden a bike before." "Let's ride bikes, then," said Dad. They then ⓑrides bikes together. The weather was great, and it was so fun. In the afternoon, Rada's family went to the beach. Jonny said to Mom, "I've never ⓒswim before." "Let's swim, then," said Mom. It was great to swim in the cool blue sea. At night, Rada and Jonny talked about ⓓlive on Earth. "It's wonderful to live on Earth," Rada said to Jonny. "Yes. it's great ⓔto been here," Jonny said.

① ⓐ ② ⓑ ③ ⓒ ④ ⓓ ⑤ ⓔ

[20~25] 다음 글을 읽고 물음에 답하시오.

The Best New Thing
Rada lived on a little world, far out in space. She lived there with her father, mother, and brother Jonny. Only Rada and Jonny were children, and they were born in space.
One day, Dad told Rada and Jonny, "We're going back to ⓐEarth tomorrow."
Rada and Jonny looked at Dad in surprise and ⓑfloated towards him.
Rada asked Dad, "What's it like on Earth?"
"Everything is different there. For example, the sky is blue," answered Dad.
"I've never seen a blue sky," said Jonny.
"The sky is always black here," said Rada.
"You don't have to wear your big heavy ⓒspace suits because there is air everywhere. (A)It's also hard to jump there because Earth pulls you down," said Dad.
"What else?" asked Rada.
"There are hills, and they are covered with soft green grass. You can roll down the hills," answered Mom.
"Dad, have you ever rolled down a hill?" asked Rada.
"Yes, (B)it's really amazing!" answered Dad.
Jonny was ⓓthirsty, so he opened a milk ⓔcontainer and shook (C)it. The milk floated in the air and formed balls. Jonny swallowed the balls.
"Jonny, if you drink milk that way on Earth, you'll get wet," said Mom.
Later that night, Rada and Jonny talked a long time about Earth. (D)It was exciting to think about all the new things they were going to see and do. There was one new thing Rada and Jonny really wanted to do. They thought about it all night and didn't tell Mom and Dad about (E)it. It was their secret.
The next day, Rada's family got on a spaceship.
"It's going to be a long trip," said Mom.
"That's alright. I'm so excited!" said Rada.

20 ⓐ~ⓔ에 대한 영어풀이가 어색한 것은? (3점)

① ⓐ the planet that we live on
② ⓑ move gently through the air
③ ⓒ clothes you wear when you travel in space
④ ⓓ eating a lot of food
⑤ ⓔ a box or bottle you use to hold something

21 위 글의 내용과 일치하지 않는 것을 2개 고르면? (4점)

① Rada and Jonny have never been to Earth.
② People in space enjoy rolling down the hills.
③ Rada and Jonny have never seen a blue sky.
④ In space, you have to wear big heavy space suits.
⑤ Rada and Jonny walked to their father to ask questions.

22 위 글을 읽고 답할 수 없는 질문은? (3점)

① What color is the sky in space?
② Why is it hard to jump on Earth?
③ How do you make coffee in space?
④ How do you drink milk in space?
⑤ What do you have to wear in space?

23 위 글의 (A)~(E)가 가리키는 것으로 어색한 것은? (4점)

① (A) 지구에서 점프하는 것
② (B) 언덕을 굴러 내려가는 것
③ (C) 우유 상자를 열어 흔드는 것
④ (D) 보고 그리고 하게 될 새로운 것들에 대해 생각하는 것
⑤ (E) 꼭 해보고 싶었던 한 가지 새로운 것

24 위 글에 나타난 우주(space)에 대한 추측으로 어색한 것은?

(3점)

① Air is not everywhere.

② It is easy to jump there.

③ It's far away from Earth.

④ It does not pull you down.

⑤ You use a straw to drink milk.

25 위 글에 나온 단어만을 사용하여 완성하시오. (4점)

Rada and Jonny were born in (A)_____, and have never been to (B)_____. They got excited when their dad told them that they'd go back to Earth.
On Earth, they won't have to wear space (C)_____, and they can roll down (D)_____ which are covered with soft green grass.

(A) _____ (B) _____

(C) _____ (D) _____

[인천 ○○중]

[26~27] 다음 글을 읽고 물음에 답하시오.

Becoming Stronger

One day, Rada, Jonny, Mom, and Dad were talking about life on Earth. Dad said to Rada and Jonny, "You have to be strong to live on Earth."
Mom also said, "Earth is a big world. It'll pull you down. You must be strong. Then you can walk on Earth."
Jonny looked at Rada and said, "Rada, let's start exercising. We have to become stronger."
Rada and Jonny went to the exercise room. There were springs on the wall. Rada and Jonny stood on the wall and pulled on the springs. They pulled and pulled, but the springs only moved a little.

"Pull hard like me," said Jonny. He was pulling very hard.
Rada said, "We'll get stronger. Then we can walk on Earth. We'll see flowers and trees there."
Dad came into the exercise room and said, "You're both getting very strong. You'll like it on Earth."

26 What were on the wall of the exercise room? (3점)

① flowers ② straps ③ trees

④ springs ⑤ planets

27 위 글의 내용을 요약한 것이다. 빈칸 (A)~(C)에 들어갈 말로 가장 바르게 연결된 것은? (4점)

Rada and her family were talking about life on Earth. Dad told his children to need to be __(A)__ to live on Earth. So Jonny said to his sister, Rada, to start to __(B)__. They stood on the wall and __(C)__ on the springs in the exercise room. After that, Rada thought they'll get stronger and can walk on Earth.

	(A)	(B)	(C)
①	strong	explain	pushed
②	strong	exercise	pulled
③	healthy	explain	pushed
④	healthy	exercise	pushed
⑤	unhealthy	exercise	pulled

[경기 ○○중]

28 다음 ⓐ~ⓔ 중 어법이 어색한 것은? (3점)

ⓐHave you ever been to Jeju-do? There are many things you can do there. For example, it is fun ⓑride horses. If you ⓒhave never ⓓvisited Jeju-do, you should ⓔgo there.

① ⓐ ② ⓑ ③ ⓒ ④ ⓓ ⑤ ⓔ

2학년 영어 2학기 기말고사(7과) 2회

문항수 : 선택형(25문항) 서술형(5문항) 20 . . .

◎ 선택형 문항의 답안은 컴퓨터용 수정 싸인펜을 사용하여 OMR 답안지에 바르게 표기하시오.

◎ 서술형 문제는 답을 답안지에 반드시 검정 볼펜으로 쓰시오.

◎ 총 30문항 100점 만점입니다. 문항별 배점은 각 문항에 표시되어 있습니다.

[영등포구 ○○중]

01 다음 빈칸에 공통으로 알맞은 것은? (3점)

• Don't _____ to your friends.
• You can _____ down if you're not feeling well.

① take   ② form   ③ float
④ lie   ⑤ pull

[충북 ○○중]

02 다음 주어진 영어 뜻에 해당하는 단어는? (3점)

to try to find someone or something by looking very carefully

① steal   ② search
③ form   ④ allow
⑤ prove

[인천 ○○중]

03 다음 문맥상 빈칸에 들어갈 말로 가장 적절한 것은? (3점)

A: Did you hear about _____?
B: Yes, I did. It's a type of ice cream.
A: Yes, and here it is. It looks good.
B: I'm really curious about the taste.

① the space station
② the space marathon
③ the new space food
④ the new book about Mars
⑤ the first spaceship that went into space

[양천구 ○○중]

[4~5] 다음 대화를 읽고 물음에 답하시오.

B: Subin, did you hear about the new movie, *Life on the Moon*?
G: No, I didn't.
B: I heard it's really good.
G: I'm really curious about the movie. What's it about?
B: It's about a man who is trying to live on the moon.
G: That sounds interesting.
B: Look. The movie is playing at the Space Theater here.
G: What time is the movie?
B: It begins at 2:30.
G: Let's eat lunch first and then see the movie.
B: OK. I'm hungry. Let's go!

*B: Minho G: Subin

04 위 대화를 읽고 알 수 없는 것을 2개 고르면? (4점)

① 영화 제목
② 총 영화 상영 시간
③ 영화 내용
④ 영화 상영 장소
⑤ 점심 메뉴

05 위 대화의 내용과 일치하지 않는 것은? (3점)

① Minho heard about the new movie.
② Subin wants to know about the new movie.
③ Minho is planning to have lunch after watching the new movie.
④ Minho knows where the new movie is playing.
⑤ Minho and Subin is going to see the new movie together.

[6~7] Read the following and answer the questions.

A: Subin, did you hear about the new movie, *Life on the Moon*?
S: No, I didn't.
A: I heard it's really good.
S: I'm really curious about the movie. What's it about?
A: It's about a man who is trying to live on the moon.
S: That sounds interesting.
A: Look. The movie is playing at the Space Theater here.
S: What time is the movie?
A: It begins at 2:30.
S: Let's eat lunch first and then see the movie.
A: OK. I'm hungry. Let's go!

*A: Andy S: Subin

06 Which of the following cannot be answered from the dialog above? (3점)

① How long is the movie?
② What is the movie, *Life on the Moon*, about?
③ Where will Subin and Andy watch the movie?
④ Did Subin hear about the new movie, *Life on the Moon*?
⑤ What time does the movie, *Life on the Moon*, start?

07 Which of the following are Subin and Andy most likely to do right after the conversation? (3점)

① They will read some books about Mars in the library.
② They will go to another movie theater.
③ They will sell their movie tickets online.
④ They will cancel the movie tickets.
⑤ They will go to eat something.

08 다음 문장이 자연스러운 대화가 되도록 순서를 바르게 배열한 것은? (4점)

(A) Did you hear about the new book, *Living in a Foreign Country*?
(B) Great. I'm really curious about this book.
(C) Me, too.
(D) No, I didn't.
(E) Look. It's right here. It's about living in New York.

① (A) - (D) - (E) - (B) - (C)
② (A) - (D) - (E) - (C) - (B)
③ (A) - (C) - (E) - (B) - (D)
④ (A) - (B) - (D) - (E) - (C)
⑤ (A) - (B) - (C) - (D) - (E)

09 다음 주어진 대화의 내용과 관계가 <u>없는</u> 것은? (3점)

G: Did you hear about the new space food?
B: Yes, I did. It's a type of ice cream.
G: Yes, and here it is. It looks good.
B: I'm really curious about the taste.

① The boy knew about the new space food.
② The boy wants to know about the taste of space food.
③ Space food looks good.
④ The boy and the girl are talking about the space food.
⑤ The girl will buy some ice cream for the boy.

[10~11] 다음 대화를 읽고 물음에 답하시오.

B: Subin, did you hear about the new movie, *Life on the Moon*?

G: No, I didn't.

B: I heard it's really good.

G: (A)_____ What's it about?

B: It's about a man who is trying to live on the moon.

G: That sounds interesting.

B: Look. The movie is playing at the Space Theater here.

G: What time is the movie?

B: It begins at 2.

G: Let's eat lunch first and then see the movie.

B: OK. I'm hungry. Let's go!

*B: Andy G: Subin

10 위 대화의 흐름으로 보아 (A)에 가장 알맞은 말은? (3점)

① I like the movie, too.

② I wonder how he can survive there.

③ I'm really curious about the movie.

④ I have already known about the movie.

⑤ I really want to tell you about the movie.

11 위 대화의 내용과 일치하는 것은? (3점)

① Andy wants to meet Subin at 2.

② Subin has seen the movie before.

③ Andy didn't hear about the movie.

④ The man in the movie wants to live alone.

⑤ Andy and Subin are going to watch the movie after eating lunch.

12 다음 대화의 빈칸에 알맞은 것은? (2점)

A: Look at this. Did you hear about the new musical?

B: _____ I heard it has great songs.

A: Oh, I'm really curious about it.

① Yes, I did.　　② No, I didn't.

③ Yes, I have.　　④ No, I haven't.

⑤ No, I don't have to.

13 다음 중 어법상 올바른 것은? (3점)

① Have you ever were to Brazil?

② Did you ever met a movie star?

③ I have caught a big fish before.

④ James has broken his arm last night.

⑤ Joe and I has known each other for 13 years.

14 다음 우리말을 영작하시오. (5점)

> • 공부하는 것은 나에게 쉽다.
> = It's _____.

> **조건**
> • 의미상 주어를 사용할 것.
> • 주어진 단어를 제외하고 5 단어로 작성할 것.

It's _____.

15 주어진 제시어만을 모두 사용하여 문법과 의미에 맞게 배열하시오. (단어 형태 변형 불가) (5점)

> (1) 밤에 운전하는 것은 어렵다.
> • is / to / it / night / hard / at / drive
> (2) 네가 그 콘서트의 표를 구하는 것이 가능하니?
> • for / is / it / to get / tickets / for / the concert? / possible / you

→ (1) _____

　 (2) _____

[16~24] Read the following and answer the questions.

The Best New Thing

Rada lived on a little world, far out in space. She lived there with her father, mother, and brother Jonny. Rada's father and other people worked on spaceships. Only Rada and Jonny were children, and they were born in space.

One day, Dad told Rada and Jonny, "We're going back to Earth tomorrow."

Rada and Jonny looked at Dad in surprise and floated towards him. Rada asked Dad, "What's it like on Earth?"

"Everything is different there. For example, the sky is blue," answered Dad.

"I've never seen a blue sky," said Jonny.

"The sky is always black here," said Rada.

"You don't have to wear your big heavy space suits because there is air everywhere. It's also hard to jump there because Earth pulls you down," said Dad.

"What else?" asked Rada.

(A) "There are hills, and they are covered with soft green grass. You can roll down the hills," answered Mom.

"Dad, have you ever rolled down a hill?" asked Rada.

"Yes, ⓐit's really amazing!" answered Dad.

Jonny was thirsty, so he opened a milk container and shook ⓑit. The milk floated in the air and formed balls. Jonny swallowed the balls.

"Jonny, if you drink milk ㉠that way on Earth, you'll get wet," said Mom.

(B) Later that night, Rada and Jonny talked a long time about Earth. ⓒIt was exciting to think about all the new things they were going to see and do. There was one new thing Rada and Jonny really wanted to do. They thought about ⓓit all night and didn't tell Mom and Dad about it. ⓔIt was their secret.

(C) The next day, Rada's family got on a spaceship.

"It's going to be a long trip," said Mom.

"That's alright. I'm so excited!" said Rada.

(D) "Dad, it's difficult to walk on Earth," said Rada.

"I know. Earth is pulling you down," said Dad.

Rada and Jonny couldn't float anymore. That was the first new thing.

"What's that sound?" asked Rada.

"A bird is singing," said Mom.

"I've never heard a bird sing," said Rada.

"And ㉡저는 바람을 느껴 본 적이 전혀 없어요," said Jonny. These were all new things.

(E) Rada and Jonny ran up the nearest hill. At the top, they looked at each other and laughed. Then they lay down on the soft green grass and rolled down the hill. That was their secret!

"This is the best new thing of all!" shouted Rada and Jonny.

And they ran up to the top of the hill again.

16 What is the best place to put the given sentence below? (3점)

> The spaceship finally landed.

① (A) ② (B) ③ (C) ④ (D) ⑤ (E)

17 According to the passage, why don't Rada and Jonny have to wear space suits on Earth? (3점)

① Because the sky is always blue on Earth.

② Because there is air everywhere on Earth.

③ Because they lost their space suits on Earth.

④ Because space suits are too big and heavy.

⑤ Because they can jump easily on Earth without space suits.

18 Match the given definition with the correct word. (3점)

to move slowly through the air

① float　　　② shake　　　③ pull down
④ form　　　⑤ swallow

19 위 글에서 아래 밑줄 친 it과 문법적인 쓰임이 같은 것은? (3점)

· It's good to eat a lot of vegetables.

① ⓐ　　② ⓑ　　③ ⓒ　　④ ⓓ　　⑤ ⓔ

20 According to the passage, the best new thing for Rada and Jonny on Earth was ... (3점)

① to walk on Earth
② to hear a bird sing
③ to see the blue sky
④ to swallow the milk balls in the air
⑤ to lie down on the soft green grass and roll down the hill

21 위 글의 밑줄 친 ㉠that way가 의미하는 것이 무엇인지 본문에서 찾아 우리말로 쓰시오. (4점)

→ _____

22 Unscramble the given words matching with the translation, ㉡. ※Change the form of the given words if necessary. (5점)

· ㉡저는 바람을 느껴 본 적이 전혀 없어요.
(the wind / I / feel / never)

→ _____

23 This is the conversation between Rada and Jonny one day after they arrived on Earth. Which of the following is grammatically incorrect? (4점)

Rada: ⓐTo walk on Earth is very hard because Earth is pulling me down.
Jonny: But ⓑit is fun to live here, isn't it?
Rada: Yes, it is. Also, ⓒit is nice to live with no space suits.
Jonny: ⓓI'm difficult to believe we are on Earth now. Do you miss our life in space?
Rada: A little bit. ⓔTo see many beautiful stars in space was really good.

① ⓐ　　② ⓑ　　③ ⓒ　　④ ⓓ　　⑤ ⓔ

24 Read the summary and fill in the blanks with the words from the passage above. (5점)

Rada's family lived in space. One day, they decided to go back to (A)_____. Rada's family talked about life on Earth. They talked about the blue (B)_____ and hills which are covered with green (C)_____. The next day, Rada's family got on a (D)_____. It was a long trip to Earth. When they arrived on Earth, Rada and Jonny ran up the nearest (E)_____ and rolled down it.

(A) _____, (B) _____, (C) _____,
(D) _____, (E) _____

[대구 ○○중]

25 다음 글에서 전체 흐름과 관계없는 문장은? (4점)

ⓐLater that night, Rada and Jonny talked a long time about Earth. ⓑIt was exciting to think about all the new things they were going to see and do. ⓒThere was one new thing Rada and Jonny really wanted to do. ⓓThey thought about it all night and didn't tell Mom and Dad about it. ⓔThe pilot wanted to answer in the same way as others.

① ⓐ　　② ⓑ　　③ ⓒ　　④ ⓓ　　⑤ ⓔ

[26~29] 다음 글을 읽고 물음에 답하시오.

Rada lived on a little world, far out in space. She lived there with her father, mother, and brother Jonny. Rada's father and other people worked on spaceships. Only Rada and Jonny were children, and ⓐthey were born in space. (A)
One day, Dad told Rada and Jonny, "We're going back to Earth tomorrow."
ⓑRada and Jonny looked at Dad in surprise and floated towards him. (B)
"Everything is different there. For example, the sky is blue," answered Dad.
"I've never seen a blue sky," said Jonny. (C)
"The sky is always black here," said Rada.
ⓒ"You don't have to wear your big heavy space suits because there is air everywhere. ㉠It's also hard to jump there because Earth pulls you down," said Dad.
"What else?" asked Rada.
ⓓ"There are hills, and they are covered by soft green grass. You can roll down the hills," answered Mom.
"Dad, have you ever rolled down a hill?" asked Rada.
"Yes, it's really amazing!" answered Dad. (D)
Jonny was thirsty, so he opened a milk container and shook it. The milk floated in the air and formed balls. Jonny swallowed the balls. (E)
"Jonny, ⓔif you drink milk that way on Earth, you'll get wet," said Mom.

26 위 글의 (A)~(E) 중 다음 문장이 들어가기에 가장 적절한 곳은? (3점)

> Rada asked Dad, "What's it like on Earth?"

① (A) ② (B) ③ (C) ④ (D) ⑤ (E)

27 위 글에서 ㉠의 It과 쓰임이 같은 것을 고르면? (3점)

① It is hard to fix a bike.
② It is so cold outside.
③ It is so good for you.
④ It is about a man who is trying to live on the moon.
⑤ It weighs 20kg.

28 위 글의 밑줄 친 ⓐ~ⓔ 중 어법상 쓰임이 어색한 것은? (3점)

① ⓐ   ② ⓑ   ③ ⓒ   ④ ⓓ   ⑤ ⓔ

29 위 글의 내용과 일치하는 것은? (3점)

① Rada has seen a blue sky before.
② The sky is sometimes blue in space.
③ Rada and Jonny should wear space suits on Earth.
④ Rada's father has rolled down a hill before.
⑤ Jonny got wet when he opened a milk container and shook it in space.

30 다음 주어진 문장이 들어가기에 가장 적절한 곳은? (4점)

> It was exciting to think about all the new things they were going to see and do.

Later that night, Rada and Jonny talked a long time about Earth. (A) There was one new thing Rada and Jonny really wanted to do. (B) They thought about it all night and didn't tell Mom and Dad about it. (C) It was their secret. (D)
The next day, Rada's family got on a spaceship. (E)
"It's going to be a long trip," said Mom.
"That's alright. I'm so excited!" said Rada.

① (A) ② (B) ③ (C) ④ (D) ⑤ (E)

◎ 선택형 문항의 답안은 컴퓨터용 수정 싸인펜을 사용하여 OMR 답안지에 바르게 표기하시오.
◎ 서술형 문제는 답을 답안지에 반드시 검정 볼펜으로 쓰시오.
◎ 총 31문항 100점 만점입니다. 문항별 배점은 각 문항에 표시되어 있습니다.

[인천 ○○중]

01 다음 영영풀이가 올바른 것은? (3점)

① pride: to show that something is true
② result: something that happens because of something else
③ publish: to do something that you tried or aimed to do
④ continue: the amount of money that something is worth
⑤ prove: a feeling of satisfaction and pleasure in what you have done

[대전 ○○중]

02 다음 중 단어의 뜻이 올바른 것은? (2점)

① publish - 출판하다　② search - 연구하다
③ proud - 자부심　　④ succeed - 성공
⑤ prove - 증거

[전북 ○○중]

03 다음 빈칸에 들어갈 표현으로 알맞은 것은? (3점)

A: What's this? I've never seen any food like this.
B: Oh, it's Tteok, a Korean dessert.
A: _____
B: Sure. Go ahead. It's really delicious.

① Can you try it on?
② Is it OK to try some?
③ It doesn't look delicious.
④ Can you tell me what it is?
⑤ Why don't you take some?

[부산 ○○중]

[4~6] 다음 대화를 읽고 물음에 답하시오.

A: Excuse me, but _____ on this hanbok?
B: Sure. The fitting room is over there. (A)
A: Thanks. Wait a minute. That's also very pretty. (B)
B: Oh, the little hat over there? (C)
A: Yes. What is it?
B: It's a jokduri, a traditional Korean hat for women. It's usually worn on a wedding day. (D)
A: Really? _____ it on, too?
B: I'm sorry, but it's only for display. (E)
A: Oh. Then, I'll just try on this hanbok.

04 위 대화의 빈칸에 공통으로 들어갈 말로 가장 적절한 것은? (2점)

① is[Is] it OK to try
② are[Are] you going to try
③ are[Are] you good at trying
④ are[Are] you interested in trying
⑤ what[What] are you going to try

05 위 대화의 (A)~(E) 중 흐름상 다음 문장이 들어갈 곳으로 가장 알맞은 것은? (3점)

Trying it on is not allowed.

① (A)　② (B)　③ (C)　④ (D)　⑤ (E)

06 위 대화의 내용과 일치하는 것은? (3점)

① A는 clerk이다.
② B는 customer이다.
③ 족두리는 오직 전시만을 위한 것이다.
④ A는 한복과 족두리를 같이 입어볼 것이다.
⑤ 이곳은 전통 의상 전시실로 탈의실은 따로 없다.

[7~8] 다음 대화를 읽고 물음에 답하시오.

W: Excuse me, but is it OK to try on this hanbok?
M: Sure. The fitting room is over there.
W: Thanks. Wait a minute. That's also very pretty.
M: Oh, the little hat over there?
W: Yes. What is it?
M: It's a jokduri, a traditional Korean hat for women. It's usually worn on a wedding day.
W: Really? Is it OK to try it on, too?
M: I'm sorry, but it's only for display. (A)Trying it on is not allowed.
W: Oh. Then, I'll just try on this hanbok.

W: Woman, M: Man

07 위 대화의 밑줄 친 (A)의 의도로 알맞은 것은? (3점)

① 사과하기 ② 금지하기
③ 부탁하기 ④ 동의하기
⑤ 위로하기

08 위 대화의 내용과 일치하는 것은? (3점)

① A jokduri is a traditional Korean dessert.
② The woman can try on hanbok in the fitting room.
③ The woman will try on both hanbok and the jokduri.
④ The man allowed the woman to wear the jokduri.
⑤ The woman wants to wear the jokduri on her wedding day.

09 다음 표지판과 그 의미가 바르게 연결되지 <u>않은</u> 것은? (4점)

① No swimming here.

② Keep on the grass.

③ Don't ride a bike here.

④ No mobile phones.

⑤ No dogs allowed.

10 다음 중 자연스럽지 않은 대화는? (3점)

① A: Excuse me. Is it OK to sit over there?
   B: I'm sorry, but sitting on the grass is not allowed.
② A: Excuse me. Is it OK to take pictures here?
   B: Yes, it's all right.
③ A: How about using a flash? Can I use it, too?
   B: I'm afraid not. You are welcome to use a flash here.
④ A: Excuse me. What's this? It looks interesting.
   B: Oh, that's a haegeum, a traditional Korean musical instrument.
⑤ A: Is it OK to play it?
   B: I'm sorry, but it's only for display. Playing it is not allowed.

A: Excuse me, but is it OK to try on this hanbok?
B: No problem. The (A)_____ is over there.
A: Thanks. ⓐWait a minute. That's also very pretty.
B: Oh, the little hat over there?
A: Yes. ⓑWhere is it?
B: It's a jokduri, ⓒa traditional Korean hat for women. It's usually worn on a wedding day.
A: Really? ⓓCan I try it on, too?
B: I'm sorry, but it's only for display.
A: Oh. Then, ⓔI'll just try on this hanbok.

11 From the underlined part ⓐ~ⓔ, choose the answer that is unnatural. (3점)

① ⓐ ② ⓑ ③ ⓒ ④ ⓓ ⑤ ⓔ

12 Please choose the best answer for (A). (3점)

① hat shop
② dress shop
③ fitting room
④ display room
⑤ wedding shop

13 Which sentence is incorrect? (2점)

① Don't sit here.
② No sitting here.
③ You cannot sit here.
④ You shouldn't sit here.
⑤ You don't want to sit here.

14 다음 중 어법상 어색한 문장은? (3점)

① I'm not sure if she likes it.
② He asked me if I had any money.
③ Do you know who stole the wallet?
④ Can you tell me where is the bathroom?
⑤ I want to know how you spent your vacation.

15 다음 중 어법상 어색한 것을 모두 고른 것은? (3점)

(A) I've known him since I was a child.
(B) I've been to Jeju-do last year.
(C) I asked him who the girl was.
(D) I don't know what did he buy in the store.

① (A), (B) ② (B), (C) ③ (A), (C)
④ (B), (D) ⑤ (A), (D)

16 다음 Tom이 파티에 가지 못한 이유를 어법에 맞게 쓴 것은? (4점)

보기
• a bad cold
• the heavy traffic
• It snowed a lot.
• He had to study for the exam.
• He hurt his knee.

① Tom couldn't go because a bad cold.
② Tom couldn't go because the heavy traffic.
③ Tom couldn't go because of it snowed a lot.
④ Tom couldn't go because he hurt his knee.
⑤ Tom couldn't go because of he had to study for the exam.

[17~25] 다음 글을 읽고 물음에 답하시오.

Q1> *Can you tell me how you became interested in Uigwe*?

Dr. Park: I studied history in college. I went to France to continue my studies in 1955. As you know, the French army took many of our national treasures in 1866. I wanted to find them while I was studying there. Uigwe was one of ㉠them.

You found 297 books of Uigwe in the National Library of France, in Paris.

Q2> *Please tell me how you found them.*

Dr. Park: As soon as I became a researcher at the National Library in 1967, I began to look for *Uigwe*. After 10 years, in 1977, I finally found the books. I think I looked at more than 30 million books.

I'm sure you were very (A)_____ when you found the books.

Dr. Park: Yes, I was, but ㉡more difficulties ⓐwere waiting for me. I thought that the books ⓑshould be returned to Korea, but my bosses at the library didn't like that idea. They even thought that I was a Korean spy and fired me. After that, I ⓒhad to go to the library as a visitor, so it was not easy to do research on *Uigwe*. However, I didn't give up. For more than ten years, I went to the library every day to finish my research. I wanted to show people the value of *Uigwe*.

The results of your research ⓓpublished as a book in Korea in 1990. Many Koreans became interested in Uigwe because of (B)_____.

Dr. Park: Yes. In 1992, the Korean government asked the French government for its return and, finally, the 297 books ⓔare here now.

17 위 글의 제목으로 가장 적절한 것은?   (3점)

① Tragic History of Korea
② A Book Review about Uigwe
③ An Interview with Dr. Park Byeong-seon
④ An Interview with the French Government
⑤ History of Battles between Korea and France

18 위 글을 읽고 답할 수 <u>없는</u> 질문은?   (4점)

① What did Dr. Park study in college?
② Where did Dr. Park find *Uigwe*?
③ Who told Dr. Park about *Uigwe*?
④ When did Dr. Park find *Uigwe*?
⑤ When did the Korean government ask the French government for the return of *Uigwe*?

19 위 글의 ㉠이 가리키는 말로 가장 적절한 것은?   (3점)

① 297 books
② my studies
③ more difficulties
④ Korean national treasures
⑤ more than 30 million books

20 위 글의 ㉡에 해당하지 <u>않는</u> 내용은?   (4점)

① Dr. Park was fired from the library.
② Dr. Park's bosses didn't like her idea.
③ Dr. Park had to do research on *Uigwe* as a visitor.
④ It took 10 years for Dr. park to know the value of *Uigwe*.
⑤ Dr. Park's bosses thought that she was a Korean spy.

21 위 글의 문맥상 빈칸 (A)에 들어갈 단어로 가장 적절한 것은?

(3점)

① relaxed   ② excited   ③ sad

④ confused   ⑤ disappointed

22 위 글의 빈칸 (B)에 들어갈 말로 가장 적절한 것은? (3점)

① its return

② your book

③ the French government

④ the Korean government

⑤ the National Library of France

23 위 글의 ⓐ~ⓔ 중 어법상 <u>어색한</u> 것은? (3점)

① ⓐ   ② ⓑ   ③ ⓒ   ④ ⓓ   ⑤ ⓔ

24 위 글의 내용과 일치하도록 다음 의궤의 반환 과정에 대해 연도별로 정리한 표의 빈칸을 우리말로 적절히 채우시오. (5점)

1866년	프랑스 군대가 의궤를 가지고 감
1967년	(1)
1977년	Dr. Park이 의궤를 찾음
1990년	Dr. Park이 자신의 연구 결과를 책으로 출간함
1992년	(2)

→ (1) _____

(2) _____

25 위 글을 읽고 interviewer가 되어 Dr. Park에게 다음의 〈조건〉에 맞는 질문 2 가지를 쓰시오. (6점)

조건
• 글의 맥락에 맞는 질문을 할 것.
• 위 글의 Q1> 혹은 Q2>와 같은 간접의문문 형태로 쓸 것.
• 주어, 동사가 있는 완전한 문장으로 쓸 것.

→ (1) _____

(2) _____

[전북 ○○중]

[26~27] 다음 글을 읽고 물음에 답하시오.

Q: Before I finish this interview, I'd like to ask you about *Jikji*, a book that changed the history of (A)_____.

Dr. Park: I found it in my first year at the library, I knew right away that it was very special. I worked hard to prove its value and finally succeeded. At a book exhibition in Paris in 1972, *Jikji* was displayed as the oldest book in the world that was printed with movable metal type.

26 위 글의 빈칸 (A)에 들어갈 단어로 가장 알맞은 것은? (3점)

① world   ② library   ③ book

④ printing   ⑤ exhibition

27 위 글의 밑줄 친 *Jikji*에 대한 설명으로 알맞지 <u>않은</u> 것은? (3점)

① Dr. Park found it in her first year at the library.

② Dr. Park didn't think it was special at first.

③ Dr. Park succeeded in proving its value.

④ It was displayed at a book exhibition in Paris in 1972.

⑤ It was the oldest book printed with movable metal type.

[28~29] 다음 글을 읽고 물음에 답하시오.

> Reporter: The results of your research were published as a book in Korea in 1990. Many Koreans became interested in *Uigwe* ⓐ_____ your book.
>
> Dr. Park: Yes. In 1992, the Korean government asked the French government for its return and, finally, the 297 books are here now.
>
> Reporter: ⓑ_____ I finish this interview, I'd like to ask you about *Jikji*, a book that changed the history of printing.
>
> Dr. Park: I found it in my first year at the library. I knew right away that it was very special. I worked hard to prove its value and finally succeeded. At a book exhibition in Paris in 1972, *Jikji* was displayed as the oldest book in the world that was printed with movable metal type.

28 위 글의 빈칸 ⓐ, ⓑ에 들어갈 말로 가장 적절한 것은? (3점)

	ⓐ	ⓑ
①	because of	Before
②	instead of	In fact
③	because	After
④	instead of	Before
⑤	thanks to	In contrast

29 위 글을 통해 답을 알 수 <u>없는</u> 질문은? (3점)

① Where is *Uigwe* now?

② Why did Dr. Park work hard for *Jikji*?

③ Which book changed the history of printing?

④ How long was *Jikji* displayed at a book exhibition in Paris in 1972?

⑤ Did Dr. Park find *Jikji* in her first year at the library?

[30~31] Read the following and answer the questions.

> On May 27, 2011, 297 books of *Uigwe*, ⓐ<u>a collection of royal books the French army took in 1866, came back to Korea</u>. The person behind this return is Dr. Park Byeong-seon, ⓑ<u>a historian who spent her whole life to search for Korean national treasures abroad</u>.
>
> Q: Can you tell me how you became interested in *Uigwe*?
>
> Dr. Park: I studied history in college. ⓒ<u>I went to France to continuing my studies in 1955.</u> ⓓ<u>As you know, the French army took many of our national treasures in 1866.</u> ⓔ<u>I wanted to find them while I was studied there.</u> *Uigwe* was one of them.

30 위 글의 내용과 일치하는 것은? (3점)

① Dr. Park studied French in college.

② 297 pages of *Uigwe* came back to Korea on May 27, 2011.

③ *Uigwe* was one of the national treasures that the German army took.

④ Dr. Park is the person who tried to find our national treasures abroad.

⑤ Dr. Park went to France to look for some Korean national treasures in 1955.

31 위 글의 밑줄 친 ⓐ~ⓔ 중 어법상 옳은 문장을 <u>모두</u> 고른 것은? (4점)

① ⓐ, ⓑ   ② ⓓ, ⓔ   ③ ⓐ, ⓓ

④ ⓑ, ⓔ   ⑤ ⓐ, ⓒ

◎ 선택형 문항의 답안은 컴퓨터용 수정 싸인펜을 사용하여 OMR 답안지에 바르게 표기하시오.

◎ 서술형 문제는 답을 답안지에 반드시 검정 볼펜으로 쓰시오.

◎ 총 27문항 100점 만점입니다. 문항별 배점은 각 문항에 표시되어 있습니다.

[경북 ㅇㅇ중]

01 다음 중 단어의 영영풀이가 바르지 <u>않은</u> 것은? (3점)

① value: the amount of money that something is worth

② research: the work of finding out facts about something

③ succeed: to do something that you tried or aimed to do

④ result: something that happens because of something else

⑤ publish: provided, especially by the government for the use of people in general

[부산 ㅇㅇ중]

02 다음 설명에 해당하는 단어로 알맞은 것은? (3점)

a feeling of satisfaction and pleasure in what you have done

① anger   ② pride   ③ nervous

④ sadness   ⑤ surprised

[전북 ㅇㅇ중]

03 다음 대화의 빈칸에 들어갈 말로 알맞은 것은? (3점)

A: _____

B: I'm afraid not. Swimming is not allowed here.

① Can you swim?

② Do you like swimming?

③ Is it OK to swim here?

④ Do you swim regularly?

⑤ What is your favorite sport?

[경남 ㅇㅇ중]

04 다음 짝지어진 대화 중 자연스럽지 못한 것은? (3점)

① G: Is it OK to take pictures here?

　M: Yes, it's all right.

② G: Is it OK to sit over there?

　M: You mean, on the grass?

③ G: Is it OK to try this Tteok?

　M: No. Go ahead.

④ G: Is it OK to use a flash?

　M: I'm afraid not. Using a flash is not allowed here.

⑤ G: Is it OK to eat food there?

　M: Yes. Eating food is allowed.

[경북 ㅇㅇ중]

05 다음 대화 내용과 일치하는 것은? (3점)

G: Excuse me, but is it OK to try on this hanbok?

M: Sure. The fitting room is over there.

G: Thanks. Wait a minute. That's also very pretty.

M: Oh, the little hat over there?

G: Yes. What is it?

M: It's a jokduri, a traditional Korean hat for women. It's usually worn on a wedding day.

G: Really? Is it OK to try it on, too?

M: I'm sorry, but it's only for display. Trying it on is not allowed.

G: Oh. Then, I'll just try on this hanbok.

　　　　　　　　　　　G: Girl, M: Man

① 한복은 착용이 불가하다.

② 족두리는 졸업식에 착용한다.

③ 가게에 옷을 갈아입는 곳이 없다.

④ 족두리는 전시용이라 착용이 불가하다.

⑤ 족두리는 서양 정장과 어울리는 모자이다.

[6~7] 다음 대화를 읽고 물음에 답하시오.

G: Excuse me, but (A)_____ this hanbok?

M: You can try it on. The fitting room is over there.

G: Thanks. Wait a minute. That's also very pretty.

M: Oh, the little fiat over there?

G: Yes. What is it?

M: It's a jokduri, a traditional Korean hat for women. It's usually worn on a wedding day.

G: Really? (B)_____ this jokduri, too?

M: I'm sorry, but it's only for display. Trying it on is not allowed.

G: Oh. Then, I'll just try on this hanbok.

06 위 대화의 빈칸 (A), (B)에 공통으로 들어갈 말로 적절하지 않은 것은? (4점)

① can[Can] you try on

② is[Is] it OK to try on

③ do[Do] you mind if I try on

④ may[May] I try on

⑤ is[Is] it OK if I try on

07 위 대화의 내용과 일치하지 않는 것은? (3점)

① 한국의 전통 의상을 볼 수 있는 곳이다.

② 탈의실에서 한복을 입어 볼 수 있다.

③ 족두리는 결혼식 전에 쓰던 모자이다.

④ 족두리는 이곳에서 착용해 볼 수 없다.

⑤ 여자는 한복을 입어 볼 것이다.

08 다음 대화를 순서에 맞게 배열할 때 4번째에 해당하는 문장은? (3점)

A: You mean, on the grass?

B: I see.

C: Yes. Is it all right?

D: I'm sorry, but sitting on the grass is not allowed.

E: Excuse me. Is it OK to sit over there?

① A ② B ③ C ④ D ⑤ E

09 자연스러운 대화가 되도록 ⓐ~ⓔ를 순서대로 배열한 것은? (4점)

ⓐ I see.

ⓑ Is it OK to play it?

ⓒ Excuse me. What's this? It looks interesting.

ⓓ I'm sorry, but it's only for display. Playing it is not allowed.

ⓔ Oh, that's a haegeum, a traditional Korean musical instrument.

① ⓑ-ⓒ-ⓓ-ⓔ-ⓐ ② ⓑ-ⓔ-ⓒ-ⓐ-ⓓ

③ ⓒ-ⓔ-ⓑ-ⓓ-ⓐ ④ ⓒ-ⓓ-ⓐ-ⓑ-ⓔ

⑤ ⓓ-ⓐ-ⓑ-ⓒ-ⓔ

10 다음 대화의 빈칸에 알맞지 않은 것은? (3점)

A: I want to ask permission if I can ride a bike at the zoo. What should I say?

B: You can say like this "_____"

① Can I ride a bike at the zoo?

② May I ride a bike at the zoo?

③ Is it okay to ride a bike at the zoo?

④ Why don't we ride a bike at the zoo?

⑤ Do you mind if I ride a bike at the zoo?

11 다음 중 어법상 옳은 문장은? (3점)

① I was late because the traffic.

② We ran away because we were afraid.

③ They stopped playing soccer because the rain.

④ She's studying because of she has a test tomorrow.

⑤ I want to go to Hawaii because of it's warm and beautiful.

12 다음 빈칸에 ⓐ나 ⓑ를 넣어 문장을 완성하시오. (4점)

ⓐ because of	ⓑ because

(1) The game was cancelled _____ the storm.

(2) He was late _____ it rained a lot.

13 다음 글의 괄호 (A), (B), (C) 안에서 알맞은 것은? (3점)

The results of her research (A)[was / were] published as a book in Korea in 1990. Many Koreans became interested in *Uigwe* (B)[because / because of] the book that she wrote.

In 1992, the Korean government asked the French government for (C)[its / it's] return and, finally, the 297 books are here now.

	(A)	(B)	(C)
①	were	because of	its
②	was	because of	its
③	was	because	it's
④	were	because	its
⑤	were	because of	it's

14 다음은 한 유명 영화감독의 인터뷰이다. 기자들이 공손하게 〈보기〉의 질문들을 할 수 있도록 괄호 안의 표현을 사용하여 완전한 문장으로 바꾸시오. (문장 부호에 유의할 것.) (6점)

보기

<Interview of the Director>

Q1: Why did you become a director?

Q2: How many movies have you made so far?

Q3: Do you have your favorite actor?

Q1. 바꾼 문장 → _____
(I'd like to know)

Q2. 바꾼 문장 → _____
(Can you tell me)

Q3. 바꾼 문장 → _____
(I wonder)

15 다음 친구에게 알고 싶은 점을 묻는 문장을 〈조건〉에 맞게 완성하시오. (3점)

조건

• who, when, where, what, how, why 중 한 단어로 시작할 것.

• you 또는 your라는 단어를 최소 한 번 쓸 것.

Can you tell me _____?

[16~19] 다음 글을 읽고, 물음에 답하시오.

On May 27, 2011, 297 books of *Uigwe*, a collection of royal books the French army took in 1866, came back to Korea. The person (A)_____ this return is Dr. Park Byeong-seon, a historian who spent her whole life searching for Korean national treasures abroad.

Q: Can you tell me how you became interested in *Uigwe*?

Dr. Park: I studied history in college. I went to France to continue my studies in 1955. As you know, the French army took many of our national treasures in 1866. I wanted to find them while I was studying there. *Uigwe* was one of them.

Q: You found 297 books of *Uigwe* in the National Library of France, in Paris. (B)어떻게 그것들을 찾았는지 알고 싶네요.

Dr. Park: (C)_____ I became a researcher at the National Library in 1967, I began to look for *Uigwe*. After 10 years, in 1977, I finally found the books. I think I looked at more than 30 million books.

Q: I'm sure you were very excited when you found the books.

Dr. Park: Yes. I was, but more difficulties were waiting for me. I thought that the books should be returned to Korea, but my bosses at the library didn't like that idea. They even thought that I was a Korean spy and fired me. After that, I had to go to the library as a visitor, so it was not easy to do research on Uigwe. However, I didn't give up. For more than ten years, I went to the library every day to finish my research. I wanted to show people the value of Uigwe.

Q: The results of your research were published as a book in Korea in 1990. Many Koreans became interested in *Uigwe* (D)_____ your book.

Dr. Park: Yes. In 1992, the Korean government asked the French government for its return and, finally, the 297 books are here now.

16 위 글의 흐름상 (A), (C), (D)에 들어갈 적절한 표현은? (4점)

	(A)	(C)	(D)
①	behind	As soon as	because
②	behind	As soon as	because of
③	behind	As long as	with
④	thanks to	As long as	because
⑤	thanks to	As long as	because of

17 위 글 (B)의 우리말을 영어로 가장 올바르게 옮긴 것은? (3점)

① Please tell me how you find them.
② I want to know how you found them.
③ You can tell me the way to find them.
④ Do you have any idea of finding them?
⑤ Please tell me if you found them in the way.

18 위 글의 각 연도에 일어난 일을 올바르게 나타낸 것은? (3점)

① 1866년: *Uigwe* was in the National Library of France, in Paris.
② 1955년: Dr. Park went to Paris to find Korean national treasures.
③ 1967년: Dr. Park began to look for *Uigwe* at the National Library of France.
④ 1977년: Dr. Park began to look at more than 30 million books.
⑤ 1992년: Dr. Park started her research on *Uigwe*.

19 위 글에서 다음 (1)~(5)의 각 어휘 풀이에 해당되는 단어를 찾아 쓰시오. (10점)

(1)_____ : to not stop

(2)_____ : the amount of money that something is worth

(3)_____ : something that happens because of something else

(4)_____ : a group of valuable things, especially gold, silver, or jewels

(5)_____ : to try to find someone or something by looking very carefully

(1)_____, (2)_____, (3)_____,

(4)_____, (5)_____

[인천 ○○중]

[20~23] 다음 글을 읽고 물음에 답하시오.

Interviewer: You found 297 books of *Uigwe* in the National Library of France, in Paris. Please tell me how you found them. (A)

Dr. Park: As soon as I became a researcher at the National Library in 1967, I began to look for *Uigwe*. After 10 years, in 1977, I finally found the books. I think ㉠that I looked at more than 30 million books. (B)

Interviewer: I'm sure ㉡that you were very excited when you found the books.

Dr. Park: Yes, I was, but more difficulties were waiting with me. I thought ㉢that the books should ⓐreturn to Korea, but my bosses at the library didn't like that idea. (C) They even thought ㉣that I was a Korean spy and ⓑwas fired me. After ㉤that, I had to go to the library

as a visitor, so it was not easy to do research on *Uigwe*. However, I didn't give up. (D) I wanted ©show people the value of *Uigwe*.

Interviewer: (E) The results of your research ⓓwas published as a book in Korea in 1990. Many Koreans became ⓔinterested in *Uigwe* because your book.

Dr. Park: Yes. In 1992, the Korean government asked the French government for its return and, finally, the 297 books are here now.

20 위 글의 밑줄 친 ⓐ~ⓔ 중 어법상 올바른 것은? (4점)

① ⓐ ② ⓑ ③ © ④ ⓓ ⑤ ⓔ

21 위 글의 ㉠~㉤ 중 쓰임이 다른 하나는? (3점)

① ㉠ ② ㉡ ③ ㉢ ④ ㉣ ⑤ ㉤

22 위 글을 바르게 이해한 학생은? (3점)

① CON: Dr. Park은 진짜 한국의 스파이였어.

② NEO: Dr. Park은 해고되자 연구를 포기했어.

③ TUBE: Dr. Park의 연구 결과가 책으로 출판됐어.

④ MUZI: Dr. Park의 상사들은 의궤 반환에 동의했어.

⑤ RYAN: 연구원이 된 해에 Dr. Park은 의궤를 발견했어.

23 위 글의 (A)~(E) 중 다음 주어진 문장이 들어갈 위치로 가장 적절한 곳은? (3점)

For more than ten years, I went to the library every day to finish my research.

① (A) ② (B) ③ (C) ④ (D) ⑤ (E)

[24~27] Read the following and answer the questions.

Q: You found 297 books of *Uigwe* in the National Library of France, in Paris. Please tell me (a)_____ you found them.

Dr. Park: As soon as I became a researcher at the National Library in 1967, I began (b)_____ *Uigwe*. After 10 years, in 1977, I finally found the books. I think I looked at more than 30 million books.

Q: I'm sure you were very (c)_____ when you found the books.

Dr. Park: ⓐYes, I was, but more difficulties were waiting with me. ⓑI thought that the books should be returned to Korea, but my bosses at the library didn't like that idea. They even thought that I was a Korean spy and fired me. After that, I had to go to the library as a visitor, so ⓒit were not easy to doing research on *Uigwe*. However, I didn't give up. For more than ten years, I went to the library every day to finish my research. I wanted to show people the value of Uigwe.

Q: ⓓThe results of your research were published as a book in Korea in 1990. ⓔMany Koreans became interested in Uigwe because your book.

Dr. Park: Yes. In 1992, the Korean government asked the French government for its return and, finally, the 297 books are here now.

24 위 글의 문맥상 빈칸 (a), (b), (c)에 들어갈 알맞은 말은? (4점)

	(a)	(b)	(c)
①	how	to look at	excited
②	what	looking for	excited
③	how	looking for	excited
④	what	to look at	exciting
⑤	how	to look at	exciting

25 위 글을 읽고 답할 수 없는 멤버의 말을 고르면? (3점)

① SUGA: I'm wondering if Dr. Park was a Korean spy.

② Jin: I wonder how many books Dr. Park looked at to find *Jikji*.

③ J-hope: Tell me what Dr. Park did at the National Library of France in 1967.

④ RM: I want to know how many books of *Uigwe* Dr. Park found in the National Library of France.

⑤ V: Can you tell me how many years Dr. Park went to the library as a visitor every day?

26 위 글의 ⓐ~ⓔ 중 어법상 틀린 세 개의 문장의 기호를 쓰고, 올바른 문장으로 고쳐 쓰시오. (6점)

(1) 기호 → _____

고친 문장 → _____.

(2) 기호 → _____

고친 문장 → _____.

(3) 기호 → _____

고친 문장 → _____.

27 위 글의 내용과 일치하는 것은? (3점)

① Dr. Park was fired because she was a Korean spy.

② Dr. Park published a book, the results of her research, in France in 1990.

③ Dr. Park became a researcher at the National Library in 1977.

④ Dr. Park found *Uigwe* at the National Library of France in 1967.

⑤ The Korean government asked the French government for the return of *Uigwe* in 1992.

정답 및 해설

Lesson 5 (중간)

01 (1) ⓑ (2) ⓕ (3) ⓐ (4) ⓔ　**02** ④　**03** ③　**04** ①　**05** ④
06 ①, ④, ⑤　**07** ③　**08** ①　**09** ①　**10** ②　**11** ②　**12** ④
13 ②　**14** ⑤
15 The soup which I had for lunch was too salty.
16 ①　**17** We call such people smombies.　**18** ③　**19** ②
20 (1) 모임이나 식사 중 휴대폰 꺼놓기
　　　(2) 문자 대신에 사람들과 대화하기
21 (A) nervous (B) sad (C) look at　**22** ①　**23** ②　**24** ④
25 ①　**26** We call such people smombies.　**27** ⑤　**28** ⑤
29 ③

01 (1) for protection: 보호하기 위해 (2) experiment: 실험 (3) creative: 창의적인 (4) cause: 원인, 이유

02 'Make sure ~'는 '~을 확실하게 하도록 해'의 의미로 상대방에게 어떤 일을 하도록 당부하는 표현이다. ④번은 '독감에 걸렸다'라는 말에 '친구들과 음식을 나눠 먹으라.'는 말로 어울리지 않는다.

03 뒤에서 'And make sure you don't text too much.'라고 한 것으로 보아 'texting thumb'을 줄이거나 낫게 할 수 있는 말이 적절하다.

04 'It's pain in your thumb. You can get it from texting too much.'라고 했다.

05 모두 무슨 문제인지를 묻는 질문인데 ④번은 '이 상황에서 무엇이 옳은지'를 묻고 있다.

06 'get it from'에서 'from'은 '원인·이유·동기'를 나타낸다.

07 'You can get it from texting too much.'라고 했다. index finger: 집게손가락(= forefinger)

08 '목이 아프고 콧물이 나온다'고 했으므로 '약을 먹어라'는 ①번이 적절하다.

09 '콧물이 나오고 열이 있다'고 하는데 '우산을 가져오는 게 어떠냐'고 당부하는 것은 어색하다.

10 People call the clock tower Big Ben. call A B: A를 B라고 부르다

11 (B) 다리에 문제가 있는지 묻자 (A) 넘어져서 다쳤다고 답하고 (E) 걸을 수 있는지 묻자 (D) 그렇다고 답하며 그런데 아프다고 하자 (C) 얼음을 좀 올려놓으라고 당부하는 순서이다.

12 Ms. Kim이 Andy에게 'I think you have texting thumb.'이라고 했다.

13 (A) 맞음 (B) 맞음
(C) talked → talked to 또는 talked with
(D) 맞음 (E) whom → who[that]
(F) will stay → stay (G) which → that

14 주격 관계대명사는 생략할 수 없다.

15 공통되는 'the soup'를 선행사로 하여 목적격 관계대명사 which나 that을 이용한다.

16 'If you are a smombie, you can have various safety problems.'라고 했다.

17 call A B: A를 B라고 부르다

18 'Another problem'을 선행사로 하고 which나 that을 이용하여 'you can have'가 선행사를 수식하도록 쓴다.

19 '스마트폰이 다양한 건강상의 문제를 일으킬 수 있다.'는 내용의 글에서 ⓑ의 '스마트폰 없이 사는 것은 요즘 많은 사람들에게 어렵다.'라는 말은 어색하다.

20 'turn off your smartphone during meals or meetings. You can talk to people instead of texting them.'이라고 했다.

21 (A) 'Do you feel nervous when your smartphone is not around?'라고 했다.
(B) 'Do you feel sad when you check your smartphone and there is no text message?'라고 했다.
(C) 'turn off your smartphone during meals or meetings'라고 했으므로 'look at'이나 'turn on'이 적절하다.

22 ⓐ 상반되는 내용이 이어지므로 However, ⓑ 앞의 내용에 대한 결과가 이어지므로 so가 적절하다.

23 (A) Living이 주어이므로 is (B) 긍정의 조건문이 나와야 하므로 If. unless = if not (C) 'may fall'에 병렬로 연결되는 '(may) get'이 적절하다.

24 (D) 다음 문장의 'too'로 보아 주어진 문장은 (D)에 들어가야 한다.

25 동명사 Living이 주어이므로 is가 적절하다.

26 call A B: A를 B라고 부르다

27 '스몸비라면, 거리에 있는 구덩이를 보지 못할 수도 있고, 그래서 넘어져서 다칠지도 모른다.'라고 했다.

28 'texting thumb'을 막는 방법을 기술하고 있다.

29 (A) 문맥상 useful이 적절하다. (B) 엄지 '대신에' 다른 손가락을 쓰라는 것이 자연스럽다. (C) 다른 손가락을 쓰면 엄지에 대한 압력은 줄어들 것이다.

Lesson 5 (중간)

2회

01 ②	**02** ③	**03** ⑤	**04** ⑤	**05** ③	**06** ⑤

07 What happened?　**08** sure you drink much water

09 ⑤　**10** ③　**11** ②　**12** ①　**13** ②　**14** ①　**15** ①　**16** ③

17 ④, ⑤　**18** ①　**19** ③　**20** ③　**21** ①　**22** ③

23 We call such people smombies, smartphone zombies.

24 ③　**25** ①　**26** ③　**27** ②　**28** ③, ④　　　**29** ⑤

30 ①, ⑤　　　**31** ①

01 순서대로 ⓐ anything ⓑ dry ⓒ stress ⓓ increase가 들어간다.

02 '걱정스러워 보인다'라는 말에 '1등상을 탔다'고 답하는 것은 어색하다.

03 'Make sure ~'는 상대방에게 어떤 일을 하도록 당부하는 표현으로 '충고'할 때 쓸 수도 있다.

04 (A) "What's wrong?"은 '무엇이 문제니?'라는 의미로 문제점이나 증상을 물을 때 쓸 수 있는 표현이다.

(B) 'be going to'나 'be planning to'는 계획을 말할 때 쓸 수 있는 표현이다.

05 주어진 문장의 'It'이 (C) 앞의 'texting thumb'을 가리키므로 (C)가 적절하다.

06 'Why don't you do some finger stretching exercises?'라고 한 것으로 보아 손가락 스트레칭 운동은 엄지손가락 증후군에 도움이 된다.

07 What's wrong? = What happened? = What's the matter? = Is anything wrong? = What's the problem?

08 'Make sure ~'는 '~을 확실하게 하도록 해'의 의미로 상대방에게 어떤 일을 하도록 당부하는 표현이다.

09 약을 먹으라고 주는데 '너무 안됐다며 물을 많이 먹으라'는 말은 어색하다.

10 'the girl'을 선행사로 하고 'rescued'의 주어가 되어야 하므로 who가 적절하다.

11 'texting thumb'인 것 같다는 말에 이어 (B) 그게 무엇인지 묻고 (D) 엄지손가락에 통증이 있는 거라고 답하자 (A) 몰랐다고 반응하고 (C) 손가락 스트레칭 운동을 좀 하라는 조언으로 이어진다.

12 What's wrong (with you)? = What happened? = What's the matter? = Is anything wrong? = What's the problem?

13 'Make sure ~.', 'Why don't you ~?'를 사용하여 충고의 말을 할 수 있다.

14 ② who → which[that]

③ her → 삭제

④ it → 삭제

⑤ whom → which[that]

15 call A B: A를 B라고 부르다

16 스마트폰 대신 무엇을 쓸 수 있는지는 알 수 없다.

17 ⓐ are → is

ⓑ to → too

ⓒ alike zombies → like zombies

18 각각 ㉠ If ㉡ into ㉢ So ㉣ while이 들어간다.

19 조동사 may가 있으므로 동사원형 have가 되어야 한다.

20 ⓒ의 'various things'는 다음에 나오는 'turn off your smartphone during meals or meetings. You can talk to people instead of texting them.'을 가리킨다.

21 스마트폰 중독을 예방하도록 노력해야 한다는 내용이다. 빈칸에는 중독(addiction)이며 ①번의 풀이가 적절하다.

22 Living과 ③은 '동명사'이고 나머지는 모두 현재분사이다.

23 'call A B: A를 B라고 부르다'를 이용하고 'smombies'와 'smartphone zombies'를 동격을 나타내는 콤마(,)로 연결한다.

24 스마트폰을 보려고 머리를 아래로 향하므로 'down'이 적절하다.

25 'You may not see a hole in the street, so you may fall and get hurt.'라고 했다.

26 스마트폰 중독을 예방하기 위해 할 수 있는 일에 대해 언급하고 있으므로 ③번이 적절하다.

27 스마트폰으로 인한 건강 문제, 특히 'dry eyes'와 'text neck'에 대해 조언하는 내용의 글이다.

28 'move your smartphone up to your eye level. You can also do some neck stretching exercises.'라고 했다.

29 'Too much use of your smartphone, for example, too much texting, can cause neck pain. We call this text neck.'이라고 했다.

30 'Another problem'을 선행사로 하고 관계대명사를 생략하여 'you can have'가 선행사를 수식하도록 쓴다. 'Another problem'이나 'Neck pain'을 주어로 할 수 있다.

31 어디가 아픈 것이 아니라 건강한 삶을 살겠다는 다짐이다.

Lesson 6 (중간)

1회

01 ①　**02** ①　**03** ④　**04** ②　**05** ③　**06** ④　**07** ②　**08** ⑤

09 ③　**10** ②　**11** ④　**12** ②

13 (1) I'm so tired that I will take a nap.

(2) I'm so full that I can't eat anymore.

14 ④　**15** ②　**16** ⑤　**17** ①　**18** ②　**19** ①　**20** ④　**21** ④

22 His songs were so sad that the gods all started to cry.

23 ⑤　**24** ①　**25** ④　**26** ①　**27** ⑤

01 myth: a story or group of stories that form part of the traditional knowledge of a society

02 • 이 도시에 살고 있는 사람들의 수가 증가했다.
• 당신의 비밀 번호 숫자를 입력하세요. celebrity: 유명 인사

03 뒤에서 그러고 싶다며 언제 만날지 묻고 있으므로 ④번이 적절하다.

04 뒤에서 매표소 앞에서 만나자 했으므로 ②번이 적절하다.

05 반 고흐 전시회에 가는 방법은 나와 있지 않다.

06 ① excuse: 핑계, 변명
② exercise: 연습, 훈련
③ excitement: 흥분
④ exhibition: 전시회
⑤ examination: 시험, 조사

07 S1과 S2는 전시회에 갈 약속을 정하고 있다.

08 5시에 만나자고 했는데 언제 만나야 하는지 묻는 것은 어색하다.

09 (B) 방과 후에 농구를 할 것이라며 함께하겠는지 묻고 (C) 미안하다며 도서관에 갈 계획이라고 하자 (D) 숙제가 많은지 묻고 (A) 자신의 동아리가 도서관에서 오늘 만난다고 하자 (E) 알겠다며 대화를 마무리 한다.

10 ① They made him the great king.
③ She let her brother carry the box.
④ He tried to make the child a soccer player.
⑤ Mom sometimes calls me by my brother's name.

11 'too+형용사/부사+to부정사'는 '너무 ~해서 …할 수 없다'라는 부정의 뜻으로 'so ~ that ... can't'와 바꿔 쓸 수 있다. 여기서 so 다음에 오는 말이 '원인'이고, that 다음에 오는 절이 그에 따른 '결과'를 나타낸다. '원인'에 해당하는 말을 because를 이용하여 절로 쓸 수도 있다.

12 ① He saw his brother wash[washing] the dishes.
③ The dog was small enough to go through the hole.
④ The book that I told about sold out in one day.
⑤ The coffee is too hot for her to drink.

13 (1) 'so+형용사/부사+that+주어+동사 …' 구문은 '매우 ~해서 (그 결과) …하다'라는 의미로 원인과 결과를 나타낸다.
(2) so ~ that ... can't는 '너무 ~해서 …할 수 없다'라는 부정의 뜻으로 'too+형용사/부사+to부정사'와 바꿔 쓸 수 있다.

14 Daedalus와 Icarus가 얼마나 오래 날았는지는 알 수 없다.

15 ⓐThey는 Henri Matisse와 Marc Chagall의 작품이다.
ⓓfly 대신에 flying을 쓸 수 있다.

16 같은 이야기를 주제로 다른 작품을 그렸다는 글이다.

17 (A) deal with: 다루다
(B) 지각동사의 목적보어로 flying
(C) 앞 문장과 대조의 관계이므로 In contrast가 적절하다.

18 주어진 문장의 Furthermore로 보아 앞 문장에 또 다른 정보를 덧붙여 제시하는 (B)가 적절하다.

19 사람들이 서로 다른 대답을 하는 것은 같은 것을 다른 방식들로 볼 수 있기 때문이다.

20 ⓑ 지하 세계에서 표면까지 얼마나 멀었는지는 알 수 없다.
ⓓ Orpheus가 어떻게 아내의 시체를 찾았는지는 알 수 없다.

21 ⓓ의 he는 Hades이지만 나머지는 모두 Orpheus이다.

22 'so+형용사/부사+that+주어+동사 …' 구문은 '매우 ~해서 (그 결과) …하다'라는 의미로 원인과 결과를 나타낸다.

23 ⓐ 같은 주제의 다른 그림들이라고 하는 것이 적절하다.
ⓑ Matisse와 Chagall이 그린 그림은 같은 그리스 신화에 관한 것이다.

24 ⓒ와 ①: 작품 ② 일 ③, ④, ⑤: 일하다

25 Icarus가 흥분을 느낀 것이므로 excited가 되어야 한다. 감정을 나타내는 동사의 경우 감정을 유발시키면 현재분사를 쓰고 감정을 느끼면 과거분사를 쓴다.

26 Daedalus가 밀랍이 녹았을 때 아들에게 무슨 말을 했는지는 알 수 없다.

27 'Icarus was so excited that he forgot his father's warning. He flew higher and higher, and the wax began to melt. "Oh, no! I'm falling," Icarus cried out. Icarus fell into the sea and died.'라고 했다.

Lesson 6 (중간) 2회

01 ②	**02** ③	**03** ①	**04** ③	**05** ⑤	**06** ①	**07** ⑤

08 I'm planning to go see the Lion King tomorrow.
09 What about 2? / Can you make it at 2? **10** ①
11 Emma was so bored that she started singing to herself.

12 ③	**13** ②	**14** ⑤	**15** ①, ④	**16** ③	**17** ①	**18** ②
19 ④	**20** so much that he wanted to keep				**21** ④	**22** ④
23 ⑤	**24** ①	**25** ④	**26** ④	**27** ③	**28** ①	**29** ②

01 'adventurous'는 형용사로 '모험심이 강한'이라는 뜻이다. 명사 'adventures'가 되어야 한다.

02 subject: 주제

03 안 좋아 보인다는 말에 '원기왕성'하다고 답하는 것은 어색하다.

04 함께 축구 경기 보러 가자는 말에 (B) 좋다며 언제 만날지 묻고 (C) 10시 반에 만나자는 말에 (A) 그때 보자는 응답이 적절하다.

05 그러고 싶다며 언제 만날지 묻는 것으로 보아 함께 가자고 제안하는 ⑤번이 적절하다.

06 Kate가 가장 좋아하는 화가에 대한 언급은 없다.

07 (A) 토요일에 만나기로 한 계획을 잊지 말라고 하는 것이 적절하다.

(B) can't wait to 동사 원형: 정말로 ~하고 싶다

08 'be planning to+동사원형'은 '~할 계획이다'라는 의미로 미래의 계획을 말할 때 쓴다.

09 'How about 2?' 대신에 'What about 2?', 'Can you make it at 2?', 'Let's meet at 2.' 등으로 쓸 수 있다.

10 Kate가 민호를 전시회에 초대했다.

11 'so+형용사/부사+that+주어+동사 …' 구문은 '매우 ~해서 (그 결과) …하다'라는 의미로 원인과 결과를 나타낸다.

12 지각동사의 목적어와 목적보어가 능동의 관계일 때 목적보어로는 동사 원형이나 현재분사가 나온다.

13 ⓐ read → reading
ⓒ surprise → surprising
ⓓ to smell → smell[smelling]
ⓔ smiled → smile[smiling]

14 (A) It rained so heavily that they had to cancel the game. (very → so)
(B) I was surprised to see him touching the snake. (he → him)

15 'too+형용사/부사+to부정사'는 '너무 ~해서 …할 수 없다'라는 부정의 뜻으로 'so ~ that ... can't'와 바꿔 쓸 수 있다.

16 미노스 왕은 다이달로스의 작품을 매우 좋아했다.

17 'so+형용사/부사+that+주어+동사 …' 구문은 '매우 ~해서 (그 결과) …하다'라는 의미로 원인과 결과를 나타낸다.

18 ⓐ, ⓑ: King Minos
ⓒ, ⓔ, ⓕ: Daedalus
ⓓ, ⓖ, ⓗ: Icarus

19 'he wanted to keep Daedalus with him forever, the King kept him and his son, Icarus, in a tall tower.'라고 했다.

20 'so+형용사/부사+that+주어+동사 …' 구문은 '매우 ~해서 (그 결과) …하다'라는 의미로 원인과 결과를 나타낸다.

21 'Daedalus then gathered bird feathers and glued them together with wax.'라고 했다.

22 (A) 지각동사 saw의 목적격보어로 동사원형이나 현재분사, (B) 조동사 Don't 다음에 동사원형, (C) began의 목적어로 to부정사나 동명사가 적절하다.

23 Daedalus와 Icarus가 날기 시작한 후에 (B) Icarus가 매우 흥분해서 아버지의 경고를 잊고 (A) 점점 더 높이 날아서 밀랍이 녹기 시작하고 (D) 추락하고 있다고 비명을 지르고 (C) 바다로 떨어져서 죽었다고 하는 순서가 적절하다.

24 'Daedalus, however, tried to leave'라고 했으므로 ⓐ를 'Daedalus tried to think of ways to leave(또는 escape).'로 고치는 것이 적절하다.

25 어느 그림이 더 인기 있는지는 알 수 없다.

26 ⓐ Matisse와 Chagall ⓑ Icarus
ⓒ their paintings ⓔ 생략 가능

27 (A) 앞 문장에 또 다른 정보를 덧붙여 제시하므로 Furthermore가 적절하다.
(B) 앞 문장과 대조의 관계이므로 In contrast가 적절하다.
(C) in addition to: ~에 더하여, ~ 이외에

28 (B) foolish
(C) simple
(D) many details
(E) some stars

29 'People will have different answers because they may see the same thing in different ways.'라고 했다.

Lesson 7 (기말)

01 ① **02** ⑤ **03** ⑤ **04** ③ **05** ⑤ **06** ③ **07** ① **08** ③
09 ④ **10** ② **11** ③ **12** ④ **13** have, finished doing
14 ③ **15** ③ **16** ① **17** ⑤ **18** ① **19** ① **20** ④
21 ②, ⑤ **22** ③ **23** ③ **24** ⑤
25 (A) space (B) Earth (C) suits (D) the hills **26** ④ **27** ②
28 ②

01 순서대로 • treasures • army • value • historian이 들어간다.

02 여기서 lie는 자동사로 '눕다'라는 뜻이다.

03 Did you hear about ~?은 상대방이 어떤 정보를 알고 있는지 묻는 표현이다.

04 'It's about a man ~.'이라고 답하는 것으로 보아 ③번이 적절하다.

05 'Let's eat lunch first and then see the movie.'라는 말에 'OK'라고 하고 있다.

06 'No, I didn't.라고 대답했으므로 'Did you ~?'로 묻는 것이 적절하다.

07 (C) 그 영화가 궁금하다면서 뭐에 관한 것인지 묻고, (B) 그 영화에 대해 설명하고, (A) 재미있겠다는 반응에 (E) 우주 극장에서 상영되고 있다고 하자, (D) 영화가 몇 시에 상영되는지 묻는 순서가 적절하다.

08 'I'm curious about ~.'은 '나는 ~에 대해서 궁금해.'라는 의미로 새로운 정보에 대하여 궁금증을 표현하거나 보다 많은 정보를 알고 싶을 때 사용하는 표현이다.

09 먹어 본 가장 맛있는 음식이 무엇인지 물었는데 타코를 먹어 본 적이 없다는 대답은 어색하다.

10 '재미있겠다.'고 하자 '그 영화가 여기 우주 극장에서 상영되고 있

다'고 정보를 주는 것이 자연스럽다.

11 화자인 두 사람이 보통 어디에서 노는지(play)는 알 수 없다.

12 가주어 it을 이용하여 바꿔 쓰는 것으로 원래 문장의 to부정사를 진주어로 쓴다.

13 현재완료의 '완료(막 ~했다)' 용법을 이용한다. finish의 목적어로 동명사를 써야 하는 것에 주의한다.

14 (A), (C) 현재완료에서 'for+기간을 나타내는 명사'나 'since+시간을 나타내는 명사'를 쓴다.
(B) just(이제 막)나 already(이미, 벌써)를 쓸 수 있다.

15 (C)의 The next day가 (A)에 이어지는 다음 날로 먼저 나오고, (C)에서 탄 우주선이 (D)에서 도착하고 (B)에서 도착한 후 언덕으로 뛰어 올라가는 순서가 적절하다.

16 처음부터 얘기해 오던 '비밀'이 곧 언덕을 굴러 내려가는 것이고 그것이 'the best new thing of all!'이라고 했으므로 'The Best New Thing'이 적절하다.

17 ⓔ는 '더 이상 떠다닐 수 없는 것'을 가리키지만 나머지는 모두 '언덕을 굴러 내려가는 것'을 가리킨다.

18 '"That's alright. I'm so excited!" said Rada.'라고 했다.

19 ⓑ rides → rode
ⓒ swim → swum
ⓓ live → living
ⓔ been→ be

20 thirsty: feeling a need or desire to drink

21 ② 우주에서는 언덕을 굴러 내려갈 수 없다.
⑤ 'floated towards him'이라고 했다.

22 우주에서 어떻게 커피를 만드는지는 알 수 없다.

23 (C)는 우유 상자를 가리킨다.

24 우유를 먹기 위해 우유 용기를 열어 흔들어서 우유 방울을 만들어 먹는다.

25 Rada와 Jonny는 space에서 태어났고, 지구에 가 본 적이 없으며, 지구에서는 우주복(space suits)을 입을 필요가 없고, 언덕(the hill)을 굴러 내려갈 수 있다.

26 'There were springs on the wall.'이라고 했다.

27 (A) 'You have to be strong to live on Earth.'
(B) 'Rada, let's start exercising.'
(C) 'Rada and Jonny stood on the wall and pulled on the springs.'라고 했다.

28 'it ~ to부정사 구문으로' ride를 to ride로 바꿔야 한다.

Lesson 7 (기말) 2회

> **01** ④ **02** ② **03** ③ **04** ②, ⑤ **05** ③ **06** ① **07** ⑤
> **08** ① **09** ⑤ **10** ① **11** ⑤ **12** ① **13** ③
> **14** easy for me to study
> **15** (1) It is hard to drive at night.
> (2) Is it possible for you to get tickets for the concert?
> **16** ④ **17** ② **18** ① **19** ③ **20** ⑤
> **21** 우유를 흔들어 방울을 형성하여 삼키는 것이다.
> **22** I've never felt the wind. **23** ④
> **24** (A) Earth (B) sky (C) grass (D) spaceship (E) hill
> **25** ⑤ **26** ② **27** ① **28** ④ **29** ④ **30** ①

01 첫 번째 문장에서는 '거짓말하다', 두 번째 문장에서는 '눕다'의 의미로 쓰인 lie가 적절하다.

02 '주의 깊게 살펴서 무언가를 찾으려고 하다'는 'search(찾다, 탐색하다)'이다.

03 'a type of ice cream'이라고 하고 'curious about the taste'라고 했으므로 음식을 언급하는 ③번이 적절하다.

04 '총 영화 상영 시간'과 점심으로 무엇을 먹을지는 알 수 없다.

05 'Let's eat lunch first and then see the movie.'라고 하자 'OK.'라고 했다.

06 영화의 상영 시간이 얼마나 되는지는 알 수 없다.

07 'Let's eat lunch first and then see the movie.'라고 하자 'OK.'라고 했다.

08 새로운 책에 대해 들어 봤는지 묻는 (A)에 이어, (D) 아니라고 답하고, (E) 여기 있다며 뉴욕 생활에 관한 책이라고 설명하고, (B) 책이 궁금하다고 하자, (C) 자기도 그렇다고 하는 순서가 자연스럽다.

09 소녀가 소년을 위해 아이스크림을 살 것이라는 언급은 나오지 않는다.

10 뒤에서 'What's it about?'이라고 묻는 것으로 보아 궁금증을 나타내는 ③번이 적절하다.

11 'Let's eat lunch first and then see the movie.'라고 하자 'OK.'라고 했다.

12 뒤에서 'I heard it has great songs.'라고 했으므로 긍정의 답이 알맞으며 Did로 물었으므로 did로 대답하는 것이 적절하다.

13 ① were → been
② Did → Have
④ has broken → broke
⑤ has → have

14 'It ~ to부정사' 구문을 이용하고 의미상의 주어로 'for+목적격'을 쓴다.

15 'It ~ to부정사' 구문을 이용하고 의미상의 주어로 'for+목적격'

을 쓴다.

16 우주선이 착륙하고 나서 지구에서는 걷는 것이 어렵다고 하는 것이 자연스러우므로 (D)가 적절하다.

17 'You don't have to wear your big heavy space suits because there is air everywhere.'라고 했다.

18 '공중을 통해 천천히 움직이다'는 'float'이다.

19 주어진 문장과 ⓒ: 가주어, 나머지: 대명사

20 언덕에서 굴러 내려온 후 'This is the best new thing of all!'이라고 했다.

21 'he opened a milk container and shook it. The milk floated in the air and formed balls. Jonny swallowed the balls.'라고 했다.

22 '~해 본 적이 있다'는 현재완료의 '경험'을 이용한다.

23 ⓓ의 I'm을 It is로 고쳐야 한다.

24 아빠가 지구로 돌아간다고 했고, 파란 하늘과 초록색의 잔디로 뒤덮인 언덕에 관해 말했다. 그들은 우주선에 올랐고 Rada와 Jonny는 언덕으로 뛰어 올라갔다.

25 Rada와 Jonny가 지구에 관해 말하면서 하고 싶은 것을 언급하는 흐름에서 조종사가 같은 방식으로 답하기를 원했다는 말은 어색하다.

26 지구에서의 생활을 묻는 주어진 문장의 답으로 (B) 뒤에서부터 설명하고 있으므로 (B)가 적절하다.

27 ⊙의 It과 ①: 가주어 ②: 비인칭주어 ③, ④, ⑤: 인칭대명사

28 ⓓ에서 by를 with로 고치는 것이 적절하다.

29 'Dad, have you ever rolled down a hill?'라는 물음에 'Yes, it's really amazing!'이라고 했다.

30 '모든 새로운 것들을 생각하는 것은 흥미로웠다'고 한 후에 '하고 싶었던 한 가지 새로운 것'을 언급하는 것이 자연스럽다.

Lesson 8 (기말)

01 ②	**02** ①	**03** ②	**04** ①	**05** ⑤	**06** ③	**07** ②	**08** ②
09 ②	**10** ③	**11** ②	**12** ③	**13** ⑤	**14** ④	**15** ④	**16** ④
17 ③	**18** ③	**19** ④	**20** ④	**21** ②	**22** ②	**23** ④	

24 (1) Dr. Park이 의궤를 찾기 시작함
　　 (2) 한국 정부가 프랑스 정부에 의궤 반환을 요청함

25 (1) Can you tell me why you became interested in history?
　　 (2) Can you tell me how many national treasures you found?

26 ④　**27** ②　**28** ①　**29** ④　**30** ④　**31** ③

01 각각 ① prove ③ succeed ④ value ⑤ pride의 풀이이다.

02 ② search: 찾다 ③ proud: 뽐내는 ④ succeed: 성공하다 ⑤

prove: 입증하다, 증명하다

03 맛있다고 하면서 'Sure. Go ahead.'라고 하고 있으므로 허가 여부를 묻는 'Is it OK to+동사원형 ~?'이 적절하다.

04 허가 여부를 묻는 'Is it OK to+동사원형 ~?'이 적절하다.

05 앞에서 'I'm sorry'라고 했으므로 (E)가 적절하다.

06 'it's only for display'라고 했다.

07 '~ is not allowed'는 '~하는 것이 허락되지 않는다'라는 뜻으로, 금지를 나타낼 때 쓰는 표현이다.

08 'is it OK to try on this hanbok?'이라고 허가 여부를 묻는 말에 'Sure. The fitting room is over there.'라고 했다.

09 'Keep off the grass.'가 적절하다.

10 'I'm afraid not.'으로 안 된다고 하고 'You are welcome to use a flash here.'라고 하는 것은 어색하다.

11 'It's a jokduri'라고 답하고 있으므로 'Where'를 'What'으로 고쳐야 한다.

12 'is it OK to try on this hanbok?'이라고 물었으므로 'fitting room(탈의실)'이 적절하다.

13 ⑤번은 '너는 여기 앉고 싶지 않다.'라는 뜻으로 금지의 뜻이 아니다.

14 where is the bathroom → where the bathroom is

15 (B) I've been → I went
　　 (D) what did he buy → what he bought

16 because 다음에는 '주어+동사'를 가진 '절'이 나와야 하고 because of 다음에는 명사(구) 또는 동명사(구)가 온다.

17 Dr. Park과의 인터뷰 글이다.

18 누가 박 박사에게 '의궤'에 대해 말했는지는 알 수 없다.

19 ⊙의 them은 앞에서 언급한 'many of our national treasures'이다.

20 ⓛ은 뒤에 언급하는 것들로 '의궤'의 가치를 아는 데 10년이 걸렸다는 내용은 없다.

21 '의궤'를 찾으려고 했으므로 찾았을 때 'excited'했을 것이다.

22 앞에서 '연구 결과가 책으로 출판되었다'고 했으므로 'your book'이 적절하다.

23 연구 결과가 책으로 출판되는 것이므로 '수동태'가 적절하다.

24 (1) 'in 1967, I began to look for Uigwe'라고 했다.
　　 (2) 'In 1992, the Korean government asked the French government for its return'이라고 했다.

25 간접의문문은 '의문사+주어+동사'의 어순으로 쓰는 것에 주의한다.

26 "직지"는 금속 활자로 인쇄된 세계에서 가장 오래된 책이라고 했으므로 'printing(인쇄)'이 적절하다.

27 'I knew right away that it was very special.'이라고 했다.

28 '~ 때문에'라는 뜻으로 뒤에 '명사구'가 나오므로 'because of'가 적절하다. instead of는 '~ 대신에'라는 뜻이다.

29 1972년 파리 도서 박람회에서 '직지'가 얼마나 오래 전시되었는

지는 알 수 없다.

30 'Dr. Park Byeong-seon, a historian who spent her whole life searching for Korean national treasures abroad.'라고 했다.

31 ⓑ to search → searching

ⓒ continuing → continue

ⓔ studied → studying

Lesson 8 (기말)

01 ⑤ **02** ② **03** ③ **04** ③ **05** ④ **06** ① **07** ③ **08** ④
09 ③ **10** ④ **11** ② **12** (1) because of (2) because **13** ①
14 Q1. 바꾼 문장 → I'd like to know why you became a director.
Q2. 바꾼 문장 → Can you tell me how many movies you have made so far?
Q3. 바꾼 문장 → I wonder if you have your favorite actor.
15 what you bought in the store **16** ② **17** ② **18** ③
19 (1) continue (2) value (3) result (4) treasure (5) search
20 ⑤ **21** ⑤ **22** ③ **23** ④ **24** ③ **25** ②
26 (1) ⓐ Yes, I was, but more difficulties were waiting for me.
(2) ⓒ It was not easy to do research on *Uigwe*.
(3) ⓔ Many Koreans became interested in *Uigwe* because of your book.
27 ⑤

01 publish: to print a book, magazine, or newspaper for people to buy

02 '해 놓은 것에 대한 만족이나 기쁨의 감정'은 'pride(자부심)'이다.

03 'is not allowed'로 금지하고 있으므로 '허가 여부'를 묻는 ③번이 적절하다.

04 '허가 여부'를 묻는데 '아니'라고 한 후 'Go ahead.'라고 하는 것은 어색하다.

05 'I'm sorry, but it's only for display. Trying it on is not allowed.'라고 했다.

06 모두 허가 여부를 묻는 표현인데 ①번은 '네가 입어 볼 수 있느냐?'라고 묻는 말이다.

07 'It's usually worn on a wedding day.'라고 했다.

08 E에서 허가 여부를 묻고 A에서 '잔디 위에서?'라고 반문하자 C에서 그렇다며 괜찮은지 다시 묻고 D에서 허락되지 않는다고 하자 B에서 알겠다고 하는 순서가 적절하다. E-A-C-D-B의 순서이다.

09 ⓒ에서 이것이 무엇인지 묻고 ⓔ에서 해금이라고 답하고 ⓑ에서 연주해 보아도 되는지 묻자 ⓓ에서 미안하다며 전시용이라고 답하

고 ⓐ에서 알겠다고 하는 순서가 자연스럽다.

10 ④번은 '자전거를 타자'는 '제안'이지만 나머지는 모두 '허가'를 구하는 표현이다. 'Why don't we ~?'는 '~하자'라는 의미이다. permission: 허가, 허락

11 ① because → because of
③ because → because of
④ because of → because
⑤ because of → because

12 because of+명사(구), because+절

13 (A) results가 주어이므로 were
(B) 뒤에 '구'가 이어지므로 because of
(C) 소유격 its가 명사 return을 수식해야 한다.

14 간접의문문의 어순은 '의문사+주어+동사'이다. 의문사가 없는 경우 의문사 대신에 if나 whether를 쓴다.

15 간접의문문을 이용하여 쓰며 간접의문문의 어순은 '의문사+주어+동사'임에 주의한다.

16 (A) behind: ~의 뒤에, ~의 배후에 (C) As soon as: ~하자마자 As long as: ~하는 한 (D) because of+명사(구)

17 I want to know. + How did you find them? = I want to know how you found them.

18 'As soon as I became a researcher at the National Library in 1967, I began to look for *Uigwe*.'라고 했다.

19 (1) 멈추지 않다
(2) 어떤 것의 가치가 있는 돈의 양
(3) 다른 어떤 것 때문에 생긴 어떤 것
(4) 한 무리의 귀중품, 특히 금, 은 또는 보석
(5) 매우 조심스럽게 봄으로써 누군가나 어떤 것을 발견하려고 하다

20 ⓐ return → be returned
ⓑ was fired → fired
ⓒ show → to show
ⓓ was → were

21 ⓜ은 대명사이고 나머지는 모두 접속사이다.

22 'The results of your research were published as a book in Korea in 1990.'라고 했다.

23 (D) 앞에서 'I didn't give up.'이 나오고 그것을 설명하는 주어진 글이 이어지는 것이 자연스러우므로 (D)가 적절하다.

24 (a) what을 쓸 경우 그 역할이 없다. (b) look for: 찾다, look at: 보다 (c) 감정을 느끼는 경우이므로 excited가 맞다.

25 '직지'를 찾기 위해 얼마나 많은 책을 보았는지는 알 수 없다.

26 ⓐ wait for: 기다리다 ⓒ 'it is[was] ~ to부정사' 구문이다. ⓔ 뒤에 '구'가 이어지므로 because of가 적절하다.

27 'In 1992, the Korean government asked the French government for its return'이라고 했다.